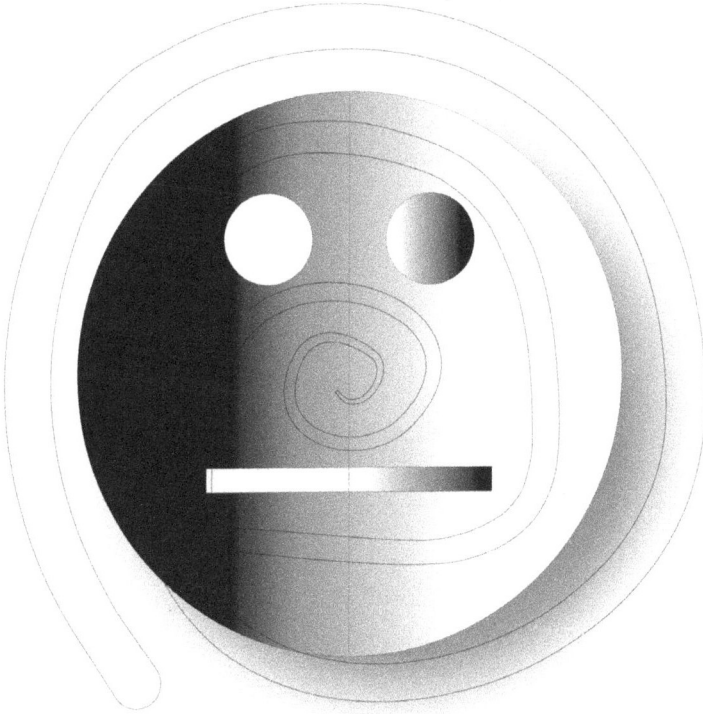

For a Minute, I Lost Myself

The Past and Present of a Schizophrenic

By Scott Gann

1

ISBN: 978-0-578-02300-7

Contents:

This book is dedicated to my parents, my grandmother, and my children, who all never stopped loving me, even in a time when I didn't love myself.

I'm serving time for a crime that I did not commit. You want the truth? Well, you know I'd do it all again. I heard a voice calling from down inside a well. So, down I fell. Down into the wall of black. My prison cell. Only the moon was shining back.

-Arcade Fire, *Neon Bible*

Prologue

What would you do if you one day realized that your brain had failed you? What if you woke up one day and realized that your brain had caused you to see and hear things that were not real? What would you do if you heard voices that came from nowhere and told you to do things that seemed right and just, but really only made a fool out of you? How would you respond to the commands of a voice that told you it was speaking to you through a tiny device in your head and was a member of a secret organization that existed to prevent the fall of man? How would you respond to the realization that all the things that the voice told you were lies? How would you respond to the realization that the voice was actually only a figment of your imagination, a product of a degenerative brain? How would you feel when you realized that you had driven away almost all the people who loved and cared for you? How would you deal with the loneliness that comes from the aftermath and stigma that is associated with the world of Schizophrenics? How would you cope with a condition that is a life long illness that can never be fully cured and could strike at any moment to send you back from sanity into the dark world, that is, madness?

The following story tells a tale about my life and how I answered all of these questions. It is a description of a descent into madness, the aftermath of that descent, and an uphill struggle to find meaning and purpose in my life after I realized that I did, in fact, suffer from a serious problem, Schizophrenia. The story begins with my childhood, adolescence, and young adult life. I wrote about those things to give a brief history of who I was before the symptoms occurred that wrecked my life. I began to write this story at a time when I had become tired of hiding from the world. As my writing began, I had grown weary of avoiding people and living with the fear of what other people might think if they knew that I was a Schizophrenic. This story was written in a time when I had just spent the better part of three years avoiding all social interaction with people. I began writing so that I could speak to someone. I did not feel able to talk to anyone about my problems, my fears, or my desire to somehow defeat the monster that lived in my head and nearly ruined my life. I began writing this story so that I could just talk to myself. I was not sure if anyone else would listen. So, through writing, I just talked to myself.

As I began to tell myself the story of what had happened that caused the tragic first appearance of Schizophrenia in my life, I realized that there may be a purpose to my story that extended beyond my personal use. I began to think that, perhaps, my family might get a better understanding of the frightening behavior that they had witnessed in me a few years earlier. I realized that since I had been silent for so many years about the subject of my diagnosis as a Schizophrenic, they might have a lot of unanswered questions that my story might shed light on. From there, I began to think that my story could be useful to other people as well. I thought about my psychiatric doctor. I thought about some of my former employers. I thought about all sorts of people who had witnessed the collapse of my mind and wondered what had happened, why it happened, and how it happened. I'm not saying that I have the answers for all of these questions, but this story is my best attempt to make a stab at answering some of those questions.

The main point that I hope this book can convey is that we Schizophrenics are not all the scary, terrible, and dangerous people that we are so often made out to be. Some of us, perhaps most of us, are just people suffering from a disease of the mind. We have to live our lives a little differently than the average "normal" person (whatever that is). Some of us have made great contributions to society. We Schizophrenics are sometimes great thinkers and doers, even though, sometimes, we think and do too much. That is the problem. Our brains don't know when enough is enough. Without the proper lifestyle, our brains will never shut off. I believe that, once a Schizophrenic has learned to control the beast, that is their brain, he or she has the potential to make wonderful contributions to the world. It is the taming of the beast that is the key factor in whether a Schizophrenic will or will not live a productive life. The purpose of my story is to shed a little light on the life of one Schizophrenic, myself. I also have tried to point out pitfalls that I think a person should avoid and things that a person should embrace as part of a lifestyle that combats the disease of the mind that is Schizophrenia.

I hope that you find my story entertaining, but most of all, I hope that it helps you understand that we Schizophrenics are not all bad people. Schizophrenics need people who love and care about them, just like anybody else. Without the love of my family, I don't think I could have survived Schizophrenia. I hope that by reading this book, you might think of someone in your life who suffers from a mental illness, and lend your love to them. That is what we all need. I know that we are a sometimes scary and even dangerous bunch, but there are some of us who can be saved from ourselves through the patience and love of those around us. Please be patient with the mentally ill. All of us Schizo's probably say and do things that really are beyond our control. We do and say things that we later regret. If you give us time, some of us will eventually come out of the darkness that our mind creates, and see things your way. I hope that this book will be helpful for both the mentally ill and those who consider themselves "normal". I hope that the mentally ill come away from my story with a better understanding of what they can do to better themselves and improve their mental health. I hope that the "normal" people who read this will gain insight into our slightly different brains, and perhaps, see some of themselves in my story; so that they make a connection and realize that, perhaps, we Schizo's are not so different from them after all.

An Introduction

As children we were told, "Sticks and stones may break my bones, but words can never harm me." Whoever came up with that little rhyme was a much different person than myself. There are certain words that possess a power unlike most others. For me, those words are: insane, crazy, and weird. Most of the time, these words are thrown around in conversation to describe someone who has done something funny or outlandish. That's fine with me. It is when these words are used with their other definitions that they get under my skin. Sometimes they are used to describe something that is unexplainable, something not understood. You might hear criminals plead insanity after they have been charged with an unthinkable crime like murder or rape. Whenever I hear these words used towards me, they cause me a little pain. They caused me to lose all confidence in my own ability to think rationally. I don't ever hear myself described with these words anymore. But a lot has changed in me since the time when I did.

For several years, those words: insane, crazy, weird; they all defined me. I really was crazy. It didn't happen overnight. I didn't wake up crazy one day. But I guess I must have been born with the brain structure that allowed "craziness" to develop. No, it took many years and many stressful circumstances to finally make me crack. But once I did break, it took a long time to piece myself back together again. That process didn't happen overnight either. I'm not fully there yet anyway. I still have some things to do before I consider myself a "normal" person again. I have yet to re-establish myself as a fully functioning member of society who contributes to the greater good of our country and handles all of life's hardships without falling to pieces and causing the people around me to suffer. Only recently have I begun to set goals and have hope of a better future for myself. It's important for me to have goals and dreams. Without them, life becomes a blur with one day slipping into the next.

One of my goals is to write this story. I hope that this story can help someone who is curious about mental illness, its causes, and how to defeat it. Maybe all this story is good for is to show someone what not to do in their life. Maybe its worth more than that though. Maybe someone can read this and learn a little about the illness that I suffer from. Maybe this story will help fight the stigma that is associated with people who have mental illnesses. That is really what I hope to do with this story. I want this story to tell people that just because a person suffers from a mental illness, that does not make them a bad individual. Some of us are bad people. But some of us are just normal people who have tried to do all the right things and ended up suffering from a defective brain. It's really no different than a person suffering from a defective heart or some other defective organ. We just have to take precautions with our lives, just as a person suffering from any other type of ailment might have to adjust their lifestyle. A person who had been told by their doctor that they have heart problems might have to adjust their diet, their level of exercise, take medications, and so on. People who are diagnosed with mental illnesses have to make the same adjustments. We all have to pay close attention to many aspects of our daily routine such as, sleep, exercise, diet, and of course medication.

This is actually the first time I have ever said most of what is in the pages that follow. Up until now, most of the events described on these pages, have been nightmares, and stressful memories that find their way into my consciousness and cause me to lie awake at night, thinking about them. There was about a year when I couldn't remember a lot of the things that made me the crazy person that I was for a time. But, over the last couple years, I have been storing memories of my times in and out of rehab centers. I also have thought a lot about what caused me to end up in those rehab centers in the first place. I wanted to write all these things down before they disappear from my memory again. If I can get all this down on paper, at least, it might offer a glimpse to those who knew me best, of what exactly was rambling around in my brain at a time when I was not myself. I did lose myself. It was more than a minute. It was more like several years. I hope that the pages that follow tell my story in a way that is easy to understand. There really is no easy way to understand a mind that has lost all ability to rationalize and interpret its surroundings in a way that is in touch with reality. That's not really what I expect to do. I just want to tell a story that shows what led up to a very strange time in my life. I hope that it will offer insight to someone who may be experiencing the same things that I did. I hope that my story can help someone who might be on a path of self-destruction. Maybe someone will read this and realize that they can find a better life for themselves. I don't know. That's just my hope for this story.

I have been told that there are lots of people out there who have my same problem, but never realize it. Some people go through life without enough stress to ever trigger the series of events that let me know, I was indeed, insane. Some people use alcohol or drugs to cover up the anxiety that my problem, schizophrenia, creates. Others wind up in the prison system. They are the most unfortunate of all. I wonder just how many people in prison suffer from my problem, but just never had the right support group to save them from themselves.

Now, I constantly evaluate my actions and thoughts to measure just how crazy I might be on any given day. I try to make sure to get at least eight hours of sleep every night. Exercise is very important, I have found. It relieves the built up tension of the day and allows me to rest easier at night. I try not to eat as much as I used to because the little pill I take every night has slowed down my metabolism enough that my old eating habits caused me to put on a little weight. For the last year and half, I have been slowly waking back up from what seems to me like a dream that occurred while I was awake. The dream lasted for about a year. Waking up from it has taken much longer and has required the help of my family, my doctors, and of course, that little pill I mentioned. This is a recollection of parts of my life that, I think, helped create that dream, which was actually more like a nightmare at times. In my waking dream I developed disturbing, frightening behaviors that drove away almost everyone I knew. This is my story, my life, the life of a schizophrenic.

Chapter 1: In the Beginning…

I was a lucky child. I lived in a nice, middle-class home in a peaceful, rural section of Polk County, Florida. Lake Buffum was where we moved to from Bartow, Florida when I was twelve years old. It is a lake that stretches about one mile from North to South and over two miles from East to West. It's one of those places that would make a perfect setting for a state park if all the land around the lake wasn't privately owned with half-million dollar houses dotting the shoreline. My two brothers, Sam and Carter, and I spent most of our free time exploring the woods around the lake and doing every water sport we could think of in the lake. My parents were teachers, so we were always home by around 4:00 and usually had a couple hours every day to play in the lake after school. We had a dock that went out about 100 feet into the lake and had a second level on the end that served as a sunshade for a boat parked under the dock and a diving platform for my brothers and myself. The neighbor's kids, my brothers, and I would play tag for hours in the summer and on the weekends, chasing each other all around and under and over the dock. It was probably some the best times we had as kids.

We also loved to water ski. We had a small boat with a forty horse outboard engine that we used to pull one and sometimes two of us behind it at a time. Once I could drive; my friend, Justin White, and I would go to Cocoa Beach and we started surfing. I found that I liked surfing more than skiing. When I was a senior in high school I took my surfboard out on the lake with a big umbrella just before a big thunderstorm. The wind was blowing strong. I paddled out a ways on the board, stood up, and opened the umbrella. The wind carried me across the water at a pretty good clip and I loved it. That was the beginning of learning to sail board.

I had seen pictures of people on sailboards and thought it looked like a lot of fun. So, I bought a book that described the concept of tacking and other sailing miscellaneous. Then I saved up enough to buy my first sailboard for about $200 complete with sails, mast, boom, etc. I taught myself how to ride the board within a week or so. The thrill of moving through the water at 20 or 30 miles an hour on a board not much bigger than my old surfboard was amazing. I could never ride for more than around thirty minutes at a time, but those were some of the most exciting thirty minutes of my life. I loved sail boarding. That's not to say I was any good at it. Half the times I went out on my sailboard I had to be rescued by boat because I had exhausted myself on just the tack out and couldn't summon the strength to hold the sail up to bring me back to where I started. This was never a big deal because somebody at my house was usually good enough to keep an eye on me when I went out on the sailboard. After realizing that I would not be able to bring myself back to land, they would usually get in one of my parents' boats and come to my rescue.

Along with all the exceptional activities we had to choose from, there were family and friends. I grew up with a close family. We spent lots of time with my grand parents, uncles, aunts, cousins, etc. I had a lot of love and respect for all my relatives and I felt loved by all of them. As far as I knew, no one in my family had even been so much as divorced. They all seemed pretty close to perfect and, to be a part of that family, I felt lucky.

My mom and dad took us to church regularly. When I was twelve, my grandparents brought me to a "revival" at their church. The preacher talked about the possibility of dying at any moment and how terrible Hell was. He made it clear that if you had not accepted Jesus Christ as your Lord and Savior you would be going to Hell when you died. The thought of dying at any moment scared me but, to think that I might spend eternity in Hell, on fire and constantly in pain; that really terrified me. I walked down to the preacher at the end of the service and told him I wanted to make Jesus my Savior and asked him to Baptize me so that I might be spared the eternal torture that was coming my way otherwise. I wonder if that is why most people decide to "get saved".

A year later my family started attending First Baptist Church of Bartow. I enjoyed it because there were a lot of other kids that were around my age and the church planned a lot of activities for the youth group. In the summer we would all go to a church camp for a week, usually out of state. It was like a vacation with all my good friends and we always ended up meeting lots of other new people at the camps as well. The main attraction for my friends and I, though, were the girls.

Chapter 2: The Alice Years

For me there was just one girl in particular that I really liked. Her name was Alice Bransen. She was a member of our church as well. She was three years older than me. I first met her when I was in the eighth grade. She was so smart and funny. I couldn't believe she would even talk to me, a lowly eighth grader, when she was a junior in high school. She had red hair and lots of freckles. I loved the smell of the shampoo she used in her hair. I loved to listen to her talk, laugh, and sing. We liked the same bands. I felt like that alone was amazing. My favorite band, R.E.M., was also the favorite band of a beautiful girl in the eleventh grade. That was what most of our first conversations revolved around; just talking about the music we liked.

A year went by and we were still just friends. I didn't think about any girl but her, but I couldn't get the nerve to ask her to be my girlfriend. I kept waiting for a perfect moment when I would know for sure that she really thought of me as more than just a friend. Then summer came and, since the second grade, that always meant going to Georgia with my parents for two months. That meant two months away from a girl I really wanted to say something to.

My parents' had a summer house, that my dad built himself, in North Georgia. It was in a sleepy little town named Young Harris, East of Blairsville and West of Hiawassee. The total population of all three of those towns was probably less than that of Bartow at the time my dad first starting building their house up there. Young Harris was not more than a couple hundred houses (if that), a small private college, Brown's Motel, the electric company, and one traffic light. There were no stores other than Brown's General Merchandise, a five and dime type store that mostly consisted of items, which probably sat in Mr. Brown's store for several years before anyone ever bought them. If you needed groceries or just about anything else, you went 8 miles to Hiawassee or Blairsville. It was an escape for my parents, a quiet place to get away from the "crowds" of Bartow. They have always preferred to be away from as many people as possible for as long as possible. Peace and quiet may be nice when you're an adult, but as kids, my brothers and I sometimes wished there was more to do.

That's not to say we were ever really bored. We spent most of our days walking through the woods, exploring creeks, and collecting beer cans from a place we found that the college kids used as their private drinking and partying spot. We appropriately named it The Beer Can Place. The ground at The Beer Can Place was covered in beer cans on top of beer cans and beer bottles on top of beer bottles. It took many summers of collecting before we moved out enough cans to notice we had made a difference in the appearance of the place. We would take the cans to a metal recycler who paid us for them. Every couple weeks we would make a trip to the recycling center and get paid around twenty dollars for our loot. The big pay outs came directly from the drunk college kids themselves. Every so often, we would find money scattered in the woods that the drunk kids had dropped and left behind. Once I found forty dollars. My brother found a gold necklace one day as well. For us, that was like winning the lottery. So, back to the main story:

Towards the end of the summer my best friend since kindergarten, Jackson Roberts, came to stay with us for a couple weeks. I was so psyched because all the company I ever got in the summer was my two brothers. Jackson and I had a great time exploring the woods around my parents' house and showing him all the things I had found to do in the summers in Georgia over the years. We swung from vines that hung in the trees. We climbed trees. We played in creeks and built dams. Then, we were walking around in the woods on one of the last days he was there and Jackson told me he had to tell me something.

Jackson Roberts, my best friend since kindergarten, informed me that he had asked Alice Bransen to be his girlfriend and she had accepted. He said he knew it would hurt me if I found out and he wanted to be the one to tell me. He said he had never thought about asking her out, but she came on to him and then he realized he liked her. He said he still wanted me to think of him as my best friend. I was stunned. I couldn't think of anything to say. I didn't think it would change anything if I did.

I couldn't believe my best friend could betray me so severely. He was the one I had told over and over again all the little things I loved about her, all the moments where I almost asked her out but could never get the nerve. He knew better than anyone how much I thought about her. He had never mentioned anything about liking her too. He had dated several other girls in the year that I spent trying to come up with a plan to close the deal. I couldn't believe that he had asked out the girl that he knew I had feelings for. Then I realized Alice must not have cared about me as much as I hoped if she was willing to go out with Jackson. Then came the sadness. That is the first time I can ever remember feeling truly hurt by something.

Jackson left a few days later. I could hardly stand to look at him and it seemed like those few days drug along like weeks. Summer ended. We came back to Florida. We went back to church, back to Alice and my former best friend. I had to see the two of them together and it made me sick. I remember coming home from school and sitting in the lake with the water just below my mouth. I just sat there all afternoon, thinking of how I had lost my best friend. Mostly, though, I kept trying to figure out how the girl who had spent so much time with me over the last year could forget me and decide she liked my best friend, all in less than two months. Obviously, the wheels had been turning for a while longer than two months, I thought. I had never been so sad and so angry in my life. I think that was when I began to lose my faith in people.

The ninth grade started and I was minus two good friends. But soon the void was filled. Jackson and I were friends with many other people at school. He was my best friend, but not my only friend. One of our friends was Justin White. He was in the ninth grade with us. We had started hanging out at lunch and before school in the eighth grade. Justin even came to church with us sometimes.

I started inviting Justin over on the weekends. We would go camping, skiing, and did just about anything exciting that we could think of. We talked a lot about what had happened with Jackson and Alice. I appreciated hearing him tell me about what I had missed while I was in Georgia. His story of how Jackson and Alice got together was a little different than what I had heard from my former best friend. Justin said that it was Jackson who was constantly flirting with Alice. Jackson always did better in the picking - up - the - girls department than me. Who knows if anything that Justin said was true or if he was just stirring a pot. At the time I took everything Justin said to be the truth and I started to think of him as my new best friend.

Justin and I spent lots of time together from ninth grade until I was in my late twenties. He really was a great friend. Justin listened when I had issues with people. I always appreciated that.

Ninth grade went on and, eventually, only about a month and a half into the school year, Alice dumped Jackson. I didn't really care. I had already blown them off in my mind and was thinking about other things, other people. It's nice how quickly you can rebound from devastation when you're young.

I did still go to church every Sunday morning and night and Wednesday night after school. So I still had contact with Alice. I tried to pretend that Jackson wasn't even there. This made things a little awkward because everyone else there still liked Jackson as much as ever. Justin usually came with me so I tried to just hang out with him and avoided a lot of the other people because I felt like they were somehow betraying me too. This didn't last long. You can't stay mad forever, especially when you're only in the ninth grade. Eventually everything at church got back to the way it had been, only Justin and I didn't have as much to do with Jackson anymore. We formed our own exclusive two man clique. Alice and I even started to become friends. Before long, it was as if nothing had ever happened. It didn't take long before I totally forgave her and Jackson in my mind and I began to think about Alice all the time. I never did bring up the fact that she dated my best friend. I just convinced myself that she must not have known how much I liked her and if she did she never would have agreed to be Jackson Roberts's girlfriend.

The youth group seemed to have something going on almost every weekend. We would take trips to the various theme parks, other churches, and sometimes meet at the houses of various members of the church. One weekend in December we had a dance at a building in a town far enough away that we didn't drive back to Bartow that night but instead stayed in the building over night and drove back the next day. That night was magical.

I don't remember what town the building was in. I don't remember what the place looked like inside. I don't even remember if Justin or Jackson were there. I do remember that was the night that Alice let me know that she had been thinking about me.

The main event was a dance. So, there was music. The lights were dim. There was a mirror-ball on the ceiling. It was loud. It was my first dance club like experience. Alice and I had been talking more and more. We would call each other almost every night and talk for thirty minutes, sometimes, maybe an hour. Our friendship was on the brink of becoming full blown dating. I still had my doubts that a now senior in high school could really have any feelings for a ninth grader. But that was the infatuation. The fact that she was so much older made her seem wiser and more mature, which made her even more irresistibly beautiful. And she had red hair to top it all off. I don't remember ever caring about the color of a girl's hair until I met Alice. I still find myself more attracted to redheads to this day. I know it's because of her.

Anyways, there we were at a dance. It was the perfect setting for what I hoped I could ask. We danced to just about every song they played. The funny thing was that this was supposedly a church function but I can't remember hearing any Christian music at the dance. I do remember dancing to a lot of our favorite songs, R.E.M.'s *Losing My Religion* was one of them. I loved any slow song they played because that gave me the excuse to put my arms around Alice. I can't remember ever being so happy or nervous before that night.

Probably around 2:00 am we stopped the music and people just started to crash anywhere they could get comfortable. Alice went over to some of her friends and started talking to them. I told her goodnight and couldn't believe I had let another perfect opportunity slip by to tell this girl what I thought about her and ask how she felt about me. Although, I was pretty sure from the way she danced with me that my prospects were much improved.

We all brought pillows and blankets so some people slept on the floor. Some people slept on top of tables. I never went to sleep but I laid down thinking I was going to, on a row of folding chairs that was long enough for me to stretch out on. Then Alice brought over some more chairs and set them up right beside mine so that we were lying right next to each other, separated only by a couple of inches. I guess the "adult supervisors" either didn't see or didn't see any harm in what she had done. Most of the lights went out and it was pretty dark. I closed my eyes and just laid there. I felt that if nothing ever came of us, at least we had had this one night. It was perfect. Then I started imagining what could possibly happen. Was she thinking the same things? I didn't know. We didn't say a word to each other. I could feel Alice breathing. I could feel her breath getting warmer. I opened my eyes and realized she had moved a little closer to me. She had her eyes closed. I closed my eyes and moved a little closer to her. Our mouths were breathing into each other. I could hear my heartbeat in my head. There was a ringing in my ears. I thought I was going to pass out.

I had kissed a few girls before Alice, so it wasn't the thought of kissing that had me so nervous. It was the fact that I was about to kiss Alice. I had imagined that I would have to somehow construct a suave statement expressing how I felt about her and that would be the beginning of our relationship. I never imagined we would begin with a kiss. I was also a little scared that the next day she would be a different person or that if we kissed she might regret it and everything would become awkward and I would lose her all over again. I was sweating. I was scared.

Then I felt her lips press against my lips. Every fear went out the backdoor. We laid there breathing into each other's mouth with our lips touching for the longest time. It was everything a kiss should be. Then I put my arm around her waist and we pulled ourselves together. Then the real kissing began. Her tongue went in my mouth. I couldn't believe this was happening. I was hearing everything I ever wanted her to say without her ever saying a word. We kissed until everyone started to wake up that morning. My mouth was so dry. I had never been happier and never felt so completely fulfilled by someone. It was total infatuation and I really loved her, more than any other girl I have ever known. A ninth grader probably shouldn't have an experience like that. It sets the bar for love too high. It raises the expectation of what a girl should be too a very high standard. It made the later relationships in my life pale in comparison.

After that night Alice was officially and finally my girlfriend. She had a car, so we could have gone on dates, but I was only in the ninth grade and my parents didn't like the idea of anything like that happening. We only saw each other in supervised locations with adults nearby except for a few times. A few times we drove around in her car for several hours listening to our favorite music and talking about nothing. She would come out to the lake house on the weekends or she would take me to her house and we would watch movies. Once she came out to the lake and went skiing with my brothers and I. I remember her walking out to the end of the dock. My brothers and I were already in the lake and getting the accessories in the boat for a ski run. She stripped down to her bathing suit and I was in heaven. She had a great body, fair skin, probably no more than 100 pounds. She looked awesome.

My parents were inside the house. It was just me and Alice and two little brothers that I wish could have disappeared. Even still, it was something just to see her in a bathing suit. She jumped off the dock and swam up to me. We were in about to our waists. I put my arms around her and just held her and we talked for a few minutes. That was the most physical contact we ever had, though I dreamed of more for a couple of years after that.

The ninth grade ended and summer began. We went back to Georgia. Alice and I talked on the phone a lot. The nice thing was that my parents and her parents had started to become friends. Our parents talked and her parents decided to come spend a week with us at my parents' house in Georgia. That week was awesome. Alice and I went on walks together, almost never alone though, always with the entourage of my two little brothers and her little sister. It was hard to have her so close and yet not be able to do the things we thought were the most fun. One time we did slip away into the woods and we talked about the fact that she was about to move to Gainesville to attend UF. She was going to become an architect. She said she would call me as often as she could and she wanted me to come see her any time I could. I was only 15 and still naive enough to think we had a future together.

The University Life began for Alice and tenth grade began for me. About a month or two into the school year my parents planned a trip to Itchetucknee Springs, near Gainesville, so that I could spend a day with Alice. My parents loved Alice too. She was so funny and upbeat that she was infectious to everyone around her. We met Alice at a Mc Donald's near Gainesville, along with a couple of her Bartow friends that were also attending UF. One of her friends happened to be my cousin, Lauren Hoks.

When my parents and I came inside the Mc Donald's, Alice, Lauren, and a couple other girls were already waiting for us. I immediately walked up to Alice and hugged her. Only she hardly hugged me back. I knew before I hugged her that it was over. When we walked in, my cousin and the other girls, who I knew from First Baptist, all smiled happily and said hello. Alice had been very reserved and calm, not like the Alice I knew. Alice went to the bathroom with one of her friends and my cousin came up to me. I asked her what was wrong with Alice. Lauren said that college was just stressful and that Alice was nervous because she was having a tough time adjusting and hadn't seen me in a while. Then she said, "but she might need to tell you something". I knew what Alice needed to tell me. I just didn't want to hear it.

We all loaded up and went to Itchetucknee Springs. Alice rode with my parents and I but only talked to my parents on the way to the springs. Itchetucknee Springs is a 2 ½ hour tube ride down a river. It was 2 ½ hours of torture. I kept paddling up to her in my tube. She would drift away. I would ask her what was wrong but she wouldn't say. She kept trying to stay with my parents or her friends. I began to feel like the butt of a bad joke. So, I just left her alone. Even though she wouldn't come out and say it, I knew we were through.

At the end of the trip from hell down the river, my parents and I loaded up and drove back to Lake Buffum. Alice went back with her friends. I don't even remember how we said goodbye. All the way home I kept replaying the day in my head and trying to figure out what had just happened. I called Alice the next day.

She answered and sounded disappointed to be talking to me. I asked her what was wrong. She said, "Nothing, college just changes people. You won't understand until you get here." I suddenly felt very small and stupid. I asked her what the deal was with not talking to me the day before. No answer. I told her that she spent more time with everybody there except me. She breathed into the phone. Then I said, "Are you still my girlfriend?" She just sat there without saying anything for a while. Then she said, "Scott, I met a guy here who is a sophomore, we've got a lot in common and he's really nice to me." I knew that was coming as soon as I saw her at the McDonald's. I mean really, how many tenth graders even get to speak to a girl who is a freshman in college, let alone have her undivided attention and affection for almost a year? Still, I was crushed and couldn't think of what to say. I wanted to cry. I had already cried the night before because I already knew this was coming. All I said was, "Well, I guess I'll see you around then." She said, "O.K., I'm really sorry Scott, once you graduate from high school and start college, you'll understand." That was the last time I ever to spoke to my beloved Alice Bransen.

18

Chapter 3: Surf's Up!

The rest of tenth grade was a daze. I remember spending several more days in the lake by myself for hours at a time wishing I could be a college student at UF so that I could have another chance with Alice Bransen. That was my first experience of what I guess you could call depression. I lost interest in most everybody at church. Church, and those people there, just reminded me of Alice. I wanted to forget about her. So I stopped going. My parents and brothers still attended pretty regularly, but they didn't force me to come along. I did still stay close with Justin. He picked up the slack that Alice had left behind and we started having our adventures.

Justin got a car that January. It was a little red Yugo. He and I toured the county in that sweet ride. Eventually we got tired of spending our weekends driving around Lakeland, Bartow, and Winter Haven. We needed something exotic. We decided we would become surfers.

Justin had some experience in water skiing and knee boarding from all the weekends he had come out to the lake and spent the days with my brothers and I. So, surfing didn't seem like that hard of a thing to learn. We had heard kids at school talk about surfing at Cocoa Beach at "Second Light". We decided we were going to find this "Second Light" and try it out for ourselves. Justin and I drove to Cocoa Beach and found the mother of all surf shops, Ron Jon's. We walked in and I instantly knew this was the sport for me. There were surfboards everywhere. Not rack upon rack of Ron Jon's shirts and shorts, sandals and sunglasses, like you see today. That stuff was all there too. It just wasn't what they were emphasizing at the time. We walked among the rows of surfboards and tried to look like we knew what we were doing. But we were really just two dumb tenth graders who had never touched a surfboard in their lives.

Then we saw a sign that said they were renting surfboards, five dollars for the day. Cha-Ching! For five dollars we could see if we had any surfer in us. Whether we did or not, the kids back at Bartow High would be hearing about how Justin and Scott had spent the weekend rippin' it up and killing those waves at Cocoa Beach. We happily donated five dollars for our surfboards and then realized we had no way of transporting them anywhere except on foot. That was just one of a million genius moments of high school. We took the boards out to Justin Yugo and tried to jam them in the back. It had a hatchback but we still couldn't safely drive with two boards in that thing. We couldn't even sit down in the seats because the boards were right where our heads should be. Luckily, Justin and I had enough money to buy a surfboard rack that went on top of the car and we were on our way.

We asked the guy who rented us the surfboards if he had heard of "Second Light". He told us that it was a great place to surf and how to get there. It was simple, "Second Light" was the second stop light in Cocoa Beach if you were headed south on A1A. We got there and unloaded our top of the line, five-dollar surfboards. They really weren't bad. They were actual surfboards at least, not the Styrofoam crap you see places renting now. We watched the other surfers for a while and decided it seemed pretty easy. Then we tried to paddle out through the breakers and nearly had our butts handed to us. By the time we got through the onslaught of white water my shoulders were burning and my nipples were already getting raw from being rubbed against the sand and wax that that covered the top of the board. We sat up on our boards and talked, trying to catch our breath and wait for the burn to go away. We felt like we had already accomplished enough to brag about when we got back to school.

Then we decided we were going to try and catch a wave. I had been bodysurfing waves at the beach since I was a little kid, so I had an idea of what to feel for. When the wave starts to tug on you, you wait. Then there's a stillness for just a split second just before the crest of the wave descends on you. That's when you dive forward and catch the wave. That's how it worked for bodysurfing anyways. On a surfboard you need to start paddling as soon as you feel that first pull because there is no diving forward. It took me a few tries to figure this out and get my timing right. Then I caught a wave. It felt a lot faster than bodysurfing, but these were much bigger waves than I had ever bodysurfed on. It was February and the peak of surfing season was near. We didn't know that there were certain times when waves were at there highest. We just couldn't think of anything else better to do that weekend. That's why we were there. The waves that day averaged around nine to ten feet.

On that first wave I didn't even try to stand up. I just coasted along and rode it all the way to shore. Then I realized I had to paddle back through all the breakers again. Eventually, I made it back. Justin had attempted to catch a wave as well. He wasn't having as much luck. Justin hadn't had the amount of time in the water or in water sports that I had. Four years of playing water tag involves a lot of swimming. And four years of water skiing and knee boarding gave me a familiarity with balance that I don't think he ever had. Never the less he was having a great time. We did not stop attempting to become surfers that day until the sun went down and by that point we had both rode several waves. We had all the material necessary for some serious B.S.'ing back at Bartow High. We felt pretty cool.

The next Monday morning before school I met up with Justin and my other usual friends for our twenty minute morning discussions about tenth grade life. It was usually gossip about who was dating who or complaints about the Big Dog Jocks of our class. If you were on the football or baseball team you were the crap and none of my circle of friends at that time were involved in either of those activities. We were mainly just the average kids. We weren't especially great in any particular area, but none of us were considered nerds, not to our faces at least. That Monday, Justin and I met our group of friends with the new confidence that came from our weekend's accomplishment. We told everybody how we had found "Second Light" and spent the day there surfin' it up. I don't know what they all thought about it, if they cared at all, but we thought we were impressing the hell out of them. We were impressed with ourselves. We were going to be known around school as "the surfer dudes".

Justin and I routinely went to back to the beach to surf every few weeks. We tried getting some of our friends to start coming with us. The problem was transportation. None of us had cars except Justin and two people barely fit in his. Once word got around that Justin and I were attempting to be surfers, kids that we never hung out with before started wanting to talk to us. A few of those kids were David Handel, Tommy Bannet, Josh Vancant, and Travis Parmer. David and Tommy were already thought of as the surfer guys. Josh and Travis were skaters. They hung around with an entirely different set than Justin and I. Their circle of friends dabbled in drinking parties. We even heard that some of them were doing drugs. I didn't hold any of that against them but I never felt like that was anything I wanted to do.

Chapter 4: The MGB and Checkers

In April I got my driver's license and that meant, with my parents, that I got a car. That meant I had to get a real job to pay for the gas. My parents paid for the insurance.

I had already received a small bit of experience with what it might be like to have a job. In the ninth grade I had been working for an old couple, The Howells, in Bartow. They lived less than a mile from Bartow Junior High, so I walked to their house after school most days and helped Mr. Howell with his yard work. It was a very simple set of things I usually did: mowing his yard, raking leaves, edging, weeding, planting, and fertilizing. His yard wasn't any bigger than the average Bartow yard, about a half acre, maybe a little more. But he always found things for me to do. Mr. Howell was Bartow High School's Agriculture teacher for years, though he had long since retired when I started working for him and was in his seventies. He and his wife were very nice people. His wife would usually have a Coke and cookies for me when I got there. They paid me $4.00 an hour for all my time I spent with them, even if I was eating their cookies and drinking their Cokes. I usually put in about 10 hours a week. It was a nice first experience for what it was like to work, though I didn't think it would afford me the income I needed once I started driving.

My dad loved to work on old cars, especially old British cars of the 1960's. In particular, he liked the Austin Healey MGB and the Triumph TR6. When I was in the ninth grade he bought an MGB that had a totally blown engine for $500. He spent a year restoring the car, rebuilding the engine, piece by piece, patching rusty fenders and floorboards, and had it re-painted a bright red. He spent a couple thousand on the all the repairs. When he finished, it was a very cool car. It was a two-seater convertible that said, "My driver is one cool cat."

Once I got my driver's license, my dad told me I could have the MGB. He had already restored another one by this time and he was driving it. My self-esteem took a big step up. Showing up at school in that thing was almost as good as showing up to school as one of the Big Dog Jock football players. All my friends wanted a ride in it. I never let any of them even think about driving it. I loved that car. It was the one and only convertible I had ever ridden in. Driving around town with the top down was like nothing else, the wind blowing in your face and the sun shining down on you, it doesn't get a whole lot better than that. A kid shouldn't have a car that nice as their first car. It sets the bar too high and everything else after feels like a disappointment. The only thing it lacked was a radio. I quickly solved that problem by setting up my old radio boom box inside the car behind the seats and running it on batteries. I even played CD's through a portable CD player that I ran through the tape deck. That turned out to be too much complication for a sixteen year old, while driving.

With the car came my first major responsibility. I had to buy the gas. So I looked for a job. I first tried Publix. My grand-dad said they had great benefits and you could work your way up in a big company like that and who knows where you might go. He had done the same thing when he was young. After a few odd jobs he made his way to Bartow and eventually was hired by IMC Phosphate, now Mosaic. He spent his entire career with that one company, working his way from a lowly laborer to one of their chief accountants. All this with NO college, not even a high school diploma. He had to quit school when he was in the ninth grade because his family needed him to work to help put food on the table. And here I was just coasting through life with a car at 16 and my reason for a part time job was because Mom and Dad said they weren't going to pay for the gas. My grand-dad has always impressed me like nobody else.

So I applied at Publix and never heard a thing from them. It was the early nineties. There was a recession and jobs were a little hard to find. I saw an ad in the paper that Checker's, fast food, was hiring. It wasn't Publix, but it was something. That was good enough. I started working at Checker's around the end of April. My first day on the job let me know that I was nobody special, just another tool that had to be trained to flip burgers and sell fries, "don't forget to try and up-sell the cheese and super-sized fries and drinks". The manager there that first night spent about thirty seconds training me how to make a Champ Burger. I won't go into the rocket science that *is* building the Champ Burger, but needless to say, even burger building required more than one thirty second tutorial. After her enlightening instructions, the manager went back to her seat at the back of the kitchen and started back on the phone to her boyfriend (or girlfriend, I was never really sure, but my Gaydar was pretty strong about her. There was a high possibility that she was playing for the wrong team). Meanwhile, I was left to interpret the smooth ebonics of the African American girl to my right who was telling me what to make. Aside from the Champ Burger, there were about a dozen other sandwiches that people ordered, and the African American girl called out to me, that I hadn't been given the first clue of how to make.

Eventually I mastered the art of burger making. Then they "promoted" me to cashier. That meant a huge ten cent an hour pay raise. The money started rolling in baby ($4.25 and hour times 20 hours a week). It wouldn't be long before they would be signing me up for the next episode of MTV *Cribs*).

The extra cash did seem like a lot compared to what I had made working for The Howells. My first financial goal was to save up enough to buy a surfboard. Only then could the status of "surfer dude" be truly bestowed upon me. After that came the clothes. Before I starting buying my own clothes, Mom always had the final say in what I wore because she, of course, was paying for all of it and did not want to go around with her son looking like the surfing hobo that he wanted to be. Now that I was buying them, I could wear what I wanted. Goodwill, the thrift store, was my favorite place to shop. I stocked up on all the old flannels and worn out jeans I could find. This was, after all, the beginning of The Grunge movement. Nirvana and Pearl Jam, on MTV, told me just how I should look. I also started to grow out my hair. The more I could resemble Kurt Cobain, the more the ladies would love me, I thought, and it worked too.

By this time the music I was listening to was changing. The abstract but usually happy sounds of R.E.M., the Talking Heads, and O.M.D., were replaced with the deranged and disturbing (now, just irritating) sounds of Nirvana, Pearl Jam, Stone Temple Pilots, and Sound Garden. I guess I was suffering the full onset of retardation that is being a teenager. I loved the sound of anything labeled "Grunge Rock". The theme songs were all so angry. That's how I still felt inside, angry with Alice for replacing me with some University of Florida douche. The band I started to love most was one that I heard while hanging around with some of the skater kids that Justin and I were starting to see more of, Nine Inch Nails.

The main theme of NIN's music is either "God, why do you hate me?" or "There is no God." I had started to think both of these things before I ever heard NIN, but having it blasted at me over catchy beats and disturbing heavy metal guitars was just the reinforcement I needed. I became a huge NIN fan, though I didn't go around announcing it to anyone because I knew it went against everything my parents and grand parents had ever stood for. My family was religious. NIN was anti-religion, even Satanic at times. I knew not to let my parents catch me listening to NIN. I would be in for a serious lecture if that ever happened, I thought. It was also around this time that my next major disaster unfolded.

Chapter 5: A Wreck!

Remember when I said that I had placed a radio behind the seats of the MGB and I had a tape deck with an adapter for a CD player running from it? Like I said, it was too much complication for a 16 year old driver. I had to reach behind me and turn on the boombox, then press play on the tape deck, then turn on the CD player just to get the first note to play out of the blasted thing. Then there was the task of selecting the proper CD for the occasion and selecting the track that I just had to hear. Well I had successfully been doing all this, while driving a stick shift, since April. It was now June. School was over in two weeks. I was coming home from school one day and decided it was time to rock with the Nine Inch Nails. I was about four miles from the house and about to go around a 90 degree turn. The road from Bartow to the lake was a treacherous set of sharp turns, especially the leg I was driving at that time. I was looking down at the CD player trying to turn it on as I was approaching the turn. The speed limit for that turn is 15 mph. I was doing around 30. This wasn't the first time I had been around that turn at that speed. My dad usually drove around it that fast every morning and afternoon when we went to and came from school. So I usually drove around the corners as fast as I thought I could. Besides, you've got to drive a sports car like a sports car, not like a granny in a Lincoln Towncar.

Well, it just so happened that a band of rain had come across the road beginning at that turn. It wasn't raining at all the whole way home. I had come from Bartow with the top down. I don't even remember seeing a rain cloud. But who am I kidding, I was so interested in the radio at that point that I could have been under a huge cloud and not known it. I looked up from the CD player just in time to see the wet road and that my car was steering off towards the right side of the road. I turned the steering wheel to straighten back up a little and pressed the brakes. When I did the tires lost friction with the road. The car started to slide and rotate counter clockwise. The general direction that the car was moving in was still forward, slightly to the left. The edge of the paving on the road had a little lip that formed a hump that stood about 8 inches high. It made for the perfect launch ramp for an out of control vehicle. The road had almost no shoulder after the turn and the ground dropped about 6 feet to a white sand covered orange grove that was just off to the side of the road. My car hit the lipped edge of the road as it was turned around almost backwards. When it hit, the lip flipped the car upside down in the air and I fell through 6 feet of air and landed about 15 feet from the edge of the road, upside down. Keep in mind the top was down, not that the top up would have saved me from any injury, it probably prevented injury having it down. I remember laying down across the gear shift and reaching across to the passenger seat while the car was upside down. Time seemed to slow down for just a few seconds. Then darkness.

The next thing I knew, I was upside down, with my head pushed into the sandy orange grove soil and all of the few dash lights that MGB had were on. All the lights were red. I remember that I could no longer hear the CD player and those genius Nine Inch Nails. They suddenly didn't seem that important to me anymore. My first thought was, "Am I still alive?" Then I figured I must be and decided I better get the hell out of that car before I suffocated or burned alive. The car had fallen upside down into the soft sand of the orange grove. It had sunk several inches into the sand, far enough down that no light was coming in from any point I could see. The doors on the MGB had windows that rolled down. In front of them were triangular shaped pieces of glass that could be tilted to let a little air vent into the car. They were perfect on a cool morning when you wanted just a little fresh air. However, they were absolutely imperfect for the situation I was in now. The triangular shaped panes were framed by a half-inch of steel. When the car sunk in the sand, and all that weight came crashing down, those steel reinforced glass daggers dug straight into the ground and didn't break. This pinned the doors closed. I was trapped in a small space that wasn't getting any fresh air. It was starting to get hot inside my new tomb as well. I sat there for a minute, upside down, pushing against the doors with my hands and feet. I then remembered that the windows had been rolled down. I started trying to dig a little hole under the top of the door. After a few scoops of digging I saw a little light coming in under the door. "At least I'm not going to suffocate", I thought. I continued digging for what seemed like forever but was probably about thirty to forty-five minutes. After that, the hole was finally big enough that I could slip under the door and escape.

I crawled out from under the car and limped back up onto the road. My thought was, "Well, I survived that, but as soon as I get home, Dad is going to kill me." I really wasn't in a hurry to head into that. I looked down and realized my knees were both bleeding and the blood had run down my knees into my socks. I wasn't hurt bad, just two gashes where the dash and my knees had met on impact. I didn't feel any pain. The adrenaline was in full effect.

I had started walking back to the house when a pick up truck slowed beside me and asked if I was alright. I guess the driver must have noticed me limping and covered with dirt and thought I might be in need of help. I told him what had just happened. He had just driven right by the flipped car and not seen it. The drop in elevation from road to grove did a good job of hiding the wreck. He asked me if I wanted him to drive me to a hospital. I said "No, but I would appreciate it if you could just take me to my parents, they're going to kill me." He said he doubted that my life was in danger and asked where I went to school. I told him and he said his brother was our school's principal, Ernie Cooper, who also happened to live on Lake Buffum. I thought, "What are the chances?, Now, there will be an announcement at school tomorrow about what has happened and all the kids are definitely give me a hard time for this." We got home and Mom and Dad asked where I had been and who's truck was in the driveway. I told them what happened and that I thought the car was totaled. Dad said, "You're kidding me right?" I said "I wish."

My dad immediately called the police and drove back to the wreck. Mr. Cooper's brother went on his way after seeing that I, in fact, was still among the living after delivering the news to my parents of what had just happened. We got back to the wreck and the car had started burning, just a little. Smoke and small flames were coming from the rear of the car. I don't remember how they got put out. I just remember my dad looking at the car, then at me, and said, "It's a miracle that you are still alive." It was. My mom said, "God must have something really important for you to do because only an angel could have saved you from something like that." I have replayed those few seconds, just as the car went off the road and flipped upside-down, hundreds of times in my head. Just inches towards the back or front of the car and my head would have been crushed and buried under the MGB. I don't know how I was not thrown from the car. I guess it was my knees against the underside of the dashboard that kept me in. The MGB didn't have seatbelts.

I remember that my parents and I were all staring at the wrecked car when the State Trooper showed up and started filing a report. He said the same thing that my dad had said, that I was lucky to be alive. Then came the wrecker. That was the worst part of it. I watched as the tow truck driver and his helpers working to flip my car back over. I knew the car was trashed, but hearing the screeching sound of failing steel, as the car was finally turned over, was more horrifying than the wreck itself. Tires snapped off their axle. Fluids ran all over the car. All of those things were worse than the wreck itself because I knew that I was seeing the end of that car's life. That was the end of my racecar driving days. That was when my self-image took its first blow. That was when I first started to defeat myself.

My mom and dad both agreed that I was lucky to be alive, but shortly after the big wreck, I started to wish other things had happened. Word quickly spread about what had happened among my family members. I didn't talk about it at school. I was ashamed that I had destroyed something my dad had worked so hard to create. I felt like crap. Eventually I had to tell my friends what happened because they noticed I wasn't pulling up in the MGB every morning at school. Nobody gave me a hard time. I think they all agreed that it was a pretty bad thing I had done, but I was giving myself a hard enough for it.

My relatives, however, took a different approach. My uncles started calling me "Crash" and gave me a pretty hard time about my careless driving. Some reminded me of how hard my dad had worked on that car and how much he had loved it. They even iterated the first thought I had after the wreck, "I can't believe your dad didn't kill you." and, "I bet he beat your butt good that night, didn't he?" These were not the things that I wanted to have to hear. I'm sure it was all in good fun, but it hurt me. It embarrassed me and I wasn't used to being embarrassed. It was a feeling that would be more common and more severe in a few years.

Chapter 6: A Pact and a Path

The school year ended and summer began. Only, this year I didn't go to Georgia. I had a responsibility to my job at Checkers and I couldn't just leave the state for the summer anymore. I don't remember a whole lot about that summer. My parents' really did not want me driving for a while, but they let me anyway. They let me drive our old Dodge Wagoneer. It was a gas guzzling machine that got about 12 miles to the gallon on the highway and less in town. Justin and I kept making our occasional trips to Cocoa Beach on the weekends. On the drives there and back, we would jam to the radio and talk about the girls we thought were hot and how we might approach them.

Justin had a girl problem of his own. He really liked a girl named Tabitha Allen. She would play him along just enough so that he thought he might have a chance, then she'd date some other guy. Justin was spending money on her, buying her clothes and jewelry. I thought he was crazy for trying to buy a girl's attention. As I have gained a little life experience, I have learned that you pretty much have to do that to an extent. No money, no ladies. That's been my experience anyways.

After several times of Justin being pulled in and pushed away by Tabitha, he started to grow tired and bitter about girls in general. I was starting to feel the same way. I didn't see anybody at school or work that reminded me of Alice. That was all that I wanted, to feel for someone the way I had felt about her. One day, on the way to the beach, Justin said, "You know what we should do? We should just start playing the girls instead of them playing us. I don't need a girlfriend. I just want to have sex with a girl." To hear such a bold, and jerk-like statement from Justin was a little shocking, but not that much.

Justin had come to church for a couple of years with me, but he was not raised in a church going home. His mother and father, in fact, didn't even raise him at all. Justin didn't like to talk about his mom or dad, who were long since divorced and saw little of him. Justin lived with his mother's sister, her husband, and their two daughters. Justin's aunt Sharon and uncle Jerry, his substitute for a mom and dad, were good people. However, they were not church people. I don't know what their religious beliefs were, but they had no interest in going to church. Justin himself only came with me to church for the social aspect. Even though he attended regularly and even went to our summer church camps, which were very inspirational to me at times, I don't think he ever got much out of any of the experiences. I think you have already developed your religious beliefs by the time you are 14 and that's how old Justin was when he started going to First Baptist with Jackson Roberts and I.

So, Justin had made this statement about not caring about girls but wanting to have sex with girls. I thought about it a few minutes and I thought it wasn't such a bad idea. Forget all the hassle of talking and spending time with someone who probably didn't care about you and was eventually going to dump you anyway. Just get straight to the heart of the matter. Even though I had always told myself, and everybody that knew me, I was waiting until I got married before I had sex; this started to sound like a good idea. Besides, we knew several guys at school who were claiming to have had sex with some of the girls. Maybe, we should see what all the fuss was about. And, there *was* that day in the lake with Alice. I had wanted to try some things that day for sure, but we had both grown up in Baptist families. Besides that, my brothers were right there watching. I don't think we would have allowed ourselves to do anything at that time anyways. I was only in the ninth grade. Hormones were already kicking in, but I hadn't developed the full onset of retardation, that is being a teenager, yet. I still felt pretty strong about the idea of abstinence, thanks to it being beat over my head time and time again at church.

But here was my best friend presenting a pretty bold idea. I finally said, "Yeah, screw 'em and leave 'em, that should be our motto." This all sounded great at the time to me. It didn't even cross my mind that we had just crossed the line to becoming full blown assholes. I felt like I sounded pretty tough saying what I had said. I thought it would be like a revenge for Alice leaving me a year earlier. A girl had hurt me and now the girls would pay. I think this shift in my view of girls was the real beginning of a walk into the downward spiral.

Chapter 7: Art, Mormons, and Gwen

Eleventh grade started. Justin and I were no longer the underdogs of Bartow High. There was a new group of tenth graders in our place and I began to feel a little confidence. That year I started Advanced Placement Art. The art teacher I had in tenth grade, Mr. Piekarski, liked my work and had selected me for the class. It was nice because the class counted as college credit if I chose to attend college after high school. I had always loved to draw as a child. My parents always told me I was very "artistic". My dad's oldest brother was a professional artist of sorts. He made his living by painting tour buses and RV's with elaborate murals, all done by airbrush. I even remember hearing, as a kid, that the first Gann's (Mc Gann at the time) to come to America from Ireland were traveling artists. So, the art bug was in our family.

I had been selecting art as an elective every year since seventh grade. It was something I enjoyed because everybody thought I was good at it. Most of my "work", until that A.P. class, was drawings of cars, monsters, and super-heroes, not exactly the work of an art genius. But college credit art required us to actually attempt to create something that had meaning, not reproduce my favorite Star Wars characters. We had to learn new techniques for sketching and painting. The actual amount of college credit I could receive was based on meeting about twenty requirements, each one being a different type of drawing or painting.

The main thing I liked about A.P. art that year was that all the A.P. kids got to sit in one of two small back rooms that were attached to the main art classroom. Each of these rooms had a door that could be closed (and it always was), so that you could feel completely unsupervised for the entire 45 minutes we were in that class. I was the only eleventh grader in the entire A.P. bunch. Everyone else was a senior. I felt pretty cool getting to hang out with kids that were older and far more respected than me, the lowly junior. In the room that I sat in most days were usually two semi-good looking girls, a skate punk kid, and Bob Mc Nedis. Bob and I got to be good friends that year. He was a really funny guy and was always complimenting my "art". His best bud was a guy named David Bingdam.

Dave was a soccer king, the team goalie, who happened to be as nice to me as Bob. Dave somehow found a way to come back and hang out with us in the A.P. backroom several times a week. Seniors at Bartow High like Dave ended up with a lot of free time on there hands because they were mainly taking electives since they had already taken most of the classes required by the state for a high school diploma. I thought Bob and Dave were the coolest seniors I knew. They were both very smart guys, Dave actually got voted "Wittiest" by the kids in his class that year, an honor that got you a special full page photo in the year book and included you in the ranks of "Most Likely to Succeed", "Best Leadership", etc. About the only thing that Bob, Dave and I couldn't agree on was the fact that I was a Baptist and they were both Mormon. They never really pressed the issue, but they did try to invite me to several church events and even gave me a copy of the Mormon Bible with a special note inside about how they hoped it would help me to find true happiness. There was another Mormon I knew who was even more exceptional than Bob and Dave, her name was Gwen Christen, but I'll get to her later. We had a lot of fun in that back room, most of the year, until it came down to the last couple months and Mr. Piekarski realized that we had been spending way too much time goofing off and were going to have trouble completing all the necessary paintings required by the class.

It was during those last couple months that art became a chore and the joy of creating something new turned into a stressful frenzy. I had to come up with about ten paintings in two months. That was a lot to me because I would sometimes spend weeks working on just one. To make matters worse, some of the paintings required had to be done using a technique called Pointillism. That meant that you had to create an image by tapping the head of a marker, pen, or colored pencil against the paper to create tiny dots. The end result was an image formed by the combination of different color dots. The process of creating an image with the Pointillism technique is very monotonous and time consuming. I did manage to complete all the required drawings and received my college credit, 1 credit hour. By the time I finished art that year I thought I had just about lost my desire to ever draw again.

Now, about that other Mormon, Gwen Christen. We were first introduced by my old friend Jackson Roberts and his girlfriend Amy. I think it was his way of trying to make up for what he had done with Alice. Jackson asked if he and Amy could come out to the lake and go skiing with me. At this point, Jackson and I were back on about as good of terms as we ever would be, though I still never really forgave him for what he had done to me. I told Jackson it would be fine if they wanted to come out. He said they wanted to bring one of their new friends, a girl who had just started attending our school and had transferred from Lakeland because her parents didn't like the friends she was hanging around with there. Her friends had all been caught doing drugs at a party and so the new girl's parents freaked out and removed her from the school. That must have been pretty tough for her to switch schools in her junior year. Anyway, that girl was Gwen. Jackson and Amy arrived at my parents' house with Gwen one Saturday. Their plan was to go skiing. Jackson and Amy's other plan was to hook up Gwen and I. It wasn't a bad idea. I have to admit. The first time I saw Gwen I thought, "Wow! She's pretty cute." She wasn't what I'd call the most beautiful girl I'd ever seen. She wasn't a red head. Her name wasn't Alice. No, Gwen was a brunette and she was a little less slim than Alice, not at all fat though.

We went inside and everybody said hello to my mom and dad. Then, we went out to the boat to do a little skiing. Gwen took off her shorts and shirt to reveal her bathing suit. It was a silver one piece that was pretty conservative, more so than what Alice would wear. All the same, I looked at Gwen and thought, "This girl's not cute, she's hot!" We started skiing and everybody took turns. This gave Gwen and I time to talk in the boat as I was pulling Jackson or Amy. I realized right away that she was smarter than me, not that that's saying much (Gwen went on to graduate with the second highest G.P.A. of our senior class). Gwen was very nice and I loved the way she laughed. It wasn't long though, before she brought up the subject of religion and the fact that she was Mormon. She wanted to know what religion I subscribed to. I told her. That pretty much set everything up right there.

Gwen and I ended up going on a couple of other dates. On our first official date, I met her at her house and was introduced to her parents. Her father shook my hand and said that Gwen had said a lot of good things about me. Then he said, "So, Gwen tells me that you're a Baptist." I felt a little nervous and said, "Yes sir." He replied, "Hmmm." He had just said everything I didn't want to hear, even though I knew that our difference in religious beliefs was a big deal.

In our summer church camps I had taken a course about cults. One of the groups that we discussed was The Mormons. We were told that the highest ranking leaders of the Mormon faith were actually Satanic followers who worshipped in secret temples with Satanic images inscribed into the walls, floors, and ceilings. We were also told that they believed that when a husband and wife died, the man could resurrect his dead bride if she had pleased him enough in his past life. Or, if his wife had not pleased him enough, he could simply be given a new one and the two of them together would be given a planet to populate. We were told that the Mormons believed that every faithful Mormon husband and wife would be the new Gods of some far off planet. All these stories about what the Mormons believed seemed really wacky to me. The impression that they made on me left me leery of the Mormon's I met in high school. I never asked Gwen if she believed in the things we were taught at that church camp. The more I got to know her, the less likely I thought it was that she could believe such things.

After that first date, I saw Gwen at school and she told me her parents didn't like the idea of her dating a Baptist. I guess the Mormons must talk trash about us Baptists too. I told her I was sorry but I couldn't see myself becoming a Mormon. She didn't press the issue, but she had put her own little special note in the Mormon Bible that Bob and Dave gave me at the end of eleventh grade. She told me that if I ever wanted to understand the Mormon religion she would love to share her knowledge of it with me and that she thought I was a really great guy.

Gwen and I went on another date but it didn't even feel like a date. We were just two friends hanging out. I don't think either of us expected anything more from the other than a friendship at that point. However, if she would have made a move on me, I would have been all over her. That's not to say I was wanting to have sex with her. She could never have been a "screw 'em and leave 'em" girl. I had too much respect for her at that point to ever want to do something like that. She was just too attractive. Her sense of humor and brains made her all the more beautiful. I could have easily had a similar to relationship to what Alice and I had if she not been a Mormon. She was a rare female. I still wonder where we might have gone if I had just agreed to explore the Mormon faith or have tried to convert her. We were told at church, however, that it was a dangerous path to ever try and date someone who didn't share our religious beliefs because so many complications would arise in the relationship and we might even end up converting to their faith. How horrible!

Chapter 8: A Lack of Faith

Eleventh grade came and went, the summer as well. By this time the routine was school or work. My free time was becoming less and less. I usually got off work on Sunday because I told my boss that I attended church and that was important to me. It was a lie.

See there had been some issues with me and my church. In my efforts to complete the painting requirements of A.P. Art, I had devoted several drawings to the subject of religion. I didn't feel like I was doing anything wrong by drawings pictures that discussed ideas and questions that I had. Then, one day I was working on one of those particular drawings, out at the lake house. I was home from school before anyone else and was all alone in the house. I was working on the dining room table and had my back turned to the front door. Then I heard the door open and assumed it was my parents, only it wasn't. It was my Sunday School teacher of the past couple years, John Johnson, and he just walked right in without knocking. He said, "Hello, Scott. What are you working on over there?" It scared the crap out of me to hear an unexpected voice. I jumped and turned around. There was John Johnson walking over towards me.

A back story on John Johnson: In the ninth grade Jackson Roberts and I had gone over to John's house one weekend to help him with some yard work. Doing chores for people of the church was one of the ways we raised the money to go on our summer church camps. Jackson had told me that he and John had been having private "Bible Studies" at John's house for the past couple months and how much he had been learning from John. John was a single man who had never been married and was in his late forties at this time. I always thought he was a little odd, but friendly enough. He was our Sunday School teacher after all. Still, I thought it was a little strange for Jackson to be spending the afternoons and evenings with this guy.

Anyways, we were raking up leaves in the John's yard when John asked if I liked to lift weights. I told him I had a weight set at home, but got most of my exercise by swimming. He then told me how he and Jackson had been working out together at his house several times a week. He told me if I wanted to come over and work out with them anytime, I was more than welcome. I tried to sound interested but I was thinking, "This seems a little odd." We kept raking the leaves and conversation shifted to other topics. When we finished with our raking, John asked us if we wanted to have a Coke, to which we told him that we were about to thirst to death. He went in the house and came back out with the Cokes and a camera. Then he brought up the weightlifting subject again. He said, "Scott, I think you would really enjoy coming over here and working out with us. I tell you what, why don't you take off your shirt and I'll take some pictures of you. That way you can have a "before" picture of what you looked like when you started lifting weights. I'll take pictures of you and Jackson every couple of months so you guys can see how you're progressing." That did it. I was ready to leave right then. I told him, "No thanks, Mr. Johnson, but if I decide to join you guys I'll let you know." Maybe that day at Mr. Johnson's house was just a case of a really nice, lonely older man who just genuinely liked teenage boys and teaching them about the Lord. But the first thought that went through my mind was, "This guy might be a child molester." For some reason, I didn't tell my parents about all this until a few years later. I think I was afraid they wouldn't believe me and then I'd end up in some conference with my parents, John Johnson, and me trying to explain why I had thought such a terrible thing.

Now, back to the day at the lake: John walked over to me at the table. I asked John what he was doing at my parents' house. My first thought was, "Oh crap, this guys about to try to make a move on me and there is no one here to help me." I was pretty scared. He said, "I just haven't been seeing you at church much lately and I wanted to have a talk with you about that." I was relieved. I told him that I was having to work on Sundays, which really wasn't the case, and that was what had been keeping me. He said I should prioritize and make church more important than work. What I really needed to do was to make church more important than going surfing at the beach. I hardly ever worked on Sundays. Remember?

John got to looking at the drawings that I had on the table. He looked at some of my drawings and said, "What is all this about?" I told him that the drawings were for my A.P. Art class and that we were required to do several drawings that had a common theme. He asked me what my theme was. I said it was religion. "Oh great! So are you going to do pictures of people from the Bible or something like that?" I told him that I wasn't really sure yet. Actually, I *was* sure of what my theme would be, I just wasn't about to get into a conversation about it with him. My theme was not going to be celebration of stories from Bible. It was going to be more like a question about whether or not to believe in all you read and hear at church. The drawing that I was working on in front of me was one of the drawings that dealt with my lack of faith in The Church. John started to look at it. He said, "Scott, what does this drawing mean to you?" The particular drawing that he was referring to was simply about a contrast between good and evil. One side of the drawing was filled with faces of happy people. In the background were religious symbols of various faiths. The other side of the drawing showed people in pain and fear. Behind them were flames and the faint marking of a pentagram. It wasn't a great work of art but I was happy with it because I thought it did have a kind of creepiness to it. John saw the pentagram and that was all he needed. "Scott, what you are drawing here is Satanic!", he said.

I wasn't sure about that. I just felt like I was exploring. I didn't see any harm in asking a question about my faith. "Mr. Johnson, all I'm doing is drawing pictures about questions that I have." He said, "Scott, that's why you need to come back to Sunday School. You can ask any questions you want. But you shouldn't be drawing pictures like these. I don't think it's good for you." He was probably right. At the time though, I just thought I was making an artistic statement. And to have him come in my house, unannounced, and start preaching to me, basically saying my artwork was Satanic; that just pissed me off. After that encounter, I felt further removed from the church bunch and cared less for them. My parents came home shortly after the last conversation Mr. Johnson and I had. He told my parents that he was just checking up on us and hadn't seen us at church lately and wished we would start coming back. He didn't talk about my drawings to my parents. After he left, I told my parents how he had just walked into the house and what he had said about my drawings. They didn't agree with him and were pretty shocked that he had just shown up at the house unannounced. They told me that they thought he was pretty weird and never pressed the issue of me attending church again.

Usually, Justin and I hung out on Sundays and did the surfing thing. We talked about how everything was coming to an end. Our senior year was about to begin and neither of us new what the heck was going to happen next. My parents had never brought up college or anything else to do with the future and I wasn't big on planning ahead unless I was forced to. Living life about a week at a time was all I cared to do. Justin and I had talked real big about how we were going to break girls hearts the year before but neither of us had really done it. He was, in fact, still chasing Tabitha Allen. She was still playing her usual tricks. Justin was working as a bag boy at Publix in Lakeland now and had even more money to blow on her. She gladly accepted everything from him except the idea of really caring about him. We still wanted to find some girls we could play our own tricks on.

Chapter 9: We're Seniors!

Near the end of the summer I got a call from one of my friends, Byron Carol. He said that the Bartow High swim team was going to start having try outs the following week and he wanted to know if I wanted to come check it out.

When I was in eighth grade my parents signed me, and my brother Sam, up with the Bartow Imperial Flyers. It was a private swim team that was run by Coach Sam Griner. He had trained Rowdy Gaines a couple of decades prior and was supposedly a very good swim instructor. I had swim practice three days a week after school at the Bartow Civic Center pool, now known as The Sam Griner Pool. After a few weeks of practice, I told Jackson Roberts about how much fun swim team was and his parents let him join also. We walked to swim practice from school every other day of the school week. We told our friends at school about being on the swim team and some were impressed. I ended up competing in several swim meets and won some races. A couple of years of playing in the lake after school every day had made me into a pretty decent swimmer. I don't ever remember disliking swim team, but after ninth grade I stopped. Jackson had quit before we ever competed in our first meet. He didn't like swimming that much.

So, Byron knew that I had swam with the B.I.F. and had been out to my house on the weekends a few times for skiing and swimming. I liked Byron and thought it sounded like a fun idea, even if it did mean wearing those ridiculous weenie wrappers. Luckily, that first try out required everybody to wear their drags, typical baggy bathing suits. I went to the try out and passed all the tests with no problem. The coach asked me why I hadn't joined the swim team two years earlier. I told him I just never thought about it. The truth was I had seen the yearbook pictures of the swim team with all the guys wearing their Speedo bikinis and thought I'd pass on looking that ridiculous.

Swim team turned out to be the defining event for the beginning of my senior year. I made friends with everyone on the team. They all liked me, partially because the coaches were giving me a lot of props, partially because I was a senior, and also because I was becoming a more confident person in general. I had no problem talking with the girls. They all seemed to have no problem with me talking to them either. My hair was getting longer, almost to the top of my neck all the way around. Being in the sun a lot gave me a pretty serious tan. I was pretty cut, not muscularly bulky though, just lean. I had the look of a surfer. The girls were starting to notice me. A lot of the girls wouldn't even look at me two years earlier, but now things had changed. I had transformed from dork to ladies man in those years since Alice. And I was starting to enjoy the extra attention.

The senior year began. We were now the top dogs on campus. I was starting to become more outgoing and sociable than ever before. Over the last year I had made friends with just about everyone at school. I didn't associate myself with any one particular group, though most people thought of me as one of the art kids. I was in another A.P. art class that year, surprisingly so, seeing as how I had barely survived the last one and thought my drawing days were over. It was the same routine as the previous year with new faces. This year there were two juniors that had been selected for the A.P. class along with about ten of us seniors. I enjoyed the class but didn't let myself fall behind the schedule like I did the year before.

I also had Physics. That was a real education, methods for predicting the forces of the real world. It was the toughest class I had ever taken and it wasn't a requirement. It was one of my electives. The only required course I had was English. Everything else on my plate that last year was an elective. I had completed all other state requirements my junior year. Another nice thing about physics was that it was the class that all the smart kids took, that and Calculus. I stayed away from Calculus because I didn't love math enough to pick it as an elective, although it would have been a big help had I taken it then. Gwen Christen was in Physics with me. She and I sat next to each other. We were still just good friends, nothing more.

Chapter 10: Drafting 101 and a Big Decision

Another class I took during my senior year was Drafting. I didn't know it, but I just stepped into my future when I walked into that class. The teacher was Mr. Harrison. He was a teacher and also a licensed Contractor. He built houses on the side in the summer. I enjoyed drafting because it was a new way that I learned to draw. I had drawn pictures of buildings in years past but never thought much about it. After a few months of Drafting, I began to think a lot about how I might use that skill to make money.

In class, we first learned about Ortho Graphic Projection. That is when you look at an object and you draw it from the perspective of looking at it on one side only, like looking at a cube and drawing only one side of it, a square. We were also introduced to the drafting table and the parallel bar. The parallel bar is the horizontal bar that slides up and down the drafting table, allowing you to draw perfect horizontal lines. We also learned to draw things at different scales. Then we started learning AutoCAD on the computers. AutoCAD is *the* standard software for most architectural or engineering firms. All construction documents are now produced on the computer using AutoCAD. I started to fall in love with drafting, especially on the computer. The computer did all the work of drawing the straight vertical and horizontal lines without having to bother with the troublesome parallel bars, triangles, and T-Squares. It also needed no erasing, just a click and it trimmed lines right to the point you ordered. This was a very cool way to draw, I thought.

Mr. Harrison told us about all the different fields that needed draftsmen: engineers, contractors, and architects. "What exactly is an architect?", I asked. "An architect is like an engineer, only he's more of an artist." I started to think about a distant relative of mine.

As a kid my mom and dad took my brothers and I to Ft. Myers to visit one of her cousins, Gary White. We spent a weekend at their place and I was amazed from the minute we arrived. We pulled up to this enormous house that sat alongside a river and had a yacht floating at the end of a dock. My mom's cousin Gary and his wife Nadine said that they were going to take us to this great seafood restaurant, only we had to get on their yacht to get there. So we loaded up in the boat. Gary and my dad went to the wheel and my mom, my brothers, Nadine, and I all went below deck in to the cabin. It was like a little house inside. There were windows looking out. There was a bed, a kitchen, and a bathroom. It was sweet. We walked back out to the deck of the ship and we could see an island in front of us. It was where we were heading.

We arrived at the seafood restaurant and ate our meal. It was a very cool place. There were live parrots on perches throughout the restaurant, a projection screen TV that was gigantic, and they had music blasting. I thought this was the coolest restaurant I had ever been to. Then we cruised back to their house and spent the night. Their house was a very modern, well furnished, home complete with a swimming pool that over looked the river that had led us to the Gulf and on to the restaurant. The next day we left and went back home. I remember asking my mom what Gary did for a living. She said, "Oh, he's an architect. He makes big money." I remember thinking, "I want to live this kind of life when I grow up."

So there it was. An architect was an artist. I thought of myself as a pretty artistic person. Architects make big money. Maybe that's what I'll do after high school. It seemed like a great idea at the time.

The other factor that helped make that decision was another childhood experience, my parents Georgia house. It was built almost entirely and exclusively by my dad. It was a two story, A-Frame house with two bathrooms, five bedrooms, a kitchen, a family room, and a great room. It totaled to around 2,500 sq. ft. of living space. It wasn't a bad accomplishment for a school teacher who only had two months in the summer and two weeks at Christmas to work on it. Of course, it took about five years to go from empty lot to finished product. Still, my dad proved himself to be a jack-of-all-trades when he built that house. Everyone in the family respected him for it too. That's what I wanted more than anything, the respect of my family.

I thought, "Architects design buildings. That's got to bring some respect. My family would definitely respect a decision to become an architect."

I went to the guidance counselor and asked him about schools that offered architecture programs. He showed me some books and I started writing down information. I looked over the courses I would have to take to receive a degree in architecture. I didn't see anything that looked like too much for me to handle. I read about what it was like to be an architect. I started to picture myself with drawings of a building I had created and instructing people around me on a construction site, orchestrating the creation of a massive piece of artwork that I had brought into the world. I was developing a plan for the future.

I told my parents about my plan to try and go to college to become an architect. They seemed impressed but told me that they couldn't afford to send me to a university. They said that if I wanted to go to college, they would help me pay for community college. Also, they wanted me to live at home instead of being off on my own at some university. They suggested I take some classes at Polk Community College.

Then, one weekend, they said they would take me to Savannah, Georgia to see an art school that was there if I was interested. I said it sounded like fun to me, so we went. We walked around the campus and met with a tour guide who told us about the programs they offered there. One of the programs was Computer Animation. She said with that degree you could go into the movie industry and create special effects for movies. I was interested. She showed us around the building that had all the hardware they used to train the Computer Animation students. We saw some the student's work. It was impressive. Computer Animation hadn't yet come along into the mainstream of movies and commercials like it is now. But the work those kids were producing was state of the art. They also had an architecture program at Savannah but we never got around to discussing that program. My parents asked the question that broke the deal before we ever learned anything about architecture.

The bottom line. Mom and Dad asked the lady what the tuition was for Savannah College of Art and Design. She said, "Oh it's about $30,000 annually including room and meal plans, but you have to keep in mind that all of our students are guaranteed job placement after graduation". That was the end of the discussion about SCAD. I don't know what ever possessed them to look at that school in the first place.

So after that ambitious effort to attend something other than community college, the college discussion quieted down. I wasn't eligible for any type of financial aid because my parents made too much money and I was still a dependant. Scholarships for architecture were slim pickings at best. I think my guidance counselor found three that he thought I should apply for. I applied and didn't get the first one. Community college here I come!

Chapter 11: Swimming and Senior Drama

It was now November and swim team was nearing an end. We had a lot of good times. Everybody on the team was now a good friend of mine. We were all close that entire year. One girl in particular, was wanting me to be more than her friend. Her name was Katherine Dunal. She was a pretty good swimmer and not bad looking. I just never felt attracted to her. It was odd, because we had a lot in common. We met when I was in the ninth grade and she was in the eighth. She was one of the people that stood around with my friends before school every morning. She had even dated Jackson Roberts when we were in the ninth grade. We liked a lot of the same music. There was just something about her that I couldn't put my finger on. I never felt attracted to her. I thought she was nice but I just thought of her as a friend.

One day, on a bus ride back from a swim meet, we were sitting beside each other and talking when she leaned her head on to my chest and just sat there with her eyes closed. I didn't do anything. I just sat there. I felt like a jerk because she was obviously trying to get me to hold her or something and I didn't want any part of it. She eventually sat back up and started looking out the window. I saw tears start coming out of her eyes but pretended not to see them. I just sat there in the quiet and felt the awkwardness of the moment. I also felt sorry for her. I thought about Alice and the way that she had rejected me. I empathized for Katy, but there was nothing more I could do. I didn't want her to be my girlfriend.

We eventually ended the regular swim meets and moved on to the County Finals. Winners of that competition would go on to compete at the State Finals. My events were the 500 Freestyle, the 400 Medley Relay, and the 100 Breaststroke. I lost both the 500 Free and the 100 Breaststroke, but we collectively killed it on the 400 Medley Relay. We got a shot at the State Finals. The girls won their relay as well. Other people placed high enough for other State Final events. About half the team ended up at the State Finals. We were psyched! All the fun we had didn't have to come to an end for a couple more weeks because now it was time to begin preparing for the State Finals in Orlando. I remember almost crying that day because I was just that happy about it.

Another girl crisis developed at the County Meet. This time it was a very good looking brunette from Winter Haven. I don't remember her name, but I thought she was hot. She was asking me all kinds of questions about myself. She was very interested in me. We were talking for probably thirty minutes when up walks Byron Carol. He introduced her as his date for the Homecoming dance that year. She admitted to it but still kept talking to me, almost ignoring Byron completely. I felt bad for Brian. I thought I had better cut the conversation off before Byron got pissed, if it wasn't already too late. So I did. After that day, Byron and I were very good friends. At Homecoming that year Byron came up to me and thanked me for not pursuing his girl. He said I could have taken her if I tried, but he was glad that I didn't because he really liked her. He told me that he really respected me for what I did.

I went to Homecoming without a date, just Justin. I left with a girl named Sue Ellen Meeds. She was a pretty sophomore that used to go to Main Street Baptist when I was a kid. Her parents knew my parents. Her grandparent knew my grand parents. I had gone to pre-school with her brother, Ryan. There was a lot of family history there. At the dance she came up to me and asked me if I would dance with her. I said, "Sure". We ended up dancing to all the slow songs that night and talked at times in between. I ended up taking her on one date afterwards. After that date I heard from her friends that she thought I was too much of a goody-two-shoes. She thought I had the looks of someone who might want to do things with her that I didn't do. I didn't dare touch her on our date because when I picked her up, her dad met me at the door and said, "Scott, remember, I know your parents and your grand parents. Don't do anything with Sue Ellen that would make me have to get your dad to beat you!" I laughed nervously and said I'd be sure not to.

With the swim team, we went on to the State Finals and had a great time. We spent a weekend in Orlando with everything paid for by the school except food. The night before the big meet, the swim team girls came over to the guy's room and said they wanted to shave our legs. I thought that sounded pretty freaky. Not the fact that I would shave my legs, that wasn't uncommon with swimmers because it gives you a little less drag in the water. The idea of six guys and seven or eight girls standing around in their underwear together, that sounded a little gay to me. I didn't want to see Byron Carol, or any of the other guys spreading their legs for one of the girls to shave their hair. The girls said they should do it because we didn't know how to shave our legs and would end up with cuts all over ourselves. I thought, "Yeah, you just want to see what color my underwear is and maybe get a little freak on. Just say it." If it had been just me, that might have been a teenage boy's dream come true, but I was not down with the idea of standing around with those other guys. And besides, imagine the crap that would start back at school when everybody heard what we had done. And if the coaches caught us, they'd probably ship us right back to Bartow without ever stepping foot into the State Finals. Fortunately, all of us guys were thinking alike. We all told them that we would pass. If anybody was going to shave their legs they could handle it themselves. The girls still said they wanted to watch. I know this is stereotype reversal, but it's the truth. We told them we didn't want to take a chance on the coaches catching us doing weird stuff and asked them to drop it. That conversation ended.

The next day we had our competition and my medley team ended up placing 13th in the state among all the competing counties, not bad, not great. We weren't discouraged. We knew this was our last hoorah. It was the getting there that was so much fun. And then you had the bragging rights that you had been to State. That was enough for me.

At the sports awards ceremony at the end of the season that year I ended up receiving a trophy for "Most Improved Swimmer" and my coach introduced me as "The guy who should have been doing this for three years now, Scott Gann." I got to stand up in front of all the jocks and for once feel like I was one of them. I was pretty happy with myself.

Just after swim season, I was getting off work one day when a car load of the Bartow High cheerleaders pulled up. One of the girls, Angie Wang, said, "Hey Scott! I know somebody who has a major crush on you. I asked who and she said, "Amber Camball! She thinks you're hot!"

I thought, "Maybe I should see where this leads." So the next day at school I saw Amber at lunch with her friends. She was a cheerleader and was a year younger than me. She was a pretty, sandy blonde haired girl with fair skin. She usually hung out with the smart kids of her class. The only problem with that was that everybody knew that all the smart kids of the junior class were also potheads. Amber was no exception. I didn't hold that against her though. I just didn't think I would ever get involved with her bad habits.

I walked up and started talking to her. It was a little awkward at first because I didn't ever associate with any of her crowd before, but they were all nice and conversations developed quickly thereafter. I remember thinking, "I bet this girl would end up having sex with me if I tried."

Shortly after meeting, we went on a date to Ybor City one night. On the drive over there we talked about what our lives were like. She was friends with some of the pothead kids in my class too. I was friends with just about everybody, so we had mutual friends. I remember her telling me that she and her friends liked to drive around town at night and pee in people's yards. I thought that was pretty weird, but hilarious. I also pictured her with her pants down. I thought that this would probably be the girl I would score with.

We listened to NIN most of the way to Ybor City. Amber said, "You seem like such a nice guy. I can't believe you listen to this kind of music." I told her I just liked the way it sounded, not the messages it conveyed. That wasn't all true. We walked around Ybor City and talked. I ended up asking her out on the way back home and she seemed ecstatic. I wasn't even nervous when I popped the question. I thought I had this one in the bag the minute I walked up and said hello to her at lunch that day. When we got back to her house we got out of the car and kissed for probably thirty minutes before we said good night. I never did anything more than hold her around her waist although we were pressed together pretty tight most of the time.

We dated for only a couple weeks. She never tried to push me into smoking pot with her. We had already had a talk about it and I let her know that I didn't want impure substances in my body. I didn't drink, smoke, or do drugs; just like I had been taught since elementary school. Her friends started to tell her that they didn't think I was so cool after all. Eventually, she told me she thought we would be better as friends. She said, "Scott, you are just too pure and perfect for me. I'll corrupt you and make you do things you might regret. I don't want to do that to you. You deserve somebody better."

I couldn't believe she had come to that conclusion. If she knew what I wanted to do with her, it would have changed her mind. I felt a little humiliated, but not really sad. She was really being honest and doing me a favor. I couldn't see myself with her five years from then. I wasn't sure if she'd even live that long with the habits she had. I did think she was a really cool person though, and we remained friends throughout the year. One day near the end of my senior year, she asked me to come into the backroom in the art class with her. It was just Amber and I. She started to cry. She told me that she was really going to miss me and that I was the best guy she had ever dated. She said she wished we hadn't broken up. The problem was, I had already met someone else. She knew that. She wasn't asking me to do anything about that. She did ask me if she could kiss me. I put my arms around her and we kissed for several minutes.

Chapter 12: Sara

At work, things were pretty much routine. I showed up after school and left by 10:00 pm each day. I was working most weekends, usually closing the store, which meant not getting out of there until 1:00 am on Fridays and Saturdays, and 12:00 am on Sundays. I usually got in about thirty hours a week. I was making $4.75 by my senior year in high school. The pay raises at Checkers were usually no more than ten cent an hour and happened a couple times a year. Working at Checkers was not a get rich quick, or ever, scheme.

I had made a few friends at work. I was liked by just about everybody, though I really didn't care for most of them. Most of the people that worked there were high school drop outs or kids that I didn't think much of at school. We even hired prisoners from the prisons-to-work program. Checkers received special funding for letting them work with us. Most of the prison guys seemed like pretty decent people until you heard about their past life. One guy was a drug runner who had been turned in by his girlfriend who received a lighter sentenced for ratting on him. He told me about all the money he used to make and the Corvette that he had given to a friend so that the police wouldn't seize it. When he finally was released from prison, he pulled up one day in a shiny yellow Corvette with a pretty young girl in the passenger seat.

Sometime in January or February of that year a new girl started to work at Checkers. She had blonde hair and her skin was a little more fair than mine. She was also a cheerleader at Bartow High and was a junior. She was pretty but she didn't stand out, to me. She was friends with a lot of the First Baptist crowd. That didn't have much weight with me though, I had hardly stepped foot in that place all year. I didn't associate with most of those people anymore. I thought of myself as different, even smarter, than they all were.

The new girl seemed nice enough though. I knew of her but didn't know her. I remembered that she had dated this guy, Jeff Brown, for years. They were now split and had been for some time. But that was the way they were, on again off again. They had a weird relationship.

Also, the new girl was good friends with a girl that I thought was the most obnoxious girl at church. The new girl's friend loved to hug everybody in the youth group as many times as they would allow. Every freakin' time we got together for Sunday school or Wednesday night youth meetings, this girl would make sure to come up and hug me. She also had the most horrible laugh and laughed at everything. So, the new girl didn't seem very promising in the way of potential girlfriend. I couldn't have been more wrong.

It turned out that the new girl's name was Sara Croan. It was soon brought to my attention, by one of my genius co-workers, in front of Sara, that she thought I was cute. I told her that I thought she was cute as well. Her pale skin turned pink. We laughed and I thought, "Maybe this girl isn't so bad after all. She has a beautiful smile." After that Sara and I were friends. We flirted back and forth at work that entire week. Finally, it was Friday. The weekend was about to start and I had Saturday off. Justin and I were going to do the usual beach routine. I thought about asking Sara if she wanted to come along.

I asked her that Friday night if she wanted to go to the beach with Justin and I. Sara could not have seemed more excited about my offer. However, I just made it seem like we were going to the beach as a couple of friends, not really a date. I really wasn't all that interested in her at that time. But I never turned down an opportunity to see a pretty girl in a bathing suit and this one seemed pretty interested in me. I remember thinking, "Well, she hangs out with a pretty obnoxious crowd, but who knows, maybe she's not so bad after all."

Saturday morning Justin, Sara, and I all met at the Bartow Civic Center. I agreed to drive. I had been given a 1986 Honda Civic by my parents a while back and that was now our usual mode of transportation for the beach trips. We piled in my car, Justin sat in the front passenger seat. Sara sat in the back seat. She barely had any room at all because we had my surfboard running down the middle of the inside of the car. I was a jerk to her from day one. Sara didn't seem to care about the seating arrangement. She got the idea that she wasn't pulling rank over Justin at that time. She was just invited to tag along while the two of us did our thing at the beach.

Once we got there, Justin and I paddled out on our boards and left Sara on the shore to lay out in the sun. I didn't stand around and watch her in her bathing suit. There wasn't any special spark that had developed on the ride over to the beach. So, Justin and I spent most of the day with just the two of us riding the waves, occasionally coming to shore to check on Sara and ask her if she wanted to try surfing. Finally, she said she wanted me to show her how to surf.

I gave her my board and we walked out into the water and I started telling her to just try to ride a wave while lying down on the board. I remember being behind her and thinking, "This girl's got the nicest legs and butt I've ever seen!" Her stomach was nice and flat too. She looked good in a bathing suit. Then we got to the part where she was supposed to lay down on the surfboard and try to paddle out a little ways. I held the board as she laid down. She had her butt pointed right at me and was about chest high on me. It wasn't hard to imagine her without that bathing suit on. I started to lust her.

Sara ended up riding a few waves while lying down on the surfboard. She seemed to be having a great time, in spite of the fact that I hadn't really spent that much time with her. The more time I did spend with her the more I started to like her. However, she still had not earned the right to ride shotgun on the trip back. Justin claimed his spot and I didn't even say a word about it, though I did feel a little guilty.

We dropped Justin off at the Civic Center and Sara asked me if I wanted to come over to her house for a little while before going home. I agreed to and followed her home.

We arrived at a small duplex apartment, in Bartow, that was Sara's home. It was dark, but you could see from the streetlight that this was not a very nice place. I immediately felt sorry for her. Sara said she didn't know if her mom was home or not because her mother had been out on a date with a guy that night. She said her mom was twice divorced and enjoyed having a new boyfriend every few months. She said that her mom, step-sister, step-brother, and Sara all lived in this tiny little duplex that we had pulled up to. I really started to feel bad for her. My parents had provided me with so much: stability, a nice home, and love. This girl didn't even have a real family. She barely had a place she could call a home. The duplex was just off of highway 60 on the east side of town. You could always hear the cars and trucks whizzing up and down the road from her house. It was sad excuse for a home.

We walked up to the front door. All the lights were off inside. Sara pulled out her house key to unlock the door. Then we heard a woman screaming inside. Only, I had never heard a woman scream like this before. Sara knew immediately what the noise was about. She grabbed my arm and pulled me away from the door. Then it registered what I had just heard. Sara walked out to the street and started crying. I walked out to her and put my arm around her. "I can't believe she is in there right now doing that. What are the chances?" We had almost walked in on her mom and her new boyfriend having sex. That was a great first impression. I didn't even know what the lady looked like, but I knew how she sounded when she was getting it on. I remember thinking to myself, "Well, if this girl's mom likes to have sex with lots of guys, she might not be too opposed to the idea of having sex herself." That was about the time I took the next step down the spiral.

Sara was crying and was saying how I probably would never want to see her again now. I told her that wasn't true. She sat there and just cut herself down over and over again and started telling me all the things that had happened that led up to her "family" living in that duplex. Not long ago, she and her mom, "Alyssa" (short for Alice, of course) Gwain, lived with Sara's step dad, Ron Gwain, in Lakeland. They had a nice home with three bedrooms and two bathrooms. Ron was a contractor who mainly did aluminum siding and screen porch enclosures. He had his own business. Then it failed. Sara wasn't sure what had happened, but that's when her mom decided she had had enough of Mr. Gwain. Sara said her mom had also cheated on Ron several times with different men that she had worked for. Sara's mom never held down a job for more than a year, or so, at a time. Then it was onto the next one. She usually worked in a dentist office as an oral hygienist or she cleaned people's houses. Sara said that she had caught her mom with a guy one time when she was still married to Ron. Alyssa told Sara that if she told Ron what she had seen her mother doing, they would end up getting a divorce and it would be Sara's fault. Sara didn't want that hanging over her head, did she? She was about 14 when that happened. Sara never told Ron. She just quietly hated her mother.

I told her I felt so sorry for her and that I thought she was different from her mother. That was Sara's greatest fear, that she would become her mother as she got older. I told Sara what my life was like and that I really loved and respected my parents. She said she wished she had my family instead of her own. I knew she meant it. I felt so bad for her. I thought that for someone to wish that they had a different family, they must have had a really bad childhood. I was just beginning to learn about the terrible home that Sara had grown up in. I had only known Sara for a couple weeks and had already experienced more drama in that one night than I had in my entire life.

Sara thanked me for listening to her and staying around after such a strange beginning to the night. It was now after midnight. I was starting to get tired and all the emotions I had felt while listening to Sara's story were now wearing me out. Then Sara told me that she really liked me and wanted to know if I would see her again. I said I would love to. Then I asked her to be my girlfriend. It was the most sudden move I had ever made on a girl. I hadn't been planning to ask her out when we pulled up in her driveway that night. And now I had just popped the question. I almost felt like I owed it to her after hearing all that she had to live with. I thought, "I need to help this girl. She's such a great person and she's got it so bad. I've got it so good. I've got to see where this goes."

She started crying again and said she would love to be my girlfriend. She said she thought I was the hottest guy at school and couldn't believe it when I asked her to go to the beach with me. I felt like a jerk. I had no idea that this girl was this excited about me. I hadn't really felt much of anything about her until now. The problem was that I hadn't started to feel so much love for her as I felt pity for her. I did find her attractive and she had made me laugh a few times that day, but the main thing I thought about as I drove home that night was just how awful her life sounded. I hoped I could be something good for her. The road to hell is paved with good intentions. Isn't that somewhere in the Bible?

Sara and I kissed before I went back home and I wasn't the least bit nervous as we were doing so. I felt very comfortable around her. When someone tells you, "You're the hottest guy at school", it has a way of creating a small sense of superiority that brought about my high level of confidence around her.

We started talking to each other on the phone when we weren't at school or work. She usually called me before I ever had the chance to call her. We would talk for hours on the phone sometimes and my parents would eventually come in and cut me off. The conversations were usually about Sara's life and how she wished she could leave it all behind. She wanted to graduate high school and move out as quickly as she could. She hated her home.

Her days after school usually involved picking up her step brother, Tyler, and step sister, Brittany, from school and then taking care of them until whenever her mother happened to show up that night. If that meant cooking supper and putting them to bed, so be it. That was not unusual. Her mother expected Sara to be the mother of Tyler and Brittany. Sara would take Tyler and Brittany to her step dad's if she had to work that night.

I came over to Sara's house one day after school and she asked me if I wanted something to eat. I said, "What have you got?". She said, "Do you like Ramen Noodles?". Then she opened the pantry where they kept their food. About ten packs of Ramen Noodles and a box of popcorn was all that was in there. In the refrigerator was a case of Cokes and a bottle of Crown Royal hard liquor. Sara and her siblings were going to be having Ramen Noodles and Coke for their supper that night. She said that was what they had pretty often unless Sara went out and bought them some McDonald's hamburgers or something like that. "How can you survive off stuff like this?", I asked. Sara said that she would go and buy vegetables and fruit when she had the money but that wasn't very often. She said her mom only ate popcorn and drank Crown Royal and Coke every night. That was her mom's supper. She would eat the popcorn and drink the Crown Royal until she was drunk enough to go to sleep. Then the next day she'd do it all over again.

Sara and I had dated about a month before we had our first disagreement. We were both working at Checkers on either a Friday or Saturday night and we both had to close the store. Closing meant you had to put away all the food, clean all the containers that had held the food, clean the grill and fryer, scrub the floor, and restock for the next day. We usually were hurrying through all these tasks because we wanted to get the heck out of there as quickly as we could, usually around 1:00 am. That particular night I was filling up the condiment bottles that we used to squirt the ketchup, and mustard on the burgers with. Sara said something like, "Geez, Scott hurry up! You're taking forever with those ketchup bottles while I'm doing everything else. I swear you haven't done anything to help out tonight!" In fact, I had already hosed down and scrubbed the floor, cleaned the grill and fryer, and washed a sink load of the dishes. I was immediately furious after her comment. "What the hell are you talking about? I'm busting my butt here! What exactly have you been doing? I can't see that you've done anything aside from talking with your buddy over there?" She fired back some comment and I retorted. It was a very stupid argument, but aren't they always.

We argued back and forth to the point that Sara got so mad that she started crying and then I felt terrible. "I was just kidding when I said the thing about the ketchup bottles. It was a joke. But you really are mad at me and I don't know why." she said.

We weren't the only ones that were closing down the store that night. There was another worker and a manager who heard everything. It was really embarrassing. I wasn't the type of person who believed in having a fight with his girlfriend in front of other people. I thought it was best to always put on your happy face in front of others and save the conflicts for private moments. But here I was making an ass out of myself in front of two people I would have to see many more times in my future. It made me even more angry with Sara.

My parents had always made sure that their disagreements took place in their bedroom when they thought my brothers and I were sleeping. Sometimes we would hear them arguing at night, but it was still nice of them to spare us the drama of watching most of their disputes.

So, here we were having our first bit of turmoil over a stupid comment that had supposedly started out as a joke in Sara's mind. I was still pissed that a way of joking to her was to insult me in front of my manager and co-worker, but I apologized for not seeing that she had just been kidding around. This all took about thirty minutes from first comment to apology, so it wasn't that big a deal, but it was the first time that I had ever argued with a girl that I was dating. It was the first time I had ever felt anger towards a girl I was dating. I didn't like it. On my ride back home I thought about calling the whole thing off. I had apologized but was still pretty aggravated with her. I didn't want a girl around me who could set me off at any given moment.

After that night, things cleared up and Sara and I quickly got back on track. People at work talked about Sara and I fighting and that made me mad at them. Then one day in art class, a girl came up to me and said, "So I hear you're dating Sara Connors. What's up with that?" I looked at her for a second and then said, "What do you mean, 'What's up with that'? Do you have a problem with it?" She said, "Well it's just that she's a total drama queen. Don't you know about her and Jeff? You could do a lot better." I said, "Well, I know she and Jeff had a lot of fights, but wasn't he always cheating on her with other girls?" She said, "Yeah, I think he was, but I don't blame him. I can't stand Sara." I said, "Sorry to offend you, but she's pretty cool to me." And with that I walked off from her and felt kind of bad for Sara that someone would go so far as to say they couldn't stand her. And just who did this girl think she was to tell me who I should and shouldn't be dating. I didn't think anything else of it. But it did make me wonder just how many other people were thinking what she had just said. I didn't know what to do about that. I decided it didn't matter what other kids thought. I wasn't trying to impress anybody by dating Sara. I liked her, that's why we were together, right?

Chapter 13: Best All Around? The End of an Era

The school year sailed on and eventually we got to the part of the year where somebody had to design the senior class t-shirt. We had a little competition in A.P. Art to see who could come up with the best idea for the shirt design. I drew a nerdish yellow jacket type figure (the yellow jacket was our school mascot) wearing his shorts jacked up above his navel, his shirt tucked in, and a big goofy grin on his face. Above him I wrote, "The Top Ten Ways To Be Mr.Cooper's Favorite Yellow Jacket"

Mr. Cooper was our school's principal. That year he had started a dress code policy. The new dress code said we had to tuck in our shirts, had to wear a belt with our pants and shorts, no sandals, no hats, no sunglasses, and no clothing that advertised rock or rap music. That was my whole image! It got stripped away because Mr. Cooper felt that all these things made the students look and act poorly. He said they were distractions that reduced the learning environment that he thought school should create. I thought he was just making us all look like dorks. I guess my opposition to the dress code was just more of that teenage retardation thing going on.

So my idea for the senior class shirt was to express my contempt for Mr. Cooper's new dress code. It was all in fun. I listed ten things that the picture of the dorky yellow jacket demonstrated. "Shirt tucked in at all times", and, "Hairstyle does not disrupt the learning process and is not a distraction", and, "Look happy for people visiting our school", etc. The yellow jacket had a little speech bubble coming from his mouth that said, "Look mom! I'm adhering to the dress code!"

On the back of the shirt was the same yellow jacket. Only now he was wearing a Smashing Pumpkins t-shirt, ripped shorts, sunglasses, and had wild hair. Above him it said, the "The belt stops here!". I thought it was pretty funny.

The class got together and we showed off our designs for the shirt. Everybody loved mine and it was selected to be the senior class shirt for that year. I was pretty proud. I thought, "If nothing else, these guys will remember me for the shirt I designed." I ended up getting a lot of compliments from people at school after the shirts came out. Almost everybody bought one. I saw people around town wearing my shirt for several years after we graduated.

I remember my art teacher, Mr. Piekarski asking me about my plans after high school. He said I should seriously think about attending an art school and at least becoming a graphic artist. I told him I didn't think that art school was for me. I told him about my uncle Stan. He had gone to art school and become a graphic artist. He even tried working for Disney. He said they made art into nothing more than a production. Everything was about how fast can you produce a required amount of drawings. He said he was always under the gun and he hated it. He left and became a freelance artist that painted tour buses for a living. He barely got by. His life, to me, looked like a struggle to pay the bills, with little time for leisure. He never made enough to even buy a home. He always rented some dumpy apartment that he was too ashamed of to ever let anyone in my family see. I didn't want to live my life like that. I thought I had found a way to do something I loved, but still make a decent living, and earn the respect of my family. I told Mr. Pie about my plans to go to school and become an architect. "An architect!", he said. "Why would you try doing something like that? That requires a lot of math and science. It's not really art at all. All you do is draw lines that tell people how to build a building. I don't think you would enjoy doing that all day." I was a little discouraged that he felt that way. My family, however, was more important to me than he was and they all seemed to think I had a pretty good plan. My grand parents even told me that as long as I went to school for architecture, they would help me pay for college whenever I needed them to. This made my resolve to stick to my plan even stronger. Now, I had a way to go to school that didn't require me to stress about how I would be able to afford it. I had my grand parents to fall back on if I couldn't pay the bills. No worries.

At work everything was just routine. I spent most of my time flipping burgers on the grill because I hated being a cashier. I didn't like having to ask people "Would you like fries with that? Would you like to Super-Size that? Would you like to add cheese for only 15 cents?" and hear them say, "No, if I wanted that I would have said it, now give me my order!" The managers always made the cashiers say these kinds of things to boost sales and I hated it.

Sara and I were fine at work for the most part but I started thinking we might be better if I worked at a different place than she did. A friend of mine, Mohammed Rathid, told me one day that Food Lion, a local grocery store, was hiring and he could get me a job there if I wanted. I told him I'd stop by that day after school and apply. They hired me and told me they would pay me $5.00 an hour. They told me I could start as a bag boy and they would train me to be a cashier. I was thrilled on several levels. I would be making more money. I wouldn't have to come home from work with grease all over my clothes and smelling like the French fries that now made me lose my appetite. Also, I would be away from Sara while I was at work. I thought this would make my life a little less stressful. It did.

A few weeks after the shirt thing had gone over, we were in English class one day and the teacher said it was time to vote for the class superlatives. These were the people who would be chosen to be "Most Athletic", "Most Artistic", "Most Likely to Succeed", etc. The nominees were decided by votes from the entire senior class. The teacher read through the list of titles and people called out student's names that they thought fit the bill. She would record the student's names that had been called out and then we would vote for our favorite. We ran down the list: "Most Likely to Succeed", she said. Someone said "Joey Siler!". A lot of people agreed and she started counting votes. She did this for all the other titles and finally came to "Best All Around". My friend Byron Carol was sitting beside me and raised his hand and said, "Scott Gann!" "Brian, what the crap are you doing!", I said. "You are.", he said. I felt like a jerk because I hadn't thought about calling out his name. I liked

Byron a lot but I hadn't thought about saying his name. Then I said, "Byron Carol!". The teacher recorded his name down as well. We took a class vote and I came out ahead of Brian. The next step was to count up all the names and votes from all the other classes. The names of the people with the top four highest scores for each title were then typed up on a ballot that was sent out to every student in the senior class. I thought it had been a really nice gesture of Byron to mention my name but that would be about the end of it. "Best All Around" usually went to the most popular jock and I figured that was just the way it always happened.

Then I was asked to meet with a photographer to have my picture taken for the yearbook. They had also asked three others to have their picture taken. The "Best All Around" category always went to both a guy and girl. So there were two of us who were having our picture taken for nothing. The girl they asked me to stand with was Brooke Hemler. She was the hilarious, and attractive, daughter of a preacher that I had been friends with since junior high. I knew Brooke was liked by everybody but I looked over at the other two who were standing there beside us. It was two other very popular students at school. The guy was a football player, who was also a very nice guy, and of course, liked by everybody. The girl was one of the really smart girls of our class and she also had a great personality. I thought, "Yep, its going to be those two for sure. Brooke and I may be liked but I don't think we're going to win any popularity contests over those two."

Then the yearbooks came out. My friends who had already received their yearbooks started coming up to me and saying, "So, Scott Gann, Mr. Best All Around! How the hell did that happen?" "What are you talking about?", I said. "You got picked as Best All Around. How the hell did that happen?", one of my friends said. "I don't know.", I said. Then I got my copy of the yearbook and saw my picture with Brooke. I couldn't believe it. I thought I had friends at school, but I didn't think enough people really liked me so much as to give me an honor like that. I was totally shocked. Brooke came running up to me after school that day and said, "They picked us! I thought they would when I realized I was going to be standing with you!" I said, "Really? I thought it would be Tavares and Neca. Everybody likes them." Sara came up to me and started going on about how proud she was that she was dating me and that she knew I would win. "I told you, you're the hottest guy in school!", she said. I had an incredible sense of pride for the rest of that year. I felt like I was on my way to big things. I thought if this was what I had accomplished in high school, there was no telling what I might have coming my way in the future. I thought, "I guess I must have a pretty good personality". I now thought of myself as a "people person". I probably shouldn't have had that experience. It set the bar too high for the future. My expectations of how I thought I should be treated by other people had grown too high. Every new group of people I found myself in after high school would seem less accepting of me than this one. I now felt that I had to be "the life of the party" in whatever new group I was in, or something was wrong with me, I must have lost my touch. This new pressure I put on myself would end up causing me a lot of disappointment in the future. It would end with me feeling like a complete failure. It would help send me further down the spiral.

The rest of the senior year was just one big party for me. I loved everything about school. I felt I was surrounded with people who really liked me. I went out of my way to ask people how they were doing and tried to live up to the title I had been given. Everybody seemed to care about me too, even groups like "the jocks" and "the cheerleaders", groups that for the most part hadn't looked my way through most of high school. The most popular and beautiful girls of my class would now greet me in the halls and ask how I was doing. Those last several months of my senior year. I felt like the most popular guy on campus. It was the high point of my entire school life. It was really one of the best times I have ever known.

The year ended and we had a tradition at Bartow High that the seniors spent the night at the Bartow Civic Center on the night of graduation. This was mainly because so many seniors in years past had gone out, after graduation, to parties and got drunk and ended up in car accidents and worse. They wanted to try to keep us in a controlled environment, without alcohol, for our own safety. This was also a last chance to be together as a class and reminisce about our years together and talk about what the future held. That's just what my friends and I did. We mainly all talked about where we were heading next. Justin wanted to go to a University and study politics. Jackson wanted to get a degree in music and become a music director at a church. Other people had other dreams. Some talked about joining the military. Most talked about college. Few ever attended. Leaving all those people the next morning, all of us going our separate ways into an uncertain future, was a very sad experience. I knew that would be the last time I would ever see most of them again.

Chapter 14: The Downward Spiral

As the senior year ended, Sara and I were still together. She genuinely seemed to love me and I really liked her. I wouldn't say I was in love with her, I liked her, but she hadn't made me feel the way I had with Alice. Like I said, the bar had been raised too high with Alice. It made my later relationships seem a little less powerful. Sara and I had occasional arguments, but they were always over petty things and never big enough for us to want to split up.

That summer Sara and I started down our path into the spiral together. The end result of our actions would seem like a miracle to her, for a time. For me it would be like a gun pointed at my head, knowing it's going to go off, just not knowing when. We began down the road to Hell without the slightest idea of where we were heading. When we first began traveling down that path, we thought we were having the greatest time of our life, in fact.

Now that school was out, I was a usual closer at Food Lion. That meant not leaving the store until 11:30 pm or 12:00 am. When I walked out to my car, most nights, there would be Sara waiting for me. She would always want me to come back to her house and watch TV with her. I liked going over to her house after work because her mom had usually either already drank herself to sleep or was not even there. It was like Sara and I had the place to ourselves. Some nights Sara's mom wouldn't be there at all because she would take her other kids to her ex husbands and sleep at her current boyfriends house. At my house, my parents had long since been asleep and never waited up for me. They knew I worked late and just assumed I was still coming home around 1:00 am. The conditions for temptation and exploration had been set. Wheels were beginning to turn. The walk down the spiral was just beginning.

Sara and I would go to her house and watch TV all the while holding each other and making out from time to time. As weeks went on, the making out sessions grew longer and bolder. It started with body position. At first, we always kissed each other either standing up, or sitting down on her couch. Then one night, she leaned against me and I fell back on to the couch. She was now laying on top of me. This was a major first step.

The next time we made out, I laid on top of her. I didn't like kissing her this way because I felt like I was probably too heavy to be putting my weight on her. We rolled over so that she was back on top of me. I put my arms around her and felt her bra pushing against my chest. This is when I realized we would eventually end up having sex. We didn't take things any further that night. The next session picked up where we left off. Now she was back on top of me. I put my hands on her butt and held it the entire time we were kissing. Every move we made in the direction of having sex, made me feel scared and excited. Each step made me feel like I was going to have a heart attack because I was so excited and scared at the same time. I had never gone anywhere near this far with any other girl. The feeling I was getting was similar to the one I had with Alice on the night we first kissed and then it also was different. With Alice there was a sense of disbelief that she would even talk to me, much less kiss me. With Sara, I had already begun to imagine that this was all possible from the first night I had brought her home and we discovered her mother having sex. I figured the fruit probably didn't fall far from the tree.

The next time we made out we went to Sara's bedroom. Her mother wasn't home. We picked up right where we had left off. Only now the thing to do was lose some clothes. I took off my shirt and she took off hers. Then she took off her bra. And then she took off her shorts and panties. She was completely nude. It was the first time I had ever seen a girl naked outside of the movies. It was amazing. All I had on was my underwear. I knew if I took that off, it would all be over. We would reach the end of the game and there would be no new things to explore. So we stopped it there that night. We agreed that we had gone too far that night. I told her I felt like what we were doing was wrong and she agreed. We were both lying to each other. We had already realized how exciting sex might be. The temptation to keep pushing the envelope was stronger than ever. We had the perfect environment for it. There was never any supervision at Sara's house. And she wanted to have sex just as much as I did. Nothing could stop what we had just started. We were on our way down the spiral.

The very next night we were back at it again. It was like we had become addicted to a drug and couldn't stop ourselves from getting another hit. Only this time we went all the way. There was a moment, after we were both naked and before we actually first had sex, that I paused and thought, "You are going against everything you have been raised to do. Mom and Dad would be ashamed of you if they knew this was what you were doing right now." But those thoughts were not enough to stop me. I had thought them every time we pushed the envelope of "expressing our love". At first, those thoughts had created the guilt and fear that had stopped me so many times before. Now, I had grown tired of worrying about what was thought of as right and wrong. Now, I knew how good it felt to be with a girl that would do these things with me and there was no more restraint, no more conviction left in me. We had crossed a line. We were no longer in a relationship that based itself on love and respect. We had become two lust filled, sex crazed, idiots; risking our future for a few minutes of self-indulgence.

I spent the entire night at her house that first night we had sex. I went to work the next morning without a shower, a tooth brushing, or change of clothes. I remember feeling disgusted with myself. Not just because I lacked proper hygiene, but because I knew I had just made a major mistake. I knew I wasn't in love with this girl I had just lost my virginity to. I wasn't sure we would even be together a month from then and I had just given her more than any other girl I had ever dated. But wasn't that the original plan that Justin and I had made over a year earlier? "Screw 'em and leave 'em.", I had said. It had sounded so gratifying at the time, the idea of getting everything I wanted from somebody without having to give them a thing. That sounded so cool and easy. Now it seemed like the stupidest thing I had ever said. I realized it wasn't so easy to for me to have an experience like that with a girl and just walk away from her. I now felt like I should be more forgiving of things about her that I didn't like. I felt like I owed it to her. After all, she had just let me do the thing I had been dreaming about doing for a couple of years now. I could at least stick around for a while and see if things got better. I wasn't going to be able to screw her and leave her, not now. Now I was in her debt and there would never be a sense that I had repaid her.

After that first night, we couldn't stop ourselves. To make matters even easier, Sara told her mom what we were doing and her mom agreed to buy Sara birth control pills. I was shocked and scared to death when Sara told me that her mom knew about us having sex. I wasn't about to tell my parents what we had been up to and I was afraid that Sara's mom now would. Sara's mom said she had no problem with us having sex. She said that she understood how my parents had a different view of the subject and that she would not tell them anything about what she was allowing me to do with her daughter. I was relieved but also lost even more respect for Sara's mom after that. I thought, "Parents aren't supposed to be O.K. with their kids having sex. What the hell is wrong with her?"

A few days after we first had sex, I asked Sara if that was the first time she had ever had sex. She started crying and said, "No." She said she was sorry but she had done the same thing with Jeff Brown, her last boyfriend. She claimed that he pressured her into having sex and she didn't want to. She said it was terrible and they only did it one time. I'm sure these are the kinds of things that anybody would tell someone who had just lost their virginity to them. I think she thought telling me a horrible tale about her first sexual experience would make me feel better about the fact that I had been a virgin and she had not. It didn't. But it did set up a new problem in our relationship, fear and jealousy, on her behalf. From that moment on she was afraid that I would somehow try to catch up to her in the sex partner department. She began to accuse me of flirting with other girls. She began to fear that I would carry on some secret relationship with another girl just to get even with her for having sex before me. I'll admit, it hurt my feelings to realize I was the only virgin in our situation. I did feel like I got cheated. Several years later, Sara revealed that she had actually slept with another guy, after Jeff and before me. Then I really began to feel like an ass. The guy she had slept with was a good friend of mine, Jackson Thomas. He and I were on the swim team together and he actually won first place in the state diving competition. He had said some strange things to me about Sara when we first started dating. He told me, "Be careful Scott, that girl will play you. She'll make you think she's in love with you, but then she'll turn cold and leave you before you know what's going on. That's how she did me." I told him I was sorry they hadn't worked out and that I would be careful with her. He wasn't the first person to give me a warning about her, but it didn't matter. I wasn't listening.

Chapter 15: Community College

Summer ended and college life began. It turned out that P.C.C. didn't offer an Architecture program so my next closest option was Hillsborough Community College, an hour and a half drive from my parents' house, one way. I started taking classes at the Plant City campus. It was forty-five minutes away, but I was only able to go there for one semester. They didn't offer the core architecture classes that I needed to graduate. I had to drive to the Dale Mabry Campus in Tampa for those.

College was different than high school. In college, the teachers didn't go off on speeches about how important it was to pay attention so we would receive our education. In college, they could care less what we were doing. We had already paid the money that paid their salaries. They didn't care if we wanted to be there or not after that. The information came at us much faster than it had in high school too. There would be no more skipping class to go to the beach with Justin. If I wanted to graduate and go on to a university, I would have to get serious fast. Another thing that was different was the type of people I was going to school with.

All my previous years, my classes had been filled with kids that were my age, many of whom could care less about being there. By the time we got to high school, a lot of the kids were more interested in anything but learning. School was just a place for these kids to meet with their friends and make plans for what kind of hell they would raise that day after school and on the coming weekend.

But in college, the kids were different. They really weren't kids at all. Some of them were five to ten years older than me. No, these were young adults who were a little more serious about the idea of education than I was used to. After all, we were now paying money just to be there, we had better be serious.

That spring, the spring of 1995, I started taking my first architecture related classes. I had already taken drafting in high school and loved it, so I was excited about what I might learn. My first experience in the world of architecture was a class called Design 1.1. I remember listening to the instructor introduce himself and tell us about buildings he had helped design. He told us that most of us would drop out before the end of the semester, two out of three, he said, would decide they didn't like the work load required by the class and would go on to other things. I remember thinking, "This guy is a jerk. If he thinks I'm quitting before the end of the semester, he's all wrong. I'm going to be the one in three that sticks around, no matter what." That class started out with about 50 students. By the end of the semester there were only about twenty of us, so he was pretty close.

He began our first classes explaining what Architecture was and how it differed from anything else in the construction field. He explained that engineers and contractors designed and built buildings out of nothing but necessity. He said that when engineers and contractors planned a building, all they did was meet the practical needs of the occupants and create a building that was as efficient and cheap as possible. He began to make engineers and contractors sound inferior to architects. He said that when an architect planned a building, the architect did all the things that the engineers did, only the architect also looked for ways to create spaces with meaning, spaces that inspired people and told stories about things or made people feel certain ways. He said Architecture was the most complex art form and was superior to sculpture and painting because it put people inside of art, surrounded them, and could make them act and feel differently than they might in other places. He said that Architecture was superior to all other art forms because people interacted with it, rather than just looked at it. I loved what I was hearing. I felt I was becoming part of something big and who knows, maybe I would one day create the kinds of places he was describing.

We also spent time talking about the idea of "The Concept". The concept is the main idea an architect tries to convey through his building. It is the form giver, the organizer. It instructs the architect how to create and arrange the plethora of decisions that must be made in order to design a building. The concept, my instructor said, is best when it is a simple idea, like "My building will be like a tree.", or something like that. The idea of creating a tree would then override all decisions about the building, from its shape and special layout to the colors chosen for the trim on the walls. The instructor said that this was how to design as a true architect. This, my instructor said, was what we would be learning and practicing.

Then we went back to very basic things. We went over the old high school, Ortho Graphic Projection methods for those who never had taken any drafting. Then we moved on to drawing with Perspective, and the realm of three dimensions. This was something I had been wanting to learn how to do for years. All my years of previous drawing in art classes left me with a recurring problem. Whenever I drew things that were at angles to the viewer, I always had trouble recreating things exactly as I saw them. An example would be a house that I drew from the view of standing at one of the corners and looking straight ahead. The walls got smaller as they got further away from me. Everything got smaller as it was further away. I knew this. It was a simple thing you learned as a child when you held up your thumb to the moon and blocked it entirely from view. You knew your thumb wasn't as big as the moon. The moon was just further away. A basic concept. However, I had never learned the rules that governed exactly how large or small something needed to be if it was to be portrayed correctly in a two dimensional image.

In that first semester of Design 1.1, we began to learn the rules that governed exactly how things appeared when you drew them in three dimensions on a two dimensional piece of paper. We learned about Vanishing Points, the idea that when looking at anything, everything in view recedes to certain focal points on the horizon. We also learned how to establish a three dimensional grid that would provide a means of drawing things at their correct sizes, no matter where they were in the drawing.

Now I could draw a building and get all the lines to be at their correct angles and lengths. I was pretty impressed with what I had learned and thought it would help me become a better, more accurate artist. We would later discover that everything we had just learned about how to draw three dimensionally, was done in seconds by a computer. The computer made the need to draw things in perspective by hand, almost obsolete. It was faster, more accurate, and could apply colors, textures, and shadows, like no human ever could.

I started learning AutoCAD in my third semester at H.C.C. Our instructor was one of the programmers who had helped design some early versions of the software. He knew it inside and out. AutoCAD was one of the few things I learned in college that had actual value when I later worked in architectural firms. A lot of the other things we had to spend our time and money to learn, I think, were only required so that the school could collect more money from you as you were forced to sign up for the class, and buy the required CD-ROM's, books, and other necessary items. A lot of Architecture School, to me, seemed a big waste of time and money. But I was determined to get through it. Every year we were given more statistics about the likelihood of failure and that just drove me further. "One in ten of you will complete this program. From there only one and ten will graduate from a university with a degree in Architecture. Of that group, only one in ten will ever become a licensed Architect.", we were told by a professor at H.C.C., and again when I was later attending university classes. It was very motivating for me. And it gave me a great sense of accomplishment every time I made it as the "one in ten". But that's moving a little ahead.

CAD: Computer Aided Drafting / Design. That was my most appreciated class of my entire college experience. We learned first how to draw things two dimensionally. Then we learned the basics of creating construction drawings: how to dimension all the important parts of buildings, how to illustrate all the various parts of a building; basically, how to fully describe a building so it could be built. This was pretty important information to me seeing as how I imagined this would be the bulk of what I did once I was actually working as an architect. After getting a grip on construction documents, we moved into the realm of three-dimensional modeling. Our instructor said this was where the future of Architecture was. "In the future, an architect will hand a contractor a computer model of a building and the contractor will extrapolate all the information he needs from the model.", our professor said. I thought this sounded really cool. I was learning a process that might be cutting edge when I got out of school and I was only paying community college prices to learn it.

The third and final semester of AutoCAD we began by creating computer models of simple objects like cups, gears, etc.; then moved on to more complex shapes such as spoons, forks, and even the computer mouse we were using to draw with. For our final project we were able to pick what we wanted to create a model of as long as it showcased all the commands we had learned to use while taking the class. I chose Darth Vader's Tie Fighter from Star Wars. I felt like I was creating special effects for a movie. It made me think about going to that art school in Savannah Georgia and seeing the work of all those kids who would later go on to work for people at Pixar, LucasFilm, and others. I sort of wished I had tried harder to persuade someone to let me go to that school. At any rate, I was sticking with the plan and having a lot of fun so, no complaints.

Two years went by and I did not have all the classes I needed to graduate. Most kids got their A.A. in two years. I was aggravated that I hadn't received mine. The problem was a lack of passing students in the Design Classes. So many people failed the first semester of the second year design class, Design 2.1, that they didn't even offer Design 2.2 for the few of us that passed. There were only about five or six of us that passed Design 2.1. The school would not pay for a teacher to teach six kids. It was all about the money and that pissed me off. I had to wait an entire year before they offered Design 2.2 and by that time I was ready to quit school all together. It was very frustrating to want to get out into the real world, after 14 years of sitting in classrooms all day, and have to be told, "Sorry, just wait until next year." I found other things to do with my new free time. However, not all of them were positive things.

Chapter 16: Big Adventures, Big Mistakes

My schedule, for that year of waiting, was mainly filled up with work. I became a full time employee with Food Lion. That kept me almost busy enough. Justin and I still saw each other from time to time. He was now working as a waiter for Chili's in Lakeland. He wasn't going to school at all but had signed up with the National Guard shortly after high school. He tried a semester at Valdosta State University taking general education type stuff and he realized he hated it. So he signed up with The National Guard and developed dreams of becoming an Airborne Ranger. He actually got selected for the training to become a Ranger and made it through 6 of the 9 weeks, but then he broke his ankle one day during a run, and was kicked out with no chance of re-entry. It disappointed him severely, but he ended up serving out his tour of active duty in the National Guard and I think he really enjoyed it.

At the time that I started working full time at Food Lion, Justin only had to serve one weekend a month and was working at Chili's, waiting tables. He had a new dream. He wanted to become a bartender as soon as he was old enough to be hired. We were only twenty and you had to be 21 before they would hire you. We talked about our past adventures and decided we needed to have at least a couple more before we settled down into the rut of work life. We decided these adventures would be big!

Our first big idea was to take a long canoe trip. It was a simple plan because we had one of the longest paddling trips in the state in my backyard. Peace River runs from Lake Hancock, near Haines City; to the Gulf of Mexico, in Punta Gorda. We decided this would be our first and maybe, last, big adventure. We loaded up my parents' canoe with all our supplies and drove two cars down to Punta Gorda, parked one there, then drove one car back to Ft. Meade to begin our great journey. The total trip from Ft. Meade to Punta Gorda is over 100 miles. It took us a day and a half to complete it. We left at 4:00 pm on a Saturday and arrived in Punta Gorda around 2:00 am Monday morning, dog tired. The trip was everything we had hoped for. The weather was great. We camped that first night in a tent Justin brought. The next day we saw lots of wildlife, including a 10 foot long gator that scared the crap out of us because he followed us for a couple miles down the river, just watching us from about 20 feet away most of the time. We were in a section that wasn't near any towns or houses and that thing just kept dragging along behind us. We kept paddling faster and faster, but he kept coming. It gave us a story to talk about for years later. On the trip we talked about all kinds of things, but I mainly talked about Sara.

Sara and I were still having sex about every time we were together. We got along most of the time, but when we argued, it was bad. On the flip side, Sara kept bringing up the subject of marriage. She said she was so tired of living with her mom. She wanted to be with me. She wanted us to get married and find an apartment together. I told her I wasn't marrying anybody until I finished college and got settled in a good job. Sara was also becoming more jealous and possessive than she had been when we first started dating. Even that very canoe trip had been a huge fight because she wanted me to spend my time with her, not Justin. She wanted me to bring her along but there was no room. And my parents would find out that we were together an entire weekend with no supervision; and they didn't want to take a chance like that (Just imagine what Sara and I might end up doing!). So, Sara coming along was out of the question and that caused a big argument.

She and Justin had already had tension building up because he felt the same way as she did. He felt like I was spending all my time with Sara and that we never got to hang out anymore. That was the main reason we had planned this trip, so that we could just have some guy time to catch up on each other's lives and pretend we were still living out our high school days.

I told Justin about how Sara resented me going on the canoe trip and about all the stupid arguments we seemed to find ourselves in more and more often. I told him about Sara accusing me of seeing other girls at H.C.C. and how I had done nothing of the sort. I explained to him how Sara's previous long time boyfriend, Jeff Brown, had supposedly had sex with her friends while they were dating and she how I thought that she was assuming that I was like Jeff. I told him it felt like a noose was tightening around my neck. I was having to defend myself against things I hadn't done. I told him that I was growing tired of the situation. His suggestion, of course, was "Dump her." I had already thought about this idea after every ridiculous argument. Every time I thought about it, I then thought about Sara's terrible childhood, of which I was reminded constantly because she always talked about it. I felt like if I were to dump her, it might just send her over the edge and she might do something terrible. I felt like it was now my responsibility to put up with all the things I didn't like about her. She had lived a terrible life as a child, but had loved me more than anybody I'd ever known. I felt that I was now obligated to keep her as my girlfriend. I hoped that our disagreements would dwindle and that she would learn to trust me and stop accusing me of cheating on her. I hoped that she would get along with Justin because she was beginning to put a strain on our friendship. I was now caught in the middle, defending Sara against Justin and vice versa. I hoped things would get better for everybody, only they didn't, they soon got worse.

After the canoe adventure, Justin and I decided we needed to do something even bigger. As adventures go, it doesn't get much bigger than The Appalachian Trail. The trail stretches from the Blue Ridge Mountains of Georgia and runs all the way up to Maine. It takes about five months for most hikers. It sounded like the perfect escape for us. We imagined ourselves spending five months together, living the life of trail hikers. To me it sounded awesome. For Sara, it was something less.

Justin and I began to plan our trip. I started saving all the money I could which was a lot to me because I was working full time and didn't have to buy books or classes. I started walking every day for several hours so that I could build up my endurance. I bought maps of the trail, books about planning hiking trips, and even a couple books written specifically about the Appalachian Trail Hike. Then I bought a pair of $300 hiking boots. I was told they would last the entire trip and were well worth the money. I believe I was an idiot and got ripped off, just a little. I was just about to start buying a backpack, tent, and other necessities when Justin called me one day and told me he had just bought a new car. He said he used the money he had been saving up as a down payment. He said that the new car payments meant he was going to have to keep working and that he could no longer afford to take our Appalachian Trail Adventure. I said, "But you didn't need a new car did you? What was wrong with your old one?" "Nothing.", he said, "I just saw this Mazda MX-6 yesterday and I had to get it. You've got to see it. It's green. It's awesome." I was totally pissed at him. It was the first time he had ever let me down. Justin was always the person I turned to if I had a problem. I could always count on Justin to come through with anything I ever asked. Now, he had made plans with me, big plans, and totally broke them without even asking me what I thought. This almost sounds like I thought we were married, pretty gay.

So that was the end of The Biggest Adventure Ever. It had ended before it ever started because my friend decided he would rather have a new car than take a once in a lifetime journey through the mountains of the eastern United States. I'm sure that we would never have made it to the end if we had started, but we never even started. It was something I regretted for years. If we had taken that trip I might have a totally different life today. I might not have made the mistake that changed everything.

One last thing happened before I made the big mistake though. The summer of 1996, my parents decided they wanted to take a family vacation unlike any other before it. They wanted to take my brothers and I on a tour of the United States and part of Canada. It would take five weeks. That meant five weeks without Sara. That caused serious fights and crying fits from Sara. She wanted to be a part of it, but my parents were trying to have a family vacation and did not want her tagging along. My brother, Sam, decided he didn't want to go. We had the room for Sara if she paid her way, but my parents did not want to be responsible for her for five weeks. I think they really wanted me to see what life without Sara was like. They knew we were having arguments. My parents no longer liked the idea of Sara and I seeing each other. My mom said, "You could do a lot better than Sara. She's just like her mother. You two are never going to be happy together. You'd be better off alone." I didn't believe her though.

At the beginning of the summer of 1996, we set off on our trip across the North West of the United States. We started in Florida then meandered our way west through the southern states of Alabama, Tennessee, and Mississippi, and then into the heartland states and eventually into the northwest, and on into Alberta, Canada. Along the way we stopped and took hiking trips, climbed rock formations, and visited several cities, towns, and state parks. We made stops in St. Louis, MI, Memphis, TN, Banff, CO, Yellow Stone CO, Mt. Rushmore SD, Devil's Tower WY, Flaming Gorge, UT, and on and on. It was the greatest family vacation we had ever taken. My brother, Carter, and I had the time of our young lives. The drastic change of scenery, from the plains and cornfields of the heartland, to the jagged, snow covered peaks of the Grand Tetons, to the dusty and dry red clay that enveloped The West; it was all incredibly beautiful. I hope I can do something like that for my kids some day.

We went as far North as Lake Louise in Alberta Canada. It was far enough North that most of the lakes were formed from glacial run off and most of the mountains were covered in snow. We went into the lands of the grizzly bear and mountain goat. It was such a different environment than anything I had ever experienced. I loved it. We had previously spent July 4th at Devil's Tower on our way to Lake Louise. Devil's Tower was incredible. The tower stood out of the ground like a giant spire right out of some Lord of the Rings movie. In fact I had seen it in a movie as a kid, Close Encounters of the Third Kind. To be right at the base of it, looking up its volcanic hexagonal prisms, was like nothing I could ever imagine. Then there were fireworks shot out with the tower in the foreground. I wished Sara was with me. I felt guilty for experiencing all these wonderful things while she sat back in Bartow with her crappy job and crappier excuse for a home.

We saw many other sights along the way and then began our journey home. Along the way we stopped at Mesa Verde. It was an ancient Anasazi Indian village that was built into and carved out of a cliff. All the buildings were actually carved from the cliff and there were probably twenty or thirty of them. It was awesome.

From Mesa Verde, NM we started to pick up the pace of traveling back home. The closer we got, the more I dreaded going back to life the way it had been when I left. I had made sure to call Sara every few days and we would talk for 15 or 20 minutes. It was nice only being able to talk for short periods, unlike our usual phone calls, which sometimes lasted a couple of hours. Those two-hour phone calls usually happened when a fight had developed over the phone. It took that long to work things out to a point where we could hang up. But on the road, calling via pre-paid calling cards, there was no time to argue. Our phone calls were always sweet, telling her how much I missed her and how much I loved her. She always told me how miserable things were without me around and how she couldn't wait for me to be back so she could feel like herself again. She said she would just sleep all the time, if she wasn't at work, because she was so depressed. I had no idea what she was talking about. I would later discover how depression works and how it really does make you tired. For me it was easier to love Sara from a distance, when I had little chance for argument and could think about all the qualities about her that had attracted me to her in the first place.

As we drew nearer to Georgia, I knew, in a few days, Sara and I would be face to face and I feared there would be retribution for me having joy in my life without Sara. We got back to my parents house in north Georgia near the end of the summer. Sara called me and said she was coming up there to meet me. She said she couldn't stand being away from me for another week and she was on her way. My parents didn't like the idea, but they went along with it.

I met Sara at the end of the road, at the bottom of the mountain, that led to my parents' house. She pulled up and got out of her car. I looked at her and realized, for the first time in a long time, that she was absolutely beautiful. I remember looking at her face and thinking how I hadn't been picturing her that way in my head. It only took five weeks of not seeing her every day to realize that I was lucky to have such an attractive girl willing to call me her boyfriend. We ran up to each other and I told her how beautiful she looked. I told her I had missed her so much. She told me the same things. We held each other and kissed with more love than I think we ever had.

Chapter 17: The Break Up

Around that time, Sara changed jobs again. She had left Checkers about six months after I did, and went to work at a little mini-golf, video game arcade-type place. She worked as one of the girls that handed out prizes to kids who turned in tickets they had won playing by playing the games. It was a simpler job than Checkers to her because she mainly dealt with children and she loved kids. During my trip across the American North West, Sara had decided she could make more money as a waitress. She got a job at a little pizza place, called Floridino's, on South Florida Ave. in Lakeland.

Sara did start making more money once she became a waitress. Like I said, she was a pretty girl. People are always more persuaded to tip a pretty waitress a little more than an average looking girl. Sara loved that job. She would tell me about all the new friends she was making and how nice all the customers always were to her. Sometimes the customers were al little too nice. She was hit on by many guys, who thought they'd take a chance on picking up a pretty blonde waitress for the night. She told me that she hated that part of the job, but I think she really liked it. Who doesn't like getting told that they are attractive? And the guys that hit on her were also her biggest tippers, just letting her know, "I've got some money to spend on you. There's more where that came from baby." One guy left her a $100 bill one night. I was pretty pissed about it. I started to wonder if some guy's money might be getting him a little extra attention from Sara. I started to wish I could have been there at the restaurant to see the interaction between Sara and her high tipping customers. It wasn't so much that I was jealous, which I was, a little; but mainly that she had now accused me several times of trying to see and flirt with other girls and it wasn't true. I wanted to see just how big a hypocrite she really was. Her new job gave her an excuse to flirt with whomever she wanted and I would never be there to see any of it. I never cared enough about it to make the drive from Ft. Meade to Lakeland to check it out. I figured if she was flirting with other guys, she would eventually end up liking one of them and leaving me. It made me a little sad but I thought that might not be the worst thing that had ever happened.

After several months of Sara working at Floridino's, she began to change. She started asking me to come to parties with her and her new work buddies. These parties always involved alcohol and drugs. Sara had never had an issue with any of these things before, but now they were something she wanted to try. Her new friends seemed cool to her and they seemed to be having a lot of fun when they were drunk or high. Sara wanted to see what all the fuss was about. I didn't. I thought her new friends were losers. One of the girls that Sara liked was even a Wiccan. She claimed she was a witch and didn't believe in God the way that Christians did. She believed in a Nature Spirit that was a woman who was supposedly the real god. She believed in spell casting and rituals that could change people's behavior or improve their luck. I thought she was an idiot. I couldn't understand how Sara would even associate with somebody like that.

Sara began to tell me I was boring. She said it was lame that I didn't want to go to these parties with her. She said they were so much fun and she had tried smoking pot at the last one. She said she didn't like it. She said it made her sick and she got paranoid. I wasn't impressed. I told her I wasn't going to any of those parties and I didn't want her there either. I told her she was hanging around with a bad crowd and they were bringing her down. She didn't agree. After all, it was the manager of the store who had supposedly given her the pot. He was actually the one who supplied a selection of drugs that people could take at his "parties". He was able to do drugs, keep a job managing the store, had a wife, and house of his own. Sara rationalized that if her manager was able to do all that, then maybe the drug scene wasn't so bad. I later found out that cops frequently barged into Floridino's and arrested people working there for dealing drugs. Floridino's actually filed for bankruptcy and closed down entirely a couple years after these "parties" had started.

One night Justin and I met up at Chili's to hang out with some of his friends. When Justin and I got there, all the others had already claimed a table and were sitting around talking and drinking beer. I was only twenty at the time and had never had a drink in my life. Justin knew I was having the usual trouble with Sara. He told me, "Tonight, you are going to get drunk and forget about her." There were a few other girls at the table as well as a guy to go with just about every one. I was introduced to everyone and then they started ordering drinks. Justin and I were not 21 but some of his friends were, and apparently the staff didn't care that these guys were ordering drinks for the table. I guessed it was because most of the people at the table worked at Chili's. I had no idea that far worse things went on with this crowd than drinking. Justin handed me a beer and said, "Try this, you'll love it." I thought about what Sara had been doing lately. And here was my best friend drinking with his friends. If you can't beat 'em, join 'em.

That's what I did. I took a drink of the beer and thought it tasted like crap. "This is terrible.", I told him. He said I'd get used to the taste after a few beers. He said that's when the fun would start. I finished the beer and didn't feel any different. Then Justin's friends ordered shots of some hard liquor, which we all drank together. That was much better than the beer. For one there wasn't as much of it, and two, it was sweet from some flavoring they added to it. A few minutes after taking the shot, I did notice a strange tingling sensation in my head. My arms and legs felt a little lighter too. I told Justin what was going on and he said, "Hell yeah! You just got your first buzz!" It wasn't long after that when Sara called Justin on his new cell phone. She was looking for me. Justin told her we were at Chili's hanging out with some friends and she hung up on him. I asked him what she wanted. He said he didn't know but she sounded pissed. Sara showed up at our table within just a few minutes. She worked just down the street and apparently had come from there. She looked at our table and saw all the littered beer bottles and shot glasses. Some of the guys had started smoking. She asked me if I had been drinking with these people. I said, "Yes, actually, I have. Is there a problem?" She picked up the pitcher of water that was on the table and dumped the entire thing over my head and said, "You want to give me a guilt trip about going to parties? You never want to come with me. But you'll go out drinking with Justin and these whores here? Screw you!" With that she stomped off and out of the building. I sat there, humiliated in front of an entire restaurant. I was soaked from head to toe from the pitcher of ice water that Sara had poured on me. Everybody at the table sat there in shock. No one said anything to me. I looked around and saw all the people at other tables who had witnessed what had just happened. I was totally embarrassed for what had just happened. Justin and I left. I told Justin that it was over between Sara and I. "I'm done with that bitch!", I told him. He acted like he couldn't be happier. He said he'd been waiting to hear me say that for a while. Justin and I rode around in his car for a while with me ranting and raving about how much I hated Sara. Then Sara called Justin's phone again and wanted to talk to me.

I told her she was literally crazy. I said there was no way I'd forgive her for what she had just done. Then she started crying and apologizing. I wanted to hang up on her, but there was something in me that forced me to listen to her. I have no explanation for what it was that kept me glued to a girl who I had so little love for. I guess it was the sex. I guess I put up with a lot of crap from Sara because I knew I could always come to her if I wanted to have sex. It seems pretty lame that I put up with so much crap for a few minutes of fun. Outside of our sex life, Sara and I were in a terrible relationship. For me, most of the time, there was little or no love, only lust.

Sara met up with Justin and I and said she wanted to take me home if I would let her. Two or three wasted hours of talking later, and we were as close to over the situation as I could get. She had apologized a hundred times over the last couple hours and was now treating me like her favorite person in the world again. I told her I hadn't intended to go out drinking with Justin, that I kind of felt pressured into it and that was the first time anything like that had ever happened. She wanted to know who the girls were. I told her I didn't know them, and how I had just met them. We left it at that. I had looked bad and she had looked worse. I didn't know how much more I would stand for, not much, I thought.

Sara and I were beginning to change as a couple. She no longer acted like she was head over heels for me. I blamed myself for this because I rarely felt that way about her. I figured a person could only give so much affection without anything in return before the well went dry. I always told her that I loved her, but I knew that I never felt about Sara the way I had about Alice. I always hoped that someday I would. The lack of feeling never interfered with our sex life however. We still made sure to take care of those needs every time we saw each other, if not several times each time we saw each other.

Then one night, Sara and I were walking around the Bartow High School track and talking. She said, "Scott, I've got a problem. There's a guy at work who has been hitting on me a lot for the last couple months. He's younger than you but he likes to party with us after work. He's a really cool guy. I still like you, but I like him too. I don't know what I should do. I thought I should tell you." And there it was. The opportunity I thought I had been waiting for. *She* was now telling *me* that she was thinking about ending the relationship. This was supposed to be just what I wanted. I could now part with her and not have to feel guilty about it in the least.

But something different happened. Once the possibility of our relationship coming to an end was in my face, I no longer wanted it. I instead thought I wanted to try and make things right with her. She was such a habit. And how many other girls would I find out there that might have the feelings about me that she once had. I started to think, "This is my fault. I have been cold to her for so long that I've finally turned her away. If I had expressed to her all the times when I actually did love her, we wouldn't be having this conversation right now. What if she's the one for me and I let her get away?" I asked Sara to think about what she was doing. I told her that it was stupid of her to walk away from me so that she could hang out with a kid who was two or three years younger than her and was already doing drugs. I told her that I thought her new "boyfriend" was a total loser and she might want to reconsider before letting me go. Then I said, "I'm not going to try and stop you. If this is what you want, then I guess you'll have to figure things out for yourself." She didn't respond. We left the track and went our separate ways. A couple of days went by and Sara never called me. I thought it was odd because she called me almost every day. So, I called her. She wasn't home. I called her work. She said she was busy and would call me later.

She and her dad spent one night a week on a bowling team where they bowled together and caught up on what was going on in their lives. I thought I'd find her at the bowling alley and we would talk there. I remember walking in and her dad and step mother giving me a look like, "Here comes trouble." Sara saw me and just kept on doing whatever she had been before she saw me. I told her that I wanted to talk to her. I asked her if her dad knew about what she had been doing and if he had met any of her new friends. Her dad was the polar opposite of her mom in the morals department. He and his new wife made sure to attend every church meeting and even home schooled their kids because they thought the public school system would corrupt their kid's values. Sara said that if I mentioned anything to her dad about what her new circle of friends liked to do, she wouldn't mind telling my parents about all of our little escapades. She said to leave her alone while she was with her dad. She would talk to me after they were done. So I waited. I talked with her dad and step mom and could tell that Sara had already told them something along the lines of us being on the split. They acted different towards me than they ever had. They usually at least greeted me and asked me questions about how things were going. Now they acted like they didn't want me there. It was really awkward. I started to feel like maybe I was chasing after Sara too hard. I thought that maybe what I was doing was considered stalking.

After the bowling ended, Sara and I got in her car and drove to a Burger King that was just up the street. I told her that I was sorry for not giving her enough attention and that I would try to hang out with her new friends if she wanted. Sara pulled out a pack of cigarettes, took one out and lit it up. I couldn't believe what I was seeing. She had never touched a cigarette around me before. I felt a little less excited about the idea of us trying to work out our problems. She said, "I'm just smoking because I'm nervous. It helps calm you down." "Whatever.", I said. Then I thought, "No, not 'whatever', this is a chance to prove how much you'll do for her." I said, "Can I have one of those?" She laughed and said, "Sure." I had never smoked before in my life. I asked her for her lighter and I inhaled my first breath of smoke.

I had just crossed another line with Sara. I always said I would never do drugs. Cigarettes had killed my dad's parents at a young age. I didn't want to end up like them. But now that wasn't important. It was important, to me, to show Sara that I cared enough about her that I was willing to change for her. I told her that I would go to one of the parties, that she loved going to, with her. She just looked at me. She said, "I don't know Scott. I think I just need some time to think about things. I don't want to break up with you, but I just need to have some experiences for myself. You and your family just had all kinds of wonderful experiences together and all I did was lie around and wish I was with you. Now, I want to have some fun, on my own. Then we'll see if we should really be together. I'll call you when I want to talk to you."

After another week and a half of Sara dodging my phone calls, I started to get really angry with her. I didn't try to see her in person. I thought if she wanted to see me, she could find me at work or home. She was the one who was having a problem with me. I thought I would let her come crawling back once she realized that she screwed up. Only she didn't. She wouldn't even talk to me. I was pissed.

I finally called her house one night, and a strange voice answered the phone. "Hello?", it said. "Sara? Is that you?", I said. "No this is Alyssa. I've just got a cold. Sara is not here right now. She's with a friend.", said the strange voice. Then I thought I heard a guy giggling in the background. I was instantly furious. I drove from my parents' house into Bartow to Sara's house to see just what was going on. If nothing else, I thought, I'd talk with her mom to see what Sara was up to and if she had said anything about the new guy she was interested in. I pulled up to Sara's house and saw that Sara's car was there. Her mother's was not. I walked up to the door and just listened for a minute. I could hear Sara and some other male voice talking softly to each other. I could tell they were watching a movie because I could hear the TV as well. All the lights were off inside the house. Then I thought I heard the sound of lips smacking together and Sara made a sound I heard her make many times before when she enjoyed the things we did together when we were alone. Everything seemed to slow down. I started to feel hot and nervous. I felt like I was about to be in a fight. The adrenaline was pumping through my veins. Yes, I thought, I was going to have to kick Sara's little punk ass boyfriend's ass.

I knocked on the door. The TV went off and everything was quiet. I banged on the door harder. Still nothing. I then said, "Sara, I know you're in there. I know your new little boyfriend is in there too. Why doesn't he come out here so I can meet him?" Nothing. Several minutes went by and I heard whispering and people walking around inside the house. "I'm not leaving until we talk.", I said. Several minutes passed and then a car pulled up next to mine. Two high school kids got out and started yelling at me to come over there and do something if I wanted to fight somebody. I started to walk towards them and the front door opened. That's when

Sara's new hero stepped out and met me. He said, "You got a problem man? I'll kick your ass. Come on, if you want some." He was suddenly very tough now that his two friends had shown up to his rescue. He had apparently called them from Sara's phone and I guess they had nothing better to do than try to jump me that night. I realized that I was surrounded by three guys, who were all a little smaller than me. Still, there were three of them. I knew I wouldn't be winning any fight that night. I said to Sara, "So this is your big new man, huh? And I guess you'd probably like to see me fight somebody over you. Well, guess what? You are not worth it!" I said to her new boyfriend, "I hope you have fun with her! She's not worth fighting for." I got in my car and drove back to the lake. I was furious. That would be the last time I would let Sara make an ass out of me. We were done and there was no going back.

After that night, I told myself that I was better off without Sara. She was going down a dark path and I had no business following her. She didn't want me following her. She had her new friends, and her new 10th of 11th grade boyfriend. She could make her own bed and lie in it. I was embarrassed that I had been replaced by a high school kid, who liked to do drugs, but I thought things would eventually get better. I told myself that I would find someone else one day. I figured that whoever my new girlfriend might be, she would have to be better than Sara. I wouldn't waste any more of my time trying to make somebody happy who never seemed to find joy in anything.

Chapter 18: For All the Wrong Reasons

A couple months passed and then it was Christmas. My family did the usual trip to the Georgia house for Christmas Break. We always spent Christmas in Georgia. That was a tradition that had been going on since my dad built the house up there. This year was different though, because for the first time in two years, I was spending Christmas without Sara. She had come up to Georgia with us for Christmas for the past two years that we had dated. She said she hated spending Christmas with her family and my family was much more normal and that she loved to be with me whenever she could. Now, she wasn't here. We had just split up. I thought about her from time to time. I remember telling my parents and brothers what Sara had been doing over the last several months since she became a waitress. I told them about how she had asked me to come to parties with her and I had refused. I even told them that she had started smoking pot. My parents said they weren't surprised but were glad that things ended when they did. They said she was not good for me. My dad said, "Well, just imagine if you had got her pregnant or something. Then you'd be trying to raise a family with that girl as your wife. You'd have her screaming at you in one ear and a baby screaming at you in the other. You got lucky to get out when you did." My family and I opened presents on Christmas day and mom cooked her usual Christmas feast for lunch that day. It was still a nice time, even if it was a little different than usual.

Then, a couple of days before we had to go back to Florida, the phone rang. My dad answered it and hung up after saying, "Hello?" I asked him who it was. He told me, "It was Sara. I didn't think you wanted to talk to her." "No.", I said. I didn't want to talk to her. In fact I believed my parents were right and the comment my dad had recently made, of Sara and I with a baby, made me sick. The phone rang several times that day, and usually it was Sara. My dad would tell her that I didn't want to talk to her, not to call back, and hang up. Then we were all about to go out for some ice cream that night and the phone rang again. I was closest to the phone so I picked it up. It was Sara. My parents and brothers looked at me, waiting for me to hang up the phone. "Please don't hang up!", she said. "I've got something really important to tell you!" My heart sank. I told my parents I would stay at the house and they should go on without me. My mom said, "What the hell? Get off the phone. Come on, you're coming with us!" "No. You guys just go on without me.", I said. After that, they all left. Then, it was just the phone and I. "What is it? I really don't want to talk to you.", I said. "I know, but I really messed up. I shouldn't have let you leave. I really miss you.", she said. "Bull crap! I thought you're new party buddies were what you needed. I thought you needed to have some experiences without me around. And what about your new boyfriend?", I said, feeling instantly back on top, she played out just like I thought she would.

74

She explained that the guy she was seeing got old pretty fast. Sara said that he was nothing like me and only wanted to get high when they were together. She said she realized she was in the wrong and would spend forever trying to make it up to me if I would just give her another chance. Then she dropped the big news. What came out of Sara's mouth next changed my life forever.

Sara had spent several minutes trying to apologize for her behavior. I sat through all of it, thinking how much I would rather be eating ice cream. I remember thinking that if this was what was so important, then I had just let her waste more of my time. I was not in a state of mind to try and work things out with her. I didn't want any more to do with her. The only reason I had allowed her to have a conversation with me was because I could hear panic in her voice when I first picked up the phone. I thought that there must be something really important, or else she would not have kept trying to contact me. Finally, I said, "So, what is it that is so important that you have been trying to call me all day? If you think that I care about your apology, you're wrong. We are through." Sara was crying. Finally she said, "I know you may not want to see me right now, but I've got to tell you something. Scott, I'm pregnant." There it was. The big news. The words that changed my entire future had just been spoken to me. My worst nightmare had just come true. Dad had just foretold the future when he spoke of the nightmare of a life I would live if Sara had wound up getting pregnant. Now, apparently, it had come to pass. I got chills all over me after I heard Sara's words. I was in shock.

I just sat there. The phone was silent for probably a minute. Neither of us said anything. "How do you know?", I finally said. "I haven't had a period in three months, so I took a pregnancy test and it came up positive.", she said. I just sat there and imagined my parents eating ice cream with my brothers, not a care in the world. Then I thought about the easiest solution to get out of this mess. "Have you thought about having an abortion?", I said. She started crying again. "Yes, but you know I could never do that. I know you don't love me but I can't just kill my baby because of that. Whether you want to get back together or not, I'm having this baby. Maybe I'll give it up for adoption. I don't know what to do. I just really wanted to call you and see how you felt about it. Now I know.", she said. She was balling. I felt like crap for suggesting the abortion. I knew how Sara felt about abortion. She was a Pro-Lifer, all the way. My suggestion was just my natural response to the situation. I couldn't think of an easier way to get out of the mess that I was now in. If she had an abortion, I would have no ties to her. We could go on living our lives as if nothing had ever happened.

I thank God that Sara had the foresight to see just how hard an abortion would really be on us. Had she agreed to an abortion, I probably would have lived with a lifetime of guilt for the sin I had committed. Even though my life was never easy after that day, I would never say that an abortion would have been the appropriate thing to do. I now agree with Sara that abortion is a terrible choice for anyone to make, under any circumstance. I don't believe that a human being should be given the opportunity to decide whether an unborn child should live or die. Whenever someone makes that decision for any other living human, who has had the chance to live for at least 9 months, it is called murder. Why is abortion viewed any differently from any other form of murder? That is what abortion is. Abortion is murder, murder of the innocent, the ones who have no voice of their own. I know that other people have formed their own logic to defend the decision they have made to kill their own child, but all that they are doing is trying to trick themselves into believing a lie so that they don't have to bear the shame and guilt that comes from the evil act that they have committed. Our society deals with all other forms of murder by strict punishment. Why is it legal for a person to murder a child?

Now that I have stood on my soap box, back to the story:

I couldn't see myself trying to work things out with Sara, especially with a kid on the way. Now, we would have to think of some way to feed, shelter, and take care of a baby; all while trying to come to terms with the fact that she had just left me for another guy. I felt like the only reason she was acting interested in me was because she knew I was her best chance of helping her support a baby. She thought of my parents as well off and probably thought they would bail us out, if nothing else.

"Look, I'm sorry that you're pregnant. I'll help you do whatever you want. I really don't know what to do either. I don't have a decent job, a house, or anything else that we need. I don't know what you expect me to be able to do.", I said. "How did this happen? I thought you were taking birth control pills?", I said. "I don't know. The pill is only 99% effective. I guess we're in the 1% that it didn't work for.", she said. "That's about our kind of luck.", I said and she laughed a little. "Scott, I really am sorry for the way I've treated you lately. I promise if you give me another chance I'm going to make it up to you.", she said. I told her that I had treated her badly too and that it was all O.K. I was really lying. It was far from O.K. I had never felt so stressed out in my life. I had no idea of what to do about the situation that I had created for myself. Just when I thought my days with Sara were done, she was back again, and begging for mercy.

I told Sara that I would need some time to think about what to do. I said that I didn't know if I could ever love her. I told her that I had never intended on marrying her, but now, things were looking differently. I had never planned to marry Sara, but I also had never planned on having a kid with a girl that I was not married to. I knew that I was going to have to choose to do one or the other. I told Sara that we could just take it slow and she shouldn't worry about me not helping her with the baby. I told her that it would take some time for me to get the nerve to tell my parents and that they didn't even want me talking to her. I told her I would see her in a couple days when we got back to Florida and we would try to figure something out.

My parents came back from their ice cream trip and asked what Sara had called about. I told them she was regretting the things she had been doing and was wanting me to see her again. My parents rolled their eyes and told me I'd be stupid if I wasted another minute talking to her ever again.

We got back to Florida and I met Sara somewhere in Bartow, I think. I was so stressed out that my memories of that time are a little blurry. I don't remember much of what was said. I know I was pissed at Sara more than anything. I had told her that I forgave her for seeing the other guy, but really, I held on to the anger that came from my true feelings about her little escapade, for years. I also blamed her for the pregnancy. I didn't tell her that, but I felt like it was her fault because she was the one who was supposed to be taking the birth control pills. Had she quit taking them while she was out drinking and smoking pot all those nights that she spent partying with her friends? I didn't know for sure, but that's what I thought. I felt like she was now probably just trying to manipulate me into helping her support a kid that might not even be mine. I had no idea whether or not she was sleeping with that new kid she was seeing. For all I knew, there could have been others. Who knows? I wasn't around at any of those parties, that were so much fun. I had no idea what went on when people started doing drugs and getting drunk. I had already heard enough stories from my friend, Justin, about parties with his co-workers where people got drunk and started screwing each other's girlfriends and boyfriends. I had an idea that people under the influence adopted a new set of morals and acted differently than they did when sober. I worried that Sara might have been the same way. Now I might be getting ready to try and raise a kid that wasn't mine with a girl who probably really cared little about me. Those days before I told my parents what was going on with Sara were very scary times for me. As the days turned into weeks, months, and years, it only got scarier. I think that my decision to get back together with Sara, for the sake of raising a child, was a move that I made for all the wrong reasons. It was the single biggest step I took down the spiral. Things were starting to become very stressful. For the first time, I began to look back on my life and wish that I could go back in time and change things. I began to have real regret for my past and real fear for my future. As far as the future was concerned, all that I could see was black. It was becoming apparent that the spiral was descending into the darkness.

Chapter 19: A Shotgun Wedding

I asked Sara whether or not she had sex with that kid she had left me for. She swore she didn't. I figured she would say that. I don't know why I bothered asking because it gave me no relief to hear her answer. I asked her if she had sex with anybody at any of the parties she had gone to. She got mad and said, "I'm not a whore. You're the only one I was having sex with. This is your baby." I apologized for asking but told her it was just something I had to know.

Within a couple of weeks of seeing each other on an almost daily basis, we were talking about marriage. I told her that if she was going to keep the baby, I thought that marriage was the best thing to do. We would figure out the rest of the details later. But I didn't want to have to live with all of my family members seeing me as the father to an illegitimate child. I didn't want to go on as boyfriend/girlfriend if a kid was now part of the picture. My family would have little respect for what we had done, but if we stayed un-married it would be completely unacceptable. So that was that. I proposed to her in less than a month after she first told me the news about her pregnancy by saying, "So, I guess I should ask you if you want to marry me.", as we were driving along the road between my house and hers. It was anything but romantic. We were just going through the motions now. We were simply trying to put lipstick on a pig. I just wanted to keep up appearances as best as I could.

I remember coming home that night after officially popping the question to Sara. I was so nervous. My parents didn't know anything about what was going on. They didn't know that I had been seeing Sara everyday for the past few weeks. And now I had to drop a bunch of bad news on them. I expected my parents would kick me out of the house. I had already told Sara that was a possibility because they now hated her. Sara's mom told me that I could stay with them until we found an apartment of our own. That was probably the only time I thought her mom was actually cooler than my own parents.

I remember walking into my parents' bedroom. They were both in there. I said, "I've got some important news to tell you." "Oh yeah? I thought something was on your mind because you've been acting weird the last couple of days. What's up?", my dad asked. I stood there for a few seconds trying to think of the easiest way to get out of the situation. Then I said, "Well, I won't be surprised if you kick me out of the house for what I'm about to tell you. Sara and I are back together. We are going to get married and get our own apartment. She's pregnant." And with that, my mom replied, "Oh crap!" I'll never forget that. I was trying my best not to smile but I wanted to break out laughing at her comment. She hardly ever cussed. This was definitely not the time for smiles or laughter though. My dad let a few seconds go by and then said, "Congratulations! You wanted to be a man and now you're going to have to start acting like one." I felt like a total idiot. He was always good at coming up with zingers that hit you hard and made you feel that way. After that my mom started in with all her comments about how Sara was no good and couldn't believe she had allowed herself to get pregnant. She said Sara was ruining me. My dad took the other tack and said that worse things have happened and that if I thought I should try to marry Sara and help her raise a baby, then he would be supportive. He didn't try to sugar coat anything either though. He warned me to think about what I was doing. He said we were going to have a tough number of years ahead of us, but hopefully I would be able to figure things out. "Did you really think we would kick you out of the house?", Dad asked me near the end of the conversation. "Yes. I have been sneaking around behind you guy's backs and lying to you about all of this for a while now. I deserve to be kicked out.", I said. "Nobody's kicking anybody out of the house tonight. You just try to relax.", Dad said.

I was relieved to get the big news off my chest but immediately felt like I had let my whole family down. I felt like this was probably every parent's worst fear for their sons; that they would get a girl pregnant. I had done just that. I felt terrible. Most of the times Sara and I had sex, behind my parents' backs, I had thought of how wrong I was acting and felt guilty. But not like this. Now, the damage was done and there was no turning back. Soon, the rest of my family would find out, and I would get to deal with their response. I feared that I would be the outcast, the black sheep of the family. In my mind, I already was.

Sara and I got married on Valentine's Day of 1997. My family all pitched in and threw us a wedding at my parents' house. My great-grandfather's brother, Uncle Otis, married us that day. Everyone in the family tried to make the best of it. I never heard the first person say a discouraging word to Sara or myself. I was surprised. Almost everyone in my family turned out for our wedding. All my uncles, aunt's, cousins, and grand parents showed up. Sara's mom, dad, step dad, and all their kids showed up along with a couple of Sara's mom's friends. We didn't invite any of our friends. We wanted to keep it very small and, besides, most of our friends didn't approve anyway.

It was a simple ceremony, we exchanged our vows and said "I do." Then we had a small reception inside Mom and Dad's house. I'm sure it was a nice time, but I felt like an idiot through the entire thing. I wasn't sure just how many details my mom had divulged to the rest of the family over the years Sara and I had dated, but I felt like everyone had a pretty good idea that Sara and I were far from the perfect couple. I felt like this was all just a big charade and everyone would go home saying, "You know that will never last."

Sara's step aunt and uncle had sent us a card to congratulate us on our marriage and to tell us they had reserved 3 days and 2 nights at the Hilton World Showcase hotel in Orlando. That allowed us to have a honeymoon. We went straight from our wedding to Orlando and checked in at the hotel. It was a very nice place. We had a room on one of the upper levels, somewhere around the 30th floor. Our room had an attached balcony that overlooked the pool/ waterslide/ tiki bar area. You could make out the Epcot globe and other Orlando destinations from our room. We had the fridge stocked with small bottles of liquor, a hot tub, and a large screen TV. That room must have cost a fortune. That night we knew we were supposed to have sex. This was when it was finally O.K. to be doing that sort of thing. But now the magic seemed lost. Every other time we had sex before there was an element of danger. I always felt like "I shouldn't be doing this" and now that was all gone. Now, sex was different, less exciting. And there was a baby growing in her belly. She was just beginning to get a little swollen around the front of her belly. She didn't look pregnant, just a little fatter in the stomach than usual, like she had just eaten a big meal. We went through the motions just so we wouldn't be haunted by the fact that we had been having sex almost daily up to a few months previous, and now couldn't bring ourselves to do it on our wedding night.

The next day we went to Disney, Epcot, and MGM. We had a great time and then came back to our hotel. We sat out by the pool. She was wearing a bikini bathing suit. I remember taking pictures of her and thinking, "I wonder if she'll ever look this good again. In a few months her belly will be twice the size it is now. I wonder if she'll become one of those girls who puts on all kinds of weight during pregnancy and then never loses it afterwards." I hoped not. I was fond of the way she had looked since I met her. She had that long sandy blonde hair, and a great body. Was all that about to change? Was everything about to change? Of course it was.

Chapter 20: Let's Play House

My grand parents owned a rental house that was right next to their own in Bartow. They offered to let Sara and I rent it for $100 a month. I think they wanted us to feel like we weren't getting a total hand out, even though we were. They should have been charging about $350 to $400 for their place. So, with an offer we couldn't afford to refuse, Sara and I moved in to that little old house in Bartow. It was a major adjustment from the comfy setting I was used to back with Mom and Dad. The house was built in the 1940's and had the original bathtub/shower, and sink. The people who had lived in it for years before my grand parents bought it were both chain smokers who smoked inside the house. All the rooms still had the smell of long ago burnt cigarettes. My grandfather's mother had actually lived in the house for a time as well. She was now dead and it kind of creeped me out to know that she had been in that house when she fell and broke her hip and eventually died from complications. But, it was a place where it was just the two of us. And that did make things seem to smooth out for a while.

Another major favor from my grand-dad, GranDaddy, as we called him, was that he arranged for me to get my first job as a draftsman. I was working in the produce department at Food Lion when he told me that he had a friend who built equipment for the phosphate mines and needed someone to create fabrication drawings of the various items they built. He said the guy would probably pay me a lot better than Food Lion and I would be getting experience I could use later. I was ecstatic. This was the perfect first step into the architecture world. And it couldn't have come at a better time. A pay raise would mean more money to help Sara and our coming baby. A few days later, I met with Julian Hazen, the owner of MetPro Steel Fabrications, Inc. Mr. Hazen told me how he admired my grand parents and how he and his wife used to attend their church. He said he was thrilled to find somebody who knew how to use a computer for drafting in Bartow. I told him about my plans to become an architect and how I knew AutoCAD pretty well but had never used it in a work environment before. He said that was no problem and if I wanted the job, he would start me out at $9.00 per hour and we would re-negotiate in a few months. So, thanks to GranDaddy, once again; I was offered an opportunity to better myself, even though I had already done a pretty good job of screwing up the next several years of my life.

At school, they finally offered the class I needed to take in order to receive my A.A. Degree, Design 2.2. It was no different than any of the other Design classes before it. I also had Physics 1 and Calculus 1. It was a pretty tough semester. It was made tougher by the fact that I spent most of my time fearing the future and imagining myself struggling through the rest of school with a wife and child.

I remember trying to CLEP my way out of college English. If you passed the CLEP test, you didn't have to sit through a semester of whatever the test said you passed. English was always my easiest subject. I thought I would have no problem passing the test. I got into the exam room and was more nervous than I had ever been for any other test. It was weird because I usually considered myself a good test taker. Some kids panicked when they had to take tests, but I was usually calm and finished most tests before two thirds of the class was done. Now that I had the constant stress of knowing that I was about to become a father at 20, everything was different. My mind was always racing. I couldn't focus on the test in front of me. I couldn't focus on the questions. I'm sure that they weren't that challenging, but I couldn't keep my thoughts from straying to things like how important it was to pass this test and the fact that I had a kid coming in a few months. The final part of the test was to write a paper that compared and contrasted TV media with radio media. I just sat there with not a clue of what to write. My mind was blank except for the realization that I wasn't going to be passing this test and that would mean summer school and possibly not starting at a university in the fall. The time ran out for the test and I barely had an introductory paragraph written. I walked out of the room knowing that something was now different about me. I was having trouble doing something that should have been easy. I knew that I was stressed out about the coming baby, but I figured that was just normal. At the time, it seemed like nothing more than just too much stress. I thought that the strange effect of racing thoughts would soon pass once I became comfortable with the idea that I was a father. I realized that I would have to take my last English class in the summer.

As hard as it was for me to deal with the pressure of school, a new job, and a new pregnant wife, things were harder for Sara. After high school, she had started taking classes at H.C.C. with me. She said she wanted to get a degree in journalism or education. She wasn't sure. She wanted to go to H.C.C. because that's where I was. She didn't have the advantage of family that helped her pay for school. Her step dad sometimes helped out with a class here and there, but for the most part, she was on her own. She had to spend her own money if she wanted to go to school. After a semester or two, she quit taking classes all together. She decided she would rather work and spend her money on other things. Probably things like food and clothes. Things no one else provided for her on a routine basis. Sara had also failed her Senior Year of High School because she skipped so many classes that her English teacher would not give her a passing grade. It wasn't that big of a deal. They let her go to summer school and she got her diploma that summer. To my parents, though, it was a huge deal. They thought that she was really irresponsible for not going to school. I did too, but I knew she wasn't stupid. I felt sorry for her not being able to walk with all of the other seniors that year. She was real upset about it. At the time Sara realized she was pregnant, she was actually taking a couple of classes, trying to get an A. A. Degree in education, I think.

All of Sara's poor performance at school came into play when we decided how we could afford for both of us to continue school with a baby. The answer was, we couldn't afford to both go to school. We would have to take turns. One would graduate first. Then the other would follow. Since Sara had a habit of dropping the ball when it came to school, I thought it would be less risky if I graduated first. Then I'd get a decent paying job and put her through school myself. If she changed her mind about what she wanted to get a degree in, or decided she didn't need to go to college at all, that was fine with me. I would be out of school, with a good paying job. She would be able to take her time deciding what she wanted to do.

But this idea was hard for Sara. She felt like she was the one making the bigger sacrifice. If we split up, she'd be left to go to college and take care of a baby on her own. I was having trouble juggling my new responsibilities and school, but at least I was getting to go to school. She would be stuck working some crappy job with no hope of bettering her situation until I graduated, and we had enough money to pay for her education. She didn't like the idea, but I eventually persuaded her. The decision was made that I would continue going to school, and Sara would wait.

I had to apply to a university by March of that year, 1997. My first pick was University of Florida. I also applied to University of Miami, and Florida A & M University, my least favorite option. In order to be admitted into any of the universities you had to do a "pin up" of all your best work. This was where you literally pinned your favorite stuff on the wall and had architecture professors come look at it and decide whether or not they thought you were good enough to be accepted into their program. The first pin up was University of Florida, followed by Florida A & M, the next day. Sara and I drove to Gainesville, did the pin up, then drove to Tallahassee the next day and did the same thing all over again. I didn't even bother with U of M because their tuition was $30,000 a year.

A month or so after the pin ups I received letters in the mail from UF and FAMU. UF said that I was not accepted into the third year architecture program, but could enter the School of Architecture as a first year student. This would mean that all my architecture related classes would not count for anything. Basically, what UF was saying was that I would lose two years if I wanted to go to their school. FAMU said that I was accepted into their third year program and they would accept all my classes from H.C.C. So, my path was set out before me pretty clearly. I would be moving to Tallahassee to attend a historically black college to receive my degree in architecture. The idea wasn't my favorite, but I would have a degree and that would hopefully guarantee a good job.

Chapter 21: The Birth of an Angel

Elizabeth Gann was born on July 28, 1997 in the old Bartow Memorial Hospital that has now been converted into a Hospice headquarters along with other medical related tenants. Sara went into labor that morning and we had Elizabeth only a few hours later. The doctors and nurses said she had a very easy labor. It still didn't look like fun to me. Sara was in a lot of pain for those few hours, I'm sure, but she was in a pretty good mood for most of the time. She didn't do the typical scream-at-your-husband-during-childbirth thing that you often hear stories about. Sara's mom was actually the first one to arrive at the hospital after Elizabeth was born. My parents were in Naples, Florida, visiting my dad's brother, David, and his wife, Pam. We called them when Sara went into labor. They got there just a couple hours after Elizabeth was born. Sara's step dad, brother, and sister showed up right about the same time, along with my brothers. Then came Sara's dad and his crew. We had a pretty big crowd. It was a long day. I was nervous and not at ease with the idea that I was now a father. I was still a kid, only 21, and now I had a baby of my own. Everybody that came oowed and ahhed over Elizabeth. They all congratulated Sara and I. After everyone had seen our new baby and told us how beautiful she was they finally left that night. After that, it was just Sara and I, and our new little girl, Elizabeth. There would never be any more Sara and I. From that day forward it would always be the three of us. That was an idea that made me a little sad, and a little worried, because I knew that Sara and I, alone, managed to find things to disagree about. Now that we had our first child, what would life be like with a baby in the mix?

The next morning we all got to go home. Not long after we arrived, people started stopping by at our house. Family and friends, Sara's and mine, all came by to see our new baby. It was nice but there was still that awkward feeling in me that I didn't belong in this scene, not yet. "This should all be happening in about five years from now. Not now.", I thought. I tried to seem excited and happy that all of it was happening, but really I was scared and disappointed in myself. I was afraid I would never be able to provide, for my little girl, the things that my parents had provided for me. This made me feel both sad and irresponsible. I'm sure it showed to everyone who came and saw us, even though I was trying to play cool.

I was thankful that we at least had a healthy baby. I didn't really care if we had a girl or boy. That didn't really matter to me. And my mom, who had only three boys, was elated that she now had a granddaughter. There was finally a girl in our family besides mom. Mom spoiled our new baby from the start. She had to make up for all the years she had wanted a little girl, and instead ended up living with three little hellion boys. Yes, I was starting to see that maybe this wasn't as bad a thing as I had previously thought it might be. My biggest fear before Elizabeth was born, was that she would be born with a defection. Sara had been drinking and smoking pot at the beginning of her pregnancy. I was thrilled to realize that we weren't punished for that. We had a baby young, and far sooner than I wanted, but she was healthy, that was a nice start.

Chapter 22: FAMU, Year 1, and the TRBC

When Elizabeth was just 2 weeks old, we moved from Bartow to Tallahassee. Sara and I had already picked out a little apartment before Elizabeth was born. It was $475 per month, The Palms of Apalachee Parkway. It was a pretty scary place really, but we could barely afford that. In fact, we couldn't afford anything at all. We came to Tallahassee with no jobs and just enough money to pay the bills for a month or so. My grand parents told us they would help us out until we could support ourselves. They started sending us a check for $1,000 every month for the first five or six months we were there. They were always the ones who bailed me out when I brought on more trouble than I could afford. I had also applied for financial aid and was told that I qualified for a Pell grant and a federal student loan. There were benefits to being a poor, married student. Financial aid was one of them. I didn't have to report my parents' income anymore and was now considered an independent. I usually received about $4,500 every semester between the grant and loan. About $2,500 of that would have to be paid back some day, as it was the loan portion of my income.

Tallahassee was bigger than any place Sara or myself had ever lived. We felt like we had moved from the country to the big city. We now lived in a town with two universities, two shopping malls, and three Wal-Marts. It was a big step up for us in the way of convenience. Everything we needed was within three miles of our apartment. It was nice.

School started a few weeks after we moved. I had already made a few trips around campus to orient myself with all the places I would need to go. It was a culture shock. For the only time in my life, I was now the minority. If I stepped outside the School of Architecture, I stuck out like a sore thumb. I could walk from one end of campus to the other and might pass one or two other white kids. Everybody else was black. Almost every car that drove by on the street was blasting rap music. A lot of the black kids stood up against buildings around campus with their own portable stereos blasting their favorite rapper's anthems. I felt totally out of place and was pretty nervous anytime I had to leave the School of Architecture.

The Financial Aid Office was one of those places outside of the School of Architecture. I went into that building several times every semester to check on the status of my grant and loan. It was almost always a nerve-racking experience. I was usually the only white kid in the building. Most kids stared at me as I walked by. Some would ask me why I wasn't at FSU. I would always try to laugh, and ask them, "Why should I be at FSU?" They would usually laugh too. Most of the kids were really nice if you had the courage to talk to them. The most courteous were usually the non-American blacks, the ones from Africa, Haiti, Jamaica, etc. They hadn't grown up with the stereotypes and ideas about whites that the American black kids had. By the time my FAMU days were over, I ended up with several good friends who were all foreign black kids.

The School of Architecture itself was a totally different environment than the rest of the school, with the exception of the School of Pharmacy. Once you walked into the School of Architecture, it was almost like walking around at any other school I had ever attended. There were mainly white kids, with a little more than average numbers of black, and Latino kids as well. I never felt uncomfortable about being white inside the School of Architecture.

I began my classes and saw some familiar faces. Jorge Magdeno and Aaron Carter were two guys that had gone to H.C.C. with me. We were the only three H.C.C. people at FAMU from our class. It was nice to instantly have friends. It would turn out to be harder to make new ones.

Jorge and I had become real good friends at H.C.C. because we were in similar situations. He was married and already had two kids by the time we graduated from H.C.C. He and Aaron also had to wait out a year at H.C.C. because they were waiting for the same class that I was. Jorge and I had a lot in common even though he was Hispanic and a couple years older than me. We both had dreams of becoming architects to support our families. Jorge was a religious guy also. I liked that about him. I felt like he was trustworthy and made a good friend. Jorge told me that he and his wife were looking for childcare so that his wife could start her job as a secretary with the Board of Regents. I thought about Sara staying home with Elizabeth and told him that she might be willing to watch his kids if they could afford her high prices. He laughed and said he would tell his wife. I asked Sara what she thought about watching Jorge's kids and she said she would love to. We decided that would be a great thing for Sara to do because not only would we not be paying for childcare, she would also be getting paid while she got to stay home with Elizabeth. It was a double win.

Jorge and his wife, Maria, agreed to the idea of $150 a month per child. It wasn't a lot of money for Sara and I, but it was a start. Besides we were rolling in the dough after my grant and loan money came in. I wanted to see what my stress level was with full time university classes, before I went out and found a job. Meanwhile, Sara had contacted one of her high school friends who was a student at FSU, Ashley Rasse. Ashley was actually one of the girls that hung out with me and my friends in the mornings before school when we were in junior high. Sara and Ashley were both cheerleaders together in high school and become good friends. Ashley had a little girl a year older than ours. Her name was also Elizabeth. Sara told Ashley about watching the two little kids at home with Elizabeth. Ashley said she wanted Sara to watch her Elizabeth as well if she thought she could. Sara agreed and now she had two toddlers and two infants at our apartment every week day from 7:00 am to 5:30 pm Ashley agreed to the same price that Jorge had agreed to. So now Sara was bringing in $450 a month and saving us a daycare bill of our own. I was bringing in

$2500 in debt every semester. My plan to support my wife and child was not yet working.

At school things were a little more stressful than they had been during most of community college. I only had Jorge in a couple of classes. The main stress maker was Design 3.1. Jorge was not in that class. I was all alone when I walked into that studio the first day. I remember feeling very out of place because almost all of the other students were from the second year class at FAMU. They all met two years previously and had all bonded together pretty well. I was an outsider. I found an empty desk and sat down and just listened to all the conversations going on around me. A guy came up to me and introduced himself as Keith Black. He asked me if I had brought a parallel bar to attach to the desk I was sitting at. I told him I had not. He showed me a desk that had a parallel bar sitting under it. "Better grab it before someone else claims it.", he said. I did. That quick move on his part had just saved me about $60, the price to provide my own parallel bar. I never had to do that before at H.C.C. Apparently at FAMU, so many parallel bars had been stolen that they no longer replaced them in the studios. If your desk didn't already have a parallel bar, you had to provide your own. I thanked Keith for the parallel bar and then he introduced me to Seth Cobin. Seth, Keith, and I would remain friends that entire semester. They were both real good guys, both smart asses, but pretty hilarious at times.

I was glad that I at least had a couple of friends at school. I wasn't sure how many more I would make though. Having a wife and kid at home made me feel out of place most of the time I was at FAMU. I couldn't stop myself from feeling like I didn't deserve to be with these other students. They were mostly all single and very focused on their life at school. I was married with child and had plenty of things at home to keep me distracted and distant from most all the other students.

After a while, I noticed a few of the students were acting like they were still in high school. There was a group of about four guys that always sat with each other in every class. They were like a group of little girls, if one of them had to go to the bathroom, the whole bunch would have probably followed along with them. I started to find these guys really obnoxious. They would usually try to blurt out some stupid comment when the instructor was trying to teach class. They thought they were filling our need to have class clowns. I wished they would have been in another studio.

They usually tried to say smart ass comments about my work and tried to make me feel like an idiot whenever possible. At first it didn't bother me so much. I figured it was just the fact that I was new and they were just having fun picking on the new kid. Then I realized they were assaulting all of three of us from H.C.C. They would make comments about how we were community college geeks. I guess they really thought that they were something because they had spent two more years at FAMU than we had. As if that were some great accomplishment. Our ideas were no better or worse than anyone else's. But these guys really tried hard to make us think otherwise. It was the first time I had felt like I was dealing with a bully since junior high. I would say things like, "You know we aren't in junior high here ladies.", to them. That was just adding fuel to the fire. They would go on and usually bring up things about me being married and "pussy whipped". They also made comments about me having a kid, "Can you imagine what Scott must be like with his kid at home? Oh my God." I eventually figured out that the best way to deal with them was to ignore and avoid them as much as possible. It was still difficult because I wasn't used to being treated so poorly. I was accustomed to people liking me and usually treating me with at least a little courtesy. That first semester at FAMU, I felt like I was the butt of a joke.

My second semester at FAMU, Ashley mentioned to Sara that she was watching kids in the nursery at Thomasville Road Baptist Church, TRBC, on Sundays and Wednesday nights. She said they were looking for help out in the nursery and loved to pay college types to help out in the nursery. Sara started going with Ashley every Sunday and Wednesday night. They paid Sara $7.50 per hour for her time, usually an hour or two at the most. Sara told me that they still wanted more help and that the lady in charge of the nursery department wanted me to come help out if I thought I could. I agreed to help out in the nursery. That was how we first got involved with TRBC.

I started going with Sara and Ashley every Sunday and Wednesday night to help out in the nursery. It was usually nothing more than an hour of holding babies, changing diapers, and talking with each other. It was a nice environment. All the people at the church seemed very nice. Mary Katherine Green was the nursery department head. TRBC was a big church with well over a thousand members in its pews every Sunday. The nursery was made up of six different classrooms that ranged from infants to about four years old. TRBC was the largest church I had ever been to. I was impressed with its size and wondered how they had attracted so many people to this one particular church. Sara and agreed it would be a good idea to start attending TRBC on Sunday mornings. We had met several couples whose kids were in the nursery and they had all asked us to try coming to a service. So, we decided to try it out.

The pastor's name was Billy Cruce. He had started the church only about thirty years earlier and had grown it into the behemoth it was when Sara and I first started attending. At the first sermon I heard Dr. Cruce give, I could understand what the draw was. He was a very articulate speaker who focused on delivering messages that instructed us how to live better lives. He never talked about tithing and rarely spoke of the terrors of Hell. His messages were always well orchestrated, positive, and left you feeling like you had just learned something you could actually apply to your life. He was the greatest pastor I have ever seen or heard. On top of that they had a music department that was more talented than anything I had ever witnessed. Every Sunday morning someone sang a solo or played a musical instrument that actually sounded great. I was used to very traditional church hymns that seemed like music from another time and whose words I had trouble relating to. The songs we usually heard and sang were moving with clear messages and beautiful instruments playing in the background. There was actually a small orchestra that played all the music we sang along to. Not just a small organ, but violins, wood winds, brass, and drums. Of course, there was also an organ. But the organ never had the over powering sound that I was used to in the churches I had attended growing up. The main instrumental focus was usually the violins, wood winds, and piano. For me, it was a nice change of style. The music at TRBC moved me.

Sara and I became good friends with one particular couple, the Hamms, Herb and Janice. They were both about ten years older than us and far more wealthy, but they never acted like it. They were both the nicest people we knew at TRBC. Herb and Janice had four kids. Herb was a pharmaceutical sales rep for Merke Pharmaceuticals. His job revolved around visiting doctors and telling them all the advantages of using Merke's products over their competitors. He was apparently pretty successful because they had a nice home in an upscale neighborhood, nice cars, and were still able to take care of four kids. Janice was a stay at home mom. She home schooled their kids. Every now and then, they would ask Sara and I to baby sit their kids on Friday or Saturday night for several hours. We didn't mind because they always paid us more than enough and provided supper and movies for everybody to watch. It was also great entertainment for Elizabeth, who was now known as Baby Liza, who loved to be around older kids even at that young age. Sara and I would usually watch the Hamm's small army from around 6:00 pm to 12:00 am, while Herb and Janice went out on a date.

Around the middle of the second semester at FAMU, an announcement was made that student's who had a G.P.A. of 3.0 or higher were eligible to attend a consortium school in Washington D.C., hosted by Virginia Tech. If we wanted to participate, it would mean spending our entire 4th year of college at the Virginia Tech Campus in D.C. We would also have to have the dean's approval before being cleared to go. I thought that sounded like a lot of fun, but didn't see how we would want to put ourselves through the stress of relocating and me joining up with yet another group of students. I asked one of my professors if we would be considered Virginia Tech students after that. He said, "No, but you can transfer into their school if you agree to get your Master's Degree with them." That got me thinking. I didn't mind having a degree from FAMU, but my family would have a lot more pride if they thought of me as a Hoakie. I mentioned it to Sara when I got home that day. I told her that the school was in Washington, D.C. I don't know if she heard anything beyond that. "D.C.? I've always wanted to go there. Oh, that sounds like something you should think about. Virginia Tech is probably a better school than FAMU too. You would probably enjoy it there.", she said. I said, "Yeah, and they said the school has a guaranteed job placement program. They say you get great work experience there. Who knows, if we went up there, we might not ever come back." And just like that, a new dream, a new adventure was born.

Sara called Justin White that very next day and told him about what we were thinking. I don't know what possessed her to tell him or if he happened to call her looking for me, but she told him about D.C. He told Sara that he really wanted to go to school at George Mason University and major in politics. He suggested the idea of us splitting an apartment for a while and all living together. Sara told me about Justin's idea. I said, "I can't believe he would suggest such a thing. You guys don't get along very well, remember." She laughed and said, "Justin is fine by me, just as long as he doesn't get you in any trouble." I thought that would be a hard thing for

Justin to do. After all it didn't require a lot of effort for Justin to be on Sara's bad side. But, I thought that if Justin and Sara could get along, it might not be such a bad idea. We would have somebody to split the rent with. We knew D.C. prices would be much higher than Tallahassee. We just didn't realize how high they would actually be. But with Sara and Justin both excited about the idea of all of us living together up there, I thought maybe things would work out. I'd be able to see my best friend and wife everyday. It sounded like a lot of fun, the more I thought about it.

At TRBC, Herb Hamm and I were talking in the nursery one night and he was asking me if I ever thought about working with a construction company. I said I would love to, that I would be able to see what the life of a contractor was like. I had wanted to do exactly that for a couple years now. He said he had a good friend that worked with Ajax Construction, one of the bigger outfits in town, and he thought they would give me a summer job if I was willing to try it out. I gave him an enthusiastic, "Yeah, that sounds great!" and my summer began to take shape.

The following Sunday, Herb introduced me to Terry Koves, a very wealthy and physically fit guy. He was as nice a guy as Herb. Herb, Terry, and I talked for a little while and Terry brought up the subject of working for Ajax Construction. He said he wasn't sure what they would have me doing but he was sure that I could have a job there if I wanted one. I told him I would love to work out in the field and get some good hands on building experience. He said that most of that most of the actual labor was done by sub-contractors that they hired. He said that they would most likely want me in some type of management or other office job. He said that since I already had a good math and science background they probably would feel like they were wasting me by putting me in the field. I said "Wherever I can help out is fine with me, any experience is good experience at this point." He agreed.

A few days later I had my interview with the owner of Ajax Construction, John Smith. He was also a very nice guy. He told me that all of his sons worked for him as construction managers. His was a family business. He said if Terry had recommended me, then I was good by him. I told him about school and working for Met Pro as a draftsman. He said they needed help in the estimating department and, if I were interested, they would pay $11.00 per hour and have me on full time for the summer. I told him that I was moving to D.C. at the end of the summer to attend the VT Consortium. He said that was fine, they just wanted to let me see what the other side of the building world was like. I thought it was very nice. They didn't really need me. They were just giving me a paid tour of life at a construction company.

I started working with Ajax as soon as school ended that semester. My first day, I was introduced around the office and shown to my immediate supervisor, Jim Marpart. Jim said that they were putting together an estimate for several schools that Ajax would be building during the summer and fall. He said that was where I would come in handy. They needed someone to help count plumbing fixtures, lights, etc. It was very basic. It only took a few days to get through that first assignment. Then they put me on tallying up bricks and concrete block. Another guy in estimating showed me how to use a program called Earthworks, to estimate the cost of grading the land, and cut/fill estimation. He showed me how to use a Laser Stylus that actually measured right off of the construction drawings. I could trace over the topography lines of a Civil Engineers drawings and it would actually draw it all up on the computer. Then I used the Earthworks software to produce a 3-D model of the building site. The model calculated how much dirt was required to be put in or taken out to achieve the designs of the Civil Engineers. I thought it was really amazing. My time at Ajax was the most fun I'd ever had working. All the people were very friendly, and Terry checked up on me almost everyday to see what I thought about the place.

One of the construction managers told me one day, "Scott, you need to get out of Architecture while you still can. Come away from the Dark Side of The Force. Step into the light.", I laughed and said I had thought about it, but was already too far down that road. "I can never be a Jedi. I am already one with the Dark powers of the Force.", I said, and he laughed. "Seriously, the only way to be a successful Architect is to either be extremely talented or be a major asshole! And still, you'll never make the kind of money you could if you got a degree in Construction Management. Construction is where the money is. We get 20 to 30 percent of the building's budget. Architects only get 6 to 8 percent. Do the math.", he said. I told him I didn't know many poor architects. The truth was I only knew one and guess what, I later found out that he had a degree in Construction Management. He, my mom's cousin, Gary; was actually a contractor and he had a partner who was a licensed architect. I didn't find this out until after I graduated from college.

Chapter 23: The D.C. Year

My time at Ajax ended sooner than I wanted it to. Summer was nearing an end and it was time to move to Washington D.C. Sara and I had already taken a trip up there to pick out an apartment. Justin said whatever we thought was nice was fine with him, just as long as he had his own room, of course. What we found was a very nice three-story townhouse that had three bedrooms, three bathrooms, a full kitchen, dining room, TV room, and an extra room that we didn't know what would be used for. The extra room was the size of a one-car garage. On some of the units it actually was a garage, but our unit was set off from the street, so they had built it as a really big extra room that would make a nice place for a home office or gym. The townhouse was in a community development that came complete with tennis courts, play ground, swimming pool, club house, and two small lakes. It was the nicest place I have ever lived to this day.

We looked all around the D.C. area with a realtor and settled on the townhouse in Woodbridge, VA. It was only about 25 miles south of D.C. and didn't seem that far away from school. I only found out, after we moved, that my daily commute to school was 1 ½ hours one way. The place in Woodbridge was cheaper than anything we saw closer into D.C., so it seemed like a good idea. We took lots of pictures to show Justin and he loved it.

So near the end of the summer, we loaded a large U-Haul truck and all moved up to D.C. with the help of my parents. We were all very excited about our new surroundings. Sara and I showed my parents and Justin around the neighborhood, pointing out all the amenities. Everybody was impressed.

Once again, we all moved without anyone having a job. Justin hoped to get on with Chili's in Woodbridge as a bartender. Sara wanted to try working at a daycare. I was planning to get a job with an architectural firm as a draftsman. Sara lined up her job first. She found a daycare right down the street from our townhouse and was hired on without any trouble. Justin applied at Chili's and they told him that they might be hiring in a couple weeks, but not at the moment. I was waiting for school to start. I was hoping the school would help place me in an architectural firm, like my professor at FAMU had told me.

So Justin and I had a lot of free time on our hands when we first got there. I didn't even have to take care of Liza, because she was going to Sara's daycare. Justin and I decided we would tour the D.C. area, before we both got too busy to appreciate it. We first drove to a Metro station. The Metro was the D.C. area public transit subway system. We hopped on a Metro train and rode into D.C. That was the first time I had ever ridden on a subway and I was very impressed. It was so nice not having to fight traffic to get from here to there. We just bought a Metro Day Pass and could then ride as much as we wanted that day. The Metro took us to anywhere in D.C. that was worth seeing. Our first stop was the Pentagon. Justin wanted to see what he would be allowed to do there with his military I.D. He was hoping we might get a special tour or something like that. It turned out that National Guard grunts got the same treatment as everybody else. We still got a free tour around the Pentagon. That was really cool. The next day we went to Arlington Cemetery and Lincoln Memorial, all for free, of course.

Sara started getting aggravated with me because I was getting to see all of this great stuff without her. She asked me to stop going out with Justin so that he could focus on getting a job. She said I should be looking around too. I told her school was about to start and I'd get one soon afterwards. We had my student grant and loan money coming in and would be able to pay the bills with no problem. That turned out to be true in fact. Justin ended up getting a call back from Chili's a few days later and started working as a bartender there.

School started. I was one of six or seven from FAMU that decided to try out the VT Consortium. That first day's first item on the agenda was a school wide meeting. We were all brought into the largest room in the school. It was only about 4,500 square feet but it was big enough to house the small group that attended the school. The entire school was all in one building in Alexandria, VA, just off of King Street. We probably totaled around 150 students all together. But the diversity of the students was like nothing I had ever experienced. We had students from schools in Germany, England, Japan, Indonesia, and of course the U.S. The United States schools were Cal Poly in St. Luis Obispo, CA, FAMU, and Virginia Tech's own. Everyone else was foreign. It was a really great environment. All the students spoke English, so you could talk to everybody. Everyone was interesting and also interested in everyone else. Each school brought along one faculty member as well. Each faculty member would pair up with another and teach a design class. The nice thing was that even though we were assigned to two instructors, they encouraged us to seek advice from the entire faculty. All the teachers there could be our personal instructor if we wanted them to. It was a totally different approach than what I had experienced at H.C.C. and FAMU. There, my only help for all projects came from my Design instructor. I couldn't expect help or advice from anyone but them.

On my first day at the VT Consortium, I was assigned to a studio. My instructors were from Cal Poly and Virginia Tech. I was hoping to get the instructor from Bau Haus, Germany. Many great architects had graduated from that school and I really wanted to see what their Design instructor was like. I was still just happy that I was going to school with people who were from the Bau Haus. I thought, if nothing else, I'd try to make friends with the Bau Haus students, just to see if any of their great talent might rub off on me.

Our first "design" project was a school wide competition to see who could come up with the best concrete object. It was a sculpture type project that had less to do with architecture and was more aimed at getting us to think about things from a different angle. In order to design an object that must be poured concrete, we had to design a mold, a form to hold the concrete while it dried. This was the main focus of the project, thinking in reverse. The mold defined everything that the concrete object was not and separated it from the surrounding space. The void created by the mold was to become the object itself. This was the new way of thinking that they wanted to introduce us to, the idea of The Subtraction.

I got the idea to make four separate objects that could be configured together in many ways to make one object. It was sort of like Lego building blocks, only more complex. Each object was basically a cube with smaller, protruding cubes coming off of it. There were also cube shaped holes, that were the size of the smaller protruding cubes in each object. The protrusions fit into the holes and allowed all the pieces to join together. The only function my object would have was that it could be used as a light, if you put candles inside some of the holes that had been created. To me, it looked really cool at night, when it was lit up and standing in our living room.

To make the objects real, I had to build their forms. I had never had any experience working with concrete, so this was all new to me. The professors told us that plywood was the best thing to use for the forms, but there was also 1 inch thick corrugated cardboard, for those of us that wanted to stick with something a little more familiar. I chose the cardboard for my form, because the shop was filled with too many people trying to use all the various tools to create their forms. I could take my cardboard to my studio and cut it myself with an Exacto knife. The problem with the cardboard was that it gave, just a little, under the pressure of the concrete, once it had been poured inside. My project still turned out pretty good, I thought, even if it didn't have completely straight surfaces. There were only a few places where any warping could be noticed and even those were minor. I was really happy with the way it turned out. I didn't get selected in the top three for my idea, but I still got an A for my attempt.

After that first project we had a couple others and eventually moved on to designing the house of a librarian who had a vast rare book collection. The book collection was to be the focal point of the house. It seemed like an interesting project. The other criteria was that the house would be situated between two historic homes, in Alexandria, that were built in the 1700's. The challenge was to design something that was modern, but somehow acknowledged these older homes, without just replicating their style of construction. I decided that my design would be of my usual Deconstructive style. That was the most popular style with all the professors at all the schools I had been to, so I figured it would work here too. Most professors seemed to hate to see us try using more traditional styles of design: Classical, Neo-Classical, Gothic, etc. They seemed to think that if our buildings looked like what the cutting edge architects at that time were designing, they were better for it. Well, the project started off fine but ended in the closest I had come to disaster at school.

The reasons for this were all at home. You see, the *House of the Librarian* project started during my second semester at VT. By this time I was working, usually around 30 hours a week. Sara had quit working at the daycare and started watching kids at our house. That was where the extra room in our house came in handy. She turned the extra room into a play area for the kids. Justin was no longer living with us. That was the biggest stress for Sara and I because we now had to come up with his third of the rent every month.

Justin and Sara had been in several arguments. Justin had witnessed Sara and I arguing as well. One night Sara found the name and phone number of a girl from school in my backpack. I told her that this girl had given me her number because she had asked for mine. She said she just wanted to have it in case she needed help with class or if she ever missed an assignment and needed to catch up. I hadn't asked for her number and only had it because she had given it to me and I had stuck it in my backpack and forgotten about it. The girl who had given me the number wasn't attractive to me at all. I never had any intention of trying to fool around behind Sara's back with this girl. I don't even remember her name. But Sara was positive that she had caught me cheating on her. She now had proof. She called the number and cussed the girl out and told her to never call my number. She also tore through my backpack and all my papers trying to find more evidence that I was cheating on her. It was crazy. She looked crazy. And that was the last straw for Justin. He told me, "I'm sorry but I can't live here with her. I don't see how you can either. I'm going back to Florida. I'll pay you my part of the rent, but I'm not living here anymore."

And a few days later, he left. This created a deep resentment in me towards Sara. I knew that Justin and Sara would have problems getting along, but I didn't think she would be able to force him out of the house. And now I felt like she had made a fool of herself and me, once again. Justin was so unimpressed with our relationship that he actually left us. I felt like an idiot. I also felt trapped. I had to stay in D.C. and finish the school year. We were only half way there at this point. And we were obligated to our lease through June. As much as I wished I could go back to Florida with Justin, I knew it would be a very stupid thing to do. Besides, this wasn't the first argument Sara and I had ever had. It was just the worst one Justin had ever seen. For me, it was something I had learned to live with, even if it was slowly eating me alive. I always hoped things would get better. I thought if we forgave each other and moved on, things would eventually settle down. The problem for me was, I never really forgave her for anything. I was keeping a mental tally of all the ways she had wronged me.

Justin left without saying goodbye. It was a very awkward situation. I noticed his car was packed with all his stuff one night. The next morning he was gone. He never called, or wrote for years after that. He never sent any money for his portion of the rent. This meant that I had to work more and Sara took on a couple more kids at home so that we could pay the bills. I remember living off of peanut butter jelly sandwiches and ramen noodles for a couple months after he left. Things were pretty tight for a while. This helped add to the stress of going to college and trying to work almost full time.

At work things weren't great either. I had taken a job as a draftsman with an architectural firm, Devenrow& Associates. It was my first experience in an architectural firm and it didn't take long for me to realize that I didn't like it. I had started out very excited. I interviewed with, not the owner, but an Associate, one of the partners in the firm. His name was Rodney. He was a VT grad who had worked with Mr. Devenrow for about ten years already. Rodney was a real nice guy and pretty funny too. I felt comfortable in the interview. After the interview, Rodney said he would call me to let me know what Mr. Devenrow wanted to do. I got a call back that night from Rodney congratulating me on getting the job and he said they would start me out at $9.00 per hour with a review in three months. He said I'd probably get bumped up a couple bucks an hour, after the review. I thanked him and told him I could start whenever they wanted me to.

My first day at Devenrow& Associates was a little nerve racking. They didn't use AutoCAD. Instead they were using a cheaper software called DataCAD. It was similar to AutoCAD but still required about a week of practice before I felt comfortable using it. Even then, I only knew how to use it for basic things. They eventually got me drawing house plans. The houses they worked on were million dollar mansions that were nothing like any houses I was used to. The level of detail that went into the drawings was way beyond the simple shop drawings I had produced for Met Pro. I could whip out all the necessary drawings for a piece of equipment at Met Pro within a few hours. Now I was working on sets of drawings, usually thirty to forty 24" x 36" sheets. We would usually spend several weeks on just one house. And that was just to produce the preliminary drawings. Then there were revisions and calls to the clients, engineers, and contractors. There was also the process of producing the specs. That was a new animal all together that we had never discussed anything about at school. The specs, Building Specifications, spelled out every last detail of the building. Drawings showed a Contractor where and how much of something. The specs said exactly who made it, what procedures were acceptable, and who was responsible for what. Carpet, for example, was shown in certain rooms in the construction drawings. The specifications said exactly who manufactured the carpet, its color, weave pattern, the amount of padding necessary, and what conditions had to be met for an acceptable installation. The specs were always hundreds of pages long. I was now learning all this new detail about exactly how architecture was practiced. I felt a little overwhelmed.

On top of that, the people weren't the greatest. The office was about half guys, half girls. They were all older than me. I was the only intern. Most of the people that worked there were graduates of VT, or other schools in the New England area. They all seemed to think highly of themselves. They did not think of themselves as southerners. They thought that people from the south were inferior to their big city hustling selves. I got a lot of comments about being from Florida. They were always brought out in a joking kind of way, but I felt like there was probably some truth, as to how they really thought of me, in their comments as well. They also knew that I had a child and that I was married. I think they all sort of looked down on that too. No one else in the office had kids except Mr. Devenrow. Everyone who worked at Devenrow& Associates was older than me, but they were all so committed to their jobs or whatever else, that none of them had kids. Only a couple other people were even married. They all drove nice cars and SUV's. I drove my little 1997 Honda Civic hatchback. Which was nice enough to me, but parked next to a Lexus or BMW, I thought it looked a little out of place. It was funny that I had not ever noticed many people at Ajax driving fancy cars, and that project manager had told me about contractors making more than architects. I wasn't sure if these people at my new firm were making so much that they could afford the cars they drove around in, or if it was just important for them to look successful. I thought it was more likely the latter.

Mr. Devenrow himself was the icing on the cake. After only working there a few days, I remember thinking, "Mr. Devenrow must be one of those architects who got successful by being a major asshole." He would make several phone calls to people everyday that would result in him yelling and cussing at them. Even when he was in a good mood, he still came across as very arrogant and full of himself. I was never impressed by Mr. Devenrow. After I had worked there for over three months, I remember asking him if I was going to be getting a review soon. That was a big mistake. He said, "You want a review? O.K., here it is. Kids like you are a dime a dozen. I could walk down to your school and replace you with ten others who would probably be happy to work for less than you do. Did you want a raise? Well, how about a quarter an hour?" And with that he walked off. He had said all this in front of the entire office. People were quietly snickering. I felt totally humiliated. I remember thinking, "That guy at Ajax was right, this is the Dark Side of the Force. These people are all assholes."

After seeing that I wasn't enjoying working at an architectural firm, I started having trouble staying motivated about school. I knew I had to finish what I had started, but was very disappointed that my first encounter with actual architects was going so poorly. "Maybe I'm not cut out for this.", I told Sara. She said that it was probably just a bad bunch of people I was working with, not to let it get to me, and to just look for something else.

After Justin left and school seemed like less of priority to me, Sara and I began having our weekend adventures. We saw everything in D.C. that was worth seeing that last semester. We went to The National Mall, of course, and visited all the Smithsonians, the National Museum of Art, The National Monument, Lincoln Memorial, The Capitol, The White House, etc. We also loved to go to the National Zoo. It was so nice because we could walk right in off the street, never pay a dime to get in, and spend the day there looking at all the different animals. Liza loved it. She had a great time pointing out all the different animals she knew. She was just starting to become a pretty good talker and she had lots of things to say every time we went to the zoo.

The thing we enjoyed most was to drive to Alexandria in my car with our bikes loaded on the back. There was a bike path that started in Alexandria and led directly into the D.C. Mall area. We would begin in Alexandria and ride the path, first to a field beside Ronald Regan International Airport where lots of walkers and cyclists would be resting, watching the jets come screaming right over our heads. It was really cool. Then we would follow the path past the Arlington National Cemetery, across the Arlington Bridge that led you to Lincoln Memorial, and on into the National Mall Area. The Mall is flanked on all sides by sidewalks that people often ride their bikes on. We would ride all over that area and would usually stop and buy lunch from one of the cart vendors that sold sausage dogs with peppers and onions. Some of my best memories of D.C. are those days when we would take our bike rides.

At school, I was told by my FAMU professor, that I was not living up to what was expected of me at the VT Consortium. She said I was representing FAMU and was making not only myself look bad, but FAMU as well. She said that my studio professors were wanting to fail me because I was missing so many Design classes and my work was poor. I told her about the situation with our roommate leaving us to pay more than what we had expected in rent. I told her I was having to work more now and that was why I had been missing so much class. She said she was sorry to hear about my situation but that I had better figure out how to juggle and re-prioritize if I wanted to pass the spring semester. I was working more, but the truth was that I was also playing more. I had missed a class or two because of things like not feeling well, or snow preventing me from driving. But I had also missed a couple classes just because I couldn't motivate myself to go. I now hated having to go to Devenrow& Associates everyday. The driving alone was killing me. I spent three hours in the car everyday driving from home to work to school and back. It was hard for me to want to get out in that traffic on days when I thought nothing important was happening in class. I never missed classes in community college or my third year at FAMU. By the second semester at VT, I was so miserable with the idea of school that I could barely motivate myself to show up at all. The realization that I might be wasting my time pursuing a degree for a job that I thought I might hate, made me lose all motivation to do well in school.

The other problem was that all of the other students were there at the Consortium 24 hours a day. If we didn't mind sharing a room with four other people, they had dorms attached to the school. Sara and I never even considered it because we had a baby. The dorms were only for students, not wives and kids. So the dorm housing was not an option for Sara and I. All the kids who lived in the dorms spent almost all their time in their studio or hanging out with faculty and each other. I was drastically different. I only came during the hours we were supposed to be there for class. After that, I was on my way back to work, or home. I didn't spend much time trying to make a lot of friends or impress the faculty by sitting at my desk and working for hours after class. I did most of my schoolwork at home. I had my own drafting table at home so I worked there. The faculty, apparently, thought that I was not showing enough effort because they only saw me during required hours and even some of those, I had missed. My Design instructors started criticizing my work. They would say things like, "This would be fine if you were a first year student, but you are a fourth year student now, haven't you learned anything?", as I presented my ideas for *The House of the Librarian*. It all ended well enough though, I busted my butt and put together a good enough project that they gave me a C. Passing was good enough for me, I wasn't trying to win any awards. I just wanted to get the hell out of school ASAP.

My only good friend at school that year, aside from the FAMU people, was a Cal Poly student who sat next to me in the Design studio. His name was Johnson Nguyn. He was a Vietnamese guy that had moved to California as a child with his family. His parents were tired of the Vietnamese government and they saw America as a better place to raise their family. Johnson was a real good guy, even if his words didn't always come out right. Sara and I would laugh at some of his expressions when he wasn't around. He liked to use words like "Big", and "Super" a lot, as in "My boss in California, he super rich guy." Johnson always made California sound like a great place to live and work as an architect. He said that a lot of the new construction around his area was Deconstructive. He loved guys like Frank Gehry, Eric Owen Moss, Architectonica, and a lot of other cutting edge types. I did too. Johnson said California was the testing ground for a lot of these guys. Some of the most state of the art stuff was out in California, according to Johnson. He said that architects were paid a lot more in California than they were in D.C. To hear Johnson talk, you'd think he had a job with the state of California to sell it to people and promote its growth.

Johnson was working with a guy named Charles Mada most of the year. Near the end of the spring semester, I think April, Johnson said that Charles wanted to find a replacement for Johnson as he would be leaving to go back to Cal Poly when spring semester ended. I told him that I had planned to stay through the summer and not leave until sometime in August. A few days later, Johnson said that Charles wanted to meet me. I liked the fact that Johnson called his boss Charles and not Mr. Mada. I thought this might be a sign of a significantly different personality than that of Mr. Devenrow. I soon found out that I was right.

My "interview" with Charles Mada was the most informal job interview I had ever done. I arrived at the address Johnson had given me and found myself not at a fancy office building, but a nice three story home in an upscale neighborhood in Arlington, VA. I thought, "Is this guy working out of his house, or did he invite me to his house for the interview?", either way, I realized that it was a totally different approach than what I had expected. Charles met me at the door of the lowest level, which was really a basement, only one side was totally exposed and had a door. He asked me to come on in and shook my hand. Johnson was inside working at a computer. I immediately felt more like I was just being introduced to a new friend, rather than showing up for a job interview. Johnson had told me how much he liked Charles as a boss, but now I was starting to see why. Charles had turned his basement into his office. He didn't have a fancy building to go to everyday. It was just Charles and Johnson, there was no need for anything more than what Charles already had.

Charles, or Mr. Mada, as I should call him, asked me to talk with him about school and wanted to see some of my past work. I had put together a small portfolio to showcase what I thought was my best work. Mr. Mada seemed to like it. He looked through my work and asked me questions about why I had done this and that on some of my projects. Then he asked if I was comfortable with AutoCAD. "Yes. But I've been working with DataCAD for the last six months now. I prefer AutoCAD though, probably just because I'm more familiar with it." , I told him. He asked me to sit down with Johnson and let him show me some of the stuff they had been working on. We looked over a bunch of AutoCAD drawings on Johnson's computer and Mr. Mada asked me if what I was seeing looked familiar enough. I said it was close to what I had been working on at Devenrow & Associates, only I liked his style of architecture better.

Mr. Mada's style was much more modern and artistic than Mr. Devenrow. Mr. Mada's houses had won several awards and he had been published in several magazines as well. Mr. Devenrow had also been in a few magazines but they were the type of magazines that published spec houses and Mc Mansion type developments, the magazines that Mr. Devenrow had appeared in were geared more towards selling houses. They were not real architectural magazines that just simply talked about great works of architecture. Mr. Mada had been acknowledged by real architectural publications that actually tried to showcase good designs, not sell them.

Once I realized that I would be offered a job with Charles Mada, I thought I was taking a big step up from Devenrow& Associates, even if I made less. But that's where Mr. Mada came through again. He said he would start me out at $13 per hour. He gave me another dollar an hour raise every month I was there. Charles Mada was what I had hoped an architect might be like. He didn't spend his time yelling and cussing on the phone. He was always very articulate and gentle when he spoke to contractors, engineers, and clients. He never allowed himself to seem upset or frustrated about anything. Also, he always commented on how fast I was at producing drawings. He and I got along great. It was just what I needed to keep me in school. I started to see that there were good and bad architects, just like there were good and bad people in every other job I had ever worked. When you have a great boss, it makes life much easier.

Another neat thing about working with Mr. Mada was lunch break. Mr. Mada was born and raised in Lebanon, although he spoke excellent English. His lunches were very unusual to me. He loved Hummus, Tahini, Tabouli, lamb, and bread with eggs, chopped parsley, tomatoes, and onions, and all sorts of other Mediterranean foods that I never learned the names of. He would always ask me to try some of his food. Sometimes I would. Sometimes I would pass. It was so nice to be able to actually have lunch with my boss and have good conversations. Mr. Mada was a VT grad himself and knew many of the faculty at the Consortium very well. He would tell me the backgrounds of some of the professors, how some had been total screw-ups in school. He told me how some had been total screw ups in their previous jobs, and on and on. Mr. Mada also liked to talk about Lebanon and his family there. And Mr. Mada talked about the fact that he had been married and had two children but was recently divorced. "Never let your job take precedent over your wife and kid. If you do, you'll end up just like me. You have to find a balance between your career and your family. Most architects put too much effort into their careers and end up in divorces.", he had told me. I thought about Mr. Devenrow being on his third marriage when I was working there, I guess he was a slow learner.

By the end of my time working for Mr. Mada, I was telling him what a great boss I thought he was and that I hoped he became the head of a very successful company. He said all he ever hoped to do was acquire about four or five licensed architects who could produce their own work. No draftsmen. A couple weeks before I moved Mr. Mada said, "You know, you really don't have to go back to Florida if you like it here so much. I'm sure you could transfer into Virginia Tech if you wanted. I could help pay for your classes if you'd be willing to work for me. Who knows, maybe you'd even get to be my first licensed architect!" He also added that I'd make a lot more working for him than some Florida firm. I told him I couldn't believe he would make me such an offer, but that I had already looked into transferring into VT and it required me to stay and get my Master's Degree. We had already had a talk about how Master's Degrees in Architecture were a waste of time unless you planned on becoming a professor. He said he understood, but to think about calling him when I graduated from FAMU. He said he would be happy to have me back if I ever wanted to work for him in the future. I was so happy to have found a good person in the Architecture community. Mr. Mada's offer gave me a sense of relief that, if all else failed in Florida, at least I had somewhere I could come back to.

Chapter 24: FAMU, Year 2, and David Bartley

In August of 1999 we moved back to Tallahassee, FL. We found an apartment online while we lived in D.C. It was in an apartment community called Banyan Bay, off Micosukee Rd. on the east side of Tallahassee. We had a swimming pool, gym, playground, and clubhouse. It wasn't a bad place, but it was nothing like our townhouse in D.C. Sara already had a job waiting for her when we got back. She had applied with Annsworth Academy, a small pre-school that took in all the rich children of people that lived in the upscale neighborhoods of Killearn Lakes. They hired her after a telephone interview that Sara did while we were still living in D.C.

I went back to register for classes at FAMU and was told that I would not be able to take the Fifth Year Design Studio class. That class was my last big hoop I had to jump through before graduation. It was just like all the Design classes before it. It ran two semesters, Design 5.1 and 5.2. The only catch was that Design 5.2 finished with a single project of my choosing that would exhibit all the things the school felt a graduating architectural student should know. I had to show that I had a basic understanding of how to heat and cool a building, how to design the structure of the building, lighting, etc. All this and also it had to have a strong concept, or statement, as well. The pressure came from the fact that the entire faculty got together and determined if you passed or failed that year. If they did not approve of your final project, you would fail and repeat the entire year. It was a very scary idea. That you could bust your butt for an entire year and then end up having to do it all over, terrified me. I had nightmares about failing Design 5.2 for about a year before and several years after actually taking the class.

So, the dean of the School of Architecture told me that I was not going to be allowed to take Design 5.1. He said that I was supposed to have taken a co-requisite, Structures 3, in D.C. and that I would have to pass that class before I would be allowed to begin my final year. I explained to the dean that they did not offer Structures 3 at the VT Consortium. I told him how I would have had to take it at another school in the D.C. area and the price for out of state tuition was more than I could afford. It would have cost me about $1,000 just to take that class alone. He said he was sorry, but I should have thought about that before I went to D.C. I told him that I felt misled because no one mentioned anything about that class not being offered at the Consortium in D.C. He said the other students that went up there had no problem taking the class off campus and that I shouldn't expect to receive special treatment just because I was trying to support a child. I thought that he was pretty cold. He also said that I would never be able to handle all the pressure of the fifth year courses along with Structures 3.

The Structures series of classes were all engineering classes that built on our prior learning of Physics and Calculus. They were more difficult than any other co-requisites. The professors told us that Structures was the weeding out tool used to separate the kids who wanted to be architects from the kids who actually could be architects. If you couldn't learn how to size steel, wood, and concrete structural members, you couldn't expect to be an architect. If you couldn't pass the Structures classes within two tries, you were removed from the program.

The dean said that if I were allowed to begin the fifth year program and take Structures 3 at the same time, I would probably end up failing all my classes and end up worse off than I already was. I thought that he was probably right, but I was still angry because when I was in D.C. I had talked with my FAMU professor up there about not having Structures 3 and she led me to believe that I would be able to take it when I got back. She just never mentioned that it would cost me another year if I didn't take it up there. It was very frustrating. I realized that I now had to figure out what to do with another year that wouldn't include full time school. On the bright side, it would make for a very easy fifth year because the dean said he would let me take all the other required fifth year classes, just not Design 5.1 or 5.2.

So, after realizing that I would spend that year with a small load of classes, I decided to pick up some more work experience. I thought that maybe I could even find the firm that I'd work at once I graduated. I was now more qualified than most of the other students who had stayed at FAMU that past year. Hardly any of them worked at all. They were mostly full time students who lived off their parents or had serious student loans.

My first class back at FAMU was Professional Practice 1. The class was supposed to teach us the details of life in an architectural firm. The class was really designed for all those students who had yet to step foot into a real firm. I felt like I was once again just paying the school for information that I already knew or didn't need. The first day of class, the instructor asked who had worked in an architectural firm. A few students and I raised our hands. The instructor knew that I had just got back from the VT Consortium. She asked me to tell the class what my experience was like. So I told them. Another student who had raised his hand, Frank Trudio, said he had worked with his father, who was an architect. Frank said he was currently working for a structural engineer.

After class, Frank came up to me and asked me if I had already found a job since I got back. I told him I was still looking. He said that the structural engineer he was working for wanted to hire a draftsman who knew a little about architectural plans and how to draw them. And that's how I started working for Bartley Engineering. I was now confident enough about my skills as a draftsman that I went to the interview without even being nervous.

I met David Bartley, the owner, and licensed structural engineer. David also had a partner, Matt Parker, who was a civil engineer. There were also two other draftsman besides Frank. David seemed nice enough, he was a little rougher around the edges than Mr. Mada, but he seemed like a guy who genuinely liked people of my age and background, even if he did call Frank and I "pencil fairies".

David had a good sense of humor and we found common ground right away in the interview when we started talking about my favorite video game at the time, Civilization 2. We both confessed to wasting hours playing that stupid game and admitted how much fun we had doing it. I think that got me the job right there, even if I was lacking any skills he needed, he seemed to like me. He went over my resume and looked through my portfolio. "This is all very nice but you won't be doing anything this fancy here.", he said, after looking over some of my renderings. "If you can draw lines and add and subtract, I think you'll do fine.", he said. Then he wanted to know how much I expected to be paid. I told him that Charles Mada was paying me $15.00 per hour when I left. David laughed and said, "Well, I'm sorry, but you're not going to get paid that kind of money in Tallahassee without a degree." I told him I understood. D.C. was a much more inflated economy than Tallahassee. I told David that I didn't expect to make what I was making with Mr. Mada. He said that was good because the most he could pay me was $10.00 per hour. He said that Frank barely made that much and he had been with him a year already, so not to talk to anyone about what he had agreed to pay me. I told him I'd be happy to start whenever he wanted, and that I could be there almost full time as I was only taking a couple classes at FAMU.

Working at Bartley Engineering was even better than working with Charles Mada. I met my best friend in Tallahassee while working there. We remained good friends for years after I stopped working there. His name was Barry Trudol. I had seen Barry around the FAMU campus during my first year there. I remember thinking, "That guy has got to have some mental issues." It was because of his appearance. Barry was about 300 lbs., had a scruffy beard, and always, always wore overalls. He looked like one of the people you might see any time you tuned in to an episode of Jerry Springer. It turned out, though, that Barry was a math genius. David had hired Barry about five years before I came along. Barry was my age. Barry was David's second employee. David and Barry were the ones that actually did all of the structural calculations for the projects that Bartley Engineering took on. David had trained Barry to be a structural engineer, only Barry was going to school for architecture. Barry was basically a qualified structural engineer who just didn't have his license. I was amazed when I realized the level of understanding that Barry had of structural engineering. Barry could imagine problems and invent his own equations to solve them. I would bring in my assignments from Structures 3 and Barry would show me two or three new ways to solve problems faster than the way we were being taught at school. He was the smartest guy, at least mathematically, that I've ever met.

Aside from Barry, there was a lot more to appreciate about Bartley Engineering. For one, David never asked me to be there at a certain time everyday. As long as you crawled in by nine every morning you were o.k. He also understood if I needed to take off a day here or there because of upcoming tests at school. Then there was just the laid back atmosphere that he created at work. We all worked hard, but David would always come in cracking jokes and just being a general wise ass throughout the day. David's personality helped make the days very enjoyable at Bartley Engineering.

One day I was telling David and Barry about playing paintball with my brothers, Dad, and his brothers, over the past weekend. I told him how much we loved playing paintball and that we didn't use guns, but sling shots. David said he thought that sounded like a lot of fun. Barry, Rebecca, and I started cracking jokes about how much we'd like to get David into a paintball game so that we could shoot the crap out of him. David said, "O.K., we'll see who gets their ass kicked. You little punks think you can whip up on the old man? Remember, I was fighting in Desert Storm, while you guys were in elementary school, barely out of diapers. You guys set up a weekend when we can all come out to my house and we'll have a real competition." I was psyched. I had never had a boss who would actually spend his free time with his employees, much less spend it by playing paintball with a bunch of college kids. I told David I was going to try to get my brothers in on the action as well. He said "the more the merrier" and that once he got a slingshot in his hand, I would need all the back up I could get.

A couple weekends after David and I had initially planned the paintball war, the whole office showed up at David's house, along with my brothers and I. Sam, Carter, and I laid out the rules of the game. We told everybody that the way we preferred to play was either two teams or every man for themselves. If you were hit by a paintball and it exploded on you were out of the game. The last man standing would be the winner. Everybody decided we would first play as two teams. We split up with Barry, Frank, and myself on one team. David, Rebecca, Sam, and Carter were on the other. To start the game, each team was given five minutes to find a good vantage point to attack from. After that the goal was to stalk down the members of the opposing team and take them out, one by one. The main focus of my team was to shoot David as many times as possible, we were not concerned with winning, we just wanted a chance to say we had torn David's butt up in a paintball game. Barry and I spotted David at the far end of a field that was part of David's property. Barry and I went running at David, firing shots as we ran. David saw us coming and started running in the opposite direction and yelled, "Run away! Run away!", like a scene from Monty Python and The Search for the Holy Grail. It was hilarious. David took off running and Barry and I each got about three hits on him before we let him consider himself "out of the game". David kept yelling "I'm hit! I'm out!". We kept saying, "What? We can't hear you." and Barry and I kept firing away. "Just wait till we get back in the office Monday. You guys are going to pay me back for that by working your butts off! I'm going to drop the hammer on you.", David said. We were all laughing hysterically. We played four or five rounds before everybody was exhausted. I think everybody had a great time. It was a great game of paintball for Sam, Carter, and I because nobody else had much experience with a slingshot. We could all take out any of the others because they didn't really have a clue of what they were doing.

Another great thing about working for David, as with Charles Mada, was lunch. With David, lunch was great because David bought the entire offices' lunch almost everyday. This usually only included David, Barry, Frank, Rebecca, and myself, but still, it was a very nice thing for him to do. David usually even let one of us pick the spot. Lunch was also great because it gave us all time to talk about problems we were having with what we were working on, or just catch up on everybody's life outside work. It was David's way of having a staff meeting without us even realizing it. I actually felt like I was working with people who cared about each other. I had never worked in a place like that.

The one thing that was not great about working for David, was that I picked up a very bad habit from him. David was a smoker and so was everyone else that worked for him. They would all go out for cigarette breaks several times a day. I didn't smoke, so I stayed at my desk and kept working while they did their thing outside. They would usually all come back in laughing from some story someone had told while they were outside smoking their cigarettes. I started to feel like I was missing out on part of the fun. I thought, "Why am I sitting in here by myself, when I could be out there talking with them." I didn't like the fact that I had to ask, "What's so funny?", every time they came back from their cigarette breaks, laughing. So I decided I would smoke a cigarette here and there just to stay close with the group and not miss out on the "important" conversation that took place at cigarette smoking time.

I was always conscious of my good health before I decided to start smoking. Now, though, it didn't seem like that big of a deal to smoke a cigarette a couple times a day. It was just a social thing. I wanted to be part of the group, even if that meant doing something that was very unhealthy. What started as a way of fitting in with my buddies, became an addiction that I have never been able to break away from for very long.

I remembered how much I did not like that first cigarette I had smoked with Sara in her car several years earlier. I knew that cigarettes had killed my father's mother and father. GranDaddy, my mother's father, had told me several times as a teenager to never pick up a cigarette. "Those things are as dangerous as a rattlesnake. They will kill you if you play around with them long enough. Once you start, it's a very hard thing to stop.", he had warned me. He had smoked from the time he was 8 years old until he was in his late 40's. It was long enough that, just like he had said, they killed him. It took about thirty years after he quit for the chemicals he had breathed in, for all those years, to do their trick on him, but they did get him in the end. And it was terrible. But all this had not yet come to pass. It would still be another 5 years before my GranDaddy was diagnosed with terminal cancer. Cancer was the last thing I was thinking about when I first started smoking those cigarettes with the guys at Bartley Engineering. Now, after seeing first hand what cigarettes will do to a person, I think about cancer every time I light up a cigarette. "One more, then I'm done forever.", I have told myself many times. But one more always somehow becomes another pack and then another carton and the cycle continues. I can think of a hundred reasons to stop smoking, but I always create an excuse for why I don't have to quit just yet. I sometimes wonder if I've already done enough damage to give myself the same kind of death I saw my GranDaddy experience. But it still isn't enough motivation to stop. I smoke about ten cigarettes a day and have been doing so for the last 9 years. Smoking has become such a habit that I am afraid stopping will be the hardest thing I have ever forced myself to do, if I can ever really stop at all.

Back to other things at Barkley. The actual work I did for David was mainly drawing house foundation plans and roof framing plans. There was a big new development being drawn up for the south-east side of Tallahassee called South Wood. It was supposed to be the new up scale neighborhood that Tallahassee's wealthy and elite would flock to, the same way they had already done on the north-east side at Killearn Lakes, where Sara worked at Annsworth Academy. Most of the time I was at Bartley Engineering, I was working on foundations and framing for all the various models of homes that would be offered at South Wood. David actually put me in charge of designing and drawing the foundations. It was really simple after he explained the rules. All the houses would receive the same types of foundations. I had to design one type that would work in Tallahassee's typical soil, and another kind that would work in pipe clay. Pipe clay was a term given for areas where the soil was very spongy and porous. When a soil analysis found pipe clay, you had to beef up the foundation so that the building would float on top of the soil, rather than sink into it. David designed the details of how the foundations would go together. All I had to do was determine where load-bearing walls were and draw the appropriate footings to support them. I had to show where footings were needed and where a small turn down in the slab would do. It was a pretty simple job. After I had been through the process a couple times, David turned me loose and let me begin meeting with the architect, who was working on the houses, by myself. That's about the time I became friends with Ann Defenbaum.

Ann was an architectural project manager that worked for Johnston Peachson Architects. We did a lot of work with Johnston Peachson. She was always in and out of our office, coordinating her drawings with ours and vice versa. I worked on a couple projects that Ann had been assigned to. I told her about being a FAMU student and wanting to work for an architectural firm when I graduated. It turned out that Ann was also a FAMU grad. She encouraged me to apply with Johnston Peachson. She said that they needed somebody who actually knew a little about how buildings went together and that she thought I would make a good draftsman. She said they had recently hired and fired a few kids that had gone to a vocational school and taken drafting classes, but that they were useless because they had no idea of what they were doing. I told her I loved working for David, but that I was planning on becoming an architect so, I should probably be working with an architect. She agreed.

Ann introduced me to Ivan Johnston, part owner of Johnston Peachson. Guy Peachson, his other half, ran the Johnston Peachson office in Sarasota. Ivan was a very soft spoken guy who seemed to have a good sense of humor. I already had the impression that I was in the presence of a great architect before Ivan ever spoke the first word to me. Many of the faculty members at FAMU had worked for Johnston Peachson. I had also seen several JP projects around town and always thought they were some of the nicest buildings in Tallahassee. The JP firm had a style that was unique and consistent in most of their projects. The JP style was always very modern, not Deconstructive. Very unusual materials and shapes were usually part of every JP design. I was really excited about the possibility of working for Johnston Peachson.

When I first walked into the Johnston Peachson office, I was amazed at what a cool place it seemed to be. I didn't know any of the people yet. I was just impressed with the architecture of the JP office. The first thing that I walked into from the main entrance was an actual art gallery, complete with all sorts of weird paintings and sculptures. Ivan rented out part of his building to a lady, Marsha Orr, who was an art dealer. She worked with artists to help them sell their stuff. Ivan let her display her artists' work throughout the office. The JP office was architecturally impressive. Other things, I would later come to find out, were less so.

My interview with Ivan Johnston went very well. I had been through the interview routine enough times now that this part of getting a job came pretty easy for me. I ran through the usual spill about my past work experience and school life. Ivan liked the fact that I was working with David Bartley. He said that he liked David and that Bartley Engineering was one of their favorite structural engineering firms. He said he thought I would be a great help in the office, but that he was experiencing some financial trouble and could only pay me $10.00 per hour to start, with the usual review in three months and possibility of a raise then. I didn't think anything of his remark about financial trouble and told him that I would talk with David Bartley and see how soon I might be able to work with JP. Ivan said that he thought David should let me go within two weeks, that was fair notice.

I talked with David about leaving and he seemed regretful but understood that I was going to school for architecture after all, and it made since to get back into architecture. He said that if it was alright with Ivan, he still wanted to have me do some work for him on the side for a while, just until all the South Wood houses were finished up. Ivan said that was no problem, and I worked a few months on the side with David while I worked full time at Johnston Peachson.

When I first started at Johnston Peachson in June of 2000, I was thrilled to be following in the footsteps of some of my professors. I imagined myself working several years with Ivan and becoming a licensed architect under his wing. Ivan had already told me in my interview that he would be happy to mentor me through the Intern Development Program. IDP is a requirement that all applicants for the Architectural Licensing Exam have to pass before being allowed to take the test that will get them licensed. IDP is a series of around 200 different tasks that all interns must spend a certain amount of time performing under the supervision of a licensed architect. The total time requirement of all the IDP hours is around 3,000 hours. That's 3,000 hours of time, logged and verified by an architect, performing specific tasks that are deemed necessary before taking the exam. A person could complete IDP training in a little over a year, if they were lucky enough to find an architect willing to be that serious about their training. Most architects I had talked to said that the IDP program was usually about a three year process for most people. When I started working at JPA, I thought Ivan would be my mentor through the IDP process. Somewhere along the way, things changed.

Everyone was very nice to me when I first started working for Johnston Peachson. There were nine other JP employees besides myself. One was our accountant, another our secretary, and everyone else was drafting and project management. Ivan was the only licensed architect. I was put on my first assignment with Ann Defenbaum acting as my go to person. She was the project manager and I was her draftsman. It was great working with Ann. She said that I was a much faster draftsman than she was. I actually knew a little more AutoCAD than she did because I had been trained more recently. She had learned AutoCAD outside of school, while working, and didn't know a few of the tricks I had been taught.

It wasn't long until Ivan, himself, started asking me to work directly with him. It started as small revisions to drawings for a project he was taking care of. He said that his last architect had left him with a mess of a project and Ivan was now having to try to straighten it out all by himself. Ann would later tell me how Ivan had withheld a month's salary to all JP employees only a few months before I started. After Ivan showed that he was a poor manager of the firm's resources, five employees left on the same day. Two of them were registered architects. That was a heavy blow to the firm. I also later found out from David Bartley that Ivan owed David over $60,000 in unpaid fees for David's structural engineering services.

I liked working directly with Ivan. It gave me a little prestige around the office. People in the office started calling me "Ivan's Boy". I liked that. I think, after a while, it also caused some tension for me, though. People started acting strange towards me a few months after I started working solely for Ivan. What I experienced was the jealousy of the rest of the office that I was becoming close with Ivan. I think a lot of people started to resent the fact that a new intern was spending so much time with the top dog of the office.

A few months after I started working at JP, Ann left too. That was a little scary to me because she told me, "I don't think we do quality work here anymore. I'm up here half the night sometimes and I still can't keep up with all the work Ivan keeps dumping on me. I'm stretched too thin and I'm not giving my projects all the attention they need. Things are going out of this office with major mistakes and all sorts of problems. I've found a new job where I hope things will be a little easier." I didn't know what to think. Was I a part of some of the mistakes she was talking about? I thought what she had told me was probably true. We now had one architect to take the place of three. There had to be things falling through the cracks somewhere.

Not long after Ann left, Ivan hired three new people in less than a month's time. One of the new hires was to become a project manager, Hugh Bozly. Another was somewhere in between a project manager and a draftsman, Carter Jameson. The third was just a draftsman, like me, Charles Di Franco. These three new guys changed the whole dynamic of the office. Hugh Bozly, in particular, would become a major thorn in my side.

Chapter 25: FAMU, Final Year, and the First Collapse

At school, I was now beginning the Fifth Year Program. I had completed my Structures class and Professional Practice. Now all I needed to graduate was Design 5.1, Design 5.2, Professional Practice 2, and Design Research. It was a light enough load that I managed to work at least 30-35 hours a week at JP, for the first semester. My Design 5.1 studio was being taught by two professors, this was a first. There had always been only one professor that taught the 5th Year Design Studio in the past. That year, my professors were Dan Donovan and Andrew Chin. Andrew was a very smart, articulate guy who always found a way to compliment my work no matter how bad it really was. Dan was soft spoken and very calm but would sometimes rip me apart if he didn't like what I were doing. Dan's style of teaching was the norm. Andrew's was something different. Dan and I got along well because we had something in common. We had both worked with Johnston Peachson. Dan knew Ivan well. In fact, Dan's relationship with Ivan Johnston eventually became a problem for me. About half way through the first semester Dan told me that he and Ivan had a major falling out and Dan quit working for him. I asked Ivan about Dan's story and he confirmed it. Ivan also added that Dan had tried to sue him for psychological distress. Ivan said that he thought Dan was gay and was a major loser. He said that teaching at FAMU was Dan's last resort because he could never work in an office for very long. After I realized there was tension between my boss and my professor I began to feel stressed. I worried that Dan might start to dislike me for associating with Ivan and vice versa. The stress associated with my fear of the repercussions of my relationships with my boss and my Studio instructor caused the beginning of my first major collapse. I think that what really caused the stress was a chemical imbalance in my brain that caused me to become paranoid about things that were not real. Yes, Ivan and Dan did have a bad past together, but I don't think that either of them were ever holding their past against me. I don't think that either of them cared that I associated with the other. I had a necessary reason to have a relationship with the both of them. The stress that came from my perception of how things were going in those relationships was what caused me to begin to show the first signs of a severe depression. However, the stress was related to a paranoia that was created by my mind. My brain was slowly beginning to play its first big trick on me. Before my last semester was finished at FAMU, I would begin to believe the biggest lie that my brain had ever tricked me into believing up to that point.

In contrast to my final semester, the Fall semester and Design 5.1, turned out to be my greatest semester of my entire architectural education. I guess that Fall, the Fall of 2001, was my first real experience with mania. My first experience with mania had no ill effect. I just remember feeling very energized and excited about architecture. I was excited about my job and especially my work at school. I became very passionate about it. For the first time, I felt like I believed in what I was doing. I felt like I finally believed in Architecture. All the years before that Fall semester, I had been plagued by doubts about how fruity and subjective Architecture seemed. I hated the fact that the real value of any Architectural work was only determined by the people who experienced it. There had been many times when I felt like I had produced something great that would only be criticized and torn down by my professors. I remember that Fall semester, I thought I had just stumbled onto some part of my brain that allowed me to produce my first truly great architectural work. My excitement, apparently, was contagious, because my professors all noticed how pleased I was with myself and how the level of quality in my thoughts had somehow been elevated. During that earliest experience with mania, I was not impaired by racing thoughts, hallucinations, or any other negative effects that would later plague me. No, that first semester of my final year at FAMU was pure bliss. I remember believing that I had finally realized my full potential as an architecture student. I suddenly had the ability to think abstract thoughts and find a way to express them through my building designs. I began to crank out work in frenzies. For the first time in my entire college education, I began to fall in love with what I was doing. It would be several years before I realized that during my time of elation, I was actually experiencing what a psychiatrist would label as a manic episode. Looking back on that last year of FAMU, I guess I really experienced my first polar swing. I went from a manic induced sense of greatness that Fall to a depression induced sense of failure that Spring. In one year's time I managed to feel the full effects, on a very minute scale, of the illness that would later shatter all of my ambitions and leave me in the dark, lonely world that exists only in the mind of a Schizophrenic.

In that Design 5.1 class, I remember noticing that something had switched on inside me, and I became serious about architecture. I drew things in frenzies. I produced more quality work for our final project than I had ever done in all my past projects. The assignment for Design 5.1 was to design a mall in downtown Orlando that had a very small footprint. The mall would be a minimum of 5 stories to meet the total space requirements. My first idea for the mall began with a simple sketch that showed oblong bubbles being held together by sticks of varying lengths. To me, it looked about as Deconstructive as you could get. My professors loved it. All the years before, I had begun my projects with a very concrete and well defined idea of what the building should look like. My professors always told me that I needed to loosen up and become less concerned with how I thought the building should look. "Let the building tell you how it should look.", they would say. I never understood what the hell they were talking about. But now, I had finally produced something that caught the attention of both my professors. They asked other students to look at what I had drawn. They said my work was a good example of good conceptual design. I remember being praised by both of my Design Studio instructors for what an excellent job I had just done. They told me that they had very high hopes for my project that semester. I felt great. Sometimes, mania makes you feel great. For me, I would later feel great, even when there was really nothing to feel great about.

That semester, I also made another good friend, Mark Ruiz. Mark played an important part in me producing more great work. Mark introduced me to a piece of software called Accurender. This software could take a 3-D model from AutoCAD and apply textures, and shading much better than the included rendering software that came with AutoCAD. Accurender also could add trees and other vegetation to an AutoCAD model so that it could actually be placed on a virtual site. Mark spent a few hours one night going over the basics of Accurender with me and I was sold. He gave me a copy of the software and I began to play with it at home. I began to think about producing my final project for Design 5.1, all on the computer. Instead of building an actual model of my project out of wood and cardboard, I would create it in virtual space, where my materials looked realistic and colors were limitless. I decided I would also do all of my drawings in AutoCAD, rather than by hand. I was now much more proficient drawing with the computer than by hand. And I had all the resources at JP to help me produce whatever I wanted. Ivan didn't mind at all.

So my final project turned out to be the big surprise of the class. I had already been labeled as an average student by my past professors. They all talked about the students in their faculty meetings and told us so. After that semester was over Andrew Chin pulled me aside and told me, "Scott, I'm really amazed at how far you have come this semester. We had been told that you under performed during your fourth year and assumed you would do the same in fifth year. Its great to see you excited about what your doing. It shows in your work. Keep it up next semester."

What caused that comment from my professor was the fact that I showed up to my final presentation with a solid project that was full of, what I thought were cool ideas. One example was that my mall was made of stores that could be moved around by a giant elevator. Tenants could choose to change their locations if sales determined the need. The entire store would roll along tracks, that it rested on, to an elevator that could relocate the store to a new location on that floor or a new level all together. The professors all loved it. To top it off, I managed to produce everything all on the computer, just like I planned. The images of my computer model were far more impressive than anything I could have ever built by hand. With the computer I was able to show a glass atrium, that enveloped the middle portion of the mall, and looked almost fluid. The atrium was a made of a warped section of glass and steel that looked like it was melting out of the middle of the mall. I thought it looked really cool. The end result of my project looked far different from the sketch of strange bubbles and sticks I had drawn at the beginning of the semester, but you could see a resemblance there as well. My professors loved that too. "Your design process clearly shows the progression of an idea. You didn't stick to a particular form. But you maintained the same concept from start to finish. Good for you.", one said. Design 5.1 turned out to be my greatest success in school. Looking back, I think what might have caused it all, was my first experience with a little mania.

See, one thing we were introduced to in Design 3.1, my first semester at FAMU, was the idea of the "all nighter". Professors encouraged us to work as long and hard as necessary to complete our work, even if it meant staying up for two or three days without sleep. They almost forced us into this habit by tearing up models and drawing over presentations we had produced. They would critique our work about a week or two from its final due date and would usually trash everybody's stuff so bad that we were forced to work overtime to make all the last minute changes that the professors told us to make. I might spend a week building a model and my professor would actually break off parts of it and re-arrange them during his last minute critique. I would then have to re-build the model all over again from scratch. It was very frustrating, but I learned to deal with it by working into the late hours of the nights just before final presentation. I started to realize that I felt a little more creative after missing enough sleep. Some of my best work usually came out when I was under the gun with only hours until final presentation. It became a routine to stay up the last couple days before a project was due, without sleep. After the final presentation, I would go home and crash. I would feel like a zombie for a couple days afterwards. I had begun to pull the occasional "all nighter" and was beginning to see what mania was like, only I had no idea what mania was. I had never heard of the word. I had no idea of what a terrible monster I was playing with. I had a lot of good reasons for staying up late on those nights before my projects were due.

With Architecture, and with all Art, I think, there is never a moment where the artist feels truly finished with their work. I know that was always the case for me anyway. I felt that way with my paintings and drawings that I had done in high school. And I certainly felt that way about all of my architectural work. The closer it came to finish time, the more pressure I felt to complete my project. It usually was not the case that I spent a lot of time slacking off, and was just putting off work until the last minute. No, the case was that I could never feel like I was truly finished with my work. As the deadline for completion drew nearer, I would always think of more and more things that needed to be done to my work so that I could consider it completed. As I completed the tasks I had set out to do, I would find other things that I wanted to tweak, and on and on the process went until finally, the deadline would arrive. Then I would be forced to quit working on my project and hand it over to my professors for their evaluation. Like I said, I always felt that my best work came out in the heat of those last few days, just before the gun that was held to my head was about to go off. I work best when under the gun. The problem is that the anxiety that comes from being under the gun keeps me from sleeping. So, I am also at my worst when I am under the gun.

I think that anxiety and the lack of sleep were what created my first episodes of true mania like symptoms that first time in the Fall of 2001. Design 5.2 started the following January of 2001. That semester would end in a complete reversal of what I had experienced in the previous one.

At work things were beginning to get a little stressful. Ivan was still using me as his personal draftsman and even let me do some small design work for him. He told me to design a sign for a government building we were working on in Alachua, FL. I did a couple sketches of what I thought looked like a good sign and showed them to Ivan. "Keep working.", he said. So, I drew some different variations of the sign. I stopped when I had come up with seven different ways the sign could look. Ivan said he liked this about one sign and that about another. He wanted me to combine the good parts of the signs I had produced and make one last effort. I did and he liked it. It became the sign by the side road that directed people to all the different government agencies that were housed in that building. The sign project was the first time I had ever had one of my architectural sketches become something real. I was pretty excited.

Shortly after the sign project, Ivan asked me to design the paint striping that would direct traffic throughout the parking lot of the building in Alachua. I had to draw up all the left turn, right turn, and straight-ahead arrows that would be painted on the parking lot surface. It wasn't a hard job, a monkey could be trained to do it. Ivan came up to me at about 5:30 pm on a Friday, after the drawing had already been sent to the signage contractor. Ivan said, "The signage contractor wants to know if you are dyslexic or something. You drew some of the arrows pointing the wrong way." He said this loud enough that the whole office heard. People laughed. I felt embarrassed. "What's wrong?", I said, in a whisper.

Sara and I had already made plans to go down to my parents' house after work that day. I told Ivan that I was sorry that I screwed up and would fix it first thing Monday morning. "Oh no your not!", Ivan said, "You aren't leaving here until this drawing is fixed and back in the contractor's hands in Alachua." More people laughed and I felt even more stupid. I ended up staying a couple extra hours that day to clear up the mess I had made. I didn't realize it, but that was the beginning of the end of my time with Johnston Peachson.

Another thing that seemed like nothing at all at first was our decision to save money on rent that last year I was in school. Our lease with Banyan Bay Apartments ended after one year. The next year's rate increased by $75 per month. We decided we would try to save some money by renting a trailer. We ended up saving about $200 dollars every month, but I ended up feeling like I was losing my sanity.

The trailer we moved into was built in the 1970's and was in pretty bad shape. The carpet had stains all over it. The kitchen cabinets were filled with dead roaches when we moved in. And everything was all fit within a singlewide width of trailer. I always felt very cramped and confined inside it. Everything was smaller than what we had been used to. The effect of living in that trailer was immediately depressing.

Just before we moved into that trailer, we adopted a dog named Pierre, from the pound. He brought his own problems to our new trailer. We would let him out for bathroom breaks and walks. He would bring in fleas. Our trailer became infested with fleas. Sara, Liza, and I would wake up every morning with bites all over us. I remember pulling off our bed sheets and finding hundreds of flea larva crawling on our mattress. It was disgusting. We had tried several times to fumigate the place with store bought flea killers. I had bought flea medication for Pierre. Nothing seemed to get rid of them for weeks. We finally had a professional come in and fumigate the place. My vet told me to stop buying the cheap flea meds at Wal-Mart and start buying Frontline from him. That solved that problem. But I still felt like we were becoming white trash.

At school pressure was building as well. I was supposed to have thoroughly researched all the necessary information for my final project, the project that would determine if I passed or failed that entire year. In fact, I had spent more time at work during my first semester than I should have. I had chosen the topic of Sustainability for my final project. My goal was to design a building that demonstrated ways to provide a functional building that was environmentally sensitive. Going Green is very popular now, but it wasn't quite as big a deal in 2001, especially in architecture. Going Green was still a fairly new idea then. Hippies had experimented with ways to conserve energy in the '60's and '70's, but now there was new technology that could be used to reduce a building's impact on the environment. I wanted to showcase some of those things in my final project. The problem was that the more I learned about Sustainable Architecture, the more I realized I didn't know enough to complete my final design project. I wanted to use solar energy, local materials, and passive thermal cooling in my design and realized that I didn't know crap about any of it. I began to imagine my instructor's asking me something like, "Explain how a solar energy collector cell works.", and I would stand there clueless. I went to websites and checked out books at the library, trying to gather all the information I could so that I would be able to talk about my project with some small bit of knowledge about Sustainable Architecture.

I started studying the work of a famous Australian architect who tried to use local materials and designed buildings that heated and cooled themselves without electricity. I mimicked his work more than I actually created something of my own. My professor's didn't have the same enthusiasm that they had about my work only a semester earlier. The combination of work, stress from the trailer life, and now a less than enthusiastic set of Design Studio professors, totaled up to some serious pressure on me. I was beginning to feel like I might not be able to keep myself together long enough to pass my final semester of Design. I was beginning to see a dark cloud forming on the horizon of my future. I was beginning to slip further and further away from the high that I had just experienced only a few months earlier. I was beginning to realize that I had really only slipped further down the spiral. Depression would soon place its cold grip on me and drag me to depths that I had never been. Soon, my brain would switch from fully on to fully off.

Just as the early signs of my first bought of severe depression were beginning to surface, Sara broke some big news to me at home one night. Sara told me that she had something very important to tell me. She asked me to come into our kitchen and sit at the table with her. I sat down at the table in the kitchen and asked her what the big news was. I could tell from the way she had set up her announcement that whatever she had to say was not going to be something I would enjoy hearing. I thought, "Oh crap, has she lost her job or something?" Finally, I said, "So, what's the big news." I waited for what seemed like several minutes. It was probably more like seconds, but the fear of what would come out of Sara's mouth made time seem to stand still. The longer I sat in the silence, the more anxious I became. I began to fear for the worst.

Finally, Sara broke the silence and told me the news that, once again, changed my world. Sara told me that she was pregnant. "What! Oh my God!", I said. I had started working less and that meant less to pay the bills with. One thing we skipped out on for a couple months was birth control pills. We had been using condoms most of the time but every now and then...

Now we would pay the price for being absolute idiots again. Sara said it was not that big of a deal because I was almost out of school and would soon be working full time. Liza was barely three years old. She had just gotten out of diapers not even a year ago. She was just beginning to be independent enough that going places didn't seem like that big of a deal. We could travel light without having to carry all the diapers, wipes, changes of clothes, and snacks. She had been through her phases of fit pitching and biting and now it was just beginning to seem like life was starting to get a little easier in the child rearing department. Now, I was being told we were about to go through it all over again. I went right to the first response I had given Sara when she told me she was pregnant with Liza, "Have you thought about having an abortion?" Sara started crying and said, "I'm having this baby. You can leave or you can stay, but you are going to have another child and you will pay to support it, with or without me. I don't care. If you think your life is hard now, just leave me and see how hard it gets." She was very angry as she said this. I was very angry with her. Once again, even though it takes two to do what we had done, I was blaming her. If it was anyone's fault is was my own. I was supposed to be wearing condoms and sometimes I didn't. I knew it was my fault for her being pregnant but I still felt like she could choose to have an abortion if she wanted to. It made me angry that she was deciding to do something regardless of what I thought. She said she would probably end up killing herself if she ever had an abortion. I believed her. So I let it go. I could leave or I could stay. She didn't care which, but she had said that she would make my life harder if I left. I had too much going on at school and work to even think about a divorce at that time, so I stayed.

Everything I did after that night seemed to be harder and take longer than it ever had before. Shortly after that night, I remember feeling like I had lost the ability to speak, not like losing my voice, no, I lost the ability to talk to someone, to pronounce words, or even think of any words to say. For the first time in my life, I was starting to shut down. I was experiencing what the psychiatrist calls "depression".

I was beginning to see myself with two kids, and a wife that now hated me, living forever in that trailer. I started to think that I was not going to graduate because I couldn't keep my train of thought focused long enough to do decent work on my final project anymore. I could sit for hours in front of my computer at home and not accomplish a single thing. I would find myself staring at the monitor with my mouse in hand, but not working on my project. Instead I was usually having wide awake nightmare visions of my future. I imagined not being able to ever hold down a job, never being happy as an architect, and some how trying to feed my two kids. I thought about how ashamed I would be to see my family once I didn't graduate and had to tell them that I was either quitting school or repeating my entire fifth year. I had just about made up my mind that if they did not pass me that semester, that was the end of the line for me. I would quit school all together and just work any job I could find. In reality, none of these things were close to happening, but I was beginning to convince myself that they would. I was sure that I would eventually be seen as a total failure by everyone who knew me. I felt like some were already beginning to have that view. The dark cloud on the horizon was growing larger.

At work things were really starting to become disastrous. I met with Ivan one day and told him that I felt like I had too much going on between work and school. I told him that I was afraid that I was going to fail my final semester of Design if I didn't cut back at work. I told him I might quit all together, at least until the end of the semester. Ivan said, "Scott, I really need your help around here. When you want to, you do good work." I told him that I didn't feel like I was doing good work for him anymore. I said that I was thinking about school and home issues when I was at work and would sit at my desk without doing anything for 15 or 20 minutes at a time because I couldn't focus on the task at hand.

The truth was that I could sometimes spend thirty minutes, or more, sometimes, just staring at my monitor, lost in the nightmare visions of my future. The fear of the future was beginning to have such a powerful grip on me that I was losing a lot of my ability to focus, rationalize, and even speak. My words began to come out in little short bursts with many pauses between them. It took my brain time to find the correct words to put out that fit the occasion that I was in. I began to notice a lot of trouble in the area of communication. The loss of ability to speak one's thoughts is a terrible thing. Without the ability to speak, I began to feel trapped by my own brain. I remember feeling like I wanted to cry all the time, but the tears rarely came. Instead, I was just trapped in the silence.

At that meeting with Ivan, I told him that Sara was pregnant and that I felt like I was freaking out. I also told him that I didn't think I was getting along very well with two of the new people he had hired. He said, "If you think you need to cut back, that's fine. Just don't totally flake out on me. Don't get wrapped up in what goes on out there in the office. There will always be problems with people anytime they have to work together. Don't let the comments of the people out there get to you. I think your just getting stressed out over nothing, but I don't want to have you fail your school because of me either. If you have to go, that's fine. We'll manage." I felt guilty for saying that I wanted to leave. I said, "Maybe I'll just try cutting back on my hours. I don't want to cause you any more problems than you already have." Ivan said, "If you can't focus on your work, and you start screwing a bunch of things up, then I have to fix it, and that would give me more problems."

Ivan said he would like to put me on the simple task of sorting through a couple hundred sets of old drawings, cataloging them, and purging any duplicate sets. He said he felt like it would be something I could do, when I had spare time outside of school, that was no pressure. He said that I could take as long as I needed to finish. It was a simple thing that needed to be done. He had been throwing all his past projects in a closet for about a year and now had accumulated multiple copies of the same drawings, and also had a lot of drawings that just needed to be thrown away. My job was to go through all the drawings, sort them into their specific projects, and build one set of drawings that contained all the final contract documents along with all their revisions. It was a very simple, but time consuming task. Anyone could have done it. If you could read dates and see where changes had been made to the

118

drawings, you could have done this. People in the office would come by and ask why I was sorting through all those drawings. I would explain that Ivan had asked me to do it and so I was. I heard somebody say, "Well, you've got to find something he can do. He seems have a hard time doing just about everything else lately." Hearing that comment drove me nuts. I remember having that comment play over and over in my head. After I realized that the office thought of me as a complete imbecile, I knew that my days were numbered, I just didn't know how many of them were left.

Another girl that worked there came by my desk one day and said, "Hey, Mad Scientist, what's up with the back up tapes of our projects?" "Mad Scientist?", I asked. "Yeah, that's your new nickname. Your desk is always a mess and you've been acting kind of weird, like a mad scientist." I felt crushed. I knew I felt weird but wasn't sure that other people were picking up on it. I didn't want to tell everybody at work that Sara was pregnant. I had been going to work for several weeks after finding out the news, with my big secret eating at me inside. I thought that once I told them, they would surely all look down on me and say disapproving things behind my back. So, I guess, to everyone at work, all they could see was that I was acting weird. When I first started working at JP, I tried to be very out going. I would take several minutes every morning to chat with everybody about how things were going and crack a joke here and there. Now, I came in and went straight to my desk, put on my headphones, and stayed in the zone the entire time I was there. I didn't want any more contact with those people than I was forced to have. This, I guess, was some of the weirdness that had been commented on. My solitude, that stemmed from my inability to speak, were what people were beginning to notice at JPA. I don't think that they had any idea of just how depressed I was. Soon, the depression would worsen. I would soon get my first taste of what deep depression can do to a person. For me, it simply shut me down. The switch turned from on to off and the power went out.

The more I worried about my future, the more I distanced myself from everyone around me. This led me to worry about what the repercussions of my new strange behaviors would be. I now also worried about what people were thinking and saying about me at work and school. This just added more stress on top of everything else. It seemed to me that everything was coming to an end, or maybe a new, dark beginning. Everything was building towards a major failure at work and especially at school. I remember taking a day off from work, when I didn't have school either, and staying home one day. I woke up that morning and watched Sara and Liza leave for the day. I then lied down on the couch and stared at the ceiling almost the entire day. The entire time I lay there, I kept envisioning my future, the one in the trailer with an angry wife, and two underprivileged kids. I couldn't bring myself to do anything. There was a load of dishes in the sink that needed to be washed. I was supposed to be working like hell on my final project. And all I could do was lie there and give up on my wife, my kids, and myself. Sara came home that day and found me laying, staring at the ceiling. "Are you O.K.?", she said. "No. I'm going to fail Design 5.2 because I can't think straight anymore.", I told her. She said she wanted us to go to a family counselor. She thought it might save our marriage and we might find out if one of us was crazy.

I had been telling Sara for years that I thought she needed psychological help because she had so many bad childhood experiences. After we got married, she never seemed to be happy with me or very happy with life in general. There would be times when I would be excited about something and she would seem to be bothered by my happiness. This had first started with her jealousy of anyone I spent time with aside from her. Then it branched out to anything in my life that brought me happiness that didn't involve her. If I was excited about something at work or school, she seemed to get annoyed, just to hear me talk about it. I told her that I thought every time I was up, she was down, and if I was down, she liked it and it made her happy. I believed that she liked me best when she felt like she could nurture me and make me better again. I told her I thought it was wrong and that she needed help. So after seeing me become more and more depressed, she finally made an appointment with a family counselor.

The first appointment she made, I cancelled on her and told her I was too busy at work and she should go on without me. It was I lie, I was hoping she would talk to someone who would tell her that she had serious problems, prescribe her some medication, and fix her. I did not consider myself to have a problem. As far as I was concerned, there was no need for me to be there.

Sara went without me and spilled her guts out to a counselor there. When I met her at home that night, she told me that the counselor had told her that she in fact was perfectly sane. He agreed that she had a rough childhood but said that her main problem was that she blamed herself for everything wrong around her. He said she did not need medication but instead gave her a book to read about how to keep a positive mindset. I thought it was a total waste of her time. The book was bull crap, the counselor was full of it, and Sara had simply charmed her way through that session with her good looks and personality. She and her mother had a way of putting up a good front for people when they wanted to. At times they could be the most hilarious, enjoyable people to be around. But when it was just Sara and I, the charisma disappeared. She usually had some gripe about something she didn't like about me or was upset by some other person in her life. I figured that she had shown her best face to the counselor and fooled him into thinking she was a sane individual. So, I asked her to make another appointment with the counselor. This time I would go.

Sara and I met with the same family counselor she had met with previously. I didn't want this to happen, but that's how it was arranged. The guy started in by telling me how lucky I was to have a wife like Sara. He said she was a very loyal and forgiving person who put too much blame on herself for things that were out of her control. I immediately felt like I had walked into a trap. This guy seemed like he was in love with my wife and was ready to drop a hammer on me before I ever opened my mouth. The counselor, a psychologist, asked me to tell him about myself after listening to Sara describe some of my recent unusual behavior and thoughts. I tried to tell him about the anxiety I was having about school and the fact that we were about to have a second unplanned child. I tried to tell him, as best I could, anyway.

My words came out with long pauses in between each of the few words that I spoke. It was the only way I knew how to talk anymore. I could speak a few words at a time and then I would have to think very hard about what I wanted to say next. I was having trouble remembering what I needed to tell him. He would ask me a question and it was a major effort for me to put together a response. I finally managed to get across enough of my ideas that he stopped me and said, "Scott, you have to think of yourself like an airplane. Sometimes you experience things in your life and you are flying way up high, other times things happen that make you fly very low. Right now you are flying in one of those very low spots." I thought, "What a stupid analogy. This is just the kind of crap I thought a psychologist might say. How does this help anything?" He said that he could recommend an anti-depressant that would help me get through this temporary low patch in my life. I told him I wasn't comfortable with the idea of taking drugs to alter my mood and would get back with him about that.

I was in shock. My worst fear was coming true. Someone told *me* that *I* needed to take medication. I kept thinking, "This is total bull crap. My wife has not only fooled this guy into thinking that she's the perfect wife, but also, that I have a mental problem. She has somehow either fooled this guy or she actually has made me into a crazy person." I started to think that all the years of her arguing and complaining had somehow changed me into a different person than I was before I met her. I couldn't believe that my wife, who had told me on many occasions, "I feel like I want to kill myself.", was deemed totally acceptable by this guy, and I was the one with the problem. The guy who got voted "Best All Around" in high school was now told that he needed to take a pill to deal with himself. It was very disturbing to me. My decision to ignore what I had just learned about myself drove me further down the spiral.

I ended up quitting my job at Johnston Peachson shortly after that day with the family counselor. I came into work one day after not being there for several days. I was supposed to be sorting the drawings still. I walked into the office without saying hello to anyone there. That was my usual routine now. I went into the closet that had all the drawings and started sorting through everything. As usual for me now, it seemed like a very hard thing to do. I couldn't stop my racing thoughts of doom and all the anxiety that came with them. The simple task that was given to me was becoming the hardest thing I had ever done at work. Hugh Bozly came by the closet I was in and said, "Well, look who decided to get back on the horse again. Are you trying to see if you can still keep your job here?", then walked off before I could respond. Not that I would have been able to say much of anything intelligible had he stayed around for a response. It made me furious. I could hear people whispering in the office and giggling. I figured that they were all making some terrible jokes about me. The idea that the entire office now thought of me as some retarded kid who didn't deserve to be working there, pushed me over the edge. I thought, "I don't need this. I can't do this. I am going to fail school anyways, so what's the point of working another day around a group of people that I can't stand and who can't stand me. I'll get a job doing landscaping or garbage collecting, anything before I step back into another damned architecture firm."

I walked back to my desk and put all my things in a box. I walked the box out to my car with the intention of going back in to tell Ivan that I was quitting. Then, as I got to my car, I decided there was no point in even having that conversation with Ivan again. I thought he might somehow convince me to stay. So, I left. Without saying a word to any of those people, including an architect who had bent over backwards to help me deal with my issues, I drove away and never stepped foot in that place again. It was a terrible thing to do. That day haunted my dreams for years to come.

At school the semester was almost wrapped up. It was time to prepare for our final presentation. By this point I felt physically sick most of the time. I either had headaches, nausea, or a slight cold for the last couple weeks of that final semester. All the anxiety had actually manifested into real physical symptoms. Now I had to try to finish my project without the resources of the JP office as well. I had to do all my work at home on my computer that was much slower than what I had used at JP to do the last semester's work. I also needed a way to print the large drawings that had to be produced for the final presentation. Luckily, David Bartley and I were still on good terms. Ivan, apparently, hadn't told David any of my ridiculous problems. I asked David if he minded me printing some of my drawings at his office and he said, "No problem, just bring me a beer, and you can print all you want." I actually brought him a bottle of Jack Daniels. He loved to drink that with Coke after work on Fridays. We had spent many Friday afternoons sitting around drinking whiskey and Coke when I worked at Bartley Engineering.

I showed up at Bartley Engineering and felt like I was back with good people again. I didn't feel like I did when I was with the people at JP. These were a group of people who I felt comfortable around and I told them about some of the struggles I was having in the most positive way I could. I didn't talk about my fear that the project I was printing would be a total failure at school. I did tell them that Sara was pregnant. No one said anything negative, but David joked, "You know what's causing her to get pregnant right?" I laughed and he said I'd better hurry up and get out of school so that I could get a real job that would pay for more diapers. It was nice to see my friends again. It was the last time I was around most of the group that I had worked with. After that, several of them went their separate ways. The next time I was at Barkley Engineers, the place had tripled in size and was a totally different animal than the one I knew.

We had our final presentation at the beginning of May in 2001. Fortunately for me, we were spared from the stress of actually having to give a speaking presentation. Had we been required to give the usual speaking presentation for that final project, I think I might have failed. My inability to recall the correct words was now in full effect. I would never have been able to stand up and defend my work against a jury of professors. I guess it must be true that God never gives you more than you can handle. Fortunately, all we had to do was display our work in the main gallery at the school. The faculty would all get together and decide our fates within a couple of days. Then it would all be over. I would find out that I failed and would become a college drop out who couldn't close the deal on getting his degree and I would go to work at some crappy job that had nothing to do with the last seven years of my life. I was sure of that.

We all displayed our work at the school's main gallery. I had several large drawings and color images that took up an 8' x 8' area of the gallery. That was all the space the school allowed for each student. I also created an animation that was a virtual walk through my 3-D model. It started with a bird's eye view that looked at my building from far away. The camera then flew towards the building, passing through a forest of pine trees, and began to walk along a trail in the virtual woods that led to my building. Then the camera walked through the building and ended up at a dock at the end of my building that overlooked a lake. I thought it was a pretty impressive little piece of video, even if I hadn't spent the amount of time that I should have on it. I was hoping that the video might save my butt if all else failed. I brought the video on a Zip Drive, hoping that I would be able to play it at the final presentation. Andrew Chin had told me that they had computers at school that he was willing let students use who wanted to display things, such as the video I had produced. There was only one other student who was attempting to do the same thing I had done, Mark Ruiz. Andrew told Mark and I that he wanted to let us display our stuff on the computers because he thought we represented what the future students would be doing as a standard in the years to come. Everyone else in the class built their models by hand the traditional way, and had no need for a computer.

I loaded my video onto the computer that Andrew let me borrow. I set up the computer in front of all my drawings that were already displayed. Then I tried to play the video. It wouldn't play on the computer Andrew gave me. "Well, here we go. Total failure.", I thought. Window's Media Player would bring up the video as just a black screen. Quick Time did the same thing. I kept getting an error message that the video was encoded with a CODEC that was not recognized by that computer. The only solution was to go back home and get my computer and play the video from it. I should have done that in the first place. I knew that when computers were involved, anything that could go wrong would go wrong. But I really didn't care enough at this point to bother bringing my computer from home. I just assumed that my whole project would be seen as a disaster. I was convinced that no matter what I did, I would fail that semester. I didn't see the use in worrying about back up plans. I told Andrew about the glitch with the computer and said I would go home and get my computer and bring it up there. "No, somebody might steal your computer or damage it while it sits out here for a couple days. Don't worry about it. Just give me a copy of the video and I'll see if I can get it to play at home.", Andrew said. "He must be planning to fail me, that's why he doesn't even care about the video.", I thought. The next day I went up to school and looked around at everyone's projects. I met a professor who had helped me when I was researching Sustainability issues for my project. He said, "Well, Scott, I guess you've heard. You didn't cut it this year. Oh, well, maybe next year you'll get it right." I just looked at him for a few seconds thinking that everything was really starting to happen, just like I thought it would. Then, after having a stone face for several seconds, he smiled and said he was kidding. He told me that they hadn't made any final decisions just yet. That didn't ease my mind any. In fact, after hearing that comment from my professor, my ears started ringing, and I started sweating from the anxiety that had come from what had just happened.

The next day we were all asked to meet with Andrew and Dan to hear the results of the faculty's review. They told us that everyone who had displayed their work received a passing grade. There were two students who did not show up at the final presentation. It would turn out that they were the ones who had to repeat the year over. I couldn't believe what I had been told. How had I convinced myself so thoroughly of an idea that wasn't true? I was sure that I would fail, and yet I passed. I couldn't believe it. I couldn't believe I had allowed myself to be so thoroughly consumed by things that weren't real. I somehow passed even though I felt like I had done a very poor job that semester. That final semester was the first time that I began to think that, perhaps, my perception of reality might be off at times. I started to think that maybe something was wrong with me after all. I still sometimes wake up from nightmares about failing that final semester and all the stress that developed from my final project in Design 5.2.

Another weird thing that I did during that time involved my dad's brother, David Gann. Uncle David called me one night before I realized that I would graduate. He told me to think hard about what my next step would be. "This is the time to think about where you want to see yourself in five years. The most important thing is where you decide to live. Don't think you have to stay in Tallahassee to have a good job.", Uncle David told me. My uncle lived in Naples, FL. He had moved his family there about 6 years earlier to start his own Air Conditioning sales and service company. He installed and repaired A.C. units in the Naples area and was starting to make a pretty decent living doing it. He told me that Naples was booming and that he knew a few architects in town, if I ever wanted to get a job down there. "If you like the beach, Naples is the place to be. Everything is growing here. Buildings are going up everywhere. I think you might really like it here. You'd definitely have job security." I told him I would think about it and call him back.

The more I thought about Naples, the more it seemed like it might be a good place to start over. I'd be closer to Mom and Dad. My aunt and uncle would be right there in the same town as me. And he said construction was booming there. After all, Ft. Myers wasn't that far way either, and that was where my mom's cousin, Gary, had made his fortune in the architectural world. Maybe this was worth looking in to. I called David back, and told him to put in a good word for me with his architect friends and give me a list of their firms so that I could set up an interview. David did his part and called me back a few days later with several firms that were waiting to hear from me. I now had a list of names and numbers. Now all I had to do was call. But then I started thinking about Johnston Peachson and all the problems I had there. I also thought about Devenrow and Associates. I began to worry about repeating a bad experience, only this time, it would be with people who knew my family. I began to worry that my bizarre behavior might be noticed by people who I might end up working with in Naples. I thought that those people might end up telling my uncle how strange I was and then he would tell my parents and then who knows what might happen. I began to think that Naples was a risk I could not afford to take. I decided that if I did have a problem, I wanted to keep it a secret from my family. I thought of the move to Naples as going from the frying pan and into the fire. I went ahead and set up the interviews though. It was the closest I ever came to leaving Tallahassee.

Even though I was already very uneasy about the idea of moving closer to my family, I went ahead and arranged several interviews. I thought that I would at least go through the interview process and then come back with a list of excuses as for why I would not be able to work for any of the firms that I had interviewed with. I arranged to do all of my interviews on the same day. The interviews all got scheduled on a day that was a couple weeks away from the day I made the calls. This gave me enough time to worry myself into a state that prevented me from doing any interviews at all. The closer the day came that I was supposed to go to Naples, the more anxious I became about the idea. I kept replaying all the bad experiences from JPA and Devenrow in my head. I convinced myself that it would be too risky for me to try and work for someone who was friends with my uncle. What if things didn't work out well? Then, what would my uncle think of me? What would he say to my mom and dad? I didn't like what I thought could happen. So, on the day that I was supposed to be driving to Naples, I called all the firms and cancelled my interviews. They all wanted to know if I had already found a job with some other firm. I told them I was still undecided but was looking around at jobs in my area. They all seemed perplexed by the fact that I had gone through the trouble to set up an interview, then backed out on going through with it. I'm sure my uncle was disappointed that he had ever given them my name.

After much worrying, I decided Naples was not an option for me. Then I thought about Washington D.C. and Charles Mada. I thought that D.C. might be my best bet. I had been my happiest in architecture while working for him. He had offered for me to come back after I was done with school. I thought it would be interesting to call him and see what he might pay me. So I did. Charles picked up the phone and I introduced myself. "Scott! It's great to hear from you. So you're done with school?" I told him I had graduated and was thinking about moving to D.C. I asked him what I could expect to make as a recent graduate with my work experience. He vaguely replied, "Well, you'll definitely make more here than you would there. But an exact dollar amount, I can't give you right now. You know I would compensate you better than others in the area. But what have you learned since you left me?" I told him about working for a structural engineer and getting a little experience in actual design at JP. He said that if I was really interested, to think about coming up there with some of my work for a little interview. I told him I wasn't that sure yet, I'd call him back. That was the last time I ever spoke with Charles Mada.

After talking with Charles, I felt a little disappointed that he hadn't just made me an offer and invited me back immediately. That was a very unrealistic expectation. How could he pull out a dollar figure without any idea of what I was like after the two years since I had left D.C.? I then thought broader. I thought about my brother, Sam, who had joined the Air Force several years earlier. Sam seemed to enjoy working with the Air Force. They were training him to become a Surveyor. He already knew AutoCAD and used it at his job. Sam had great benefits: paid housing, food, medical, and a paycheck on top of that. I wondered if I might have a future with the Air Force.

So I called the local Air Force recruiter and told him my background and that I was interested in learning about how I might fit into the Air Force. "We don't have a need for Architects in the Air Force. You could be trained as an engineer. Then you would have lots of job opportunities with us.", he said. He said if I were to enlist, I could immediately begin Officer Training to become an officer. But he said that officers who were brought in from outside the Air Force enlisted soldiers, like me, had a harder time than the ones who joined as enlisted soldiers and were promoted through the ranks to become officers. He said I would have seniority over all the regular enlisted guys, but there would be tension because they might feel like I had received special treatment. It didn't sound like an easy road to me. I didn't consider myself to have leadership qualities. I couldn't see myself jumping into a totally new culture with a new career path, and more responsibility than I already had. So, the Air Force was another very short-lived dream.

Chapter 26: A New Angel is Born

A few weeks after I graduated, my depression symptoms seemed to recede. I guess the stressor, college, was removed and my brain slowly began to regain some of its former capacities. My abilities to speak and think, were beginning to be a little more like what they had been, before the pressure of school and work did its damage, though I knew that I was still not the person that I wanted to be. I finally got myself motivated enough to set up some interviews with local architects. A few weeks had passed since graduation and I figured I should at least give architecture one more try before throwing in the towel. After all, I had spent seven years in school preparing for this career and only about two years had been spent actually working for an architect. So, I ended up getting another job in town. I became an employee of Manoda, Lerring, Dobson, Architects.

My interview with MLD wasn't as swift as some of the interviews of the past had been. I was still rattled from my experience at Johnston Peachson. I remember meeting with the owner, Trent Manoda, and a partner, Jodi Dobson. They looked over my stuff and asked questions about JPA, and why I had left. I told them that Ivan was having a lot of financial trouble and that he wasn't able to pay me what I thought was fair for someone with a degree. That was partially true, but I didn't go into the real reasons I had left, of course. I felt like I was lying to these guys and that made me nervous. I was holding back a big secret and it made me feel out of place. A comforting sight that day was to meet up with a friend of mine that I had no idea was working there, Roosevelt Biggens.

Roosevelt had graduated a year before me, the year I was supposed to graduate had I not gone to D.C. Roosevelt and I had gotten along well together when we were in Design 3.1 and 3.2 together. Seeing Roosevelt gave me a little relief. I thought it might be nice to work with a friend. Jodi Dobson introduced me to everyone else and showed me around the office. I was sure that I had the job. Then he said, "So, are you always this quiet?" I was bothered by the question. I didn't think that I had been "quiet". I had asked a question here and there, but I guess I hadn't talked enough. Now I was being described as quiet. That's what I had been at Johnston Peachson in my last few months. I had not planned to let that old persona carry over to my new job. But there it was. Someone had already noticed something odd about me, the fact that I was quiet. I couldn't stand being thought of as a quiet person. I had so many good years where I was known as a talker. To me, being called quiet, was like being called stupid. I felt insulted every time a person described me as a quiet person. I felt like I had so much to say, but the words never seemed to be able to make their way out of my mouth now. At MLD, just as with JPA before it, I was a quiet person.

After a slightly nerve wracking interview, I got the job at MLD and things started out fine. For my first assignment, I was put on a project that involved the re-roofing of a state park building at Marianna Caverns State Park in Marianna, FL. MLD specialized in roofing. They designed buildings, but they were known in town as roofing experts. Trent Manoda and Randy Lerring, the other partner in the firm, had both made it their business to learn the ins and outs of what made a good, durable roof. They were selected by FSU to perform all re-roof installations throughout the campus. After my first project as just a draftsman, roofing became my business as well. Randy Lerring told me he wanted me to start training with Roosevelt to become a roof inspector. FSU paid MLD to keep a full time roof inspector on most of their roofing jobs. The job was to simply document the process of the roof's installation as it was built. This was done by taking photographs of all the activities centered around the roof's construction and by writing reports that detailed the daily activities of the contractors, what materials they used, and whether they violated any of the contract agreements. These roof inspection reports were then sent to FSU's project administrators who kept tabs on whether or not FSU was getting what it had paid for. The roof inspector was the first and primary line of protection for FSU from getting ripped off by a contractor who might promise to do things the right way and end up doing something else when no one was watching.

It was also around this time that Sara gave birth to Gwen Gann on October 12, 2001 at Tallahassee Memorial Hospital. Around the time that Gwen, baby Gwen, was born, Sara and I were at each other's throats. I think the chemical imbalance that comes from being pregnant caused her to be more irritable than usual. She and I were in a couple of major arguments right about the time Gwen was born. I was so tired of dealing with her that after she had Gwen, I didn't even spend that first night with her at the hospital. I stayed home with Liza and my mother who had come up to Tallahassee to help out with Sara and the new baby for a few days. My mom got tired of Sara pretty fast too. She and Sara never really got along well. I think my mother held on to a lot of the things that I did, when it came to Sara. My mom had seen Sara pitch fits in front of her and pretty much lost all respect for her. My mom suggested that I stay at home with her and Liza after Sara and I got into a small argument at the hospital in front of a nurse and my mother. As usual, I don't remember what the fight was about. I just remember that it made my mom mad enough that she was telling me she didn't know how I could stand to live with Sara.

As far as Gwen was concerned, I was again thankful that we had another healthy child. I was a little disappointed that we hadn't had a boy though. I didn't ever want to have more than two kids and I thought that would be my last shot at having a son. It wasn't a big issue for me though. I was happy that Liza would have a little sister that would look up to her. They were four years apart. By the time Gwen was born, I didn't feel depressed about the fact that we now had two kids. I was actually comfortable with the idea. I wasn't thrilled about two more years of diapers and a screaming baby. But Liza was now at an age that allowed me to begin realizing the joy of having a child. By the time Gwen was actually born, I had begun to realize that two kids were better than one. I knew Gwen would be through her difficult periods sooner than I would realize. I had been through the drill with Liza already and now this time around, it didn't seem to be as big a deal. Having an enjoyable job and being finished with school didn't hurt either. We now were making more money and had more free time than ever. The other big factor was that we had moved out of the trailer and were living in a nice duplex on the east side of town. We had moved from the depressing trailer park into a quiet neighborhood that was all duplex style houses. A funny coincidence was that Ann Defenbaum, my old friend from JPA, and her sister lived only two houses down the street from us. It was nice to have them as neighbors. Yes, now that school was over, and I realized that I might be able to handle a career in architecture after all, life seemed to be getting a little easier.

Chapter 27: The MLD Experience

At work Roosevelt and I spent about a week together training for the roof inspector position. He showed me what he did throughout the day and pointed out various things that were going on at the job sites he was overseeing. He showed me how to write up the roof reports and what to photograph. It seemed like a very easy job, but a very educational job as well. I was now getting to see construction as it happened on a day-to-day basis. The things that I had been drawing in the offices, over the last several years, were now real. With the roof inspection job, I got to watch people work to transform the ideas on the paper into actual objects. It was really exciting to me to be with contractors all day and see what their lives were like.

My first project that I was placed on, by myself, was the re-roofing of FSU's Alumni Village. Alumni Village was a series of duplexes and apartments that some of the students that had families lived in. It was not the dorm room, beer party, atmosphere that the other kids lived in. It was more like a typical apartment complex. The Contractor for the job was All-State Construction. Their project manager on that job was Buster Keding. He and I spent all day, 5 days a week, together, with nothing to do but watch the day laborers and sub contractor tear off and re-roof the buildings. We spent a lot of time just talking about our lives outside of work.

Buster was in his 60's. He was a chain smoker. I had quit smoking for about 6 months before I met Buster. But after a couple weeks of watching him smoke cigarette after cigarette, I caved in. I went out and bought a pack of Sampoerno Gold, clove cigarettes. That's what I had always smoked before. The tips of the cigarettes were soaked in some sugary sweet substance that made every puff taste like candy. The cloves also added to the sweet flavor. They were very addictive. I went from smoking a few a day to about 10 a day. That got expensive so I switched to regular cigarettes, Marlboros.

Aside from all the smoking and chatting with Buster, I really was learning a little about roofing. For me, there was a whole lot to learn. I got familiar with how hot the tar should be before it was applied to the roof, nail fastening patterns, and the general process of how a single ply roof membrane is installed. After a couple of weeks, I got tired of just sitting around all day and just watching the guys work. I told the Sub-Contractor, Wendell Parner, owner of Parner Bros. Roofing, that I'd be glad to help actually do some of the work with his guys. I didn't know it, but that was crossing a line that was not supposed to be crossed according to the guys back at MLD.

Wendel said he appreciated all the help he could get and I started helping tear off old roofs and install new ones. Wendel wasn't my boss, so I could help out if I felt like it or I could just stand around and tell guys they weren't doing something right if I felt like it. Correcting the mistakes was supposed to be one of my main priorities anyway. The Parker Bros. workers loved me for helping them out. I was supposed to be the guy who reported them to FSU when they screwed up and here I was helping them do their job. It never occurred to me that I might be setting myself up for a conflict of interest type situation.

Alumni Village wrapped up and I was put on a new job, Re-roofing of the School of Communications at FSU. I picked up right where I had left off at the last job. The General and Sub Contractor were the same as Alumni Village. All-State Construction was again the general contractor and Parner Bros. Roofing actually performed the work of tearing off the old and installing the new roof. I was with all the same people that were at Alumni Village, except All-State had a different project manager, Carter Jameson. Carter wasn't as talkative as Buster, so I spent most of my time talking with the guys at Parker Bros. By this time, Wendell Parner, and his brother Dave, had asked me if I wanted to join their softball team and play a couple nights a week with them, Roosevelt, and some of the other Parker Bros. guys. I told him it sounded like fun to me and started adding softball to my after work schedule. I also started working out at the gym with Roosevelt three nights a week. Basically, I was never home, except to go to sleep. I'd wake up the next morning and be out the door in thirty minutes. I thought the best way to stay married to Sara was to just avoid her as much as possible. Sara would later tell me that she thought that was the first hint of mania she ever saw in me. She and I had no idea of what mania was at the time. To me, it was a great time in my life, even though I was avoiding all my responsibilities to my wife and kids.

Another thing that started about this time was the occasional drink with the guys from work, not the MLD guys, the Parker Bros. guys. It was usually just me and another guy who worked for Parker Bros. His name was Kenny. He was a Jamaican and had a great sense of humor. Kenny was married but liked to go out and drink a few beers every now and then. He and I started going to a couple of the FSU bars and pool halls about once a week. We would play pool, drink beer, and stare at all the hot college girls that hung out at these places. That's about when I started thinking of actually doing what Sara had been accusing me of all those years earlier, cheating on her. Up until that time, I had never thought about trying my luck with another girl. Now that Kenny and I had started making our trips to the various bars and pool halls, the girls were everywhere. Also, we were in the heart of the FSU campus all day long working at the School of Communications. I had never felt tempted before, but now there were a few girls who had flirted with me here and there. I thought about taking a chance.

One of the girls I started talking to, I met at a hot dog stand at the School of Communications. The hot dog stand was operated by a guy named Scott, and his wife. I would sometimes eat lunch right there at the hot dog stand. This girl was usually there for about an hour everyday talking with Scott, his wife and myself. She was a Communications major and seemed like a very smart and funny girl. She asked me lots of questions about myself and that got us talking. I told her about being married to a wife that I didn't think I loved anymore. I told her about a lot of our problems and that I was thinking of leaving her. She agreed that it was better for both of us to separate if we didn't get along. One day I asked her if she wanted to go have lunch somewhere off campus sometime. She said that she didn't want to become the person that split up my wife and I and that she would stay out of the picture until I was divorced and happy about it. Attempt to cheat one, swing and a miss.

The next girl I thought about trying to get to know better, worked as a waitress at the pool hall that Kenny and I went to about once a week, Hobbit Hoagies. She was a very pretty FSU student who was working nights at the pool hall. She did about the same routine as the other girl. We started talking about things, only I didn't elaborate as much about Sara as I did with the first girl. I actually stayed with her at Hobbit Hoagies a few nights after they closed and helped her put up chairs on the tables. I pulled the same we-should-get-together-for-lunch-sometime-routine as I had with the previous girl. She said she had a boyfriend and that he would get mad at her if he knew that she was going out with other guys. Attempt two. Another failure. After that, I figured I was no Romeo and had better just leave other girls alone and be happy with what I had. I felt guilty about trashing Sara to other girls and started to think what I had done was pretty stupid.

At home Sara had actually become less abrasive, even though I was always gone. I think she was beginning to think she had finally pushed me away and was starting to regret it. I don't remember any more fights between Sara and I after Gwen was born. We just started to either get along or love each other so little that fighting didn't seem to have a point anymore. I'm not sure which. One thing that Sara did, that made me very happy, and her very worried, was that she agreed to get her tubes tied. I told her that I didn't want any more kids, especially accidental ones. She said that I should have a vasectomy because it was supposed to be less painful and require less healing time. I told her that she was already off work on maternity leave and why should I put myself out of work for a couple of days if she was already not working. She reluctantly agreed to have the surgery. I feel guilty about making her do that now. Not that she needs any more kids, but still, I could have just as easily had the surgery myself. At the time I felt like her doing that for me was a very nice gesture. Now I feel like I was a bit of an asshole for making her do that. On the other hand, if neither of us had the surgery, and we had more kids, I don't know what I'd be like today, probably not as well off as I am.

One day at work, Randy Lerring called me into his office and told me that my roof inspection reports were not as thorough as they should be. He also said, "Remember, you're not in school anymore. You've got to take what you do seriously. This isn't fun and games here. I hear you're hanging around with Parker Bros. after work. You need to stop doing that. It doesn't make us look good to FSU. Those guys aren't your buddies. You are supposed to be reporting them if they try to screw FSU. How are we supposed to believe that you're doing that if you are best friends with them?" I apologized and said I hadn't thought about it that way, that they were just very friendly to me and I was just being nice back. "These guys are not your friends. They will try to pull the wool over your eyes. That's all they are doing.", he said. I felt pretty stupid, but didn't really believe him.

It wasn't long after that when I told Wendell Parner about the fact that the roof on my duplex apartment was leaking and he should try to talk with my landlord about replacing the roof. I had already called my landlord and told her the ceiling was leaking and that the shingles looked like they needed to be replaced. She agreed and I brought up Parker Bros. She and Wendel worked out a deal and Parker Bros. re-roofed our duplex one weekend. I helped out, of course. I wasn't paid a dime, of course. That weekend was also Sara's birthday. I remember all of the guys that were helping put the new roof on were drinking some Jamaican beer that Kenny had brought, Red Stripe. I sat up there drinking beer with the guys as we were putting on the new roof. I started to get drunk. I had bought a birthday cake for Sara and invited all the guys to have some cake with us. I'm sure that she loved that idea. We all sat out in the yard eating birthday cake and drinking beer. Then I got nauseous and threw up all over the yard. Happy Birthday Sara, I love you! This was still the period that Sara says she thinks that she saw her first glimpse of mania in me. She says that she really started to worry about me during this time.

We had a Christmas party at the MLD office that year, 2001. It was a very simple affair, just a few appetizers in the conference room. We had to give up our lunch break to have our "Christmas Party". The choices for lunch that day were crackers and cheese, boiled shrimp cocktail, and some fruit. I can't stand shrimp, so I had the fruit, cheese, and crackers. I felt very uncomfortable during our little get together. I spent so little time with the office people that I didn't get any of the inside jokes that people cracked here and there. I was always by myself at FSU and only rarely saw Randy Lerring. Now I was sitting with all the office types and it was awkward. Nobody seemed to have anything to say to me or care about anything I said. Something was up.

On my last day of work before I planned to take off for a few days of Christmas vacation, I was called into the conference room by Randy Lerring. He asked me to sit down. I was thinking, "What the hell is this about? Is he about to dump some assignment on me that keeps me here through Christmas?" Randy said he had bad news. "What is it?", I asked. "I hate to be the one to tell you this Scott, but we're going to have to let you go. We have lost our contract with FSU for Minor Services. That means that we have less money coming in now. Also, I've asked you to get serious about your position here and you haven't. Your roof reports are poor. You aren't showing up at FSU when you are supposed to. You act like you are still in school. I can't repeat myself over and over. Trent, Jody, and I have all met and agreed that you can gather your things and turn in your key. We'll send you a check for your last months pay." I just about started crying. I could barely speak with a crackling voice and I said, "Is there any way I could have another chance? I didn't realize things were so serious. I need this job. How am I going to explain this at my next job?" Randy said, "Look, I feel bad. I like you. You are a nice guy, but we can't have you running around with Parker Bros. and working for us. I'll talk with Trent and Jody and let them know that you want them to reconsider, but don't hold your breath. When Trent makes up his mind about something, that's the end of it. I recommend that you start looking for a new job and take it seriously. We'll give you a good recommendation. We aren't out to get you."

And that was that. I left the room feeling like a total idiot. Everyone else already knew. Roosevelt saw me gathering my things and said, "I'm sorry Scott. I don't really know what's going on, but I might be next." I left and cried when I got in my car. I thought I had been a pretty good employee. Sure I was hanging around with Parker Bros. too much, but I didn't realize I was putting my job in jeopardy. I never understood his comments about my inspection reports. I compared my notes to Roosevelt's after my first warning and our reports were almost identical. Roosevelt said that he thought they really just wanted me to cut off my dealings with Parker Bros. and that he had gotten a lecture as well. Roosevelt was our only black employee and had been there a year longer than me. I think that's why they spared him and made an example out of me. I remember thinking, "All right, I'm giving this architecture thing one more try, and if it doesn't work out this next time, I'm done forever."

I had to go home to mom and dad's for Christmas that year and pretend that nothing was wrong. I couldn't bring myself to tell them I had just been fired. They knew I was acting very strange around the time I left Johnston Peachson. I didn't want to worry them. I did feel like I could tell my brother, Carter, who actually rode with me down to their house from Tallahassee. Carter had moved to Tallahassee to live with a girl he met, Sue Smith, a while earlier. Sara and the girls had already gone down to my parents' house. So it was a six-hour car ride with just Carter and I. I felt like if I didn't tell him, he would notice my acting strangely and wonder what was up. I told Sara about it when I got there. She said she could tell something was really wrong as soon as she saw me. She said, "Don't worry about it. You'll find something better. Let's just forget about it and try to have a good Christmas." It was a very kind moment from her. I really appreciated the way she took the news. I'm sure it scared her, but she was a champ that whole Christmas. She was very loving towards me. I think she felt sorry for me. She was always at her best whenever things seemed at their worst for me.

After Christmas was over we went back to Tallahassee and I tried to once again pick up the ball and keep moving. I felt like this was my last attempt to keep striving towards a dream I had when I was in high school of someday being a successful architect. I thought if I got one more job with a firm and it failed to work out the way I wanted, I would quit on my dream. I started to think about other things I might try doing. There was a new stipulation though. Sara wanted to go back to school and get a degree in education. She wanted to be a teacher. She said if she could become a teacher, then I could have another chance to try something else out that required training. I needed to either stick to the plan or find a job that paid well enough but didn't require anymore school. School was the last thing I wanted more of anyway. I thought about going in to landscaping, or becoming an employee of Parker Bros. roofing. But I thought I'd first just do the easiest thing, try for another architecture job.

Chapter 28: Intro to ETO and the Last Stand

When I applied for my job at MLD I also interviewed with another firm, ETO/Architects. I interviewed with an architect named David Barthowe. I thought the interview went well enough but never heard back from them. Then I met Warren Eto, the owner of ETO/Architects at a 5k run that I just happened to run in one weekend. Warren was an avid runner and was in that race as well. I signed up for the race because it seemed like a fun thing to do. I heard about it at The Downtown Get Down, the pep rally held before every FSU home football game, that was a town wide festival. Some FSU girls were going around asking people to sign up for the race and I thought it sounded like fun. I had no idea that running that race would result in me landing my last architecture job in Tallahassee. The way it all came about was this: I saw Warren at the race warming up for the run. I remembered him from my previous encounter with ETO/Architects. I introduced myself and told him I had taken a job with MLD Architects and was now one of their roof inspectors. He was very friendly and apologized for not hiring me at the time. He said that they were hoping to get a job that fell through and they couldn't afford to hire at the time I had interviewed. He said if I ever became available again to give him a call. We talked for several more minutes and then the race began. Warren and I jogged together for a while and then he said, "Well, I've got to pick up my pace. I'm practicing for the Boston Marathon and I've got to get moving if I want to have a chance at that." Then Warren took off at a pace I couldn't keep up with. After the race, I felt like I had just made an important contact and would remember what he said if the time ever came.

Now, after being fired from MLD, I needed a job again. I immediately thought of Warren. So I called ETO/Architects and asked them if they might be interested in hiring me. I interviewed again with David Barthowe. He gave me the same story that Warren had about not getting a job that they needed to afford a new person. He said they were currently about to get a contract with FAMU to design a building for them and that if they got it, I was hired. Two weeks went by and then I got the call that I was hired at ETO/Architects. It was the first week of January of 2002. In total, it was less than three weeks after I had been fired from MLD. I felt vindicated. I was scared about the possibility that people at ETO would find out about why I was no longer working at MLD, but I was more scared about not paying my bills, so I did what I had to.

My first day at ETO was, as first days usually are, very nerve racking. Lots of new people, a new set of responsibilities, and now I had another big secret to hide. The nice thing I noticed about jumping from firm to firm was that my salary went up every time I made a switch. Now at ETO, I was starting out at $2,000 dollars more than I was making with MLD. I was to be paid $30,500 annually. It seemed like pretty good money to me.

The office at ETO staffed about twenty people when I started. It was the largest firm I had ever worked for. ETO/Architects was actually two companies. There was ETO/Architects and then there was ArC/ Masterbuilders. ETO was the architectural firm. ArC/ Masterbuilders was a general contracting company that Warren also owned and operated. ETO/ArC was a design-build firm. This was the same type of company that my mom's cousin, Gary, owned. We had three registered architects and three licensed contractors under one roof. ETO did not specialize in any one particular type of building. Nor did they specialize in any particular area of a building like MLD had done with roofing. ETO didn't try to have a unifying style that marked their work. We did everything from the very traditional to the slightly modern. Nothing we did was really "out there", or mind blowing, but I thought it was all nice stuff. ETO's main clients were FSU, Capital City Bank, and FAMU. We also did some houses, some city of Tallahassee buildings, and other things.

My first assignment was to design a library for FAMU. The library was an addition to an existing library at a little elementary school that was owned by FAMU. The elementary school, like FAMU, was predominately African American. There were a few white kids that went there, but mostly, it was just like FAMU, only elementary school style. David Barthowe was the architect for the project. I was to function as a project manager in training. My duties were mostly drafting related, but also included meeting with FAMU's project manager for the job, as well as all the consultants: electrical, mechanical, and structural. For that project, we did our own civil engineering. The FAMU Media Center Addition project was a nice way to get familiar with how my job would be with ETO. I had told Warren in my interview how much I loved being out in the field and he had said my job would include some of that as well, just not at the level I was used to at MLD. The FAMU Media Center was not one of those projects with a lot of field experience. But it was the first time I had that level of involvement in a project.

The first day of the Media Center project started with David Barthowe showing me his sketches for how the overall layout of the building might work. He had some very rough floor plans and elevations. I got the chance to refine his sketches into working drawings that met the space requirements of the program. I also created elevations that resembled his sketches but still had a little of my ideas in them as well. It was the most actual design work I had ever done up to that point. From the beginning, I felt like I was a part of the design process. The project was set up so that it would be my baby as much as it was David's, even though it would all go to his credit. My name would appear on the project as Draftsman. It was still very exciting to me. I was in and out of meetings with David, the client, and all the consultants. I started to feel pretty proud that I seemed to be doing a good job for once. I tried to take what Randy said about "getting serious" and apply it as best I knew how at ETO/ Architects because if this gig failed to produce a positive result, I was done playing architect.

The Media Center project took about two months to take from those first sketches to final contract documents. Then it was time to build it. By the time we finished the Media Center, I had developed my own details for how the building went together and felt I had played a major part in the end result. It was very satisfying. And David congratulated me on the success and quick speed that we had finished the project with. We completed the project ahead of schedule and under budget. David told everybody one day, "Scott, here, has just completed his first project with us. He's faster than any of you guys and he doesn't bitch and moan about everything I ask him to do like you guys either. You better watch out for him." We were all in the break room after work on a Friday drinking beers when David made this announcement. That was our usual way to end every work week, Beer Friday. Someone would usually make an announcement over the intercom that, "It's beer o'clock, please, everyone gather in the break room for an important meeting." It reminded me of David Bartley's after work Coke and whiskey days. Eventually, I liked the fact that we could all hang out for a few minutes after work and just bull crap about other things outside of our office life. It was similar to our after work ritual with David Bartley, also, because all the big dogs of the office usually participated for a few minutes as well, even Warren, though he never drank beer with us.

Even though I later grew to appreciate "Beer Friday" as much as everyone else, at first, I hated having to be forced to spend time with my new co-workers. I guess I was just so nervous about some things that I didn't like being in a group environment any more than I had to. For the first several months that I worked at ETO, I tried to stay at my desk as much as possible. I didn't want to make the effort to get to know the people in the office because I assumed that once they got to know me, they wouldn't like me. I thought it was best to just cut them off before they had the chance to hurt me.

After the Media Center, I was put on several other projects. Florida Surplus Lines was an office building complex that drug on for about a year. Capital City Banks, our bread and butter client, always had some work we were doing for them. I started my first C.C.B. assignment with a guy who worked there named Mark Lambert. Mark was a former UF student who had taken architecture and construction courses there. I think he had a degree in Construction Management, but not Architecture. He seemed like a pretty nice guy. I could tell he was very smart and knew that Warren liked him a lot. Mark said that ETO was the only architectural firm he had ever worked for. He had started about five years before I did and never left. Mark was only a couple years older than me, but he had far more experience than I did. He was handling the Capital City Bank projects almost by himself, with Warren assisting when needed. He seemed like a really sharp guy. But something about him rubbed me the wrong way. I think it started one day when some funny e-mail was being passed around the office and Mark said, "Just don't let the new guy see it. He hasn't earned his e-mail privileges yet." So, this e-mail joke got passed around the office and everyone but me received it. They were all talking about whatever was in the e-mail and I had no clue of what was actually so funny. I think that Mark probably just thought he was jerking my chain for being the new guy, but I never liked to be the butt of a joke. And his sense of humor seemed to revolve around making me the butt of the joke anytime he could. It was probably just his way of breaking the new guy's balls. But like I said, I was weird about people using me as material for their jokes, so I started to dislike Mark Lambert not long after starting work there.

The problem I had with Mark and the fact that I already felt like I was hiding a big secret (the fact that I had just been fired from my last job), made it hard for me to be outgoing at my new job at first. I soon picked up my old routine I had learned in my days at Johnston Peachson: come in to work and go straight to my desk with as little contact with my coworkers as possible, and put on my headphones to further reduce the chance of getting into a conversation with anyone. If I wanted coffee or water from the break room, I usually tried to make sure I didn't see anyone in there before entering, again, to avoid as much contact as possible. There were times when I had to speak with people, however. I was still new so, there were always questions about things I was working on, where certain things were kept, and so forth. It was also taboo to leave without at least acknowledging everyone in the break room on "Beer Friday". For a time, I tried to act like I was just so dedicated that I needed to continue working through the time that everyone else gathered in the break room on Friday afternoon. No one usually hung around for more than thirty minutes after they went back there. I could usually leave the office by 6:00 pm on Fridays if I sat at my desk, working until almost everyone else had left. Staying late set up a routine that would eventually become my typical work-day. Warren noticed me working late several times and said that he appreciated my efforts. That was about the time that Warren and I started working very closely together.

When I first started working at ETO, a guy named Carter Christen was the go to for all renderings at ETO. Carter did an O.K. job, I thought, but Carter seemed to have a pretty bad temper. One day the office was nice and quiet. We were all working as usual. Then Carter burst out in a tantrum about something that was going on between himself and one of the contractors in the office. He started yelling and cussing about Bill Moore, the head of ArC/ Masterbuilders, and said that Pat Huy, a licensed architect and contractor, needed to get him under control before Carter lost it with him. I thought the whole thing was very bizarre. I had never seen someone lose control of themselves in an office before. Carter sounded crazy as he yelled and stormed around the office to Pat Huy's desk. Pat closed the door to his office and I heard both Carter and Pat yelling at each other for several minutes. Then Pat, Warren, Bill, and Carter all went into the conference room together. They were in there for about a half hour. Carter came out looking like he was about to cry. He gathered his belongings and left. He had just been fired. That was the strangest event I had ever seen take place anywhere I had previously worked. Warren called a staff meeting that afternoon and announced that Carter had been let go because he was making too many mistakes on the Florida Surplus Lines project. Warren also added that he had displayed a very poor attitude and apologized for Carter's rant that happened earlier that morning. Several people made comments about Carter at lunch the next day. They were all saying that what had happened to Carter was messed up because the real problem was that Carter had been given too much work to complete by himself and had been working serious overtime just to try to keep up. They also said that Pat Huy and Bill Moore had hurt Carter too by not giving him the help he needed to do his work. I didn't know what to think because I had no idea of what had happened with Carter, and I wasn't about to say something against two of the partners of the firm. I just kept my mouth shut and took it all in and wandered whether I had made a mistake by deciding to work with ETO.

Chapter 29: The Beginning of Marketing Days

With the office's artist out, there was no one who could do the color renderings anymore. Warren asked me to take a shot at filling Carter' old spot. I also inherited Florida Surplus Lines. That was a nightmare. The more I got familiar with the drawings, the more I realized that Carter had definitely brought some of his problems on himself. There were all kinds of contradictions in the drawings. One drawing might show the length of the building to be 250' and the next page might read 250'-6". Those kinds of errors in construction drawings produce major headaches for the architect and contractor. These were the things that Pat, Bill, and Warren were very pissed about. The drawings had already gone out of the office as 100% Contract Documents, meaning these were the working drawings that Florida Surplus Lines would be built from. Now the sub contractors were all out in the field scratching their heads about how big something was intended to actually be or where to actually locate various parts of the building. The only way to fix the mistakes that were in the Florida Surplus Lines drawings was to issue Supplemental Drawings, about 50 in all, that dealt with each error as it was discovered. These drawings added to the cost of the project and cut into our profits. The whole time I was working on Florida Surplus Lines with Pat, Bill, and Warren; people in the office would say to me, "You better be careful. They're setting you up to be the next Carter. It won't be long before you start running around the office cussing at everybody. Better cover your ass big time while you're working on that project because Pat and Bill will screw you over if you aren't careful." I appreciated the warning, but I never felt like I was being led into a trap. The comments made me a little wary, but I felt like Pat, Bill, and Warren seemed to really want to help me in every way they could. I thought the other people in the office were just a little on the paranoid side.

So Warren also had asked me to try my hand at producing some of the more artistic drawings that we needed to have done. I did a color rendering of a 24" x 36" Capital City Bank elevation using markers. I had seen lots of renderings over the years I had worked with architects, but had never been allowed the chance to work on one. I still thought of myself as pretty artistic, so I told Warren that I thought I could do the rendering with no problems. It actually turned out that Warren really liked what I did with the Capital City Bank elevation. From then on, I was the new go to guy for all office renderings. I did elevations, site plans, and master plans of a couple of really big projects that we were trying to get. Then I upped the bar by trying to do a site plan rendering not with marker, but with AutoCAD and our own office plotter. After I discovered the method for creating colored renderings with AutoCAD, it ended up becoming the standard way to produce site plans for any project. I ended up becoming the instructor of the office for how to use AutoCAD to produce some decent colored drawings. I showed all of the production people how to use AutoCAD to draw their colored site plans and elevations.

With AutoCAD, I didn't need to worry about running out of markers or streaking the colors as I applied them to the paper. AutoCAD produced a very slick looking image for site plans. The colors were always uniform. I even added shadows in the trees and buildings to make things pop off the page a little. I might spend several days working on a rendering when I worked with markers. Now with AutoCAD as my tool, I could produce a rendering within a matter of hours. AutoCAD was a major improvement over the old "by hand" method. And my effort to increase productivity won me a few bonus points with Warren.

After about six months after I had started working with ETO, Sara and I had saved enough money to make a down payment on our first house. We also had a little help from my grand parents, as usual. Sara and I started looking all over town and even as far away as 20 miles outside of Tallahassee. We started hunting first with the internet listings. After a few wasted weekends of driving from one bad neighborhood to another in search of the homes we saw listed online, we decided to meet with a realtor. About a month after we first met with him, he found a little place that had three bedrooms, two bathrooms, a small kitchen, dining room, living room, laundry room, and a garage that had been converted into an extra room. The house sat on an acre of land that was heavily wooded on the back of the lot. The place was built in the '70's and the owner was asking for $95,000. We worked out a deal that knocked off $6,000 from what the owner was asking and she included all the kitchen appliances. We were very happy to now have our own home. We could finally stop paying rent and start paying ourselves. It was very exciting and gave me a sense of relief that we had moved up a little in the world. We were now the new owners of 4525 Autumn Woods Way.

After Sara and I bought our house, everyone at ETO got together and donated $200 dollars to Sara and I as a house warming gift. I felt very appreciative of everyone's generosity. I never expected people at my work to care about my housing situation. After that, I started to think that the people at ETO were a pretty good bunch. I was very thankful to be working with such a great employer and a group of people that cared enough to give their own money so that Sara and I could have a few things for our new house. It was the nicest gesture anyone I ever worked for had done for me.

As far as what I was doing at work goes, I had been hoping that Warren might let me do some virtual models of some future project. I loved building things in three dimensions. For me, I felt more familiar with a project once I saw what it looked like three dimensionally. I thought that probably applied to everyone else as well. For years I had imagined that one day I would put myself in a position where I worked for a firm as a virtual model builder. The models I had built in school were my most favorite work. I felt like I really understood what I was doing when I built my buildings in three dimensions on my computer. When I began working at ETO as a rendering specialist, I waited for something small to come my way where I might get to test out my virtual model-building dream.

One day, Warren gave me a house addition to design for a family in town. This project became known as The Smith-Schoenwalder Residence project. It was just a minor addition of a couple bedrooms, a bathroom, and a staircase. I thought it would make a great project to try my luck with a three dimensional model. Warren gave me the original drawings of the Smith-Schoenwalder house and said they were done by a famous architect, whose name I don't remember. He wasn't that famous to me. Warren said he would see how well I could design. He said he wanted me to try and match the addition to what had previously been done so that the finish product appeared to have all been built at the same time. It was a design project as far as space layout was concerned, but the appearance of the building from the outside would match the existing design. I drew up the floor plans and elevations for a few different ways the house could be done. We met with the Smith-Schoenwalder's and they seemed to like all the options. They weren't really making any decisions for us. It was because they really weren't seeing what was in front of them. They had trouble imagining what the two dimensional drawings were really showing. For a lot of people, that is a very common problem. A lot of people have trouble taking the two dimensional drawings of floor plans, sections, and elevations and building them into a three dimensional picture in their mind. The husband seemed to be getting a little idea of what the final result might look like, but the wife admitted she wasn't very good at imagining what the actual spaces might be like when all she had to look at was the sketches that I had put in front of her. I thought, "Here's my chance to build a model for Warren. I'll build a virtual model of the Smith-Schoenwalder house so that they have a full understanding of what we are proposing for their house."

I took the drawings that I had done in AutoCAD and started building a model of one of the concepts for the house. Warren came by my desk one morning and said, "Is that the Smith-Schoenwalder house?" I told him it was. "When did you do this?", he asked. I told him I had just started on it about 30 minutes ago. "We've got to use this at the next meeting. Do a model of all your concepts. Way to go!" And that was the beginning of my model-building career with ETO/ Architects.

Warren was very happy about the models I was building for the Smith-Schoenwalder house. He was telling people in the office to come over and check out what I was doing. He started to get me excited, because he kept acting like it was such a big deal. "This is the future. Maybe one day we'll be creating models of all our projects.", he told me. He also told me I was turning into a really big help for him. I started to feel confident that I might make a decent architect one day after all.

Eventually, the models were all built and Warren asked the Smith-Schoenwalders to come see their house in virtual space. We had the meeting in the conference room, as usual, only this time we weren't sitting around sheets of paper. No, this time, we were all gathered around my computer that I had set up in the conference room. It was really neat to me, even though Warren did most of the talking. He explained to them all the different things that were going on in each concept. These people were friends of his and he was a much smoother talker than I was anyway. So, Warren handled most of the actual communications with the client. The Smith-Schoenwalders seemed to like the models better than the drawings. They now fully understood what they were looking at and even started making sketches of their own for changes they wanted to make to one of the concepts that they liked the most. The model idea was another big hit. Warren was very happy that I had created them, even if it did mean more changes to the drawings. That project finished up shortly after that meeting. Now, I had a house that would be built according to a design that started as just ideas of Warren and myself. That project gave me more sense of accomplishment and self-pride. I felt like I was finally starting to grow as an intern architect.

Not long after my virtual model building duties began, Warren and I had a talk about starting the IDP process of logging hours in all the specific categories required by the licensing board. He said he would be glad to help me through the process. He told me that I should do some research and see about ordering study guides for the Architectural Licensing Exam. He said he would buy them for me. Then other projects came up. I never got around to buying the study guides. I never even registered with NCARB to start the IDP training process. I always spent my time working on whatever current crisis popped up on my desk and never set aside a time to simply spend a couple hours researching and ordering all the things I needed to get started towards my own license. I think Warren figured that when I wanted to do it bad enough, I would make time. I just never did.

At home, Sara started watching kids again. She had a falling out with several people at Annsworth Academy and felt like it stressed her out too much to be there anymore. We decided she would have less headaches and more money if she started watching a few babies at home again. It would also save us a baby sitter bill that we had been paying for Gwen since she was just a couple months old. We had been taking her to spend the workday with an older woman who watched little babies. She was a very nice lady, but we paid about $600 a month to watch Gwen, and with Sara at home with Gwen, we now pocketed that money every month. Sara eventually started taking care of three other children, and Gwen, for about a year.

Around this time was when work started to become my life. I wasn't trying to avoid Sara anymore. I had simply taken on a lot of responsibility at ETO and was starting to have to work a little unpaid overtime to keep up with everyone's demands. I usually had to juggle three or four projects at a time. I might spend a few days on one project and then be pulled of to work on something else. Some days, I would find myself spending time on several projects in one day. This meant meeting with several different people everyday. I was being pulled between David Barthowe, Pat Huy, and Warren Eto. It started to get a little stressful because they would all want to know when they could expect certain things from me. I would have to give them times and try my best to stick to it. That's where the overtime came in. I never seemed to have everybody happy by five o'clock. I would usually end up working a couple hours late just to keep someone off my back. Things really picked up when I began the next phase of my life at ETO/ Architects, Marketing.

My Marketing Days began when Warren started having me spend less time working on the actual production of contract drawings and more time involved with the conceptual designs of our proposal work. In order to win a bid for a job as an architect, you have to present a Conceptual Design. This is the first rendition of any project. The Conceptual Design is the architect's first ideas for how a project should develop. A lot of time goes into conceptual designs for projects that architects may never actually end up working on. At ETO, our success rate was usually around one in ten. That means for every ten jobs we attempted to land, we got one. You have to exert the same amount of effort for every proposal. Its very frustrating knowing that you are spinning your wheels and may not end up going anywhere. I would spend 60+ hours on some proposals and it would all end up being for nothing. We would end up losing the bid for the job to another firm. Very disappointing. But I was paid the same whether we got the job or not, it was Warren's loss, not mine. And when we did end up winning a project, Warren would usually take me out to lunch or dinner or give me gift cards to take my wife out on a date to some of Tallahassee's fanciest restaurants. She loved that kind of stuff. I could have just as easily eaten a cheeseburger at McDonald's. We would have never gone on some of our more extravagant dates if it were not for Warren footing the bill. Yes, Marketing had its perks. But it also had its down side.

The main problem with the job was that I really loved what I was doing too much. I would get so wrapped up in what I was working on that I would sometimes stay at work for two days without ever going home. No shower. No change of clothes. No sleep. Just 30-40 hours of nonstop computer banging. The first time I did this was when we were putting together the proposal to bid for FSU's Parking Garage 3.

Parking Garage 3 at FSU was about my third or fourth major model-building job at ETO. We decided that we were going to show up to the presentation with photo quality, realistic images of the parking garage we had designed. This required me to build a model in AutoCAD and render the final images using Accurender. I had already sold Warren on Accurender by doing a couple models of Capital City Bank projects. He loved the way you could fly around the project in Accurender and how it could produce views of how the project would actually look when it was complete. As far as the parking garage was concerned, we started out by having a little design contest between David Barthowe, Ken Curring, and myself. They let me play along as a designer, I think, because they knew I was the one who was going to get stuck with the bulk of the work. I had to produce most of drawings and renderings that were used in the final presentation. David and Ken had already worked together to design Parking Garage 2 at FSU, so they were the real experts. I was just along for the ride.

Never the less, I ended up with the most amount of hours involved in the conceptual design part of that project because, like I said, I was responsible for creating the model, the renderings, and a load of drawings that went to the final presentation. We worked like crazy for a couple weeks to get through the design part of the process. We decided on going with mainly all of David's ideas, of course. Ken had some of his design work included in the final product as well. Very little of my design work was used for the final product, just my idea for how the parking spaces laid out inside the garage, I think. The overall imagery of the building was mainly

144

David Barthowe. He just mimicked the Jacobean Gothic style that was so popular with all the project managers at FSU.

After the design was hammered out, it was time to produce all the final drawings and the model that would produce the renderings. I was the first person to see exactly what FSU's Parking Garage 3 would look like once it was built. That's because I'm the one who put all the 2-D sketches together to build the virtual 3-D model. I added cars driving around the parking garage, and trees, and other landscaping. Then I had to use Accurender to apply all the textures to all the model surfaces. I had to make parts of the model appear to be made of concrete or brick or metal. I also had to create the site that the parking garage rested on. This was tough because we didn't have civil engineers for the project yet. I had to play civil engineer and design the slopes of all the land around the parking garage and model it as well. On the day before the presentation, I ended up working all night and into the next morning to complete everything in time. Everyone else working on the project had long since gone home. But I had to stay up there by myself and finish the model. No one else knew how to do that except me. So I had to stay until all of it was done. This set the new precedent for how far Scott would go to make sure the job got done right.

We ended up winning that job. Warren and David were my new best buddies until the next crisis developed. That was the way office life was. I was only appreciated until the next crisis hit. That usually only took a day or two. There was always a state of emergency for almost everything I worked on once I started doing most of ETO's marketing.

During those last few hectic days with Parking Garage 3, I got a call from my wife while I was at work. It was probably around 7:00 pm. Sara sounded very weird on the phone. I asked her what was wrong. She said, "I think you need to come home. Something is wrong with Pierre. I keep trying to get him to come out of his doghouse, but he keeps laying there. I think he might be dead." I felt sick at my stomach. I tried to remember the last time I had fed him and given him water. Had it been yesterday, or the day before? "Have you fed him today?", I asked. "Yes. He was eating his food earlier this afternoon." That was a relief. Pierre was usually my responsibility. I always walked him and was usually the one to give him food and water. Sara was home all day every day, but usually assumed I was taking care of him. Since all the pressure had built up with the Parking Garage, I hadn't even thought about Pierre. I hadn't taken him on a walk in two days, I knew that much.

I told the guys at the office I would be right back and that I thought I had a dead dog at home that I had to go bury. David said, "Sorry to here that. But try to get back up here if you can." I went home and sure enough, Pierre was dead. I knew that he was dead the second I saw him. He was lying down in his dog house. He never moved as I approached him. I knew he was dead because Pierre always came running out of his dog house as soon as I opened the back door of our house. I stood there looking at him and almost cried. I felt like I had been neglecting him lately and he could have died from lack of exercise or food or water. I wasn't sure.

Pierre had severe heartworms when we adopted him from the pound. They told us there was about a 30% chance he would survive the heartworm treatments. But he was such a sad looking, gentle little dog that I loved him from the start and thought I'd take a chance on paying for him to receive heartworm treatments. If he died in the treatments, I wouldn't feel too bad, because the heartworms were going to kill him anyway if he was allowed to live with them. Pierre was really great with Liza too. She could pull on his ears and fur and he hardly ever seemed to mind. Every now and then he would whimper, but he never bit Liza. There were a couple of walks I had recently taken Pierre on where he stopped walking and started making a terrible rattling coughing sound.

I convinced myself that Pierre probably died from the damage that the heartworms had done to his heart. But I still wondered. I stood there looking at him for several minutes with my flashlight in the dark. I thought about all the great times we had all had with him. I knew I would miss him. I had brought a trash bag with me to put him in and bury him. I couldn't bring myself to do it that night. I went back to work hoping to get my mind off of him. I left him there in his doghouse for one more day before I buried him. I thought about Pierre for several months after he was gone. I really missed not having him around to sit in my lap when I was at home. He wasn't the first dog I had ever lost, but he was the most recent. And I always hated to lose my dog.

At work things went on as usual. After that first all-nighter, it became the routine to spend the last few days of every proposal practically killing myself to see it through to the end. I never felt finished with my work. It was an experience that had carried over from school to my work ethic. We had been trained to pull the all-nighter since third year Design. Now I saw how all of our training with the all-nighter fit into the workplace.

Chapter 30: Someone Needs an Attitude Adjustment

People were hired and fired at ETO on a pretty regular basis. I had now been there two years and was on my way to becoming one of the old employees. I was now receiving stock contributions from Warren, $1,000 dollars every year. I saw many that were hired before me get canned, but I never worried about myself. I knew as long as I went the extra mile for Warren, he had my back. He told me so at every evaluation. Pat Huy told me that I was one of Warren's favorite employees because I came in, did my job, and never complained about it. That would all soon begin to change.

Monty Stern was hired some time after I hit the two-year mark. Monty was in his mid-40's and was a licensed architect in Texas who had recently moved from there with his wife and her children. Monty was not yet registered as an architect in Florida. He was an amazing illustrator, the best I had ever seen. His renderings were all done by hand and were beautiful. They were artworks to me. I would frame and hang any of his sketches on my wall at home. Monty was a very upbeat, positive guy who always had a great sense of humor. He was a real light in the dark for me at ETO. When Monty started working at ETO, Warren decided to pair the two of us up together. He moved my desk to one right across from Monty's office. I could turn around in my chair and have a conversation with Monty anytime I wanted, although the best conversations usually took place in his office, with the door closed. I told Warren that I appreciated his idea to have me work with Monty. Warren said, "Monty is a very accomplished architect. Learn everything you can from him." Monty had designed buildings for Cingular Wireless in Texas. In Tallahassee he had designed the Challenger Learning Center and IMAX Theater. The Challenger Learning Center and IMAX Theater was a huge project that ETO had tried to get but failed. Monty was the guy who stole the project from us. He stole it with his talent and personality. Monty had a style to all his work. He could be almost Deconstructive at times, but he could play around with more traditional architectural imagery as well. I thought everything he did was pretty awesome. I was happy to have him as a mentor and friend.

Once Monty and I teamed up as the Marketing Department, the pace really quickened. We started going after bigger jobs, and more of them. Things started to get hectic. Once Monty and I became the Marketing Department, I would usually do an all-nighter almost every week. Every week at least one if not two or three proposals were due. They all required serious man-hours to produce. The nice thing was that Monty was usually right there with me the whole time. He was able to do a lot of the things that I could. He also knew a lot that I didn't. About the only edge I had on him was that I was more proficient with AutoCAD and knew how to build the elaborate virtual models. Monty more than made up for that with all his years of experience dealing with consultants, designing buildings, and of course, his wonderful artistic abilities and personality.

Monty and I spent many nights working together at ETO with no one there but the two of us. We got to know each other pretty well. It was during those late hours that I started complaining about the fact that it was always the two of us working there long after everyone else had gone home. I started to feel like I was pulling more than my share around the office. I would tell Monty, "This crap has got to stop! Warren's at home watching TV and David will be out playing golf tomorrow. And we're here busting our asses so that they can keep their comfy schedules. Doesn't that bother you?" He said, "You've just got to pay your dues." I said, I already have! I've been doing this crap for over a year now! When will it be said that I have paid my dues? Never." I thought it was getting ridiculous because the workload kept building, never letting up. Monty said that we really needed the work, and that eventually, he thought we'd land some big jobs and things would ease up a bit. I doubted it.

In December of 2003, we had our usual Christmas get together at my parents' house in Georgia. My grandparents came to spend about a week with us as usual. I remember GranDaddy taking Tylenol every couple hours. He said his back had been killing him and that he thought he had pulled something when he was out doing work in his yard. I said, "You better go to the doctor because you probably shouldn't have to take that many Tylenol for this long." He was popping Tylenol every couple of hours the entire time he was there.

When he got back to Florida, he went to his doctor and they discovered a tumor growing on his spinal cord. He had cancer. The doctors told him he would need to begin chemo-therapy to destroy the tumor. They weren't sure if the cancer was localized in the tumor or if it had already metastasized and spread to other parts of his body. Granddaddy's wife, Nanny, had a brother who had already been fighting Leukemia for several years and was beginning to have severe complications from it. Once I heard that GranDaddy had cancer, I began to fear for the worst. I had no idea of just how horrible the last couple years of his life would be.

Sometime around six or eight months before I had my first encounter with the milder effects of Schizoaffective disorder, Sara began to have a lot of trouble at her job at Annsworth Academy. Sara had been having a lot of bad days at work. She would come home and cry to me about the terrible things that a few girls who worked there said to her during the day. Every day I came home from work, I had to hear another sob story about how someone at work had mistreated her, insulted her, or did something to piss her off. The really dicey part of all this was that one of the people who Sara was having trouble with was Sue. Sue was my brother, Carter's, girlfriend. Somehow, Sue and Sara started butting heads at work. To make matters worse, Sue was backed by two other girls who joined up with her, and verbally beat up on Sara. According to Sara, they all made sure to give her a hard time every day. So, every day I came home from work and heard stories of how Sue and the other two girls had picked on Sara. Sara would cry and complain about how much she hated her job. I felt terrible for Sara but was really just becoming annoyed with her for not taking

148

action for herself. I had told her several times that she needed to call these girls and try to talk out her problems with them. I told her that if she just talked with them, they might listen and understand her side of whatever their problems were. After weeks of spending hours every night listening to Sara's problems, I blew a fuse. I told Sara that I was tired of hearing her complain about problems if she was not going to do anything to resolve them. I told her that I wanted her to call Sue that night and tell Sue the things that she had been telling me. Sara wouldn't do it. She asked me if I would call Sue for her. She said that she would get on the phone after I had spoken with Sue. So, like an idiot, I called.

Sue picked up the phone and said, "Hello?" I said, "Sue, this is Scott Gann." She said, "Oh, hey Scott how are you doing?" I said, "Not good. Sara keeps telling me stories about you, Karen, and Carol picking on her at work." Sue seemed a little nervous on the other end. I went on to tell Sue that I wanted the harassment to stop. The more I talked, the more Sue defended herself and said that Sara was the one who was causing all the problems. That just made me angry. I didn't want to hear anyone else's side. All I wanted to do was bark at the people who were making my wife miserable. I was tired of seeing Sara so upset. She had worked hard at Annsworth and I didn't feel that she deserved to be treated the way that she said she had been. As soon as Sue would try to say something, I would cut her off. The longer I talked, the angrier I got. I began to threaten Sue. I don't remember what my exact words were, but I think I cussed her out. After that, I hung up the phone on Sue or she hung up on me. I don't remember which. I was so angry that I can't really remember exactly how the whole thing ended. I just remember the rage. It was unlike anything I had ever unleashed on anyone. After I got off the phone, I remember feeling very proud of myself for what I had done. I knew that I had probably scared Sue. That was what I wanted. I actually scared myself a little too. But that didn't stick around long because Sara was so grateful for what I had done. To her, I had just defended her honor. She was so pleased with me. It made me feel good. It wouldn't be until much later that I would realize how wrong what I had just done was. I still have deep regrets about making that phone call. My brother ended up marrying that girl. That phone call was not a decent thing to do. I am sure that it has changed the way that Sue sees me. She probably has that phone call in the back of her mind every time she sees me. I know I do.

Sara stopped working at Annsworth shortly after that phone call. She began watching kids at home. She watched Gwen, and three other babies. It was nice because she made a little money, and we avoided a childcare bill for Gwen. After she left Annsworth, she became much happier.

The last big project that I completed before I became a total pain in Warren's ass was Capital City Bank's Palatka Branch Bank. I was supposed to build a model of the interior and produce renderings of how it would look in the lobby and from a secondary entrance hallway. It was a simple enough job. I had to build the model and take two pictures of it, basically. The problem was that Warren, Monty, and Mark Lambert kept making changes to the interior. They changed lighting, wall colors, carpet, and even the layout of some of casework in the lobby. In all, the renderings went through about thirty changes. Each time required work on the model and then a big wait for the computer to produce the rendering. Rendering was always a time consuming process. By this time Warren had purchased a top of the line computer and a second monitor for me. I now had a screaming fast computer and worked from two monitors simultaneously. I should have been very happy. Instead, I was beginning to develop a very poor attitude.

I finished the two renderings of Capital City Bank Palatka with a lot of grumbling and moaning. Mark Lambert also got to have a say in how the bank's interior turned out. "Why in the hell is he getting to have his two cents in about all this?", I thought. Mark would come by my desk and ask when he could see the latest renderings of the bank and I would feel like I wanted to punch him. I couldn't stand the fact that I could walk by his desk and find him surfing the internet for a guitar he wanted to buy, and then, several minutes later, have him come over to my desk asking how much longer it was going to take me to finish my work. "Why don't you learn how to do this yourself, Mr. Bigshot? Then you might have something to do other than surf the freaking internet.", I thought. By the time those renderings were completed, I was starting to hope that I wouldn't have to do another model for a while. The whole process of having to take orders from three people, one whom I couldn't stand, made me tired. I was no longer in love with the idea of model building. I felt like my desire to build a decent model was being pushed too far and that I was being used and thought of as nothing more than a dog who could bark on command. I thought that I had been asked to bark a few times too many.

Chapter 31: Blue

Speaking of dogs, we got a new one at home. We had now gone almost a year with an empty dog house in the back yard. We all missed having a little creature around who was always in a good mood. In February of 2004, Sara, the girls, and I all went to the mall one day just to get out of the house. We walked around for a while and then stopped at a pet store there. We hadn't talked about getting a new dog. But there was a most unusual looking puppy at that pet store that day. It was spotted all over with browns and whites and tans, almost like a calico cat. It had pale blue eyes. It was an Australian Shepherd puppy. The puppy was four months old. We asked the girl working at the pet store if she could take the puppy out of its cage so that we could see how the little dog was with Liza. The girl brought out the puppy and we all went into a little cubicle type area that was set up for people to play with the animals in. That little dog got so excited when she was playing with Liza that she actually peed on the floor a little. The owner said that dog had a habit of doing that every time they let her play with new people. The little dog wanted to lick all over anybody who put their hands near it. It seemed very friendly. Liza, Sara, and I all took turns holding her as she tried to lick all over us. We thought she was a nice looking dog, but then they told us the price, $700 dollars. That was $675 dollars more than our last dog. I said we couldn't afford that kind of a dog and so we left. The girl said that if we changed our mind, we would have to act fast because that dog wouldn't be there long. She said they had sold all of that dog's siblings within days and she was the last one left.

After meeting the little dog, we went home that day. Liza was very disappointed that we didn't get the dog. I told her we would keep looking and find a cheaper one. But in my mind I was thinking about what a cool looking little dog we had just seen. I thought it would be neat to have a dog that people did a double take on when we walked it around at parks and other places. I had never had a $700 dog before. We had two chows when I was a kid and I'm sure they were expensive dogs at the time, but those weren't really my dogs, they were my parents' dogs. Sara said that she really liked the little dog too and that we had the money if we really wanted to get it.

The next day we all went back to the pet store without ever looking for any other dog. There was the puppy still sitting in its little cage looking out of through the glass at everybody that walked by. I told the girl working there that we wanted to buy the little Australian Shepard puppy. And that's how we got Blue. We named her Blue for her unusual pale blue eyes. She was a nice little thing to have around the house. She was great with both the girls. Gwen was still only two years old, so Blue's small size was perfect for her. They told us at the pet store that she would grow to be a medium sized dog and weigh between 40-50 lbs. as an adult. But when we got her, she fit in my two hands put together. She was only about 10 inches long and 8 inches tall. She was a very cute puppy. I had no idea at the time I bought her that there would soon come a day when she was about the only thing that could stand to be around me. Blue started out as just another dog. I thought that she was a nice looking dog, but could never replace Pierre. I had no idea that she would one day be my only friend. She would become the best dog I've ever had.

Chapter 32: The Brain-Intestine Connection

The last thing that happened before the real scary stuff started, was that I got sick. I got really sick. Sara and I went to eat lunch at a Mexican restaurant in town one day and I ordered some very greasy tacos. I went back to work and not long afterwards, my stomach began to cramp up. It felt like I needed to use the bathroom but when I tried nothing happened. I stayed at work the rest of the day and just ignored the abdominal pains. I went home that night and told Sara, "That Mexican food had really messed me up. I feel like crap." That evening, I started to get chills, so I decided to take a bath. I never took baths, but I just wanted to lie down in some hot water and see if that got rid of the chills and cramps. It actually seemed to help. I went on to bed that night and on to work the next day. The only problem was that the pain never went away and kept getting worse. I ended up leaving work a little early that day. By the time I got home I was having some of the worst pain I could ever remember having in my life. I was sweating and felt cold. The abdominal pain would come in waves. There would be a period of maybe thirty minutes where I didn't have much other than a slight discomfort, but then a major cramping sensation would start in my abdomen. It was severe enough that once one started I had to lie down and clinch my fists to get through the pain. I tried taking another bath. It helped for a short while, but the cramps quickly came back. They felt like the kind of pain you get if you have gas building up in your intestines, only far worse than anything I had experienced, and I never had any gas. Sara said, "Why don't you go to Urgent Care and have somebody look at you instead of just sitting here complaining about how much pain you're in." I was hoping to wait until the morning. It was already about 8:00 pm and my insurance charged me about $15 more if I went to their Urgent Care facility rather than my doctor, who was now long gone for the day.

An hour or so later I decided I had better do something. I couldn't sleep because I was in so much pain. I decided that $15 was worth getting some antibiotics or something to get rid of my pain. I didn't really know what was going on but I thought that it might be a severe case of food poisoning. I drove myself to Urgent Care and could barely walk from the car to the inside of the building. Every step I took made my abdomen feel like it was going to explode. I was sweating but still kept getting chills. I checked in with the lady at the front desk and felt exhausted as I sat in the waiting room. It was about an hour before they finally called me back to see a doctor. By that time I felt like I was about to die. I had been lying in bed all that time at home. By that point, simply sitting there in that waiting room chair was causing the most excruciating pain that I had ever experienced. The abdominal pain was constant at this point. What had started as waves of severe pain was now just constant severe pain. I wanted to scream.

After waiting for what seemed like hours, the doctor called me back to an exam room and asked me to lie down on the little table there. He pressed down on my abdomen slowly and said, "Does this hurt?" "Oh yeah.", I said. Then he removed his hands and my abdomen popped back up. When that happened, I passed out. The pain was so sharp and I was already so weak that it just knocked me out. I could still hear him but my vision was all gone. He was telling the nurses to quickly bring him an I.V. with some solution in it. They hooked up some painkillers and something else that I don't remember. I started to get my vision back as they were hooking everything up. There were about 4 or 5 people in the room with me by that point. After a few minutes, one of the nurses said, "We've got to take some of your blood. Are you feeling better? You aren't going to pass out on us again are you?" I said I was feeling better. The painkiller went to work immediately. They took my blood and came back several minutes later and said my white blood cell count was over 10,000. They said that meant my body was fighting a severe infection. The doctor said he thought my appendix may be about to burst from infection and that it would be very bad news for me if it did. He said I needed to get to the emergency room at Tallahassee Memorial Hospital and have them look at my appendix immediately. He wanted an ambulance to drive me from Urgent Care to TMH, which was only about 3 miles away. I told him I didn't want to pay for an ambulance and that I could drive myself. He said that he would give me some more pain meds and have me rest a few more minutes to make sure I was able to drive myself.

I left about 15 minutes later and went to the hospital. The painkillers worked well enough that driving was no problem. I checked myself in and called Sara. She apologized for not realizing how serious my problem was and said she would be right there in a few minutes. She took the girls to spend the rest of the night with a friend of ours and met me at the hospital, around 12:00 am, before I had even been called to see a doctor.

The doctor there at TMH said that I had to have a scan done of my abdomen. He said that they were going to have to inject Barium Solution into my intestines through my butt and do a CAT scan of the abdomen. He said it would be very uncomfortable but it had to be done. I felt very nervous, but thought if it was a matter of such serious importance that I was now in a hospital emergency room, I could survive being raped by a doctor.

The doctor did his thing and looked over the results of the CAT scan. He came back to me about an hour after we had been through the fun time of getting butt raped and he said it appeared that my appendix was not the problem. He said that it was my intestines. He said that I had Diverticulitis, the inflammation of the diverticuli. "Diverticuli are small sacks that form, with age, in the intestines of just about everybody. Most people don't get as many as you have until they are in their 70's or 80's. You have the intestines of an 80 year old man.", he said. I was shocked. I had always eaten pretty healthy, I thought. He said, "Your problem is probably genetic. Someone in your family probably has this problem and it got passed on to you. Fast food and heavily processed foods don't help though. Do you eat a lot of fast food?" I told him I ate hamburgers and fries a couple times a week, but usually had pretty healthy meals. He said, "Then your condition is caused from genetics.

154

You'd have to eat fast food for about every meal of your life to have the amount of diverticuli that you have." He said there was no cure for my condition. He said that I now had to be careful about what I ate, or I would end up in the E.R. again. He said if things got too bad, they would end up removing parts of my intestines and that could have serious long-term effects. But he assured me that I was no where near that kind of shape yet and that if I made sure to eat a high fiber diet, with lots of fruit and vegetables, I would be able to go on with little or no more abdominal pains. He said that fiber was now the biggest concern I should have about my diet and to avoid lots of highly processed foods. After that night in the E.R., I felt a little older. I realized that I now had a health problem that would be with me the rest of my life.

It took several days for the antibiotics to do their trick and knock out the infection. I only missed one day of work because I knew the crap would just keep piling up at my desk and there were always deadlines. I didn't want to let Warren down and end up on his bad side, so I went to work as soon as I felt rested. Everybody at work joked with me about my condition. "So…Diverticulitis, isn't that like Irritable Bowel Syndrome? You aren't going to be crapping in your pants are you?", David Barthowe said to me. We both laughed and I told him, "You are such an asshole David." He laughed and said he knew that I was just trying to get out of any work I could, even if it meant coming in and telling stories about having intestinal problems. That was David. He was always very abrasive and always quick to jump your butt if you screwed up. But really, he was one of my favorite people in the office. He really was the most honest guy there. He didn't go behind your back and say things about you when you weren't around. He told you to your face if he had a problem with you and I appreciated that. Fortunately, David rarely had problems with me and we usually got along really well together.

Pat Huy told me about a good friend of his that had died from complications that started with Diverticulitis. He said his friend didn't take his condition seriously and ended up having a lot of his intestines removed. "You better take this seriously Scott. I know its probably embarrassing to talk about having intestinal problems. But if you don't eat right, you might end up like him.", Pat said. That scared me a little. I didn't know much about my new illness and hadn't been told that people actually died from it. After that episode in the hospital, something changed inside me. I now felt a little less invincible. I thought I had better get right with God.

Chapter 33: The Switch Turns to "On"

My mom's cousin, Hank Hollings, had moved to town about three years before my first episode with Diverticulitis. He had tried to get me to take a job with his company when I was looking at working with MLD. Hank worked for an office furnishings designer and supplier. He thought I might be interested in getting a job with his company as a draftsman / designer and eventually training to become a salesman like himself. The job was all about selecting office furniture and creating the interiors of office buildings. I spent a day with him at his job and decided it was less interesting to me than architecture. Just after that first episode of Diverticulitis, Hank called me one weekend and asked me if I wanted to come to church with him and his family. Hank went to TRBC. I was the one who introduced him to TRBC when he first moved to town. Sara and I now rarely went to church. A lot of the people we had been friends with had moved away and I didn't want to give up my Sundays to sit at church and listen to the pastor. The old pastor, Billy Cruce, was now too sick to preach and had been replaced by a new one that didn't make the same impact with me that Dr. Cruce had.

But now Hank was inviting me to come to church with him. For some unexplained reason, I actually wanted to, and told him so. Hank said that he was teaching a Sunday School class for young married couples and that Sara and I would fit right in. So we went to church that next Sunday with Hank as our Sunday School teacher. It was great. Hank made the best Sunday School teacher I ever had. He was an excellent speaker and always had well planned out bible study sessions every time we went. I liked that the people in our class all talked about the problems and good times they were having in their lives at every class. Hank would always pray for each person in the class. He was so sincere and intelligent. I felt very proud that he was my cousin.

I remember telling my mom, on the phone, about Hank and going back to TRBC again. I told her I felt like I had put God back in my life and felt more positive about the future than I ever had before. She asked me what had brought about all this positive change and I said, "I don't know. One morning I woke up and it was like a light turned on in my head. Like a switch inside me went from off to on. I now feel like I am 'On'." Looking back it now, I think what happened was that somehow, through the infection my body had just fought off due to the Diverticulitis, something happened in my brain. I think it had probably tried to produce chemicals to fight the pain and infection, but also produced something that was now making me feel almost euphoric. I felt like I had more energy. Everything seemed more special and important to me than it ever had before. After that first bought of Diverticulitis, I would lie awake and night and my thoughts would race about all the things I needed to do. "Manic" is the word a psychiatrist would use to describe my new state of mind.

After I got over the pain of my first episode of Diverticulitis, I began to be very positive about everything in my life. I started to try to be a better husband to Sara and a better father for the girls. I felt like I didn't know what the future would be like, but I had better try to make things right if I was going to get to be around for a while. I started trying to spend more time with Sara, and the girls. I did little things, like making sure I always opened Sara's door when she got in the car. I also told her how much I appreciated her and that I loved her. I told her that I felt like I had been treating her badly for all the years I had known her but she, for some reason that I never understood, still stayed with me. I told her I would try to be more like the husband she deserved. Then I made a major mistake, I told Sara about my past true feelings for her.

I told Sara that I had mostly felt sorry for her when we first started dating and that I never really felt 'in love' with her all the years we had been married. She started crying. I told Sara that I wasn't trying to hurt her feelings, I was trying to express what I felt and that my point was that I was promising to make things better for her. I wanted her to know that I really felt like I was in love with her and that if she stayed with me, I thought we had a great future together. She said she felt stupid because she had always assumed that I felt about her the way that she had felt about me. She said she had always loved me and looked up to me. I told her, "Maybe you thought more of me than I deserved. Maybe you created a better image of me in your head than I ever really was. I think I have always been a worse person than you have ever imagined me to be. I think you thought of me as someone that I am not." She said she now felt like a fool for thinking that I loved her as much as she loved me all those years. I thought she would be happy to hear that I was in love with her. Instead, it seemed to make her very uneasy about me. After we had that conversation, she seemed to love me less.

That summer, in late July of 2004, a major hurricane hit my parents' house on Lake Buffum. It forever changed me. After that first hurricane, I began to experience the life of a schizophrenic.

Chapter 34: The End of My Old Life

My parents' had just spent a couple of weeks of the summer of 2004 in Alaska with my two brothers. They were now back in Florida at their home. In late July, the news showed a major hurricane that would probably pass over central Florida in a couple of days. I remember going online to the NOAA weather alert website and closely watching the forecast track for Hurricane Charlie. It didn't look good. Every time I checked the website, my parents were in the middle of the cone of error. I remember calling them and asking if they were planning on leaving the area a couple days before the storm hit. They said they had been through many bad storms and this would just be another. They would ride it out at their house like they always had before. I thought they were probably right, but the news kept talking up the potential dangers of the approaching hurricane and I really started to wish they would get out of its way.

To complicate matters, GranDaddy was in severe pain a lot of the time as well. That was the main reason my parents stayed put. He was already too sick to travel. He was having serious back pain because the vertebrae in his back were disintegrating. The doctors had been through several types of treatments and nothing was working. He had just recently had a surgical procedure where doctors inserted a balloon in his spine and filled it with a type of cement. The cement would take the place of his disintegrated vertebrae and hopefully relieve some of his back pain. As for destroying the cancer itself, they weren't having any luck. GranDaddy was in pretty bad shape and this made my parents feel like they needed to stay close, in case something happened to him.

I called my parents on the day the storm was approaching their house. I was at work and just wanted to hear that they were O.K. My grandparents had come to ride out the storm with my parents. They thought that my parents house was a safer place to be than their own. I remember talking to my dad and GranDaddy and it sounded like they were having a freaking party down there. I could hear my mom and Nanny talking and laughing in the background. Dad said the wind was really picking up and it was raining real hard but nothing major had happened. GranDaddy said jokingly, "Don't you have better things to do at work besides check up on us?" Everything seemed normal. No worries.

That night Hank Hollings called me and asked if I had heard from my parents lately. I told him that I had talked to them at work that afternoon and that it sounded like they were riding out a pretty bad storm but everything seemed fine. He said he had called his mom and dad, who lived only about 20 miles from my parents, and that they were talking on the phone. Hank said that his dad said, "Yeah, it was really bad here a little while ago, but now its calmed down quite a bit." He said that they talked for a few more minutes and then his dad said that the winds were picking up really fast. Hank said his dad told him that the screened end porch roof was starting to come apart and then the phone went dead. Hank said that he tried to call his parents several times afterwards and couldn't reach them on their cell or landline. He was very worried. That made me very worried. Hank was about as level headed of a guy as you could meet. To hear panic in his voice made me very nervous. We hung up and I immediately called my parents. I got the same problem. Their landline and cell phone gave a message that the call could not be completed. Then I saw the news and they were showing all the devastation Hurricane Charlie had caused in its wake. They said that several tornadoes had spun out of the hurricane and caused a lot of serious damage. It looked like Punta Gorda got it really bad. That was a good ways from my parents' house, but I started to fear for the worst. I called Carter and told him I was going down to Mom and Dad's to check on them. He said he wanted to come along.

The next morning I started loading up a lot of things that I thought I might need once I was down there. I also realized that we didn't have a lot of money in our account. I decided to go to a Cash Loan place and get a quick few hundred bucks, just in case I needed it. It was a really stupid thing to do. The interest rate on that money was something like 200%. I paid back the money as soon as I got back from Lake Buffum and I think I already owed $330 dollars for a $300 loan. I had only borrowed it for about a week. I also called Warren before I left. I couldn't get a hold of him. I wanted to tell him that I probably wouldn't be back to work on Monday and that I thought my parents might be in trouble because Hurricane Charlie had gone right through their area. I decided to call Pat Huy. I thought I'd leave a message with him instead and he could tell Warren.

I called Pat and told him what was going on and almost started crying. The crying came as a surprise. I was talking one minute and then the next, I could barely speak a word because I became so upset at the thought that I may never see my parents alive again. I felt pretty stupid for getting emotional on the phone with one of my bosses. He said not to worry about missing work and that he would get in touch with Warren. Then Warren called me and asked if everything was O.K. I told him it was far from O.K., it was terrible. I told him that I had just tried to round up a few extra bucks at the Cash Loan place and that I was about to leave. He said, "I wish you would have called me before going to a Cash Loan store for money. Do you have time to swing by the office?" I thought, "Yeah, I've really got time to deal with work stuff right now." I asked him why he wanted me to go to the office. He said, "I'll get Tammy to meet you there. She'll give you all the cash we have in petty cash. If you give me your bank account number I can deposit however much money you need into it. That way if you have to make some kind of major purchase, I'll cover you. You do what you have to. Don't worry about us."

I was stunned. My own boss was totally giving me a blank check for any expenses I might incur while I was down there. It was above and beyond any kindness I had ever had displayed towards me. I immediately felt like I would be paying Warren back for the rest of my life for the favor he had just offered. I told him how much I appreciated his offer. "I'll pay you back with whatever interest rate you want Warren.", I told him. "Don't worry about it. Anything I can do to help. You just go down there and help your folks. Forget about us. We will be fine.", he said. Again, I almost cried. I was absolutely at a loss of words for how much I appreciated that man. I told him he was the best boss I had ever known and that I would be back as quickly as I could.

Carter and I didn't end up leaving town until after 4:00 pm. I had run to the office to meet Tammy, our accountant. I had also spent way more time than necessary trying to think of everything I might need as I headed into a disaster area. I didn't know what to expect, so it was hard for me to think of everything I might end up using on my trip. The main factor that had wasted so much time, I'm sure, was that I was now becoming more manic. My thoughts were racing through my head so fast that I could hardly focus on any one thing for long. Never the less, we finally left that afternoon.

The drive down was fine. Everything looked normal until we got into Polk County. We started seeing billboards alongside the interstate that had been blown apart or bent over. As we got closer and closer to our final destination, things started to look pretty scary. Once we got about 15 miles away from my parents' house, we really started to worry. A tree was laying across the road that we needed to go down. The only way around it was to go off the road and into the soaked mud and grass. I was driving a two-wheel drive Chrysler Town and Country mini van that was Sara's usual ride. I was afraid that we were going to end up stuck on the side of the road and not make it to my parents' house. We got around the tree and kept moving. Power lines were down everywhere, poles and all. There were hundreds of power line poles that were either completely blown down or bent about 45 degrees over. And then there were more trees and debris blocking the road the whole way out to Lake Buffum. I just kept dodging my way around them, going off the road almost as much as I was on it. It took us about an hour and a half to make it through that last 15 miles and out to Lake Buffum.

We finally reached my parents house around 10:30 pm. All the lights were out, of course, because there was no power. It was dark but you could see that the trees had been stripped of every leaf. Debris was scattered all over my parents' yard. There were palm limbs, branches, and all sorts of things scattered everywhere. The first sign of life was the sound of a generator running by the garage. I immediately felt relief when I heard that sound. Carter and I walked in and found everyone gathered in the living room trying to sleep with no A.C. on a hot Florida summer night. My dad's two brothers were there, Uncle Mark and Uncle David. They woke up when they heard Carter and I come in. I had been holding a flashlight and was pointing the light around the house to see what it looked like inside. We asked if everybody was O.K. and they said that they were. Nanny and GranDaddy had gone back to Bartow to check on their place and were no longer at the lake. They saw the devastation that had occurred at Lake Buffum and wanted to get back to assess their own house.

Once we arrived at Lake Buffum, I was so happy to find everyone O.K. It was the biggest sense of relief I think I had ever felt. It was like waking up from a terrible nightmare only to realize that you were safe in your own warm bed. All was well. Mom and Dad might have some work to do, but at least they were alive. Thank you God.

The next day we were up with the sun. I walked outside and got my first look at exactly what had happened. Now I could see all the bare trees. It was eerie. Even in winter, trees don't lose all their leaves in Central Florida. Now all the trees were bare, the ones standing, that is. My parents had three large oak trees in their yard. Luckily, not one of them fell down in the storm. Several large branches had though. There were scattered limbs all over the place. The worst damage was to the roof of the house. A lot of shingles had been blown off in the high winds. There were even a couple of spots where large areas of bare plywood were now exposed. That meant that water had traveled into the attic space and was probably ruining the insulation.

Two houses down from my parents, there was a large oak tree that had fallen right into the house. A few houses down the other direction was a house that's roof had been totally blown off. The new SUV in the driveway had an oak tree sitting on top of it. The car was totaled. Its wheel wells were pressed against the top of the wheels from all the weight from the tree. The top of the car was sunken in where the tree was now resting. So, my parents didn't get the worst damage, but they didn't fare well either. They also lost their dock. It was now completely blown away and was lying in pieces in a neighbor's yard. Later that day we also found an aluminum boat that was picked up near the lake, lifted up over the houses, and deposited about 400'-500' away from its original location. It was wrapped around a tree in the woods across the road from my parents' house. It belonged to Terry Mann, my parents' next door neighbor. He asked if we had seen his boat and we showed him right where it was. There was another boat on shore that no one knew who it belonged to. Attached to the boat was a 15' x 15' piece of a dock. Someone's dock had obviously been blown apart and the boat just drifted away with it. A couple of days later, some people came to us, who lived on the other side of the lake, and said that the mystery boat that had floated to shore near my parents' house, was their boat. After seeing the damage that Hurricane Charlie did to Lake Buffum, I realized that was the biggest disaster that I had ever witnessed.

Dad said that ten-foot high waves had crashed up over the dock at one point during the storm. He said one second the dock was there. Then a big wave came up over the dock and enveloped it so that it disappeared from view. Then the wave passed and the dock was gone. He said waves from the lake were hitting the glass windows on the front of the house. Their house was about 100' from the shoreline at the time. They also had a 3 ½ foot tall sea wall that acted as a barrier from wave action. The waves came up over the sea wall, into the yard, and hit the house, which was elevated another 1 ½ feet off the ground. Dad said that the rain had blown across the lake horizontally instead of falling from the sky. He said they saw a water spout, a tornado over water, coming across the lake. Dad said that he thought that was what had done the damage to the houses down there that had lost their roofs. He admitted that the whole ordeal was very scary.

I told mom and Dad about Hank's parents, Uncle Harold and Aunt Nancy. I told them how Hank had been trying to call them and couldn't get through. After seeing that Mom and Dad were O.K., I decided to check on Uncle Harold and Aunt Nancy. Mom said she wanted to come with me. The decision to check on Harold and Nancy would turn out to be a serious mistake.

We drove over there and it was the same routine that Carter and I experienced on our drive from Bartow to Lake Buffum. We had to go off the road at several places to get around fallen trees and power line poles. We went through Ft. Meade and saw destruction everywhere: A church with it's steeple knocked off, all buildings boarded up and closed down, more downed power lines and poles, and devastated trees that were completely uprooted or missing all sorts of major limbs. Another thing we saw in Ft. Meade was the Salvation Army and National Guard troops patrolling the town and passing out emergency supplies. The town looked like a war was being fought there and it had suffered heavy losses.

On the way to Bowling Green, the town Harold and Nancy lived in, we noticed that every gas station had National Guard troops, with M-16's, standing outside and making sure no looters tried to vandalize anything. Bowling Green was just like Ft. Meade. It was a total disaster. Fire hydrants had been opened along the streets so that people could have access to drinking water. The water just sprayed out of the hydrants continuously. The gas stations were all closed and guarded by the military. The town was another war zone. To add to the effect, military helicopters were flying all over the area. We could see and hear helicopters flying around during that whole first trip Carter and I made down there.

We got to Uncle Harold's house and had to stop before we got to his property because a major tree in his yard had fallen across the road leading up to his house. We walked the short distance to his house and saw that his screened in porch was a twisted pile of aluminum and screens. It had collapsed and was strewn across the backyard. Other than that, his place was fine. There was no structural damage to the house. The roof even looked pretty good, compared to Mom and Dad's. Uncle Harold asked if I would help him cut up the tree that was blocking the road leading to his driveway. They couldn't leave their house until that tree was moved. So, I got a chainsaw and started cutting. After working on Uncle Harold's tree for a couple of hours, a man pulled up in a pick up truck and yelled, "Harold! Harold! I need your help! My house is going to be ruined if I can't get some help over here!" Uncle Harold went over and talked with the panic stricken old man for several minutes. He then asked me if I would go with the guy back to his house and see what the problem was. I thought, "I came down here to help Mom and Dad, not some stranger. This isn't right. I should have stayed with Dad. Now I'm about to waste time helping some guy I don't even know."

I followed the guy in my van and drove to his house with him. He lived about five miles away from Harold. We got to his house and I could see why he was panicking. He had a tin roof that had been blown off completely in sections. Other parts were bent up. He also had a tree leaning against one side of his house. He took me inside his house to see all the water that had come through the holes in his roof, through the ceiling (which was now collapsing and bulging from the water above), and onto the carpeted floor. A lot of the pictures on the walls were smeared and the colors had run down the page because they had been soaked too. He started crying and said that one of those pictures was of his wife who had now passed away. He said that was the last nice picture he had of her and it was now ruined. I felt really bad for that guy. Then I thought, "You know, Jesus would help a stranger before a friend, I'm sure. I should probably help this guy. It's the right thing to do. He has more damage than anyone I know." So I decided to sacrifice my Dad's house for this friend of Uncle Harold.

Uncle Harold's friend said that he had already bought some tarps to put over the holes in his roof. He said he wasn't steady enough to climb a ladder and walk around on the roof himself. He needed me to do that for him. I decided I couldn't do it by myself and told him I was going back to Harold's to get someone to come back with me and help me out. I went back and discovered that my dad and his brothers had now come over to Harold's house also. Harold was having them fix his barbed wire fence in sections that trees had knocked down. My dad and his brothers were helping Harold put up a fence while my dad's own house was needing a tarp on the roof and all the debris cleaned up out of the yard. I didn't realize how ridiculous it all was at the time because I assumed my dad had somehow already taken care of enough of his damages if he was now helping Harold. Everybody was in such a state of panic that I don't think anyone was thinking very clearly. We were all tired. Dad had already been doing this drill for two days before I showed up. I know he had to be exhausted.

At one point, I asked Harold if his phone was working and he said it was. I asked if I could use it to make a quick long distance call. He said that was fine. I called ETO with what I thought was a revelation. Charles Di Franco picked up the phone. It was Sunday afternoon and he, Pat Huy, David Gurthwade, and Monty Stern were there trying to put together a proposal that was supposed to be done by Monty and I. It was nice to see that somebody else was killing themselves over a project besides me. I told Charles, "Listen, put Pat on the phone I've got to tell him something!" Charles started to say something and I interrupted him, "Charles put Pat on the phone! This is important!" "Hang on I'll put you on speaker.", he said. Now I could hear Pat in the background asking how I was doing and what things were like down there. I said, "It's a freaking war zone down here! There are damaged buildings everywhere. ETO needs to send one of you guys down here! Warren could make a killing from doing all the repairs, demolition, and new construction that's going to have to be done around here. If nothing else, get a few of you guys together with some chainsaws and pick up trucks and you could make a killing from just cutting up all the trees that have fallen down!" Pat started laughing and said there was no way that Warren would even try to get involved with any projects down there. He said it would require too much driving and that all the work would end up being done by local people anyways. Pat said that Warren had no contacts in that area and wouldn't be a likely candidate to receive any work from there. I felt like Pat was being very closed minded. I felt like he had just laughed at a big opportunity that I had presented to him. He was missing the boat. I said, "I don't know Pat. You should see how much needs to be done around here." He said he had seen it all on the news. He said that he understood what a hurricane could do. He changed the subject and asked about my mom and dad, the reason I had come down in the first place. I told him they were fine and then said, "Pat someone needs to at least come down and see this!" He said, "Scott, you're probably exhausted. You need to calm down and just help out your parents and get back up here. We've got to have this proposal in by Wednesday. We should be able to make it, but it would be easier with you here. Don't worry about it though, just do what you need to and get some rest. Then get back up here." I told him I would. I didn't tell him that I was helping complete strangers and that I had abandoned my mom and dad to do so.

So I got to Harold's and asked my brother if he could come with me to help Harold's friend. Uncle Frank, my mom's brother, also came with us. Uncle Frank, Carter, and I worked as fast as we could to cover the guys roof with tarps and nail them down. We nailed down 2x4's around the perimeter to hold down tarp. Before we could finish, a strong storm approached and the wind started picking up. We worked as lightning crackled around us and the thunder kept getting louder. Then came a very heavy rain. We had covered everything except a section over the guy's living room, the area that was already ruined. We decided to stop because the lightning was so close. I felt really bad for that guy. I told him I would come back the next day and finish what we had started.

After the rain started pouring, Carter and I rode back to Mom and Dad's and everyone went straight to bed. I actually slept that night, a little. The next morning, Carter and I went to Wal-Mart in Bartow before going back to Harold's. I wanted to get some groceries for Harold and Nancy because they still weren't able to get out of their driveway yet. They didn't need the groceries. That trip for unnecessary items was part of my mania that was just starting to kick in. Unnecessary spending is one of the things psychiatrists say that people do when they become manic. I checked out my groceries with the cashier and she told me that her house was badly damaged in the storm. I handed her a $100 bill and told her to keep it. "God bless you.", she said. I'm sure she thought I was the most generous guy she had met that day. Little did she realize, I was also the craziest. The mania was playing a part in that little exchange of money as well. I figured that Warren had given me that $300 from the petty cash for a reason, I felt like God wanted me to give that lady that money. I have never given a stranger money in my life except on that day.

We got to Harold's and I gave the groceries to Aunt Nancy. She thanked me but told me they had plenty of food and that I should take it back to the store. "Maybe someone will come by here who needs them. I'm sure you can find some use for them.", I said. Then Harold, Hank, Carter, and I all went back to Harold's friend's house. We finished putting all the tarps on in a few hours. Then we went to my parents' house again. My mom and dad were now sleeping in their R.V. because they could run the air conditioner in it and stay cool. The next day we went to see my grandparents' house in Bartow. Bartow was spared from a lot of the storm's worst force. There were several badly damaged homes, but most of the town was in much better shape than the towns south of there. Bartow even had power. My cell phone worked in Bartow also.

Later that day, I called ETO to see how things were going. Pat Huy told me that they were really at a place where they needed my help and if I could get back up there…. "Damn it! These guys can't make it more than three days without me! I never miss work. Now I've got a major crisis going on and they are asking me to come back! Assholes!", this was all in my head, of course. I told Pat that I would leave that day and be back there that night. I drove back to the lake, packed my things, drove back to Tallahassee, dropped Carter off, and then went straight to the office, grumbling and moaning the whole way. When I got there I was pissed. I felt like the guys at ETO couldn't relate to what I had just been through at Lake Buffum. They had laughed at my idea to come down there and collect some new work, and had now asked me to come back after only missing one work day. I felt like they were being ridiculous for asking me to come back and finish a proposal for a job that we probably would not get.

I walked in and everybody greeted me with enthusiasm. They all wanted to know all about what I had just done and how things were when I left. Pat said, "What are you doing up here? I didn't mean for you to come straight to the office from your parents' house. You need to go home and get some rest. You've got to be tired." I told him I was fine and that I was already there so I might as well do something. He hesitated and asked me to go home again. I told him I just wanted to see where they were at in the proposal and how much still needed to be done in the next two days before it was due. Pat, Monty, and Charles all showed me what still needed to be done and it looked like they were in pretty good shape. I was thinking, "Why in the hell did Pat say he wanted me back up here? They would have probably been fine without me." Monty later told me that at the time I had talked to Pat on the phone, in Bartow, things were not looking as good and that Pat was starting to freak out about not meeting the deadline. After seeing that all seemed to be going smoothly, I went home.

I got home and wanted to sleep but also wanted to tell Sara about all the things that had happened while I was gone. I felt like I couldn't convey the things I had seen enough to get the proper reaction from her. The more I talked about Lake Buffum and my experience down there, the less interested she became. She seemed concerned about what had happened, but I didn't feel like she acted concerned enough. She didn't want to here all of the details, she just wanted to know if everyone was alright. After that, she wanted to talk about what a rough weekend she had with the girls by herself. I said, "Well, I'm sorry that I had to leave you by yourself, but if you had seen what it was like down there, you would understand how I feel." I told her I wanted to go down the next weekend as well and that I didn't think she should bring the girls down unless they had power and water working again down there. She didn't say anything but I could tell that she didn't like my idea.

At work, the proposal got finished with the usual routine, only this time it took Monty, Charles, and myself working at the ETO office all night that last night before it was due. I was now burning a candle from both ends. I was exhausting

165

myself on the weekend at my parents' and then I was further wearing myself down by staying up all night and into the next day at work at least once a week. The funny thing was, I rarely felt tired. I was in a serious sleep debt, but I couldn't tell that it was having any effect on me. I was the only one who couldn't see how it was changing me though. Everyone else was starting to see warning signs. My family was beginning to see troubling behaviors develop in me: a short temper, excessive and rambling speech. I was oblivious to these things though. I just kept on moving.

I think Hurricane Francis came over my parents' house that week while I was at work. I don't really remember. Memory loss is, I guess, something that happens from my brain experiencing a little too much stress at one time. I couldn't talk to my parents because the phone lines and power were all still out. I worried about how well Mom and Dad were coping with all their problems. I talked with Nanny and Granddaddy to see how things were with them and asked about Mom and Dad. Nanny said that they were alright but that the ceilings in the lake house were all starting to bulge and sag because water had come in through the roof and built up in the attic. She said that Hurricane Francis had torn off the tarps that my dad had put up and the rain came right into the house. I decided I definitely needed to go back down that following weekend.

I drove back to my parents' house that weekend. Carter didn't come this time. It was just me, and Blue, our dog. I walked into the house and saw the ruined ceilings in the dining room, living room, and my parents' bedroom. The carpet was all soaked. There were buckets throughout the house, collecting the water that was now dripping from the ceiling. Some of the drywall at the bottom of the walls was bulging too. A lot of work was going to need to be done to repair the damage. They now needed a new roof on the main house and the guesthouse, as well as new drywall and insulation throughout several rooms of the house. When I got there, Granddaddy's sister, Aunt Emaline, and her son were there helping my parents take out sections of the ceiling that had already fallen on the floor. It looked like the carpet was probably ruined too because all the drywall mud and acoustical ceiling treatment was all over the carpet. My parents' ceiling had that sprayed on 'popcorn' type ceiling. The little Styrofoam balls that were once stuck on the ceiling were now all in the carpet. Mom was trying to clean and dry the carpet. The place was a bigger mess than it was when I had left the previous weekend.

We spent the weekend hauling drywall and insulation out of Mom and Dad's house. We also put a new tarp on the roof. This time we used 2x4's around the perimeter to hold down the edges of the tarp. After that first hurricane had struck Lake Buffum, my dad and his brothers had just tacked down a tarp, over the badly damaged roof, with roofing nails. They didn't do anything around the edges to keep the tarp from blowing off other than tack it down with those roofing nails. Like I said, everybody was panicking after that first hurricane and I don't think that anybody was thinking at their clearest, myself especially. I think that Dad and his brothers probably rushed through the job of putting on the original tarp because they wanted to see how bad Uncle Harold's place was. Uncle Harold fared well through Hurricane Francis. After all the help that he received from my family assisting him, his place had been well taken care of. Mom and Dad's place had not. After that first storm,

Mom and Dad had received no help except from my Dad's brothers. And now Hurricane Francis made a bad situation worse.

I remember telling my dad how angry I was with everyone at work for making me leave him with so much to do. As my dad and I tacked down a new tarp over his roof, I spent the entire time complaining to him about how some people in the office had nothing to do while a few of us were always asked to work overtime. The more I talked about it, the angrier I got. I remember telling him that I was thinking of moving back to Polk County because I didn't want to ever find myself so far away that I couldn't help out in situations like the one he was now in.

Another thing we did that weekend was help Mr. Pren cut up some of the trees in his yard. My dad and I used our chainsaws to cut off limbs of a tree that had fallen against his house. We also cut up another tree that was laying down on the other side of his house. The $250 Echo chainsaw I bought, was another one of those manic purchases. Along with it I bought a $300 Echo leaf blower and a $150 Echo weed trimmer. I was now spending well beyond my means, but felt like it was all justified because I felt at the time that all those things were suddenly necessities.

While I was cutting limbs from one of the trees at Mr. Pren's, I took off my gloves to tighten the chain on my chainsaw. I laid them down and brought the chainsaw over to my parents' shed. When I got back to the fallen tree, I noticed one of my gloves was missing. Blue, the dog, was standing there looking at me. I said, "Blue! Where is my other glove?!?" I held up the glove that I still had left, and asked her again, "Where is the glove Blue?" I had never talked to Blue like she was a person before. I was just really angry that my dog had now probably eaten one of my gloves. I was simply yelling at her because I was angry. After seeing me get upset with her, Blue took off around Mr. Pren's house and disappeared from view. A few minutes later, I was already back to cutting on the tree when I felt Blue nudging the back of my leg. I turned around and Blue was standing there with my other glove! I couldn't believe it. I had just uttered that question to her, about where she had put my other glove, out of anger, but she understood enough of what was going on that she knew to go get that other glove from wherever she had laid it down. I stood there for a second thinking she had picked up the glove that wasn't missing before. Then I saw it still laying right where I had put it. I said, "Blue, you are a smarter dog than I have given you credit for!" I had never known a dog to have that kind of brain power. I had trained her to sit and stay within about 30 minutes, but I never would have guessed that she would be able to do what she had just done. After that day, I realized that Blue was a pretty special dog.

I went back to Tallahassee on Sunday, exhausted. I went back to work on Monday and asked Warren if wanted to see some of the videos that I had taken from the weekend before last. He said, "Maybe after work. I've seen enough of that kind of stuff on TV for now. I'm sure it's amazing though." I felt disappointed that he wasn't willing to see what I had experienced. I brought up the video tape again before I left that day and he said he had to leave too, maybe another time. I got the point. For some reason he was not interested enough to see my video of the destruction. I don't know if he was trying to tell me in a subtle way that I was going overboard about all of it or what, but it made me feel like he didn't care as much as I thought he did just a week ago. I also tried to give Warren back the $300 dollars he had given me from petty cash on that day I first left to see my parents. Warren said he wouldn't let me pay him back. He said that was just his way of helping out. He said I had more than earned that $300 and I could use it for whatever I needed. I insisted that he take it back, "I didn't ask you to give me money Warren. I agreed to borrow this from you. Please take this back. I don't need it." Warren wouldn't listen to me. He just laughed and said, "I'm sure you can find something, just hang on to it for another rainy day, if nothing else." I thanked him and again felt very grateful towards him. He asked a lot out of me when it came to my time, but here was one of the benefits. Since I had gone above and beyond what the typical ETO employee did, Warren offered me another perk. It was a very nice gesture on his part.

Warren also gave me a $3,000 raise that year. I was now making over $36,000 in salary, plus a $1,000 annual stock contribution, plus a $1,000 Christmas bonus. Life seemed to keep getting better. Warren told me that he wanted me to start thinking of myself as a project manager that would soon be a great architect. He said that he thought I had displayed a lot of leadership qualities over the last year and would soon have people working under me. He said that I needed to start to think about how I would act towards someone who worked for me, and be that way all the time. He said he wanted to see me present myself to everyone at the office as a leader. That was the best review I had ever received from Warren. Things always went well in my reviews with Warren, but I had only received a $1,000 dollar raise each year before. After that review in 2004, I felt like I was really becoming a major player at ETO/Architects.

With my mania beginning to influence more and more of my decisions, I thought the first thing I needed to do to show I was now a 'leader' was improve my driving situation. I had been driving a 1997 Honda Civic hatchback since 1996. It was now 2004. I thought I should step up my ride. I spent about a week looking at different cars on the internet and decided that I needed a Subaru Forester. I went to a Subaru dealership on my lunch break. I told Warren that I might be buying a car that day and might be back a little late from lunch. He said that was fine and to be sure to show him what I got if I decided to get anything. I arrived at the Subaru dealership and met Sara there. She agreed that I needed a new car. She had now been driving a new van, that we bought from my grandparents, for about a year. The Civic was too small for all of us to fit in very comfortably. She wanted me to get something that we could all ride around in. The salesman showed me all the Foresters that they had on the lot. I told him that I had already researched the market value of the Forester and had an idea of what I was willing to pay. I didn't tell the salesman, but I thought I'd have a good deal if I paid around $22,000 for a new one. He showed me a white 04 Forester that came with a lot of factory upgrades. It was priced at $18,500. I drove around town for a few minutes with Sara and the salesman. The Forester was a standard transmission. I was sold. I told him I would buy it if they gave me a good price for trading in my Honda Civic. They gave me $3,000 for it. It had about 200,000 miles on the odometer. I thought that was a pretty good deal. So I bought the 04 Subaru Forester. I now felt that I appeared more like a 'leader' at the office. Ridiculous, I know.

On that next weekend, I drove down to my parents' house again. This time Sara and the girls came along with Blue and I. Now, my dad was preparing to tear off his old roof in preparation for a new one. My dad's brothers came over, along with my cousin's husband, Billy. Together we all tore off the old shingles and tar paper. We covered the bare plywood roof with a new layer of tar paper and new shingles. I think I was getting on everyone's nerves that weekend. I kept talking about my experiences working on roofs at FSU. As my dad's brothers and Billy worked on the roof, I would say things like, "That's not how we would do it at FSU." , when I saw something that didn't look right to me. I spent an excessive amount of time trying to correct my dad, his brothers, and Billy. I felt like I was the expert of the bunch. Never mind the fact that my dad and his brothers had built the house in Georgia and had helped build the very one we were all working on now. I'm sure they were all about ready to throw me off the roof by the end of that day. I remember saying some smart ass comment to my dad and one of his brothers said, "You have to take whatever help you can get, right Byron(My dad's name)?" My dad said, "Yeah, I guess, but damn this worker is mouthy!" It was all a joke, but I'm sure they were trying to tell me to shut up.

The incident that I remember showing what a complete asshole I was becoming, occurred between my cousin's husband, Billy, and myself. Billy was making a joke about the way I was tearing off the old shingles from my dad's roof. Billy said something like, "Scott, that's not the way to do that. Let me show you how we used to do it when I used to work as a roofer." I think he was making a joke about how I kept trying to correct the "mistakes" that I thought were occurring with the re-roof. I immediately took offense to Billy for making his little comment. I said, "Yeah, Billy, why don't you show me how to do this because I'm sure you've got a lot of experience re-roofing houses. I'm sure that you're a real expert.", with as much sarcasm as I could possibly put into my words. After that, I stomped over to a different section of the roof so that I was away from Billy. I don't think that we spoke again that entire day. That little episode of aggression was just one of the first of many that would soon occur between several of the other people in my life and me. The mania gave me an arrogance unlike any I had ever known. The cockiness caused me to be very short tempered with everyone around me. As the days went on my self-esteem soared to uncharted levels, even though my world was quickly beginning to collapse around me.

One other thing that I remember about that weekend was a drive that my dad and I made from the lake house to Bartow. My dad and I were driving along in my new Forester when a crop dusting plane flew over us. The plane was spraying a mist that covered my windshield as it flew over. As I saw the plane approaching, I quickly rolled up my windows and turned off the air inside the car. I was in a panic. I thought that the pilot of the plane could be a terrorist and that we might have just been sprayed with some form of chemical or biological weapon, possibly Anthrax. I told my dad what I thought had just happened. I don't think that I was being too paranoid because the date on that day that my dad and I got sprayed by the crop duster plane was September 11. I remember getting a little paranoid every September 11 that passed after the attacks on New York and Washington D.C. in 2001. I told my dad that I thought we might want to see what the early symptoms of anthrax were and that we should report the plane to some government agency. My dad said that he thought that I was over reacting. He said that the plane was just spraying some chemical on the fields that bordered both sides of the road that we were driving on. Dad said that he had seen crop dusting planes there many times before and that I was being too paranoid. The way he dismissed my paranoia made me angry. I felt like he was not being concerned enough about a potentially life threatening situation. I think that incident with the crop dusting plane was my dad's first glimpse of the growing effects of mania that were beginning to change my entire personality.

Sara, the girls, and I all went back to Tallahassee again on Sunday. The next week at work I decided to tell Warren that I was thinking about moving back closer to my parents. He said, "You know, there are advantages to being this far away from your parents. You don't want to be too close." I told him that I did want to be close because my grandfather was also dying of cancer and that I was worried about what would happen to my grandmother after he died. I worried about how she would be able to take care of herself after living so long as a married woman. She was now in her 70's and I thought I might be able to help her with things if I was closer. Warren didn't seem to like what I told him. I was surprised that he almost seemed agitated at my news. I had imagined that he would be understanding of what I wanted to do. I was wrong.

After Warren knew that I no longer wanted to be one of his employees, he began to act different towards me. All the time I had worked there before, Warren would make a trip to my desk every morning. He would usually sneak up behind me, as I was sitting in my chair facing my computer, and put his hands on my shoulders and say, "Good Morning 317." "317" was my nickname with Warren. The name came from an incident where I received a phone call from an engineer who asked if I had a direct extension to my phone at my desk. I told him my extension was 317. He called the office later and told the secretary he needed to speak to extension 317. The secretary came over the intercom and announced that extension 317 had a call on line 1. Everyone in the office laughed because no one had ever actually given their extension number to anyone before. I thought we had extension numbers for that very purpose, but apparently no one ever used them. Everybody started calling me 317 after that for a while. Warren never let it down. After that incident, I was always referred to as 317, by Warren. I also called him 314, his extension. A typical phone conversation with Warren would go like, "317, I need to see you in my office." I would respond, "Yes, 314. I am on my way." It usually got a couple laughs when Warren and I did that routine. After Warren realized that I might soon leave him, I was never called 317 again. He also stopped greeting me in the morning when he came in.

I quickly grew tired of the cold shoulder from Warren. I also began to have worries that he might try to fire me rather than let me quit. It was strange. I thought once I told Warren that I needed to move closer to my family, he would tell me that he appreciated all my hard work and that he was sorry to see me go, but that he understood why I needed to leave. Instead, it seemed like once Warren realized that I would soon quit, he began to make things hard for me. He started acting like I was spending too much time to complete my work. He would come by my desk and ask why it was taking so long to do this or that. It started to make me angry. I told him, "Warren, I have two speeds. I have my usual speed and then I have the speed that comes from you harassing me about when I'm going to be finished. That speed is much slower than my usual speed because I waste so much time trying to explain to you why it takes me as long as it does to complete something." Warren didn't like to hear that.

Either one or two weeks after the tension started to build at work, I went down to Lake Buffum again for the weekend and stayed until Monday night. That weekend, my family had the first meeting with Hospice, that I was involved in. They had already been meeting with the Hospice people for a few weeks, I think. That weekend was just the first time I had ever met any of them. There was a man one night at Nanny and Granddaddy's house. He was a Hospice worker who was evaluating the level of care that Granddaddy would need. He told me that his last name was Studebaker, as in the old car company Studebaker. He told me that it was actually a great uncle of his that had started the Studebaker car company. The guy who was there at my grandparents' house looked to be in his early seventies himself. I found him to be a very interesting man. He told me how, as a child, he realized that he had a way of calming animals when they were stressed. He said that he knew, from a very early age, that he wanted to go into the medical field, because he found out that he had the same calming effect with people. He said that he knew how to talk with people under stress, like my grandfather. He said that he enjoyed the work that he did because he felt like he was helping people ease their mind at a time when their life was ending. I thought he was a very kind man. He went on to talk about the proof of God. He said something that I had never thought of before. Mr. Studebaker said that there had to be a God, because the universe was too perfect to just form from some coincidence or natural process. He said that the greatest example he could think of to prove that there must be some divine creator, is the fact that the sun and the moon appear to be exactly the same size from Earth. He said that he did not believe that was a coincidence. Mr. Studebaker said that he felt like that was a sign from God to let us know that He was out there and that He had created the Heavens and the Earth, just as the Bible says.

That theory was a little mind blowing to me. I had seen the eclipse of the sun several times, but never thought about the fact that the moon and sun appear exactly the same size from our perspective on Earth. I told Mr. Studebaker that I believed he was correct. I told him that there had to be a Creator for something like that to happen. I really enjoyed talking with Mr. Studebaker. We talked until midnight or later. After that, I went to sleep on a couch at my grandparents' house.

Chapter 35: The Secret Society

On that same weekend, I drove over to Chili's to see my best friend, Justin White. I met Justin at Chili's and hung out with him until he was able to get off work. Afterwards, we drove over to a restaurant that he wanted to show me. It was a place that was very similar to Chili's to me, but he really liked it. Justin and I walked in and sat at a bar. I remember getting an attitude with the bartender, for reasons that I can't remember. I do remember Justin trying to calm me down and figure out what had caused me to get so snippy with the bartender. I don't remember what I said to the bartender, but I know that it was very confrontational and was completely unprovoked. Shortly after the bizarre encounter with the bartender, Justin said that he wanted us to leave. So, we did.

We drove back to Chili's, where I had parked my car. I wanted to show Justin a little of my work from ETO/Architects. I had been telling Justin how I was going to quit ETO and move back to Polk County. I told Justin that I had been working on a little slideshow that I would use at my job interviews with the Polk County firms that I planned to interview with. I remember showing Justin my slideshow on my laptop and noticing a group of girls that were standing outside of Chili's that seemed to be noticing what I was doing. I thought that I heard one of the girls say, "I am so glad that he is on our side." I had no idea of what they were talking about, but I got an impression that I was somehow connected to these girls.

It was around this time that my manic symptoms were beginning to peak. My paranoia was beginning to change the way that I saw the world. It was around this time that I first began to suspect that the world was filled with secrets. I began to think that there might be a secret society of people who did things and knew about things that I did not. At first, I just had a suspicion that there could possibly be a secret society. I had not gone so far as to try to understand what this secret group thought, did, or how they were related to me.

My first realizations of this secret group's existence were brought on by watching television. My paranoia began to develop when I realized that I could watch FOX News and CNN and get two totally different perspectives on the events that were happening around the world, especially when related to national politics. At first, I think, my suspicions of a secret group were basically well founded. At first, I was not thinking of a secret group, per say, but really just that there was definitely a biased opinion in the way that FOX News and CNN portrayed their stories. I noticed that FOX seemed to present the news with a right winged agenda, while CNN, ABC, NBC, and especially NPR, all seemed to present the news with a very liberal slant.

This realization made me sure of the fact that the media was trying to influence the outcome of the 2004 elections. I was sure, and rightly so, that the majority of the media outlets wanted to sway public opinion to vote for John Kerry instead of George Bush. With the majority of Hollywood and the media outlets pushing the people to vote for John Kerry, I realized that the media was trying to brainwash the public. I began to be suspicious about the existence of a secret group who worked behind the scenes of the nation's eyes, and worked to bring about things that met with their secret agenda, of which I had no idea. At first, all I knew was that there were definitely powerful people who wanted to sway voters to vote for a Democrat instead of a Republican. This realization scared me, but that was really the end of it. At that point I did not feel that the secret group had anything to do with me. I just believed that there was probably a group of powerful people who had an agenda that was represented through the stories of the news outlets. That was it. I think that my first thoughts about a secret society were really not far from the truth. However, I would later take these ideas to new levels and find new implications for the way the secret group impacted my life. My relationship with the secret group would soon become very personal. The secret group would one day wreck my life.

As for that night with Justin at Chili's, for some reason, I thought that those girls must be members of the secret society. I thought that they were making the comment that they were glad that I was now a member of their group. I had no idea of what they were talking about. I wondered if I had just overheard a conversation that had nothing to do with me, or if the girls were actual members of a secret society that had somehow included me as one of its members with out me ever being aware of the fact. I looked at the girls and smiled. I remember wandering if I just seen some members of a secret society. I didn't let Justin in on what I thought might have just happened. I just kept on showing him my portfolio of work.

Chapter 36: A Conspiracy! The Last Days of ETO

On Monday, I went job hunting. I posted my resume with four different firms in Lakeland and tried to set up interviews. I actually interviewed with one that same day. The firm was Straughn & Trout Architects. I thought the interview went well. I explained to Mr. Straughn and Mr. Trout all the drama that had occurred with my family in the last couple months and told them that was why I felt I needed to move back to Polk County. They said they preferred to hire people like me who were grew up in the area. They even knew some of my relatives. They took me on the office tour and introduced me to everyone in the office. The secretary was the mother of a kid I had gone to high school with. She seemed to like me for that alone. I thought I had the job in the bag. I went back to Tallahassee feeling like I was ready to pull the plug on ETO/Architects. All I needed was to hear that phone call from Straughn & Trout telling me when I could start. My mom called me later that week on my way to work. I now had a cell phone and talked to people on my morning commute. Mom told me that she and Dad wanted to let Sara and I buy their lake house and move in. She said they were going to retire soon and didn't need such a big house. She said she thought it would be perfect for us when we moved back down. I couldn't think of a more perfect place to live than my childhood home. This just excited me more about moving down. I felt like everything was coming together. I thought everything was happening for a reason. It was God's will. His perfect plan for me was falling into place.

At work I began to feel like a short timer. I no longer cared about holding back my opinions on what I thought about everyone in the office. The people I didn't care for, and even the ones I did, soon would all know what I thought of them. I started to get angry with Mark Lambert. In the time I had worked at ETO, I had come across several drawings with his name on them that were filled with errors. In fact, they were the same kinds of errors that had caused Carter Christen to lose his job shortly after I started. I thought it was odd that one guy could get fired for making AutoCAD mistakes and another could be Warren's pet. I would always try to reason to myself that Mark was not as well trained in AutoCAD as I was and that he had made the mistakes on accident. I told myself it wasn't a big deal to Warren because Mark did a lot more than just draw on the computer. He spent most of his time dealing with the construction side of projects. I think, partly because, that was Warren's remedy for Mark not being the world's greatest draftsman.

On my last project with ETO/Architects, I found myself working on a proposal that required me to use one of Mark Lambert's screwed up drawings. The drawing was of a school. We were going to use a school we had previously done as a starting point for a concept of a new school at FAMU. Mark's drawing was filled with lines that didn't fully intersect and lines that were not perpendicular to each other that should have been. These kinds of errors cause major headaches when a proposal gets turned into construction drawings for a project. Those errors cause the incorrect measurements and other problems that had plagued Florida Surplus Lines and cost Carter Christen his job. I started to think that maybe Mark wasn't making these errors on accident. I started to think there was a conspiracy going on and I needed to get to the bottom of it.

Mark Lambert primarily worked on Capital City Bank projects. They were our bread and butter client. We had an hourly contract with them. Every month we billed them for the hours we had spent on their projects and they paid without question. I started to wonder if Warren might be letting Mark screw up drawings, just so they would have to be fixed and we would be able to bill more time to the Capital City Bank projects. That was the conspiracy. ETO was bleeding Capital City Bank for way more time and money than we actually deserved. At first, I thought that maybe Warren wasn't aware of what Mark was doing. At first, I thought that I needed to tell Warren about the mistakes Mark had made so that he could do something to remedy the situation. I started going in Warren's office and showing him all the errors I had found with Capital City Bank projects. Warren seemed to get angry with what I was telling him, but not at Mark. Warren was getting angry with me. "Scott, quit bothering me with all this stupid crap about Mark and Capital City Banks. I know you don't like Mark. You and Mark have different personality types. He is a number-cruncher. You are an artist. You two will always clash heads. You both have two very different brains and personalities. Quit wasting time trying to dig up dirt on him. He does his job well and I don't need you tattling on him and giving him a hard time!", Warren told me.

From then on, I felt like Warren was now part of the conspiracy too. I began to think that he was masterminding a scheme to steal money from Capital City Bank. I realized that I had just made a major error. I had just revealed myself as a whistle blower. I felt like I had just caused myself to be fired. I started to become very paranoid. I thought that Warren was talking about me to everyone in the office and slandering me somehow. This made me even more angry and even more paranoid. I really wanted to get that call from Straughn & Trout now. I called the secretary at Straughn & Trout and asked her if she knew anything about whether or not Mr. Straughn had made a decision about hiring me. She said she was pulling for me, but that he had not yet made up his mind and would call me as soon as he did. This worried me as well. At that point, it seemed like I might be burning a bridge in Tallahassee a little too soon. I knew that it is never a good idea to burn bridges anyways. I hadn't planned on screwing things up so badly for myself at ETO. I thought Warren would thank me for letting him know about a problem in the office. Instead he was now becoming angry with me, and things didn't look so promising in Polk County yet either.

The straw that broke the camel's back occurred just a few days after my meeting with Warren about Mark and Capital City Bank. I was working on the proposal for the new school at FAMU. Despite the tension, Warren had made me the lead designer for that proposal. He told me to get help from Monty Stern when I needed it, but that I would be allowed to develop the master plan for the school by myself. I think he was trying to throw me a bone to see if it might change my mind about moving to Polk County. Warren told me that I was the designer. I was given two draftsmen to do any production work that I needed, David Gurthwade and Charles Di Franco. They were supposed to do what I told them.

I didn't feel comfortable giving orders to guys that were both older than me. David was in his 40's and Charles was about five years older than me. Charles and I had been friends since we worked together at Johnston Peachson. I actually helped him get the job at ETO by giving him a good recommendation to Warren. I felt very awkward about the idea of now acting like his superior. So, I did most of the work myself and passed off as little as I could to Charles and David. Friday came around and Warren said that we would have to work through the weekend to meet the deadline for the proposal. Before that, Warren trashed a couple of my ideas for the school and said I was wasting too much time on one of my concepts that he didn't like. When Warren said we would be there all weekend I said, "You mean, Scott will be here all weekend. You'll be at home watching football as usual. I'm sick of this. I'm not working this weekend. I have things I need to do. We aren't going to get this job anyways. FAMU will probably pull the plug on this job before it ever gets into construction drawings." FAMU had already wasted a lot of my time by advertising jobs in the paper and then announcing that they realized their budget for that year could not afford the project that we had just dreamed up. We might spend three weeks putting together a design for them and they would just cancel everything on us. We wouldn't get paid a cent. That didn't matter to Warren though. He said that was just the way the game was played. He said it was important for us to keep showing interest in their projects so that when they actually did have work, we would get it.

After I made my smart-ass remark to Warren, he stood up. "Scott, come with me to my office. The rest of you listen to Monty. He is now in charge of this project. Scott you are no longer the lead designer for this proposal. Let's go have a talk." I followed Warren to his office. He walked calmly and gave no indication of what was about to be unleashed. He stood at his door and I walked in. He then slammed the door behind me. "What the f@$! is wrong with you?!?", Warren yelled at me. "You are screwing up everything. I gave you this project as a chance to shine and you decide to spit in my face in front of everyone out there! You must be out of your f@$!ing mind! Who do you think you are?...." He went on a tirade for about five minutes. His face was red and the saliva in his mouth was becoming thick and foamy. To me, he looked like the crazy person in the room. He ranted and raved about how he had tried to be understanding of what my family had been through but I that was taking everything way out of proportion and really starting to really piss him off. He said that he didn't understand why I had such a problem with Mark Lambert and that was also another thing he was sick of hearing about. The weird thing was that all his screaming and yelling didn't scare me. In fact, I can remember trying to keep myself from smirking at him. I felt like he was making a complete idiot of himself and I felt nothing but sorry for him for letting himself get so worked up. I felt like I was in a dream the whole time he stood there yelling at me. "So, this is the real Warren Eto.", I thought.

After he finished his tantrum, I tried to speak as calmly and politely as I could. Normally I would have been crying if something like that had happened to me. Instead, I felt like I needed to calm Warren down before he had an aneurysm in front of me. "Warren, I am so sorry for getting you this mad at me. I am just tired of being one of the only people in the office who has to work so much overtime. Its not like I'm getting paid extra for it. That's one of the reasons I have a problem with Mark Lambert. He comes in at 8:00 and leaves at 5:00. He takes an hour or more at lunch everyday. I see him goofing off on the internet all the time. Why doesn't he have to work as hard as I do?", I said.

"Why do you have a f@$!ing hard on for Mark Lambert? Plenty of other people in the office do just what he does. And how do I know why it takes you so damn long to do your job? For all I know you could be screwing around all day too. I see you up from your desk talking to other people throughout the day. That's time you could be spending working. I'll tell you what, from now on, I don't want to ever see you here before 8:00 or after 5:00. If that's what has you acting like such an asshole, then don't ever work late again. You will also never work another weekend. Other people will. But I won't let you. Will that make you happy?", Warren said. "No, Warren, that won't make me happy. I don't mind working overtime every now and then, just not all the time. I'm sorry for complaining and having a bad attitude. I appreciate all that you have done for me and I don't want to leave here on a bad note. I will work this weekend. I'm sorry.", I told Warren.

Warren said that he really didn't want me up there that weekend if I was going to go around bad mouthing everything like I had been doing so often lately. He said that I was counter productive and was bringing down everyone's moral. He said Monty was still in charge of the project now and that if I wanted to come in and help him that was fine, but that he better not hear another complaint out of me. He should have fired me that day. I thought he was going to. Things would have been easier for the both of us if he would have.

Instead, I went back out to the conference room and met with Monty, Charles, and David. They all gave me a very strange treatment. It was as if I was carrying an infectious disease and they were afraid that they might catch it. They didn't want me to be in there. They didn't want my help. They didn't want my disease. They had heard Warren yelling and knew that I was in deep trouble with him. To associate with me now was like joining sides with the enemy. Everybody talked specifically about the project and anytime someone said anything to me, there was a derogatory tone in their voice, like they were letting me know they were no longer on my side. I volunteered to help Monty produce a couple of concepts that he whipped up for the school in a matter of minutes. I was once again just a draftsman, adding the details that the architect left out, trying to make a quick sketch become a working concept. I would get no recognition for creating the design for that school now. Now, it was Monty's baby and I was just Monty's tool.

I came in that Saturday and started working on Monty's sketches, turning them from streaks of ink on scrap paper into real, hard line AutoCAD drawings that had the buildings at their correct sizes with a working parking lot scheme. The more I worked, the more I began to change what Monty had sketched. By the time I was done, my AutoCAD drawing looked nothing like what Monty was proposing. The proposal for the school was filled with my ideas again. It wasn't one of the earlier concepts that Warren had trashed. This was a new concept. I thought, "Maybe Warren will like it. If he doesn't, then I'll do Monty's ideas, just like he sketched them." I spent all day Saturday on the drawings and never even started doing the concepts that Monty had sketched up. I figured I was up there on my time and if I wanted to take another shot at coming up with a decent concept, I was entitled to it, even if Warren had told me I was no longer the designer for the project.

I went home Saturday night and told Sara that I was tired of working for Warren. I had already told her about all the things that had happened recently. She seemed very worried. I told her I was going to quit working for Warren and make him pay me for all the overtime I had worked while I was there. Then I panicked. I thought Warren might be up there at the office editing my timesheets so that all my overtime was erased. I had copies of all my time sheets in a folder at my desk. I thought that I better go down there and bring them home before Warren destroyed them, if he hadn't already. My paranoia was peaking. It was around midnight when that thought popped in my head. Sara and I were in bed talking before we went to sleep. I got up and got dressed and drove to the office. I'm sure Sara was beginning to think something might be wrong with me.

I got to the office and realized that no one was there. I went in and found my timesheet folder. I started looking through it to see if anything was missing. I thought Warren might be a step ahead of me, but I was wrong. They were all there. I grabbed my folder. Then I thought, "You know what, I might just walk out of here Monday. I should go ahead and pack up all my stuff to save myself the embarrassment of cleaning out my desk. I grabbed all my things and loaded them into boxes and carried them out to my car. My desk was empty except for my ruler, calculator, and a few pens and pencils. I thought I could grab that last handful of stuff if things got bad on Monday.

I remember walking into the office that following Monday morning around 8:30 am. I had thought about just quitting my job and not showing up ever again. I was so mad at Warren. I was tired of feeling over worked, under appreciated, and now like the target for Warren's wrath. I was sure that if I continued to work there much longer I would soon find myself as a scapegoat for some error filled project that Warren would pin on me and blame me for. I thought that would be the way that he would have me fired, just like poor Carter Christen.

When I walked in that morning, I immediately realized that Monty, Charles, and David, had already assumed that I had quit. I had cleared my desk of all my things. It was bare. So, they had already seen my desk and come to the conclusion that I would never be back. When I walked in, there was a look of surprise on their faces, but nothing was said. Monty was handing the sketches that he had given me Friday, to Charles. When he saw me come in, he asked if I had worked on his sketches over the weekend. I said, "Well, sort of, but not exactly. Look on my computer and I'll show you what I've got." I showed Monty my design for the

FAMU DRS School proposal. He quickly realized that what I had done looked nothing like what he had sketched. He made no comment. He just looked over what I had done, and walked into his office. I'm sure that in his mind, he was cussing me out for leaving him hanging. A few minutes later he got his sketches from Charles and asked me if I could quickly draw them up in AutoCAD, before Warren showed up.

That Monday morning, we all met with Warren in the conference room to go over what still needed to be done before the deadline. Warren asked to see what I had worked on over the weekend. Monty immediately told Warren that I had not done the sketches that he had given me, which I had said I would do for him. Warren ignored me and asked to see Monty's sketches. He looked over them and then asked to see what I had done. I showed Warren my proposal for the FAMU DRS School. He was once again furious with me. This time he didn't bother sparing me the embarrassment of being yelled at in front of everyone. He just yelled at me in front of everyone. He told me that I had wasted the entire weekend and probably ensured that they would not be able to meet the deadline for that proposal. I tried to defend the concept that I had drawn. Warren told me to leave the room. He said that he didn't want me working on that project anymore. He said that I had screwed it up badly enough already.

After listening to another of Warren's tirades, I was now the one who was furious. I had just pissed away another weekend working on one of his projects. "So what if I wasn't doing what I was told. Monty can do his own damn drawings. Maybe then they'll see just how much they need me.", I thought. Everybody in the office was now avoiding me. Nobody would even make eye contact with me when I walked right by them. I thought about telling everybody to kiss my ass and just walk out.

Warren came to my desk and said he had an assignment he thought I could handle. Of course he said this with the most derogatory tone so that everyone in the office would know that he was sick of me. Warren told me to go to FAMU and take pictures of the school that I had done the Media Center Addition to. He said he wanted pictures of that school to use in the proposal. I grabbed a camera and took off. I was thrilled to get out of the office after what had just happened. I called my grand parents on my way to FAMU. "GranDaddy, I've got great news! I think they are going to fire me at ETO and give me a severance package. I heard somebody talking about giving me $8,000 I think.", I told them.

My hearing was one thing that I remember somehow being elevated during those last few weeks that I worked at ETO/Architects. I remember overhearing lots of whispered conversations that I sometimes thought were about me. I remember several people acting surprised when I would comment on something that they were whispering about at a level that they thought I would not be able to hear. I later learned that heightened senses is a feature associated with mania.

So, one of those whispered conversations that I thought I overheard was a conversation between Warren and Bill Moore about how they could get rid of me. I thought I heard Bill tell Warren that $8,000 seemed like a fair amount of money to give me after they fired me. I thought they were getting me out of the office so they could discuss what to say to me and start doing the paper work that came along with my termination. Once I thought I had overheard that conversation, I wanted to tell my grandparents. I was so whacked out that I was actually happy about what I thought might be about to happen when I got back to the office that day. I had already told Warren that morning that I had friends who were lawyers. I told Warren that I would use them if he tried to fire me unjustly. "Scott, you are absolutely scaring me. I don't want you to be around me right now. Just stay away from me. Go home. I mean it.", Warren had said. I told him I wanted to help out on the project somehow and felt bad that my good intentions were misunderstood. Shortly afterwards he came to me with the assignment to photograph the school. He just wanted me out of the office. I guess that all my bizarre behavior had frightened him that much. He just wanted to get me out of his hair until he could figure out how best to deal with my situation.

I got to the school and took a lot of pictures. I talked with several of the people that worked there that I had met when I was working on the Media Center. They all told me how much they loved the new building and what a good job I had done. I told them that I was mainly just the draftsman, that David Barthowe and Warren Eto had done all the great design work. I told them that Warren and David really wanted to get the chance to design the new school at FAMU too. I tried to praise Warren, as much as I could, to everyone I talked with. In reality, Warren had never done the first thing on the Media Center. It was all David Barthowe, not Warren. David Barthowe was not involved in the proposal for the new school, so I tried to tie Warren in because he would be the chief architect involved for that project. One of the guys I was talking to asked me if we had any paper that they could use for a float they were building for the upcoming Halloween parade. I told him that I thought we did and would ask Warren if he would give them some of our paper from the office. I thought I was playing the role of an office diplomat, bartering services for a chance at one of their projects. It was totally ridiculous. The guy I was talking to probably had nothing to do with the decision making process of who designed the new school. He was FAMU Elementary's P.E. Coach.

After all my gallivanting around the FAMU Elementary School, I got back to the office and found that Warren was the only one still there. I told Warren that I had lots of pictures and had been promoting ETO/Architects to everyone I met over at FAMU. "I'm sure you are my biggest cheerleader, Scott.", Warren said sarcastically. I honestly don't remember what I said to him after that, but what ever it was it sent him over the edge. All I remember is that he was walking towards me and I was walking in his direction to get to the desk that I had to hook the camera up at to download it's pictures onto our server. "What the hell are you doing?", Warren said. "I'm downloading these pictures.", I told him. "Get out of this office and give me your key.", Warren said. "Warren you can't make me leave. I'm trying to download these pictures for you.", I said.

Warren grabbed me by the collar of my shirt and started pulling me away from the computer and towards the back door. I walked along as he pulled on my shirt and pushed me out the door. I laughed at him. "Thanks a lot Warren. Now you just gave me the physical abuse card. I'm going to sue your ass.", I told him. Warren was standing at the door and said, "Scott, I'm going to pay you to take some time off. Something is wrong with you. You need to go see your doctor and get help. Don't come back up here until I call you and ask you to." With that he slammed the door shut and locked it.

I drove off and felt like I had just achieved a victory. Warren had now physically removed me from the building and pushed me out the door. "I will have his ass in court. He's going to pay for what he just did to me. You lose Warren.", I thought to myself.

I got home and saw Sara. She looked scared to death. Apparently Warren had called her and my parents while I was at FAMU taking pictures. Warren told Sara and my parents that I was acting like a crazy person and that they better get me to my doctor ASAP. Sara told me that she had called my parents and told them she didn't know what to think or do. My dad said that he was coming up to Tallahassee to see what things were like, personally. Sara said my dad was already on his way and would be at our house in a couple hours. I was stunned. My boss had now attacked me by trying to turn my own family against me. I was once again furious. I told Sara that Warren was the one who needed to see a doctor. He was the one who had screamed and yelled at me a couple days ago. Sara said that Warren cried when he talked to her on the phone about me. I didn't know what to think of that. I felt like that was probably just another indication that he was the one who needed help. Sara and I talked for a while and I told her that Warren was giving me a paid vacation. I said that I as going to use the time to get a job in Polk County and that I was never going back to ETO/Architects ever again. I made some joke about how stupid the whole thing sounded and we were both laughing when my dad knocked on the door.

My dad walked in and Sara and I were sitting on the couch watching TV and laughing at whatever I had just said. "Well, I'm glad to see you're not rolling around on the floor crying.", my dad said. He said he had been standing outside the door for a couple minutes just listening to us to see if everything was O.K. I told him it just turned out that I was working for a crazy person and soon everything would be resolved. I told him that I was planning on coming down to Lake Buffum to do more job hunting. He told me that my mom and grandparents were very worried because Warren had said a lot of strange things about me. I reassured my dad that he had just been pulled into a big misunderstanding and what was really going on was that I had uncovered a conspiracy in the office and Warren was trying to make me out to be crazy so that no one would believe my story about what he had been doing to one of our best clients. The more I tried to explain to my dad the details of the Capital City Bank Conspiracy Theory, the more he seemed to doubt my story. This started to make me angry with him. Dad finally said that if what I said was true, even though it didn't really make sense to him, Warren would win in court because he would hire a better lawyer and drag the case out so that I could never afford to pay the bills to win the case. "How would you pay for a lawyer to begin with?", he asked. Dad said the best thing to do would be to never contact Warren again and just start lining up a job in Polk County.

That night I wrote an e-mail to Pat Huy at ETO telling him that I appreciated what Warren was doing, but that I would never see a psychiatrist because I felt that psychology was just voo-doo magic. I said that every culture in history had a way of explaining what was right and wrong. I felt that psychology was just another pop-culture phenomenon that was nothing but a false religion. I thought it was wrong to see a psychologist. I thought that the person I should talk about my problems with was my pastor at TRBC. Pat never replied back from my e-mail. My dad said it was a bad idea to be talking to anyone at ETO. He said they were all Warren's employees and would never take my side in a fight with their boss.

The next day I drove my dad to FSU to show him some of the buildings I had worked on there. We went to the job site for Parking Garage 3. It was now under construction and Ken Curring was our full time office representative on site. Ken and I had become good friends, I thought, over the years that I had worked with ETO. I thought that if anybody would hear my side of the story, it would be Ken. I walked into the job site trailer with my dad and introduced him to Ken. Ken seemed very nervous the whole time I talked to him. I asked him if he had heard anything about what happened between Warren and I. He laughed nervously and said he had. I told him that Warren was giving me a paid vacation and that I was taking my dad around to see some of our work. Ken quickly came up with an excuse as to why he had to leave us. I thought it was very odd. I felt disappointed that my closest friend at ETO was now giving me the cold shoulder as well. After Ken walked out on me, my dad and I left. Dad told me that he expected that would happen. He said that was why I needed to cut myself off from the ETO staff and quit trying to contact them. He said, "Its all about self-preservation. These guys aren't going to sacrifice their jobs for you. They are only going to do what's best for them. They don't care if you're right."

I agreed with what Dad said and thought that the people I had worked with were now useless to me. I felt sad that I had spent so much time with them and now they acted like I was dirt because I had a falling out with the boss. It amazed me that people would turn on me that quickly. It was all about self-preservation, just like Dad said. They could no longer associate with me. I was dangerous. I was now the enemy.

Dad decided to go back to Lake Buffum that afternoon. He said that I needed to forget about Warren and the others and start focusing on looking for a new job. I kept telling him that I wasn't through with ETO just yet. I told my dad that Warren hadn't fired me, he was just giving me a paid vacation. Dad told me that my time with ETO/Architects was over. It was. I just refused to believe it. I was so delirious that I didn't know what was going to happen next. All I could think about now was how I was going to have my revenge on Warren Eto for messing with me and my family.

I called Warren at some point that day and cussed him out. I told him he had picked the wrong person to screw over. I said I was going to sue him for slandering me to my family and roughing me up when he threw me out of the office. I also told him that I was going to go to the president of Capital City Bank and would tell him everything I thought Warren was doing to him. I told Warren that I would tell the president of Capital City Bank that Warren had been stealing money from him. Warren hung up on me.

That evening, Sara and I decided to take the girls to Chuck E. Cheese, just to get out of the house. Sara called her friend, Crystal Mathews, to meet her at Chuck E. Cheese. My dad called me on my cell phone as we arrived at Chuck E. Cheese. My dad was so upset that he was crying on the phone as he pleaded for me to leave my boss alone. Dad said that he had told me not to call Warren again. He said that Warren had just called him and said that he was going to have me arrested for harassment if my dad did not come back to Tallahassee and force me to see my doctor. I told him that there was no way I was going to see a doctor and started trying to explain how this was all part of Warren's plan to slander me so that I couldn't appear in court against him. "Stop talking about taking Warren to court. You have to let this go. Please don't call anyone up there again. They are going to arrest you if you do.", Dad said. "You don't understand. If I let him get away with this, he wins.", I told him. "Nobody is winning or losing anything here. You have to stop thinking that you are winning or losing something here. You've got to stop harassing those people. Don't call anyone else that works at ETO.", he said. I told him I wouldn't and that I was sorry that Warren had made him so upset. My dad never cries. For him to be emotional on the phone took a lot of trouble on Warren and my behalf. I told Dad that I wanted to kill Warren for what he was doing to him and Mom and Sara. He said to be careful of what I said. I told him I didn't mean it, but that's how angry I was at Warren for manipulating my family. I told Dad that Warren was just playing all of them like a game and that they were all doing exactly what he wanted. Dad didn't say anything. He said he was on his way back up. I said that was fine but unnecessary.

I decided to go watch a movie at the theater next door. I got about thirty minutes into the movie when I realized that I was supposed to be at a meeting at the TRBC for volunteers to help out with media related projects with the church. They had asked for people with backgrounds in art, photography, and computer graphics; to volunteer to help out with several projects at church. I volunteered. The meeting was supposed to give all the volunteers a chance to introduce themselves and be assigned to specific projects that the church had going.

When I arrived at TRBC, my brother Carter pulled up beside me. Carter said that Dad had called him and told him to meet up with me and follow me back to my house. I was pissed that Dad was now telling me what to do. It was as if Dad thought that I was a little kid again. And on top of it, he brought in my little brother to act as an escort to make sure that I did what Dad said. I told Carter that Dad was totally stressed out about all the damage that had been done to his house. My parents had now been living with my grandparents for several weeks because their home was ruined after all the hurricanes. I told Carter that the stress from the hurricanes and then Warren calling and making up lies about me was making Dad act weird. I asked Carter if he wanted to come to the meeting I was about to go in. He said that he would because Dad asked him to follow me. At the meeting I introduced Carter and told everyone that he had come along because he was also an artist. No one seemed bothered by that and in fact seemed more interested in Carter' artistic abilities than my experience putting together proposals for ETO. After the meeting, Carter followed me home and we met Dad and Sara, who were already there.

Chapter 37: Crazy? Who? Me?

We walked in and Dad started asking me questions about why I had called Warren after I told him I wouldn't. He said he left because he thought I was going to be able to calm myself down and deal with things on my own. He said that after Warren called him that last time, Dad knew he had to come back and get involved. I told Dad that this wasn't his problem and it had nothing to do with him. I said I couldn't believe he was letting Warren scare him into thinking he could actually have me arrested. I hadn't done anything wrong, I told him. Then Dad told me to explain to him again how this conspiracy idea went. I felt like I was going to have a heart attack. My chest was hurting because I was so stressed by the idea that no one believed me. I started to realize that they all believed Warren over me. I was panicking. I knew I had to tell The Conspiracy story in a way that somehow made sense to them. They couldn't understand how lines in a drawing that didn't fully intersect or weren't exactly parallel or perpendicular could cause such a big deal to me. I tried drawing a few things on my computer in AutoCAD to illustrate the problem. I showed everyone how if I drew two lines that appeared to intersect but actually did not, it created a gap between the two lines that might not be visible if you looked at it at one particular scale on the computer screen. When I zoomed in on the intersection the gap between the lines was apparent. Then I measured the lines. The first measurement was from the end point of one line to its other end. Then I measured from the apparent intersection and showed them how the two dimensions were different. The gap between the lines caused the difference in the measurements. I couldn't think of any better way to explain how this caused problems in construction drawings. I might as well have been speaking to them in a foreign language. The above description should probably be written in a foreign language too, I'm sure. I know it probably doesn't make sense to anyone but me. But that's the best description of the problem I can give.

Everyone sat there looking at me like I was crazy. I tried to explain how when different measurements come up for the same wall of window in a set of construction drawings, it causes huge problems. You can't tell one guy a wall is 10 feet long and another guy that same wall is 10 feet and 2 inches long. Nobody knows how long the wall should really be. Then the wall either gets built as 10 feet long or 10 feet 2 inches and somebody ends up having a problem. Calls get made to the architect to explain why the drawings are screwed up and the architect has to remedy the situation by either redesigning things that are related to that wall, like windows, doors, trim, etc.; or the wall gets torn back down and built to the architect's real intention. It causes extra costs from the architect and the contractor. I tried to explain to everyone that ETO was the architect and the contractor for several Capital City

Banks and that all this extra cost meant extra profits for Warren Eto. Still, everyone sat there looking at me like I was crazy. I guess I was. Still, I wonder…

Dad said, "Let's go sit down at the kitchen table and talk." Dad, Carter, and Sara all sat on one side of the table. I sat alone on the other side. I felt like I was sitting across from three judges that were deciding whether or not I was sane. That's exactly what was going on. They were all beginning to think that I needed to see a doctor to make me sane again. They all kept asking me questions and would sometimes laugh at my responses. I became angry with all of them. Finally, I said, "You know what? I'm tired of trying to explain myself to you. I'm wasting my time talking to people who have no idea of what I am saying. Dad, you are a school teacher. Sara, you have watched babies all day for most of your career. And Carter, you are a house painter for God's sake. What in the hell makes you think you have an understanding of what goes on at an architecture firm? You are all sitting there judging me and acting 'better than thou' towards me. I'm sick of this. My chest hurts and I'm tired. I'm going to bed. You can all leave. I don't care what you think."

Dad said, "Scott, you can go to bed if you want. But, in the morning you are going to see your doctor and I'm coming with you." I laughed and told Dad he was crazy if he thought he could come in my house and tell me what I was going to do. I said, "What if I don't go? Are you and Carter going to try to physically put me in my car and drive me down there?" He said, "If that's how you want to do it." I walked on to my room and felt like crying. My own father and brother were now in my house along with my wife and they were all trying to force me to do something that was against my will. I thought about getting in my car and just driving far away to somewhere that no one would ever find me. I thought about leaving them all for good and never seeing any of them again. I was so disappointed in all of them. I couldn't believe that they were believing the words of a stranger, my boss, over me. The only contact my dad ever had with Warren was those few telephone calls. He had known me my whole life. How could he be convinced to do the bidding of someone he didn't know over his own son? I didn't understand. It just made me sad and angry with all of them. Especially Sara. She was supposed to be my partner, the one who trusted and believed in me when no one else did. And now I knew that she had actually masterminded the whole night that had just taken place. She called my dad and asked him to come back to Tallahassee and figure out what was really going on between Warren and I. I was most disappointed in her. She had upset me many times in the past, but never had she done anything that upset me the way that I was that night. I felt totally betrayed by her. I thought about divorcing her, "I can't keep someone around who will turn on me like this. She doesn't love me. If she did, she never would have allowed any of this to happen. She knows what's going on at ETO better than anyone and she doesn't seem to care. All she's worried about is that I won't be getting a paycheck. She's trying to make me look crazy so that if we end up divorcing, my family will take pity on her for having to put up with me for so many years. She is just looking out for herself. Its all about self preservation, like Dad said."

That next morning I woke up with a new plan. I decided I was going to call one of the associate pastors at TRBC that I knew pretty well. I called him and told him that my dad was trying to force me to see a psychologist because he thought that I was crazy. I gave him a very abbreviated story of what had transpired in the last few days. I told the pastor that my dad was actually the one who needed help because of all the stress he had been under since the hurricanes tore up his house. I also added that my dad was a science teacher and that he was not a very religious person. I said, "My dad sees the world as a problem that can be solved through science. He doesn't understand that religion is actually the way to deal with life's problems." I asked the pastor if he could meet with my dad and I before my dad tried to force me to see my doctor. My pastor said, "Scott, sometimes its better just to let someone have their way. Maybe after you see your doctor, your dad will feel like he has done everything he can to help you and then you can get him to meet with you and I. I think the best thing for you to do is just listen to what your dad and doctor have to say. I'm not an expert in the type of situation you are describing. I think your doctor will be more able to calm your dad down than I can at this point." I thanked him for his advise and hung up. I felt like everyone was letting me down. I thought the associate pastor would surely have been able to fix this dilemma. Instead he said himself that he was not qualified to solve my kind of problem. I thought church was supposedly able to solve all of life's problems. This was the first and only time I had ever asked anyone at a church to help me with a problem in my life, and here I was being told to go to a secular doctor and let him fix me. The church just let me down. Maybe they weren't the answer to all of life's problems after all.

After being let down by my pastor, my dad said he wanted me to see the doctor. I said, "Fine. If that's what it takes to make you happy, then I'll do it, even if I think it's a complete waste of time." Dad said I had nothing but time now and what harm could come from spending a few minutes talking with my doctor. "This isn't any bigger of a deal than you make it out to be.", he said. I thought that was the biggest understatement I had ever heard. This was the most stressful, bizarre thing that I had ever experienced. My dad, brother, and wife, were all suggesting that I needed psychological help. I couldn't believe it! All the people I worked so hard to please were now telling me to do something that I was completely against. I didn't know what else to do other than keep on trying to please them. I decided I would go to see my doctor as my dad had asked. My dad and Carter got in his car and I got in mine and we all drove to the Capital Health Plan clinic on Magnolia Drive in Tallahassee. That was where my doctor was. Dr. Stan Curio was the doctor who had seen Sara, the girls, and myself for the last few years. He was a nice guy who told me that he wanted to be an architect when he was in college too. He said he switched his major to medicine at some point and became a doctor instead. He liked to talk with me about projects we were working on at ETO and told me about the house he was building for himself. I thought we had a pretty decent relationship. I figured he would hear my story about what had happened over the last month or two and understand that I was just stressed out. I thought he might even tell my dad that he needed to take something to calm his nerves too.

We walked in to Capital Health Plan and asked to see my doctor. We only waited about thirty minutes or less and were called back to meet with Dr. Curio. We all walked in to one of the exam rooms and Dr. Curio came in shortly after. My dad immediately introduced himself and started telling Dr. Curio that I had been acting strange and was under a lot of stress at work and away from work because of all the things that were going on between Mom and Dad and my grandparents. Then Dr. Curio started asking me questions. I really don't remember specifically what he said. I was so stressed out because I felt like I had just walked into Warren Eto's trap. I started to think that Dr. Curio might be in on the whole thing too. I thought Warren could have talked with him and told him to get me on some type of medication so that it appeared I was crazy and would not seem like a plausible person to listen to in court when I tried to sue him for what he had done to me, my family, and Capital City Bank. Warren was the one who paid for my insurance. I figured it was likely that he could have enough pull with people down at Capital Health Plan to get them to slander me and help him out. Capital Health Plan was our HMO. Under my insurance with Warren, I could only see CHP doctors. They could refer me to other specialists, but I always had to start with them. I thought it was very likely that Warren could be friends with some of these people and was now using them, just like he was using my own family, to destroy me. I believed Dr. Curio might be part of Warren's plan to make me out to be crazy. I believed Warren was behind all the new trouble in my life. I was growing more paranoid by the hour. It was at that doctor's office that I began to fear Warren.

Dr. Curio asked me to explain exactly what I thought was going on at ETO/Architects. I knew this was a slippery slope. My explanation had not convinced anyone close to me. How could I make sense of everything to my doctor? I started talking and telling Dr. Curio the whole story, beginning with the hurricanes that destroyed my parents' home and ending with why I was now there in his office. I thought I was probably talking for about 30 minutes. My dad later told me I was rambling for over two hours. Time has a funny way of blurring and going by faster when you lose enough sleep to go into mania. I don't know if I slept the night before, but I know I had been going for days without sleep many times around the period when all this trouble started. Hours might fly by in what seemed to me like minutes. It's similar to how time seems to fly by when you sleep, only you're wide awake, living in a dream.

By the time I thought I was done with my story, I could tell Dr. Curio seemed very skeptical. I then decided to tell him how I thought he fit into this whole scheme as well. I accused him of working for Warren to help slander me. I said to my dad and brother, "Warren is paying this guys paycheck! ETO employs over 20 people who all have Capital Health Plan as their medical provider. Warren is probably paying Dr. Curio to lock me up in some insane asylum! Don't you see that you've led me straight into a trap!" My dad and brother were crying. Dr. Curio said, "Scott, I don't even know Warren Eto. Do you realize how many people are covered by Capital Health Plan? ETO/Architects is just a drop in the bucket. There are so many more people with far larger companies than the one you work for! Why would you ever think Warren Eto could have enough power to make me do something like this to you?" Dr. Curio walked out of the room and partially closed the door. I could hear him whispering to some people outside. I saw a nurse come and stand by the door, almost like she was guarding it. After a short while, Dr. Curio came back in and said that I was about to be taken to Tallahassee Memorial Hospital to see a psychologist.

"You're getting ready to have me locked up in a Looney Bin, just like Warren told you to, right Dr. Curio?", I said to him. "No, Scott, you are experiencing a chemical imbalance in your brain and you need to see someone who is more familiar with your condition than I am. We are all just trying to help you.", Dr. Curio said.

"Why don't you help my dad? He's been crying a lot lately and that's not like him. He is under a lot of stress right now. He doesn't even have a home to live in. And Carter, you are a pothead! You smoke marijuana all the time! How is it that you don't need help? You guys both think that you are fit to judge me? You guys are both the crazy ones! Not me!", I said to all of them. My dad and brother were still crying. Even Dr. Curio seemed to be getting a little emotional. I couldn't believe that this was actually happening. I knew things in my life would never be the same after that day at Dr. Curio's office.

Someone knocked on the door of the exam room and Dr. Curio went out and started talking to them. I heard walkie-talkies chattering outside the room. The door opened and two police officers came in and told me to put my hands behind my back. I was scared to death. What crime had I committed? Why were police officers handcuffing me? I hadn't done anything. One of the officers told me to remain calm and they would escort me out of the building and into a police car that was going to take me to Tallahassee Memorial Hospital. "Why are you handcuffing me?!?", I yelled at them. "I hope you guys are all happy now! Is this what you thought would happen when I went to the doctor, Dad? This is crazy! Warren is winning and you guys just all helped him out!", I yelled at my dad. The policemen took me away and we started walking out of the CHP building. In the lobby, we passed my mom. What was she doing there? She hadn't come up with Dad. She drove separately early that morning after Dad called her and told her he thought she should come to help Sara and the girls. I saw my mom and said, "Thanks a lot! You are ruining me! Warren Eto has used all of you to ruin me! I hope you are all happy now! Apparently I'm now a criminal!" The police were making me walk quickly and didn't let me stop to talk to her. I was just yelling this at her as they marched me through the lobby. There were other people there, waiting for appointments, too. I didn't care. I just felt so disgusted with all of them that I decided I was going to let them have it. I didn't care who heard. After all, I was already being escorted out by two policemen, one on each arm, with my hands in handcuffs. It couldn't get any more embarrassing than that. The nurses who had seen me many times over the last several years, all looked at me with fear in their eyes. I was now a criminal who had never broken the law.

The policemen told me to watch my head as they put me in the back seat of the patrol cruiser. I had never been arrested before. I had never seen the inside of the backseat of a police car. I remember being very uncomfortable. The handcuffs were tight and pressed against the bones in my wrist. My weight was pressing against the handcuffs because my hands were behind me and I was forced to sit back against them. The seat of the patrol car was hard plastic and very uncomfortable as well. I kept asking the officers why they had just hand cuffed me. They said it was standard procedure for The Baker Act. I asked what The Baker Act was. They said it was a way for people to have someone committed to a psychiatric care facility against a person's will. If someone was acting strange and appeared to be in danger of harming themselves or someone else, they could be "Baker Acted". The officer said I had just been "Baker Acted" by Dr. Curio because he felt that I was a threat to myself and might try to hurt someone else. They said I seemed O.K., but that I needed to listen to whatever the doctors at TMH told me to do, or else things might get worse.

We arrived at TMH and the police took off the hand-cuffs. I had tried my best to seem polite and as all together as I knew how to be. They wished me luck and turned me over to an orderly at the hospital. They explained to the orderly what had happened at CHP and said that I had been calm on the ride over and shouldn't be much trouble. The orderly walked me to a hospital bed in a hallway and told me to put on a hospital gown. I had to give him all my clothes, my wallet, car keys, and cell phone. I realized I was now surrendering to a higher authority. I was no longer a free citizen. I was now something less. I had lost my right to do what I chose, when I chose. I realized that I had just lost my freedom.

I thought about trying to run out of the hospital. I thought I might be able to escape into the woods near the hospital and maybe make my way to my house eventually, even though I had just given my wallet and car keys to the orderly. I wanted to get up and run, but I didn't think I would have much of a chance of getting past all the people in the hospital. Even if I did escape, what would I do? If I showed up at my house, Sara would probably turn me right back over to the people I was now with. So, I just laid there in the hospital bed and awaited my doom.

A doctor came to see me and asked me to follow her to a room that had padded chairs and a couch. She asked me to sit down and tell her what had caused me to be Baker Acted. I started to tell her my story and she cut me off. She asked about my sleeping habits. She asked if I felt more energized than I normally did. After only a few minutes she told me that I was in a state they called mania. I told her that she was mistaken. I told her that I was voted "Best All Around", by my fellow students at Bartow High. She said, "Big deal. My good friend was one of the most popular people when he was in high school. He committed suicide. I'm trying to prevent you from doing something like that. I think you may have a mental disorder. Let's have you go lay back down in your bed while I take care of some things, O.K.". She said all of this without any inflection of sympathy. It was as if she was just telling me about some small detail that required no extraordinary inflection in her voice as she broke the news to me that I was officially "crazy".

The doctor walked with me to my bed and told me to just wait there until someone asked me to do something else. As I was laying there, I saw a familiar face walk in. It was Paul Mathews. Paul was the husband of Crystal Mathews. Crystal was Sara's best friend in Tallahassee. Paul and Crystal had three kids who were close in age to Liza and Gwen. We had gone out to eat with The Mathews and had each other over at our houses several times. Paul and I had become good friends as well. He was a very funny guy and he liked to play video games even more than I did. Paul and I would get together and play games sometimes when Sara and Crystal wanted to hang out. Paul was a paramedic. He was delivering a patient to the hospital that day

190

and happened to walk in right where they had my hospital bed in the hallway. He saw me and did a double take. "Scott, what are you doing here? Are you alright?", Paul said. "Of all the days for me to be here and I have to be here when Paul Mathews shows up.", I thought to myself. I told Paul that I had just been Baker Acted. I said I thought that my boss was trying to smear me because I had caught onto a conspiracy in the office and my boss was stealing money from a client of ours. I told him how Warren had talked to Sara and my dad and convinced them that he was going to have me arrested if I was not taken to see my doctor and get some help. Paul seemed to believe me. "Scott, I am so sorry this is happening to you. It sounds like you're in some big trouble. The only thing I can tell you is that if the doctors tell you to take medication, just do it. They will let you go sooner if you cooperate with them.", Paul told me. Paul said he had to process the person he had just delivered to the hospital but he would come back to see how I was doing.

Another guy came up to me while I was lying there in that hospital bed in the hallway. He was another orderly who worked in that portion of the hospital. He looked at my chart and said, "Man, I hate to see this kind of thing happen to people." I asked him what he meant. He said, "It looks like you probably had a normal life up till now. Things like this tend to change people. You are going to have a tough time ahead of you. Just try to keep your chin up and don't let things get you down. Things always get better." I had no idea what he was talking about. All I knew was that my boss was hell bent on destroying my reputation with my family for some reason. I didn't think I had a problem. I thought I was being mistreated and I wasn't sure just how far Warren Eto's will had stretched into the people I was now meeting. I still thought this was all part of some scheme Warren had created to ruin me for threatening that I was going to tell Capital City Bank that he was stealing money from them. Most of my thoughts were focused on how I was going to get out of the mess that I was in and get revenge on Warren Eto.

A nurse came up to me and told me to get up and go to a bed that was in a room with some other people who were also waiting around. I followed the nurse to my new bed and she showed me which bed to sit at and then walked off. There were two other people in that room. They were both also laying in beds and wearing hospital gowns. One was a woman in her forties. The other was a guy who looked and sounded absolutely insane. He had shaved parts of his head and then other parts were covered with hair that was probably eight inches long. He looked and talked very weird. He kept saying things that didn't make any sense. I don't remember what he was saying. I just remember knowing that I was in a room with actual crazy people. After a while, the nurse came back and took me to a room where there was a bed and a door. She closed the door behind me and said I would be staying in that room until I was to be delivered to TMH Behavioral Health Center. I asked why I was going there and when I was going to get to go back home. She said she didn't know. She said the people at the Behavioral Health Center would determine when I could go home. I didn't know it, but the Behavioral Health Center was a fancy name for an insane asylum.

My mom and dad came into the room where I was now waiting. I told them to leave. I said I didn't want to talk to them or see them. My dad said, "Scott, all I'm trying to do is help you. That's all anybody is doing. Nobody is helping Warren Eto. You've got to get that thought about him and this conspiracy business out of your head. If you would have just calmly told the doctor your story, you wouldn't be here now. I only took you to him because I thought he would prescribe you some medication that would help you calm down. But you always did like to do everything the hard way." I told him to leave and that I was sick of hearing what he had to say. He said, "I'm just trying to help you. You have to believe me. One day you are going to thank me for doing this. Just wait." I said, "I've already thanked you. Now leave. You have 'helped' me enough already. Just go before you screw me up worse than I already am.", I said to him with as much hate and sarcasm as I could. After that bit of verbal abuse, he and my mom left.

A little while later Paul came by. He said that he just wanted to see how I was doing. I told him that I was fine but that I was just sick of Sara and family trying to "help" me. I told him how I felt that Sara had betrayed me by calling my father and asking for his help to deal with me. I told him I couldn't believe that my wife would believe my boss over me. Paul said he wasn't sure exactly what was going on, but that he knew Sara cared a lot about me. He said he didn't think she was intentionally trying to hurt me. I told him I wasn't sure. Paul reminded me again to do whatever the doctors at the hospital said. "The more trouble you give them, the harder they will make life for you while you are here.", Paul said. He also stressed the importance of taking whatever drugs they gave me. He said, "If you want to get out of here fast, take whatever pills they give you. They probably don't know what's going on with you. But just do what they say. At least until they let you leave. Then once your out, nobody can make you take anymore pills. Just hang in there and be nice to everybody. They really are trying to help you, even if you don't believe it." After a while of talking to Paul I told him I was just exhausted and he said he would leave me. He said he would visit me again later. I thanked him and asked him not to tell anybody about running into me at TMH. He said he wouldn't and left.

I don't remember ever seeing or talking to Sara during that entire day. Sara had conveniently gone to class or something that morning when my dad said it was time to go to my doctor. She was taking classes at Tallahassee Community College and was working part time near TMH with a physical therapist. Sara had recently decided she wanted to become an occupational therapist. She went to school several times a week and usually worked on the weekend, during the day, with the physical therapist. Sara had either gone to class, work, or both that day and I had not seen or heard from her all day. She also had to take care of the girls. I'm glad she didn't bring them around while I was at the hospital. That would have just made matters worse.

Chapter 38: The BHC

I think it was around 7:00 pm when a nurse came to my room and said there was an opening for me at the Behavioral Health Center. She said that some people were on their way to take me there. I asked her where the BHC was and she said it was not far from the hospital. Two guys showed up shortly afterwards and said to follow them. They walked me to a van parked outside the hospital. I got in and they drove me to the BHC. I don't remember even talking to those guys. I was just so sick of trying to explain myself to everyone. I thought I would do best to keep my mouth shut.

We arrived at the nuthouse and they brought me to a lobby where a nurse started asking me a bunch of questions. I started to tell her how this was all just a big misunderstanding and that I did not belong there. I explained that I was an intern architect who had helped design parking garages for FSU and banks for Capital City Bank. She didn't seem affected by my words. She just calmly asked me to have a seat somewhere and let her do her paperwork. Another nurse came up to me and asked me if I had eaten supper at TMH. I told her that I hadn't eaten anything since breakfast that morning and that I was starving. She said they had already eaten supper at the BHC but she would go see what she could find. She came back with a salad with a piece of chicken breast on top. It wasn't great, but I was hungry. I ate everything.

A girl who looked like she was about 15 or 16 walked out into the lobby where I was. She started asking the nurses if she could go home. They told her to go back to her room. Then an older woman who worked there told her she had brought her dog and the girl could pet the dog if she wanted. The lady brought out an Australian Shepherd that looked similar to my dog, Blue. I walked over and petted the dog and told the old lady that I had an Australian Shepherd at home too. I told her that my dog looked a lot like hers. She gave me a strange look and said, "Really? You have an Australian Shepherd?" She asked the question in a way that made me think she didn't really believe me. I think she thought I was lying. It made me mad. I said, "What? Do you think I'm making this up?" She said, "I don't know. Are you?" I just laughed and said, "Yeah, I'm lying to you about having a dog. I'll have somebody bring her up here if you don't believe me." She said maybe that would be a good idea. She said she would at least like to see a picture of my dog. It was like she absolutely thought I was lying to her. I had never had an encounter with a person where they thought I was lying about something so simple. I thought, "I am dealing with a bunch of idiots. These people are probably all bigger screw balls than I am. And they are now going to judge whether or not I am sane. This is totally stupid."

After a while I was shown to my room. I shared a room with another guy. I don't remember his name or hardly even speaking to him for a while. I think I eventually told him my story and that my wife had betrayed me and I was now planning on divorcing her when I got out. I don't remember anything else about that first night except that they asked me to take some pills and I refused to take them. No one forced me to take anything. They just said it was for my own good and that things would be easier for me if I just took the pills. I still refused and they let it go at that.

The next day I met with my assigned psychiatrist, Dr. Veneble. It made me think "Venom Abled", as in, able to produce venom. It fit right into my belief that psychology was just a false religion. I thought that it was nothing more than a 21st Century religion that manipulated its members with mind altering drugs. I thought psychology might be a new weapon used to do away with certain people in society. Sort of like the way Hitler killed many of Germany's most intelligent and influential people during his time. I thought psychologists were the new weapons being used on people. They were falsely diagnosing people with problems that didn't really exist. At the very least, I thought, psychologists were the tools of drug manufacturers who wanted to find more and more people to sell their drugs to. I thought the psychologist was just a tool on the payroll of the pharmaceutical companies and that they were hired to make people believe they had a problem that could only be cured by some miracle drug that happened to be made by some drug manufacturer. I also thought that psychology was the antithesis of church. Everything that psychology stood for made a mockery of religion, to me. So when I met Dr. Veneble, I immediately despised her and thought she was part of Warren's plot to slander me.

To my surprise, Dr. Veneble came across as a very nice lady. She asked me questions and actually seemed to care about what I was saying. She didn't act like I was telling the tale of a crazy person. She just listened and would offer a comment here or there, but never in a derogatory type of tone. She told me she wanted me to take some tests to further evaluate me. I said that was fine. She handed me two tests. One was about thirty questions long. The other was over 300 questions. The questions were like, "Spiders make me nervous." , and, "I like to be around children." They weren't really questions. They were weird statements. I was supposed to bubble in a number from 1 to 5 that expressed how much I agreed or disagreed with the statement. I finished the short test in just a few minutes. I think it took me a couple days to read through the longer one though. People were always interrupting me when I was trying to work on that test. They kept us very busy the whole time I was at the BHC. We went from meal to class to class and meal with very little down time in between. They told us we would be able to leave sooner if we attended all the classes they offered. So I went to every one. If you didn't go, you had to stay in your room.

I called Sara several times from the phones they let us use at the BHC. I don't remember what I said to her, but I know it wasn't nice because I can remember that she would usually cry and hang up on me. One time my mom got on the phone and told me to stop calling Sara and upsetting her. I think I was usually telling Sara that all this was her fault and that I would never forgive her for what she had done.

194

A couple days after I arrived, I was walking to see Dr. Veneble. She had asked to speak with me and I was going to her office. A beautiful red haired girl walked out of Dr. Veneble's office just as I was getting close to the door. The girl smiled at me and said, "Hey.", in a very soft, sad voice. I smiled and said hello to her and walked into Dr. Veneble's office. Dr. Veneble asked me more questions and then let me leave. Soon afterwards, I was eating lunch in the day room where we ate all our meals and had free time. One of the orderlies came up to me with that pretty red head standing beside him. He said, "Scott, this is Le Anne Bener. She says she goes to your church. Do you two know each other?" I said I didn't know her but would be glad to get to know her. She asked if I minded if she sat by me while we ate lunch. I told her I would be happy for her to sit with me. I introduced myself and told her why I thought I was there at the nuthouse. She seemed to believe my story. I asked why she was there. She told me she had just tried to kill herself by swallowing a bunch of pills. She said that she had been in a huge fight with her fiancée and she got so upset that she decided she didn't want to live anymore. I thought about all the times Sara had threatened to kill herself after we had a big fight. Even though this girl had actually gone through with the act, I wasn't bothered by it. I immediately felt very sorry for her. "Why on earth would a beautiful girl like you get so upset over some guy? You could probably have any guy you want. I can't believe you would let a person affect you that much. Please don't ever do something like that again. You are too beautiful. Someone out there will find you someday and make you happy.", I told Le Anne with all the sincerity I could.

Le Anne told me that her fiancée was very immature and liked to party and do drugs way too much. She said that she wanted to find someone who had better values. She said that's why she started going to TRBC. She wanted to find someone there who was more like the type of person she wanted to marry. I thought it was strange that she had allowed herself to get engaged to a guy that she seemed to now despise, but I didn't ask questions. I wanted to like Le Anne. I didn't want to find out something that I might not want to know. I told Le Anne about Sara and how I felt like she betrayed me. I told Le Anne that Sara and I had always had a lot of trouble from the beginning of our relationship. I told her about Sara being pregnant with Liza and partying with other guys then asking me to get back together with her. Le Anne said that Sara sounded like her now ex-fiancée, Mark. I didn't think Sara was anything like what Mark sounded like, but I played along. I was interested in letting Le Anne know that I was available. If it meant trashing Sara even more than she deserved, so be it.

After that talk at lunch that day, Le Anne and I tried to stay close to each other the rest of the time we were there at the BHC. I thought, "This is God's will. God knows that Sara and I are not meant for each other. God has brought me to this place to meet this beautiful girl. Maybe this is the reason I am here. Maybe this was all God's plan to introduce me to a new person that I might be more compatible with." I thought Le Anne was beautiful. I also thought she had a great personality. I think I was just delirious and trying to find meaning to why I was at the nuthouse.

195

One day, Le Anne's friends from TRBC came to visit her at the nuthouse. We had an outdoor area where there were chairs and grass to sit on and get some sun. Le Anne asked me to meet her friends. I immediately recognized one of them. She was the daughter of one of the associate pastors. Her father had held the meeting, with all the volunteers who wanted to help with media related projects, the night before I ended up going to my doctor. I introduced myself to all her friends and they all greeted me. We all sat together on some lounge chairs and Le Anne and her friends started talking. Two of her friends were girls. Two were guys. One of the guys and girls were dating each other. The other guy and girl were single. The associate pastor's daughter was the girl dating one of the guys. He was a black guy and looked a little shady to me. I wondered if that girl's dad knew she was with this guy. After listening to them talk for a while I began to get irritated with Le Anne. She sounded so immature when she was talking with her friends. The main problem was that all her friends looked to be about 5 to 7 years younger than Le Anne and I. They were kids. And she was acting like one of them. Le Anne's friends were telling her about some party that they were at a couple nights earlier and how drunk they all were. They were saying how they wished she was there and she was saying that she wished she was there too. They were also talking about all kinds of stupid TV shows. I remember Le Anne saying that's what she hated most about being at the BHC, she was missing her favorite show, The Sopranos. "I gots to get my Sopranos!", Le Anne said. All her friends laughed. I just acted like I was asleep. At this point I wanted to tune all those people out. I wanted them to leave so that I could be alone with Le Anne again. I didn't like the way she acted with her friends. I thought they were part of her problem. Finally, somebody asked Le Anne if I was asleep. I just laid there with my eyes closed. Le Anne said, "I guess so. They give us all some pretty strong drugs in here. It's probably made him drowsy."

Another guy walked up who was also a patient at the nuthouse. He was openly gay, but I didn't care. I actually thought he was pretty funny. I wasn't trying to judge anybody at this point. I figured if I could get thrown into a place like this, anyone could. The gay guy started talking with Le Anne and her friends. The conversation was all about alcohol and partying. I tuned it out. Then I realized at some point that they had all started talking about me. I wasn't sure what was being said, but I remember hearing the gay guy say, "Oh yeah, Scott is definitely a breeder." I sat up and said, "I don't know what the hell a breeder is, but you guys can all screw yourselves if you're over there talking crap about me. I haven't been asleep. I've just been listening to all the stupid crap you are all talking about." I told the pastor's daughter he would be real proud of her if I told him all the things I had just heard her say. I got up and left Le Anne with her crappy friends. The gay guy said, "Scott! We weren't saying anything bad about you! A breeder is just a straight person. All I was saying is that I think you are straight." I walked inside and let the door close behind me. I figured Le Anne was probably more screwed up than Sara and that I was going from the frying pan to the fire if I tried to have a relationship with her.

That next day Le Anne came up to me and told me that she thought I was a control freak. I said I didn't know what she meant. I told her that her friends were a bad influence and she needed to separate from them and stop partying if she really wanted the things she claimed she was looking for that day at lunch when we first started talking. I told her that just because those people went to TRBC, didn't make them true Christians. I said that they did not seem like people who were wanting to live a Christ-like life. I told her that she was only hurting herself if she was doing the kinds of things that they were talking about. After that, I went to my room and didn't speak to her for several hours. I remember crying in my bed. I was realizing that I had been chasing after another girl that was probably worse for me than Sara. I began to think that my experience at the BHC couldn't be God's plan. I felt totally confused. Why was I so quick to try to chase after this girl when it seemed like I might have a good one at home. I began to think that maybe Sara had done all that she had done recently with the best of intentions. Maybe she really was trying to help me, like Dad said. I didn't know what to think. The main reason I think I started crying was because the drugs were starting to affect me.

I had refused to take any drugs for several days after I got there. Then one day, I was in the day room watching a movie with a group of patients. This weird looking guy across the table from me was drawing a picture and he kept looking at me and smiling. He finally said, "You are that architect guy right?" I said, "Well I worked for an architect, yes." He said, "This is for you." He handed me the picture he had been drawing and smiled at me. I looked at the picture and was a little scared at what I saw. It was a crappy drawing of a tree with a person hanging from it by a noose. He said, "Do you know who that is in the picture?" I said, "No. Who is it?" "It's you!", he said, with a big grin on his face. I felt terrified. He said, "You want to go outside?" We had an attached outdoor area to the dayroom where people could go outside and smoke. The area was totally fenced from floor to ceiling, but you still felt like you were as "outside" as you could be at the BHC. That weird guy was asking me to go out to the smoking room with him. I didn't want to, but part of me felt drawn to do what he said, and I knew that we were being supervised, so I decided I would go and try to talk to him and see why he was threatening me with pictures of me being hung from a tree.

We went out to the smoke room. We were all alone. I said, "Why would you draw a picture of me like that?" He said, "Because that's what I'm going to do to you.", and smiled. After the crazy guy made that statement, I got chills all over me. I thought that Warren must have sent this guy here to kill me or at least scare the hell out of me. I asked the crazy guy why he would want to kill me. He said, "Let's just say that I work for some people who are not very happy with you. I will tell you this, after I'm done with you, no one will ever find you. I'll even let you pick the place, under a pond, way out in the woods. I could even bury you in concrete under some building and no one will ever find you." He also told me not to be worried because when he killed me it would be at a time when I did not expect it and it would be quick. He said I probably wouldn't even realize what had happened. He said he had done this kind of thing many times before. I had never been so scared as I was when that guy told me all this. I thought I had just met the guy that Warren had hired to kill me. I was now absolutely terrified of Warren.

I thought about a project at ETO that was being held up by two people who jointly owned a piece of property. One of the owners wanted ETO to develop the land and build several office buildings on it. The other guy didn't like the idea of office buildings on his land and was causing the whole project to come to a halt. Then, that guy died one night. The project went on ahead, even though the owner ended up using a different architect than ETO. I now wondered if Warren had something to do with that guy's death. I couldn't remember what the story was on how the guy died, but I started to believe that Warren was involved. They even joked about it at the office, saying that Warren had hired a hit on that guy because he was causing us too many problems. I now thought the joke was probably fact.

So I was here with this guy who claimed he was going to kill me. I asked him if there was anything I could do to prevent him from killing me. He said it was all about money and named some price I could pay him to make him go away. I don't remember his number but it was a ridiculous amount of money and I told him I didn't have that much. Then he told me that he really was looking for a job and asked if I knew any architects that were hiring. I thought, "What the hell is this guy talking about? One minute he's talking about killing me and now he's asking me to help him find a job? This is crazy!" I told the guy that I did know of a structural engineer that was hiring, David Bartley. The guy told me that he knew Barry Trudol and had met him at a job site that he was working at. I wondered how I was going to refer a guy to David who had met me in a nuthouse and threatened to kill me. I told the guy that if he left me alone I would put in a good word for him with David. He said that sounded good to him. I left it at that. Up to that point, my meeting with my killer was the most frightening thing that I had ever experienced in my entire life. Little did I know, there would soon come a day when I would one day find myself even more terrified. There would come a day when my meeting with a killer seemed like a walk in the park.

After I felt I had smoothed things over with the crazy killer, I immediately went to one of the nurses and told her what had just happened between me and that crazy guy. She said that he had threatened another person there as well. They moved him out of our unit and put him in a different part of the facility where I never saw him again. The weird thing was that he called me at my house after I got out of the BHC. He was asking me if I had talked with David Bartley about him. I told him I had not. I never did. I wasn't going to introduce David to a guy that I was sure was crazy. A month or so later I was talking with Barry Trudol about what had happened to me. That was probably a big mistake. I mentioned the crazy guy. His name was Pat something. Barry said that he knew who I was talking about after I described him. Barry said that he had met him at a job site, just like Pat had said. Barry said Pat was a day laborer working for a concrete company that was pouring the foundation of a house that David was working on. Barry said that the guy seemed really weird. Barry said that he thought the guy was an idiot. He said I shouldn't worry too much about his threat to kill me. He said that the guy probably just heard my story from someone there at the BHC and decided that he was going to try to scare me. He said that he doubted that Warren Eto had anything to do with Pat. Barry said he thought Pat was probably just some lunatic that I had let get under my skin.

As far as how Pat managed to call me at my house, I don't remember giving Pat my phone number, but I wouldn't be surprised if I did. I don't remember a lot of things that probably happened while I was there. The drugs they had me start taking, after I ratted out my killer, had a way of blurring my memory and made me feel very tired for several days after I started taking them. After my experience with Le Anne Bener and Pat the crazy guy, I decided I would take whatever drugs they told me to, just so I could get out of there as quick as possible.

Chapter 39: Stumbling Into a Secret

Another bizarre experience that happened at the BHC was with the woman who I first met when I was at Tallahassee Memorial Hospital and was put in that room with my first two crazy people. She was the lady in her 40's that was laying in one of the beds beside the really crazy guy. I remember talking to her at the hospital and she told me that she was a free-lance writer who wrote pieces for magazines like Time and couple others that I wasn't familiar with. She seemed pretty normal when I talked to her at the hospital, even though she did yell at the nurses who came in and tried to make her take pills. She came to the BHC on the same night I did. Her name was Pam.

One day Pam and I were putting together a puzzle in a room that had games and blank paper to draw on. Pam told me that there was a reason why I had met her. She said it was destiny. I had already told her about why I was there and she seemed to believe my story as well. Pam said that there was a much larger conspiracy that she was involved in. She started telling me that the reason that she was in the BHC was because she was attempting to assassinate an associate of Dick Cheney, as in Vice President Dick Cheney. She said she had a loaded gun and was about to shoot this guy who worked for Dick Cheney when she was caught and abducted by people who brought her to the BHC. She said this wasn't the first time she had been put into an asylum. She said it was something that this corrupt organization within the government was doing to people who fell out of line with their agenda. She said that she believed that this secret organization was actually planning the way for the Anti-Christ, and that it was their mission to bring him to power in the United States. She said Dick Cheney was one of this organization's members. Then she started to sound even more bizarre.

She said that the Death Star from the Star Wars movie was a real weapon that the United States had developed and secretly built in space. She said that Dick Cheney was usually on this "Death Star", when the news talked about him being at an undisclosed location. She said that Dick Cheney was like a real life version of Darth Vader. She said that he had all kinds of blackmail on President Bush and that's why Bush had chosen him as Vice President, just so Cheney wouldn't spill the beans on some bad secrets about President Bush. She said Cheney was going to become the next president and that he would lead the way for the Anti-Christ. She said that she wasn't sure how all the details worked. She said that she just met with people on her computer and they told her these bits and pieces of information. Pam told me that the entire Bible was actually a secret code. She said that computers had been used to crack the secret messages that were contained in the Bible. She said that once you read the Bible's true message, life had a new meaning. She said that after reading the deciphered version of the Bible, you knew what God's true message for us was. One of the things I remember her saying was that God didn't care about whether a guy liked a woman or another guy. God wanted everyone to love each other. That was all. She said homosexuality was something that people started to look down on thousands of years ago because they realized it caused disease. She said God didn't really care if people were homosexual or not. She said that all the plants and animals were actually trying to tell us God's true message but that nobody paid any attention to it. She said that if you watched how things in nature existed in harmony, you would see how God really wanted us to behave. I thought about all the violence in nature, animal eating animal to survive. To me, nature was a struggle of life and death. I didn't see any harmony there. But I just listened to Pam because I had never heard such wild ideas.

Pam went on to say that the Rapture had already happened and that all the people who were true believers in God had already been taken off the earth. She said that we were now living in the time just before the final confrontation between God and Satan. She said that there were people who had already realized this and chosen to fight for good or evil. She said that she was working for the group that was fighting for good. Dick Cheney and the organization that he was a member of were fighting for Satan. I thought, "This is some real out of the box thinking. I wonder if any of this is true." Pam finally told me that I could join the group that she was a part of. She said that the first thing I had to do was get out of the BHC. She said to just play along with whatever they told me to do so that I could leave. Then she said I needed to get to my computer. She said that if I typed the correct sequence of letters, symbols, and numbers, I would receive the deciphered version of the Bible. She said that only the chosen would get the real version. She said every computer already had the whole deciphered version of the Bible on it. She said that each person's code was different and that she could not tell me what mine was because she didn't know it. She said I would be the only one who would be able to enter the correct sequence for myself. I asked her how she found hers. She said she started writing letters and numbers and those became new symbols that were not actually letters or numbers at all. She started drawing some of the symbols she said she had entered into her computer to make it spit out the deciphered version of the Bible. What she wrote on a piece of paper looked like Egyptian or Hebrew letters or something like them. She explained what each one meant as she drew it.

I told Pam that I had never heard such strange stories from anyone that I had ever met. She warned me to be careful who I talked to about the things she had told me. She said I would be surprised to find out just who was working for Satan's secret army and I might end up dead if I told the right information to the wrong person. I told her I wasn't going to tell anyone. I also told her that I would try to play around with my computer when I got home and see if I had any luck getting it to spit out the deciphered Bible. I still wonder if there was any shred of truth in that conversation with Pam at the BHC. The things that Pam told me that day at the BHC ended up re-shaping my perception of the world. That conversation haunted my thoughts and dreams for several years afterwards. I still sometimes wonder if any of what she said could be true.

Aside from those two strange encounters, most of my time at the BHC was pretty normal stuff. Most everybody there seemed like a totally normal person who had just experienced a stressful time in their life or had been using drugs and done something stupid. Aside from Pam and the guy who threatened my life, everyone else seemed pretty sane, for the most part. Most of the girls there were around my age and had a case of depression. There were a few other guys as well. One of them was a teenage kid whose parents caught him smoking pot and had him Baker Acted to teach him a lesson. I guess he must have had other issues if he was there, but he never talked about them, and was really pretty hilarious. One lady had this habit of cutting her arms with a razor blade. She said she wasn't suicidal. She said she felt like it relieved her stress to cut her arms sometimes. I thought that was a really weird thing to do. I tried to avoid her. I thought she was a little too weird for me.

Chapter 40: The Beginning of My New Life and the End of My Grandfather's

One of the last things I did at the BHC was write a letter of resignation to Warren Eto. Sara came up there to visit me and said that Warren wanted me to resign. I thought that after I had met the guy who I believed Warren had hired to threaten or kill me, resignation was probably a good idea. I hoped that if I resigned, Warren would leave me alone and that guy would go away. I wrote an apology to Warren for my behavior and told him how much I appreciated him. Then I ended the letter with my resignation. At that point, I finally realized that my time with ETO/Architects and Warren Eto was over. It made me sad. I never could have imagined that I would end up in a psychiatric facility because of a falling out with a guy that I once thought was the best boss I had ever known. How did things get so out of control? I couldn't explain it. I still thought that Warren was orchestrating all the things that led up to me being at the BHC; although, as the drugs began to do their work, I did start to have my doubts.

After two weeks of listening to people talk in classes about the importance of taking medication, stress management, negotiating problems with other people, and a bunch of other garbage; they let me go home.

The last thing I did was have a group meeting with my parents, Sara, Dr. Veneble, and myself. Dr. Veneble explained to everyone what she thought my condition was. I don't remember much about what she said, because my opinion was that it was all garbage. I didn't want to listen to her. I just wanted to get the hell out of there. The words I remember hearing are Bi-Polar Disorder. Dr. Veneble was telling everyone that I suffered from Bi-Polar Disorder. She said that Bi-Polar Disorder had caused the racing thoughts that led to the sleepless nights that led to mania. She said I was in mania when I came in. She said I had also shown signs of depression. She said that made me Bi-Polar. I thought, "O.K., so if I'm happy you call me manic, if I'm sad you say I'm depressed. Never mind the fact that there are reasons for why I get happy and sad. What a bunch of bull crap."

My parents met me in the lobby and handed me the key to my Subaru Forester. It was the first taste of freedom I had in two weeks. I remember feeling the coolness of the fall air as I stepped outside of the prison that I had been held captive in for over two weeks. I remember watching all the leaves that were falling from the trees that surrounded the parking lot. It was so nice to be outside again. I had been cooped up inside that terrible asylum for too long. That day was the first time that I had been able to see a wide-open space since the day that I had been brought there. I was so happy to just be able to see my former prison from the outside and know that I would not be forced to go back inside of it. I thought that my life was about to return to normal. I was given all my clothes and belongings. I packed them into my Forester and followed Mom and Dad back to my house, driving all by myself. It felt great to leave the BHC. I was so happy to be out of there. I told myself that I would do whatever my family wanted me to, just as long as they didn't send me back there again.

I drove from the BHC to my house. I don't remember if Sara was there when I arrived or not. I guess that shows how little I really cared about her at the time. I really don't remember much of anything else about that day. I remember being tired from the drugs. I just wanted to sleep. Mom and Dad eventually went back to Lake Buffum. It was just Sara and the girls and myself again. After I was released from the BHC, things were very different between Sara and I. I had told her all about Le Anne Bener while I was at the BHC. I told Sara that she could only blame herself if I fell in love with another girl because I never would have met her if Sara had not started the ball rolling that ended with me in the nut house. Sara didn't really even try to stop me from carrying on a relationship with Le Anne. Sara probably hoped I would leave her at that point. I verbally abused her every chance I got and blamed her for every problem in my life. I treated her very poorly. I deserved to be left. She had simply been overwhelmed by my strange behavior and called the only person she thought could help talk sense into me, my dad. I hated her for that. I didn't see that she was probably trying to help me because she loved me. I thought she was trying to destroy me and had been brain washed by Warren Eto. I told her that I thought she was stupid for listening to Warren and for calling my dad. I think Sara's love for me died in those weeks that I was at the BHC and especially after I came back home. I don't think anyone can love someone that treats them the way I treated Sara after I came back from the BHC. She eventually got a gut full and said she thought I needed to work things out on my own. She took the girls and moved down to Lake Buffum to live with my parents. I was glad to see her leave. I could now focus on fixing up the house so that we could sell it. I could also talk to Le Anne anytime I wanted without having to see Sara start crying.

I talked to Le Anne on the phone a few times and even invited her to come by my house. She had moved to North Carolina to live with that ex-fiancée of hers, Mark. She said he was the only one who would help her. She said she didn't love him, she was just using him for a place to live until she could get out on her own. The more I talked to Le Anne, the less attractive she seemed to me. I started to wonder when she was telling the truth and when she was lying. She told me that she had a little girl. Le Anne's mother was raising her kid. I thought that probably said a lot about Le Anne that I didn't already know. Le Anne was in North Carolina with some guy she claimed liked to do drugs while her mother was raising her kid in Florida. I decided Le Anne was too much of a risk. I thought the best thing for me to do was to mend my relationship with Sara, if that was possible. I certainly didn't deserve her anymore. I still hoped that maybe she would come back around, just like she had so many times before.

After Sara left, I started working on the house as best I could. The problem was that the medication I was taking was causing me to sleep for 12 to 14 hours a day and that left me with very little daylight to get things done. I wanted to paint the house and build a circular retaining wall around a tree in the front yard and surround it with flowering plants. Those two projects took me three weeks, I think. I remember my mom calling and asking why it was taking me so long to get the house ready to sell. She thought I was stalling because I didn't want to move down there anymore. She said moving down there was my only option because the doctors at the BHC had told my parents that I would need close supervision for a long time and that meant I needed to move down there with them. I really didn't want to move in with them. I wasn't stalling on the house because of that though. Before the crap hit the fan, I had imagined that Sara and I moving down there would allow us to be a big help to everyone. Now, the tables were turned. Now, it would be Sara and I moving down and my parents and grandparents helping us out, as usual. The thought of it made me depressed. It probably did cause me to work slower, but it wasn't intentional. I eventually got everything fixed up and we got a realtor to put the house up for sale. After a few weeks of living like a bachelor, Sara, my dad, and his brothers, all came up and packed our things and we left Tallahassee forever. I remember pulling out of the driveway for the last time. Sara was crying. I wanted to cry too. I knew life would never be the same and wondered if things would ever be as good as they were before those hurricanes hit my parents' house and turned my world upside down. We pulled out of the driveway and stared at the house for several minutes from the street. We knew we would never see the inside of it again. It was terrible.

The closer we got to Lake Buffum, the more the reality of what life was going to be like started to set in. I wanted to turn the car around and go back to Tallahassee. I felt like I was driving myself to a new prison. I realized that we weren't going to our new home. We were going to be moving in and imposing on my parents, who now thought of me as less capable than I once was. I was now a person with a mental disability, in their eyes. I had no idea of how I would be treated. I had already had a small taste of it when Dad came to my house that night and treated me like a child, ordering me to see my doctor against my will. The entire ride from Tallahassee to Lake Buffum was so depressing. I remember thinking, "I will never pass this way again. No more trips to Mom and Dad's for the weekend. Now, its Mom and Dad's place all the time and forever. Good-Bye Tallahassee. Good-Bye old life."

There was a lot of tension when we first moved in. New rules had to be established as to who had the authority in the house. In all the years of their life before, my girls knew that I was the top authority figure in their life. Now, I was replaced by my mom and dad and lastly, Sara. I was at the very bottom of the authority totem pole. Mom and Dad were the new top dogs in my girl's lives. Mom and Dad provided the roof over their heads and the food they ate. I went from providing everything to nothing. This caused a lot of confusion for the girls. They didn't know who to listen to. I might tell them to do one thing and my parents might contradict me and tell the girls to do something different. Sara also had her opinion. As I said, my opinion was now the least important in the house. So if I ever told the girls to do something that was in contradiction with what Mom, Dad, or Sara wanted,

I was always over ruled. Sara was also always over ruled by my mom and Dad. This caused a lot of new problems for Sara and I.

Another source of friction was that Sara was now going out with her old friend Ashley Rasse, at night. Ashley had moved back to Bartow to live with her parents several years earlier. She now had a new husband and was spending a lot of time introducing Sara to people she knew. Mom said Sara was dressing differently and was always gone at night since she came down to live with them. Mom said she thought Sara was trying to find a new man. This worried me. I felt like I probably deserved whatever Sara wanted to do, even if that meant leaving me for good. I hoped I could talk to her and get her to give me another chance.

Sara was getting ready to go out with Ashley one night when I asked her to stay and talk to me. I hadn't hardly spoken a word to her since we had come back from Tallahassee on that last trip down. I told Sara that I really wanted to just talk. She said that was fine. She called Ashley and told her that she was staying out at the lake with me. Sara and I talked for hours that night. I told her that I realized Le Anne was too much of a risk for me, even though I still had feelings for her. I told Sara that I really did want to try to just work things out between us. I said I realized that I had been mistreating her and that I was going to stop all that. She didn't seem very emotional about anything I said. I told her that I understood if she didn't love me anymore. I said that I deserved that for the way I had treated her. I asked her to give me some time and see if we could learn to love each other again. I told her that I knew I had made a lot of mistakes with her over the years, but I was going to try to be the person I promised her I would be before all the trouble had begun a few months earlier. Sara said she didn't know how she felt about me anymore. She said she just didn't feel much of anything at all. She said that all the stress from my episode at ETO, the Behavioral Health Center, and now living with my parents, had just caused her to not care much about me or anything else anymore. She said she was sorry but she was just being honest. I told her I understood. I asked her to please stop going out with Ashley and try spending time with me instead. She agreed that she would. We went to sleep in the same bed together that night. That was the first night we had slept together in over a month. We didn't even touch each other. We just went to sleep. That was a major step for me. After that night, Sara and I started to get along again. I made extra efforts to be as kind and loving towards her as I knew how. She started to do the same in return. Within a couple weeks, things seemed to be improving.

Once we moved in with my parents, Sara had no idea of what to do about getting a job. Neither did I. Sara was taking classes in physical therapy and working part time with a physical therapist before she left Tallahassee. She had to quit her classes and her job. She was very upset about having her plans wrecked because of me. I'm sure that she was under an incredible amount of stress, but she held together and decided to get a job as a waitress until she could find something better. I dropped the ball and Sara picked it up and kept it moving. Sara saw an ad for Curly Tails in the paper and went down to the restaurant to get an application. She talked with the owner and he hired her on the spot. I didn't like the idea of Sara waiting tables. I remembered all the trouble she got into back when she was a waitress at Floridino's in Lakeland all those years ago. But we had bills and I wasn't working yet, so I didn't say anything.

After a few weeks of living in a daze, I decided to apply at several more local architecture firms. I had already told myself I was never going to work for an architect again if my job at ETO didn't work out. Now, I thought it was the only way that I would ever have a chance at putting our life back together. I sent out resumes to several Polk County firms and even to firms as far away as Orlando and Tampa.

I interviewed with the firm in Orlando first. It took me over an hour and a half to get there with good traffic. I thought that my commute would be a nightmare if I tried to work there. I went ahead and interviewed and was offered a job on the spot. I asked the guy to give me a chance to interview with some other firms and told him I would get back with him within a couple weeks. I hoped I could find something closer to home, even though I loved the firm I had just interviewed with. The place was as well designed as JPA and they had done some impressive projects for Disney, and other big time Orlando clients. They even had a small gym inside the building for the employees to use. They shared the building with a couple other tenants. One of the tenants took photographs for magazine covers. According to the guy who interviewed me, they had celebrities in and out of their building all the time.

I also interviewed with a three Lakeland firms. I canceled all my Tampa interviews. There were three of them as well. The interviews in Lakeland all went well. Two firms offered me a job right away. The one I decided to go with was called Swiley, Curtis, Mundy, & Honeycutt Architects. That's a mouth full. I met with three of the four partners at my interview. I was very nervous before I got to the office for my interview that day. I knew I couldn't tell my interviewers about what had happened at ETO. They wouldn't give me a chance if they found out about what I had done in Tallahassee. Luckily, Warren had written me a very good recommendation letter. He wrote me the letter after I had resigned. I couldn't believe that he managed to find so many good things to say about me after the way I treated him. But, I guess that was the real Warren. I started to think that maybe he really didn't want to ruin me after all. I gave copies of the recommendation letter to all the firms I interviewed with. I think that was probably the most influential thing I had that helped me get a job.

Once I arrived at the office of SCMH Architects, I sat in my car for several minutes and thought about canceling the interview and going back to my parents' house. I finally convinced myself that I could at least get through the interview. No harm could come from lying in the faces of my potential new bosses, right? Somehow I managed to get through the interview well enough that the partners all seemed interested in me. It didn't hurt that I now presented my past work on a laptop and also brought along one of my best full size 24" x 36" renderings. The partners all seemed impressed. After the interview, I mentioned to Mr. Mundy that my dad said that he knew him as a kid. Mr. Mundy asked which Gann was my dad. "Byron Gann", I told him. He smiled and said, "Byron is your dad? We grew up together. I lived just a few houses down the street from your dad and his brothers. How are David, Mark, and Stan?" I went into a little detail about everyone of my dad's brothers. Mr. Mundy told me some stories about things they had done as kids. After that, I think I had sealed the deal.

I got a call a few days later from SCMH Architects. They offered to pay me $34,500 with an instant $2,000 sign on bonus that I would receive on my first day of work with them. It sounded like an offer I couldn't refuse. I thanked Mr. Curtis, who had called me, but told him I was still waiting to hear back from one other firm I had interviewed with. I asked him if I could call him back in a day or two with an answer for him. He sounded a little disappointed, but said that was O.K. The other firm I interviewed with had seemed just as excited about hiring me as SCMH, so I wanted to hear their offer before I made a final decision. They ended up offering me $35,000 to start with no bonus or anything else. I decided to call back SCMH and tell them I would love to have the job. I called Mr. Curtis and told him my news. He seemed very happy about it. He said that they had tried to come up with an offer that I would be interested in. He said that they thought I could probably use the $2,000 bonus right away because I had been out of work for so long already. I thanked him but told him that I wasn't struggling financially because I had saved a lot before I left ETO. That was a lie. We weren't able to pay the bills we had. That was the whole reason I was attempting to work, even though I was scared to death at the idea of going back to another architectural firm.

Mr. Curtis told me that I could start after New Year's day. That's how long I had been out of work at that point, from October 8, 2004 to January 2, 2005. My start date was still over a week away. That gave me plenty of time to get myself worked up about all the possible things that might go wrong at my new job. The night before my first day at work, I could not get myself to go to sleep. I was lying there in bed with thoughts racing in my head again. All I could think about was what had just happened at ETO/Architects and the BHC. I couldn't turn off my brain. As 6:00 am rolled around on the morning that I was supposed to get up and begin my first day of work for SCMH, I was still just lying there in panic. I remember sweating and feeling absolutely terrified. Sara woke up around that time. I told her that I hadn't been able to sleep all night and that I thought I was going to cancel my job with SCMH. I told her that I didn't think that I would be able to handle my new job. She looked at me with an expression of total disappointment. "Why don't you just go on in today and see how things work out.", she said. I told her that I was still thinking about doing that but was afraid I might do or say something weird because I had gone all night without sleeping. I got up and told my parents about how scared I was to start my new job. I told them I was thinking about canceling with SCMH. My dad said, "Don't push yourself too hard. If you don't think you can start right now, just call them and tell them that you can't do it right now. Make up some excuse and leave it at that. Nobody is telling you to go back to work yet. You have been through a lot and it might take some time before you are ready to work again." That was all I needed to hear. I had already been thinking the same thing Dad said. To know that my parents didn't care if I started working right away gave me relief.

I called Mr. Curtis at around 7:50 am. He answered the phone. I said, "Mr. Curtis, I have some bad news. I'm not going to be able to start working with you guys today. I don't think I will be able to work for you at all." He asked me why I had changed my mind. I said, "I'm sorry but I've got a lot of things going on with my family still. My grandfather is dying from cancer and I think he might need my help. I don't think I am in a state of mind that would make a very good employee for you." I said all this with pauses between every few words. I was so nervous that I couldn't speak properly. He said, "Well, I'm sorry to hear this Scott. I hope everything works out for you." He may have said something else, but I don't remember. I was just so relieved that I had ended what might have been a very terrible day at SCMH. I told Mr. Curtis that I was sorry I had waited so long to tell him my decision. I told him I hadn't made up my mind until that morning. He didn't respond. Then he said, "All right, well, good-bye Scott.", and he hung up. I felt relief but also was totally ashamed of myself. I knew I was letting Sara and the girls down. We really needed me to get a job so that we could start trying to get our life back together. Our house in Tallahassee hadn't sold yet, but we did have a person who was very interested in it.

The realtor in Tallahassee was a guy who was like a grandfather to Crystal Mathews. His name was Mr. Gaskin. He and his wife had known Crystal since she was a child and knew Crystal's mother and father before they died. Crystal's parents both died young and Mr. Gaskin and his wife acted like Crystal was their adopted child. He was a very nice man. We chose him to be our realtor because Crystal had told us what a great person he was. Mr. Gaskin found a young guy who was interested in buying his first house. He was a single guy in his twenties, Mr. Gaskin told me. It took several weeks for the prospective buyer to get all the approvals for a loan and reach an agreement with us on the price. I wanted to sell our house for $130,000. We had only bought it less than three years earlier for $89,000. I felt like I had made enough improvements to the place to justify the new price. The housing market was also booming. Everyone's house value was going up by leaps and bounds. I drove around our neighborhood and looked at several houses similar to ours that were asking for $125,000 to $129,000. I thought I would raise the bar a little higher and see what happened. The guy who wanted to buy the house said that he would agree to the price if we had a new roof put on it. Mr. Gaskin worked out all the details of hiring a roofing contractor to replace the roof and it only cost us about $8,000. Mr. Gaskin said the cost of the new roof would be subtracted from the price of the house. Once the guy's bank loaned him the money to buy our house, the cost of the roof would go directly from the guy's loan to the roof contractor. We never had to put up any money at all. So, we ended up selling the house for a little under $122,000. Mr. Gaskin only charged us a fee of 2.5% for his services. That was less than anyone else would have charged. I thought that he was very generous.

In the end, we received a little over $25,000 dollars from the sale of the house. It was money we needed to pay off bills that were piling up. My Forester had not been paid for in several months and I was starting to get threatening letters in the mail from the bank telling me that they might reposes my car. I had called them and told them that I was waiting for my house to sell and would soon be able to catch up on my payments. They gave me an extension, but kept adding late fees. We also had credit card bills that were collecting interest and were several months past due. Once the house sold, we paid down all our accumulating debts and spent about $5,000 just to clear our credit cards and catch up on car payments. In a perfect world the extra money would have been set aside as a down payment for our next house. With me not working, the money we received from the sale of our house slowly began dwindling away to pay the bills. I was causing us to lose everything we had. I felt terrible. I began to go into a deep depression.

My grandmother, Nanny, asked me what I thought about helping her take care of Granddaddy, since I was not jumping into a new job. I told her I thought I could handle it. Granddaddy had already been to Lakeland Regional Medical Center for the last time in the middle of all the hurricanes. His health was just another dimension of stress for me. I knew he was dying, but the doctors still hadn't given up hope for him until after that second hurricane came through Lake Buffum. Granddaddy was in so much pain that he had to be taken to the hospital so that they could give him some medication to relieve him. They put him on Duragesic. It was a morphine patch that slowly absorbed into the skin. The drug relieved his pain but also ate away at his ability to reason and act like himself. It made me very sad when I got my first glimpse of what Granddaddy would turn into. Granddaddy called me on the phone one day, when I still lived in Tallahassee, and said, "Scott, I left the gate open at the pasture. Do you know where I put the key?" Granddaddy was calling me from his hospital bed phone at Lakeland Regional Medical Center. He was having some kind of delirious moment and got the idea to call me and ask about locking a gate at his pasture. He hadn't owned any cows or had a cow pasture in several years. I knew what he said made no sense at all. I just said, "No, Granddaddy, I don't know where the key is. Don't worry about the gate. I'll close it for you." I had already heard stories from my parents that Granddaddy was starting to lose his mind. They told me that the best thing to do when he said something odd, was to just play along, or he would become confused and upset. That phone call from Granddaddy came just a week or so before I was committed to the BHC. Like I said, Granddaddy's health was just one more element of stress that helped send me over the edge.

Granddaddy was a very important person in my life. He and Nanny were the ones who took me to church that night that I decided to get Baptized when I was 12 years old. He gave me my first experiences of what it was like to do hard work. He would take me out to his cow pasture and let me mow the fields with his tractor. We also put up barbed wire fence, fed the cows, and helped stack hay bales in his barn. I had spent a lot of quality time with Granddaddy as a kid. When I got into high school, Granddaddy was the one who told me to focus on my grades so I could go to college and get a decent job. Granddaddy was the one who offered to pay for my college. He had lined up my first drafting job. He and Nanny had baled Sara and I out of countless financial tight spots. He was a very important person to me. With the realization that he might not be around much longer, I feared for my future and the future of my immediate family and especially for Nanny. I knew she loved Granddaddy and didn't know how she would cope with losing him. These fears caused me a lot of worrying and stress. When Nanny asked me if I thought I could help take care of Granddaddy as he died, I told her that was the least that I could do. He had helped me out my entire life, I could never repay him and Nanny for all the good things they had done for me. I hoped that helping take care of him, as he died, would somehow help pay back a little of the debt that I owed him. It was a funny thing. Before I went nuts and got myself locked up in an insane asylum, one of the primary reasons I wanted to move down to Polk County was to help Nanny. In a strange series of events, I ended up doing just that. Maybe God does work in mysterious ways after all.

I agreed to make Granddaddy my new full time job. Instead of working in some office, I went to Nanny and Granddaddy's house every day. I eventually started living there throughout the week and trading places with my parents on the weekends just so I could see Sara and the girls for a little while. All that time away from Sara and the girls made Sara and I start to have less and less of a real relationship. She spent most of her time with the other people that worked at Curly Tails. I started to wonder if she was going to change again and be like she was when she worked at Floridino's. Sara would stop by Nanny and Granddaddy's house at night after she got off work. She would usually talk to Nanny and spend very little time talking to me. It started to bother me. I asked her if she would spend the night with me at Nanny and Granddaddy's house every now and then. She did on a few occasions. It was usually very frustrating for me when she did. At night when we would lie in bed together, she wouldn't talk to me the way she always had. I would try to put my arm around her or lie next to her and she would say it was making her uncomfortable and unable to sleep. She asked me not to touch her. She said she just didn't think we should be having any physical contact because she didn't think of me the way she used to. This just made me more depressed.

Sara did have a short conversation with me one night that I remember. She told me that there were times, recently, when she had thought about leaving me. She said that she wished she would have left me when I was having my little thing with Le Anne. She said that everyone would understand her leaving me for cheating on her. She said that if she left me now, she knew my family would all hate her because I was under a lot of stress taking care of Granddaddy. She said that she hoped things would change for the better soon. She said she didn't think she could live like she was having to for very long. But she said she couldn't think of a way to fix anything either. I just laid there and didn't say anything. I was afraid that if I talked, I would start crying.

After Granddaddy went to the hospital that last time, between the second and third hurricanes that hit Lake Buffum, the doctors told us all that Granddaddy would die from the cancer he had. They said he was not responding to the radiation and chemotherapy. The tumor that was in his back was still spreading. They had also found a tumor in one of his lungs. They said that the cancer had already spread into his bones and was causing them to disintegrate. They said he would most likely have a very slow and painful death. The doctor told us that Granddaddy now had two options, Home Health Care or Hospice Care. He said that Home Health Care would do everything they could to prolong his life. They said he would end up coming back to the hospital at some point and would be hooked up to respirators, feeding tubes, and drugs that would keep him alive for as long as they could. The doctor said he didn't recommend this because Granddaddy would just be suffering and would probably just spend most of his time unconscious and on life support machines that did all of his breathing and feeding. He said that scenario was usually harder on the patient and the family. He recommended Hospice Care. He said Hospice had a different agenda. He explained that Hospice Care is "End of Life" care. He said the goal of Hospice was to make the patient as comfortable as possible as their body went through the natural process of shutting down. He said this sometimes took weeks, sometimes months, or even years for people in Granddaddy's condition. He said he couldn't give us a timeline for when he thought Granddaddy would die. He said everyone was different, but that Granddaddy would definitely die from his cancer. The doctor went on to explain that Hospice Care allowed Granddaddy to come home and die in his own house. He said that nurses would come and bathe him and give him drugs to keep his pain levels low. The doctor said that Hospice Care was a more humane way of letting a person die. I wanted to cry as I heard the doctor speaking so calmly about all this. He was talking about my grandfather's death as if it were a matter of fact now. He gave us no hope that Granddaddy could be cured. It was very upsetting for everyone.

The worst moment was when this news was delivered to Granddaddy himself. The doctor let us tell Granddaddy about the conversation we had just had with him. Mom and Nanny broke the news to him. Nanny couldn't hardly even talk. I tried to say a few things to Granddaddy about what the doctor had said about Hospice Care. I can't imagine what it must have been like for Granddaddy to hear his family telling him that he was surely going to die from cancer. Granddaddy said he wanted to hear this news from the doctor. The doctor came in and spoke with Granddaddy. Then the reality set in for him. Granddaddy started saying that he wanted a new doctor and that he didn't like the doctor who had just told him the horrible news. It was very sad.

Granddaddy said that he wanted to go home if no one there was going to help him. So, he and Nanny decided they would begin the process of Hospice Care. Hospice Care started about two weeks before I ended up at the BHC. So, by the time I started spending all my weekdays with Nanny and Granddaddy, they had already been doing the Hospice routine for about a month or two, I'm not really sure exactly, because Hospice took over for my grandfather during the time when my life became a blur.

During the day, my routine was very simple. All I had to do was sit in the room where Granddaddy now had a hospital bed. It was his old TV room. The TV was still there. There was also a couch and chair. We moved out two of the chairs to make room for his hospital bed. The only thing I did was help change Granddaddy's diaper and get him something to drink when he was thirsty and feed him when he was hungry. Granddaddy had to wear a diaper because he could no longer get out of bed. He was too weak to get up and walk to the toilet that we had set up in the TV room. I tried to help him out of bed several times when he asked me to. I would get him out of bed as carefully as I could. He would be moaning and complaining of pain the whole time. It took several minutes to get him situated from a lying down position to the point where he was standing up on the floor. It was scary because I was afraid he would fall and hurt himself. I pretty much carried him to the toilet, supporting as much of his weight as I could, while still letting him stand on his own two feet. His legs had shrunk to the diameter of my arms. All the muscles had been eaten away by the cancer. He couldn't support his own weight. Eventually Granddaddy would manage to sit down on the toilet. Then he usually wouldn't be able to do anything. He would sit there for a few minutes and tell me, "I swear I thought I had to use the bathroom." Then he would complain that his back was hurting and we would begin the process of getting him back in the bed. This usually took several more minutes because it was just the reverse of everything we had just done.

After going through the bathroom process many times with Granddaddy not doing anything, Nanny and Peter, Granddaddy's nurse, said that I should just let him stay in the bed. Peter said that it was too dangerous for Granddaddy to be getting up now. He said his bones might fracture of his skin might tear and bleed profusely. The medicine they were giving Granddaddy made his skin thin and fragile. One time I was just helping him sit up in bed when a section of skin on his arm peeled off. The area was about as big around as a small apple. I wanted to throw up when I saw what I had done. Granddaddy just said, "Owey! I think you just pinched my arm Scott." His arm started bleeding and some of the skin that peeled off his arm was stuck to my hand. It was a scene straight out of a horror movie. That spot on his arm never fully healed before he died.

The most humiliating thing for Granddaddy, and me, was definitely the process of having to clean up his mess after he went to the bathroom. The reason I kept trying to put him on the toilet was because I didn't want him to have to use the bathroom in his diaper. I knew that would be a very difficult thing for anyone to have to do. I felt so sorry for him. He had been one of the greatest people I knew all my life, now he was having to lie in a diaper full of his own crap and let me and Nanny clean up the mess. It was the most terrible thing I have ever had to do. I haven't had to experience many people dying, but cancer has got to be one of the worst ways for a person to die, the humiliation and the slow process of the disintegration of the body, it is all so horrible. The cancer slowly ate him alive.

The best thing for Granddaddy was that he wasn't usually aware of what was happening to him. The drugs that Hospice provided him seemed to do away with most of his pain. They also made him delirious. It seemed like he was having dreams while his eyes were open. He would see things and hear things that weren't real. Sometimes he would sit in his bed and think he was out in the woods hunting rabbits or deer. He would even hold out his hand like he was holding a gun and make the sound of a gun going off. "Did you see that? I got him!", he would say. Most of the time he thought he was either fishing or at his pasture with his cows. It was scary to me at first. After a while though, there were times when I couldn't help but laugh at some of the things he would say. He was very different from his old self once the medication took hold of him. He would say things that he would never have said before the drugs. One time he was telling my dad that he saw Nanny running around outside the house streaking. We all started laughing. My grandmother is the most reserved person I know. Streaking is definitely not something she would ever do. It was pretty funny. We had to try to find humor in the situation because most of the time spent with Granddaddy could be very depressing.

One of the things that I really didn't like to see was how Granddaddy talked to Nanny sometimes. He sometimes thought she was forcing him to lay in his bed all day. He would tell me, "Your Nanny thinks I can't walk around anymore. She likes to keep me here in this bed and make me crap in my diaper. You've seen me walk around. Remember yesterday when I walked around the house." This would usually lead to him asking me to help him out of bed. Sometimes I would, just because it killed me to tell him that he couldn't walk and that he had not walked yesterday or the day, week, or month before. He hadn't been able to walk for months. Like I said, his legs were about as big around as my arms. They were mainly just skin and bone. His feet looked like those of a corpse. They were almost white and the toenails were a yellow color. I have had dreams about seeing Granddaddy walking around with his legs looking the way that they did before he died.

The thing I disliked the most about taking care of Granddaddy was having to visit with all the people that came to see him. I was very depressed during the time that Granddaddy was dying. I didn't want to be around any more people than I had to. When people came to visit, I usually grabbed a newspaper and pretended to be busy reading it while they were there. Most of the people that visited were family members. I knew that they probably all thought I was crazy and that Nanny was just trying to keep me busy so I wouldn't do something else as stupid as what I had done in Tallahassee. People would tell me that they appreciated what I was doing for my grandmother, but I didn't believe them. I figured that they were probably just trying to be polite. I figured that they really thought of me more like they might think of a retarded person. They knew I had a mental disability. So I figured they probably just associated me with crazy or retarded people. It made me not want to be around any of them. I tried to do whatever I could to minimize my conversations with them. Sometimes I would actually want to talk, but would never feel like I had anything worth saying. So, most of the time, I just stared blankly at a newspaper and kept reliving all the things that happened at ETO and the BHC.

About the only person I liked to see come over was Granddaddy's nurse, Peter. Peter was a very likable guy and always treated me like I was anybody else. We never had any real conversations other than things related to Granddaddy's condition, but I still felt like I was able to talk to him better than I could talk to just about anyone else.

A few months before Granddaddy died, Sara and I were out at the lake house one weekend and she revealed some disturbing news. Sara had been very cold and distant towards me for quite a while. I remember that the girls had gone to bed and I was outside sitting in front of a fire in my parents yard. Sara came out and sat on the opposite side of the fire from me. I started talking about how I was sick of hearing her tell stories about this chef that worked at Curly Tails. I said, "You've got something going on with this guy don't you?" She just sat there and didn't say anything. Then after a couple minutes she calmly started telling me about her and the chef. She said that the chef had made several moves on her and that she had refused him each time. She said one night he brought a guitar to work and sang a song to her after work that night. He told her that he wrote the song for her. Sara said that was when she started to like him. She said that was why she had not wanted me to touch her for the last few months, because she was beginning to have feelings for the chef at a freaking barbeque restaurant. She said she felt like she was falling in love with this guy at work and didn't think she loved me anymore. I thought, "This is a total repeat of the time she worked at Floridino's". Sara went on to tell me that she had given this guy a ride to his house one night. She said they both got out of her car and kissed in his driveway. She said she came to Nanny's house that same night after dropping him off. She said she felt very guilty about what she had done and never did it again. She said she now wanted the chef to leave her alone and that she wanted me to forgive her. I didn't even feel angry about it. I even laughed and said, "Well, it sounds like you've got a pretty big problem to take care of." I told her that I didn't blame her for liking someone else. After all, I had recently done the same thing while I was at the BHC. I said, "I guess we are now even." She laughed a little and said, "So, you aren't mad at me?" I said, "No. I don't deserve you anymore. It means a lot to me that you would even tell me about what you did. Thanks." After that she came up to me and hugged me. That was the first time she had touched me in months. She started crying. She said she never would have believed that our lives would be this screwed up just a year ago. I apologized. I told her that it was all my fault. She said it wasn't anyone's fault.

It was around this time that I started to see a psychiatrist again. Just before Sara told me the news about her and the chef, I told Nanny that I thought Sara was going to leave me. I remember crying in front of her as I told her that Sara didn't care about me anymore. Nanny said I should see a psychiatrist that she had used years earlier when she had her first episode of severe depression. Nanny said that she would pay for it. She said I had earned it from all the help I had given her with Granddaddy. She set up an appointment for me to see Dr. Barnes.

My first meeting with Dr. Barnes was very different from my meetings with Dr. Veneble at the BHC. With Dr. Veneble I was always upbeat and very talkative. I was in mania when I met Dr. Veneble. When I met Dr. Barnes, I was in depression.

Sara came with me to my first appointment with Dr. Barnes. Sara and I walked into a room with Dr. Barnes and she started asking me why I needed to see her. I told her that I thought my wife was going to leave me and this was what my grandmother had recommended that I do. I started crying again. I tried to explain to Dr. Barnes how I felt worthless and knew I didn't deserve Sara. I told her about my episode with ETO and the BHC. I told her that I didn't have a job and all I did was sit around my grandparents' house all day, doing very little to nothing. It was hard for me to talk because all I could do was cry. I have never been the type of person to cry often. I had been to funerals for my great grandparents and felt like I should be crying, but couldn't bring myself to do it. Sara and I had been through several near break ups and I never cried. I didn't cry when I realized she had left me for that kid at Floridino's all those years ago. Why was I so upset now? It was because I felt like Sara was the only person on earth who really understood what I had been through and now she was abandoning me. I felt like if she didn't care about me anymore, then no one did. That's why I was so upset.

Dr. Barnes said she couldn't stop Sara from leaving me. Sara never said that she would or would not leave. She didn't say much of anything. She just sat and watched as I made a fool of myself. Dr. Barnes said that I needed to take an anti-depressant. She asked if I was taking any medication. I told her how I had stopped taking the pills that they gave me at the BHC shortly after they let me out because they made me tired and I didn't think they were helping me. She said she was going to prescribe me a medication and that it was very important to keep taking it until she told me I could stop. She prescribed Lexapro. It was a mood-stabilizing drug that was supposed to help lift me out of my depression. Dr. Barnes wanted to see me every other week. Each visit cost about $180. Nanny wrote me a check every time I saw Dr. Barnes. So, by that point, not only was I not much of help to Nanny, I was costing her money on top of it. My dream to come down to Polk County and help my family had now totally backfired. Instead, I was becoming the usual problem that I had always been. My family was taking care of me once again.

I told Nanny that Sara was getting stressed out from having to take care of the kids by herself at night. Nanny said that I should start spending the night at the lake again and have my mom or dad stay with her at night. So, that's what we did. I started going back out to the lake most weeknights and all weekend. Sara and I now got to spend as much time together as we used to when we lived in Tallahassee. It was nice, but I also felt like I was letting down my parents and grandparents. My only responsibility was to help take care of my granddad and I was now failing at that too.

Still, it was nice to get to pretend that life was a little more normal. Mom and Dad usually both slept at Nanny's house; that left Sara and I with the lake house to ourselves most nights. Life was almost normal for us when Mom and Dad weren't around. We could cook our own meals and tell our kids what to do without having to be overruled by what my parents thought we should do. We could talk to each other the way we usually talked. When my parents were around we didn't discuss personal issues. Now we could talk about problems or whatever we wanted to, without having to worry about my parents listening in. It was nice, for a while.

One day I made the mistake of telling Mom about Sara and the chef. She was instantly furious about it. She said that Sara had a lot of nerve to cheat on me while Mom and Dad were helping put a roof over her head and raise our kids. The topic of Sara and the chef came up because mom was complaining to me about Sara. She was listing all kinds of things about Sara that irritated her. She mentioned that Sara never seemed to talk about me or want to be around me. That's when I tried to explain to Mom why Sara had been acting so different. I tried to explain that Sara had gone through a period where she felt like she had fallen out of love with me (for good reasons) and was beginning to have feelings for another man. As I said, telling this to my mother was a big mistake.

I thought I could tell Mom the story and once she heard the part about Sara apologizing and wanting to be with me, Mom would be understanding and let the topic go. Instead she got very angry with Sara. Mom said she couldn't believe that Sara would add to my stress at a time when Mom thought I was already dealing with too much. Mom said that Sara didn't love me. She said Sara was just biding her time until something better came along. Mom said I needed to tell Sara that she needed to get her act together or move out. Mom said she was tired of feeling like Sara was just using everyone. She said Sara had better act like she wanted to work things out between us or Mom and Dad were going to kick her out themselves.

The next day I told Sara about what my mom had said. I told her that I agreed with my mom. I said that if she didn't love me, she should leave me. I said I wasn't mad about her and the chef. I was mad at how cold she had been towards me for the last several months. I said, "I know you don't love me because I don't have a job. If I was working, you would be a different person. You wouldn't have cheated on me. You would keep trying to work on our relationship because I would be providing things for you and the girls. You have given up on me because I don't feel like I can work right now. If you have given up on me, then just leave. You can leave right now. I won't try to stop you. I'll even pack your things for you." Sara started crying hysterically. She said she was trying to work on our relationship. She said that was the whole point behind telling me about her and the chef. She was mad at me for bringing my parents in on it. She said she couldn't leave because she had nowhere to go. She said that now she wanted to leave, not because she wanted to get away from me, but because she didn't know how she was going to face my parents after knowing that they knew what she had done.

The next night I spent the night with Nanny and Granddaddy. Nanny and I were watching TV in her living room. We couldn't watch TV around my granddad anymore because the things he saw on TV caused him to have hallucinations and he would either get scared or angry. As we were watching TV, the phone rang. It was Sara. She was crying and I could hear my parents yelling at her in the background to get off the phone. Sara ignored them and told me that I had to come out to the lake and put an end to a fight between Sara and my parents. She said that they were lecturing her about her bad behavior and she was sick of them. She cussed at my mom while she was on the phone. Keep in mind that my two girls were also in the house. It was well past their bedtime, but I bet they heard everything that was said.

Sara was begging me to come out to the lake. She sounded hysterical. Then my dad got on the phone. He said that they were just having a little chat with Sara and that I didn't need to worry about a thing. He said for me to stay at Nanny's house. He said that Sara needed to work out a problem she had created for herself and it wasn't my job to rescue her. I asked him to please just try to give Sara a break because I had just reamed her out the night before. I said I thought she was going to try to work things out with me and that he and Mom should leave her alone. He said that Sara had shown a lot of disrespect towards them and that was the main problem they were having with her. He again said that I needed to stay with Nanny and let them work out the problem on their own. I said I would.

I saw Sara the next night and she cried to me about how my parents had threatened to kick her out of the house and take her girls from her. I assured her that nothing was going to happen. She said that we had to find a place of our own if we were ever going to work things out between us. She said she thought my mom was hell bent on getting rid of her. I said that she probably was, because Sara had cussed her out. I told her my mom was not the type to forgive and forget. I told Sara that she had probably just made her life a lot harder than it needed to be. I told her that she should just try to stay away from Mom for a while and be as nice to her and my dad as she could. Sara said that she wanted to get an apartment and all of us move into it so that we could leave my parents and just work on being a family. That was probably a very good idea. Had I agreed to do that, Sara and I might still be together today. But, at the time, I didn't think it was a good idea at all. The main reason was the obvious one, we couldn't afford to live on our own. I couldn't see the point in trying to struggle and make our kids suffer just because Sara could not figure out how to get along with my mother.

Not long after that night of the big fight between Sara and my parents, my mother retired from her job as a teacher at Lewis Elementary School in Ft. Meade. Mom said that she had just become too exhausted of her work and she was ready to retire. I think what really happened was that she became too stressed out by all the things that were going on outside of her job. She had to deal with a house that was still in disrepair from the hurricanes. Her father was near death from cancer. And then to top it all off, she had to deal with my wife, who she despised, on a daily basis. I think the combination of all those factors is what made my mom retire. I don't think she retired from too much stress at work. She retired because she had too much stress at home.

On Thursday night, June 30th, 2005, Sara and I had put the girls to bed and were watching TV when Nanny called me out at the lake house. She said, "Scott, your Granddaddy just died." I said, "I'm sorry Nanny. Should we come in to town?" She was crying and said, "No, your mom and dad and your uncle Larry are here right now. I'm fine. People are already on the way to take Granddaddy. He won't be here by the time you get here." I told her that I loved her and would see her the next day. Then I hung up the phone. The thing I felt most after getting that call was relief. We had watched Granddaddy deteriorate from a witty, vibrant man into a living corpse that was asleep most of the day and existed as a mockery of his former self.

Cancer is cruel. It changed my grandfather both mentally and physically. Even when he was asleep and looked peaceful, I felt so sorry for him. He had lost so much weight and his body was covered in sores and red splotches caused from the medication he had to take. He never talked much the last few weeks he was alive. He usually slept day and night. When he did open his eyes, he usually just stared straight ahead and didn't acknowledge anything that anyone said. We had to try to force him to drink and eat. The catheter bag that hung from his bed was filled with urine and what looked like mucus that was draining from his bladder. In the weeks before he died, his urine became almost a dark brown. He would go for days without ever having a bowel movement. We knew his body was shutting down.

Peter had been telling us for weeks that he thought my grandfather would die in a few days. Peter told us that Granddaddy's breathing and heart rate showed that his body was finally shutting down. He said that Granddaddy was a very strong man. He said most patients didn't live as long as he had with that level of cancer. Every day Peter came by and announced that my Granddaddy was going to die within a few days, a little countdown would begin in my head. I checked on him all the time when I was at his house. I remember watching him lie there with his eyes closed. I was watching to see how long he took between each breath. One time he went several minutes without ever breathing. Then he took several short breaths in a row, like he was trying to catch his breath. Nanny said she had seen him do the same thing several times before. Peter said that was one of the last things a patient did before they died. He said Granddaddy's heart rate was so high that I would have to run as fast as I could for several minutes to make my heart behave the way his was while he was just lying there.

All the weeks of anticipating Granddaddy's death, at any moment, made the actual event less emotional. I had already cried many times over the last year as I thought about life without my Granddaddy. Now that I knew he had finally died, I felt happy for him. I thought, "If anybody deserved to go to heaven, it was Granddaddy. I hope I get to see you again one day Granddaddy. I love you."

I was glad that he had spent most of the end of his life imagining that he was in the pasture with his cows or fishing in some lake. I thought that was a much better way for a person to die than to suffer and know just how bad things really were. Hospice is definitely the better way to let a person die. I think we would all have had a much harder time if Granddaddy was actually aware of what was going on and we had to keep trying to explain everything to him. And to think that he would have ended up with tubes going down his throat for food and air with machines pumping drugs and breathing for him, if we had chosen to go with Home Health Care. He might have lived as a vegetable for a couple more years if we had taken that route. I was thankful that it ended when it did. Now Nanny could begin to mourn and have closure. She had not hardly left her house in almost a year. She could now move on with her life. She had done her very best to comfort her husband right up until his death. She had endured months of verbal abuse from him. She had cried many times in the last year. Now it was her chance to find some peace, if that was at all possible.

We had the funeral for Granddaddy a few days after he died. All of his family and Nanny's family showed up along with most of the people from Main Street Baptist Church and other family friends. We had his service at Main Street Baptist Church. The building was filled to capacity. My cousin, Shane, gave a speech about Granddaddy and how he had led the life of a true Christian. Shane was also a preacher. He was a very good speaker. His speech about Granddaddy was very well done. Shane talked about how my grandparents had lived their whole life helping everyone they could. He talked about how generous they were with their time and money. He mentioned how my grandparents had lived their entire life together in that little house in Bartow, on Mc Addo Lane, where Granddaddy died. He said everyone knew that they could have afforded to live in a much fancier home, but that wasn't Granddaddy's style.

Granddaddy was a cowboy, who grew up poor, on a farm that his parents' did not own. Granddaddy's parents were sharecroppers. They worked another man's land to make their living and had very little for themselves. Granddaddy worked hard his whole life so that he could help his parents and Nanny's parents. Once they had kids of their own, they raised them to be strong Christians. I've already talked about all the things that Granddaddy did for me personally. I can't imagine how much good he did for everyone else. He loved his family. He always gave us good advice and lived a life that showed us how a person should be. He was my hero. I will always be in his debt. The only way I know to ever repay him is to try and raise my girls as best as I can by his example. I know I'm not doing that good of a job. But I'm trying to.

I remember going to my Nanny's house for the first time after Granddaddy had died. The Hospice workers had already taken away his hospital bed. Now the TV room had a big empty spot that reminded us all that a great man had once laid there for a year and died. It was weird to be in that room without Granddaddy. I had spent so many hours there listening to him talk about the hallucinations he was having and just watching him sleep. Now there was just a big empty floor. Granddaddy would never be there again. I started to wish he was still alive, even if he was so sick that all he could do was talk about the dream he was living in. I missed him dearly. I think that was what sent me over the edge for my next big trip.

Chapter 41: The Switch Goes Back On

I remember having a dream myself one night shortly after Granddaddy died. In my dream I was standing beside Granddaddy and he was lying in his bed. I was crying. I thought he was dead. Then he opened his eyes. Then he sat up, got out of bed, and began to walk around. He said, "Scott, why are you crying about me? I'm all right now. I can walk again." Then he walked around the house. Then he said, "I've got to leave you, but you'll be fine without me. I'll see you from time to time." After that, he walked out of the house. I woke up and I was crying. My pillow was wet from tears. The dream seemed so real. I felt comforted by it. I felt like I had just spent time with my granddad that was as real as if it had actually happened. I wondered if I had just somehow received a message from Granddaddy. I couldn't forget that dream and how real it seemed to me.

A couple weeks after Granddaddy died, I decided I would try to get a job again. I thought I would try to do something other than work at an architectural firm. I had fantasized for years about working at some job that required manual labor and let me be outside most of the time. Being trapped indoors and staring at a computer screen all day was the main thing I disliked about working for an architect. The monotony of office life had worn thin with me. I thought about how nice it would be to have the job of a plant nursery worker or a landscaper. I thought that if I did something like that, I would be outside and with nature all day. I always loved to be outside as much as I could. That was one of the things I loved most about my job as a roof inspector with MLD Architects. When I was working that job I could spend all day in the sun if I wanted to. If I wanted to do some hard work, all I had to do was help the roofers. I decided I would try to find a job that let me be outside and do some hard physical labor. I went to a local temp worker agency and filled out an application.

I received a job in just a few days after applying with the temp agency. I liked how simple the process was. There was no interview. No dressing up to impress people. All I had to do was fill out a form that showed my work history and stated how little I was willing to work for. I filled out the part about my wage as "No minimum". I wasn't concerned with how much I would make. I was just exploring what other jobs I might be able to work. I just wanted to see what it was like to work a labor type job. I felt like I had my fill of sitting at a desk all day. I wanted to see how other people worked to live.

The temp agency got me a job with a company that produced chemicals that were used by the local phosphate mines. The company was Arr Maz Chemicals. The temp agency called me and told me when I could start and what I needed to have with me when I showed up. It was simple. The girl from the temp agency told me, "You need to wear blue jeans, a t-shirt, steel toe boots, and a hard hat. Come by the office and we'll give you a hard hat." That sounded like my kind of dress code. I hated having to dress up for work every day; the dress shirts and slacks, the tie, and dress socks and shoes. Those things made me uncomfortable. Now I was going to be wearing nothing but t-shirts and blue jeans. That seemed good to me. "What's the pay like?", I asked the girl from the temp agency. She said, "It's a lot less than what you are probably used to, $8.50 per hour. I said, "That's not a problem for me. I'll take the job. Anything is better than staring at a computer all day."

My first day at Arr Maz was very easy. I walked into the front office building and met with the secretary. She told me to go outside and find Sam Houston. She said he would be at a building that was behind the main office building. She pointed out a window to it. I walked outside and realized that there were three other buildings on the Arr Maz property and about 15 giant silos that stored the chemicals that they made. I found Sam and introduced myself to him. Sam was a big fat man in his 50's with the look of a person who had endured a life of hard labor. His hands were calloused. He had a deep voice and he used it to scare the crap out of people when he was angry with them. Sam said hello and that was about it. He was busy doing some paperwork. The building Sam was in was really just a giant metal frame with a roof and two walls. The other two ends were open. At night they closed giant gates that swung shut and secured all the equipment that was inside. Just to try and start a conversation, I asked Sam, "So what kinds of chemicals do you guys make here at Arr Maz?" He looked up and said, "We make several different chemicals. Go sit over at that picnic table until I can find Melvin. Melvin is going to be training you today." I thought, "This guy seems like an asshole. Maybe he is that way because he probably has to deal with a lot of stupid people. He probably assumes I'm just another idiot."

After about ten minutes of waiting at the picnic table, a black guy in his forties came walking up and started talking to Sam. Sam said, "Melvin, take Scott here. He's going to be your help for the day." That was my introduction to Melvin.

Melvin seemed to be a pretty friendly guy. He shook my hand and introduced himself. He told me to follow him and said, "Well we've got it easy today. All we have to do is get some water out of the area around these tanks over here." Melvin and I walked to a group of 7 silos that were surrounded by a low wall that stood about three feet tall. The silos were on a giant slab of concrete that was probably about 200' x 100'. Rain water had been collecting in the low spots around the tanks. There were drains that water was supposed to drain into. Pumps were supposed to pull the water through the drains and pipes and into a retention pond. A couple of the pumps were not working, so we had to take giant squeegees and push the water into one of the drains that had a working pump. It ended up taking us all day to get all the water out. I loved it. This was exactly the type of mindless job that I was hoping for. All we did was walk around with our squeegees and push water from one spot to another. Melvin and I talked the whole time we were working. That was another thing I loved. In all my past jobs, I always sat in a cubicle that separated me from everyone else. The offices I had worked in did not invite a lot of chatter between the employees as they worked. The office was usually quiet except for the sounds of mice and keyboards clicking away. You might have a few minutes here or there when you went back to the water cooler or on Friday afternoon when we usually had "Beer Friday". Now I could talk as much as I wanted and whenever I wanted. It was just Melvin and I. There were no bosses within hearing range to worry about.

My job at Arr Maz was always manual labor. We were either sweeping floors, scrubbing out the inside of the chemical silos, breaking down metal crates that were used to transport chemicals, or moving things around with forklifts and Bob Cats. That was another thing I like about Arr Maz. I learned how to use a forklift and Bob Cat in my first week. We used the forklifts to carry off the metal crates that had to be thrown away every few days. That was something that baffled me. I couldn't believe that it was more cost effective to cut up and recycle these metal crates than to re-use them. Sam said it was. That's why they did it. The metal crates were large enough to hold four large garbage cans. They actually held giant plastic containers that were filled with chemicals. The containers went inside the metal crates and were loaded onto semis and trains for transport. Some of the companies that used the chemicals sent the containers and crates back. It was one of my jobs to use a Sawsall to cut up the metal crates and take out the plastic containers inside them. The metal was taken to a metal recycler. The plastic was also recycled. I had to take the plastic and the metal and put in giant dumpsters that were hauled to recycling plants every few days.

We used the Bob Cats to move around dirt and whenever we needed to haul off a load of something that was too heavy to carry from one end of the facility to the other. The entire Arr Maz plant was probably around 15 acres. It was a big place. Other things we did in my short time there were: dig trenches for underground utilities to be laid, and move out the office furniture of one building and put it in another. Arr Maz had just bought a building that was adjacent to their property. The former owner had us move his belongings to a storage building that Arr Maz owned. The furniture-moving job was my last task before I quit Arr Maz. I only worked there for five weeks. During that five weeks I went from acting pretty normal to behaving like a full on lunatic.

The first thing I remember that was strange was a morning after I had been working at Arr Maz for about a week. I had to take the girls from the lake house to Nanny's house every morning before I went to work. Mom and Dad were still spending the night with Nanny. They were still sleeping in Bartow at Nanny's, partly because they didn't like the idea of Nanny sleeping in a house all by herself at night, partly because Mom and Dad wanted to give Sara and I as much time alone as possible, and partly because Mom and Dad didn't want to be around Sara any more than they had to.

Mom took Liza with her to the school she had taught at in Ft. Meade, Lewis Elementary. That was where Liza started going to school after we left Tallahassee. Liza went to first and second grade at Lewis Elementary. My dad took Gwen to a pre school in Bartow that I went to when I was her age, First Methodist Pre School.

I remember driving to Nanny's house with the girls one morning and thinking of all the stress I had caused my parents since we had all moved in with them. They were providing us a place to sleep and were buying some of our groceries too. They did all this, but couldn't feel comfortable enough in their own house to sleep there at night anymore. The tension between Sara and my parents was too much for them. They preferred to stay away from us as much as they could. It made me feel terrible. I also felt guilty for being angry with my dad for so long. I had partially blamed him for causing me to go to the BHC. He was the one who forced me to see my doctor. I had a hard time forgiving him for that. I still didn't believe I actually had a problem. Still, I decided I needed to forgive my dad and apologize to him for letting things get so chaotic.

I remember dropping the girls off at Nanny's, and Dad was standing outside in her driveway. I walked up to him and started trying to apologize to him and thank him for putting up with all the crappy things I had done over the last year. I was trying to tell him these things and I just started crying. Dad hugged me and said, "Don't worry about it. None of this is your fault. Things are getting better. You are making a lot of progress. Don't start beating yourself up now." I finally got a hold of myself and thanked him. I told him that I hoped I could pay him back someday for all the good things he had done for me. He said, "You just take care of these two girls. That's your job." After that, I drove on to work and cried on my way there. It was weird to me that a flood of emotion would hit me so hard. I had been feeling guilty about all the things I had done since I had worked at ETO, for over a year. I never talked to my dad about any of it until that morning. I didn't expect that I would end up too choked up to talk. I felt good that I had made a first step towards a better relationship with my dad. But I knew it wasn't like me to go around crying. I was taking an anti-depressant that was supposed to stop that kind of thing.

Not long after that morning at Nanny's, the day that changed everything happened. A few things had happened leading up to that day. One thing was that Sara and I started to go back to church. I had thought about going to church over the last year since we left Tallahassee, but I was too ashamed of myself to show my face around people who knew me. We were now living in the area where I grew up. I didn't want to walk into Main Street Baptist or First Baptist of Bartow and have to tell everyone that I had fallen so far since my time in Tallahassee. I figured that most people had probably already heard about me anyway. I didn't want to have to face them and see how differently they acted around me now that they knew I had a mental disorder. After I started working at Arr Maz, I thought, "I've got a job. I can take a chance on running into someone I know now. It won't be so tough. I'll just tell them that I didn't enjoy my job in Tallahassee and that I have started a new career with Arr Maz."

So, Sara and I started going to First Baptist of Bartow. That was the church I had gone to as a teenager. That was where I met Alice. I still knew a lot of the people that went there. Alice was not one of them. I wasn't going there hoping to run into her anyway. I had gotten over her years ago. Now I loved Sara. I wanted to go to church so that our girls would be in a Christian environment and have the same kind of experiences that I had as a child.

Sara and I went to Sunday School that first Sunday we attended. We met up with my old Youth Minister, Frank Brooks, who was now the associate pastor. He took us to a class that was geared for married people that were our age. We walked in and recognized almost everyone in the class. We had gone to high school with most of them. They all acted glad to see us. Several asked questions about what we had been up to and why we were there. I explained that I had been working on becoming an architect in Tallahassee and got tired of the job after several years. I told them that I decided I wanted to get away from a desk job and try working a labor type job for a while. I remember seeing suspicious faces in the room as I told them these things. It didn't bother me. I was just happy that I could say that I was working. I remember the Sunday School teacher going over the day's lesson and how I had several things to say about the topic he was talking about. I don't even remember what the topic was. The unusual thing was that I was being so outspoken. I usually never felt like I had much to say in Sunday School. But that particular Sunday, I was with a new group of people and felt like just rattling off whenever a thought struck me. I remember Sara getting embarrassed at some of the things I said. I don't remember what they were. To me, that's just another indication that the chemicals in my brain were beginning to go out of balance again. Sara and I only went to Sunday School and church together for two or three weeks. After that, she was no longer with me.

At some point Sara and I started having arguments again. We only had a couple before the last big one. I don't remember what any of them were about. My mind was slowly leaving me again. I was becoming more assertive and felt like I had more energy again. I was quick to snap at Sara if she did something to offend me.

Chapter 42: Good-Bye Wife

The last morning that Sara and I were together as husband and wife was a morning that occurred after I had worked at Arr Maz for about three or four weeks. I remember Sara and my dad were having a tense conversation when I got out of bed that morning. I don't remember what she and Dad were saying but I somehow thought that they were talking about me. I thought I heard her say something derogatory about me to my dad. I don't remember what exactly. I just remember that I instantly thought that she was probably saying all sorts of bad things about me when I wasn't around. I wondered just who she talked to and what kinds of things she said about me to them. I knew she wasn't happy about me working at Arr Maz. She thought I was working a job that was beneath me and that I was wasting my time. I wondered what she told people about me working there.

When I thought I overheard her saying something negative about me to my dad, it was very similar to the times I had thought I overheard conversations about me at ETO. The words were always too quiet to catch all of them. I would just hear a phrase here and there and think that I heard my name being mentioned from time to time. I would extrapolate my own ideas about what people were really talking about from these bits and pieces. It was paranoia. Paranoia was now striking me again. Only this time I thought it was my wife and Dad who were having secret conversations. No one, except Sara, usually talked to me about the things that had happened in those final days in Tallahassee. Sara and I talked about it all the time. That was almost all we ever talked about. The fact that no one ever talked to me about that time made me think that they all probably talked about it when I wasn't around. I had spent many hours over the last year wondering what kinds of things people had said about me when I wasn't around. Now I thought I had stumbled in on one of those conversations. I thought that I had caught my wife complaining to my dad about me. It made me furious.

I remember yelling something at Sara. She then went into the girl's room and I followed her, yelling at her the whole time. I don't remember what I said. It was probably something terrible. I said a lot of terrible things when the mania started having its way with me. I remember Sara was crying and asking me to stop yelling at her. The girls were both right there. They were both crying as well. My dad came in and grabbed me by the arm and pulled me out of the room. I don't remember much of anything he said either. I do remember one line. He said, "Don't you ever do that again!" I really don't remember what I said. I'm not trying to save face by pretending to have selective memory. I just have blank spots in my memory when I try to think back on certain things that happened. As I said, I'm sure whatever I was saying to Sara was terrible. The fact that Sara and the girls were crying, and that Dad removed me from the room, let me know that much.

After having a fit on Sara and getting everyone in the house upset. I went on to work and worked the whole day as if nothing had happened. I usually picked up Gwen from pre-school after work everyday. I drove to her school and went to pick her up from her teacher. Her teacher said that Gwen had not come to school that day. I thought that was odd. I called Sara but she didn't pick up the phone. I drove on out to the lake house and no one was there. I looked in the girl's room and noticed that things were all tidy. I went to the room where Sara and I slept. There was a note on the bed. I picked it up and read it. It read as follows:

Dear Scott,

I love you very much and I hope you can understand why I will not be at the house with you tonight. I know that you may not be able to control your thoughts or what you are saying right now and I understand. But, the kids do not understand. I can't bear to see them hurt anymore. I am not leaving you. I am simply taking the girls out of a situation that I see as emotionally damaging. We are staying at my dad's (Ron) house tonight. Please understand how painful this is for me. I hate this illness. I love you Scott and I will continue to pray for God's healing.

Love,
Sara

That was the last time Sara ever wrote me a letter. I still have it. That's how I was able to include it here. I knew, when I read that letter, we were through. I put the letter away, knowing that I would never receive any more letters from Sara again.

I read the letter and just stood there for a moment in shock. I knew I had left her on a bad note that morning, but we had fought before in the past and nothing like this had ever resulted from it. She had left the house before when we lived in Tallahassee. We had a big argument and she got real upset and said she was leaving and never coming back. She stormed out of the house and drove off. She was back thirty minutes later and was crying about how she was sorry about whatever we were arguing about. This time was different though. This time she had actually taken some of her clothes and the girl's clothes and all their toothbrushes and hairbrushes. I knew she meant business this time. At first I was a little sad, but it quickly just turned into anger.

I thought, "That bitch! All the things I have put up with over the years from her, and now that I have a problem, she runs away. If she can't support me by being with me, then I am going to get rid of her. I can't have someone around who is only my friend when times are good. We are through."

I didn't even try to call her that day. I think I let several days go by before I tried to call her. When I finally did call her, I let her have it. Again, I don't remember the details, but it was along the lines with what I had thought after reading the letter. I remember her crying and hanging up on me. I called her several more times over the next few days. Each time I did the same routine. I would start cussing her out and yelling at her about what a terrible wife she had always been and how she was only having a tough time dealing with my issues because I wasn't giving her a big paycheck anymore. She would usually hang up before I could get much out. After a while she stopped answering. Then Ron, Sara's step-dad, called me and asked me to please stop calling her. He said, as politely as he could, that all I was doing was making her more upset and making matters worse. He asked me to just give her some time alone and let her figure out what she should do. I told him that I thought we should get a divorce. He didn't say anything to that. A few days later I was at Arr Maz and a group of guys and myself were cleaning out one of the chemical silos when the next strange thing happened.

Cleaning the silos was hard work. You had to wear a special rubber suit and rubber boots. You also had to wear a mask to keep from breathing in all the fumes inside the silo. We had to clean the inside of the silo with high pressure scalding hot water. The water was so hot that it made the air inside the silo very hot as well. We only worked inside the silo for five minutes at a time. After that we got a ten-minute break. We worked in groups of four. One or two guys would go into the silo at a time while the others rested outside and tried to cool off. The other thing we had to do inside the silo was shovel out all of the residue that fell from the walls of the silo onto the floor. We would haul out 50-60 buckets of this crud that was stuck on the walls and floor of the silo. It was exhausting work, mainly because it was easy to get over heated. It was August in Florida. That means the daytime high is already close to 100 degrees. Add to that the fact that we were wearing rubber suits that trapped all our body heat, face masks that kept hot air around our faces, and hot humid air inside the silo that was heated from the scalding water we were using. The air temperature in that silo was probably 120-130 degrees if not hotter.

So, the point to all this, is that I was physically exhausted at the time my next weird episode came along. I remember being the only white guy in the bunch that day. All the other guys were black guys who were a little younger than me. They all knew each other pretty well from school and working together at Arr Maz. No one talked to me the whole time we were working. They were all talking to each other, but not me. I felt out of place. I would make a comment here and there and would usually get no response from any of them. I remember sitting outside the silo, taking a break. I was sitting there thinking about what a mess my life had become. I had not talked with or seen my girls in several days. I thought about what a pathetic excuse for a father I had been most of their lives. I wondered what I should do about Sara.

One of the guys I was working with started asking me a few questions about what I was like in high school. He was a much younger guy than me. He had probably graduated high school five years ago or so. He and the other guys were reminiscing on some of their high school days and he tried to bring me into the conversation. He said, "Did you ever play football in high school Scott?" I looked at him and thought about how many people liked me when I was in high school. I also thought about how no one liked me now. Not even my wife. I tried to answer him, "No, I didn't play.." After that I started to cry. I couldn't talk anymore. I was too choked up. I just turned away from him and put my head in my hands and sat there trying to make myself stop crying. He didn't say anything. After a couple minutes I got myself together enough to apologize to the guy for being weird. I told him that I just had a lot of crazy things going on in my life lately and left it at that. He said, "Man, are you alright?" I told him I was fine and tried to play it off as best I could. I didn't want to tell him that my wife had just left me and that I was just thinking about her. I definitely wasn't about to go into the story about the BHC and ETO. That was a secret that I thought I would never tell anyone. I went back into the silo and started working. I tried my best to act chipper and comment on things that they were talking about. I hoped that the guy who had seen me cry wouldn't tell anyone what I had just done. I think he probably did. He and his buddies probably got a laugh out of it after I wasn't around.

Chapter 43: A Voice in the Silence

After Sara left, things quickly spiraled more and more out of control. The first thing that was hard to cope with after she and the girls left, was having to sleep by myself at night. For the last eight years I had slept beside Sara every night. Now there was an empty side of the bed where she used to lay. I always slept on the left side of the bed and she slept on the right. Now it seemed weird to sleep on the left side when no one was there with me. But that's what I did. I started putting a pillow on the right side of the bed and I turned it so its length ran with the length of the bed. I would put my arm around the pillow, the way I had always slept with my arm around Sara. It was the way I was comfortable sleeping. The pillow was a sad excuse for a beautiful girl who used to lay in its place.

The other thing I hated was that it was so quiet at night. Sara and I usually talked, sometimes for an hour, in bed before we went to sleep. Now, I had no one to talk to. The girls weren't even next door snoring away anymore. It was totally quiet. I now had to be totally exhausted before I would even try to go to bed. I didn't want to have to lie there, awake in the silence, anymore than I had to. It was one of those silent nights when things shifted from stressful and depressing to frightening and bizarre.

One night, I had another vivid dream. I dreamed that I was asleep in my bed at the lake house and I woke up to find people standing over me. I could here a buzzing sound and the people that were standing over me looked like doctors. In my dream, they put something over my mouth and I went back to sleep. Then I woke up from the dream. I couldn't figure out if I had just dreamed that people were standing over me or if it had actually happened. I remember being sweaty when I woke up, like I had just woken up from a nightmare. I went back to sleep and woke up the next morning with that vision of people standing over me, in my bed, fresh in my mind. I didn't know what to think about it. I just figured it was another weird dream, like the one I had after Granddaddy died.

Shortly after that night that I had the weird dream, I started to think I was hearing conversations of people talking very quietly. I couldn't figure out where the conversation was coming from. I remember being out at the lake house the first time it happened. That first time I heard something peculiar was just a few seconds of someone talking very quietly. Then there would be nothing for maybe a minute or two. And then I might here another few words here and there. I couldn't make out what was being said. I thought someone must have left the TV or the radio on at a very low volume. I went and checked the TV and radio and they were both off. I remember putting my ear as close as I could to them to figure out if the noise was coming from them. I couldn't tell. Then I went outside to see if someone was talking out there. I couldn't see anyone. But then I heard someone whispering again. I still couldn't figure out what they were saying. It scared me. I couldn't figure out how I could be hearing someone talking and not know where it was coming from.

After a day or so of not being able to solve the mystery of the whispering voices. I began to suspect that something extraordinary had happened to me. I thought about the dream of the doctors standing over me while I was sleeping in my bed. I began to think that some group of people had come into the lake house at night, while my parents and I were all asleep, and performed some type of surgery on me. I began to think that the dream was not really a dream at all. I thought I must have woken up during the middle of that surgery and they must have put me back to sleep. My jaw had been hurting for a couple days. I wondered if they had done something to my jaw. I remember looking at my face in the mirror and wondering if those doctors had somehow operated on me and healed all the incisions before I woke up. I started to think that they had placed some type of implant in my ear that was causing me to hear these weird whispers of a conversation from time to time. I thought about what that lady, Pam, had told me about at the BHC in Tallahassee. I thought about her story about a secret group of good and evil that was working to bring about the end of days. I wondered if I had just been made a new member of one of those groups. Her story seemed fantastic at the time she told me. I thought it was interesting, but I never really believed any of it. Now I was hearing these whispers and had that strange "dream". The best explanation I could come up with was the one I just described. I started to believe that larger powers were at work in my life. I wondered if I was some type of secret military experiment. I started to think that even though I thought my life was ruined, someone might have big plans for me after all.

Once I made the connection between the whispering voices, the dream, the pain in my jaw, and my theory of an implanted listening device in my ear; my life quickly spiraled out of control. My ability to explain the strange phenomenon of hearing things that had no real world source gave me a sense of importance. The sense of self-importance quickly grew into arrogance. The arrogance quickly led me straight into trouble that caused me to be placed back into a psychiatric facility. During my days before my second stay in a psychiatric facility, the switch in my brain that turned to "On", let a flood of chemicals loose that impaired my ability to reason, communicate, and interpret the world around me as a rational human being. During those days after Sara left and before I was admitted into the psychiatric center, I was not only in mania, but was also getting my first experience with hallucinations. From that time on, whenever my brain switched to the "On" position, my world was filled with delusions of grandeur and hallucinations, no illegal drugs required! My brain could now send me on a trip whenever it chose without the stimulation of foreign substances.

I remember that once I had the idea that someone had planted some type of device in my ear, I knew I had better not tell anyone. I thought I might be involved in some secret operation and I might jeopardize my safety or the safety of whomever I told my secret to.

Chapter 44: TV and Secret Messages

One morning I was all alone at the lake house and I was watching the news on TV. One of the newscasters said, "Good morning", and winked. I thought, "Holy crap! She just winked at me. She just winked at me like she was talking to me and realized that I now knew she was talking to me." I remember just sitting there in awe. I thought, "Whoever put this phone device in my ear must also be able to talk to me through the television. Maybe they've been trying to tell me something and I just haven't heard it yet." I sat there and listened intently to everything they said. I don't remember any of it. I just remember that I kept thinking they were somehow talking about the news and there was also this little subtle joke going on between the two news casters that I had just become aware of the fact that they could talk directly to me through my television. Every time they made a smirk or a little giggle, I thought they were doing it because they knew that I now realized that they were watching me and had something to tell me. I sat there and watched the newscasters. I was absolutely shocked at what I thought I had discovered.

I remembered seeing a movie, *The Game*, where Michael Douglas played a character who got involved with this organization that would sometimes talk to him through his TV. There was a scene in the movie where he was watching the news and his TV's picture starts to become a little distorted. The picture then clears back up and the guy who was just announcing the day's news starts talking directly to Michael Douglas. I remember thinking that was a mind-blowing scene in that movie. Now I believed it was actually happening to me. My mind was completely blown.

I thought if somebody had gone through the trouble to put some kind of implant in my ear and was now trying to talk to me through my TV, I must be a more important person than anyone I knew. I was also afraid, but excited about what the future might hold for me. I started to think I might be a type of secret government agent in training, or something like that. I thought I would soon figure out what I was suppose to do with this new technology that I was being introduced to. I believed that my best chance of finding out what the secret orders were, would be to watch as much TV as I could, and also try to figure out what I was hearing when I was somewhere quiet enough to hear the whispering in my ear. I wondered if there was some type of malfunction with the phone implant that was making it so that I couldn't hear what someone might be trying to tell me. I thought that maybe the people who had put it there were fine tuning it, remotely somehow, and that maybe I would soon start hearing the whispering voices clearer.

Once I had come to believe that I was walking around with a phone implant in my ear and could now receive special messages through my television, I then began living the life of a total lunatic. I was now convinced that this secret group had selected me, for reasons I did not know, to play a part in some future mission of theirs. I also began to wonder if anyone else might be involved with the group who had now "contacted" me. I remember hearing my mom and dad talk on their cell phones and listening intently to what they were saying. I began to suspect that Mom and Dad were talking with some government agency as well. I started to think that maybe I had somehow been flagged as an important person when I was at the BHC in Tallahassee. I thought that maybe the government had people there that had noticed something special about me and contacted the group that sent the doctors to the lake house and had them place the implant in my ear. I wondered if those same people were now in contact with Mom and Dad. I started to think that Mom and Dad might know a lot more about what was going on than I did. I would listen to their phone calls, only their end of the conversation, and wonder who they could be talking to. Also, I noticed that my dad would go out to his shed and listen to the radio out there by himself. I started to think that maybe he was actually getting messages from this secret group, telling him information about some secret that I was dying to figure out.

I remember Dad being on his cell phone and talking to someone. I don't remember what he was saying, but I started to think that he was talking about me to one of those secret government agents. After he got off the phone I said, "Who were you just talking to on the phone?", accusingly. He looked at me funny and said, "That was your Aunt Janice.", with a very suspicious tone. He was probably trying to figure out why I had just seemed so bothered by the fact that he was talking to aunt Janice. I said, "Really. That was Aunt Janice. Huh.", with a strong tone of sarcasm, like I didn't believe a word he had just said. Dad asked, "Who do you think I was talking to?" I wondered if this was some trick question that if I answered right, might begin to unravel the new conspiracy that I seemed to be involved in. I looked at him and grinned. I said, "I don't know who you were just talking to. But I know that wasn't Aunt Janice." After that, I think I walked off. I didn't want to reveal to him what I actually thought was going on. I started to wonder if maybe Mom and Dad were not involved with the same secret group of people as me. I wondered if Mom and Dad might be in contact with a different group of people than the ones who I thought were trying to communicate with me. I started to wonder if one side, a good side, had contacted either my parents or myself; and another side, a bad side, had contacted the other. I started to think that two groups were involved in this conspiracy that my family and I were becoming a part of. I believed that there was a good group and an evil group. I wasn't sure just what that meant yet, but I remembered what Pam, at the BHC, had told me about these secret forces of good and evil. I started to wonder if Mom, Dad, and I were all being pulled by one of these groups, being persuaded to join their cause.

I remember watching TV at Nanny's house one weekend and Dad was in the room with me. I had already decided I was going to reveal a big secret to Dad. We were sitting there and Dad was flipping through the channels. I kept noticing that a symbol would pop up in the upper right hand corner of the screen as we passed by certain channels. I thought, "That symbol might mean that channel is one of the channels I should be watching to receive a message from these secret people." The symbol was the letters "e" and "i", inside of a circle. It's the symbol for educational programming. At the time, I had never seen that symbol before. I thought that symbol was the sign of the secret group who wanted to talk to me. I remember telling my dad to stop on one of the channels with that symbol. He did, and I began to listen to everything that was being said on the show we had stopped on. It was some cartoon. I thought that there was probably a coded message in what was being said on TV. The cartoon was about some aliens and they were talking to each other and flying around in a space ship. I didn't think much of it at the time, but the alien theme would soon be a major part of my new delusions and paranoia.

I remember deciding to let Dad in on my secret. I said, "Do you know what that symbol in the upper right corner of the screen stands for?" He gave me a weird look and said, "What does it stand for?" I said, "Think about it, there is an 'e', an 'i', and an 'o'. E-I-E-I-O." Dad looked at me with a totally puzzled face. Then I sang, "E-I-E-I-O." like the nursery rhyme song about the farmer in the dell. I said to Dad, "The farmer in the dell, as in 'the farm', as in the C.I.A. of the F.B.I." I knew I had heard one of those agencies referred to as "The Farm" before. I thought the "E-I-O" symbol was their secret way of letting me know that the station it appeared on was one that they could communicate through. Just seeing that unfamiliar symbol on the television screen was all it took for my mind to put together all the ridiculous connections that led me to the train of thought that I was now either dealing with the F.B.I. or the C.I.A. My mind was now able to make these fantastic new ideas up in just seconds. It only took a few seconds from the time I saw the symbol on the TV screen to the moment that it hit me that E-I-O somehow stood for the F.B.I. or the C.I.A.

Dad looked at me and laughed. He said, "You think that symbol has something to do with the F.B.I. or the C.I.A.? Why would they put a symbol like that on the TV screen?" I said, "I think that they might be sending secret messages to me through the TV. I'm trying to figure out what it is that they are telling me." He laughed again and went to get Nanny. He told her, "Scott thinks that he is getting messages from the TV." Nanny and Dad started asking me a bunch of questions. I think I had probably just scared the hell out of them. I don't remember what they were asking me. I just remember getting angry because I could tell that they didn't believe me. I realized that they thought I was just losing my mind. For me, though, there was not the first thought that I might be losing anything. No, to the contrary, I was sure that something big was going on and I was about to become a part of it. I also thought that Dad and Nanny might already know about the secret TV messages and were trying to down play what I had just told them because they had already been in on whatever big secret was out there for a long time. I began to think that they might all be working for the other group that was secretly planning to do something that I still wasn't sure about.

The reason that Dad and I were at Nanny's house was because we were supposed to replace some old siding and trim that were rotted on her rental house next door. That was the house that Sara and I had first lived in after we were married. Nanny had asked me to look at the siding and trim and see what needed to be replaced a few days earlier. I had found several panels of T-111 plywood siding that needed to be replaced as well as some fascia boards along the roof. She also had a beam, that was supporting a part of the roof, that needed to be replaced. I tallied up all the materials that she would have to buy to fix the areas with wood rot. She gave me some money and I went to the hardware store and bought all the materials to replace the affected areas. Dad and I were there that weekend to perform the task of actually replacing everything. Dad looked everything over and said, "You don't have enough plywood or fascia boards to replace everything that needs to be replaced." I said, "What are you talking about? I have everything right here." He counted up everything that I had bought, and sure enough, I was short by two sheets of plywood and a couple 2x6 trim pieces. I immediately suspected that he had hidden the missing pieces somewhere. I was sure that I had bought everything I needed. I said, "Did you move something and put it somewhere else?" He said, "I haven't been here since you bought all this. Why would I have moved anything? You just didn't buy everything you needed. No big deal. We'll just go back to the hardware store and get what we need." I still thought that he must have taken away some of the things I bought and hidden them somewhere. Why he would do that I wasn't sure. I thought he might have just wanted to make me look bad in front of Nanny. It was just more of my paranoia and delusions. I don't know why I seemed to find fault with my dad every time the mania came around. I don't know how he can stand to put up with me. I'm afraid I would have a tough time dealing with my kids if they ever treated me the way I treated my dad during the times that I went into mania.

One day, not long after I began to have the delusions of people secretly whispering to me in my ear, my parents and I went to McDonalds. We ordered our food and sat down at a table to start eating. As I was eating, I overheard a conversation between two guys who were sitting within earshot of us. I couldn't make out everything that they were saying but I could tell that part of what they were talking about was George Bush. They were speaking negatively about him. I was beginning to be under the impression that there was a connection between the secret group, who had planted the little phone in my ear, and the President. I had begun to be very defensive of anything to do with the President. I thought that he himself might be somehow monitoring all that I was doing. I wanted to be sure that I made a good impression with him if he was. So, when I heard the two guys complaining about George Bush, I took offense. I had a very short fuse during that time and was easily agitated into a confrontational mode. When I heard the complaints that the guys were making about Bush, I decided to go have a talk with them. I walked over to the guys and asked them why they had a problem with the President. I'm sure that whatever I said was very confrontational because I remember the guys being agitated by whatever I said. There was an exchange of words between the two guys and myself that grew heated. I don't remember what exactly was said. I just remember getting angry enough with the guys that I was ready to get physical with them. I'm sure that they did nothing to provoke it. I remember one of the guys saying, "Hey man, it's still a free country. We can have whatever opinion we want." I remember the guys getting up from their table and walking out to their car. I followed them outside and kept badgering them. I wanted to start a fight with them, just because I had overheard some negative remarks about the President. I had grown tired of hearing criticism of the President before I was manic. But once the mania set in, I was ready to fight anyone who disagreed with the President or criticized anything that he did. I felt connected to him by the little phone in my ear. I felt it was part of my new responsibility to defend his reputation wherever I went.

Chapter 45: Mission Katrina

During that time when the delusions had just started and I was trying to figure out what message the secret organization was trying to convey to me, Hurricane Katrina struck New Orleans. Every time I turned on the news, that was all anyone was talking about. I saw the devastation that Hurricane Katrina did to New Orleans. It made me think about what had just happened a year earlier in Polk County. I started to wonder if that might be what my calling was. I remember a news commentator saying, "If you can donate your money or time to the people of New Orleans, please do so. They really need your help."

Just after the newscaster made his request, I received the same request from another source. The request came from the voice that I had heard whispering so many times recently. Up until that point, The Voice had never spoke in a way that I could actually make out what it was saying. But that day, The Voice spoke to me. I remember what it first told me. It said, "Go to New Orleans. We need your help there." I had lots of questions for The Voice but did not think that I could ask them. I didn't think that The Voice would be able to respond to my questions. But after it made that request, along with the newscaster who I was certain had also just spoken directly to me, that was all it took. I thought, "That's it! They want me to go to New Orleans and help out some people there. I have the experience. I just lived through three major hurricanes. I'm probably better qualified than most people to help in a situation like that. This must be my first mission." I remembered how good it felt to help out my mom and dad when their home was ruined a year earlier. It was the first and only time I ever felt like I was of any use to them. I was very proud that I was able to help them at a time when they needed it. I realized that I could get that feeling back if I went to New Orleans and helped out those people who were going through a very tough time. I didn't know what I would end up doing. I just knew I had to go there. I had just been ordered to go by the secret organization that had planted a phone in my ear and talked with me through my television.

I remember a weird thing about one of my last days at Arr Maz. There was a day, just before I left to go to New Orleans, when I noticed some very peculiar bugs around Arr Maz. They really were just ordinary bugs, but to me, they were something more. One of the bugs that caught my attention was a large praying mantis. It was a bright green and was probably two inches long. I had only seen a praying mantis of that size a few times in my life. It was sitting on top of a barrel of chemicals that was in a room I was sweeping. I watched the praying mantis for several minutes. It always had its front arms situated in a praying posture, just as the name suggests. The Voice told me that the bug had been placed in the room as a sign of the always present, but never seen, secret group. I began to believe that someone at Arr Maz must be connected with the secret group. I had no idea of who that might be. Later that day, I began to be suspicious of one of the workers. I found evidence that I thought might link him to the secret group.

I was sweeping in another building later that day when I came across a white moth. The moth was also about two inches long. It was pure white. It caught my attention because I had never seen a moth like that before. After seeing the praying mantis just a few hours earlier, and The Voice telling me that it had been placed there by the secret group, I was sure that the moth was just another bug that had been placed by the secret group. I thought that they were playing some game with me, just letting me know that they were around, but I would never see them until they wanted me to. In the room where I found the moth was a guy who I had never seen at Arr Maz before. I immediately assumed that he was the one who had put the moth in the room. I thought that he must be the agent from the secret group who was disguised as an Arr Maz employee.

I walked up to the guy. I said, "So, are you the bug man?" He looked a little puzzled. He smiled and said, "What do you mean?" I thought that his smile was an indication that he knew exactly what I meant, but he was not about to reveal himself so blatantly as to tell me that he indeed was the one who placed the bugs at Arr Maz and that he was indeed a member of the secret group. I said to the guy, "I have found a couple of unusual bugs around here today. Have you seen this moth over here?" He said, "No. Let me see it.", and walked over to it. I thought the whole routine was an act. I thought that he really was an agent of the secret group, but was just playing dumb. I showed him the moth and said, "I've never seen a moth like that. I also found a large praying mantis earlier today. It was a bright green. It was very unusual. I think that someone is placing weird bugs around here today." He said, "Well, I don't know, but it wasn't me.", and laughed and walked off. I followed him back to where he had been when we first started talking. I said, "So, I have never seen you here before. What do you do here?" He told me that he was a floating mechanic who repaired the equipment at the Arr Maz location that I worked at as well as the equipment at other Arr Maz plants. He said that he traveled between all the Arr Maz facilities in central and north Florida. I didn't believe his story, but I didn't let him know that. I just said, "Well, from now on, I'm going to call you Bugman, because I have never seen such strange bugs here until you showed up." He laughed and said, "That's fine. Do you really think that I brought those bugs with me?" I smiled and said, "No. I'm just messing with you." The truth was that I really did think that he was responsible for the bugs. I just didn't want to run the risk of looking like an idiot if I was wrong about him placing the bugs there. I decided that I had done enough to let the agent of the secret group know that I noticed what he did. I didn't expect him to admit he was an agent of the secret group. I just thought that it was a good idea to let him know that I had noticed the strange bugs, in case he was an agent of the secret group.

My idea about a connection between the secret group and bugs developed further as the days went on. After I had already quit Arr Maz, there were a couple of other strange bug related events. One occurred as I was on a drive in my car. I was driving down the road when a strange, wasp like bug flew into my car from outside. It hit me right on the arm and then bounced into the passenger seat. I looked over at it and thought that it looked very unusual. It was a red and black wasp like bug. It did not look like the typical wasp. This bug was a darker black all over and had bright red stripes running down its back section. I looked at the bug and The Voice told me that it was an agent of the secret evil group. The Voice said that the evil group used these bugs to spy on me. The Voice told me to smash the bug so that it would stop transmitting information about me to the evil group. I looked back to where the bug had been sitting only seconds earlier, and it was gone. I kept driving down the road ad looking around on the floor and behind me to see if I could spot the bug. The Voice said, "You are too late. It has already disappeared." The Voice told me that the evil group could make things become invisible. The Voice said that the bug had done that very thing. I drove on down the road with goose bumps on my arms. I believed that I had just witnessed my first real encounter with an agent of the secret evil group. I also believed that I had just seen a bug vanish right in front of me. The thought that the secret evil group could send invisible agents to spy on, or harm me, caused me to worry. My paranoia was soon put to rest by The Voice.

A few days after the wasp incident, The Voice called my attention to a bright green dragonfly that was hovering around me one day. The Voice told me that the dragonfly was an agent of their group. The Voice said that they used bug like robots to spy on all sorts of people, including the agents of the secret evil group. The Voice said that the dragonfly that I had noticed was transmitting my image to computers run by the secret group. I looked at the dragonfly in amazement. The Voice said that even if I caught the dragonfly and examined it, I would never be able to tell that it was actually a robot. The Voice said that the secret group had mastered nano-technology to the point that they could create artificial life forms that completely resembled their living counterparts. The Voice said that the dragonfly was built to appear identical to a real dragonfly, guts and all, but that it actually was a robot. The Voice said that they had sent it to me to show me that they were always looking out for me and would protect me from any danger. That made me feel at ease and it lessened my paranoia that the secret evil group was always ready to pounce on me when I least expected it.

On my last day at Arr Maz, I told the secretary and Sam Houston that I was going to leave for a couple weeks to go help out hurricane victims in New Orleans. They said that they thought that was a very noble thing to do and I was welcome back when I decided that I wanted to come back. I thanked them and left Arr Maz with the intention of coming back in a couple weeks. I never worked another day at Arr Maz again.

I told Mom and Dad about my plan to go to New Orleans. They didn't think it was a good idea. Mom asked me not to do it. She told Nanny what I was planning to do and Nanny begged me not to go. She said that New Orleans was not safe and she didn't like the idea of me being so far away, all alone. She cried as she pleaded with me not to go. I think she was scared that she might not see me again. She and Mom and Dad all knew that I was not well. They told me to talk with Dr. Barnes and see what she had to say about going to New Orleans. I called Dr. Barnes and explained to her why I wanted to go to New Orleans. I didn't mention anything about a secret group talking to me through my TV. I just told her that I felt like I could be of use to those people and I felt like that was a more important thing for me to do than work a low paying job in Bartow. She said that as long as I was taking my medication, she didn't see a problem with me going. I had tried my best to get her to say just that. I told her that I was still taking my meds and that I had enough to last me while I was away. I don't think I was taking anything at all. I think the drugs she had given me probably helped push me into mania. She was having me take an anti-depressant. I was now far from depressed. I was peaking on the other side of the spectrum. I was now totally manic.

I spent about a day gathering up all the things I thought I might need on my adventure. I packed a bunch of old clothes, food, yard tools, a chain saw, my roofing tools, and loaded three red, plastic gas tanks on top of the Forester. I strapped them down to the roof rack. The last thing I gathered was a bag of toys to take to some children I might meet in New Orleans. I thought that it would be a nice thing to give a homeless child a new toy, if nothing else. I went into Liza and Gwen's room and started looking at their toys. I thought, "You girls don't need all this stuff. Some little kid in New Orleans would probably love to have a stuffed animal or doll." I loaded an entire trash bag with Liza and Gwen's toys. One of the things I took was a frog pond terrarium that I had just bought Liza before Sara took her away. Liza had been so excited about it. I was supposed to send in a coupon in the mail for a delivery of tadpole eggs that we would raise into frogs. Liza really liked the fact that she was going to have her own pet frogs. I remember seeing that terrarium and thinking, "Liza probably doesn't love me anymore after seeing me yell at her mom. She won't care if I take this terrarium." So I loaded it in the bag with all the other toys that belonged to Liza and Gwen. That was a terrible thing that I did. At the time I was doing it, though, I felt like I was doing something good. After I saw how disappointed Liza was that I had taken her terrarium and given it to a stranger, I knew I had messed up. Liza was only 8 years old. She didn't understand why a stranger would be more deserving of her toys than she was. That was just one of many terrible things that I did, as far as the girls were concerned. During the time that I did these kinds of things, it never struck me that I was doing anything wrong.

After loading all my stuff, I started to make my way to New Orleans. Mom and Dad still disapproved of what I was doing, but I went on regardless of what they thought. They had not been ordered to go there like I had. I didn't tell them about the news anchor asking me to go to New Orleans. I had already had enough of them laughing when I told them what I thought was going on. I got in my car and started heading north. I drove towards Tallahassee. I thought I would spend the night there and leave the next morning to head to New Orleans.

On my way to Tallahassee, I stopped at a mall in Gainesville. I had no reason to stop in Gainesville. I just wanted to parade around in a town that I felt had rejected me one time in my past. When I applied at UF, after I finished Community College, I was basically rejected. So, Gainesville was always a town that had a sore spot in the back of my mind. Now that my mind was beginning to collapse, I thought it would be a good idea to prance around at the mall, just to rub my "success" in the faces of, what I considered to be, a bunch of snobs. I believed that I had a type of celebrity status. I believed that if the secret group had gone through the trouble of placing amazing technology in my body, then I must be a very important person. I wanted to walk around the mall a little, just to see if I noticed any rubbernecking from the people who saw me. I wasn't sure, but I was beginning to believe that other people might have already heard about who I was. I thought that there may be a lot of other people who might know more about what I was about to be involved with than I did. My trip to the mall was an attempt to see if I really was some type of celebrity like figure.

I walked in the mall and purchased some items that would become essential parts of my daily attire. I bought a straw hat that resembled a cowboy hat, and a pair of camouflage sandals. Those two items became something that I began to wear almost everywhere I went. I felt like the hat was a little throw back to Granddaddy. It sort of looked like a hat that he used to wear when he worked in his cow pasture. The camouflage flip-flops were a symbol of who I felt I was working for. I was sure that I was being trained to be some type of military spy agent for the secret group. The camouflage flip-flops were my little secret about who I really was. I knew that only the secret group would appreciate why I had bought them. I wore them to honor their organization, in the way that a person might wear their favorite football team's logo on their shirt. My flip-flops were my statement of who my favorite team was, the secret group.

I walked around the mall for a while after making those purchases. I kept looking for people who seemed to be checking me out. I never could be sure, but I thought that there were people who were doing just that. I'm sure it was just my imagination, but I felt like a lot of people were noticing me as I walked around the mall. I would try to listen in on what people were saying as they passed me. I thought I heard one person say, "He's got *Hard Candy*? Oh man!" *Hard Candy* was the name of a Counting Crows album that would end up reshaping the way that I viewed the world around me. I had recently purchased it, but had not spent much time listening to it. There were other people talking as they passed me, who I thought were talking about me. The whole experience at the mall in Gainesville just added to my swelling ego. By the time I left that mall, I was beginning to be more sure of the fact that I must be some type of celebrity. After leaving the mall, I drove on to Tallahassee.

I arrived in Tallahassee late that afternoon. As soon as I arrived, I started reminiscing about how life used to be. I decided to drive by ETO/Architects and see what the place looked like. I drove by the side of ETO/Architects on 5th Avenue, and didn't stop. I just looked at the building and all the cars parked in the parking lot. I could tell who was still working there because I recognized most of the cars in the lot. As I turned onto the street that ran perpendicular to the one I was on, I noticed there was a wreck just past the ETO office. It was a gray Subaru Forester that was identical to mine, except the color, of course. The traffic was backed up on Thomasville Rd. That was the street that ran right in front of the ETO office. Once I turned onto Thomasville Rd. I crept past the ETO office and saw several people I knew looking out through the storefront glass, on the front of the office, at the wreck just up the street. I thought, "That is really odd that a Subaru Forester would be wrecked right in front of the ETO office. I wonder if the secret group is behind this." I drove past the wreck and felt a little scared about what I thought I had just seen. I thought that the secret government group was somehow making a statement to Warren. I didn't know what the statement was. I just thought that the chances of a Subaru Forester being wrecked outside of ETO/Architects at the moment I happened to drive by, had to be very slim. The group that I had come into contact with was somehow behind what I had just seen. It scared me because I felt like it was just another statement about how powerful this group must be.

I drove from ETO/Architects to a hotel. I got a room at the Microtel on Monroe St. in north central Tallahassee. After I got my room, I thought about trying to meet up with Barry Trudol to catch up on what his life had been like in the last year. I called Barry on my cell phone and got his voicemail. I left a message telling him that I was going to go to a bar/ pool hall where we used to go and play pool on occasion, Pockets Pool. It was just down the street from the hotel. I thought it would be a nice place to hang out for a couple hours, even if Barry never showed. I had never been to a bar by myself before. I had never wanted to. That was just another effect of the mania. I wanted to talk to as many people as I could. Normally, I never had a thing to say to anyone.

I walked in Pockets Pool and went to the bar. A beautiful girl was the bartender. I told her that I wanted a sweet tea. She smiled and said, "Sweet tea? That's it?" I said, "Yeah, I'm by myself. I have to drive back to my hotel. I don't want to take a chance on getting caught driving drunk." She said, "Well, you're probably the smartest guy in here tonight then. There are lots of other people who will leave here drunk tonight." She handed me a sweet tea and asked me my name. I told her and asked what her name was. She said her name was Jen. I said, "Jen, you are the most beautiful girl I have ever seen here. What are you doing working at a place like this?" She said she was a communications major at FSU and was bartending at night because she made good money and was easy work. Jen came over and talked to me every time she had a free minute between making drinks for all the people at the bar. I thought, "This girl is interested in me. I wonder if she would go out with me after they close." After an hour or so, Barry Trudol showed up with a friend of his that I didn't know. I walked over to Barry and thanked him for showing up. We talked for several minutes and sat down at a table that was pretty far away from the bar. I told Barry that I thought the girl at the bar liked me. He said, "Damn! She's hot." Barry's friend said he knew her. He said, "Be careful with that girl. She is a big time player." He said she had tricked several friends of his into thinking the same thing that I was. He said she was all about trying to find ways to get you to spend money on her. I just ignored him. After talking with Barry a few more minutes, I told him that I was going back to the bar and I left him.

I went back to sit at the bar. Barry left at some point and I never spoke to him. I was too busy trying to score with Jen. We kept having quick little conversations between her drink orders. I stayed until 2:00 am, when the bar closed. I asked Jen if she wanted to go walk with me around a lake that was just down the street. She said it was too late and she had class the next morning. I said, "Would you like to just hang out in the parking lot for a little while? I'll wait for you out there." She said, "Hmm. I don't know. Maybe." Then I said I was going to wait for her in my car outside. As I left, I noticed that she had walked over to another guy who was at the other end of the bar and they were talking and he was staring at me. I wondered if she was saying something about me to him. I had seen her talk to the guy a couple times over the night while I was sitting there. He would say things to her and they would laugh, sometimes he would look at me. It made me wonder if he was talking about me too.

I went out to my car and waited for about thirty minutes. Then a guy came up to my car. He said, "Are you waiting for Jen?" I said I was. He said, "Man, you need to leave. She left half an hour ago. She said that you scared her. She's not interested in you." I thanked the guy for letting me know and just sat there for a minute. I drove out of the parking lot and started crying. I thought that the guy at the bar must have been a member of one of the secret organizations. I thought he must have told her something to make her scared of me. I thought that the guy had just ruined my chances with her. I wasn't sure if he was on my side or a member of the other secret group, but I was angry either way. I thought I had just had a beautiful girl start to like me and that guy said something to change her mind. I pulled over into a parking lot just up the street from the bar. I just sat there and cried. I wanted to find a quick replacement for Sara. I realized that I wasn't going to have one that night. A police car pulled up behind me and turned his lights on. An officer walked up to my car and I rolled my window down. "Have you been doing a little drinking tonight?", he asked. I said, "As a matter of fact, I haven't drank anything except sweet tea tonight because I knew this very thing would happen to me." He laughed and said, "You didn't even drink one beer?" I said that I had not and would take a breathalyzer to prove it. He said that he believed me. He said, "Why are your eyes bloodshot and watery?" I told him I had just been crying because my wife had left me recently and I was at the bar talking with a girl who had just stood me up. He said to just drive home safe and left me alone. I went on to the hotel after that and went to sleep.

The next morning I was up with the sun. I probably had only slept three hours or less. I felt great and ready to head on to New Orleans. In the lobby was a rough looking man whose skin was very red. He was sitting in front of the TV watching the news run clip after clip of the horrors that were taking place in New Orleans. I told the guy that I was heading to New Orleans. He said, "You won't be able to get into the city. All the roads are closed to the public. Only emergency vehicles and military are allowed in." He told me he had just left New Orleans. He said that was where he lived. He started complaining about how the government was doing a really crappy job of assisting the people there. He said that President Bush was an idiot and didn't know how to do anything right. I said, "Well, when the hurricanes hit us in Polk County, FEMA and the Salvation Army were there right away. They helped provide food, water, and ice to people for weeks." He said that none of that was happening in New Orleans when he left. I said, "Maybe its because New Orleans has a lot of bad things about it. Prostitution is big in New Orleans. I think Bush figures that New Orleans just got what they deserve." That was a really stupid thing to say, but I was full of nothing but stupid things to say. The guy got really angry with me. He said, "I've lived in New Orleans all my life. It's a great town. You are full of crap and don't have any idea what you are talking about." I got up and left. I went back to my room and packed up my things and started driving to New Orleans.

The drive from Tallahassee to New Orleans was just a six-hour trip down I-10. Along the way I noticed several strange things. The most common strange occurrence was that I believed that the secret group was communicating to me through the license plates and things written on the vehicles that passed me. This was something I had started to believe before I left for New Orleans as well. I started to read meaning into certain cars that passed me. I thought that some of the bumper stickers I saw on them were a message for me to figure out. The main message I thought I had figured out was that this secret group wanted me to join the military. I kept seeing stickers for the Army and Air Force. I thought about my brother, Sam, who had now been in the Air Force for about five or six years. I wondered if this secret group was in contact with him and was trying to train me, perhaps the way that they had already trained him. I started to associate the color blue with the Air Force. Every time I drove anywhere, I thought that I was noticing a lot more blue cars and trucks than I had ever seen before. I'm sure this was just another delusion. There were probably no more blue vehicles on the road than there had ever been. I was just trying to find a secret meaning behind everything around me. I figured that the secret group was sending me a subtle message by having all these blue cars around me all the time. It was almost like they were letting me know, "We are everywhere, and we are watching and protecting you." I felt comforted by the idea that some people were going through so much trouble for me. It made me a little less scared and it made me feel like I must be important.

Chapter 46: The End of Days

On the way to New Orleans I noticed a semi truck pass me that had the word "Warren" painted across the back of it. Someone had written, "Here, Kitty, Kitty.", with their finger in the dirt that was on the back of the truck. I saw the truck and started laughing. I interpreted this as a message to me that the group I was now following orders from had just let me know that they had no love for Warren Eto. I interpreted the "Here, Kitty, Kitty.", as a statement someone might say to Warren just before they beat his ass. I thought it was funny. Like I said, my mind could put together strange new ideas from just a little new information in seconds. This was just one of hundreds that came to me in the next several weeks. And they only got more and more bizarre.

The next thing that happened was I thought I discovered a secret message hidden in some songs that I had been listening to for a month or so. The album I was listening to was *Hard Candy* by the Counting Crows. There was a song that said, "It looks like darkness to me, drifting down into Miami." Then the real mind blowing part came, "Make a circle in the sand. Make a halo with your hand. Make a place for you to land. The bus is running. It's time to leave. Summer's gone. So are we. So come on baby, let's go shut it down...In New Orleans. Lets go shut it down in New Orleans." I got chills all over when I heard these lines as I was driving to New Orleans. I had bought the CD a month earlier and never paid any attention to that song. Now it was full of messages to me. I immediately put together an idea that, first of all, something bad was going on in Miami, Florida. I had no idea of what that was, but I thought the "darkness drifting down into Miami" line was a secret message that evil forces were at work in that city. I had no idea of what they may be up to, but it scared me to think that I was living so close to a place where I now thought a powerful evil force was operating. The main thing that scared me was the line, "Lets go shut it down in New Orleans." I thought this was an invitation to stop some evil force that was in New Orleans. I began to wonder if Hurricane Katrina was not a natural disaster, but a weapon that had been used against the city. I wondered if our own government had unleashed some secret weapon that could create a hurricane to level a city. I thought, "New Orleans is a very corrupt place. Maybe the government knew about something that was going on there that had to be stopped. Maybe the only way to stop it was to level the city."

I thought about the girl in the rehab center who told me that God had used natural disasters to take the chosen people to heaven. She said that natural disasters like floods and earthquakes, where hundred or thousands of people died at a time, were the Rapture. She said, "Remember the Bible says that in the twinkling of an eye the chosen will leave this life and be with the Lord." She said that those disasters were Gods way of secretly removing his true followers and leaving behind those that would have to live through the time when Satan ruled the earth. She said that we were the ones living in that time and that we would be the ones fighting in the Apocalypse.

I now felt scared to keep driving to New Orleans. I was afraid of what might happen to me there. I began to think that maybe Hurricane Katrina was just the beginning of the end of the world. The line "Lets go shut it down in New Orleans.", told me so. The Counting Crows had just revealed themselves to be a part of the conspiracy as well. I thought that they had been used to convey the order for people to come to New Orleans to fight in the ultimate battle of good and evil. I wondered if I was supposed to take part in it. I listened to all the other songs on that album with a new attention to the words. I realized that I had to crack the code again. Every line might be a secret message for me to decipher. I felt like I had a lot of work to do. I listened to that album over and over my whole ride to New Orleans. I thought that I discovered a lot of information about the present and near future on it.

A couple other things that happened on my way to New Orleans occurred at a rest stop and as I drove closer to New Orleans. I pulled into a rest area. I got out of my car and saw a sign that had a diagram of the rest stop building it was in front of. It was like a floor plan of the building. I looked at the shape that the floor plan made. The building had been designed in a cross like pattern. Cross patterns are very common in buildings, especially Catholic churches. This was a state owned building, however. The thing that struck me was the fact that the diagram of the building showed the cross shape of the building, up side down. The building was a cross but it was situated on this diagram as an upside down cross. I thought, "These people are blatantly Satanic. Why else would they have an upside down cross as the shape of this building." That was the first bit of evidence, to me, that there definitely was an evil power at work in New Orleans.

To further reinforce this idea, I passed under a bridge that crossed the interstate that actually had a pentagram sprayed on it. There was a message written across most of the length of the bridge as well, "Sons of The Confederacy, Go Home!", it read. I wondered if The Sons of The Confederacy was the name of the secret group that I thought had told me to come to New Orleans. I thought that graffiti that had been spray-painted on that bridge was the most concrete evidence that evil was at work in New Orleans. I thought it was a threatening statement written by people who worked with the other secret group of evil that was at work in New Orleans. The delusions had now totally consumed me. I was living in a fantasy world. My life was slowly was becoming another waking nightmare.

The last thing I saw that helped me believe that I was surely heading into an evil place was along side the interstate. I had been driving through an area with clear signs of storm damage for probably 30 minutes. The thing that struck me as odd was all the dead animals that I kept seeing along the side of the interstate. I passed several dead deer and two dead hogs that were on the side of the road within 30 minutes. There were also several dead birds scattered along the way as well. I thought, "I bet that some of the people who work with the evil group in New Orleans sacrificed those

246

animals and placed them on the side of the road to hex or scare people." I was sure that was what had happened. It never occurred to me that those animals might have been panicked during the hurricane and got hit by cars on the interstate. My mind never put together logical explanations for anything I saw now. Every experience had a connection to the supernatural secret forces of good and evil now. I was sure that I had seen enough evidence to prove that I was right about everything I had suspected. I believed that I was about to become involved in a battle between good and evil. I had seen the signs and deciphered the code. The message was clear.

As I approached New Orleans I started to see the familiar signs that I was in the wake of a major storm. The billboards went from having the signs ripped off to being blown down all together. Even the steel beams and columns that served as the structure of the signs were blown over. All the trees were bear. I knew I was getting close. I pulled off I-10 into a small town when I was about 60 miles away. I wanted to find out if there were any hotels with vacancies. I quickly found that all the hotels were being used to house military, FEMA, power line workers, and emergency rescue types. I talked with a guy who told me to go back to Mobile, AL if I wanted to find a hotel. He said that was about as close as I would be able to get. Another guy told me about a church that was only 10 or 15 miles back from where I had just came. He said that the church would let me pitch a tent there. He said he had done that for a couple nights before he got a room at the hotel. So, I followed the guy's directions and found the church and asked if they minded me spending the night in their parking lot. They said it was no problem and they were happy that people were willing to help. They were collecting food and clothes for people in the surrounding area who had lost their homes in Katrina. I gave them my bag of Liza and Gwen's toys. They took them and thanked me. I felt like I had just done my first good deed.

A lady came up to me after hearing me tell some of the people their that I had helped replace a couple roofs after the hurricanes hit Florida a year earlier. She asked me if I would mind following her to her house to look at her roof. She said she had been spared from a lot of damage, but some of her shingles had blown off. She wanted me to look at her roof and see what I thought she should do. I told her that I would be happy to follow her. We drove back to her house, which was only a few miles from the church. The drive to her house looked very familiar. People were out clearing all the debris from their yards and piling it into little mounds alongside the road. Some people had already put up the blue tarps over their roofs. That was a scene that occurred for months after the Florida hurricanes.

We got to her house and she grabbed a ladder and we climbed up to her roof. She showed me the places where the shingles had blown off. She asked me how she could replace them, or if she needed an entire new roof. I told her that I thought she should just replace the missing shingles because there were only a few missing and those that were there didn't look that old. She asked me how to go about replacing the missing shingles. I told her she would probably have to pull up a couple rows of shingles above all the missing spots and re-nail the existing shingles after she replaced the missing spots. She thanked me and I left.

I left the church with the intention of coming back there to spend the night. I wanted to see how close I could get to New Orleans. It was only about 2:00 pm. I thought I still had plenty of time to figure out what I might do to help out the people of New Orleans. I drove as far as Slidell, LA and was forced to exit I-10 because the interstate was closed after that point. Just like the guy at the hotel in Tallahassee had told me, all roads into New Orleans were closed to the public.

I drove into Slidell and saw the familiar sights of a town that had felt the destructive power of a hurricane. Buildings were damaged with broken or missing windows. Power lines were down. A lot of buildings had no roof. All the traffic lights were out. Military guards were out directing all the traffic. There were a lot of military vehicles and police cars roaming the streets. It was similar to what I had seen in Polk County after the hurricanes, only on a much larger scale. The military presence was much more pronounced than anything I had ever seen in Florida after our crisis. They were running everything.

I went to a grocery store in Slidell before I ended up at my final destination that day. I walked in to find a newspaper. I found some at the front of the store. On the cover of one of the local papers was the picture of a starved looking black man, standing on the roof of his house that was surrounded by water. The old black man in the photograph looked like a living corpse. His face was very drawn and his skin sagged. His eyes were sunken deep into their sockets. But they were open wide with lots of white showing around the pupils. The article was about all the people who were waiting to be rescued from their homes in New Orleans. It talked about how hundreds of bodies were floating in the water that covered the houses and streets in some neighborhoods. It scared me. The picture of the old black man scared me too. He looked evil to me. In reality, he was a helpless flood victim, who was probably starving as he waited to be rescued. The picture was probably shown to create sympathy for the situation he was facing. To me, however, it created fear. I thought that the old man looked evil and wondered what he was like. I wondered if he had been a member of some voodoo cult that existed in New Orleans. The girl at the rehab center in Tallahassee had told me that voodoo was a big subculture in New Orleans. She said that the voodoo cults that existed there practiced witchcraft and worshipped Satan. She had told me that she had fought with voodoo cult members several times in her life. I now wondered about her stories. I thought maybe there was some truth to them. Maybe there was a voodoo presence in New Orleans. The old man in the photograph looked like what I imagined a voodoo cult member to be. The thought scared me. I bought the newspaper so that I could have a record of what I thought was going on. After that I left and started exploring the town a little more.

Chapter 47: The Slidell Supply Line

I drove around for a short while and noticed a line of cars going into a Wal-Mart. I decided to get in the line. I could see that the parking lot was filled with semi trucks and military vehicles. It looked to me like the Wal-Mart had been converted into a place where supplies were being distributed to disaster victims. It turned out that I was actually right about that. I drove up to the point where people were waiting to give me ice, food, and water. A guy asked me how much I needed of all the supplies. He said, "How many people do you need ice, water, and food for?" I said, "I'm not here to take anything. I have some things I would like to drop off for you, though." He looked at me funny and said, "Well, pull up ahead and lets see what you've got." I pulled up and out of the delivery line. The guy I had just spoken with went over to a couple military guys in uniform and they came over to me. They asked me what I had brought. I told them that I had brought some food and water. They said that I didn't need to give those things to them. I said, "I have driven all the way from central Florida to help out up here. Please take this stuff. It will make me feel like I helped out." They said that was fine and thanked me. I asked, "Do you guys need any help here?" One of the military guys said, "Yes we do. Wait here for a minute." The military guy walked over to another guy who was talking with a group of people. The guy that he started talking to looked like he was an administrator or something. He looked my way and smiled at me.

Then he came over to me and introduced himself. He said, "Hello. I'm Byron Harvey. So, you came all the way from Florida and want to help out here?" I told him I did. He said that he worked with some federal agency, that I can't remember, and was helping coordinate the supplies for that area. I told Byron about my experiences with the Florida hurricanes. I didn't mention that they had caused me to end up in a psych ward. I just tried to promote myself as someone who had experience with what needed to be done after a storm like the one that had just hit New Orleans. I told Byron that I would be glad to help out in anyway that he could think of. I also asked him about getting closer to the city. He said, "This is actually the first checkpoint for getting into New Orleans. If you want to do something further in, you will have to talk to some of the higher ups and see if they will let you go with them." Byron told me that I had to receive a clearance through people that were higher up on the administrative list than he was, if I wanted to do anything in New Orleans. He said that they would be glad to have me help out on the supply line though. I told him that sounded great to me.

Byron introduced me to a group of people that were working at one of the supply delivery stations. There were about 15 stations all together. Each station had a group of around 5 or 6 people that were loading ice, water, and food into people's cars. Some people were actually loading the supplies into the cars. Others were unloading the supplies from pallets that were being taken out of the semis that were constantly coming in. One guy served as a flagman that told the car where to drive to and stopped them when they arrived at the right spot. Once they were stopped another guy would ask what supplies they needed. Then he would call out the order to the loaders and they would load everything up in seconds. The whole process took less than a minute for each car. Byron said that I could work with the group of people that he introduced me to and then walked off. He was always talking on his cell phone and walkie-talkie. He looked like a pretty busy guy most of the time.

I talked with the guys who were loading the cars at the station Byron had brought me to. They told me that I could unload ice, water, and food from the pallets and stack them up beside the road where they would load them into the cars. The job took no explanation. It was just the simple task of moving things from one place to another. So, I started unloading pallets right away. I talked with the guys as we worked. There was a few seconds between loading each car, where they would come up and chat with me before filling the next car.

Byron came back over to me after I had been working for about an hour. He said, "Scott, put this on. You are our honorary volunteer for the day!" He handed me a neon orange plastic strap to wear over my shirt. The strap was like the one you would see a policeman wear as he directs traffic. It had a badge that said, "Volunteer", and had a number on it. The number was "1". I looked at the number one that was written on the badge. It made me wonder why I was given something with the number one on it. I took it as a compliment.

Later in the day I noticed another young guy that I had not seen before. He had started helping the group in the supply station next to the one I was at. He also was wearing the strap and badge that I had on. Only the number on his was "3". My brain never put together the obvious fact that I had probably just received the badge with No. 1 on it because I was the first volunteer to show up that day. Or it may have been a totally arbitrary and coincidental thing that I had received the badge with No. 1. But to me there was never anything that happened by chance anymore. Everything had a meaning. I thought that since I had received a No.1 badge and the other guy had received a No. 3 badge, I somehow had a higher rank than he did. I wondered if he was jealous of me.

One of the guys working in my supply group would talk with the young guy at the station next to us. I could tell that they knew each other. I started to think that maybe the two were father and son. I remember hearing the older guy that was working at my station say to the younger guy at the other station, "So, what took you so long to get here?" I thought that maybe the older guy was upset with his son for getting to the supply station so late. It was probably 4:00 pm or later when I noticed him show up. The supply line stopped at 7:00 pm that night.

I remember wondering if the older guy at my station was upset with his son for not getting the badge with No. 1 on it. I asked the young guy if he wanted to trade badges with me. He looked at me strangely, which he should have. It was an idiotic question to ask, I'm sure. He said, "No. My badge is just fine." I said, "O.K., its just that mine has a No.1 on it and yours had a No.3. I didn't know if that bothered you." He laughed. He probably thought I had just tried to crack a joke with him. I was serious though. I thought that there may be some significance to the numbers on our badges. I realized that he thought I was joking, so I just laughed with him.

I spent the rest of that day unloading pallets and felt pretty tired by the time we shut down for the day. Byron came up to me and asked where I was staying that night. I told him about the church I was going to drive back to. It was over an hour away. Byron said that the Salvation Army had set up a camp there in town and I could probably stay with them. He told me how to get there. So, I drove down the road to a little church in Slidell that had been set up as the temporary headquarters for Salvation Army in that area.

I had joined the Salvation Army when I was in Tallahassee. It was one of the last things I did before I was forced to resign from ETO. I remember being so pleased with all the good things I had seen them do in Polk County during the hurricanes. I wanted to join so that I could take part in their activities in the future. They sent me several e-mails about places I could go and help as a Salvation Army volunteer. I never got the chance to do any of it. I was removed from the office only a few days after receiving some of those e-mails.

I pulled into the parking lot of the church in Slidell that was serving as the Salvation Army camp. There were tents set up all over the place. I had to park on the street because there were no empty spots in the parking lot. I walked inside the church and saw that sleeping bags were everywhere on the floor. All the pews had been moved to the sides of the room in the sanctuary. The sanctuary was now just a big area for people to sleep. There were also all sorts of supplies stacked up inside the church and outside the building as well. I introduced myself to some people who were standing around inside. I told them my story about coming from Florida, helping out during their hurricanes, and being a Salvation Army member myself. I asked if they minded if I slept there that night. They told me that was no problem and asked me if I had eaten anything. I told them I had.

I ate some army rations back at the supply line for supper that night before I left. That was the first time I had ever eaten army rations. I had heard stories about how terrible army rations were. I thought they were pretty good. One of the guys that was eating with me said, "Yeah, they're not so bad until this is all you eat for a week. Then they start to taste like crap." I said that I could see how they could get old but I was surprised at how good my first one tasted to me.

A lady at the Salvation Army told me that I could go with her and a group of others to her house and take a shower. I told her that I appreciated the offer and that I would follow her in my car. She said it would be a little while before they left. I went outside and sat in my car, waiting to see her leaving. I turned on my car stereo and began to play the Counting Crows songs that I thought delivered a secret message. I turned the volume way up so that people standing around the Salvation Army could hear. I just sat there blasting the Counting Crows for probably thirty minutes. No one ever came over and asked me to turn it down. But no one came up to me at all. I noticed people looking at me. I would just smile and keep sitting there. I'm sure they thought I was being really obnoxious, at the least. The lady who had invited me to take a shower at her house never came and got me. I wonder why. I never saw her leave, but there was several minutes when I was laying there with my eyes closed. She probably left during that time and figured that I had changed my mind about coming or was too scared to ask me after hearing the music that I was blasting.

Eventually, I walked back inside and asked if the group heading for the shower had already left. I was told that they had. Another lady told me that they had a camping type shower set up outside. It was just a bag filled with cold water that ran through a little showerhead. They had set up a curtain around it and placed it outside, behind the church, for privacy. I told them that I didn't have to take a shower. They asked me what my plans were for the next day. I said I was going to go back to Wal-Mart to help out on the supply line again. They said that I was welcome to help them if I wanted. They were running a similar operation, only on a much smaller scale. They weren't being backed by disaster relief funds and the federal government. Their operation was based solely on whatever people donated to them. The operation at Wal-Mart was much more elaborate than what the Salvation Army was doing. I decided that I wanted to go back to Wal-Mart and help out there. They said that I was still welcome to stay there as long as I needed to. I thanked them.

I brought in my pillow, backpack, and sleeping bag. In my backpack were all my toiletries, my medication that I was hardly ever taking, and a Bible. There were also a few other small things. One of those small things ended up causing me trouble. Somehow, one of the Salvation Army guys found a ring that must have fallen out of my backpack. The ring was the "One Ring" from the *Lord of the Rings* movies. My brother had given it to me as a joke of a birthday gift. The ring looked exactly like the ring in the movies, with the weird inscriptions written around the outside of it, just like it had in the movie. The guy who found the ring asked, "Who lost a ring?" Everybody looked at it. I saw it and recognized it immediately. I said that it must have fallen out of my backpack. He said, "Where did you get this ring? Isn't this the ring from the *Lord of the Rings* movies?" I said it was. He said, "Why would you have a ring like that? Those movies are Satanic." Several people were looking at me with suspicious faces. I felt angry and a little scared. I said, "My brother gave this to me as a joke. Those movies aren't Satanic. They are just movies. You are reading way to much into a little ring." I took the ring from him and walked away from the group that was standing around and had heard the whole conversation. I was pissed at that guy for trying to make me feel bad because I had that stupid ring. I honestly don't know what it was doing in my backpack. I probably put it there with some crazy idea in my head at the time I put it in my backpack, but I don't remember it.

I remember walking around the rooms in the church and feeling very out of place and paranoid. I started to think that I should leave. Then I saw an older guy talking with one of the ladies who was in charge of the Salvation Army camp. He was talking to her and smiling. He looked at me a couple times and smiled. I thought he was telling the lady in charge bad things about me. I thought that the older guy was doing the same thing that the guy in the bar had done to the bartender after I thought I had made such a good impression. I thought that the older guy was telling the lady some lies about me so that they would become scared of me, the way that Jen the bartender had become scared of me. I saw the lady pick up a telephone and start talking to someone. I tried to hear what she was saying. I started to think that she had called my parents or Dr. Barnes and was telling them that they needed to come pick me up because I was acting crazy. I felt like I needed to leave immediately. I went and gathered my pillow, sleeping bag, and air mattress that I had brought in with me. I told the people there that I was not going to sleep there that night. I said it was too noisy and I thought they probably didn't want me there after seeing the ring that was in my backpack. After that I left. I forgot all about grabbing my backpack. All the paranoia and lack of sleep made me very forgetful when it came to doing things that should have been simple. My attention to the delusional ideas distracted me from doing most anything that I should have done.

I left the Salvation Army Camp and drove to the church that was an hour from Slidell. When I got there I realized that I had left my backpack with my toothbrush and medication. I started to think that maybe I should take my meds, because I was getting so scared from all the ideas that were constantly in my head. I set up my tent and planned to get up early the next morning to go back to the Salvation Army and get my backpack. As I was setting up my tent, I thought I heard people whispering in the woods near the church. I listened closely. I thought I was hearing a conversation between two people about what I was doing. I thought, "There must be people out there in the woods watching me." It scared me. I just stood there and listened. Every now and then I would hear a whisper here and there. I don't remember what they were saying, but I could make out some of the words now. I heard enough to believe that what I was hearing was two people talking, who were watching me in the woods. I figured that they were military guards who had been sent to watch over me. I looked out in the woods. I couldn't see them. I figured it was too dark and that they were probably well hidden. I realized that I must be hearing them through the listening device that was in my ear. The secret group, The Sons of the Confederacy, had somehow tuned in the device to let me hear the two guys talking out there to let me know that I was being protected. It made me feel safe. I continued setting up my tent and blowing up my air mattress knowing that two guards were out there in the woods watching my back. I felt like I was on display now. I had an audience of two guards who were watching my every move. In reality, I was all alone in a church parking lot, over an hour from Slidell, building on to the growing fantasy world that was consuming me. Still, to me, I had just realized that I wasn't alone, no matter where I went. The Sons of the Confederacy were always watching over me.

I laid there that night listening to the whispers of the guys out in the woods, the voices of my own imagination that had tricked me into believing that I was a VIP being protected at every moment from the great danger that was everywhere around me. Every now and then I would hear a little laugh after some comment. It made me feel like those guys out in the woods were nice guys. I was happy that they were there protecting me while I slept. Eventually, I did sleep. But I was wide-awake by 6:00 am. I probably slept for two or three hours that night.

I got up that morning and took down my tent, packed everything up, and headed back to Slidell to work on the supply line. I remember one of my shoulders being very sore that morning. On my drive back to Slidell, I passed a sign that said, "Shoulder Work Ahead". I thought that it was a message from the secret group. Of course, it really was just a standard road sign for work being done on the shoulder of the road. I knew that, but I thought that the sign had a double meaning. The Voice had told me about the secret groups mastery of nano-technology. The Voice had told me that I had tiny machines running around inside my body that were making repairs, fighting off viruses and bacteria, and just generally making my body stronger. When I saw the sign that read, "Shoulder Work Ahead", I thought that the secret group had sent me a message to let me know that the little robots inside me were repairing my shoulder. The weirdest thing is that I can remember rubbing the muscles in my shoulder and feeling a little bump. It freaked me out at first, but then I remembered what The Voice had told me about the robots inside me. I just assumed that the bump was one of the little machines working away on my shoulder. Later that day, I could no longer feel the bump. I figured that the little machine must have moved on to some other internal area. It still amazes me at how comfortable I was with some very bizarre ideas. In a normal state of mind, I think I would be very uncomfortable with the idea of tiny machines crawling around inside my body. But during that time, whatever The Voice told me was fine with me, no matter how strange it was.

Before I arrived at the supply line, I stopped by the Salvation Army camp to get my backpack. I drove up and saw a commotion of activity going on outside the church where the camp was. People were pulling up and taking supplies. Salvation Army volunteers were working as fast as they could to hand them out. I walked past all the activity and into the building. I saw some people inside and asked them if they had seen the backpack that I had left there the night before. No one knew what had happened to it. I thought, "They're lying. They have probably hidden it somewhere and just don't want to give it back to me." I showed the people where I had set it down and they told me to ask a guy who was working outside if he had seen it. They said that he had been sleeping where I had left my backpack. I walked outside and found the guy. It just so happened to be the older man that I had seen chatting with the lady who ran the place the night before. He was the one who I saw talking to her and smiling at me. I thought that he was the one who was saying some lie about me, to the lady in charge, to scare her and either force me to leave or somehow call my parents or Dr. Barnes and tell them that I was acting crazy. I walked up to him and said, "Well, so you're the one who knows where my backpack is. What are the chances?" He said, "I'm sorry? What are you talking about?" I said, "You know what I'm talking about! I'm talking about the backpack that was on the ground where you slept last night! Where did you put it?" He said, "There's no reason to have an attitude with me. I don't know anything about any backpack. I don't know what you're talking about." I said, "Damn it! That backpack has medication in it that I need! Just tell me where you put it so I can get my medication!" He said, "Do you know who you are talking to?" I said, "Do you know who you're talking to? You don't want to piss me off, but you already have. Give me the f@$!ing backpack!"

He said, "I'm not going to talk to you. You can't talk to me like that. I don't know where your backpack is. Just look around, someone has probably moved it somewhere. I never saw a backpack last night." I said, "I know you're lying! I don't know why you guys are trying to make my life miserable! I need that medication!" He said, "You definitely need something. I'm sorry but I can't help you." I said, "Fine! Just keep lying. You'll get what you deserve someday." After that I stomped off and yelled, "I *was* a member of the Salvation Army! Not anymore! I officially resign from being a Salvation Army volunteer! Screw you guys!" In actuality I had never done the first thing to help the Salvation Army. The only thing I ever did was sign up and receive their e-mails, which I never responded to. I thought I had just gotten even with that guy, whoever he was. I didn't believe that he was actually just a Salvation Army volunteer. I still thought that he was working with the secret evil group that was making my life hard and planning to do terrible things in the future. In reality I had just made a total ass out of myself. I'm sure everyone who saw me at the Salvation Army camp that morning knew that I was a raging lunatic. I was becoming dangerous. I never did get my backpack, even though it had a bible with my name on it, and my prescription pills that had my name and address. I have no idea of what actually happened to that backpack.

After my fit at the Salvation Army, I calmed myself back down and drove on to the supply depot. I got there and ate another military ration for breakfast and started working again. On that day, a group of National Forestry workers from Utah had shown up. They were almost all Native American Indians. Two of them were working at the station that I had worked at the day before. I saw Byron and asked him where I should work. He said I could work at the same place I had worked at the day before. So I walked up to the group of people at the station I had been at the day before and asked them what I could do. They had me start unloading pallets again. I went to work with a frenzy. I started stacking up packs of water bottles, military rations, and ice as fast as I could. I soon had built a wall about four feet high, of all the water, food, and ice; between me and the guys who were loading the cars. One of them said, "You can take it easy for a while. We can't keep up with you. It's going to take us a while to load all the stuff you've piled up. Thanks."

So, I went to the other side of the wall and started helping them load the things into the cars. I started talking with the guys who were working in my group. I told them where I was from and about the hurricanes we had a year earlier. I asked them about their jobs. They were all National Forestry workers who had volunteered to help out in New Orleans. They said they were getting paid extra for their work, but they felt like they were on vacation. One of the Indian guys was my age, maybe a little older. He was the flagman that directed the cars into our station. He was comical to watch because he put a lot of flare into his flag routine. He would wave his flags around like he was a NASCAR flagman. He would whip one of them back and forth very fast to direct cars to come into the loading area. When he wanted them to stop, he blew a whistle and held out his flags in a cross and stood in front of the vehicle. I'm sure my description doesn't do justice, but he was very animated and funny to watch. He was always saying funny things as well. He would ask the people in the cars, "One family?", meaning "Do you need supplies for one family?" The people would hesitate for a second and then respond. Some times they would need supplies for more than one family. The guy acting as flagman would say, "We've got a 'two family' here guys. That's a 'two family'. Copy? Lets do this!", or something of that nature. I thought he seemed pretty witty.

After a while he traded spots with one of the guys who was loading the cars with me. We started talking as we were loading the cars. He said his name was Cody. He was also with the National Forestry Department. He reminded me of my dad's brother's son Mark Gann. Mark was a very smart guy who had graduated Valedictorian of his class in high school. He was always witty and usually could deliver a smart-ass comment on demand. I told Cody that he reminded me of one of my cousins. He asked for his name. I told him and he gave me a funny look. "Don't tell me you know him.", I said. He said that he didn't and laughed. I said, "You do know him, don't you." He said, "No. I'm just messing with you." Mark had gone to school at University of Florida and had done a little traveling. I wondered if Cody really did know Mark and was just keeping that a secret. I just kept on loading cars and talking to him. He kept calling me Jack every time he said something to me. "So, how you doing over there Jack?", he would say, or something like that. I kept saying, "The name is Scott." He would laugh and keep going with his routine. I finally started calling him Dick. I would say, "Need some help over here Dick.", and he would laugh. He said, "Dick. You got me there. That burns." We laughed and I felt like I had just made a friend.

Later that day a news reporter came through our supply station. She had a cameraman following her as she talked to several people that were working there. I saw her talking with Byron Harvey for several minutes. Cody said, "You know who that is don't you?" I said I didn't. He said, "Look at the camera. That's CNN." I looked at the camera and, sure enough, there was a CNN logo on the side of it. I felt pretty cool to be at a scene where CNN was doing a story. Later that day I felt even more proud of myself. A white helicopter flew over and landed just down the street from where we were working. Some of the guys said, "I think that was President Bush. That was a White House helicopter." I walked out to the street to see the helicopter. It had gone down behind the trees. I wondered if that was him. I felt sure that it was.

I remember waving at the helicopter as I saw it go down behind the trees. I felt like my new boss had just come to see what I was up to. I was sure that the secret organization that had told me to come to New Orleans had ties to President Bush. I wondered if he might already know all about me. I also wondered if that badge that said, "Volunteer No.1" on it was something that he had told the people there to give to me. I started to think that maybe I was in some sort of training to become a president myself some day. I wondered if I was part of a secret competition that was being held to select possible candidates for some special program that President Bush had created to train people to become high-ranking leaders. I thought that part of the reason I had received the message from the television was to get me to come to New Orleans and earn some points in this competition. I thought that by my willingness to volunteer at a time when people needed so much help, scored me some kind of points in a rating system that was being used to qualify candidates for this secret program that President Bush was running.

Every time I saw a low flying helicopter or jet pass over, I wondered if it was flying over to send me a message. I would look at the helicopter or jet and read a message from what I saw. One time I saw a jet flying over that had two objects hanging from the back of it. I'm not sure what they were. All I could tell was that it looked like two balls being suspended from the back of the jet by long pipes that connected to the back of it. One ball was larger than the other. I looked at it and thought, "That is a symbol of President Bush and one of his trainees flying through the air together." I thought that the larger ball represented President Bush. The smaller ball was a symbol for one of the candidates who would be chosen from the competition that I thought I was now a part of. I wondered if the smaller ball represented me. I thought that maybe I had just seen a message from the president that I was his new apprentice. The jet flying over told me that it was the President and I now. I was his new apprentice. There might be others all over the world, but he had just sent me a special message by having a jet fly over with two balls suspended from the back of it. I figured that he knew if I could break the codes that I had deciphered to get to that point, then I would easily understand the message that he had just sent me.

Another message I got was from the military helicopters that passed over throughout the day. I'm not that familiar with many military helicopters but I do know the Apache and the Black Hawk. I saw both of them flying around many times, as well as the types that have twin rotors on top. I saw those types of helicopters flying all over the place. I remember watching a Black Hawk helicopter fly around us one day. I thought to myself, "Maybe that's my codename, Black Hawk." After that, I thought of myself as "Black Hawk". That was the new name that I decided the secret group must have given me. I figured that they told me this by flying that Black Hawk helicopter around me that day. I remember feeling very cool to now have a code name. It made me feel like I was definitely part of the secret group now, even though I had never received the first piece of mail, or phone call from anyone. I figured that they didn't communicate in those ways. That was too obvious and traceable. I believed that whenever they wanted to tell me something, it was always in the form of a code that required me to break it to understand its meaning. I didn't think I would ever get an actual phone call or letter from anyone. I was too "Top Secret" for anything like that. Everything was about secrecy with me now. I knew I shouldn't tell anyone what I thought was going on. The things that I believed I was now involved with were too important and confidential to share with anyone. I had to put on my best normal face around everyone I knew, and hold on to the secrets that I was learning until the time was right to act on them. The only problem was, even when I thought I was acting normal, everyone else probably quickly realized that I had a problem.

Another person I met that second day at the supply depot, was a woman named Trudy Salbury. She was a very friendly lady who was always talking with everyone and usually laughing at jokes she cracked. She helped out at the supply station where I was working. I remember asking her what she did for a living. She said that she worked for the state of Louisiana. I asked her what her job was. She seemed very evasive in her answer. She just said that she helped people do certain things. I thought that was a pretty vague answer. I kept trying to get her to explain her job and she would just change the topic or crack a joke. With my brain beginning to find more and more outrageous explanations for my experiences in the world around me, I started to wonder if she was being secretive about what she did because she was a high ranking Louisiana public official. I thought, "Maybe she is the governor." That's how ignorant I was about Louisiana politics. I didn't know the name of their governor. I was pretty sure that the governor was female. I had no clue of what she looked like. But I started to think that maybe this woman was her, or at least someone who worked very closely with her. I quit trying to pry with Trudy Salbury. I figured she was a friendly lady if nothing else, and I would leave it at that. I had heard that people were saying that the governor of Louisiana was corrupt and was responsible for a lot of the problems that New Orleans was having. I wondered if this friendly lady was afraid to tell me who she was because she knew that most people thought poorly of Louisiana's governor and she didn't want me to know that she was either the governor herself or closely connected to her. Even though I suspected that she was connected, I still treated her very kindly and we got along well. She even told me that she had 'adopted' several young people as her 'kids' and that she thought I might be her newest 'adopted kid'. I thought that was a nice thing of her to say.

That night, I went back to the church that was over an hour away. I set up my tent again and started hearing the whispers from the woods. I didn't even try to acknowledge the people that I thought were out there. I figured that they probably didn't want me to act like I knew that they were there. I just set up my tent and tried to sleep. I listened to the whispered conversation that I thought was taking place in the woods near my tent. I still couldn't make out what was being said all the time. But I thought I would hear things like, "I can't believe that's him." and other comments that made me think that whoever was watching over me felt like they were protecting a celebrity of sorts. Eventually I went to sleep. I have no idea of what time it was when I actually did fall asleep. I was up the next day by 5:00 am. I packed up and headed back to Slidell for day three. As usual, I felt great.

Chapter 48: The Rise of the Undead Army

On my way to and from Slidell I had noticed a large refrigerated storage warehouse. I noticed how many semis I passed that were cold storage types that I thought might be making deliveries to the warehouse. I wondered why so many refrigeration trucks would be on the road. I also noticed that Red Cross trucks were parked at the refrigeration warehouse. Then The Voice told me, "There are bodies inside those trucks. The refrigeration warehouse is being used as a big morgue and all the refrigeration trucks and Red Cross trucks are going around and collecting bodies to put in that warehouse." I listened to the radio as I drove to Slidell. I heard a report that the death toll numbers were not as high as what they had once thought they might be. Then The Voice enlightened me with a more disturbing thought. The Voice said, "We think that the Red Cross is somehow bringing people back to life that died during the hurricane. They are bringing people back to life so that the government will not be blamed for allowing so many people to die." The Voice didn't go into the details of how this miracle procedure was being performed. All I knew was that maybe the Red Cross was bringing bodies to that warehouse and inside they were injecting the bodies with some kind of new drug that brought the dead back to life. I thought that maybe the Red Cross was creating real life zombies that had died and been brought back to life. I thought that maybe the Red Cross had secretly collected the bodies and the goal was to resurrect them and put them back into society without anyone ever knowing that they had died. I thought that the Red Cross might be secretly creating an army of undead that would one day fight in a terrible battle of good versus evil. I thought that maybe the zombies would look and act like normal people, but one day would reveal their true purpose, to kill the living. So, as you can see, my mind was beginning to make up its own horror movies. Only I thought it was all very real. It scared the crap out of me. I imagined that I would one day have to fight against an army of undead zombies. I thought that maybe I had been called to New Orleans to witness their creation so I could warn others about them. I thought that I might be one of only a few people who realized what was going on. I didn't know what details the secret group knew about what was happening in New Orleans. I thought the zombie army had to be a sign of the end of days. The Bible said that the dead would rise from their graves and roam the earth in the end times. I thought that this might just be the beginning of how it would happen.

Chapter 49: A National Celebrity

Another thing I heard on the radio that morning was the morning talk radio guys talking about local things happening in the area. One of the things I kept hearing them talk about was "The Rooster". At this point my attention span only lasted long enough for me to hear pieces of information. I never listened to everything I heard. I kept hearing them talk about "The Rooster" and all the things he was doing around town. Whoever "The Rooster" was, it sounded like he had done some good deeds. I thought I heard them saying something about "The Rooster" doing some of the things that I had been doing. I think they mentioned something about "The Rooster" helping out Katrina victims. I thought, "My Forester is white with those red gas tanks on top. Maybe they have given me this nickname because my car is white with red on top, like a rooster's head. Maybe I'm 'The Rooster'. Maybe they know about that secret competition that President Bush is holding to select an apprentice. Maybe there are other people out there that know about this competition and they are hearing about me on the radio. Maybe a lot of people have been hearing about me for a while and I just don't realize it."

The thought added to my already swelling ego. I now started to believe that I might be a celebrity and not even know it. I thought I might be like Jim Carey's character in the movie, *The Truman Show*. The movie was about a boy who lived inside a town that had been created as a set for a TV show. The TV show was a reality show about the boy's life in that town. There were hidden cameras everywhere in the town that recorded the boy's every move. The boy was the only one who didn't know that he was actually the star of a TV show. He just thought that he was living a normal life. Only, the whole nation watched him all the time just like they would watch a reality TV show. The boy never knew he was in a make believe town and was actually living with actors who were reading scripts and causing him to live a life that was created by some writers who directed his every move. I remember thinking that was another mind-blowing movie when I saw it. Now I wondered if I was discovering that I was in the same situation that the boy in the movie was in. I wondered if people had been secretly watching me for some time without my knowing. I wondered if my life had been broadcast on some website or secret TV channel that I didn't know about. I wondered just how many people might be watching my every move. It made me paranoid. I thought that there might be a camera on me no matter where I was. I thought that the internet, newspapers, radio, and television might all be secretly telling my story to people who were interested in me. I started to wonder just how many people were tuning into this information. The paranoia made me become aware of my every move. I didn't want to act up if I might be on camera. I thought I had better start acting like someone that people would respect if they saw me on camera.

Chapter 50: Last Days at the Supply Line

In contradiction to how I thought I should behave, I went nuts on my drive back to Slidell that morning. An SUV passed me, on my way into Slidell, as I drove along I-10. I can't remember what exactly happened between the driver of the SUV and myself, but something he did triggered some serious road rage from me. I remember pulling alongside the SUV and shooting the guy a bird and yelling cuss words at him through my rolled down window. He yelled back at me. I remember pulling ahead of him and swerving into his lane. Once I got in front of him, I slammed on my brakes, hoping that he would hit me. Had he hit me, I'm sure I would have gone to jail. I was driving like a maniac. Fortunately, the guy was more level headed than me. He pulled off to the side of the road and somehow contacted the police. I kept driving towards Slidell. Within ten minutes of the road rage incident, I was being pulled over by a state trooper.

The state trooper got behind me and turned on his lights. I pulled off to the side of the interstate and sat in my car. I remember thinking that once the state troopers saw who I was, they would apologize and let me go. I rolled down my window as one of the state troopers walked up to my car. He said, "We just heard from the gentlemen in the (whatever car he was driving). He says that you pulled in front of him and slammed your brakes and just about caused him to wreck. I said, "Oh, I'm sorry. I didn't mean to cut him off. I was switching lanes. But I know who you are talking about because that guy was shooting me a bird and cussing at me when I went by him. I think he has some serious road rage problems." I told the officer that I was on my way to help at the supply line in Slidell. I told him that I understood how people could be stressed out from the hurricanes that had hit the New Orleans area. I told the officer that I thought the guy might just be one of the many people who were at their wits end from trying to deal with the stress brought on by the storm. The officer said, "Well, I didn't see it. I've just got your story and his story. I don't feel like writing a bunch of tickets. Just drive careful, O.K. I've got enough to deal with without having to take care of problems like this." I thanked him and started to drive off when the most unusual thing happened.

Just as I was about to start my car, I heard one of the state troopers yelling. I looked behind me and saw a flaming bottle fly through the air and land in the grass right between the police car and my own. The grass started burning and I saw the state troopers running over to the fire and stomping on it with their boots. I thought, "That must have been the secret group looking out for me again." I believed that agents of the secret group came along, just as I was talking with the police, and threw a Molotov cocktail at them. The bottle must have been filled with gasoline or some other flammable liquid because when it hit the ground, fire spread very quickly from it. I didn't get out of my car to help the police officers. I just drove off, thinking that the secret group had made sure to distract the police so that I could get away without any further trouble from them. I guess the people who threw that flaming bottle were some seriously disgruntled residents of the area who had real problems with the police. I'm sure that the state troopers got them because as I drove on to Slidell, I was passed by the same state troopers who had just spoken with me. They had their sirens blazing.

After the incident with the state troopers, I eventually arrived at the supply line. I got there that day and jumped right into the same routine I had been doing the past couple days. I unloaded pallets, loaded cars, and even directed traffic into our station. I talked with all the people that were at my station. It was the same group that I had worked with on the day before. Cody and Trudy were both there again. Towards the end of the day a bus arrived at the supply depot. It was filled with a National Guard platoon from Pennsylvania. They all piled out in their camouflage uniforms with M-16's and helmets, the works. It was pretty impressive, to me, to see all those soldiers arrive. It made me wonder if something big was about to happen. Most of the National Guard guys started sitting under some trees, near the first supply station, in the Wal-Mart parking lot. A few of the guys went and started talking to some of the administrative types that walked around all day and coordinated where to deliver the pallets of supplies and which truck to unload next. After a while, the National Guard troops started coming into the supply stations and working alongside the National Forestry guys. We now had more help than we needed at the supply line. We had two people doing the job that one person had been doing the last couple days. The National Guard guys were all very friendly and talkative. I remember several of the guys having skull tattoos on their arms. They looked like they thought they were real bad asses. I thought they looked like kids whose parents probably didn't like the fact that they had such morbid tattoos on their body. Most of the guys were very young. They looked like they were probably only a few years out of high school. Most of the guys my age were the superiors of those young kids that were helping us. Most of the older guys just sat under the trees in the parking lot and talked to each other. There wasn't enough work to be done to keep everyone busy. They didn't see the need for them to work just to be busy.

That night as I was getting ready to leave, Byron came up to Trudy and I and asked us what we were doing for dinner that night. I said that I was just going to take one of the rations back with me and eat it when I got back to the church. Byron said that he wanted Trudy and I to come to a military function that was happening that night at the place where they all went to sleep every night. I said it sounded like fun to me. I asked him how late he thought it would be when it was over. I told him I still had to drive all the way back to that church once we got back. Byron said that I could just set up my tent at the supply line and no one would mind. He said he would tell the guards that I was going to stay there that night. There were about 10-15 armed guards that kept watch over the supply line all night once everyone left. Byron told some of them about me spending the night there and that took care of it. After that, Trudy, another guy, and myself loaded up in her SUV and followed Byron and some other guys to their camp.

Byron's camp was actually a mall that had been shut down temporarily to house a lot of military and government agency workers. It was about 45 minutes away from the supply depot. All of the National Forestry guys, and the National Guard guys that had just shown up that day, were sleeping at the mall. The inside of several of the stores had been emptied out. In place of all the merchandise that would normally have been there, were cots. It was odd because there were still some display cases and counters where you could tell that jewelry or perfume was sold. But they were all empty and surrounded by those cots. The entire usable floor area of those stores were filled with rows and rows of cots. In the parking lot around the mall was a make shift village. There were trailers that were giving out food and drinks. There were temporary laundry houses. And there were rows of portable toilet stalls. They had also set up a covered outdoor eating area. There was also a place for a band to play or a speaker to make an announcement. Byron showed us around for a little while and then said we should go get something to eat. I was glad that he said that because I was starving. It was after 8:00 pm and I hadn't eaten since lunch, which had been another military ration. Trudy, Byron, the other guy that had ridden with us, and myself; all went to one of the food trailers to get something to eat. The meal was steak, potatoes, and some vegetables. It tasted really good to me. We went to another trailer and got our drinks. They had everything you could want except alcohol. I got a sweet tea. While we were eating, I remember there was a band playing at the makeshift stage area. Someone would get up and say a thing or two between songs. At one point we all stood up and said the Pledge of Allegiance and sang The National Anthem. Most of the songs were patriotic. Most of the speaking was congratulating everyone for the good work that they were all doing.

At one point this old woman who had been helping out at the supply line came up to me and asked me to go dance with her in front of the stage. Several people were already up there dancing. Trudy said she would go up there with us. So we all went up to the area where people were dancing and Trudy and the older lady started dancing. The older lady grabbed my hand and tried to get me to dance with her. I played along for a little while but didn't really get very animated. I think she was a little disappointed that I hadn't tried to have a better time with her. The problem was that I had suspected that there was something strange about this lady. I had seen her several times at the supply depot. Once, she even brought me a bowl of some stew that she said she had made at home and brought for us to eat. I remember already being paranoid about what I put in my mouth. I had already started to believe that someone might try to poison me. It was just another part of my delusional thinking that evil forces were all around me and might try to kill me when I least suspected it. When that lady handed me the bowl of stew, I thanked her and told her that I was going to let it cool off a little. As soon as she walked away, I threw it in the trashcan. I didn't want to take a chance on her stew being poisonous. I didn't know the lady and I thought that she might be working with the evil group that I thought now may be out to get me.

When she asked me to dance with her, I felt like I was socializing with someone who might be a threat to me. I wondered if she was trying to get me to feel comfortable around her so that she might be able to harm me. There was a time after we danced when Trudy, the older woman, and I walked around the parking lot of the mall and watched people scurrying around the laundry facilities. I remember facing the lady as she was talking to Trudy and I. Behind my back, I was making a gesture with my hand like it was a gun and I was pulling the trigger. I was hoping that some of the military people were watching my hand gestures and could understand that I thought that the older lady was a threat and needed to be dealt with. I thought it was my mission to point out people who I thought were working for this secret evil organization and let the people who were watching over me deal with them, whatever that meant. I was trying to tell the military people, who I thought were probably watching my back now, that this lady was a member of that evil group and they needed to get her out of there.

After a while we walked back inside the mall and through the area where everyone had set up their cots. We walked past all that to an area where a map of the United States was set up on a corkboard. A young lady walked up to Trudy and I. Her name was Sue Gillis. She was another one of the administrative types that worked at the supply depot. I had spoken with her briefly a couple times over the days that I was working there. She said, "Hey Scott, why don't you put a pin on the map. We are all putting a pin on the map where we live." Sue showed me where she lived, most of the time, in Colorado. I noticed that there were pins all over the country. People that were sleeping at that mall had come from just about every state in the nation. There were already several pins in Florida. Nobody had placed a pin near my area though. So, I put a pin right in the center of the state. That's about where Lake Buffum is, almost dead center in the state of Florida. Sue asked me for my telephone number. She said that she never knew when we might run into each other again, but that she thought it would be nice to have my number, so she could keep in touch with me. She said that it took a certain type of person to work in a disaster area and she loved doing it. She said she had been to areas that were struck by fires, floods, and just about every type of natural disaster there was. She said she appreciated that I had come all on my own and was not affiliated with any agency. She said that she thought it showed I was a very caring individual. Sue was probably ten years older than me, but I thought she was pretty attractive. I thought it was neat that she wanted my number. I got hers as well. I never called her after I left New Orleans.

Not long after that, we loaded up in Trudy's car and drove back to the supply depot. I said goodbye to everyone and started setting up my tent. That night I didn't hear any whispers or other noises. I think I went right to sleep.

Chapter 51: Revelations

The next morning I woke up and didn't feel so well. My throat was a little sore and I felt a little lethargic. I remember thinking that all the hard work and stress had caught up with me and that I was probably about to get sick. I walked over to the supply station and started doing the usual routine. I looked around and noticed how many National Guard guys were already sitting under the trees and talking. I thought, "There are too many people here now. I don't think I'm needed here anymore." I decided I would head back home to Lake Buffum. The National Forestry guys were also going back that day as well. I told Cody goodbye and went over and thanked Byron and Sue Gillis for letting me help out on the supply line. I said, "I know I didn't do anything important, but thanks for letting me help here. I feel like I did something." Byron said that they appreciated all the help I had given them. Sue told me to keep in touch with her. Like I said, I never called her. I don't think she ever called me either. I had told Byron about Sara leaving me just before I came up. I didn't tell him about being in the rehab center in Tallahassee or the fact that I had not held a job for almost a year. I just told him that Sara and I had a lot of problems and that I wasn't sure about the idea of divorce. Byron told me, before I left, to pray about my problems. He said that God would help me through my trouble. He said that he didn't think that divorce was the answer. He said that divorce hurt everyone, especially kids. I told him that I agreed with him and thanked him for his help. He told me to call him some time after I got back to Florida. I never called him. I do have his number and the numbers of all the other people I have mentioned in New Orleans. That's the only way I was able to remember their names to write in this story. I looked in the cell phone I was carrying at the time I was in New Orleans and found their names.

After saying my goodbyes to everyone, I loaded up my car and started to drive back to Lake Buffum. I figured I would do a reverse of the routine I had done getting to New Orleans. I planned to go back to Tallahassee and spend the night, then drive down to Lake Buffum the next day. The drive back home was filled with more fascinating and terrifying visions of the future.

The entire time I was in the car I had my radio blasting. I kept listening to The Counting Crows most of the time, along with Radiohead, and a few others. The Radiohead album *Hail to the Thief* gave me new ideas about the future that were further from reality than anything I had ever believed before. I'll start with other things I thought I heard on the Counting Crows album *Hard Candy*.

One story that I thought the Counting Crows were telling was in a song about "The gentleman with the collar and the blue suede shoes. He don't know what to do. He just wants to look good for you. So he rushes in to tell you what he did today. But he can't think of what to say. I think you'll listen anyway. So you watch him as he stutters over what to say. Its just a little game we play. Its no easier for you somedays…He wants to have a good time, just like everybody." I somehow interpreted this man in the song to be President Bush. My mind could now read a story into just about anything I saw or heard. I had already been thinking that I might be secretly associated with The President. So, at the time I was listening to this song, my mind just jumped on those lines about a guy in a collar and blue shoes, who stutters over what he says. I don't know that those words really describe President Bush, but that's the connection that I made. Another line that helped me come up with the idea was, "I just want to have a good time. I'm just another boy from Texas. I really want to have a good time. I really love the girls from Texas." I thought that the fact that the guy was from Texas, nailed it. The song was definitely about President Bush. It didn't matter to me that there was no message in the song about something President Bush might do. It just made me feel like he was probably a very good guy. The song by the Counting Crows described a decent person who "just wants to have a good time". That's all I ever wanted. I think that's all anyone really wants, to have a good time, whatever that means, whatever that takes. It may mean that you have to work hard and sacrifice things at times in your life. But really, aren't we all just out to have a good time? Some people hope that by struggling in this life, they will end up having a good time in the next life. But still, the end game is just to have a good time.

Another song that really blew my mind again was a song that started out with a guy saying "Big children run to God." I thought this was a powerful statement in itself. It made me think that the Counting Crows were at least somewhat religious if they had made a statement like that. It helped me to feel like the things they said were probably true and good. The rest of that song gave me new ideas about technology that might be out there that I did not yet know about. The song says, "I've got a home with electrical air and I live in a world that is smaller than anyone. I've got a lot on the new frontier. I've got a lot on the new America. All of the people are vanishing here. I could be huge if I could just get from the outside of everything, to the inside of you." Adam Duritz goes on to talk about, "The purest of no men, people are walking, the streets of America. It's so hysterical. Nobody here gets a word that I say. And the problems, I'm told, are more than medical. Well, I've got a friend from the new frontier. And Galatians says, this is not America. You need a girl with electrical hair and the word that you wanted was 'Al-u-minium. I was in bed with a girl at the end of the world. She said, 'I'm going home. You should come home too.' Well I'm at the end of a new frontier, here at the edge of a flower bending. I'm getting off, to get lost in the air at the end of the world, where the light is bending." These lines said a lot to me.

The first part about "the purest of no men" walking the streets of America, and problems that were "more than medical"; said something to me about my theory about a zombie army that would secretly live among us. I thought that the "purest of no men" were the zombies. The part about problems being "more than medical", reinforced the idea that whatever brought the dead back to life, was more than just a medical miracle, it was something evil. The "friend from the new frontier", I assumed was President Bush himself, or maybe even a higher authority that I did not yet know. I recognized the Galatians reference as some mentioning from the Bible about how corrupt our country had become. The "girl with electrical hair" reference left me guessing. I wondered if there was some group of special people who had received some new technology that I had never heard about. I wondered if the girl that Adam Duritz talked about was one of these people. I thought that maybe she was a type of new soldier that possessed special technology that somehow would help fight the coming battle that I thought would soon take place. I hoped that I might soon meet a person like the one he described. And finally, "I'm at the end of a new frontier, here at the edge of a flower bending. I'm getting off, to get lost in the air at the end of the world, where the light is bending." I thought this was an obvious statement about the end of the world coming soon. I thought that Adam Duritz already knew exactly what was about to happen and this was his warning for everyone to get ready. Exactly what we were all supposed to do, I wasn't yet sure. I just knew that The Counting Crows must have put out this album to tell everyone that the end of the world was now upon us. There were other songs that told me other stories about the mysterious present and near future.

Another song, I thought, was all about the reality of human cloning and advanced surgeries. "Surprise, surprise. You miss your hair. I miss my eyes. So we slide inside of someone's mouth, someone's eyes, until there's the sound of something internally exploding. But it's all inside of you. It's all inside of you. I wished that I was anesthetized and sterilized and then we wouldn't have this evidence congealing. Surprise! Surprise! Another pair of lips and eyes. And that is the consequence of actually feeling. But it was all inside of you."

This song seemed, to me, to be an obvious description and argument for human cloning. I imagined that Adam Duritz was describing a procedure where a human body was cloned so that a person might have a longer life expectancy. I thought that maybe, doctors might transfer a person's brain into a cloned body, at a point when the body was breaking down, so that they might continue to live. I thought the part about "we slide inside of someone's mouth, someone's eyes, until there's the sound of something internally exploding.", described what it was like to under go this procedure. I thought that maybe Adam Duritz himself had undergone the procedure and that was how he was able to describe it. The line about, "It was all inside of you", told me that Adam Duritz was trying to let everyone know that cloning wasn't something to be feared, it was just the process of taking a part of our own body to recreate a new part from it. That was an interesting argument to me. I had thought of cloning as being something that was potentially dangerous almost evil. I was frightened by the idea of people being created by scientists. After hearing The Counting Crows statement that, "It was all inside of you", I felt that maybe cloning wasn't such a bad thing after all. If scientists had discovered a way to produce new body parts, or new bodies all together, to prolong the life of the living; then maybe that was actually a good thing. All the rest of the lines, I thought, just reinforced the argument for human cloning.

Another song on the album that had a message to me was one that said, "Fading everything to black and blue. You look a lot like you, shatter in the blink of an eye. But you keep sailing right on through. Every time you say your learning, you just look a lot like me; pale end of the blistering sky; white and red, black and blue. You've been waiting a long time. You've been waiting a long time to fall down on your knees. Wait for everyone to go away. And in a dimly lit room where you've got nothing to hide, say your good-byes. Say your suffering in a note that says 'I'm tired of feeling nothing, good-bye."

I thought this song might be a description of what I needed to do to truly enter the realm of the secret group that would fight for good in the coming battle. I thought that the song described a way to make everyone think that I had disappeared forever. I thought that once I did that, the secret group would collect me and take me under its wing, finally showing themselves to me, and begin my training to prepare for the coming battle at the end of the world. I thought that all I needed to do was leave a note to my parents and Sara that made it appear that I had committed suicide. It seemed like a terrible thing to do. I imagined that Sara and my parents would spend the rest of their lives blaming themselves for my death. I thought this might not be the best way to disappear from my family.

The last song on the album that gave me an assurance that I was on a path to bigger things was one that said, "Is everybody happy now? Is everybody clear? We could drive out to the dunes tonight, because summer's almost here. I've been up all night. I might sleep all day. Catch your dreams just right. Let them slip away. When the roads are clear, head on out of here. If you're coming back, I'll see you in the morning. I'm just staring at the ceiling staring back at me, just waiting for the daylight to come crawling back on me. It's too late to get high now. It's too late to get high now."

I felt like this song described the way that I felt when I was working in New Orleans. I had been staying up until the early hours of the morning and wished that I could have slept all day. The part about heading out after the roads were clear was what I was doing at that very moment. I was heading back to Lake Buffum to rest and figure out what I needed to do next. And the part about "Its too late to get high now.", had nothing to do with smoking marijuana to me. I thought this was Adam Duritz telling everyone that it was now too late to try and act like you loved God. I thought that "get high" was a reference to getting holy, or religious. I thought that he was letting everyone know that God had chosen his followers now. A line had been drawn. It was now too late to try and switch sides. If you were living a life that reflected evil, you were now doomed to become a follower of Satan. If you had been fortunate enough to live your life according to God's will, then you were safe. I felt like I was on God's side. I was ready to find out just how I had to serve Him. I thought that probably had nothing to do with showing up at church or reading the Bible at this point. I thought that the way God was asking me to serve him was to find the secrets that were all around me and find the secret group who had asked me to come to New Orleans. So, those were the things that I thought I had learned from listening to The Counting Crows album, *Hard Candy*.

Radiohead had released an album a couple years earlier called *Hail to the Thief*. For me, it was filled with disturbing ideas about what was happening in the present and what would soon happen in the future. The first song on the album started me thinking. I thought it said, "Are you such a dreamer to put the world to ruin. I'd stay home forever but two and two always makes a five. I lay down the tracks, sand bags, and all. January was April showers but two and two always makes a five. It's the devil's way out. There is no way out. You can scream. You can shout. It is too late now. Because I might have been paying attention. Paying attention. Yeah, I might have been paying attention. Either I'm jealous or I'm horny... but I'm not. No I'm not. I'll swallow my pride... Oh hail to the thief, hail to the thief. Over my dead! Over my dead! Don't question my authority or put me in a box because I'm not it. Oh hail to the king and the sky is falling on me! But it's not. No it's not. No I'm not! Maybe not!"

The lyrics to this song seemed so vague to me and yet I thought I understood some of their meaning. I thought that Radiohead was saying something about a path that led a person straight to Hell. I thought Thom Yorke was saying something about when things in your life didn't add up to what they should, when you thought you had more or deserved more than you actually did, you were on your way to Hell. I thought that the line about "two and two always makes a five" said that. How I arrived at that idea, I don't know. Like I said, my mind had a way of reading something into nothing at all. I have no idea if those lyrics are even close to what Thom Yorke was really saying. I just heard what I wanted to hear and made up a story to make it have a meaning for me. The part about "I might have been paying attention!", I thought, was an announcement that Thom Yorke was also paying attention to the secret messages that were all around us. I thought that I too was now paying attention to everything much more closely than I ever had. My new attention to nuances and subtle things that happened around me, allowed me to discover the things that other people might not ever know, at least not until it was already too late for them. The part about, "Hail to the king and the sky is falling on me! But its not." Made me believe that people would soon worship a new leader, who might be the Anti-Christ, and they would feel like they had to worship him because if not, the sky would fall on them, they would be doomed. I thought that I would not find myself in that boat. I would be one of the people who fought against the Anti-Christ and helped the forces of good fulfill the destiny that was written in Revelations.

The next song begins, "Sit down. Stand up. Sit down. Stand up. Walk into the jaws of hell. Walk into the jaws of hell, anytime. Sit down. Sit up. Sit down. Stand up. They can wipe you out anytime. They can wipe you out anytime." I thought that this song described work life. For me it was how I felt when I worked at ETO/Architects. I was always being told what to do. "Sit down. Stand up." And after all my hard work, they did away with me, just like Radiohead said: "They can wipe you out anytime." The song later took on a different meaning to me. After I got back to Lake Buffum and had heard the album over and over. I began to re-translate what I thought some of the songs really meant. The new meaning was more incredible and terrifying than the previous. For now, this song was just about a terrible work environment.

Another song on the album said, "We're rotting fruit. We're damaged goods. What the hell, we've got nothing more to lose. One gust and we will probably crumble. We're back drifters. This thought, put no further. I'm hanging off a bridge.

269

I'm teetering on the brink of heart so sweet so fall asleep. I'm backsliding. You fell into a hose. We're traveling and there was nothing we could do. All evidence has been relieved. All tapes have been erased, but your thirst has given you away. So you're back tracking. You fell into a hose. You fell into a hose."

I thought this song described me, and what I was going through. I was "rotten fruit, damaged goods" because I had been labeled as a person with a mental disability. I felt like society did not view me as anything more than damaged goods. I thought that the process of getting labeled was also connected to how the secret group had found me. I thought that they might have interests in the people that society had set aside as mentally challenged in some way. I thought that they knew that I saw the world differently from most people and that's why they had chosen to contact me and bring me into the process I was now involved in. "I'm teetering on the brink of heart so sweet so fall asleep", described the way I now felt. I felt like I was overjoyed that I had been selected as a person of special interest. I was scared, but happy to be doing what I thought was God's good work. The "heart so sweet so fall asleep", line, to me, was a good description of how I felt. I thought it was a description of the peace, I thought I had, from knowing that God was watching over me and had surrounded me with his helpers to fight for Him. I thought that the "back drifters" were what I was a part of. I thought that was a name Thom Yorke had given to the group that I thought I was now a part of. The line about "You fell into a hose.", I thought, was a description of what had just happened to me. At one point I had lived a fairly normal life. Then I had a break down. I thought that fall into a breakdown was my fall into the hose. I thought the hose they talked about, was my journey from being someone who was normal, to someone who now knew all the secrets that I was learning. The "hose" was the portal that I had traveled into that was leading me to discover all the secrets that were hidden from normal people. I thought that my new keen perception of reality was what had allowed me to fall "into a hose" that was a path that led straight to the secret group that I was now a part of. I thought that I had been discovered by this group just as the line in the song said, "your thirst had given you away". I thought that because I had been seeking to find a reason for why I had been allowed to have that breakdown in Tallahassee, I had a thirst for meaning that was above the average person's desire and ability. I thought that the secret group had somehow discovered me while I was at that rehab center in Tallahassee. My thirst had given me away. I might have appeared normal before that time. But, once I was put in the rehab center, someone noticed something unusual about me. I was revealed as a person of exceptional skill in some area, I thought. I had no idea of exactly what that skill was. I just figured that there must have been a reason why I had been selected by this secret group. I thought that, in time, I would learn exactly what was so special about me to deserve this earpiece that was in my ear and to receive special messages from my television. You might think it seems crazy that a person could develop so many wild ideas from listening to music, but that's what I was. I was crazy. That's the only word I know to describe my thinking during that time.

Another song that got the wheels spinning was one that said, "Cheer right up. Cheer right up. It is now the witching hour. Close your eyes. We are not the same as you. Cheer right up. Its funny how the walls bend, when you breathe in.

They will suck you down to the other side. Do the shadows bloom? Do the shadows bloom? It's pure alarm bells. They should be ringing. And this is the code…" After that last line there is about a minute or more of electronic beats that, to me, might have been a secret message hidden at the end of that song.

The impression that song made on me was intense. I thought that I might have just discovered some real information that I needed to decipher to understand what Radiohead really wanted me to know. The beats at the end of that song were what really had my attention. All the lines that led up to the last one, "And this is the code.", described what, I thought, was a picture of the time we were living in. "the witching hour", I believed was a reference to the terrible times we lived in. I thought that the end of the world was near. I wasn't sure about walls bending when I breathed in. I later came to have a better understanding of what I thought that line meant. Getting sucked down to the other side, was what I thought would happen to most of the people I knew. I thought that they would be deceived by Satan's followers and would end up joining their fight against God and his followers. The alarm bells were what were going off all around me. All of the strange things I had seen in the past couple of weeks, I thought, were alarm bells, warning about the danger that was imminent. And the last line, "this is the code". That line blew me away. I wondered if the series of electronic beats that followed after that line, were "the code". I wondered if Radiohead had placed a secret message in that song that could be read only by some computer program. I wondered what the message was. I thought it was probably something related to the end of the world, and that I needed to figure out how to decipher that message. I remember listening to those electronic beats and feeling sure that I was hearing some computer language, like the noises you hear when a computer modem talks to the network before letting you log on to the internet from a dial up connection. It fascinated me to think that I had an actual secret message in my hands. I just had no idea of how I would decipher it. I never did. I got distracted by all the other things I thought I should do and soon ended up in another rehab center.

There was another song that I thought said, "Dinosaur, breathe in. Come on back. Come on back. Heaven sent you to me. Come on back. Come on back. We are actually waiting. Waiting. Come on back.", and then the guitars actually sounded as if they were making the sounds that I imagined a dinosaur might make. The really disappointing part about all this is that I actually read the lyrics to this song, years later, and found that what Thom Yorke was actually saying had nothing to do with dinosaurs. The word, dinosaur, wasn't even in the lyrics. I don't remember the actual lyrics now. It's irrelevant anyway. The point is that I could think I had heard something and my mind would instantly produce a story or explanation to go along with it. The song ,to me was, Thom Yorke, telling me that scientists had produced a living dinosaur. I had seen Jurassic Park. I'm sure this helped me feel like the creation of an actual dinosaur was possible. I started to think that the dinosaurs would once again roam the earth. I imagined that they might also be a new weapon that the military was developing to unleash on our enemies, or on our own people in the near future. I imagined living in a future where Tyrannosaurus Rex might be lurking in the woods, waiting to eat his next victim. I imagined a future where battles were fought with soldiers using giant monster companions to aid them in their fight. The wars of the future might involve our military unleashing these dinosaurs on people in foreign countries. Or maybe they might be used against us. Maybe the people who had learned the secret of bringing a dinosaur to life were actually the secret evil group. Maybe the dinosaurs would be used to strike fear in all who opposed the rule of the Anti-Christ. I wasn't sure. The song didn't tell me one way, or the other. So, I felt scared about the possibility of having to deal with a dinosaur in some upcoming battle. I just took this idea in stride with all the other things I thought I had learned. Now, information this bizarre didn't phase me like it had when I first started having this unusual experience. I was scared but also felt a sense of calm. I thought I was on God's side, so, no one could stand against me.

Another song that registered with me said, "I will lay me down, in a bunker underground. I won't let this happen to my children. Because white elephants are sitting ducks. I will rise up. Little babies eyes. Little babies eyes."

I thought that this song was probably like a message from Osama Bin Ladin. I didn't think that Radiohead was supporting Bin Ladin. I just thought they had written a song to describe his mind set after the life he had to lead following September 11th, 2001. I thought that the message was pretty clear. Osama was living in an underground bunker and was saying that he would not let this happen to his children. Osama said he would rise up, one day. The thought that someone like Osama Bin Ladin might rise up and kill more innocent Americans, terrified me. I knew that there were plenty of other terrorists out there who wanted to destroy our country. But the fact that Radiohead had written a song that I thought was almost like a quote from Bin Ladin himself, worried me. I wondered if they knew something that I didn't. I wondered if the events that occurred on September 11th, 2001, were just the tip of the iceberg and if the United States would soon find itself a conquered nation. I wondered if I would soon see a day when America had become a new nation that no longer was free, but instead was overrun by the terrorists that sought to destroy us. I wondered if the near future might involve another genocide. Only this time the genocide would be Muslims killing off all the Christians in the U.S.

The last bit of information that I gleamed from Radiohead's *Hail to the Thief* album was one of the most fantastic ideas that I had received up to that point. The song that really got me wondering about what was really happening around me said, "I'm walking out in a forced gale. The roof is hanging on by its fingernails. Your voice is right. Yesterday's Heaven is blown by the wind. Yesterday's people are scatterbrained. Any fool can, it's easy, peek a hole. I only wish I could fall in. I'm moving inside it, far away. Somehow I'll get out. Scatterbrained. Somehow I'll get out, I'm just scatterbrained. I can feel his power card, scatterbrained."

Again, those words are my interpretation of Radiohead's actual lyrics. I'm sure that I don't even have half of them correct, but that was what I thought I heard when I listened to that song. The one line that really had an impact on me was the one that said, "Yesterday's Heaven is blown by the wind." That got me thinking about the possibility that the very nature of what Heaven was had changed. I wondered if God was actually an alien from another planet that had created all the life on earth. I wondered if Heaven was actually another planet where all the souls of the departed went to after they died. I wondered if the people who lived their life according to the Bible went to this planet, Heaven, after they died. I thought that maybe Satan was another alien who had fallen from God's graces and was condemned to spend eternity on Earth. I thought that maybe Earth was Hell. I thought that the people who did not live their life according to the Bible, would be punished by having to live for eternity with Satan on Earth. I thought that once Satan was allowed to transform the Earth into what he wanted, then the planet would become the Hell that the Bible spoke of. I wondered if, maybe, Satan now lived in the center of the Earth. I thought that maybe the hot, molten core of the Earth was actually Satan's temporary prison. I thought that was where all the people who had been damned to Hell might be with him now. So, I now had an idea that Heaven and Hell were actually just planets. One was some far away place that had not yet been discovered by scientists. The other was actually our own planet, Earth. I thought that God, Satan, the angels, the demons; were all just aliens fighting for followers. We humans were just pawns, being used like cattle, to satisfy the desires of the aliens that had created us. I thought that this was pretty unsettling information that I couldn't tell anyone. It was my new religion. I now thought of God as an alien being who had decided to create our universe long ago. The alien theme was one that grew to be my wildest idea of all. I started thinking about the possibility that the God we worshipped might not be the only God out there. I wondered if the being that we worshipped was something that had fought other beings in the past to achieve the status he had come to bear on our planet. I wondered if other aliens had visited Earth in the past. I wondered if those aliens were what ancient civilizations had worshipped. I thought about the Egyptians, the Greeks, the Romans, with all their ideas of polytheism. I wondered if at one time these beings that were worshipped as gods had fought each other or reached some kind of agreement that they would let only one of them rule the planet. I wondered if that being that had somehow been chosen was the one that we called God. I was now inventing my own version of history, the Bible, and my own religion. Things were starting to get really weird.

Yes, the trip back from New Orleans was when most of the first really disturbing ideas came to me. These were just the beginning though. As the days went on, my mind kept topping itself to come up with more bizarre and fantastic explanations for what I thought was going on around me. It started to become hard for me to hold all this information to myself. I really wanted to tell someone. I thought someone should know about what I was discovering before it was too late. I just couldn't think of anyone I could trust. I now felt like my parents and grandmother might be working with another group of people that could be in conflict with the group I thought I was working with. I wasn't sure who they were associated with, yet. I just felt suspicious about them because they seemed to downplay everything that I talked about. It made me think that they either just didn't believe me, or that they were hiding some secrets of their own. I had not told them very much yet. About the only thing I had mentioned was that I thought that the television might be able to send messages as well as view what the person in front of it was doing. I had told this to my dad when we were at Nanny's house that day, before we started working on her rental house. I had told Dad that I thought the television had a camera behind the screen that was sending a video of the view from it to some secret group who was monitoring people. Dad had acted like that idea was absurd. I felt like he seemed to be hiding something that he knew about what I had just told him. I thought his acting like what I had said was ridiculous, was just a cover. He had laughed when I told him that I thought I was receiving messages from the television. I thought that too, was just part of his cover up.

There was a particular commercial that I remember seeing one day as I watched television. It was a commercial for a phone company. There was a voice that said, "Hello, Hello, Hello." The voice had an inhuman tone. I guess it sounded like the voice of a cartoon character. To me, though, it sounded foreign. It sounded alien. The voice, saying, "Hello, Hello, Hello.", in my mind, was the voice of an alien. In my mind, that was a message from the aliens who were about to make themselves known to us. The message that I received from that commercial was that the aliens were greeting us. I thought that the commercial was a sort of first contact between the aliens and us. The commercial even ended with a message that said, "Coming soon." I thought that was a clear indication that the aliens would be coming to present themselves to us soon. That commercial had a big impact on my thinking. I was sure that it was proof that my ideas of aliens about to change the way that everyone saw the world and themselves, was imminent. After seeing that commercial, I was sure that aliens were talking to me through the television.

It never occurred to me that maybe what I was thinking and saying was ridiculous. I felt like I had seen and heard things that had no other explanation. The people around me were the ones that looked crazy to me. I couldn't understand why they seemed so adamant to deny anything that I suggested might be possible. I figured that I probably should not share any more information with them. They couldn't be trusted. If they had trouble believing the few things that I told them before, there was no way that they could handle what I knew now. I was on my own. But I still wanted to tell someone.

The person I finally started to tell a little to, won't talk to me anymore. He hasn't spoken a word to me since the days when I tried to let him in on the secret danger that we were all in. I scared him so bad that he won't even return my phone calls and has hung up on me when he accidentally picked up the phone and realized it was me. Having that kind of effect on people damaged me for a long time. The person I finally tried to tell some of my secrets to was Justin White, my best friend. He and I have not seen each other or spoken since the days when I tried to let him in on what was going on. The fact that I lost my best friend really hurt me for many years. Now, I have learned that I have to move on. People can judge me, fear me, or whatever else I may cause them to do. I can only keep on living and try to never allow myself to get that far from reality again.

Chapter 52: The ARMY

I arrived in Tallahassee on my way back from New Orleans at night on the day that I headed back. I got a room at the Microtel again. I decided not to go to Pocket's Pool again that time. I just went to my room and slept. The next morning I drove back by ETO/Architects. It was just before 8:00 am when I got there. I saw someone I knew standing in the parking lot. There was Charles Di Franco, getting out of his car to start work that day. I pulled into the parking lot. I got out of my car and said, "Hey Charles! I hope I'm not getting you into any trouble by being here talking to you.", and laughed. Charles looked very nervous to see me standing there. He said, "No, I'm not going to get in trouble. Who cares anyway? What are you doing here? What is all that crap on top of your car?" I told Charles that I had just come back from New Orleans and was helping hurricane victims there. I told him that I had now volunteered with FEMA, The Department of National Forestry, and the National Guard. I said I had no idea of what might come from that, but that I felt pretty good about what I had just done. I told him that I was working with Arr Maz. I described the company to be similar to 3M. I told him that they made chemicals that made products work better. I said that they were a big company with plants all over the world. This was all true. The part that I didn't tell him was that I was basically a janitor there. I just told him that I planned to work my way up through the company from the bottom. I didn't tell him that I was making less than half of what I made when I worked at ETO. Charles seemed impressed by what I had told him. He probably just wanted me to shut up so he could get away from me before someone saw us together. That didn't happen though. Buster Cardar pulled up as we were talking. I greeted Buster with the same enthusiasm I had given Charles. Buster shook my hand and asked me how I had been doing. I gave him the same story I had just told Charles. Before I left, I wrote down a quick note on a sticky note that I asked Buster to give to Warren Eto. I wrote, "Warren, I love you! ETO/Architects rules!" and signed my name. Buster looked at it and laughed. He said, "O.K., I'll be sure he gets this.", and walked inside. After that, I headed back out of town, on to Lake Buffum.

I did one last stupid thing before I left Tallahassee to head to Lake Buffum. I called a florist in Tallahassee and asked them to send a $60 bouquet of flowers to Jen at Pocket's Pool. The lady asked me what I wanted to say on the card that came with the flowers. I said, "Write: Jen, you are #1!, and sign it from Scott Gann". The lady said she would and asked for the address of Pocket's Pool. I said, "I don't know the street address, its on Monroe Street. Can't you look in the phone book and find the address?" The lady hesitated and I said, "Look, if that's too much trouble then I'll just call one of your competitors and get them to send the flowers for me." The lady quickly said, "Oh no, its not a problem. We'll take care of it." Then she asked for my credit card number and I gave it to her. It was just one of many unnecessary purchases I had made. The list of ridiculous purchases would soon grow larger by leaps and bounds. I soon started spending money like I never had before. I thought that my future was bright and money would soon be something that I had an unlimited supply of. I figured that the secret group that I was associated with would probably start sending money to my bank account. I had no care about how much I spent or how little I needed an item.

On my way back to the lake house, I drove through Lakeland. There were a couple of strange things that happened that day as I made my way through town and on to Lake Buffum. The first was something so strange that I have no way of explaining it to this day. I was driving my car down South Florida Ave. I was near the Family Fun Center in South Lakeland when The Voice said, "Get ready. Here we go!" Right after The Voice said that, a Honda Civic driving alongside me wrecked into the back of the car in front of him. I could not believe what had just happened. I had been having thoughts about how evil every non-American product was. I included foreign cars as part of the evil, even though I drove one myself. When the Honda Civic wrecked beside me, I pulled into a gas station that was nearby. I got out of my car and laughed. I could not believe that the secret group had just allowed me to see such a powerful display of their capabilities. I believed that the secret group was behind the car wreck. I believed that they had somehow caused the car to wreck because it was a foreign car. When The Voice said, "Get ready. Here we go!" I had not even noticed the car beside me. The wreck happened only a few seconds after The Voice said that. It all made perfect sense to me that The Voice was letting me know that they were about to display their force, and then they did it. I was amazed. I stood at the gas station and watched the car that had been wrecked. By that point, the driver had stepped out of his car and was talking on a cell phone. The car he hit was stopped and its driver was also on the phone. I looked at the wreck and just laughed. I was stunned that the secret group could pull off such an outrageous stunt. I knew that the drivers of the wrecked cars had no idea of what had just happened. I believed that I was the only one who knew what had actually just happened. It made me laugh. I am sure that I looked like a psychopath as I laughed at the scene of a car wreck. I remember seeing people at the gas station who were giving me dirty looks. I didn't care. They did not know the things that I knew. I was not one of them. I was something much more special.

The next weird thing that I did took place only a few miles further down the road. After I finished staring and laughing at the wreck that I had just witnessed, I got back in my car and headed south towards Hwy. 60. As I was just about to leave south Lakeland and enter into Mulberry, I saw a sign on the side of the road. The sign read, "Over the hill!" It was a small homemade sign that was probably announcing someone's 40th birthday party. Any other time, I would have seen the sign and thought of it as just that. But in my delusional state, The Voice told me that the sign that read, "Over the hill!", was a statement made by someone who was "over", or tired of, Capitol Hill. I saw the sign and believed that it was a protest statement against George Bush's administration. I had already heard a lot of complaining from people on TV and the radio about things that they thought were wrong with the Bush

276

administration. Once The Voice clued me in on the true meaning of the sign, I became furious. I turned my car around and headed back up the road to find that sign. I pulled off the road in front of the sign. I got out of my car, walked over to the sign and pulled it out of the ground. Then I threw it out into a nearby parking lot. I thought that I had made a big statement about how loyal I was to the Bush Administration. I believed that the cameras that the secret group always had pointed at me, were probably sending footage of what I had just done, back to them. I thought that they would be proud once they saw what I had just done. After that, I got in my car and continued on to Lake Buffum.

I got back to Lake Buffum at some point that day. The thing I remember about coming back to Lake Buffum was the sky that day as I neared the lake house. The sky was totally overcast. It looked like a major storm was about to hit. The sky around me was filled with clouds that seemed to be swirling around the town of Lake Wales, as I drove through. I remember seeing this band of low clouds that seemed to be moving in a circular motion. It looked to me like the clouds were actually moving out of my way as I drove towards them. I wondered if the secret group was trying to show me another trick that they could do. I started to think that they were showing me that they could control the weather. I could not ever remember seeing clouds move the way that they seemed to be moving that day. I was convinced that the clouds were actually moving *around* me. I drove on to Lake Buffum thinking about Moses parting the Red Sea in the story from the Bible. I wondered if the same force that had helped him part the sea, was now helping disturb the clouds around me. I felt like I was now something more than an average human being. I began to realize that if I was connected to a group that could actually change the weather, then I might be something more than the average Joe.

I got to the lake house and found that no one was home. The wind was blowing hard and the sky looked ominous. Those clouds that had seemed to swirl out of my way on my ride out to the lake had now formed a ring in the sky that made a calm center in the middle of a dark looking ring of clouds. It was very strange looking to me. It looked like a terrible storm was about to occur all around the lake. But right over the lake, the clouds had parted, forming an almost circular opening where the sky was much brighter. It was not a clear sky in the middle of the circle. But there was a drastic difference between the light color of the sky over the lake, and the very dark, heavy clouds that surrounded it on all sides. I could never remember seeing the sky look that way. I'm sure that I wasn't hallucinating. It was just a weird weather phenomenon. Of course, I assumed that there must be a meaning to why the sky appeared so strange. I began to worry that I was being given a message that my parents were in trouble. I called Nanny and asked where Mom and Dad were. She said that they had gone south to see my uncle Mark and aunt Janice for the weekend. I thought, "All right, maybe they are O.K. Maybe I'm just getting worked up over nothing." After that phone call to Nanny, I just went outside and stared at the sky. I kept thinking, "These guys are amazing. How are they able to control the clouds?" I just kept staring at the weird sky and imagining that this was all a show that had been put on by the secret group to let me know, "We're still here. We're still watching over you." The sky looked frightening, but I felt safe. I now knew that I was backed by a force that could control the weather itself. It made me feel powerful to think that

I was associated with such a group of people. I figured that the secret group must be using the device they had used to create the hurricane that had destroyed New Orleans. They were just showing me that they were still with me. Knowing that I had such powerful people on my side gave me a sense of calm.

I don't remember anything else about that weekend. I do remember that when Mom and Dad came back from seeing Dad's brother, the real trouble started brewing. After Mom and Dad got back, I wanted to tell them all about what I had done in New Orleans. I had no intention of sharing my crazy ideas with them. I just wanted to tell them about all the things that I had done in New Orleans. I wanted to describe the devastation. I wanted to tell them about handing out food and water to thousands of people. I wanted to tell them about the Department of Forestry and the National Guard people that I had made friends with. I thought that those were important stories that I had to tell them about. Mom and Dad acted like they didn't want to hear anything I had to say about New Orleans. Every time I started to talk about it, they would start talking about something that related to them. They always stopped me and changed the subject. I could tell that they had no interest in hearing about what I had done in New Orleans. It made me very angry. I knew that I had left for New Orleans against their will, but I was 29 years old. I felt like I had a right to do what I wanted, even if they were the ones who bought my groceries and put a roof over my head. Still, I had done something that they were against, and now, I thought, they were letting me know it. Eventually, I gave up on trying to talk to them about New Orleans. I started trying to figure out what my next step should be.

I thought about how important I felt while I was helping people at the supply line. I thought about seeing those National Guard troops and the Department of Forestry guys working in their uniforms and looking very official. I liked how they were part of something big. I thought I was part of something bigger, but no one else knew that. I wanted to be part of something big that everyone could appreciate. I remembered seeing all the advertisements for the military, before I went to New Orleans, and how I thought that they were actually messages from the secret group. I decided that what I should do was, join the Army. I thought that was probably what the secret group wanted me to do. I felt like they had been putting me in contact with the military to let me see how my life could be. I thought that once I joined, the secrets that they were still hiding from me would be revealed. I thought that I needed to join the military so that I would be escorted to the people there who were working with this secret group. I thought that the secret group was probably heavily involved in the military. I thought that they wanted me to join so that I would receive the special training that they wanted to put me through so that I could become one of them. So, I decided to go see a local Army recruiter.

I went to the Eagle Ridge Mall in Lake Wales. Inside was a recruiting office for the Army. On my drive from the lake house to the mall, I kept noticing all of the blue cars that were around me. I thought these were cars driven by members of the secret group who were escorting me on my way to make my big commitment to the Army. I remember looking at the people driving the blue vehicles, as I passed them, or they passed me. I would smile and wave at them as they went by. Some would smile and wave back. Others wouldn't notice me or would see me and not acknowledge me. I thought that all of them were definitely members of the secret group. I felt like I was moving closer to my destiny.

I walked in wearing my new usual attire. While I was in New Orleans, I started wearing the straw cowboy hat that I had purchased in Gainesville. Along the way back I picked up a pair of sunglasses that were pretty flamboyant for me. They were clear plastic and had very large lenses. Kurt Cobain, from Nirvana wore similar looking sunglasses in some pictures I had seen of him. I thought they looked really cool. I thought that, with the straw cowboy hat, they made me look like a bit of a celebrity. I also wore the camouflage sandals that I had bought in Gainesville. So, I walked into the Army recruiter's office wearing a straw cowboy hat, Kurt Cobain sunglasses, t-shirt, shorts, and flip-flops. I remember talking to one of the recruiters and he asked me, "Who are you working for?" He thought I was not really someone off the street that wanted to join the Army. He thought I might be with some agency that was reporting how good of a job he was doing, I think. I could be totally wrong. I just remember that he was laughing at me as I said some of the things that I told him. He didn't think that I seriously wanted to join the Army. I told him about volunteering in New Orleans and how I realized that I really liked helping people who were in a crisis. He started to take me a little more seriously. He told me to take a practice test for the ASVAB. I completed all the sections and they graded it right there. He said that I would likely be able to pick most any field that I wanted because I had scored a 93 out of 100 on the ASVAB practice test. He said to take the ASVAB and then I would be able to determine what field I wanted to go into. Then I slipped up.

The recruiter asked me about my medical history. I started to tell him about my time in the rehab center in Tallahassee. His eyes got a little big as I told him what had happened to me. He said, "Well, you shouldn't have told me that because now that complicates your situation." I told him I knew I probably wouldn't be allowed to join. I told him that was why I had come clean about the rehab center. I didn't want to waste a lot of time jumping through hoops to find out that they were going to turn me down. The recruiter said, "You didn't have to tell me that though. That's confidential information that I'm not required to know. But now that you have told me, I have to get a bunch of paper work from your doctor and your parents, about why you were admitted to the rehab center, before I can let you even try to join the Army." The recruiter said that I would not be allowed to have any medication if I went to boot camp. He said that I should stop taking my medication to see how I did without it. I told him that I hadn't been taking my medication for several weeks. That wasn't entirely true. I had taken some of my pills before my backpack went missing in New Orleans. I wasn't taking them regularly, like I should have been, but I hadn't completely stopped either. The recruiter told me that my best chance of being admitted to any branch of the military was with the National Guard. He said that if I worked 6 months with the National Guard and all went well, I could then transfer into the Army. He referred me to a recruiter for the National Guard in Haines City. He told me that when I spoke with the National Guard recruiter, not to mention the things I had told him about the rehab center. He said that if I wanted to pursue going directly into the Army, that I would have to get my parents and all the doctors that I had been involved with in Tallahassee and Bartow, to write letters explaining what had happened that got me put in the rehab center and how they felt I was now fit to join the Army. I told my parents about needing them to write me a letter so that I could join the Army. They didn't seem to like that idea any more than my idea to go to New Orleans. It never occurred to me that they probably saw me as the last person who should be joining the military. I just thought that they were giving me a hard time for no good reason. I never thought about how telling my dad that the television had talked to me, might cause him to see me differently. I didn't spend much time dwelling on how other people might see me. I only focused on what I needed to do to become a part of the secret group. Whatever ideas other people had about me: what I was doing, saying, or what I was capable of, was irrelevant to me.

Since Mom and Dad didn't seem to want to write any letters for me, I decided to see the recruiter for the National Guard. Mom and Dad kept asking me when I was going to go back to work for Arr Maz. I told them that I didn't think I would go back to Arr Maz because my new plan was to join the military. They didn't like the sound of that idea. I didn't care. I figured that once I was under the military's wing, I wouldn't have to worry about what they thought I should be doing anymore. So, I went to Haines City to talk with the recruiter.

I met with a man at the National Guard armory in Haines City, who was their recruiter. He was a very friendly guy. He asked me if I liked to smoke. I said, "I'm trying to quit. I haven't smoked in a few weeks." He said, "Well, I like to smoke NewPorts." That was my favorite brand of cigarettes. He lit up a NewPort and started smoking as we talked. He said, "Sure you don't want one?" I said, "What the hell. Yeah, I'll smoke one with you." So, he gave me one of my favorite cigarettes. I lit it and started smoking and telling him about my experience in New Orleans and my score on the practice ASVAB. He showed me a few fields, in the National Guard, that he thought I should think about going into. I told him that I was interested in going into an intelligence type position. I told him that I wanted to get myself into a field that would allow me to eventually work with the C.I.A. The recruiter said that those types of jobs were something I could do once I joined the Army. He pulled up some information on his computer about possible fields that I could go into with the National Guard. I don't remember being very interested in any of them. The one I thought I would probably do, was a field that involved the coordination of supplies to various bases within the National Guard. It seemed more like the job of a FedEx worker than a military job. The job involved transporting supplies and accounting for supplies stored in warehouses. The job didn't sound interesting at all. It had nothing to do with my dream of getting into military intelligence. The reason I said I was interested in that job was because I would be working out of an armory in Lake Wales. I thought that would make my life easier while I waited to join the army. I figured I could work six months at a job that didn't seem very glorious, if it allowed me to join the Army and get to my real goal.

The real goal was to join the military and become an intelligence agent. I thought that if I did that, I might get access to top-secret information that might prove some of the wild ideas I had in New Orleans and on my way back from there. I thought that the secret group probably wanted me to get involved with intelligence so that I could learn these secrets and so that I could learn new information for them about the other group that was plotting to bring about the end of the world. Of course, I didn't reveal any of this to either of the recruiters that I talked to.

The National Guard recruiter set up a date for me to take the ASVAB in Orlando a few days after our meeting. I went to Orlando and took the test. I thought it was a pretty easy test. I bet I did very well. I don't know. I never found out my score. I never talked to the recruiter again. Before I ever got the chance to do any of that, I was locked up in another rehab center. After my second lock up in a rehab center, I knew that the military was not going to be the way that I met up with the secret group. I tried to find another way.

One evening, at dusk, I was walking along Orange Street (the road that leads to my parents' lake house) and I had a very frightening encounter. I walked to the end of Orange Street to where it meets with Lake Buffum Road. As I approached Lake Buffum Road, I noticed a man walking down it. I stopped and watched the unusual way that the man was walking. I thought that his walk resembled the way that I had seen zombies walk in horror movies. He had a slow stride and he limped on one foot. He was also leaning to one side a little. It looked very odd to me. The man was a good distance away, but was close enough to observe his unusual stride. The Voice affirmed what I was already thinking. It said, "Congratulations, you just saw your first zombie." I got chills after hearing that news. I had already been imagining the horrors that I thought were taking place in New Orleans. I had not thought that the zombie problem was something that was occurring in my neck of the woods. I stared at the strange man for several minutes and wondered what I should do about him. I began to walk towards the strange man. I didn't walk fast. I walked just fast enough to get a little closer to him. I was unarmed and did not want to take my chances with the undead. I had no idea of what the strange man might be capable of. I followed him for several minutes and then watched him walk off towards a house that was just off of Lake Buffum Road. I thought that there was a chance that I had just seen a zombie, or maybe there was a chance that The Voice was just screwing around with me. I wasn't sure.

One last incident that I remember happening, before that second lock up in a psychiatric ward, was a drive from Lake Buffum to Lakeland. I remember driving to a gymnastics practice for Liza and Gwen. Sara had put the girls in gymnastics. I drove on to their practice listening to the Counting Crows album, *Hard Candy*. There was a song that said, "Make a circle in the sand, make a halo with your hand, make a place for you to land." The Voice told me that the halo symbol was a form of communication with the secret group. I was not sure about what the circle in the sand part was about. I had heard of certain cults who believed in making magic circles. I remembered hearing about a group that believed that by making a circle in the sand, and chanting the correct phrases, a person could make a circle for them to stand inside of that protected them from evil spirits. In my delusional state, I wondered if the magic circle had real powers that might protect me from the forces of the secret evil group. After hearing the Counting Crows talk about making a circle in the sand, I wondered if the magic circle was what they were referring to. As I drove on towards Liza and Gwen's gymnastics practice, I kept making hand signs that I thought communicated messages to the secret group. The Voice and the Counting Crows had told me about the halo. I figured that was a sign that told the secret group that I was definitely wanted to be one of them. To me the halo represented the holiness of the secret group. I was sure that they were a force of good. The halo also was a sign for a hole. I felt that I had slipped into a hole that led me to the mysterious world of the secret group.

As I drove on to the gymnastics practice, I made other hand signals that I felt told the secret group things that I was thinking. One thing I did was make my hand into the shape of a gun. I pointed it out of my window and pretended to shoot all the foreign cars that passed by me. After seeing the secret group wreck that Honda Civic, I was sure that they meant business about foreign cars being terrible for the safety of our nation. The Voice had told me how we were giving so much of our money to foreign auto makers and that it was very dangerous because we were importing more than we were exporting. I shot my imaginary hand gun at almost every foreign car that passed by. I also made a hand signal that represented the jaws of a dinosaur. I made my hand into the shape of what I imagined to be the head of a Tyrannosaurus Rex. I moved my fingers so that it appeared that the head was moving its mouth open and closed. I drove along imagining that there would soon be a time when dinosaurs roamed the Earth. I made all these hand signals with my hand hanging out of the window of my car as I drove down the road. I am sure that people passing me must have thought that it was odd to see me driving down the road, making all these strange gestures with my hand.

After the gymnastics practice, I stopped at a gas station on my way home. I went in wearing my straw cowboy hat, my camouflage flip-flops, and my Kurt Cobain sunglasses. By this point, I was beginning to believe that I was a type of National Security agent. I felt that it was part of my duty to call out any people that I felt were a threat to the safety of our nation. To me, that included most people that worked at gas stations. Every time I saw a Middle Eastern person working at a gas station, I made sure to give them a little attitude. That day at the gas station was no exception. I walked in and noticed the Middle Eastern man behind the counter. I took off my sunglasses and shot him my best tough guy stare. Then I walked over to the candy aisle and picked up a pack of gum. I remember picking up a pack of Eclipse gum. I thought the name of the gum was symbolic for the situation. I thought, "Eclipse. Like the Bush Administration is about to eclipse the Middle East and send them back to the stone age for what the terrorists did to us in New York and Washington D.C." I thought that the gum made a subtle statement to the gas station worker, who I am sure thought nothing of the candy that I put on the counter in front of him. He said, "Will this be all?" I said, "Yes. That's it." I stood there for a few seconds and then said, "Don't think that we aren't watching what you and your friends are up to.", and then walked out. I'm not sure what the guy thought about my weird comment because I didn't stick around to hear it. I just calmly walked out with the best bad-ass routine I could come up with. I looked back at the guy as I walked out to my car and saw that he was watching me. I got in my car and kept staring him down as I drove out of the parking lot. I bet he wondered who I was and what provoked the comment that I made to him. I hope I didn't cause him too much worry. I doubt that I did. I'm sure gas station employees are used to dealing with whack jobs.

Chapter 53: The Path to the PRC

The day that I got put away in the rehab center started out like a good day, I thought. It was a day just a few days after I had taken the ASVAB in Orlando. My dad had asked his brothers and I to help him put a new roof on the guesthouse. That was what we called the other house that was on my parents' lot. The guesthouse roof had been damaged during the hurricanes the year before. It just didn't get damaged enough to need an immediate replacement. Dad, his brothers, and I, had replaced all the shingles on the main house with green shingles. He wanted the guesthouse to match it. Dad and I had already torn the shingles off of the guesthouse to get it ready for a new roof. That was a couple days earlier. I remember that day because that was the day that I thought I would share a new piece of information with Dad.

A couple of days before getting thrown in the psych ward, I remember tearing off shingles from the roof of the guesthouse. I remember as I worked to tear off the shingles, I kept hearing people whispering. I thought I was hearing the conversation of some people watching me from somewhere near the house of one of our neighbors, Mr. and Mrs. Pren. I remember stopping what I was doing every now and then and staring out at The Pren's house, looking for someone who was talking very quietly. I realized that what I was hearing was a conversation about me. It was very similar to the whispers I had heard when I tried to sleep in my tent at night, near New Orleans. The conversation was something like this, "Can you believe that's him.", and, "I know, he is amazing." It was the same kind of flattery that I thought I had heard in New Orleans. Somewhere, some people were watching me and were amazed that they had the chance just to see me. I thought I was hearing the conversation of two new guards that had been sent to watch over me at the lake. I thought that they must hold me in the same high regard as the guys who had watched over me those nights I slept in the tent near New Orleans.

To hear people sounding excited just to see me, as if I were some kind of celebrity, added to my enormous ego. I remember smiling and looking towards The Pren's house as I threw shingles off the roof. My dad noticed my strange behavior and asked why I was smiling and staring at the neighbor's house. I thought about what I should tell him. I decided that I would see how he handled my news about having a tiny phone in my ear that he couldn't see. I said, "You've seen those hands free headsets that people walk around with now haven't you? You know, the ones that let you talk on your cell phone without having to hold a phone to your ear?" Dad said, "Yes.", with a tone that let me know he was wondering what in the world was going to come out of my mouth next. I said, "Well, what if I told you that I have one of those in my ear. Only you can't see it. It's been put somewhere so far into my ear that it isn't visible." Dad said, "How did you get something like that?" I told him that I thought the military had put it there when I was sleeping one night. I told him

283

that it allowed me to hear people talking and I thought it allowed the military to listen to what I wanted to say to them too. I explained that it was basically like a tiny cell phone, only I didn't have to dial any numbers. I could just talk and they would hear me. I told him that sometimes I would hear them. Then I told Dad that I had been hearing two people talking about me that had to be somewhere that they could see me. I told Dad that I thought that two guards were watching me from the bushes at The Pren's house.

Dad played the situation with his usual cool. He just said that he didn't see anyone over there and that he doubted that anyone had put something in my ear. If I had been in his shoes, I would have had me Baker Acted right there on the spot. I think he had been told, by the police, that there was nothing he could do to me if I wasn't harming anyone else or myself. So, he had probably wanted to put me back in a rehab center for a long time, but they wouldn't help him. There was no cause to Baker Act me, because I had not threatened anyone, that they knew, or myself. After I told Dad about the cell phone, we just kept on working. I thought he would be filled with questions about how such an amazing piece of technology had come to be placed in my ear. I thought he would want to know about the people I said had placed it there. Instead, we just kept on working. I thought that he was either jealous that he didn't have this new technology himself, or maybe he already had it too, and didn't think that I should have it. I wondered if he was working with the people who were associated with the evil group that wanted to bring about the end of the world. I didn't think my parents were evil. I thought that something had happened that put them in a situation where they were being forced to work for this evil group. I thought that they either didn't realize the true agenda of the secret group that they were working for, or they were being forced to associate with them, against their will. It still made me paranoid of them. I couldn't understand why they seemed so distant and unimpressed every time I told them a bit of the incredible secret world that I was now involved in. The idea that they must be working for some other group, was the only explanation I could come up with to explain their disinterest in me. What I was really seeing was my parents struggling to figure out what the hell they should do with their crazy son before I hurt someone or myself and ended up in jail. None of that occurred to me at the time though. Everything was a delusion.

So, back to that last day of running around as a free, crazy person:
We had removed all the shingles from the guesthouse a few days earlier. Dad knew that I was nuts. I didn't know that. I just thought he was being an asshole for reasons I couldn't be sure of.

My dad's brothers were at the lake house. They had arrived the night before. I remember waking up at around 4:00 am and drawing pictures of the things I wanted to tell my dad about. I drew a picture of me riding on a small, friendly looking dinosaur. I drew another picture of our solar system. I drew all the planets spinning around in orbit. I drew another dot far off in the corner of the page. It represented Heaven. It was just my first sketch to record my new thinking about The Creator. After I got done sketching, I took out some old Star Wars action figures from my collection of Star Wars toys. I was 29 and I decided to play with my old Star Wars toys. I didn't really play with them. I arranged them to tell a story to whoever saw them. I grouped several of them together on a table that was in my room. I had them all standing up and facing the same direction, almost like they were a group of students. I made sure that everyone that was standing in that group was a human. There was Luke Skywalker, Han Solo, Princess Lea, and other human characters from the movies. At the front of the group I placed Yoda, the little green, sage like, alien character from the movies. I had him facing the group of humans. Behind Yoda, I placed a few other alien characters from the movies. The story I was trying to tell with the characters was this: We humans were being taught how to live by aliens. The aliens represented my new idea of what I thought that God and his angels really were. The humans represented all of us. I hoped that if someone saw the arrangement of figures, they might ask me about them. I don't know if anyone ever saw them. No one ever commented about them to me. Whoever saw them, probably just figured it was another of my deranged behaviors and gave it no further thought.

After I had done the sketches and played with the Star Wars characters, I decided to do one last thing. I laid out a CD insert that belonged to an album I had been listening to. It was the insert that came with the Beck album, *Guero*. The music had not given me any secret messages but the insert that came with the CD did. The insert folded out to reveal a series of images. One image showed a group of people, of different ethnicities, gathered behind a man like figure with the head of a monster. The figure also had bat wings hanging from its arms and connecting to the sides of its torso. Some of the people standing behind the monster were wearing military uniforms. Other people were dressed in civilian clothing. There were also women and small children gathered behind the monster. What I took from the picture was an image of the leader of the secret evil group, possibly Satan himself, standing in front of a group of his followers. The image was disturbing to me. The winged monster looked grotesque and made me fear the fact that I believed I was going to have to fight against creatures like the one in the drawing.

The other image that had an impact on me was a picture of three men, dressed in white clothing, who were being lifted up on a rope that ran off the end of the page. The rope was being suspended by something that was out of the picture. One man was on the ground, holding the end of the rope. Another man was climbing up the rope. At the very top of the picture were the feet of another man, who I assumed was also climbing up the rope. The man on the ground was surrounded by creatures that were not human. I assumed that the creatures were aliens. I believed the picture to be a secret message of how to escape the coming trouble that would ultimately plague the world. I thought that the picture showed humans being rescued by aliens. I thought that the rope in the picture led to a spacecraft that would carry the humans away from the dangers that, in the near future, would threaten to end life as we knew it. I thought that the rope was a symbol of escape. The people climbing up the rope were escaping the problems that would soon develop on Earth.

I wanted to lay out the CD insert so that my dad and his brothers would see it when they woke up that morning. I was hoping that it would start a conversation about the things that I thought were being discussed by the images on the CD insert. After having it sit on the kitchen counter for about thirty minutes, all unfolded so that everyone would see it, I decided that it would be best to have that discussion another time. I thought that Dad would probably just make fun of my ideas or get irritated with me for talking about them. So, I folded the insert back up and put it in my room. The ideas that the insert gave me about an escape route would later develop into a more complex thought. There would soon come a time when I really wanted to find the aliens that would give me an escape from the terrifying world around me.

Shortly after putting up the weird CD insert, everyone else was waking up. I walked out of my room and started talking to everyone about nonsense, I'm sure. I don't remember what I said to them. Eventually, we started working on the guesthouse roof. My dad and his brothers and I pulled off all the tarps that were used to keep water off the roof. Then we started putting down the tar paper. After we finished that, we started on the shingles. My dad's brothers, Mark and David, started working on one side. Dad and I worked on the other. The whole time Dad and I worked together, I was a total pain in the butt for him, I'm sure. I remember giving him an attitude about everything we did. I kept pointing out how Uncle Mark and Uncle David seemed to be working so well together. They were working faster than we were, I kept telling him. My dad was probably ready to throw me off the roof and put me out of my misery. But, he just kept taking the abuse and trying his best to hold his tongue and not beat me senseless. I was already lacking enough sense as it was. I guess he figured that I didn't need to be beat for it. I remember at one point Dad was laying down shingles and I was nailing them in. I kept placing nails very closely together. Dad would say, "I think you can spread them out a little more than that." Then I would place nails much farther apart than I knew they should be. I was just being a total pain in the butt. There was no reason for it, other than I thought he had given me a lot of hard times lately. I still blamed him for getting put in the rehab center in Tallahassee. So, I felt like all that had happened to me over the last year, all that I lost, was his fault. So, every chance I got to show him how dissatisfied I was with him, I showed him. It was a very terrible thing to do to the person who had done nothing but try his best to help me. I can't believe that he was able to deal with me as long as he did. I spent most of that day doing one disrespectful thing after the next.

Another thing that I was doing, that was unusual for me, was blasting my radio at my parents' house. I kept trying to get my dad and his brothers to hear the messages in the songs I had listened to lately. I kept playing The Counting Crows and Radiohead. I had it blasting from my car stereo. I didn't want to come out and say what I thought each song was talking about. I wanted them to hear the words and see what conclusions they came to. My mom came out several times and turned the radio down. Every time she went back inside, I would jump down off the roof and turn the volume back up. Both albums had songs with the "F-word" in them. Normally, I would never listen to a song with that kind of language in front of my parents. Now, I didn't care. It was more important to me that they all heard the messages in those songs. Nobody ever clued in on any of the "secret messages" that the songs were talking about. I thought that surely, once they heard the words, something might pop in their heads that I had thought. Nobody seemed very impressed with anything that I played. I decided to tell them about some of the less bizarre ideas I thought some of the songs were talking about. I mentioned the song that I thought was a description of President Bush on The Counting Crows album. I also tried to explain how one of the songs talked about something bad happening in

Miami and New Orleans. Nobody seemed to agree with me. They acted like I was reading a little too much into some songs written by a rock band. I just ignored their disagreement and kept explaining. I put in the Radiohead album again and pointed out the song that I thought talked about Osama Bin Laden. There was just more of the same reaction from everybody on the roof. They just acted like I was a little paranoid and was studying the lyrics a little too hard.

After we finished putting on the shingles that day, we sat around under an oak tree in my parents' front yard. I remember talking to Dad and my uncles but have no idea of what I was talking about. The thing I do remember about sitting around under that tree was that I decided to smoke a cigarette in front of them. I had never smoked a cigarette in front of my dad or my uncles. It was just more of my bizarre behavior. I remember telling my dad and uncles that I could look like I was smoking, but not actually be smoking. I said, "Watch this.", and I drew in a breath of smoke from the cigarette. I made my chest look like it was expanding, but I didn't inhale the smoke. I said that was a trick I had learned lately. That was probably the stupidest thing I had ever done in front of them. They all looked at me, and each other, with strange faces. I just kept doing my fake smoking routine. Eventually, they all went inside and left me by myself. I think that they got a gutful of my weirdness. I sat there by myself under the tree and wondered why they all seemed to be avoiding me as much as possible. I thought, "They don't mind using me when they have work for me to do, but otherwise, they act like they can't stand to be around me." I started to feel a little sad. I thought about the girl I had met at the bar that night in Tallahassee, Jen.

I had called her a couple days earlier at Pocket's Pool. She actually answered the phone. I said, "Hey Jen, its me Scott Gann. Remember, I'm the guy that you talked to a lot that night when I was up there at Pocket's? I asked you if you wanted to walk the lake and you disappeared. I heard that I had scared you somehow. Did you get the flowers that I sent you?" Jen said, "Yes. I know who you are. I got the flowers." I said, "Was that odd to send you flowers?" She said, "Yeah. A little weird. I don't get the note." Then she said, "I've got to get back to work. See you later.", and hung up the phone. I realized that I had wasted my time and money on her. I thought she seemed interested in me. I was wrong. I wondered what her last name was. I thought, "I'll bet it begins with an 'H.'" Everything had to be symbolic to me somehow. My dead grandfather's initials were J.H., for James Hollings. I thought, "Jen H., that's got to be it. Someone put me in the place to meet her because her initials are J.H., we must have some future together. Maybe she likes me, but is afraid to let me know because that other guy at the bar told her something to make her scared to tell me that she likes me." I took the white tank top that I had been wearing and got a red and a black permanent marker. I drew a heart on the shirt and wrote "I" above the heart, and "J.H." below it. The shirt now said, "I (heart) J.H." I hung it on a cable that stretched between two trees that Blue was sometimes tied to. I looked at the shirt as it hung there. I thought, "Maybe the cameras that are always watching me will record this and show it to Jen. She'll know what the shirt means. No one else will but her. Mom and Dad will think that the letters stand for Granddaddy's initials." Then I decided that I wanted to add some blue to the shirt so that it would be red, white, and blue.

I went inside and grabbed a bottle of blue dish washing soap. Mom said, "What are you doing out there?" I said, "I'm just cleaning the shirt I was wearing.", and walked back outside. I took the bottle of blue soap and squeezed it all over my tank top. It now had blue streaks of dishwashing soap all over it. I thought it looked pretty cool and was very patriotic. Mom came out and asked why I was pouring soap all over the shirt. I just said that I thought it looked cool. She said I needed to stop wasting soap and went back inside. I put down the soap and got angry. I thought, "I am tired of them telling me what to do every minute they are around. And I'm sick of them making me feel like what I talk about is crazy." I started to get myself a little more worked up. I thought, "Mom and Dad are probably in the house right now telling Mark and David all kinds of bad stuff about me." Then I thought, "Why would mom not like a patriotic shirt? I wonder if it's because Mom and Dad don't believe in what this country stands for. I think that maybe the group they are working for might even be against the idea of democracy. Maybe Mom and Dad are working with a group of people that are socialists or even communists. Mom and Dad might be communists. They work for the public school system. They get paid from people's tax money. Maybe they would support the idea of a government that paid everyone with taxes, like a socialist or communist type of system."

The thought that my own parents might be working with a group that supported to revolutionize our government, made perfect sense to me. I thought that probably was the explanation for why they seemed to shoot down everything I said. I thought that they wanted to keep me in the dark about what was about to happen because maybe they were being promised some position of power in the new system that would be created after our government was overthrown. The ideas kept spinning, wilder, more paranoid than ever before. Now, I was sure that my own parents' had a secret agenda: to help destroy the nation. It made me scared of them and angry for keeping such big secrets from me. The thing that kept giving me a lot of these ideas now was the whispers in my ear. I kept hearing the quiet voice suggest the ideas that my parents could be associated with a group that threatened the future of a democratic United States. The Voice was now telling me things that I could understand and react to. I decided I had to do something.

My genius plan was to vandalize their property. I started with a bottle of some chemical that I found in the shed. I opened the bottle and started pouring it all over the driveway. Then I started drawing symbols on their driveway with the liquid that poured out of the bottle. I think I drew a pentagram, a cross, an eye, and maybe some other symbols. I can't remember what the other things I drew on their driveway were. By the time I finished my driveway graffiti, I had emptied a couple bottles of anti-freeze, and a few quarts of motor oil. Then I decided to dump motor oil on Dad's car, the TR6. I took a quart of oil and emptied it all over the back of his car. The oil ran all over the trunk and down the sides of the back of the car and onto the concrete floor of the garage. Then I started dumping oil all over the back of my mom's van. There was a sticker on the back of her van that had an American Flag and the Dodge Ram logo on it. I peeled off the part that had the American Flag and left the part that had the ram. I thought, "You guys are working for an evil group, so let your car show it. Let the ram stay on the car and get rid of the flag. You aren't a patriot. You can't

288

display the flag, but since you are working for evil, let the ram show your true allegiance."

After that, my dad walked outside into the garage and saw the oil on his car. He said, "What are you doing?!?" I said that I was tired of having to put up with them and hear them tell me that they didn't believe the things I told them. Dad said, "Get out of this house. Just leave here. Pack a few things that you need and leave. Don't come back." I said, "That's fine with me. I can't stand living here anyways.", and started to gather up things. After a few minutes Dad came into my bedroom and said, "Get out of here. I want you out!" I said, "I'm working on it. Let me get some of my stuff." He walked off and I could hear him telling my mom and uncles about what he had just seen on the driveway. He saw the cross, the eye, the pentagram. They all went outside and looked it over. After that Dad said, "If you aren't out of here now, I'm calling the police." I said, "Good. I'll call them for you. I want to report a couple of communists anyways." Dad said, "No, I'm calling them. Just leave and I won't call them." I told him I had decided I wasn't leaving right away because I didn't trust that he wouldn't destroy all my things before I was able to come and get them. Dad said that I had no reason to worry about him messing with my stuff. He said, "Just leave. Your things will all be here when you can come and get them." I said that I didn't believe him and that he should call the police because I wasn't going to leave. So, with no other options, Dad called the police. I remember listening to him make the call. I just sat calmly at a distance from him while he, my mother, and my uncles all gathered in the chairs under the oak tree in the front yard.

I decided to tell Mr. and Mrs. Pren that Dad had called the cops on me and that I probably wouldn't see them again. I went over to their house and told them my news. Mrs. Pren said, "I'm sorry to hear that Scott. You take care of yourself now.", and closed the door. I felt like I should tell them because I had felt close to Mr. Pren since those hurricanes. My dad and I had helped him remove a lot of the debris from his yard. Mr. Pren always asked me about my grandfather when he was dying of cancer. I always thought Mr. Pren was a very nice man. I just wanted to say good-bye to him, because I didn't think I would ever come back to my parents' house again. Telling Mr. and Mrs. Pren that I was about to be Baker Acted was a very poor decision. But, again, that's all I did was make one poor decision after the next. The lack of sleep, the paranoia, and the whispering voices, all took their toll on my brain's ability to function properly. I don't think I ever had a rational thought pass through my mind in those last few days before I got sent away.

The police arrived at my parents' house about 20 minutes after my dad called them. Two officers got out of the car and started talking to my parents. I just sat there and listened. My dad showed the officers what I had done to the driveway and to his cars. One of the police officers said, "This is oil. Did he try to light it and start a fire?" Dad told him that he didn't think I had any intention of starting a fire. I remember thinking, "Holy crap! I hadn't even thought about motor oil being able to catch on fire. I hope they don't try to make me out to be an arsonist." I had never intended to burn anything. The thought never crossed my mind. Dad blew the whole idea off and that let me relax a little. I remember my dad telling the cops about all the strange things I had said and done in the past few weeks. He told the cops that he had asked me to leave his property and I had refused. They said that they would Baker Act me if I volunteered to do it. They said that if I allowed them to Baker Act me, things would be easier for me: I would have a place to stay. I would be given food. I could get help with my problems.

I told the police that the Baker Act route was fine with me. I told them that my dad was over reacting, but I didn't want to be around him anymore than he wanted to be around me. So, the cops let me pack a bag of clothes and personal items to take with me. As I was packing, the phone rang. I picked it up. It was Uncle Mark's wife, Aunt Janice. She asked me how I was doing. I said, "I'm fine, but Dad is having me arrested at the moment, so I can't really talk right now." Aunt Janice said, "What? Why is he having you arrested?" I told her that we had just had a fight and that he wanted me to leave and I wouldn't. She said, "Put me on the phone with your Uncle Mark." The cops said they would take care of the phone and for me to finish packing my stuff so that we could leave. They were very patient and calm the entire time. They didn't cuff me or put their hands on me the way that the cops did in Tallahassee. I tried to just stay calm and relaxed and talked with them as I gathered my things. I packed everything up and they opened the back door of the patrol car and asked me to get in. The whole process of, basically getting arrested, seemed a little familiar now. I didn't even mind this time. I felt relieved to be getting away from my parents. I was now afraid of them. I thought that they might be working for an evil group and I couldn't trust them anymore. It was a relief to be with the police. I felt like they were on my side. Wherever they were taking me, had to be an improvement over where I was coming from.

I don't remember having any conversation with the police on the ride to the rehab center. They just told me where they were taking me and that I would be able to stay there for a couple weeks, most likely. I said that was fine. I had no plan for what I would do after I got out. I just hoped that the secret group would rescue me and take me to wherever it was that I was supposed to go. I thought that the police who were taking me to the rehab center might be part of that secret group. I thought, "Maybe this is part of the plan. Maybe I'm supposed to go to the rehab center so that I can be removed from Mom and Dad and then taken to whoever it is that keeps talking to me on this little phone in my ear."

Chapter 54: The PRC, Round One

The police took me to Bartow, to the Peace River Center. It was a mental institution. At the Peace River Center, were holding cells for all types of people who had been removed from society because they had a mental illness and had been seen as a threat to the safety of someone or to themselves.

The police officers let me out of the back of the car and walked with me to a door on the side of one of the buildings at Peace River Center. A nurse came to the door and the police introduced me to her and told her that I had volunteered to have myself Baker Acted because my dad and I had been in an argument and I had vandalized his property. They said that I had seemed calm the whole time they were with me. The nurse asked me if I was feeling alright. I told her I was fine. She brought me into the facility and said, "Don't worry, we're going to take good care of you." I thought she was kind of pretty and hoped that she stayed as friendly as she was when I got there.

We walked in through several doors that all had number combinations and keys to open them. Then we arrived in the area where I was to spend my time. She told me to sit in a chair that was in a hallway. I remember sitting there and looking around. There was a dayroom, similar to the one we had at the rehab center in Tallahassee. There were people sitting in there watching TV and just staring at the walls and ceiling. There were also two hallways. One hall was the guy's hall. The other was the girl's hall. All the bedrooms led off of those two halls. There were no phones on the walls like we had in Tallahassee. That didn't matter to me. I had no one to call. Still, I got the impression right away that this place was a dump compared to the place I had been sent to in Tallahassee. All the people that were patients looked a little scary. I didn't see anyone that looked like the somewhat normal people I had met in the BHC in Tallahassee. Everyone had some quirk about them that was immediately obvious. These people were all much worse off than the ones I had met in Tallahassee. I began to think I had made a mistake by allowing myself to be placed at the Peace River Center.

I don't remember a whole lot about my first experience with the PRC. I know that there was a point where I got so out of control that I had to be sedated by having a shot put in my butt cheek. I remember ranting about something and two of the orderlies grabbed me on each arm and took me from my room. They dragged me down the hallway, through a double door, and into an isolation room. A nurse came in right behind them with a needle in her hand. The two orderlies told me to lie down on a bed that was in the room. I refused. They grabbed me and forced me onto the bed. They turned me on my stomach and the nurse gave me the shot. After that they all left. I was in the room all alone. There was a room attached to the one I was in. I walked over to it and saw a bed that looked like a cross. It had a place to lie down on, and a piece that came out on either side for an arm to be put on. It looked like the type of bed you see a prisoner strapped to when they are about to administer a lethal injection to him. I remember laying on the bed and putting my arms on the pieces that stretched out on both sides. I was laying there in a crucifixion pose, I thought. I felt that I was like Jesus. I was being punished because people did not understand me. I thought it was ironic that I was now laying on a cross like bed. I just laid there and thought about the mess I was in. I remember wondering if the PRC had actually killed anyone on that table. I began to imagine that, perhaps, when a patient became too unruly, they were brought to that table and administered a lethal injection. Then I heard a voice in my ear. I thought I heard it say "Scott, this is your Uncle Mark and David. I don't know what's got into your parents. We're going to help you get out of there." Another thing I thought I heard them say was, "We've seen Stan. I don't know how they did it, but he's back." After that, I couldn't make out what they were saying, but I kept hearing a voice, very quietly, too quietly for me to understand.

I thought about that last comment that I had heard my Uncle Mark say very hard. I didn't know what to make of it. Stan had died a couple years back. My dad and his brothers had found Stan in his house after he had not been seen at work for a few days. Someone from Stan's work called my dad and said that they didn't know where Stan was and they had not been able to reach him on his cell phone. Dad and his brothers, Mark and David, went to Stan's house to see if he was alright. Dad told me that as soon as they opened the door to Stan's house, they knew something terrible had happened. Dad said the smell of a dead body was so strong that, after walking into Stan's house, he went back outside and threw up. One of them went in and found Stan lying in bed. He had died a few days earlier in his sleep. The autopsy showed that he had a massive heart attack.

It was summer and Stan's air conditioner was not running for some reason. His body had started to decompose and the smell of his rotting body had absorbed into every fabric in the house, my dad told me. They actually burned everything that Stan had in the house. They said that it all smelled so bad that there was no way it could be salvaged. It sounded like a really bad experience for my dad and his brothers. They had to see their brother's decomposing body and take care of removing all of his things from that house. Most of the things that they decided to keep had been brought to the guesthouse at the lake. I remember going in there when Sara and I and the girls came down from Tallahassee to attend Stan's funeral. The smell of Stan's belongings made the guesthouse wreak of death. Dad said that the things they kept were the things that didn't smell so bad. They still smelled very bad to me. I remember getting a little scared when I saw his things piled up in my old bedroom. The smell added to the weirdness of having a dead man's possessions in my old room. I looked at the piles of boxes and things and walked out. I didn't want to know what they had saved. I hoped that they would figure out what to do with it soon. I didn't like seeing all his stuff in that guesthouse.

Now I wondered if the comment that I thought I heard my Uncle Mark say, in my little phone implant, about seeing Stan was true. I wondered if Stan had been brought back to life, like the people I thought had been revived in New Orleans. I knew that it had been a couple years since he had died, but I still thought that it could be possible. Maybe Stan had been resurrected for some reason. Maybe he was just one of the first of many who would be brought back to life. I didn't know. I was sure that I had just heard my Uncle Mark talking in my ear. I thought about the fact that he and David had been in the military when they were young. They had fought in Vietnam. David was even an intelligence type who listened in on conversations of people talking to each other in Turkey. I thought, "They must be a part of my group. Maybe they've been with the secret group all along and were just waiting to see where Mom and Dad stood. Maybe they now realize that Mom and Dad are working against me. Maybe Mark and David are going to help take me to wherever I'm supposed to go."

A little while later I thought I heard a banging sound and I thought I heard people screaming. I thought the sounds were coming from outside of the PRC. I thought that maybe people were trying to get into the PRC because something terrible was going on outside. I wondered if Bartow was under some kind of a terrorist attack and people realized that the PRC was a safe place to retreat to. I imagined that the people in the PRC were trying to keep everyone out. I thought that it sounded like a riot was going on outside of the building. I was scared. Then it got quiet. I wondered if there were dead bodies on the ground outside of the PRC. I imagined that someone or something had come along and silenced all the people that I thought I had heard screaming outside. It was terrifying.

After a while, a lady came in and asked me if I could behave myself if they let me back out of the room. I told her I could. She let me go out to the dayroom and I sat on one of the hard plastic "couches" that was in there. That night, I went to my room and went to sleep. I had another vivid dream that night. It was probably caused from the drugs that they had injected into me earlier, and my thought about the PRC killing some of its patients.

The dream was short, but I thought it delivered a powerful message. In the dream, I was a slug like creature crawling along on the ground. I don't know how I knew that the slug in my dream was me, but I did. I was sliding along and a giant foot came along and squashed me. The foot rose back up and there was a splattered mess of guts and slime on the ground where I had just been. Then ants came crawling out of the slime and guts and I woke up with sweat all over me. I remember feeling like I had just had a dream and that I had died in my dream. I remembered hearing an old urban legend that if you ever died in your dream, you died in real life. How anyone could ever prove something like that, don't ask me, but I was sure that after having that dream, I had certainly died. I felt like I had actually died and come back to life. I started to believe that's what actually happened. I believed that the drugs they had injected into me had killed me that night while I laid there asleep. I thought that either the doctors there had given me something to bring me back to life, or someone from the secret group had come into my room and brought me back to life. I wasn't sure of the details of what had just happened. But I knew that I must have died and rose from the dead that same night. I now believed that I had just experienced what Jesus had experienced after he died on the cross. I thought that the foot that had squashed me in the dream was Satan himself. I thought he and his followers, the staff of the PRC, had killed me. I figured the good forces that I was now associating myself with had somehow saved me. This made me feel even more unstoppable. I realized that not even death was an end for me. I thought that if I was ever to die again, the same group who had just brought me back to life at the PRC would come to my rescue again and repeat the process.

Every morning we had to get up at 6:00 am and stand in a line to receive our medication. I remember standing in line one morning and seeing a guy who had just been brought into the PRC. He was wearing a military camouflage jacket and looked like a homeless person. He had long hair, pulled back in a ponytail, was bald on top, and had a short beard. He reminded me of my Dad's brother Stan. The guy looked like he could have been Stan, after some sort of medical procedure had been done to bring him back from the dead. The guy had sores all over him. He was being led around by some orderlies. He seemed confused and I heard him mumble something to one of the workers. When he tried to talk, it sounded like the way that I imagined a person might talk if their brain was not operating fully. I thought that maybe this guy was my dead uncle and that some medical miracle had brought him back from the dead. I thought that the way he looked and acted, was probably because the procedure was not a perfect process, especially when performed on a body that had been buried in the ground for two years. The really ridiculous part is that I knew that Stan had been cremated. That meant that my uncle was now just ashes. I thought the story about him being cremated must have been a lie. I thought that maybe his body had been saved and brought to the people who had performed the procedure to bring him back to life. I kept thinking about that last message I heard in my ear. The one that I thought was from Uncle Mark, where he said, "We've seen Stan. I don't know how they did it, but he's back." I knew that this guy must be Stan. Someone had brought him here so that I could see just how powerful the secret people were. They wanted me to see that death was no longer the end for people on Earth. Now, people could be resurrected, just like Jesus had done after he died on the cross. Someone had discovered a way to bring the dead back to life. I just got my first bit of proof.

So, now here was this guy who looked like my dead uncle, Stan. I looked at him and got chills. I thought, "I should try to talk to him. I wonder what he's like now. I wonder if he remembers me." I never got a chance to talk to the strange man that I saw walking through the halls that morning, while I waited for my meds. I don't know what they did with him. They probably moved him into another section of the PRC and that was why I never saw him again. I don't know.

There was another guy there that I noticed, after I ate my breakfast that same morning. He didn't have long hair, or a beard. His hair was very short, but he was bald on top. His face was clean-shaven. I thought that he looked like Stan, perhaps after he had his hair cut off and his beard shaved. I wondered if this guy was the same one that I had seen come walking in that morning several hours earlier. I wondered if they had done something to him to change his appearance and give him more mental capability. I watched this guy talk to a few other people and I was sure that he seemed much more mentally capable than the thing I had seen walking the hallway that morning. I began to suspect that this guy was indeed the same person I had seen just hours earlier. I had never seen him before that morning either. I thought that somehow, the people at the PRC had made some improvements on the zombie like man that I saw earlier that morning. I thought that I was supposed to see all this and realize exactly what I was now thinking. It was just another demonstration of the secret groups power. I was amazed.

I decided to try to talk to the guy, who I believed was very likely, my Uncle Stan. It was very weird. I actually thought that I was about to have a conversation with my Uncle Stan, who had been dead for two years. I also figured that he probably had not been dead for that long. I figured that he had been resurrected a short time after his death, and had spent most of the last two years in some facility where the doctors who had revived him performed tests on him and tried to teach him to be like a normal human being. I figured that the brain must have been damaged due to the decomposition. I imagined that they must have spent a long time trying to reconstruct his brain, so that he functioned as normally as possible.

So, I watched the guy go into his bedroom. I walked over to his room and stood outside his door. The door was open, so I could see him as soon as I walked up. He was sitting in his bed. I said, "How are you doing?" He said, "I've been better." I laughed a little. I remember being very nervous and excited. I was sure this was actually Uncle Stan that I was talking to. I said, "Do I look like someone you know?" He said, "Yes, actually you do look familiar. Where do I know you from?" I said, "Well, I'm not sure. But you remind me of an uncle that I used to have. He had long hair and beard, but I bet he looked a lot like you when he shaved his beard and cut his hair." I was hoping that my comment might jar some memory that he might still have about me. Instead, he just sat there looking a little confused. He said, "What's your name?" I said, "I'm Scott Gann. Do you remember me?" He said that he couldn't remember ever knowing anyone with that name. I felt a little sad and disappointed. I said, "Well, I'm sure that you aren't who I thought you were. But you sure do remind me of my uncle." He said, "What's your uncle's name?" I told him, "Stan Gann". He said that he thought he might have known a Stan Gann at one time. It was very possible. The guy said that he lived in Auburndale, FL. Stan used to live not far from there. He may very well have run into him at one time.

I still wondered if that guy really was Stan. I wondered if maybe he just had no memory of who he was before he died and was brought back to life. I thought that maybe his memory loss was due to the fact that his brain may not have been able to be completely salvaged. I was sad that this guy might actually be Stan, but not have any clue that he was. I talked with him a little longer and never let him know who I really thought I was talking to. I felt a little unsure of whether or not that guy was Stan. But I still had my explanations for how I thought it could be him. It was still comforting to me to think that I might have just had a conversation with a person that I once cared a lot about and missed.

I remember asking for paper and a pencil every time I had a free moment while I was at the PRC. I would have to go up to a glass-enclosed booth, where all the nurses sat, and ask them for a piece of paper and pencil. They always acted like I was asking them for money. They would roll their eyes and ask why I wanted it. I would say that I wanted to draw because I was bored. They would usually eventually end up giving me the paper and pencil, but it was always an ordeal. Sometimes they wouldn't even let me have a piece of paper or a pencil. I thought that was really crappy. Most of the time we had absolutely nothing to do. We just sat around waiting for our next terrible meal. A couple of times during the day they had us go to a classroom where we usually listened to soft, elevator type, music and were allowed to draw, write, or color with crayons. Sometimes a guy would talk to us about the importance of taking our medication or eating a balanced diet or getting enough sleep everyday. The routine was not nearly as busy as it had been when I was at the BHC in Tallahassee. There was a lot of sitting around and wishing that I had never allowed myself to be brought to that place. There was not the first attractive girl there. All the guys seemed like they had serious problems. I guess I probably fit right in. But, I didn't see myself as one of them. I still held strong to the idea that a secret organization was out there waiting for me to find them. It confused and disappointed me that they had not come to rescue me yet. I started to think that maybe the trip to the PRC was not part of their plan after all. I couldn't see any good coming from my experience there so far.

One day we were having a class about the importance of nutrition. The guy who taught the class passed out a folder to me that had contact information for the Department of Nutrition and Fitness. The guy who taught the class talked about the importance of eating well and the food groups, etc. At some point I started asking him about working for the Department of Nutrition and Fitness. He said that they had jobs that had to do with developing nutrition plans and exercise programs that helped a person live a healthy life. He said that I should go to their website and research any information about job possibilities, if I was interested. I took this as a direct order from the secret group. I thought, "Finally. Now I see why they had me come here. They want me to join this government agency. Maybe this will be my cover to allow me access to secret information that they want to give me." I remember listening to the guy talk and being so happy that I started crying. I was getting so worried that maybe I really was crazy. Now, though, I thought I had just realized why the secret group had allowed me to be placed at the PRC. My next mission was to get a job with the Department of Nutrition and Fitness. I started imagining myself working with super healthy people who were probably all very intelligent. I wondered if maybe I was supposed to meet my next wife there.

The people that were patients, more like prisoners, at the PRC, were all very far out of touch with reality. One guy would walk around and start pissing on himself several times a day. He also could not speak well. He was mentally challenged. Everything he said sounded mostly like the gibberish of a retarded person.

Another guy there was the craziest person I had ever seen. I was walking down the hall to my room one day and this crazy black guy popped his head out from behind the door of his room. He said something to me that I didn't understand. Then he held out his hand. In his hand was an actual piece of human feces. He smeared it all over his head. I thought I was going to throw up. I ran back to the nurses' station and told them what the guy had just done and they went and took care of him. After that experience, I really wanted to leave the PRC. The problem was that event happened only a couple days after I got there. I think I was there for over two weeks before they let me out.

There was also a fat black woman there who was totally crazy. She might have had five teeth in her mouth. The teeth that she had were all rotten. She looked like she was only about 40 years old. Her skin was dry and flaky. She would usually be babbling some nonsense. Most of the things she said were sexual in nature. She talked about how she had invented a certain type of condom. She also would ask me if I wanted to see her vagina. I was totally repulsed by her and always tried to avoid her. She would usually come up to me when I was in the dayroom and start babbling to me about all kinds of weird things. A nurse would usually come over and take her away when she started talking about all her foul things that she liked to do. She also liked to talk about all the drugs she liked to take. She mentioned about every illegal drug that I knew of, and others that I didn't.

I remember listening to her one time and having my back facing towards the nurses station. I started making the gun gesture with my hand. I acted like I was pulling the trigger. I was hoping that someone was watching who knew what I was trying to say. I was trying to send a message to the secret group that this lady should be put out of her misery. I thought that she was a waste to society. I thought that she should be killed, so that taxpayers didn't have to pay to keep this lady housed and fed anymore. I was hoping that someone working at the PRC was a member of the secret group and was able to see my hand gesture and know what I meant. I thought that maybe this was a part of my training with the secret group. I thought that maybe they wanted me to realize that there were some people who did not deserve to live. They may not have committed a crime, but they were a burden on society and had to be done away with. I thought that the secret group had allowed me to meet this woman so that they could see how I would react to her. They wanted to see if I had the ability to determine when someone's life was not valuable enough to allow them to live it. This was the first time I had actually thought that a person didn't deserve to live. At that instant, my values had changed. Before I became manic, I would have probably felt sorry for this woman. She clearly was not all there. Now, I felt like she was just too big of a burden on society and she was killing herself anyway. I thought that there was no harm in putting down a sick animal. That's all I thought she was. My dad could have easily taken the same view of me. That thought never occurred to me though. I wasn't sick. I was special. The secret group just had not told my parents how important I was.

There were a few people that I did end up talking to. There was one guy there that had long hair and was covered in tattoos. After speaking to him a little bit, despite his rough appearance, I thought he seemed like a pretty normal guy. I remember looking at his face and thinking that he almost looked like he could be related to the girl I had met at the bar in Tallahassee, Jen. I started to wonder if he was, perhaps, her brother. I wondered if he had been sent to the PRC to tell me some message from her. I remember asking him, "So, how is your sister?", and smiling. The weird thing was that he just gave me a smirk and said, "She's doing well." After he said that, I was sure that this guy was Jen's brother and he might be a member of the secret group as well. I think I asked him a couple more questions about Jen and he always had an answer for me. I don't know if he actually had a sister and he was just talking about her, or if he was just having fun messing with a crazy person. The fact that he seemed to know who I was talking about, made me sure that I had found a person that I could trust. I decided to tell him some of my strange ideas about God, Satan, the angels, and the demons. I also told him about being in New Orleans and seeing the refrigeration trucks carrying dead bodies to the warehouse to be brought back to life. None of these things seemed to phase this guy. He just listened to my wild ideas and acted interested in everything I said. I told him about the secret group that I thought I was in contact with. I asked him if he was a member of that group. He said, "No, not that I'm aware of anyway. But I think what you are saying is possible."

Another person that I talked to there at the PRC, was an overweight girl with a slightly disfigured face. She looked like she had been through some type of surgery on her head. Her face had scars across it. She had a couple bald streaks across her head where scar tissue had formed and hair would not grow. She sat beside me in one of the classes we had at the PRC. She started drawing a picture on a piece of paper. She wrote, "Jen" above whatever she drew. I asked her why she had wrote, "Jen" on her paper. She said that was her name. I looked at her and thought, "This is a really odd coincidence to be sitting next to a girl named Jen." I started to talk to her and I started to get the idea that I was actually talking with the same Jen that I had met in Tallahassee. The Jen that I met in Tallahassee was a beautiful girl with brown hair and a perfect body. This girl at the PRC looked nothing like the Jen from Tallahassee. But, I still thought this girl must be her. I started to wonder if the girl I had met in Tallahassee had been in some terrible accident and the same people who brought my dead uncle back to life had placed the brain of the Jen that I knew from Tallahassee inside of the body of this disfigured girl that was sitting beside me. I listened to her talk and realized that she seemed a little intelligent. I still felt like the person I was talking to was a few fries short of a happy meal. I thought that maybe the procedure that had been done on the Jen from Tallahassee had damaged her brain, similar to how I thought my uncle's brain may have been damaged when he underwent his procedure. I thought that perhaps the secret group was letting me see another example of what they could do to prolong a person's life. I thought that maybe their ultimate goal was to repair Jen's body and make her look the way she did when I met her at Pocket's Pool that night in Tallahassee. Again, I didn't feel sure of any of these ideas. I just wondered if that could possibly be what was going on.

Another guy there that I had a talk with was an older man. I heard him telling one of the workers there that he had found a cure for cancer. He was telling the worker that someone had taken all his money. He said that his bank accounts had been emptied by someone and he was now completely broke. He said he used to be very wealthy and now was poor. I listened to the guy talk about how he could smoke as much as he wanted because he knew the cure for cancer. Because of his reference to a cure for cancer, I somehow connected this guy with the secret evil group and started to wonder if this guy was an agent of theirs. I also got the idea that this guy might be Jen's grandfather or father. I don't know how I came to this conclusion. It was just another case of my brain making up whatever story it wanted from just a little new information.

I remember asking the guy if he had a daughter or granddaughter. He said he had both. I said, "Is her name Jen?" He looked at me funny and said, "No. Why do you think you know my daughter or granddaughter?" I said, "I know her name. I met her in Tallahassee. You may not realize it, but she has been in a terrible accident." The guy just stood there and said, "Really?", as if he believed every word I had just said. Then, The Voice hit me with a new idea.

The Voice told me that this old guy had been involved with some type of cure for cancer. He had discovered how to cure it and now held the power to conquer cancer. I already suspected, for some reason, that this guy was associated with the secret evil group. The Voice told me that the secret evil group had brought harm to Jen because they found out that she had come into contact with me at the bar that night, and expressed an interest in me. The Voice said that because Jen had come into contact with me and because she was the granddaughter of this old guy, the secret evil group had made an attempt to kill Jen, before she was able to reveal secrets about the evil group to me.

I said to the poor old man, "Do you know what your people have done to your granddaughter?" I just assumed that Jen was this guy's granddaughter. The guy said that he had no idea of what I was talking about. I said, "They have killed your granddaughter. The people you were working with when you thought you had discovered the cure for cancer have had her killed! Its your fault." He looked terrified. He asked me how I knew this. I said, "I have people that I work for, who let me know about things like this." He just stood there looking very afraid of me. I said, "They are probably also the ones who took the money out of your bank account. You won't ever see that money again, unless you help your granddaughter." I told him that his granddaughter was here at the PRC. I said that she didn't look the way that she used to. I didn't explain to him how I thought his granddaughter's brain had been transplanted to a host body. I just told him that some people had saved his granddaughter and were planning on doing some more operations on her to make her look and act like her old self.

The old man just took all this information in as if it were fact. He asked me what he could do. I said, "The best thing you can do is just talk to Jen and tell her that you love her. And don't ever get involved with those people you were working for when you developed the cure for cancer." He asked me if I could talk to the people that had taken his money. I said, "I can't really talk to you about that. I will see if there is anything I can do to help you. But you will first have to prove to my people that you are not working with the people you used to work for." The old guy just stood there and seemed to believe everything that I told him.

That was probably one of the most terrible things that I did when I was at the PRC. This poor old man was probably delusional himself. All I did was add to the stress that he was probably already under. If he believed everything that I told him, the way that he seemed to, I'm sure that he was scared to death. I remember feeling like I had just tapped into a little of my new power. I felt like telling this guy that he better get his act together, or else the people I worked for, the secret group, would continue to make his life miserable; I felt like that was my first real exercise in demonstrating just how powerful this secret group really was. I knew that I had scared the crap out this guy. I felt good about it. Now, I feel sorry for that poor old man. I hope that I didn't cause him to go around worrying that some unknown group of people had actually stolen his money. I don't know if the guy ever really had any money to begin with. I just hope that, maybe, he didn't really believe everything I told him, or if he did, he soon realized that he had just had an encounter with a person that was absolutely insane.

Another guy that I talked to at the PRC was a Latino. His name was Jose. He spoke English, just not very well. He was near my age. He told me that he was from Columbia. He seemed very friendly and was actually the most normal person that I had come across at the PRC. I didn't ask him why he was there. We just had little conversations about how bad it sucked to be at the PRC and things of that nature. I thought that he was a very nice guy.

Shortly before I had been placed in the PRC, I started to see little flashes out the corner of my eyes every now and then. I also would sometimes see little red dots bouncing around in my field of vision at times during the day. These were the first visual hallucinations that I started having. At first, I thought that the little dots and flashes were just caused from lacking so much sleep. Then I began to think that something else was going on. I could never keep a reasonable explanation for anything very long. Everything that happened to me, I thought, was something that the secret group was responsible for. After those little flashes and dots began to pop up in my field of vision, I started to think that, perhaps, the secret group had also done something to my eyes. I thought that maybe there was some implant in them as well. Maybe these early flashes and dots were the beginning of a new technology waking up inside me. I thought that there may be some sort of communication device in my eyes that they might use at some point in the future to beam me an image or video that only I would be able to see. I imagined that there might be some little device in my eye that allowed me to receive a special transmission from the secret group.

When I met Jose, for reasons that I can not remember, I suspected that he might be one of the people that was responsible for my new vision. I thought that maybe he was some secret Columbian doctor that performed the type of surgery that had been done on me. I thought that maybe he was there at the PRC, posing as a person with a mental disability, so that he could monitor me while I was there. I also had started to think that those flashes might be something more than just an illusion.

I remember one time I saw a flash of a person in the corner of my field of vision. It was just a white silhouette of a person that only appeared for an instant. When I tried to move my eye to see it better, it vanished. I thought, "There are people around me that I can't see right now." I began to believe that there were invisible people who were following me and watching over me. It made me feel safe. I felt like the people might always be around me, waiting to protect me if harm should come my way. I thought that they were probably using some new type of camouflage device that bent the light around them and made them invisible to the human eye. There was a Counting Crows song that had mentioned something about "getting lost in the air at the end of the world where the light is bending.", I think, when I heard that song and listened to those lyrics, I had already had a few times where I saw the flashes and spots. I think those lyrics helped me come up with the idea of light bending to create invisibility. I had also seen TV shows on Discovery Channel or Nova on PBS, where they talked about what would be needed to make something invisible. So, once I saw the flash of a person, I thought that I had just seen a malfunction in the technology that allowed me to see that person for just a split second. I remember talking to the air, hoping that the person would say something back to me.

Well, when I met Jose, and thought that he was some secret type of eye doctor, I also assumed that he might know something about the invisible people. I remember mentioning little things to him about what I thought he did. I remember thanking him for what I thought he had done to me. I also thanked him for providing me with invisible guards, who I thought, were watching over me while I was at the PRC. I imagined that they might be walking up and down the halls, with no one but Jose and I knowing that they were there. Jose didn't speak English that well. I don't think he understood any of the subtle little comments I threw at him. I would never come out and say, "I know you're some type of secret ops eye doctor. Thank-you for putting the device in my eye that lets me see things that other people don't. Thanks for giving me invisible bodyguards that watch over me." I never said anything that obvious and direct. I would just make subtle remarks about there being other people around us at times when it was clear that it was just Jose and I, and things like that. I don't know if Jose even understood the English words that were coming out of my mouth. He probably just assumed that I was speaking in phrases that he didn't understand. He always seemed to like me. He even thanked me one day. He said, "Scott, thank-you for being my friend." I told him that I was more appreciative of him than he was of me. I said it was so nice to have someone to talk to who didn't have something weird about them. Jose became my closest friend while I was at the PRC. I had a lot of respect for him and I wanted to let him know it. I believed that he was the one who had given me my new vision and provided me with a secret force of bodyguards who were always waiting to pounce on anyone who tried to harm me.

The last odd thing I remember about that first visit at the PRC was a day when Jose, the weird, long haired, tattooed guy, who I thought was Jen's brother, and the old man that I had terrified, and myself were all standing around talking in the dayroom at the PRC. I remember that at this point I felt like the old man was now one of my friends, even though I still didn't totally trust him. I thought, that he had at one time, worked with the secret evil group. I wasn't sure that I could ever really trust him. Anyway, we were all standing together in the dayroom talking about the problems of the world.

We talked about the hurricane that hit New Orleans. We talked about the war in Iraq. We talked about other things as well. The thing I was interested in talking about was that I wanted to know if they had seen or heard about any unusual events that would give me more information about what the secret forces of good and evil were up to. We were talking about something along the lines of the voodoo cult that I thought operated in New Orleans, when the crazy black lady came over. She was the one who I had talked to and made a hand gesture of a gun behind my back. She said that she was one of the members of that voodoo cult. She said that she knew all kinds of magic. She said she could curse people to death if she wanted to. I asked her to please not put a curse on any of us because we were busy talking at the moment. I didn't take her very seriously and was trying to get her to leave us alone.

I felt like I was having a very important conversation with people who might have major roles to play in the battles that I thought would soon be taking place. Instead the crazy black lady kept babbling about voodoo related topics. Then I heard her say, "Just wait until November. You'll see what I'm talking about then, for sure." I said, "What's happening in November?" She started acting very scared and she yelled, "I didn't say nothing!" Then some orderlies came in and took her out of the room. I heard her screaming and yelling as they walked her down the hall to her room. I thought, "She just blurted out some kind of important date. She probably wasn't supposed to be talking about it. That's why she got so upset. That's why the orderlies took her away. They're all in on it. The orderlies and the crazy lady all know about something that is going to happen in November. I wasn't supposed to hear that." Then I wrote down "November" on a piece of paper that I had with me. I thought she had just revealed the month that some major attack was going to happen. I thought that maybe she was a voodoo cult member. Maybe she had been here all along to keep an eye on me, as a representative of the evil secret group. Maybe she had been spying on me the whole time I was at the PRC. I felt like I had just cracked a big case. I hoped that the secret group that I was a part of had seen or heard what I just heard about November. I hoped that they were one step ahead of whatever the secret evil group was planning on doing in November.

Chapter 55: Still Crazy, But Free

I started taking my meds right away when they put me in the PRC. I remembered what had happened the last time I was at the BHC in Tallahassee and how refusing to take my meds just slowed down the whole process. So, after having good behavior for about two weeks, they told me that I was free to leave.

They handed me all my things that I had arrived with. It all went into my backpack. They asked me if I wanted to call someone to come pick me up. I told them that my dad worked at Bartow Middle School and that I was just going to walk over there and see if he would let me stay with him again.

So, that's what I did. I walked out of the PRC and started heading to Bartow Middle. It was only a couple miles from the PRC. It may have taken me an hour to get there on foot. The whole way I thought about how I really had no choice but to come crawling back to Mom and Dad and see if they would let me stay with them again for a while. I tried to think of somewhere else that I could go. I couldn't come up with any other idea than to start living on the street. I knew that I at least needed to get my car and some of my things from Mom and Dad's house. So, I kept walking to Bartow Middle. I walked right into Dad's classroom. When I arrived at his class, he had another lady who was talking to the class and he was sitting at his desk. I walked in and smiled at him. He had a look of shock and disappointment on his face. I went to the back of his classroom and waited for the class to be over.

After everyone left, it was just Dad and I. He asked me what I was doing in his classroom. I said, "They let me out of Peace River. They said that I'm alright as long as I take my medication. I was hoping you would let me come back out to the lake house with you." Dad looked at me for a moment and then said, "If you promise that you will stay on your medication, then you can come back out there." I said that I would take whatever I was told. So, he agreed to let me ride home with him. I don't remember anything about the drive home or arriving at the lake house. I just know that I still believed that he and mom were wrong about me. I thought that I was still associated with the secret group. I knew I couldn't ever talk about it with them again. So, I just acted like that was all part of the past. I didn't tell them that I still heard voices in my ear. I didn't talk about how I could communicate with the television. I just pretended that I was as normal as I had ever been. The act didn't hold up for very long.

I still was not convinced that Mom and Dad were not associated with some other secret group. I just didn't talk about anything to do with conspiracies or secret organizations anymore. I knew that if I started talking about those things, they would probably kick me out of the house again or force me to go back to the PRC. Even though I didn't talk to them about these things, the ideas and delusions kept on coming. Apparently, whatever drugs I was taking at that time, were not yet doing their job. To help lessen the effects of any medication, I stopped taking my pills altogether, shortly after being released from the PRC. I just kept telling my parents that I was taking my pills so that they would leave me alone. I was still convinced that the drugs, the rehab centers, the doctors; all of it, was just part of a plot to destroy me. I kept all that secret though. I knew that if I discussed anything about the process of rehabilitation in a negative sense, that would only alarm my parents and they would eventually bring me back to the PRC. So, I kept on pursuing the secret group, only with much more caution.

One Saturday night Dad and I were watching television in the living room. The living room had lots of windows that looked out onto the lake. At night you could see the lights of all the houses on the other side of the lake. I remember looking out the window at the lake. I looked at the lights reflecting on the surface of the water. I remember noticing a series of light flashes that seemed to look like something other than reflections on the water. I started to stare at them. The light flashes began to look like tiny lights under water that were almost like runway lights at an airfield. I started to think that there were divers in the water sending me a signal. The lights were very faint. Sometimes they would disappear and then come back on again. I'm sure that all I was seeing was the reflection of the lights across the lake bouncing off of waves in the water, but that never registered to me. Instead, my mind put together another fantasy. I thought that divers were out in the lake signaling for me to notice a certain light on the other side of the lake. The series of small flashes in the water seemed to be making a line that pointed towards a light on the opposite side of the lake. Sometimes the light on the other side of the lake was on. Sometimes it went out. I thought that someone on the other side of the lake was trying to get my attention. I didn't mention anything to Dad. I tried to just appear interested in whatever was on the TV. What I was really doing was trying to figure out how I could get over to that light on the other side of the lake. I thought that someone over there wanted to see me. I thought that it might be the secret group, finally wanting to meet with me face to face. I decided to wait until morning. In the morning, I thought, I would paddle across the lake in my Dad's kayak and investigate what was going on where I had seen the lights that night.

The next morning I woke up around sunrise and ate breakfast. I told mom and Dad that I was going to get some exercise by paddling across the lake and back. I went out to my Dad's kayak and put it in the water. I started paddling out across the lake. The whole time I paddled, I wondered if the divers that I thought were in the water the night before, were still out there, following me as I made my way across the lake. I got about ¾ of the way across the lake and then I felt a bump hit the bottom of the kayak. I thought that one of the divers had just let me know that he was below me. It scared me, but I also now felt sure that I had been right about people being in the lake the night before. I paddled a little further and felt another bump on the bottom of the kayak. It felt just like someone had punched or kicked the kayak from underneath. I stopped paddling and just sat there. I was hoping that someone would surface and show themselves. Nothing happened. I just drifted along with the waves, wondering what the bump was about. I said, "I know you guys are out there. Just come up and talk to me." Nothing. Just me and the lake.

I started to wonder if that was all they wanted me to do. I thought maybe they just wanted me to come out to into the water and acknowledge that I had seen their signal the night before. "Maybe I just passed another one of their tests.", I thought. I thought about paddling on towards the house where I thought I had seen the light turning off and on the night before. I stared at the house. I was very close to it now. I couldn't see anyone walking around outside. I had imagined that at this point someone would have come out to meet me, if there was anyone waiting. Then I thought, "Maybe there would have been someone here if I had paddled over here last night. Maybe they have already left. Maybe I should just go back to the house now." So, that's what I did. I turned around and paddled back home. I looked at my watch and realized that if I hurried back, I could make it to church at First Baptist in time for worship service. I decided that I would do just that. I paddled back to the house, wondering what might have been waiting there for me the night before. I thought that maybe I had partially failed their test. Maybe they had really wanted to tell me something the night before, but since I had not come when called, they had already packed up and left long before I actually came to meet them.

I can't imagine what would have actually happened if I had tried to paddle across the lake in the middle of the night. Lake Buffum is filled with alligators. They always feed between dusk and dawn. If I had paddled out there on that tiny kayak that night, I might have ended up as another missing person, a rotting body buried at the bottom of the lake, waiting to be a gator's next meal. Or maybe I might have made it to the other side and actually walked up to that person's house, expecting to find a member of the secret group, waiting there for me. I might have even tried knocking on the door and talking to whoever lived there and been arrested for my weird behavior. Who knows. I'm just glad that I didn't do it. That was one stupid thing that I actually did not do. Thank God.

After I got back from my little adventure with the secret group, I got dressed up and went to First Baptist of Bartow. I got there in time for worship service, which started at 10:45 am. I felt great. I remember listening to the preacher and thinking that he was delivering a sermon about me and was speaking directly to me. He talked about this guy who had spent a short time working at a factory, operating a forklift, and moving around barrels of chemicals. I thought, "He is talking about my job at Arr Maz." The preacher went on to say that this guy was someone that everyone thought was a nobody. Once he started working at that factory, though, he caught on to all the responsibilities he had, quickly. The preacher said that the guy proved himself to be a fast learner. He then said that the guy went on to become one of the heads of that company. That was the part that I couldn't understand. I thought, "I didn't move on to be the head of Arr Maz. Why would he say that? Maybe he is speaking figuratively. Maybe he is talking about something that will happen in my future." The rest of the sermon, I don't remember. What that story had to do with the sermon, I don't remember. I was still only able to take in a few minutes of new information at a time. After that, my brain would start processing the little bit I had just learned and would make up a story that made whatever I saw or heard fit into my totally twisted view of what I thought was going on around me.

I remember the music director choosing to sing "How Great Thou Art" at the end of the service. I remember we were all standing as we sung the song together. I started crying as I sung along to the familiar song. I thought about all the unexpected things that had happened over the last year and how I still realized that God was great. I thought that he was greater than I had ever imagined. God himself was the one behind all the strangeness that was now my life, I thought. I had now seen and heard things that no one else could believe or understand. God was great in my life.

After church, I ran into Susan Prevaughn. She was the girl's P.E. coach when my Dad had taught at Union Academy in Bartow years ago. She was the girl's P.E. coach the year that I was there in 7th grade. She and my dad had been good friends. She asked me how I had been doing and said, "If you don't have any plans for lunch, I would like to buy you lunch today. I'd like to hear what you and your parents have been up to." I told her that sounded great to me. So we went to Crisper's in Bartow. It's a little soup, salad, and sandwich restaurant that has some really good food.

Susan and I went into Crisper's and ordered lunch and started talking. I decided to tell her an abbreviated version of everything that had happened up until that day. I didn't talk about all the weird ideas that were in my head. I just talked about the things I did: the things that had happened before and after the hurricanes, losing my job at ETO/Architects, the conspiracy that I thought happened there, Mom and Dad losing their house, Granddaddy dying, Sara leaving me, Hurricane Katrina in New Orleans; that kind of stuff. I did tell her about Dad having me Baker Acted twice and how I thought that I was just totally misunderstood. I didn't tell her about being diagnosed as bi-polar. I didn't tell her that I was supposed to be taking medication, but was now lying to my parents about taking it. I talked for probably an hour, almost non-stop. Susan just listened to all the horrible stories that I had to tell her. She said that she was glad to hear me talk about my problems and that I could call her anytime that I wanted to and talk some more. I thought that was very nice of her.

While Susan and I were talking, a girl walked in and stood in line to order her food. She was beautiful. She was wearing a tight tank top shirt and shorts and had a camouflage hat that said "ARMY" on it. I thought she was one of the most beautiful girls that I had ever seen. She had an awesome body and a gorgeous face. She was very young, maybe twenty years old, if that. I was now 29. She saw me staring at her and smiled at me. She said something to a girl that was with her. I assumed that the girl was probably her little sister. She looked like she was probably in junior high. The girl's sister looked at me after the really good looking girl had said something to her. The girl's sister looked at me and smiled, and then said something back to the hot girl. I said to Susan, "I think those girls over there are talking about me." Susan looked over and waved at them. She then turned back to me and laughed. She said, "Oh that's Rachel Smitten. She works over at Beef

306

O'Brady's. She is one of my former students. She was a great soccer player. I looked at the girl's legs and thought, "Yeah, I could see her playing soccer. She looks really athletic." I told Susan that I thought she was really cute. I asked Susan if she knew Rachel's phone number. Susan said, "I think you better get that kind of thing from her.", and laughed. I said, "Yeah, I guess you probably shouldn't give out confidential information like that, huh?" She said she didn't know her number anyway, but that I should go over and introduce myself to her. I said that I might, whenever we left. We decided to leave shortly after that. We walked right by Rachel's table and I smiled at her. She smiled back. I said, "Hello. How are you?" She said, "Fine.", and her sister giggled. I got nervous and decided to cut the conversation right there. I said, "See you later.", and walked out. Susan and I walked on out to her car and then I decided I would go back in and tell Rachel my name. I said, "I'll be right back Susan.", and walked back into Crisper's. I walked back up to Rachel and said, "Hey, my name is Scott Gann. I just wanted to introduce myself. I was just eating with Susan Prevaughn. She said you were one of her former students. I like your hat." Rachel shook my hand and said, "Hi, I'm Rachel. Its nice to meet you." I said, "Well, I just wanted to tell you who I am. I'll see you around maybe." She said, "O.K. Thanks." Then I walked back out to leave with Susan. Susan drove me back to my car at First Baptist. We talked a little more on the ride back. She told me again to call her and keep in touch and tell my parents that she said hello. I thanked her for listening to me at lunch. She said she was always glad to here about what my parents and I were up to. After that I left and went back out to the lake. I remember thinking about going back up to Crisper's to see if Rachel was still there, but I didn't. I just started to plan how I would make her my new girlfriend. I thought that the fact that she was wearing an ARMY hat gave me a sign that she had been chosen for me by the secret group. It was now my mission to get to know her better.

A few days after my "encounter" with the military personnel that were hiding underwater in the lake, I saw a large gator that had been killed and set out on the side of the road. The Voice told me some startling news about that alligator. The Voice said, "We had to kill that gator because it was put out in the lake to try to kill you. It's a man-eater. It had been trained to eat people. The evil group placed it out there in the lake to take out some of our men and you." I was a little alarmed, but grateful that such measures had been taken for my security.

The Voice went on to tell me that ever since I had been discovered, assassins had been coming out to the lake to kill me. The Voice said that they had already been prepared for such events and had their people secretly hidden in places all around my parents' house and throughout the lake and surrounding properties, waiting to eliminate any agents of the secret evil group who came to harm me. The Voice said that, late at night, they disposed of the bodies of the evil agents, either by dumping them in the lake or hauling them off in vehicles when no one was around. This disturbed me very much. Now I had to believe that people were being killed for my safety. I had already become comfortable with the idea that the evil agents might be trying to harm me, but this was the first I had heard of people actually dying. And it was all because of me. Eventually, I told myself that it was better to have the assassins killed than me. I began to shift from pity for the assassins to anger towards them. I couldn't believe that people were being sent to kill me when I had not yet done the first thing to provoke such action.

I remember walking down Orange Street one night and challenging someone to come out and face me. I was trying to get one of the assassins to show themselves to me, if for no other reason than to bring proof to what The Voice had said. I remember walking down Orange Street and yelling as loudly as I could, "Come on you bastards! Show yourselves! I'm here! If you think you can take me out, then come try it! Show yourselves!". Of course, I was only speaking to the wind. I stood there on the road for probably thirty minutes, listening for some sound that would give away anyone who might be hiding in the dark. My adrenaline was pumping. I was sure that I had just provoked a fight for my life. No one ever came.

A couple days later, I got a call from Sara. She said that she was moving into an apartment. She said that she was going to come out to the lake, with some friends of hers from work. Sara started working for a chiropractor a couple months before she left me. She was still working for the chiropractor when she called me that day. She said that some of the people from the chiropractor's office were coming with her to help her load up her things to take to her new apartment.

Later that afternoon, Sara arrived with three other trucks following her. They were all driven by people from her new job. I had already made up my mind that I was not going to be around while she took all of our things. I didn't want to fight with her about what she could and couldn't have. I felt that she could have whatever she wanted. I didn't feel attached to any of it. Besides, I thought, it would be easier for me to forget about my life with her if I didn't have to look at all the things we had owned when we were together. And, she had the girls. I wanted the girls to have as easy of a time as they could, now that their mom and dad no longer lived together. I knew that they were probably hating me for not even talking to them. I figured that Sara had probably filled their heads with all kinds of negative things about me. She would have been justified in doing so, I thought. I knew that I had never treated Sara the way that she deserved to be treated. I thought that if I just let her take everything that she wanted, maybe that would make her happy. I hoped that by taking our things, she would feel like she had won. So, when I saw her pull up, I started getting ready to leave. Sara's boss got out to the house a few minutes before she did. He knocked on the door and I asked him if he would like to come in. I tried to be very cordial with him. He seemed like a very nice man. We talked for several minutes. I don't remember anything we said.

Once Sara and her other friends started showing up, that was all I could take. I got my car keys and walked to my car. Sara didn't even acknowledge me. I could tell that she was nervous and was making a point to avoid even looking at me. I got in my car and drove off. I remember seeing her laughing as she stood in the yard and talked to the girls that came out there with her. I think she probably wanted to have all those people with her because she was afraid that I would give her a hard time about taking things that weren't just hers. I think she had planned to intimidate me with her group of new friends. I didn't feel intimidated. I just felt a little sad. I realized that I might have made a mistake to let her go. I wondered if I should have tried a little harder to patch things back together after she left. She had told me in her letter that she didn't want to leave me. I was the one who overreacted and started telling her that I wanted a divorce. Still, I thought I had already found another girl who was probably better than Sara. I was a little sad to know that things were really coming to a close with Sara and I, but I was mostly focused on forgetting about her and moving on to getting to know this Rachel Smitten.

After I left the house, I drove to somewhere that I don't remember. I have no memory of what I did during the time when I was trying to avoid Sara. At some point, I went back to the house. I was gone long enough, because when I got back, everyone had left. I walked into the guesthouse, where all of our things from Tallahassee had been stored. The guesthouse was almost completely empty. Sara took almost everything. She took all of our furniture, dishes, appliances, a new laptop, a new video camera, everything of value. All that was left in the guesthouse were a few boxes that were filled with my old Star Wars toy collection. She also left the two old desktop computers that we had. I walked into the main house and saw that she had taken furniture from there as well. She took our couch, our bed, and the girls beds. I figured that she needed everything she took. It still hurt me to see all these empty spaces where our things used to be. It made me realize that my time with Sara was over. She had no intention of ever coming back to the lake house. If we were ever going to live together again, it would be somewhere other than my parents' house.

Another few days passed and mom told me that I had received a check in the mail from a disability insurance that ETO/Architects had given me. Mom said that Warren Eto had told her about getting me on the disability insurance after I resigned over a year earlier. Mom said that she had been fighting with the insurance company about getting me a check for quite a while now, and that they had finally sent me my first check. The check was for $16,000. It was a total of all the payments that I should have received up to that point. After that check, I started receiving $1,800 every month from the disability insurance company. The policy was only good for two years, so I knew the money wouldn't keep coming forever. When mom told me the news about the insurance money, it hardly phased me. I remember her being very excited when she told me the good news. I just said, "Thank you for going through all that trouble. I don't really need that money though." Mom said that I did. She said to just hang on to it and save it for a rainy day. I remember wondering if that check might actually be my first payment from the secret group. I thought that perhaps the secret group had some connection to the insurance company and that they had made the push to get me that money.

I wish that Mom and Dad would have taken that money from me and set it aside until they were sure that I was stable and clear headed enough to handle having that much money. I guess I had put on a good enough front to make them believe that I was stable. The $16,000 check would soon disappear. I quickly found things that I felt like I couldn't live without. I burned through most of that money in a matter of weeks.

Chapter 56: The Last Great Adventure

I remember getting in several arguments with my parents during the time after I got back to the lake house, after I was released from the PRC. I don't remember what the arguments were about. I'm sure that they all stemmed from the fact that I had a very short fuse still, and could snap at anyone, especially my parents, over the slightest of things. I remember one night, Dad said, "Are you still taking your medication?" I said, "Yes, twice a day, just like you want me to." That was a total lie. I had stopped taking the medication again for over a week at that point. Dad looked at the bottle of pills that I was supposed to be taking. I said, "What are you doing? Are you checking up on me now?" Dad said, "Yes I am. I have trouble believing you because this bottle still looks as full as it did the last time I looked in it." He said, "You aren't taking your pills. You are lying to us." I said, "Fine! You caught me! I'm not going to let you force me to take some drug that does nothing for me and is probably doing me more harm than good!" Dad and I had this discussion several times in the past. I would always tell him that in school we were always told, "Just say no to drugs". And now here he was telling me to take drugs. I said that the drugs that they wanted me to take caused diabetes and who knows what else. I told him how they just made me tired and made me have trouble speaking. Dad would always tell me that the drugs were for my own good. I thought it was ridiculous. I thought that he was ridiculous. I told him several times that when he started taking drugs, then I would. I would always tell him, "You love to tell people that they need to take drugs. You've got mom convinced that she needs Prozac. Nanny thinks that she needs anti-depressants, but I don't see you taking anything yourself. Why is that? I guess you don't believe that you have a problem. You just like to tell everyone else that they have a problem."

Dad finally said that if I was not going to take my meds, then I couldn't live at the lake house anymore. I said that was fine. I told him that I would rather live on the street than have to take a pill that I didn't need. The next day I packed up a bunch of my stuff and decided I was going to take a little vacation. I figured that if I left for a couple weeks and had no problems, Mom and Dad would probably see that I was just fine, and let me come back to the lake house. I also thought that I might not ever come back. I thought that there was a good chance that this was all part of the secret group's plan. I thought that they might contact me, while I was having my little vacation, and whisk me away from all my hardships.

I remember telling Dad that I was tired of being mad at him. I said, "I refuse to let myself get angry with you anymore. I'm not leaving because I am angry with you or mom. I am just going to go on a little camping trip. Maybe I'll come back here one day. Maybe I won't. Either way, I'm not mad at you. I just don't want to take a pill to live my life the way that you think I should." Dad said that he was not mad at me either. He said that he loved me and wanted me to be careful while I was gone. He told me to call them every few days to let them know that I was O.K. I told him that I would.

I decided that I was going to drive up to Dunnellon, FL and spend a few days camping at Rainbow Springs State Park. That was a place that my parents, Sara, the girls, and I used to meet up on the weekends when we lived in Tallahassee. It was a beautiful place that had water that was clearer than any water I had ever seen. We used to take my dad's kayaks and paddle up the Rainbow River, from the campground, to the headsprings. Then we would tie our kayaks to our ankles with a thin rope, and snorkel back down the river, drifting along with the current. We all had a lot of great times at Rainbow Springs. It was one of my favorite places. I decided that I would go there and just relax and try to forget all the nonsense that had happened with Sara and my parents.

I remember thinking about Rachel Smitten on my way out from the lake. I decided that I would go to Bartow, to Beef O'Brady's and see if she was there. I hoped that she would be there. I wanted to see if I could talk her into coming to Rainbow Springs with me. I remember pulling into the Beef O'Brady's parking lot and writing a note to Rachel. I said, "Rachel, I'm going to be doing a little camping for the next few days. I wanted to see if you might join me for an adventure. If you want to come, bring the things on the back of this note. Give me a call and I'll let you know where you can meet me." I wrote the note, and my phone number, on the back of a list that I had made when I was packing all of my things to go to New Orleans. The list included all kinds of things that no one would ever need if they were just planning on doing a couple days of camping. I'm sure she saw the note and realized that it was a note from an idiot. To make matters worse, I went into a Dollar General store that was just a couple stores down from Beef O'Brady's, and bought a beach ball that I included with the note. What I thought the beach ball was supposed to tell her, I have no idea. I just remember thinking that it seemed like a cool idea at the time. I'm sure that she took a look at the note and the beach ball and wondered what kind of crazy stalker she was dealing with. I remember going into Beef O'Brady's and asking the bartender if Rachel was there. The bartender told me that Rachel had the day off. I handed the girl at the bar my note and a bag that had the beach ball in it. I said, "Could you make sure that Rachel gets this?" The bar tender asked me what it was. I said, "Its just something for Rachel. She knows what it is." The girl gave me a weird look and said, "Yeah, I'll make sure that she gets it." I thanked her and left. I was sure that I would soon be getting a call from Rachel, letting me know that she wanted to meet me. That never happened. Instead, I got a call from Rachel's dad. It wasn't pretty.

After leaving my note for my new sweetheart, I started making my way to Rainbow Springs. Before I arrived at Rainbow Springs, I made a stop at a Wal-Mart in Bushnell, FL. I walked into the Wal-Mart with my usual level of cockiness. I remember that I wanted to transfer some money from my checking account to a Wal-Mart debit card, so that I could save 3 cents per gallon on gasoline every time I filled up at a Wal-Mart gas station. I went over to a cashier and asked her about getting a

Wal-Mart debit card and transferring money to it. She handed me one of the debit cards and told me to swipe it through the little card reader, then swipe my bank debit card, then punch in the amount that I wanted to transfer from my bank to the Wal-Mart card.

I went through the process of transferring money a couple times with no success from the machine. It kept screwing up and asking me to swipe the cards again. I got frustrated and asked the cashier if she could do it for me. She tried doing everything except entering in my pin numbers and had no success. Then, The Voice told me that this was just the beginning of the dark future that lay ahead. The Voice said that once computers had replaced a lot of the tasks that people used to do, the world would suffer for it. The Voice had already warned me that computers would become a force that would rival humans and would eventually try to destroy us, as in the story from the Terminator movies. I remember saying to the cashier, "Have you seen the movie, 'Kill Bill'? That's what I want to do, kill Bill Gates, for creating such crappy software for you guys." I had noticed that the Wal-Mart cash registers all operated on a Microsoft platform. So, when I saw the little card reader screwing up my transaction, I figured that I was experiencing a Microsoft software glitch. I told the cashier, "This is just the first wave of attacks from the Techno-Union Army. Things are only going to get worse from here." The cashier had no idea of what I was babbling about. I had given a name to the technology related problem that I thought would soon threaten the very existence of human life. I had named the group responsible for the creation of the evil machines, The Techno-Union Army. I got the name from *Star Wars, Revenge of the Sith*. I thought it was a fitting name for the group who I thought were hard at work building the machines that would rise up against us. I eventually had to go to the Customer Service desk and have a lady there make the transfer to the card for me.

After my little run around at Wal-Mart, I got back on the road and headed to Rainbow Springs. I got there a couple hours later. I think it was late afternoon when I arrived. I went into the head office and got a campsite. Then I started setting up my tent and gathering firewood from the debris that I saw laying around in the woods near my campsite. As I was gathering firewood, a skinny, long-haired guy came walking over to me. He said, "Hey, I'm the campground host. I just wanted to let you know that you aren't supposed to be taking wood from the forest there. The state doesn't want people disturbing that area. Sorry." I told him that I had camped there many times before and never had anyone tell me anything about not gathering dead wood laying on the ground. The guy said that since the state had taken over ownership of the park, they started enforcing this rule. He said that I could take any wood from the abandoned fire pits around the campground that had no one camping at them. He also said that I could take any branches that I found laying around outside of the forest. I thought it was a ridiculous rule, but I dropped the wood that I had collected and went back to my tent. I thought, "What a bunch of crap. I wonder if that guy is just making up his own rules and trying to give me a hard time." After the guy disappeared from view, I went back into the woods and collected the wood that I had just dropped. I figured he wouldn't know what I had done, and I didn't care about his stupid rule. What harm was there in picking up dead wood off the ground? I was a member of a secret group that had a little more authority than the stupid state

312

park campground host. I didn't care what he wanted me to do. I figured I was a little more important than he was. I could do whatever I wanted. So, I did.

That night, there was a guy and a girl camping in a tent beside me. I heard them talking and laughing. I also thought that I heard other people over there that I couldn't see. I thought that I could hear several people talking. Every time I looked over there, though, all I saw was the guy and the girl, sitting at their fire. They were camped out at the closest site to the river. I wondered if they were talking with people who were in the water. It was nighttime, so I thought that it was weird that people would be out in the river. Then I heard something in my ear. It was another one of The Voice's soft whispers that I had heard many times now. It said, "Go over and talk to them. They are talking with a real live monster. There is a vampire down there in the water. You should go talk to her." The Voice scared me. I thought that I was being asked to walk into a trap. I thought that there was actually a female vampire waiting out there in the dark. I imagined that she was swimming in the water. For some reason, I imagined that she was naked. I thought that she was probably a beautiful looking woman who might try to seduce me, if I went and talked to her.

I walked over a little closer to the campsite where the guy and girl were still sitting by the fire. I was trying to listen to what they were saying and see if I could still hear anyone else talking to them. The guy and his girlfriend saw me and asked me if I wanted to come over and talk with them by their campfire. I went over there and we started talking. As I walked over I tried to look out to the water to see if I could see anyone out there. I asked them, "Do you guys have some friends out there in the river?" They laughed and said that they didn't. They said that it was just the two of them. I wondered if they were lying. I kept thinking, "Any minute now, someone is going to come out of the darkness and scare the hell out of me."

I started talking to the couple. They told me that they had just left New Orleans and were planning to move to Florida. They said that they had lost their house in the hurricane and also lost their jobs because the places that they worked at were also destroyed. The guy said that he was a cook at a restaurant. I don't remember what his girlfriend did. I thought, "This is not a coincidence to meet two people from New Orleans. The secret group must be behind this too. Maybe the vampire is still just waiting for me out there." I remember telling the couple that I thought I heard them talking to other people at their campsite. They said that they had been listening to the radio. They said that I probably just heard people talking on the radio and thought that was some other people at their campsite. I'm sure that was the case. But I still believed that they were making up a story to hide the fact that there were members of the secret evil group out there in the water. I kept looking out into the darkness, trying to spot someone swimming around. I never could see anyone. I figured that they must have swam on down the river, out of sight. The couple offered me a sandwich that they cooked in a campfire toaster. I thanked them and ate it. It was really good and really simple. The guy showed me how he made it. He just took pepperoni, cheese, and pizza sauce and put it between two pieces of heavily buttered bread. Then he put that into the little campfire toaster and held it over the fire for a few minutes. The heat toasted the bread and melted the cheese. It almost tasted like a really good pepperoni pizza. I told the guy that his little trick was delicious. He thanked me and then I told him that I was getting tired and told them good night.

When I woke up the next morning, the couple was gone. They had already packed their tent and left. They had told me the night before that they were planning on leaving the next day. So, after realizing that the couple that had been very nice to me, despite my strange behavior, was gone; I decided that I would go get some breakfast in town. I drove into Dunnellon, which is only a few miles from the campground. I went into Wal-Mart to see what the little restaurant inside had for breakfast. The restaurant inside the Wal-Mart was a Blimpie sub shop. I don't know why I thought I would find anything good for breakfast there. So, I looked at the menu and saw that they had a couple of breakfast type sandwiches that were just slices of ham on a little roll. They didn't look too great to me. But, I didn't feel like driving anywhere else just to get something to eat. I decided that I would have a hot dog. It was about 7:30 am. I ordered a hot dog and the girl laughed at me. She said that she had never had a person order a hot dog that early in the morning. I said, "Well, I'm hungry, and those little ham sandwiches don't seem much worse to me than a hot dog." She laughed and handed me my order. I loaded it up with mustard, ketchup, pickles, and onions. It tasted pretty good, considering that I was eating a hot dog for breakfast.

After my breakfast, I decided to look around the store to see if I could find a lantern. I wasn't able to get a lot of wood the night before, so I thought I would just buy a lantern to avoid bothering with a fire. I found a lantern that I liked pretty quickly. Then I started looking at all the other camping gear. It all started to look like something that I needed. I picked up a couple tarps, some rope, a machete, one of those campfire toasters that I had seen the guy the night before using, and a bunch of other little camping related items that I didn't really need. Then I decided to look around at the rest of the store. I ended up looking at sunglasses in the sporting goods section. They had several pairs that I thought looked pretty cool. I bought four or five pairs of sunglasses. I had never bought more than one pair at a time before. When I was picking them up and putting them in the buggy, I was thinking, "I'll use all of these, eventually." I also bought a fishing rod, and some tackle to go along with it. Then I made my way around the rest of the store. I saw a jacket that I liked. I put it in the basket. Then I decided to look around the electronics department. I saw a Palm Pilot that had been marked down to $90. It was originally $200. It was on a clearance shelf. It had been discontinued. I thought it was just what I needed to keep up with all my wild ideas and I imagined myself writing down all the important revelations that had occurred to me recently. I thought that it was another thing that I needed. So, in the cart it went.

Then I looked at the cell phones. I already had one cell phone. I didn't need another one. But, I had come up with a theory that Sprint, the carrier for my phone, was associated with the evil secret group. The Voice had told me that my calls were being monitored on the Sprint network. The Voice told me that I needed to switch to Nextel. The Voice said that the Nextel network was owned by the secret good group. Their network was safe for me to talk on. I thought that if I got a Nextel phone, I would probably start receiving calls from people who were wanting to talk to me, but had been afraid about calling me on the Sprint network. I thought that once I got the Nextel phone, I would be able to talk to anyone and not be monitored by the secret evil group. So, I looked for the cheapest Nextel phone they had and got the cheapest plan available. The phone was free and my plan was $40 per month. I thought I had just bought the most important item I had found up to that point. I imagined that I would soon hear from the secret group on my new phone. Of course, I never did. I tried to find a way to communicate with them, and at one time, I actually thought that I had discovered the way to do it, but that was just another delusion.

After that purchase, I decided to look at the Star Wars toys. The Star Wars movie, *Revenge of the Sith*, had just come out in the theaters not long ago, so the store shelves were filled with Star Wars merchandise. I started looking at the action figures. I decided that I could stand to buy a few of them. I think I ended up buying about 15 of them. I also saw a Darth Vader helmet. It was a pretty good replica of the real thing. It was a two-piece helmet, just like the one he wore in the movies. I thought that I had to have it. So, in the buggy it went. There goes another $50, no big deal. I also bought a black cape and a light-saber toy that was a full size replica of the ones from the movies. I walked back over to the clothes to see if I could find any Star Wars related T-shirts. I was in luck. I found four different shirts that I had to have. After I had found all the things that I couldn't live without, I proceeded to the check out line. My bill totaled up to over $600. I thought, "That's a lot of money, but I might as well get used to spending like this. I'm sure that the secret group will be sending me a lot more money in the future." That trip to Wal-Mart was just the first of many. Each time I went, I usually spent more than I did the time before. I started to chew away at the $16,000 check I received pretty fast. It was all gone within a month. Big spending is just one of the signs of mania. I managed to spend all of the money I had and then some. I ended up maxing out my credit cards before my shopping sprees ended. I couldn't even tell you where most of the money went. I was delirious at the time I was spending it. Most of the things I bought were frivolous items like the ones that I just mentioned. Some of it is still packed away in boxes. Every time I open those boxes and look at that stuff, I wonder, "What was I thinking when I bought this?" The fact is, I was not thinking at all. I had just started to believe that I was going to have an endless supply of money coming to me from the secret group. If I saw something that even remotely looked like something I could use, I bought it.

After my big shopping spree at Wal-Mart, I headed back to the campground. I unloaded all of my new purchases and started looking at all my new gadgets. I believed that I had just purchased some state of the art technology from Wal-Mart that day. I remember The Voice telling me, "Just stay in one place. We will bring the technology to you. We will make all the technology you need available to you at Wal-Mart stores. We will guide you to the items that you will need." After hearing that from The Voice, I made sure to always go to Wal-Mart for everything that I needed. I never knew when The Voice would tell me about something that I would eventually need. The Voice helped spur many shopping sprees. As my level of insanity increased, The Voice managed to convince me that I needed all sorts of things that were absolutely unnecessary.

When I got back to the campground, the first thing I did was try out my new phone. I turned it on and it started talking to the network. It kept saying that it was downloading the T9 text input software. I figured that this was probably some state of the art software that the secret group was going to be using to communicate with me. It sat there downloading all this information for several minutes. Then it turned itself on and was ready for use. I looked at the screen. I was waiting to get a call from the secret group. I knew that they would call me any minute now. I figured that it was the secret group who had just sent the T9 text input software on my phone. I had no idea of what the software was. It was actually just some crappy text messaging software that the phone used to help guess what it was you were trying to type whenever you entered text into the phone, I think. Maybe there was more to it than that, but that's the only thing I ever found that it could do. I never read any instruction manuals. I just figured that the only reason I had bought the phone was to communicate with the secret group. I reasoned that they wouldn't be putting instructions for how to communicate with them in the manual that came with the phone. I figured that the information in the manual was all irrelevant to me. This phone was now more than an average phone, it had the T9 text input software on it. I had no idea of what that was. But I knew it was something from the secret group and it was probably some top secret software. I figured that I would probably have to discover how to use the phone on my own.

After a while of pushing buttons to see what happened, I got bored and decided to do something else. I looked at the Palm Pilot. I never opened the case. I just looked at it and thought about writing some stuff down. I never did. I knew that it would have to be charged before I could use it. So, I just left it in the case until I could think of how to charge it up. So, then I decided to look at the Star Wars toys that I had bought. I looked at the Darth Vader helmet. I thought that it was very cool. Halloween was only a couple weeks away. I figured that it would make a great Halloween costume, if nothing else. Then I looked through the action figures that I had bought. I had bought a few other action figures over the years. I always left them in their packages and thought of them as a collectible. I looked at these though, and thought that they were tools for communication. I thought about setting up another scene like the one I had made in my bedroom, on the day that I got sent to the PRC. I took out several figures from their boxes. There was Darth Vader, Emperor Palpatine, a woman, some alien girl, and several other figures that I don't remember. The other's left in their packages. I thought I had selected the right ones to set up and tell a story with.

I placed Darth Vader on a picnic table that was at my campsite. Behind him I placed Emperor Palpatine. Then I stood the figure of the lady beside him. She had red hair and looked stately. I think she was one of the Rebel commanders in *Revenge of the Sith*, I don't know for sure. These three figures, I thought, were the main focus of the story. The lady, to me, represented Laura Bush. The Emperor, was George Bush. Darth Vader represented me. I saw myself as George Bush's apprentice, the way that Darth Vader had been the apprentice of The Emperor. I knew that no one else would ever arrive at that conclusion if they saw the Star Wars figures on the picnic table. I just placed them there to help remind me of who I was now. I felt like

316

I had a good and an evil side, just like Darth Vader. I thought that in the end, my good side would prevail, just like Darth Vader. But for now, I thought of myself as a bad ass. I thought that the secret group wanted me to present myself this way. That's why I started wearing the straw cowboy hat and the over sized sunglasses. I thought that those things made me look different from everyone else. I thought that it showed people that I was a different type of person than they were. I definitely was different, just not in a good way. The idea of being Darth Vader soon became a strong concept for me. I began thinking of ways that my life resembled the life of Anakin Skywalker, who would become Darth Vader, in the movies. I felt like I had lost people who were important to me, just as Anakin had lost his mother, as a young boy. Mostly, though, just as Anakin Skywalker experienced the loss of his closest friends, I knew that the people who had been closest to me, were now the most afraid of me. I realized that I was losing the trust and love of all the people who, at one time, were the closest to me. I felt like I was misunderstood, just like Darth Vader. It was pretty wacky thinking, but that was how my brain worked at the time. I was looking for anything that I could find to give me a framework, a reference, that would explain the weirdness around me.

Later that day, I went over to a little shop at the campground that rented kayaks. I rented a kayak for a few hours. I paddled up the Rainbow River and snorkeled back down, just the way I had done with my family many times for many years. Only this time, for the first time, I was all alone. It was strange to me to be floating down the river and seeing all the beautiful water, the fish, and the birds; and have no one to share the experience with. I felt lonely. I realized that even my favorite place in the state was not as fun when it was just me. Still, I floated along, watching the fish, turtles, and birds; and tried to tell myself that this was all the fun I needed. "I don't need anyone. I would rather be alone for the rest of my life, than have to be around people who want nothing but to see me drugged up all the time.", I tried to tell myself. I knew that this was probably the least enjoyable time I had ever had snorkeling down the river, but it was still pretty nice.

When I got back to the campground, two girls were setting up a tent at the spot where the couple had been the night before. They weren't all that great looking, but they weren't totally ugly either. I said hello to them as I walked by their campsite. Then I went to the camp store to get some firewood. I had bought the lantern so that I wouldn't have to rely on a campfire for light. But, I decided that I still wanted to have a fire, just so it felt like I was camping. I decided that I better not collect any more wood from the forest because I didn't want to take a chance on getting caught by that stupid guy again. So, I went to the camp store and actually paid for firewood. I realized that this was the reason the state didn't want anyone to gather wood from the forest, they had a little racket going on firewood. It was $3.00 for 5 pieces of wood. That wood only lasted a couple hours. Yes, the state was making a little fortune by forcing people to buy their wood. Oh well.

I bought my high quality, high priced, wood from the store and went back to my campsite. I decided to listen to some music and see if I could charge my Palm Pilot up from my car. I put in some Radiohead and started jamming. Then I looked at the back of the box that the Palm Pilot was in, I could see that it came with a wall type adapter, but nothing for charging it in the car. So, it stayed in the box. I decided to draw some sketches in a notebook that I had with me. So, I sat there and drew God knows what while I blasted the campground with Radiohead's *Hail to the Thief* album. After a while, one of the girls at the campsite next to me came over and said, "Hey, would you mind turning your music down just a little." I said, "Sure. Sorry, I didn't realize it was that loud." That was a lie. I knew it was loud. I wanted them to hear it. I was hoping that they might come over and tell me that they were Radiohead fans too. The plan backfired.

Later that evening, once the sun was starting to go down, I started to build a fire. I had just a few little scraps of paper and some empty boxes from the garbage I had bought at Wal-Mart that day. I got the fire started with that. Then I built it up with some smaller sticks that I went into the forest to collect. I looked around for the campground host before I went in and didn't see him. I didn't see him when I came out either, so I figured I was in the clear. The pieces of wood that I had bought from the camp store were so big that it was hard to get them going. I had to have some smaller pieces of wood from the forest, or else I would never have been able to get them lit, unless I doused them with lighter fluid or gasoline. I don't know how the state intended for people to make a fire using only the wood that they sold at the store. I remember watching the two girls next to me try to get their fire going. They had also purchased wood from the store. That was all that they had to start their fire. I could tell that they must not have started too many fires before in their life. It was funny what they were doing. They kept squirting lighter fluid on the logs and trying to get them to burn. The lighter fluid would burn up in seconds and the fire would go back out. They would then start the process over again. I walked over to their site and told them that they probably needed to start a fire with something a little smaller than those logs they had bought. They asked me if I had anything. I gave them all the little scraps of paper and twigs that I had left, and told them about the camp host getting on to me for going into the woods to gather deadwood there. They agreed that it seemed like a stupid rule and said that they were going to go into the woods and get some wood of their own. After that, I went back to my campsite and sat by my fire. I also turned my car stereo back on. This time it was quieter than it had been that afternoon, but I'm sure it was still loud enough that those girls could hear it.

Later that evening, I was still listening to the Radiohead album and I started to sing along to some of the songs. I was probably singing loud enough for other people to hear me. That was something that, before I was manic, I never did. I remember getting a little choked up on one of the songs. The lyrics said, "She said, baby, I think you're crazy'. But we'll see who's crazy, in the next life." The song made me think about Sara and how so many times over the last year, she had doubted my mental state. I thought about the time in Tallahassee, when Sara, Dad, Carter, and I were sitting at the table in the kitchen and they were questioning me about all the weird things I had done recently. I felt like the song was a little picture of a very bad time in my life.

At some point that night, one of the girls hollered something over to me. I walked over towards their camp and started talking to them. One of the girls told me that she was a psychology major at FSU. I don't remember anything about the other girl. After that girl told me that she was a student at FSU, I told her all about my years in Tallahassee. We talked for a long time. I told them about going to New Orleans and helping out on the supply line. I don't remember anything that they told me. I just remember wondering if these girls knew Jen, the girl from Pocket's Pool. I wondered if Jen had somehow heard about where I was and sent some of her friends to check up on me. I remember talking to the girls and thinking that it sure was another odd coincidence to run into more people that had been in an area where I had lived for so many years. I was sure that this was no coincidence. I thought that, once again, the secret group was involved somehow. The girl that kept speaking to me was a psychology major, to top it off. I wondered if she was able to realize that she was talking to someone who had been diagnosed as bi-polar. I never mentioned anything about the BHC or the PRC. I just tried to make myself seem as normal as possible. I'm sure that I wasn't doing a very good job. Like I said, even when I thought I was normal, I'm sure everyone else still thought that the things that came out of my mouth were odd.

One thing that I told the girls, that I know was strange, was about the voodoo cult working in New Orleans. I had asked the psychology major if she had taken any classes on religion. She said that she had. I asked her if she knew much about voodoo. She said that she really didn't know much about that. I told her that I was sure that there was a voodoo cult operating in New Orleans. I told her that I had met some people who actually practiced voodoo. What I was referring to was the lady that I had met in the PRC; the crazy, fat, black, lady who told me that she was heavily involved with voodoo and could curse a person to death. I didn't mention to the girls that I had met this lady at the PRC. I just told them about her but didn't reveal how I knew her. Then I told them some real disturbing information. I said, "Do you know what is the most disgusting thing about these people who practice voodoo?" The girl said, "What?" I said, "They like to, well, recycle their own bodies waste, if you know what I mean." The girl looked at me and laughed. She said, "I hope you don't mean what I think you mean." I said, "Yes. They actually eat their own poop and pee." The girl said that made her nauseous and we needed to change the subject. I just laughed a little and said that it was all true. She said, "I'm not saying that I don't believe you. But, I don't need to know about that kind of stuff. I like to hear about happy things." I apologized for talking about gross stuff and we changed the subject. I think that was probably one of those conversations that I should never have had with anyone, especially someone that I had just met. I was talking about the subject as if it were a confirmed fact. It was all based on what I had heard the crazy lady at the PRC talking about. I don't know anything about voodoo. I sure hope that the people that practice it aren't as gross as I made them out to be. I talked with the girls for a little while longer and then went back to my campsite. I sat by my fire and listened to more music for a little while and then decided to go to sleep.

That night, I laid in my tent and listened to the sound of those girls talking to each other in their tent. I could hear them giggling a lot. I thought that they were talking about me. I thought about going over to their tent and asking them what was so funny. I wondered if they wanted me to come over to their tent and ask them just that. I remember thinking, "Jen, you have got some crazy friends." I was sure that those girls were Jen's friends. I never asked them if they knew her. I just assumed that they would deny knowing her if they did. Also, I didn't even know Jen's last name. I didn't want to mention someone to them who I didn't even have a last name for. I just laid there in my tent and thought about how Jen had sent two of her friends to meet me and check up on me. I figured that they would probably report back to Jen after they left. I didn't even think about my theory that Jen was the girl in the PRC; the disfigured, heavy girl, that looked nothing like Jen, but had the same name. I just believed that I was either wrong about that girl at the PRC or that Jen may have already been put back together to look the way that she did that night when I met her. As far as Rachel was concerned, I started to think that she was too immature for me. She hadn't called me. So, I just felt like she must not be mature enough to see what a valuable catch I was. Never mind the fact that I had now been in two rehab facilities, had no job, lived with my parents, who had kicked me out. Hey, I was still a good catch, in my mind! I was a member of the secret group. I was a super spy with technology that no one had ever seen. It didn't matter that all these things appeared to be wrong with me. What was important was the secret world that I was involved in. I knew that once the rest of the world caught on to the things that I had already realized, I would be seen as the intelligent, charismatic type of guy that I knew I was.

That night, I eventually fell asleep. I woke up at some point in the night, thinking that I heard someone walking around my campsite. I listened closely and thought that I heard someone breathing right outside my tent. I laid there and tried to think of what I should do. Then my memory flipped to a strange character that I had seen earlier that day.

I remembered a strange looking guy who was camping in an R.V. not far from my campsite. I remembered walking up from the kayak rental shop and passing his R.V. He was sitting outside of it in a camping chair. He had long hair, a wild beard, and several tattoos. I remembered smiling and saying hello to him as I walked by his campsite on to my own. He just sat there in his chair and didn't smile or say a word to me. I thought it was a little odd. I don't know if I had already pissed him off by playing my loud music or what, but I got the impression that the guy was not happy with me. When I heard the noise outside my tent, I immediately wondered if that strange guy was walking around my campsite, possibly stealing some of the stuff that I had left on the picnic table.

I laid there for several minutes and then didn't hear anymore noises. I got out of my tent and grabbed a knife that was on the table. Then I grabbed the machete that I had bought earlier that day. I thought, "If that dude is crazy enough to come walking around my campsite in the middle of the night, there is no telling what he might do to me." So, I now had some protection. I decided to get out my flashlight. That was another purchase from earlier in the day. I had bought two Mag Lights. They were very nice flashlights that used four D batteries, had an aluminum casing, and a lifetime warranty. I turned on the flashlight and looked around the campsite to see if anything looked out of place. I couldn't see that anything had been touched. I checked the ground for footprints that weren't my own. I saw some that didn't match my shoes. I figured that those belonged to the guy in the R.V. I shined my light over to his R.V. The light was very bright and I pointed it right into every one of his windows for several seconds. I was hoping I would see him pop his head up, or that maybe he would even come out and start yelling at me. I felt like I was ready to fight the guy. I had no proof that he was ever at my campsite. I just assumed that it was him, and I was ready to kick his butt. It's a good thing that he never did come out of his R.V. that night, because I would have probably ended up going to jail for what I planned to do to him. I didn't plan on really hurting the guy. I just hoped that he would come out so that I could threaten him and scare him half to death. After walking around for several minutes with no proof of anyone at my campsite, other than some mysterious shoe prints, I decided to try to go back to sleep.

I laid down in my sleeping bag and started to go back to sleep. Then I thought that I heard someone walking around outside again. I listened closely. Then I thought I heard a click. I thought that it sounded like the kind of click I might hear if someone was pulling the safety off of a gun, or cocking a gun to get ready to shoot. I laid there in my sleeping bag feeling absolutely terrified. I thought that the weird guy had come back to my tent and now had a gun with him. I thought he was planning to shoot me right there in my tent. I just laid there and said a prayer. I asked God to please forgive me for all the wrong things that I had done. I told Him that I knew that there were times when I had not been a Christian. But I begged Him to forgive me and allow me to go to Heaven if I died that night. Eventually, after a long time of laying in my sleeping bag in a panic, I calmed down and decided that the guy had either changed his mind about shooting me, or was never really there at all. I thought that maybe I had heard some other sound, and got myself all worked up over nothing. (What I probably heard was raccoons checking out my campsite for food.) I eventually went back to sleep. But the next morning, I was up at sunrise.

I decided it had been a rough night and I needed to unwind a little before starting the day. I turned on my car stereo and started playing a little Radiohead. It was probably 6:30 am when I first started blasting the campground with another round of Radiohead. I was listening to Radiohead loud enough that the girls in the tent next to me woke up. One of the girls came over to my campsite. She said, "Do you hate us or something?" I said, "No. Why would you say that?" She said, "Because its not even 7:00 in the morning and you are blasting your radio. We came out here to get some peace and quiet. We have to hear that kind of noise all the time at our dorm. Could you just turn it off so that we can have some quiet?" I said, "Sorry, I didn't realize that it was too loud." I turned off the radio and thought that the girls were being a little snotty. I had listened to them talking and laughing until the early hours of the morning the night before. I didn't think that it was so rude to play my radio once the sun had already been up for 30 minutes. But in reality it was a very rude thing to do. Normally, I would never have been that obnoxious, but the mania allowed me to behave in ways that I never would have before.

I decided to drive over to Dunkin Doughnuts and get some coffee and a breakfast sandwich. I went in, ordered my breakfast, and ate it. As I was sitting there, I thought about how my daughter, Gwen, was about to have a birthday in a couple days. I thought that I better go to Wal-Mart again and get her a gift. I left Dunkin Doughnuts and drove over to Wal-Mart. I walked around the toys and couldn't see anything that I thought she might like. I decided that instead of buying her a gift, I would send her everything she needed to have a birthday party. I went over to the section of the store that carries all the party favors and party related items. I bought plates, napkins, cups, and several bags of party favors. Almost everything I bought was Star Wars merchandise, just what every 3 year old girl going on 4 wants, right? Maybe not. Definitely not Gwen. My kids could not have cared less about Star Wars. Buying Gwen a bunch of Star Wars birthday party stuff was about as appropriate as buying a little boy a bunch of Barbie birthday party items. However, the thought never occurred to me. I loaded up enough stuff to fill several Wal-Mart shopping bags. I also bought her a card that had Yoda on the front. I decided that I needed to mail all these wonderful things to her so that she would get it in time for her birthday.

I went to the post office and stood in line to mail my bags of junk to Gwen. I stood in line and started whistling. I was whistling the Imperial March song from Star Wars. It's the music that you always here when any scene dealing with the Empire comes on, you know, Darth Vader, The Emperor, those types of people. People in line would look at me and smile. I would smile back at them and then keep right on whistling. I'm sure they thought that was a little strange. I was just trying to get myself noticed. I figured that most people probably knew who I was by now anyway. I assumed that people were probably watching me on some secret website or reading about me in some newspaper that I could never find. I was just trying to give them a little show.

I mailed Gwen's package and then decided to take a look at some kayaks that were for sale at a store that was owned by the people that rented the kayaks at Rainbow Springs. The name of the store was Dragon Fly Water Sports. They sold mainly kayaks and kayak related gear. I walked in and asked about buying one of their used kayaks. They sold the kayaks that they rented at the springs. The guy that owned the place walked me outside to several kayaks and gave me a run down about each one. I decided that I really liked one made by a company called RTM. It was called the Tango. It was bright orange and yellow. It was an ocean going kayak that was also well suited for paddling down rivers like Rainbow River. I asked the guy how much he wanted for it. He told me it was $650. I told him that I would buy it. Then I had to buy all the other gear. I had to buy a padded seat to put in the kayak, $50. I had to buy a paddle, $110. And then I asked him about a rack for the kayak. That was another $200. I decided to pass on the rack. I can't believe I didn't buy that as well. So, I had to load the kayak on top of the Forester without a rack for it. Luckily, the Forester had a roof rack, it just wasn't made to specifically hold a kayak. I just put the kayak on top of the rack and used some ropes to tie it down to the rack and to the front and rear of the car. I thanked the guy and drove on back to Rainbow Springs with my newest purchase.

I got back to the campground and decided that I definitely had to try out my new kayak. I loaded up all of my snorkeling gear and dragged the kayak down to the river. It was much heavier than my dad's old kayaks. My new kayak was built with thick plastic and was a larger vessel than the white water, fiberglass kayaks my dad had. I was very proud of my new kayak. I thought it was the coolest one I had ever seen. I got down to the water and saw the girls who were camping next to me, standing in line to rent a kayak for themselves. I thought, "They must want to hang out with me, so they're getting some kayaks to paddle up the river with me." I waited for them to bring their kayaks down to the river. I started talking to them a little and they said a few things and then started paddling up the river. I followed along behind them. Then one of the girls said, "Are you following us Scott?" I said, "I can if you want me to." She said, "It doesn't matter to me, but we didn't know that you were following us." I decided that they must not want me around after all. So, I drifted along with the current and let them get some distance on me. I let them get almost out of sight, then I started paddling. I slowly made my way up the river, thinking that it would have been more fun if they had wanted me to tag along with them. Then I decided I would see if I could catch up with them. I started paddling as hard as I could. I caught up with them in no time. As I got close, I decided I would just blow on by them. I figured I would just show them how fast I could go and also show them that I wasn't trying to stalk them. So, I kept paddling as hard as I could, like an idiot, and went flying by them. I paddled hard all the way to the headsprings. Then I put on my snorkeling gear and tied my kayak to my ankle. I started floating down the river, watching the white sandy bottom and all the fish that swam by. It was very peaceful and very quiet. It was quiet enough for me to hear the whispers again.

I thought I heard a conversation between, what I guessed, were military administrative types. I could hear someone saying what a remarkable job I had done paddling up the river. I heard them saying that I was a very impressive swimmer as well. Then I heard someone say that I would make a great frogman, as in, Navy SEAL type diver. I thought that I was hearing some conversation among members of the secret group who were trying to figure out what to do with me. I thought they were discussing what type of training I was best suited for. Hearing how impressed everyone sounded, made me want to impress them more. I started going under water and holding my breath as long as I could. Then I started swimming as fast as I could. Then I thought I should demonstrate my balance. I climbed into my kayak and stood up and walked up and down the length of it. I stood near the front and started paddling along. Then I thought about doing a flip off the front of the kayak into the water. I didn't even notice that the girls from the campsite next to me were approaching me from the opposite direction that I was heading in. I flipped off the front of the kayak into the water. When I came up I saw that those two girls were almost right up on me. One of them said, "Are you trying to impress us Scott?" I said, "No, I'm just having fun. But are you impressed?" She said, "Oh yeah, I'm very impressed.", and laughed. The other girl laughed too. They both kept on paddling in the opposite direction, away from me. I thought, "Those girls are a couple of little bitches." And I did a couple more flips out of my kayak and then figured that I had done enough things to impress the secret group who was somehow watching over me. After that, I paddled the rest of the way back to the campground. I didn't see the point in drifting along with the current and enjoying the view underwater. I just paddled back, the whole time, a little angry about the sarcasm I thought I heard in those two girls as they paddled away from me.

That night I had another fire and played more loud music. I didn't go over and chat with the girls that night. I figured that they had let me know what they thought about me. I no longer thought that they were Jen's friends. I didn't think that her friends would act so rude towards me. I just figured that they were a couple of snotty college girls who were now getting on my nerves. I didn't think about all the obnoxious things that I had done to them already.

At one point I decided that I would walk around the campground dressed as Darth Vader. I put on my Darth Vader helmet, and cape. I also grabbed my flashlight. I thought of it as my light saber. I remember walking around that night with the helmet and the cape, swinging my flashlight through the air and watching its intense beam cut through the air. I don't remember exactly what I was thinking when I walked around that night. The only people that saw me were the girls next to me. One of them said, "Oh boy! Darth Vader is camping with us tonight!", and laughed. I didn't say anything to her. I don't know if she knew that it was me in the costume or not. I was not at my campsite when she saw me. I was walking around by the canoe launch area. I saw that girl and just kept walking. I didn't say a word to her. I was even doing the Darth Vader breathing as I walked around. I know it was very bizarre, but at the time, I thought it was a very cool idea. To become Darth Vader, I thought, was my mission. I thought that my new image should put fear into people. Most of my life I had tried to be as gentle and kind towards everyone I met, as I possibly could. At that point, I had decided that I had wasted a lot of time being nice to people and nothing good had ever come from it. I decided that I wanted to see what happened when I made a point to scare the hell out of people. Walking around that night in the Darth Vader costume, was my first effort to do that. I think that if more people saw me, the effect would have worked. Luckily, the only ones that saw me that night were the girls next to me.

I made a few laps around the campground, flailing my flashlight around as I walked as Darth Vader. Other people might have seen me from their campsites, but it was dark. I don't think that anyone could make out what I was wearing. After a few laps, I walked back down to the canoe launch area. I stood there for a while and then heard some noise coming from up river. It was music. I could also hear people talking. I couldn't make out what was being said, but I got the impression that I might be about to make contact with the secret group. The Voice whispered to me in my ear, "Go to them. They will take you away." I then realized that this was the moment I had been waiting for. I thought that this was the moment when the secret group had finally decided to meet me, face to face. I believed that the noises I was hearing in the distance were coming from people who were involved with the secret group. I stood there for several minutes, wondering how I could get to where the sound was coming from. Then I realized that the sounds were getting closer to me. I then realized that I was hearing the sounds of music and people talking on a boat that was coming down the river. Another whisper came to me, "You have to make it look like you drowned. Leave your things behind and swim to the boat." I believed everything I heard from the whispering voice. It was the secret group talking to me, after all. They were telling me how to disappear completely. I knew that if I left my Darth Vader things behind, along with some of my clothes, that eventually someone would realize that those things belonged to me. I imagined the police and my parents trying to figure out what had happened to me. I would be long gone. I imagined that I would be whisked away on that boat and taken to some secret base where the secret group would begin informing me of just what my next step was.

I took off all my Darth Vader stuff and stripped down to just my shorts. I left behind my shirt, my sandals, my car keys, and wallet. I was about to go for a swim in the late hours of the night. I stood there and waited to see if the boat was still coming my way. It was dark and I knew that there were gators in that river. I didn't want to take any more chances than I had to. Then I saw the boat coming down the river. I got behind some bushes to hide myself, just in case I was wrong about this being the secret group. I guess I didn't have 100% security in what The Voice had told me. It had already told me something that I now knew could not be true: The idea that the girls next to me were Jen's friends. I now believed that the voices might be messing with me sometimes, just to test my ability to figure things out on my own. But usually, if the voices gave me an outlandish idea, I jumped all over it. Like the one I was about to respond to now.

The boat passed right by me very slowly. I could hear a couple guys talking and could also still hear music coming from a radio on the boat. I tried hard to hear what they were saying. I thought I heard one of them say, "All you have to do is swim out here.", but I wasn't sure. I wasn't sure if he was talking to me either. He didn't say my name or my codename, Black Hawk. So, I just sat there in the bushes and watched the boat go by. I waited for the boat to pass by a little and then I walked along the shore behind it. I followed the boat, walking through the woods, with bare feet and no shirt. After several minutes of following closely behind the boat, I stopped. I thought, "O.K., if these guys want me, they can come and get me. I've left behind my things. I'm right here in the woods, all alone at night. No one else is going to see them if they come and get me." So, I sat down on a log in the woods. I had no shirt or shoes to keep me warm. I started to get cold. The ground was wet and mucky. My feet were covered in mud. I just sat there for probably thirty minutes, expecting the boat to come back and take me away. Then I started to realize that no one was coming. It was very quiet again. I kept listening to hear a person walking towards me, or something. Nothing.

I thought, "I was either supposed to swim to that boat, or maybe this whole thing was just another game that they played with me. Maybe these guys are getting a kick out of seeing what they can get me to do." I started to feel angry. I felt like the secret group was playing a trick on me. They had told me to leave behind all my things and I did. They had told me to swim to the boat, but I didn't. So, I wasn't sure if I had just failed another of their weird tests or if this was all just a game. I decided to walk back to my things, gather them up, and go back to my campsite. I was several minutes into the woods, so it took only a short while to make my way back, in the darkness, to my things. Luckily, no one had stolen my stuff. It could have easily happened. People walked down to the canoe launch at night often. There was a little dock that people fished off of at night there too. A lot of people could have walked right by my stuff while I was out there in the woods. Fortunately, no one took my things. I put my shirt and sandals back on and grabbed my wallet and car keys. Then I grabbed my Darth Vader outfit and walked back to my campsite. When I got back to the campsite, I realized that the power had gone out at the campground.

I realized that the power was out when I tried to plug in my lantern to a power outlet at my site. I had just realized that the outlet was there and working that afternoon. I plugged in the lantern and it wouldn't come on. I looked around the campground and noticed that no lights were on anywhere, except the inside lights of the R.V.'s that were running their generators. I saw some people with flashlights walking around the campground bathhouse. Then The Voice talked to me again. It said, "We've placed a body in the bathroom. It looks like you. We are going to make it look like you killed yourself. Then we are going to take you away." I thought that sounded like a terrible way to disappear. I asked The Voice, "How did you get a body?" It said, "We got it from a morgue. We just needed someone who looks like you so that we could fake your death. We are coming to get you soon. Get ready." I sat there at my campsite feeling very awkward about what I thought was going on. I thought that it was very morbid of the secret group to go and take a dead person from the morgue and place them in the bathroom at the campground to make it look like I had killed myself. But, I thought that they probably had done this kind of thing with other people before, so I should just relax and get ready to meet the people that I had been hoping to meet for quite some time now. I sat in my chair and watched the people walking around with flashlights. The Voice said, "They just found the body. They'll be calling the police soon. We are on our way to get you." I just kept watching the guys walking around the bathhouse. I tried to hear what they were saying. I kept seeing people walk in and out of the bathroom. I could see flashlights shining through the windows of the bathhouse. I imagined that I was seeing the police walking around inside and examining the body that had just been discovered. I could hear people talking on walkie-talkies or Nextel phones. I kept hearing the little phrases being said and then a beep, just like the Nextel phones made when you used the two-way communication button on the phone. I knew that a lot of emergency workers used those types of phones to communicate, so this just helped reinforce the idea that The Voice had given me about a body being in the bathroom. I decided to walk over to the bathhouse and see what was going on. I wanted to see if what The Voice had told me was true, or if this was just another game that it was playing with me.

I walked over to the bathhouse and could see that there were several guys walking around outside it with their flashlights. There was also a truck parked beside the bathhouse that had its lights shining on it. It was a state park ranger vehicle. The people walking around were state park rangers and another guy who was not wearing any type of uniform. I watched them from a distance for several minutes. I tried to hear what they were saying. I could tell that they were not saying anything about a dead body. I walked up to the bathhouse and asked one of the guys what was going on. He said that they were trying to figure out what had caused the power to go out. I thought, "It's the secret group. They have turned off the power, but I'm not telling you that." I asked him, "Is there anyone in the bathroom?" The guy said, "No, but you can't go in there right now. We're still trying to fix the circuit breaker. You'll have to wait until we're done. We should have everything back on in a little while." I thought, "There is a body in there. He's trying to cover it up for some reason." I wondered if I was actually talking to a member of the secret group. I said, "Well, I just wondered what was going on. I thought that something bad had happened in the bathroom. I just wanted to check things out." He said that it was just a power outage and there was nothing to worry about. So, I went back to my campsite. I just knew that I had seen some cover up operation. I kept watching the bathroom, waiting to see

326

some people come walking out with a body bag. A van pulled up and had its lights pointed on the building. I thought that the van was either my ride out of the known world or that they were going to get rid of the body by putting it in the van and driving off with it. I thought that maybe the body had been placed there when they thought that I was going to swim to the boat. Since I didn't swim to the boat, maybe they had a change of plans. Maybe they decided to cancel the plan to take me away to their secret base. Maybe they were now planning on taking the body back to the morgue and scratching the whole idea of escorting me to the secret base that night. I didn't know what to think. I just sat there and waited.

Eventually, the power came back on. I kept waiting for someone from the secret group to show up at my campsite and take me away. No one ever came. I sat there for several hours, listening to my car stereo, too loudly, I'm sure. At one point I decided to go take a shower at the bathhouse. I wanted to see if I could find any sign that a body had been in there. I walked in and looked around and couldn't see any blood or any other strange looking things in the bathroom. I went ahead and took a shower. I started singing one of the Radiohead songs very loudly as I showered. As I was walking out of the shower stall, I saw the campground host standing there in the bathroom. He said, "Are you having a good time over there?" I said, "Yeah, just doing a little singing in the shower.", and walked out. I felt a little embarrassed that the campground host was in there and I had not realized it. I thought, "Whatever. I don't care what he thinks. That guy doesn't like me anyway."

The next morning I ate breakfast at the campground. I had bought some eggs and bacon from the camp store, so I cooked that up. The girls next to me started packing up their things and left a little while after I woke up. They never said anything to me. I guess they were tired of asking me to turn the radio down, because they never said anything to me the night before, or that morning. Another person did come over and talk to me about my radio though. It was the campground host. He came up to me and said, "I've had a couple people ask me to tell you that you are playing your radio too loud." I said, "Oh really? Is it those girls that are beside me?" He didn't answer. He looked at my fire pit and saw some of the branches that I had drug out of the woods. He said, "So, I see that you are still taking wood out the forest. I asked you to please stop doing that." I said that I would. I told him that I just needed some little stuff to get my fire started. He said that if I needed kindling that he would give me some from his own stash. I asked him where he got his kindling from. He said that he brought it with him. I said, "So, you took your wood from some place where the state allows you to gather dead wood on the ground, huh?" He looked at me with a little displeasure in my smart ass little comment. He said, "Yes, I brought it from my house. Please, if you need any wood to get your fire going, just come over to my camp site and I'll give you as much as you want." I thanked him and said that I was planning on leaving the next day anyways. I told him that I wouldn't even have a fire that night, so he didn't need to worry about me going back into the woods again. He said, "O.K. Do whatever you want, but if you decide to have a fire, come to me for the kindling, don't go back into the woods." Then he walked off.

I decided that I would snorkel down the river one last time before I took off for my next destination. So, I loaded up my gear and drug the kayak to the canoe launch. I paddled up the river and went to the headsprings. I decided to eat lunch at the snack bar that they had there. I ordered some food and ate lunch. Then I walked around the park. The headsprings area was an old Florida amusement park at one time. It had closed down in the 60's I think. The state bought the land and developed it into a state park. Now, all that remained of the old amusement park were the sidewalks that had been converted to nature trails that wound through the woods and went by some of the man made water features that had been part of the old amusement park. There was even a waterfall that was several stories high. I walked around the park for about an hour or so, and then went to the headsprings. The headsprings had a swimming area where lots of kids played around in the water. It was the middle of October, so it wasn't a really warm day. It was probably in the upper 70's when I was there that day. I decided that I would go for a swim at the headsprings. I put on my fins and jumped in. I think there was one other person actually in the water besides me. I swam around as fast as I could. I did several laps around the swimming area. I thought that I was showing off, for the secret group who were probably watching me, and for the people standing on the little dock, who were watching me and probably thinking, "This guy has some kind of problem."

After swimming for maybe a half hour, I decided to head back to the campground. I went back to my kayak. I started to untie it from the landing, and one of the state park workers came up to me. He said, "Is this a rental kayak?" I said, "No. I bought this yesterday over at Dragon Fly Water Sports." He said, "Yeah, I see their logo on the side. That's why I'm asking. We've had a lot of people try to steal their rentals." I said, "No, I'm not stealing this. I own this now. I'll give you my information if you don't believe me." He said that he believed me and let me go. So, I started paddling down the river, back to the campground. It was overcast and a little cool. I didn't feel like snorkeling down the river again, all by myself. When I got back to the campground, it was around 4:00 pm. That was when I got a little surprise.

I got back to my campsite and started unloading all my gear from my kayak. I turned on my car stereo and started playing more Radiohead. A park ranger pulled up to my site as I was unloading my things. He said, "Are you camping at this site?" I said, "Yes." He told me his name and said that he was the head park ranger. Then he said, "I've had several complaints about you from some people in the campground. Several people have complained to me about your music. Could you turn off your radio please." I went over and turned off my radio. Then he said, "I'm afraid that I'm going to have to ask you to leave, because you have made a lot of people upset around here." I said, "All I've done is listen to my radio. Is that really a big deal?" He said, "Well, you have also been asked not to take wood out the forest and you kept gathering wood after you were told not to." I said, "Ah, well, I guess you have me there." He said, "I'm sorry, but you need to be out of here as soon as you can get your things packed." I said, "That's fine. I was planning on spending the night here, but, I'll just go somewhere else." He said, "Thanks.", and drove off in his golf cart.

I started packing up my stuff. It was about 4:30 pm. I decided that I would just go on to Tallahassee. I was already planning on doing that the next morning, but to pack up and start heading that way at 4:00 pm was a little inconvenient. I thought, "What a bunch of tight ass people. All I did was play some music a little too loud. Other people sit at their campfire at night and sing and play guitars. If I had played country music, I bet that no one would have said a thing." I was pretty pissed off. I took down my tent and grumbled the whole time I was doing it. There was an older couple at an R.V. next to me. I thought that they were probably some of the people who had complained about me. I decided that since I was already getting kicked out, I would play my radio as loudly as I wanted to while I got ready to leave. So, I cranked up some more Radiohead.

I saw the older couple walk over to the side of the R.V. that faced my campsite. They stood there and looked at me. I remember saying something sarcastically to them about how I hoped that they were happy that I was leaving. They didn't say anything. I kept packing up my stuff. Then the park ranger came flying back up in his golf cart. He got out and said, "I told you to turn off your radio! Turn it off!" I said, "I'm just listening to some music while I pack up, why don't you calm down." He said, "Turn the radio off now!" I walked over and turned it off. He said, "You are not allowed to come back to this park. Don't think about camping here again." Then he drove off. I thought, "Yeah right, and just how are you going to stop me from camping here again?" I loaded up the rest of my stuff in the quiet. I could hear the old couple next to me talking about me. I wanted to go over and cuss them out. I remember grumbling under my breath that they would all be sorry for what they had done. I thought that since they had all wronged me, the secret group was going to do something to scare the hell out of them. I saw the old man looking at me. I said, "Just wait until tonight. You're in for some real fun." I bet that comment kept that old guy up for a little while that night. After threatening the old couple, I drove out of the campground.

When I got out onto the road that leads from the campground entrance to the highway, I saw a sign that said, "Detour Ahead". The Voice said, "They're redirecting traffic so that you can get out of here safely." I already had a feeling that I might be in danger, after the park ranger got angry with me and I threatened the old couple. I thought that members of the evil secret group might be coming to harm me. The Voice had told me that as well. The Voice said that the old couple were members of the evil secret group. The Voice told me that they were in their R.V., contacting people to come and harm me that night. The Voice said that was the reason that I was being forced to leave. It said that the park ranger was actually working with the good secret group and that he was just getting me out of there before the real trouble started for me.

I remember overhearing some conversation that the old couple was having at the campground. I don't remember what exactly it was that they said. I just remember overhearing them say some thing about a squid. I remember hearing the older woman in the R.V. talking to her husband and mentioning something about a squid. At the time that I overheard the mentioning of a squid, it made no impression on me. There is something funny about how the subconscious brain of a schizophrenic operates, because when I overheard the word, "squid", it made no impression on me at the time, but only a couple of days later, the word, "squid", would end up being something that was associated with the most horrible thing that I had ever imagined. My brain subconsciously held on to that word and used it later to terrify me with a message from The Voice.

So, back to me leaving the campground. I got to the intersection of the road I was on and the highway. There was a police car with its lights on and two policemen were standing on the side of the road. One of them walked up to my car and said, "Which way are you heading?" I said, "I need to make a left here." He said to the other police officer, "He's going to make a left." Then he said to me, "O.K., you can go." I drove on into Dunnellon and got some gas at the Wal-Mart gas station. On the way there The Voice said, "That detour was also set up because The President was coming to see you, before you messed things up. He was going to visit you tonight at the campground. They were going to re-route traffic while the President visited you at Rainbow Springs." I thought that was amazing. I had been hoping to meet with someone in the secret group. I had not expected that The President himself would be the one to contact me. I also felt like The Voice could be lying to me again. It had already now told me about the boat in the river and the body in the bathroom. I had never been able to find evidence to prove that either of these things were true. I thought that The Voice might not always be telling me the truth. Still, I thought that if what it had told me about George Bush wanting to come see me was true, that was pretty amazing. I said, "Sorry George, maybe I'll meet up with you sometime soon." I believed that I could talk to the air and the secret group could hear me. Whenever I was alone in my car, I would have conversations with just me and The Voice in my head. I don't remember the details of many of our conversations. Most of them were like arguments about why I had not seen any proof of their existence yet. I kept getting angry with The Voice after it told me about things that never ended up happening. At least, I couldn't prove that they had or had not happened, that is. So, it was around this time that I began to become irritated with The Voice. I was beginning to grow tired of the wild goose chases.

I don't remember much about the drive from Rainbow Springs to Tallahassee. One thing I remember was hearing a new voice in my ear. It said, "Scott, this is George Bush. You are screwing things up. You have got to settle down son." I said, "I'm sorry sir. I will try to do whatever you say." And kept driving down the road. I remember calling Sara shortly after hearing that voice. I told her that I was wondering if she had already started the divorce process. She said that she had not. I told her to wait just a little longer. I told her that I thought I was about to become a member of one of the branches of the military or the C.I.A. I said that if she waited until I joined up with one of those groups, she and the girls would receive benefits from them, as long as we were married when I joined. I got this idea from the National Guard recruiter in Haines City. He had told me not to divorce my wife until I joined the National Guard. He said, that as long as we were still married when I joined, she and the girls would all receive benefits like insurance and a monthly check, even after we divorced.

Sara said that she agreed that we needed to get a divorce. She said that she no longer felt like she and the girls were safe with me. She said that she thought I was dangerous. I said, "I'm not dangerous. But I am in a lot of danger at the moment." She asked what I was talking about. I said, "I can't really tell you a whole lot about what I'm involved in. I'm a sort of spy now." She said, "What are you talking about?" I said, "I know that you probably don't believe me, but I have talked to some very powerful people lately." She said, "Really. Like who?" I said, "You wouldn't believe me if I told you." She said, "Its not that I don't believe you, its just that this is all very confusing to me. I don't understand how you are now a spy." I said, "O.K., I'll tell you this much. The person that I just talked to a little while ago was George Bush." Sara said, "You just talked to George Bush?", with suspicion. I said, "I told you that you wouldn't believe me." She said, "I don't know Scott. I just can't believe that George Bush called you. Why would he call you?" I said, "I can't talk about that with you." She said, "This is what I'm talking about. I can't be with you when I don't know if you are telling the truth or lying to me." I said, "I understand. I'm not lying to you. But for the safety of you and the girls, I think it is best that we get a divorce. I don't want to have the people that are after me come and get you and the girls." I thought I heard Sara crying. Then she hung up. I didn't call her back. I just kept on driving to Tallahassee.

On the way to Tallahassee, The Voice had told me, "Jen is waiting for you at Pocket's Pool. She knows that you are coming. They are going to be having a little welcoming party for you at Pocket's Pool tonight. She is going to be wearing a disguise, but you will recognize her."

As I got close to the city, The Voice said, "There are people here who want to harm you. You need to disguise yourself. Put on the Darth Vader helmet." So I did. I drove down U.S. Hwy. 27 North while I put on my Darth Vader Helmet. I put the helmet on and said, "It's a little hard to see with this thing on." It was already dark outside, and looking through the eye pieces of the helmet was like looking through dark tinted sunglasses. The Voice said, "Then put on your other mask." I had another little Darth Vader mask that was a cheap little kids Halloween type costume mask. I had bought this at the same time that I bought the nice helmet. This cheap mask just had holes cut out where the eyes would be. So, I put that one on instead. I could now be in disguise, but still see clearly. I drove into town with the mask on. As I got into town, I realized that all the streetlights made it bright enough that I could put the cool helmet back on. So, I did. I drove down Apalachee Pkwy. with the real Darth Vader helmet on. I remember people at stoplights looking at me when I pulled up beside them. I was quite a sight, I'm sure. Its not everyday that you see Darth Vader driving a Subaru Forester, with a bright orange kayak tied to the top. One car was filled with a group of college kids. They started laughing and hollering at me, "Darth! What's up Darth?" I looked at them and waved. I had several other cars honk their horns at me as I drove through town. I felt a little like a celebrity. I'm sure that most people thought I was a little odd, at the least.

I decided to go to the Microtel that I had stayed at a couple times now already. I pulled into the parking lot and decided to keep the Darth Vader helmet on. I walked right up to the front desk with the helmet on. The guy behind the counter said, "Are you practicing for Halloween or something?" I laughed and took off the helmet. I said, "Yes. I'm just filled with the Halloween spirit. And I love Darth Vader." He gave me a look to let me know that he wasn't very impressed with my little entrance. Then he asked if I needed a room. I told him that I did. He gave me a room on the first floor. The other two times that I had been there I had stayed on the third floor. I thought, "I guess I'm moving up in the world. Now, I'm on the first floor." The first floor was no more or less prestigious than the third. I just found ways to tie everything that happened to me to the idea that I was now a sort of celebrity.

I went to my room and unloaded a few of my things. I realized that I needed to use the bathroom. The Voice told me, "They are going to collect your DNA to make a clone of you." I said, "Who is going to make a clone of me?" The Voice said, "There are people here at this hotel who are going to try to get a sample of your DNA while you are here." I thought this seemed like a pretty wild idea, but it was no less crazy than some of the other things that I had already been told by The Voice. I thought about the guy at the front desk. He had a strange accent and I asked him where he was from. He said he was from New Zealand. I thought about Star Wars and the character that was used to create the clone army in Attack of the Clones. The character was named Jenga Fett. The guy that played him was actually from New Zealand. I immediately made a new Star Wars connection in my life. I thought that the people who were running the Microtel were from New Zealand, based on meeting one guy who worked at the front desk. I then thought that maybe George Lucas, the creator of Star Wars, had put out a little secret message in his film, that the New Zealanders were cloning humans. It was another of those little bits of information providing me with a radical new theory. As I went to the bathroom, I wondered if my pee was going to be collected and used to gather my DNA. I'm not even sure if that's possible, but at the time, I just knew it was. I flushed the toilet and said, "Well, New Zealand, you're welcome." I imagined that there were some scientists right there in the hotel who had somehow routed the plumbing from that toilet to a collection area where they would be able to get a sample of my DNA from my pee. Another genius idea, I know.

After my little cloning theory had developed, The Voice spoke to me again. The Voice reminded me to go over to Pocket's Pool to check out the little welcoming party that was supposedly being held there for me. So, I decided to go to Pocket's Pool to see what was going on there and to see if I could find Jen again. I drove down the street and walked into Pocket's Pool. I remembered what The Voice had said about Jen being in disguise. As I walked in, I looked around at the people. I seemed to notice a lot of them looking at me too. I thought that they probably all knew who I was, even though I did not recognize any of them. I just tried to be cool and walked on past all the people standing around and went up to the bar. I looked around for Jen, or someone who might be Jen in disguise. I did not see her, or anyone that even resembled her. There was another cute bartender girl there that night, but she was not Jen. I asked the girl if Jen was there. She said, "No, she's off tonight, she already worked this afternoon." Then I realized that The Voice had lied to me again. After realizing that I had been tricked once again, I became angry with The Voice. I was getting tired of feeling like I had been tricked. Every time The Voice told me something, I took it as fact. Now, I had acted on several things that The Voice had said, and things never turned out the way that I had imagined that they would. I asked the girl if she knew whether or not Jen might be coming up there that night. She said,

"Oh, I don't know. How do you know her?" I told her about meeting Jen there a while back. I didn't tell her how many times I had fantasized about getting to know Jen better. I just told the girl that I thought Jen seemed like a very nice person, and I was just curious about her.

After realizing that Jen was not going to be showing up, I decided to just stay around and chat with the new girl at the bar. She seemed as friendly as Jen, although she was not as cute as Jen. The girl was cute, just not as cute as Jen. I don't even remember her name. I talked with her for a little while. The whole time I was there, I drank sweet tea again.

A guy brought me a sweet tea one time after I had already drank a couple glasses full. He handed it to me and smiled and said, "There's your sweet tea buddy." I thanked him and thought, "That guy seems suspicious to me." I took a drink of the tea. It tasted different from the stuff that I had been drinking. The Voice said, "You have just been poisoned. Don't drink anymore." I put the tea down and told the bartender girl that I thought someone had spiked my drink. She said, "What do you mean?" I said, "This tea tastes totally different from what I was just drinking. I think that someone put something in it." She said, "Maybe they accidentally gave you a Long Island Iced Tea. They might have thought that's what you were drinking." I thought, "All the liquor is right out here at the bar. That guy came with my tea from inside the kitchen. Why would he be putting alcohol in my drink in the kitchen?" I told the girl that I didn't think that was the case. I told her that I thought that guy had put something in my drink while he was back in the kitchen. She went back and talked to the guy. He came back out and apologized. He said, "He man, I didn't put anything in your drink. I'll make you another one if that one tastes weird, but I didn't add anything extra to that tea.", and smiled. I didn't believe him. I just said, "Could she (the bartender) make it for me this time?" He said, "Sure.", and walked off. The girl at the bar gave me a weird look and said, "I don't think he put anything in your drink, but I make the best drinks around here anyway. I'll make you a tea, but I'm just going to be pouring it out of the same container that he did. It'll be the same stuff you just had." I said, "Then I'll just have a water." She said, "I can make that right in front of you.", and she squirted in some water into a glass from a little hose that poured the draft beers and other liquids that she used to make drinks. I thanked her and started drinking my water.

Then I got an idea. I thought about The Voice telling me about there being people who wanted to harm me in Tallahassee and needing to wear a disguise. I decided to go out to my car and put on a disguise. At first, I thought about wearing a pair of sunglasses and a different hat, maybe even changing my clothes. Then The Voice said, "Give them a show. Wear the Darth Vader outfit. So, just like every other time The Voice told me to do something, I did it. I put on the helmet and grabbed a light saber. I thought about putting on the cape, but decided that would draw too much attention, as if walking around with a Darth Vader helmet and light saber wouldn't draw attention. I walked back into the bar with my new outfit on. People looked at me, but didn't say anything. I went up to the bar and sat back down where I had been sitting. I placed the light saber on the bar counter. I thought that if nothing else, I would get some laughs. No one talked to me. No one laughed. Not even the girl at the bar. I saw her go back into the kitchen and talk to some people who looked at me. Shortly afterwards a big guy in a shirt that said, "SECURITY", came up to me and said, "Hey buddy, you can't wear that kind of thing in here." I said, "I'm just wearing this because I don't want someone to recognize me." He said, "Sorry, we don't allow masks in here." I said some smart-ass comment to him and he got angry with me. I also told him that he couldn't tell me what I could and could not wear. I said, "This is a free country, and I've been ordering drinks from you for a couple hours now. I'm not taking this thing off until I want to." He said, "All right wise ass, get up. Your out of here." I said, "What are you talking about? I haven't done anything. You can't make me leave." He said, "If you don't leave on your own, I'll force you out of here myself." I said, "Fine. I'm leaving. Even though I haven't done anything and you are just an asshole, I'll leave." After that, I got up and walked out. I went back to my car and took off my helmet and put up my light saber. I decided that I was not going to be run out of the bar that easily, however. I decided to wear a new disguise.

I put on a baseball hat and changed my shirt. I also put on some sunglasses. It was around midnight at this point. I thought that I had changed my look enough to be able to walk back into the bar and not have the bouncer realize who I was. It was just another very stupid idea. The sunglasses alone probably tipped off most people that I was a little wacky, as if the Darth Vader outfit had not already done that. I walked back in and sat down at the car. The bartender girl said, "What was up with the Darth Vader mask?" I just laughed and said, "I'm just getting ready for Halloween. Is that a crime?" She didn't think that I was very funny. She said, "You should probably leave before you get kicked out again. I said, "I'm not going to cause any trouble. I just wanted to talk to you some more." The girl didn't seem to want to talk to me anymore, though. I guess I had already scared her, the same way that I had scared Jen. The thought never occurred to me though. I just sat there and tried to get her to talk to me more. Not long after I came back in, the bouncer came back up to me. He said, "Aren't you the guy that I just told to leave?" I said, "No. I just got here. You must have me confused with someone else." He said, "No, you're the guy. I recognize your voice. Get out or I'm calling the cops on you." I said, "What are you going to call the cops on me for. I haven't done anything." He said, "We have the right to refuse service to whoever we want, and I've already told you to leave. Now you're back. I can call the cops and have them arrest you." I said, "I would love to see you try." He said, "Look man, I don't want to have to deal with the police. Please just leave or I'm going to take you outside myself." I said, "Go ahead." So, he grabbed my shoulders and marched me out the door. This was now the second time that I had ever been physically removed from a building. The bouncer and I walked past a lot of people on our way out of the bar. I was laughing the entire time the guy was walking me out of the building. People were looking at me and shaking their heads.

We got outside and the guy said, "Are you going to leave or do I have to call the cops?" I said, "You might want to go ahead and call the cops, because I haven't done anything wrong. I'd like to see just what you can do to me. I want to see you have me arrested for drinking sweet tea at the bar and not harming anyone. He said, "You are a dumb ass. I'm telling you that if you will just leave, I won't call the cops." I said, "No. Go ahead and call them. Besides, one of your guys put something in one of my drinks tonight. I want to tell them all about that." That was all he needed. Now, I guess, he felt like he had to call the cops. I was being belligerent. He had run out of options, and I wasn't budging. He said, "O.K., you just wait here a minute.", and went back inside. A few minutes later, a patrol car pulled up. I was sitting on the sidewalk in front of the entrance, smoking a cigarette. The bouncer and the owner came outside and started talking to the police. They walked out of earshot of me so that I could not hear what they were saying. I thought, "What a couple of assholes. They are probably over there lying about what happened so that they can try to arrest me."

I figured that what none of them knew was that I was actually above the law. I was a member of the secret group. I figured that the police would quickly realize who I was, and would either take me to meet up with the secret group, or at the least, just let me off with no problem. Then The Voice said, "One of these cops is working with the evil group. He's going to try to break you. Get ready for a long night. They might even torture you. Just don't reveal anything that you know."

I sat there and waited for the cops to come talk to me. Eventually they did. There was a young black officer and an older white officer. The black guy seemed pretty nice. The white guy, I figured was the one working for the evil group. The Voice had told me that he was the one who was going to break me. The older white officer actually never talked to me. He just sat back and let his partner handle me. The black officer said, "Sir, would you mind putting out your cigarette." I said, "No problem.", and did. He said, "So, the owner tells me that you were asked to leave the premises and you refused. Tell me your side of the story." I said, "I haven't done anything. That's the problem. All I did was sit at the bar and drink sweet tea. I never said anything rude to anyone. I didn't do anything." He said, "They said that you were wearing a costume and they asked you to take it off and you refused." I said, "Yes I did. It was just a Darth Vader helmet that I'm going to wear for Halloween. Is there a law against that?" He said, "Some people don't like you to conceal your face. If they wanted you to remove your mask, you should have done that." I said, "Look, the main thing is that before all that happened, someone spiked one of the sweet teas that I was drinking. A guy handed me a tea that tasted totally weird. There was something in it. I don't know if they were trying to get me drunk or if there was something else in that tea, but that definitely was not just a plain sweet tea." He said, "Let me see what they have to say about that." He walked back over to the owner and the bouncer and talked with them. After several more minutes, he came back over to me. He said, "O.K., here's what we're going to do. They want to ban you from coming to this bar. That means that you can't set foot on this property for three years. If you are caught coming back up here, then you will be arrested. Do you understand?" I said, "What exactly did I do? This is bull crap!" He said, "I understand that you are angry, but don't use foul language with me." I said, "Sorry, but this is not fair. I haven't done anything wrong. They are the ones who are handing out spiked drinks. What are you going to do to them?" He said, "We don't have any proof of what you are saying. Do you want to take a breathalyzer to see if you have alcohol in your system?" I said, "No. I don't think it was alcohol that they put in that tea." He said, "Alright, then you need to leave. Don't come back here for three years. Remember they have a restraining order against you. If you come back, they can have you arrested." I said, "This is totally unfair." He said, "Just go to your car and calm down. Then go home."

I went to my car and sat there for a few minutes. I thought, "Alright, you bastards may be able to keep me out of the building, but you can't stop me from driving around the parking lot." So, I drove through the parking lot and slowly crept by the front entrance. I wanted the people inside to see me and see that I had won. I had not been arrested. I could sit out in front of Pocket's Pool and there was nothing they could do about it. Then the police officers pulled up beside me. The old white man said, "Do you want to go to jail tonight?" I said, "No. I'm leaving." He said, "The restraining order includes loitering in the parking lot. Don't let us find you driving around here." I said, "Are you telling me that I am banned from all of the buildings in this plaza? What if I want to see a movie at the theater over there?" He said, "If you want to see a movie, that's fine. Just don't let us find out that you're sitting here in front of Pocket's Pool." I said, "Alright. Thanks.", and drove off.

After nearly getting arrested, I decided that I would go for a jog around Lake Ella, and wind down a little. Lake Ella was the little lake that I had asked Jen if she wanted to walk around with me after I met her that night on the last time I was in town. Lake Ella was also a place that Sara and I used to take Elizabeth to when she was little. We would feed the birds and fish and walk around the lake. We went there many times over the years that we lived in Tallahassee. It was one of my favorite places in town, because it was close to my work and not far from where we lived.

When I got to the lake that night, it was already around 1:00 am. Surprisingly, there were several other people still hanging out at the lake as well. Some of them were couples that were making out on benches by the lake. Others were homeless people who slept on some of those benches at night. I didn't mind being in a sort of dangerous environment. It didn't seem that dangerous to me anyway. I had the protection of the secret group. I could do whatever I wanted, when I wanted. So, I started jogging around Lake Ella at 1:00 am. I remember seeing a Ford Explorer that looked like the one that my old boss, Jodi Dobson from MLD Architects, used to drive. I watched it drive by me very slowly. I thought, "That's Jodi. He's probably heard about me being in town. He must have come down here just to see me." The car drove on by and went out of sight. I was sure that Jodi had come to spy on me because he had probably heard about me from one of those secret web sites or newspapers that I thought lots of people must be reading.

After jogging for a little while, I got pretty hot. I decided to take off my shirt. That's something I never would have done in my old life. But, I also never would have done most of the things that I had in the last few months. I jogged a few laps around the lake with my shirt off and noticed a group of college kids that kept looking at me and smiling every time I passed by. The group of college kids consisted of about 3 or 4 girls and a couple of guys. I passed by them my last time and said, "I hope I'm not offending you guys by jogging out here with my shirt off." One of the girls laughed and said, "You're not offending me at all. I like guys with their shirt off." I laughed and kept jogging. I can't believe that I didn't try to hit on that girl. I guess that I didn't hit on her because I was beginning to get a little frustrated with my encounters with girls over the past month. First Jen, and now the other bartender girl, had both become afraid of me after only talking with them for a few hours. I just assumed that if I stopped to talk to that girl, something would happen that scared her. I figured if nothing else, the secret group would somehow interfere with my attempt to get to know her and would screw me up, the same way that I thought they had screwed me up with Jen and the other bartender. So, I just jogged back to my car and left. I got in my car and decided that I needed to take a shower. So, I went back to the hotel.

I drove back to the hotel, went straight to my room, walked in, and took a shower. It was now around 2:00 am. As I was in the shower, The Voice said to me, "You have to leave. People are going to come in your room and kill you if you stay here tonight. Leave the hotel immediately." I thought about the cop that The Voice had told me about, the one that The Voice had said would break me. I wondered if he had contacted some other people who were on their way to kill me. I got out of the shower and grabbed my things and checked out of my room. I asked the guy if I could have a partial refund of money since I had not actually slept in the room. He said that was not possible. So I just left.

I got in my car and started driving. I wanted to get the hell out of the hotel as fast as I could. After all, people were coming to kill me. The Voice had told me so. It was a fact. I drove away from the hotel trying to think of somewhere else that was safe for me to stay. I didn't want to pay for another hotel and have The Voice tell me that people were going to kill me there too. The Voice said, "You will be safe at the homeless shelter. The bartender from Pocket's Pool is staying there tonight too. She would like to see you. Go there."

I thought about what The Voice said and wondered if the homeless shelter would still take someone at the late hour that it was. I drove by the spot where the shelter used to be on Tennessee Ave. and remembered that it had been relocated further out of town, off of Tennessee Ave. a few miles west of FSU. I drove on down Tennessee Ave. to where I thought I should turn to find the shelter. I couldn't find it. I was wearing down and could barely keep my eyes open, much less remember exactly how to get to the new location of the homeless shelter. I decided that since I was unable to remember how to et to the shelter, that was all I needed to keep from going to there that night. I figured that if I was supposed to find it, the secret group would lead me to it. Since they had not led me to it, I decided to not look for the shelter anymore. I had already been imagining what it would be like to have to sleep with a bunch of homeless people. I also had a thought that someone might stick me with a hypodermic needle or something. I didn't want to take a chance on getting HIV or some drug injected into me while I slept. I had already survived being killed by chemical injection once at the PRC, I didn't want to take a chance on that happening again. So, I decided to give up on the homeless shelter plan and just wait out the last remaining hours of darkness by walking around Wal-Mart for a while. I hoped that once the sun came up, I would be able to just park my car somewhere and sleep in it for a few hours.

By the time I got to Wal-Mart, I was absolutely exhausted, but I decided that it would be the safest thing for me to just walk around the store for a while to see if I could just stay up until daylight. I walked in Wal-Mart and started looking around. Amazingly, I started to find things that looked like stuff that I could use. So, being totally exhausted, I began on another Wal-Mart shopping spree. I saw some hats that I thought would make good disguises. I had already tried switching a few of the things I was wearing at the bar earlier that night, in an attempt to disguise myself. That was a total failure. So, why I thought that by simply changing my hat or sunglasses had anything to do with disguising myself, I do not know. My brain was not always putting together the smartest ideas I had ever had. The disguise thing was one of many not so smart ideas.

I bought 4 or 5 hats and then saw some shirts and a sweater that I thought were nice. I loaded those in the buggy. I then decided that I needed some protection against people who were trying to harm me. I didn't want to get a conventional weapon though. I wasn't sure of exactly what would be coming to harm me. And I didn't want to get pulled over by the police and have them find a gun or a large knife in my car. So, I went to the lawn and garden section of the store. I decided that the weapons that I would use on my enemies would be cruel, terrible weapons that would slowly maim and disfigure my victims before I delivered them a death blow. I thought that the lawn and garden center made a perfect weapons department for these types of weapons.

I started looking at garden tools as weapons. I saw a pair of large pruning scissors. I thought, "I'd love for someone to try to mess with me. I would tear someone apart with these." I was beginning to have more twisted thoughts about what I would do if someone from the evil group crossed my path. I imagined myself coming across a zombie or some other less than human creature that I might have to kill. I saw a little hand saw and thought that looked like a good weapon. Then I grabbed a pair of hedge clippers, a medium sized knife, and a couple of metal rakes that could be held in one hand and had 6, ¼ inch steel teeth that made up the raking end. I thought that those two little rakes could do some serious damage to somebody if they tried to get too close to me. After those items, I felt like I had covered myself in the inconspicuous weapons department. All it would have taken for me to kill someone was for The Voice to identify a person as a threat and for me to believe it. I was now armed and was just one erroneous thought away from committing the most atrocious act that a person can commit, murder.

After looking for monster killing weapons, I thought about getting a digital camera. I wanted something that I could use to photograph all the bizarre things that I saw. I had many encounters where I wished that I had been able to get a picture. I wanted to photograph a lot of the cars that passed me on the road, the ones that I thought were sending me little messages through bumper stickers, license plates, or things written in the dirt on the car. I really wished that I had a camera when I was in New Orleans. There were a lot of things that I wanted to photograph there. I actually brought a video camera with me and recorded a lot of things that I saw. I even got some film of some of the people I was working with on the supply line, even though they acted like they didn't want me filming them. Still, I wished that I had a camera many times in New Orleans, just so that I could have something that easily documented things when I saw them. So, I went over to the electronics department and started looking at cameras. They had a pretty decent selection of cameras ranging in price from under $100 to over $300. I saw a Kodak EasyShare camera that looked really nice to me. My brother, Carter, had bought an EasyShare a few years earlier and I was always impressed with the quality of the pictures that he took with his camera. The EasyShare was $250. I thought that was a good price for a camera that took such great pictures. I got a girl to come over and get one out of the case for me. I put it in my buggy. Then I asked her about printers for the camera. She had no clue of anything to do with electronics. She was just a worker from some other department filling in for a person that was supposed to be there. I'm sure that the regular electronics person knew about as much as she did. I haven't met too many Wal-Mart employees who know much about the things that they sell. I decided to get a printer that was a Kodak EasyShare printer. I assumed that it would be compatible with my camera since it had the same name. To this day, that printer has never even been opened out of the box.

After the camera and printer purchase, I went and bought other things that I don't even remember. I had enough crap to fill up another Wal-Mart buggy. My car was already overflowing with crap that I had bought since I left the lake house. This trip pushed my car's storage capacity to the limit. Once I unloaded all the crap that I had bought into my car, I had things stacked up from the floor to the ceiling throughout the entire car. I don't even remember what the total was on that bill, but it was the most expensive Wal-Mart trip I had taken up to that date.

As I was getting ready to check out, I noticed a Wal-Mart employee who looked half dead. He was covered in sores and had very red skin. His eyes were also blood shot. He looked homeless. He probably was. He had a beard and scraggly hair that he wore under a hat. He looked like he had not taken a shower in days. I thought that he might be an agent of the evil group. I thought that he might be carrying some disease that was meant to be transmitted to me. I stayed far away from him and hoped that he did not try to come near me. He looked at me with a blank stare and just kept on walking past me. I kept watching him the whole time I was waiting to be checked out at the register. I remember mentioning the strange guy to the girl at the check out counter. I said, "That weird looking guy that just walked by a minute ago, does he actually work here?" She said, "I don't know who you're talking about." I said, "That guy who just walked by with the long hair, beard, and sores on his arms and face." She said, "I don't know anybody who works here who looks like that." That just fed into my suspicion that I had just seen an agent of the evil group. I wondered if he might be one of the people who had been sent to kill me. I thought that, perhaps, he was an evil agent sent to the Wal-Mart, disguised as an employee. I imagined that he was carrying some terrible infectious disease that was going to be used as the weapon that would kill me. I actually started to itch as I walked out of the store. I remember scratching my arm and thinking, "I've got to wash my arms, I think that guy somehow put that virus on me. That's what's causing me to itch." I put my stuff in my car and went back into Wal-Mart to go to the bathroom and scrub my arms with hot water and soap. I went in the bathroom and no one else was in there. So, I got some soap out of the little dispenser and rubbed it all over my hands and arms. Then I used hot water to rinse it all off. I hoped that I had done enough to fight whatever germs that weird guy had somehow put on me. After that, I went back to my car.

I sat out in my car and saw that it was a little before 4:00 am. I thought about sleeping right there in my car at the Wal-Mart parking lot. But then I thought about the weird guy and thought that I might not be safe there. So I left. I drove back down Tennessee Ave., towards down town. I only went a few blocks up the street when I noticed a little church. I thought about how I had camped at the church outside of New Orleans. I remembered how I had been safe there. I said, "Is it O.K. to sleep at this church?" The Voice said, "Yes. We'll send people to watch over you." So, I pulled into the church parking lot. It was right off of Tennessee Ave. I decided that I didn't want to break out my tent and all of that gear. I decided to just get out my sleeping bag and pillow and lay down on the sidewalk in front of the church. I thought of it like a little camping trip, just without a tent. It was actually as close as I have ever had to come to sleeping like a homeless person. As I was setting up my sleeping bag on the ground, I felt something sting the back of my neck.

The sting felt like that of a mosquito bite, only worse. The Voice said, "You have just been shot with a poison dart. There is a member of the voodoo cult out in the woods. They just shot you with a tiny dart. Don't worry. The microscopic robots inside you will take care of what was in the dart. You will be fine." I felt a little panicked. I looked around to see if I could see someone in the woods around the church. I couldn't see anyone. I decided not to worry about it. I believed The Voice. I had faith that there were little machines in my body that were placed there to improve the function of my body's systems.

I laid out my sleeping bag and pillow on the sidewalk and said a prayer. I asked God to please protect me as I slept. I laid down on the hard concrete and was so exhausted that it actually felt good. I was inside my sleeping bag and had all of my clothes on, but the ground was still much harder and colder than anything I had ever slept on. Still, I actually managed to fall asleep. Cars were whizzing by along Tennessee Ave., but all the noise quickly disappeared from consciousness and I fell asleep. I woke up a couple hours later and the sun was coming up. I thought that I should leave before someone from the church came and found me there. I didn't want to have to explain why I was sleeping on their sidewalk. Instead, I left a note on the door, telling whoever found it, that I had slept there that night and was very grateful that no harm had come to me. I put a few dollars worth of change on the ground in front of the door and left.

I don't remember what I did for breakfast that morning but I did something to pass a little time and then I decided to go through with an idea that I had a few hours earlier. When I was loading my things into my Forester at Wal-Mart at around 4:00 am, I thought, "This Forester doesn't have enough storage room. I need something bigger." I had seen an ad on television about a new vehicle that Subaru was making called the Tribeca. I thought about that car and wondered how much it cost. I decided that I would go to the Subaru dealership and check out the Tribeca the next day. So, that was my plan for day two in Tallahassee. After doing whatever I did that morning, with about 2 hours of sleep, I decided to go car shopping.

I drove to the Subaru dealership and started walking around, looking at the new models. Shortly after I arrived, I was met by William. William was the guy who had sold me the Forester over a year and half earlier. He came up and said hello. I asked him if he remembered me and he said that he did. He said, "Are you thinking about trading in that Forester already?" I said, "Yes I am. My wife and I are now separated and I just want to get rid of it because every time I look at it, I think of her." He said, "Well, what are you interested in getting?" I said, "I love the Forester, but it is a little small. I was thinking about getting something a little bigger." He said, "Well the only larger vehicle that Subaru makes is the Tribeca. Are you interested in that?" I said, "That's exactly why I'm here. I wanted to look at one of those." He said, "Alright, we've only got a few of them. We just got them this month. These are the first Tribecas we have received." and he walked me to three Tribecas that were all blue. I said, "Man those things are awesome." He said, "Yeah, but they cost a lot more than your Forester. If you are about to go through a divorce, do you think you would be able to afford the payments?" I told him that money wasn't a problem for me and he said, "Alright, then why don't you take one for a test drive?" I said that I would love to. So we got into a Tribeca and he let me drive it off the lot and down Tennessee Ave. He told me all the features that were included with the one that I was driving. It had all wheel drive, like the Forster. It got less gas mileage than the Forester. It was slightly roomier than the Forester. He told me about the Boxer engine that was in the Tribeca. It had a 260 hp engine that had a lot more pick up than the Forester. The one thing that I did not like about it was that it did not come with a standard transmission. It had a stick on the floor that you could shift through several gears, but it was really just an automatic. The only thing you really ever used the stick for was to put the car in drive, park, and reverse. William told me that you could put the car in Sport Mode and the stick would actually let you shift through 5 gears, but there was no clutch pedal. All you did was push the stick over to the left to put in Sport Mode. Then you could push the stick up or down to make the transmission shift a gear. I thought that was a little lame, but I still loved the car. It had power everything and a very cool cruise control. It had a sunroof and a neat display for the stereo. The center console had all kinds of buttons that took me a while to figure out what they all did.

We got back to the dealership and William said, "Let's see if we can get you approved for a loan." I said, "Sounds good to me." So we went in and he had me start filling out all the loan paperwork. He said, "How much do you make with Arr Maz?" I paused for a second and then he said, "Let me ask you this, do you make more than $70,000 annually?" When he said this he had a smile on his face and he winked. I took this as his way of saying, "Just tell me that you make this amount and I'll take care of everything else." I thought, "William might be connected to the secret group too. He must be trying to let me get approved for this loan because they want me to have this vehicle." I said to William, "Um. Yes, I make around $70,000 now." He said, "Alright, I'm just going to write $70,000 for your income." I thought, "Yes, William must be working for the secret group too." I thought that my purchasing the car was just one of many great things that the secret group had in store for me. I thought that they were allowing me to get set up as a big shot. The vehicle was just the first step towards becoming the incredibly wealthy secret agent that I thought I was about to become. I think that William was actually just another sleazy car salesman who was willing to put down a little lie on paper so that he could sell cars. He could have cared less what I was making and whether or not I could actually afford the payments. He was just interested in making a sale. That was his job after all. If he could sell me a car, he would get a slice of the money too. I think its people like William who have caused our country to get into the mess that it is now in. Greed is the powerful engine that has driven our economy into a state of depression.

So, after filling out all of the paper work, I had to wait around a while for William to talk with the bank to get my loan approved. He came back up to me after a while and said that everything had been approved and that I just had to come up with a $3,000 down payment for the vehicle and it was mine. He went through how much they were going to give me for trading in the Forester. I don't even remember what that amount was. I was very tired the entire time that I was doing all this. I had been going for days again with little sleep. I was in the worst mental state a person could be in when making a major purchase like a car, but I was convinced that I needed to do this. William had me meet with a guy who discussed the terms of the loan and what my payments would be, the trade in value of the Forester, and what the grand total for the Tribeca would be. I remember that it came up to over $32,000 after the trade in amount for the Forester had been deducted. I didn't even blink. I just agreed to everything that the guy told me and signed all the forms that he put in front of me without reading the first word. The guy said, "Some people like to read over the fine print of everything I give them. I can see you are not one of those types of people." I said, "Normally I am, but I'm just really tired. I only had about two hours of sleep last night. I just don't feel like reading through all this right now. I'll look it over later." and I kept on signing away.

After signing all the forms, the guy started trying to sell me different insurance type plans and extended warranties. I passed on everything. I told him that I would just go with whatever warranties that Subaru had for the vehicle when I purchased it. I didn't want any more cost added onto the huge amount that I realized I had just agreed to pay. The guy had already told me that my monthly payments would be over $550. I was used to paying around $400 for the Forester. My insurance was going to go up too, because I was driving a vehicle that cost almost twice what I had paid for the Forester. With the Forester I had financed for 4 years with the bank. With the Tribeca, I financed for the longest time that they would allow me to pay back the loan. I think it was a 6 year payment plan.

After finishing my meeting with the finance guy, I waited around for them to get the Tribeca ready for me to drive off the lot. William suggested that I look at the accessories that were available for the Tribeca. He said, "They have a lot of cool features that you can add on to the Tribeca. You should check these out." and he handed me a catalogue of accessories. I looked through it and, just like every time I walked in to Wal-Mart, I started to see things that I had to have. There was a cargo rack, a bike rack, a kayak rack, front and rear mud flaps, a dog fence that set up between the back seat and the trunk area, a flashlight that plugged into the power outlet in the back of the car, and a sun roof bug guard. I got it all. There were a few other accessories that I did not get, but I decided that I had to have about 75% of everything that I saw. I asked William how I could order the accessories. He said, "Just go back to the parts department and they'll take care of you." So, I did.

I went back to the parts desk and showed the guy all of the items that I wanted to have installed on the Tribeca. He said, "Well, since we just got those Tribecas, we don't actually have any of these parts right now. But I can order them for you and put them all on when they come in." I said, 'Well, I live about six hours from here, but I guess I could just make another trip back, whenever they arrive." He said, "Alright then, I'll put these on order and call you when they come in. Just go over to the girls next door and they'll take care of billing you." So I walked over to the cashier's desk and gave them the parts list that the guy had just printed up for me.

There was a lady working back at the cashier's desk who looked like she was probably in her 40's. She was still pretty good looking, just a lot older than me, older than any woman I had ever thought about having a relationship with. I gave her my bill from the parts desk. She asked me how I wanted to pay. I told her that I would just put it on my debit card. She said, "Wow, you're going to actually pay for all this and not put it on credit? That's pretty rare." I said, "Well, that's what you can do when you make the big bucks like me." She said, "So you just bought the Tribeca?" I said, "Well, I just agreed to go into debt for it anyway." She laughed and told me her name. She started to get a little flirty with me. I thought, "This lady is almost old enough to be my mom and she's trying to hit on me." After paying my bill, I went outside to see what they were doing to the Tribeca. I stood out there and talked to the guys as they were detailing the car and putting on the plates. The lady from the cashier's desk came out and started talking to me. She said, "That is one nice car you just bought yourself there." I said, "Yes it is. I love it. I'm going to look good in it." She laughed and we talked a little more. I thought, "This lady is old, but she's not bad looking, and she seems pretty nice." Before I left, that lady gave me her name, home phone, and cell phone number. I guess the ladies love a guy who appears to have money, even if he is actually crazier than a bed bug.

After the Tribeca was ready to go, I started unloading all of the stuff out of the Forester. It was a lot of stuff. I had bags and boxes of crap, a lot of clothes, my camping equipment, and there was also the kayak on top. A lady walked up to me when I was unloading all my gear. She said, "Man, they should be filming a Subaru commercial right now. You've got the camping gear, the kayak. It looks like you've been on an adventure." I said, "Yeah. I've been doing a little camping for the last few days. I decided to upgrade my vehicle while I was on vacation." She said, "Well, good for you." Little did she know that I was actually jobless, homeless, and out of my mind. Purchasing a new vehicle was the last thing that I should have done or could have afforded. But, mania is a very expensive problem. It can make a person do things that they never would have done when they thought rationally. Rational was the farthest thing I was from at that point. I could put on a front for a short period of time, but it never lasted long.

At one point, while I was unloading the Forester, I noticed a couple of well dressed guys watching me from the dealership. They were talking on cell phones. Somehow, I got the idea that they were talking about me. One of the guys kept looking at me and smiling when he talked. He kept talking to someone named George. I wondered who he was talking to. I kept hearing him talk about what sounded like movie business related stuff. I don't remember exactly what he was saying, but I heard enough to trigger The Voice to fill me in on who the guy was talking to. The Voice said, "He's talking to George Lucas about you. George Lucas is interested in hiring you to work on one of his next movies." I immediately began imagining myself working as a computer graphics illustrator with LucasFilm. I thought that George Lucas must have seen some of the work I had done on the computers at ETO/Architects. I thought that he must be a member of the secret group and he was going to have me work with him to produce his next movie that would offer more secret information about the near future, the way that I now thought that the Star Wars films had done.

I walked over to the guys in the nice suits and introduced myself. I wasn't sure what to say to them. I just wanted to see if they would mention anything about George Lucas. I don't remember what I said to them or what they said to me, but I quickly realized that if they were from LucasFilm, they weren't going to be mentioning anything about it to me there. After talking with them for a few minutes, William came out and said, "Scott, are you still unpacking your car?" I said, "Yes." He said, "Well, I've got a lady who wants to look at it. Could you finish up so that I can let her see the inside of it?" I said, "Sure. Sorry, I've just got a lot of stuff in there." He said, "I know. Have you been living out of your car or something?", and laughed. He didn't know how true his little joke was. I said, "No, I was just camping for the last few days. I brought everything I needed and then some. I'll be done in a few minutes." So, I went back to unloading my car.

The last thing I had to do was get the kayak off without scratching up the paint. William had said he would help me get that off. My car was now the dealership's car. They didn't want it to get messed up as I got all my things out. So, William came over and helped me lift it off and put it on the Tribeca. Then I loaded all my things up in the Tribeca and tied down the kayak on top.

As I was loading the Tribeca, it occurred to me that William had told me that the price of the vehicle was over $32,000. I thought about how I had traded in my Forester and the total was still over $32,000. I immediately felt like I had just been taken advantage of. I had felt comfortable dealing with William. I felt like he was a trustworthy guy. He had helped me get my loan approved with no problem. And he had given me a great deal when I bought the Forester from him. I just assumed that I was probably getting another great deal when I bought the Tribeca. After I thought about how the total cost of the car had not come down after I traded in the Forester, I started to think a little less of William. I thought that he had just ripped me off. Now I wanted to go back in and change the agreement.

I went inside and found William. I said, "William, I have a question for you. You said that the Tribeca sells for $32,000. I traded you my Forester for the Tribeca.

Why is it that my total is still $32,000?" William said, "Well, you'll have to talk about that with the finance department. I don't know what you owed on your Forester and what you added in warranties and that kind of stuff." I said, "Well, I've changed my mind. I don't want the Tribeca. I want my Forester back. I think you guys just ripped me off." William said, "Calm down Scott. We didn't rip you off. Go talk with finance. They'll explain to you the cost breakdown again. You already signed the agreement for the price and I've already sold your Forester to the lady who was interested in it. I can't give you your car back. Its already been sold." I hadn't left the Forester in William's hands for more than an hour and said that he had already sold it. I didn't believe him. I said, "You have already sold the Forester?" He said, "Yes. That lady loved it and she's already bought it." I said, "Well, thanks a lot William. Let me speak with that guy in the finance department. I've got to get clear on why I am paying you guys the exact amount that you said was the price of the vehicle before a trade in." He said, "Alright, come with me. I'm sorry that you aren't happy with your contract, but you did already sign all the papers. I don't think they're going to change anything now. This has all gone through with the bank. We would have to start the whole process over if you changed your loan amount." I said, "I've got the time. It won't bother me to do everything over again."

William brought me back to the finance guy. William explained to the finance guy that I was confused about what I was paying for the Tribeca. He asked the guy to go over all of the paper work with me again. The finance guy and I sat down in his office and he explained how I had owed this amount for the Forester and how that had been subtracted from the trade in value of the car and then there were fees for this, that, and the other. None of it was making sense to me. I'm sure the main problem was the fact that I was just too exhausted to concentrate on the numbers that he kept going over. He showed me on paper how everything added up. But I still kept pointing out that the vehicle sold for $32,000 without any trade in. I had paid about a third of the Forester off. I didn't understand why that amount was not reflected in the total amount for the Tribeca. I didn't understand how, after trading in the Forester, the Tribeca was still $32,000. The guy showed me paper after paper that I had signed and agreed to. He said that we had agreed on a contract. I had signed it. That was final. I could not change the agreement that I had already signed my name to. I said, "That's fine. You guys took advantage of me when I wasn't paying attention. I shouldn't have trusted you. It's my fault. I'm not mad at you. I'm mad at myself for letting you trick me into paying too much for this car. I should be paying at least $5,000 less. But it's my fault. I signed the papers. You win." The guy apologized and said, "Scott, I'm sorry you feel like we're cheating you. We aren't. That's what I'm trying to explain to you with these papers." I said, "I know you're here to make money. I like what you sell. I'll probably make sure that my next car is a Subaru too. But I don't think you'll ever see me in here again." After that I walked out and got in my car and drove away. I was starting to develop a pattern of leaving on a bad note. I had done it with my parents several times now. It had happened at Rainbow Springs. And now I did it again at the Subaru dealership. The pattern would continue and only get worse before it was all over.

By the time I had exhausted myself at the Subaru dealership, it was around 4:00 pm. I decided that I would drive around town a little longer and see what happened. I was trying to decide whether to start heading back towards Lake Buffum or if I should go somewhere else. When I drove through downtown, I found my answer. I remember looking at a building that was under construction in downtown. There was a large crane on top of a skyscraper that was going up. The crane was sitting there motionless when I first started watching it. Then it started to turn very quickly. It turned itself so that the long arm of the crane was extending to the south, in the direction of Lake Buffum. I thought, "There's my sign. The secret group wants me to go south so that's where I'm heading." I actually believed that the secret group had staged that crane's movement to point south at the moment that I was watching it. I believed just about everything was revolving around me. I was totally self absorbed and lost in my fantasy world. There was no coming back now. The secret group was becoming less mysterious and more real than ever. They had just moved a crane to tell me where to go. I was on my way.

After seeing the sign from the crane, I headed out of town on I-10. I remember stopping at a gas station on my way out of town. The gas station had the radio playing at the pumps and the song said something about, "baby please come back soon". I didn't recognize the song, but I laughed when I heard it. I thought that the secret group was playing a little joke on me. I thought that they had selected that song so that I would hear it and realize that the secret group agents in Tallahassee were telling me to come back soon. I was just amazed at how the secret group seemed to be everywhere and nowhere at the same time. I never knew when my next encounter with them would be. I loved it.

I drove on out of town and stopped at a rest area just before I got to I-75. As I stepped out of the Tribeca, I felt like a super star. People really were looking at me now. They were noticing the unusual vehicle that I was driving. A couple people asked me what I had pulled up in. I told them, "It's a Subaru Tribeca. This is actually one of the first ones sold from the dealership in Tallahassee. They're brand new from Subaru…" In mania, I could have been a salesman if I wasn't so freaking weird all the time. Everyone I talked to seemed very impressed with my new ride. Eventually I made my way to the bathroom. When I came out, there was a guy sitting on a bench in front of the building. He started up a conversation with me. I don't remember what we were talking about. What I do remember is that another guy walked up and started talking to us. He was an employee at the rest stop. The comment I remember him making was this, he said, "Yeah, they used to tell me that I was going to be a big timer. Now look, they got me working as a janitor at this rest stop." I don't remember what the context of that statement was. I do remember what I thought about that statement though. I thought that he had just told me that he had been promised big things from the secret group and that he now worked as a janitor at the rest area. I thought that he had either not performed to the standards of the secret group or they had tricked him into becoming a janitor. I thought about how many times the secret group had told me to do something and I ended up in trouble because of it. I wondered what my fate with the secret group was. I hoped that I was not being tricked into going down a path that I thought led me to greatness but instead led me to become another janitor at a rest area, like that poor guy.

After talking with those guys for a few minutes, I got back on the road. I started heading south on I-75. I made it to Gainesville and decided to stop again for some gas and something for supper. There was a gas station that had a Hardee's inside. I decided that I would stop there. I went in and ordered some food and sat down to eat. I remember having this idea that Gainesville was also a bad place, like Miami and New Orleans. I think the idea just came from the fact that I had applied to UF and they had basically turned me down. Now that I was crazy, I had come to believe that bad things were going on in Gainesville. I wasn't sure exactly what those things were. I just had a feeling that there were people in the area who were members of the secret evil group and that they were up to no good. When I walked into the gas station / fast food restaurant, I looked around at the people inside. There were several college kids, dressed in somewhat preppy clothes. I thought, "Look at all these little snotty college kids. I bet their parents' are all paying for everything they have. They probably all come from upper class families. These kids make me sick."

My jealousy for all people who attended UF had now grown my dislike of their kind from a slight annoyance to total hatred of them. I sat down at a table and heard a couple guys and a girl talking at a table near me. They were talking about how much they disliked President Bush and how the war in Iraq was about blood for oil. I remember that at one point I started commenting on things that they were saying. At first I was just thinking how much I disagreed with what they were saying. But after a few minutes I started actually speaking loud enough that they could here me. I started by just saying a thing or two to the air. I don't know if they heard me or not. At one point I saw them start looking at me. Then I started let them know that I was talking to them. I don't remember exactly what I said, but it was something along the lines of telling them that I thought they were a bunch of idiots. I told them that they were wrong about Bush. I said that he was a great man who had good intentions but was smeared by the press. I said that after 9.11.01, everybody wanted to go fight whoever was responsible for the Trade Center attack. I told them that they were just fickle, narrow-minded people who were being told what to say and think by the media. They were just repeating what they had heard people on the news say. The people just sat there and stared at me. I was totally worked up. I was actually almost yelling at them before I was done with my tantrum. After I said my piece, I grabbed my tray and walked off.

I went over to the gas station side of the building. I saw a pack of M & M's and decided that I wanted to get them for a snack on the road. I grabbed them and got in line. I was standing in a line with four or five people in front of me. The Voice said, "Don't let the cashier touch your M & M's. She's going to try to poison them." I got to the cashier and she tried to take the M & M's so that she could ring them up. I said, "They're 85 cents." She said, "Well, I need to scan them." I said, "No. I don't want you to touch them." She said, "I have to scan them if you want to buy them." I said, "Well then, I don't want to buy them." and I put them on the counter in front of her and walked out.

When I got outside, there was a girl, who was very cute, standing outside of a car. I put some gas in my car and watched her as my car filled up. She noticed me looking at her and smiled at me. She said something to me that I don't remember.

Then some other people came out of the gas station and started talking to her. I listened to them while my car was filling up. I thought, "That girl seems like she has a very cool personality." She was laughing a lot about whatever was being said between her and the people she was with. She was very animated when she talked. At one point, a lady she was with said, "Alright, get in the car. We're leaving." The girl was laughing and said something to the lady. The lady had noticed me watching them and smiling at them. She said, "Would you take her off my hands. She is too wild and crazy for me to deal with." I laughed and said, "I would be happy to." The girl and the lady laughed and got in their car. As they drove off they passed by me and the girl rolled down her window and said, "Good bye my future husband." I laughed and said, "See you soon." If she only knew that she had just invited a crazy person into her life, I'm sure that she never would have been so flirtatious with me. The Voice said, "That was George Bush's daughter. He wants you to watch over her. She is very wild and parties a lot. He wants you to get her to settle down. He wants you to tame her, like he would tame a wild horse." As usual, I believed everything that The Voice said. I couldn't remember what George Bush's daughters looked like. I knew they were around my age, a little younger than me actually. I couldn't remember seeing any pictures of his daughters though. I thought, "Man , I don't remember hearing that President Bush had a daughter as good looking as that girl."

I got in my car and started following the car that the girl was in. I was about to leave when they passed by me. So, after the girl made the comment about me being her future husband, I jumped in my car and took that as an invitation to follow them. The Voice said, "President Bush wants you to marry his daughter. They are leading you to the place where you will be married. You are going to get married tonight. President Bush has planned an entire ceremony for you. He is giving you his daughter as a gift because he likes you that much. He thinks that you are perfect for his daughter." Since The Voice had said this, it was fact.

I followed the car for probably fifteen minutes. Then The Voice spoke to me again. This time it said, "Don't follow her. Meet her at the location of the ceremony. She's going to meet you there later. You need to go back to Gainesville and wait for her there." So, I turned around and started heading back towards I-75. Again, that was another of those moments where, say if she had happened to turn into the driveway of her house, I might have actually followed her and got out of my vehicle. I might have totally freaked her out after she realized that I had followed her and her family back to wherever they were heading. By turning around and ceasing to follow her, I might have just avoided another run in with the police and not even realized it. The Voice got me into trouble most of the time, but sometimes it actually made me do something that would have prevented me from getting myself into more trouble.

I drove back to I-75 and got back on the interstate. I remember realizing how tired I was. I felt like I could barely keep my eyes open. But I had also just been told that I needed to show up at a wedding ceremony that had been arranged for me and the President's daughter. As I thought about it a little, I started to think that the idea of marrying a girl that I had never spoken to was a bad one. I remember saying, "I'm sorry, Mr. Bush, but I don't think it's a great idea for me to marry your daughter. I don't know her. And if she is wild and crazy, then she's probably not anything that

I can handle. I've already had one wife who I thought was a little crazy. I don't want to do that again." The Voice said, "You don't want to piss off the President. This is what he wants you to do. He needs you to do this. His daughter has given him a lot of trouble. He thinks that you could help her learn how to behave better." I said, "I don't think that should require me to marry her. If he wants someone to be his daughter's friend, that's fine. I'll talk to her and see just how wild and crazy she is. If I think I can tell her something that might help her out, I will. But, I don't really think that I'm the right person for that kind of thing." The Voice said, "Just play along with Mr. Bush's idea. You don't want to piss him off."

As I drove down the road, arguing with The Voice in my head, I began to realize that the signs that listed the mileage to the nearest towns were all talking about towns that were north of Gainesville. I said, "Damn it! Have you guys let me get on I-75 North?" The Voice said, "No, we have changed the signs on the interstate to keep out all the people who are not attending the wedding ceremony. Keep heading the way that you are going. You are actually heading south, into Gainesville." I said, "Why does the compass on my car say that I'm heading north then?" The Voice said, "We are using a device that messes up everyone's car compasses too. We don't want to take a chance on people from the evil group showing up at the ceremony. There will be a lot of VIPs there. We can't take a chance on any of them getting killed." I thought, "These guys are going through a lot of trouble for me. How long would it have taken for them to switch all the road signs so that they are sending everyone in the wrong direction?"

I drove for probably 40 minutes and then started to realize that I was getting near Lake City. That's about 40 miles north of Gainesville. I said, "O.K., you got me again. I'm getting tired of you guys playing tricks on me. Please stop. I'm tired and I want to find somewhere to sleep. I'm not going to any damned ceremony tonight. I don't care who wants me to show up. You guys have made me drive 40 minutes in the wrong direction. You lied to me. You didn't change the street signs. I actually was heading north, just like I thought. I'm tired of this game. I'm tired of getting lied to."

I turned around and stopped at another gas station to get a Red Bull because I was so tired. I was hoping that the Red Bull drink would perk me up enough so that I could make it back to Gainesville and find some place to sleep for the night. I think it was around 9:30 pm by this time. I pulled up at the gas station and decided to put on my Darth Vader helmet when I walked in. I don't remember what possessed me to do that. It was a really bad idea. I walked into the gas station with the helmet on. I went over to get a Red Bull. I also saw a box of fire works that I thought would be a nice thing to do with Liza and Gwen someday. I picked that up as well. I walked up to the cashier and put my things on the counter. I didn't speak a word to her. I also saw a few fake dollar bills that they were selling that had pictures of George Bush on them. I thought that they were neat, so I also bought them too. I just handed all these things to the cashier and stood there. She said, "Is that all?" I shook my head to say, "Yes". She looked like she was pretty scared of me. That was just what I wanted. It never occurred to me that, with my Darth Vader helmet on, I probably looked like someone who might try to rob the store. I can't believe that she didn't do something to have me arrested right there. It turned out that it just took her a few minutes to take care of that.

I walked outside and thought about how the Middle East had total control of everyone's gas prices. I had already had the idea that most gas stations were tied to the Middle East. I thought that most of the gas station owners were people from the Middle East who were probably happy when they heard about the terrorist attacks on 9.11.01. I stood there outside my car and looked around at the gas station for a minute, thinking of what I could do to let them know that I was onto their secret plans to take down the country. My genius idea to give the Middle Easterners a message, that there was a new lawman in town, was to cut off a limb from one of the little palm trees that was growing there at the gas station. How I thought that made an effective threat to the Middle East, I can't tell you. It was just another of the genius ideas that my brain was so full of.

I opened the trunk of my car and got out the little pruning saw that I had bought at Wal-Mart. I walked over to the little palm tree and started sawing on one of its limbs. I hadn't even managed to cut one of them off when I saw police lights coming my way. The car pulled into the gas station and drove up to me. I put the saw in my car as I saw them coming towards me. The cop rolled down his window and said, "What are you doing?" I said, "I'm just doing a little trimming on this tree. The limb was sticking out a little. I just wanted to cut it down so that it didn't scrape anyone's vehicle." The policeman said, "Just stay right there." He pulled into the gas station and he, and his partner, got out of their car and walked over to me. I took off the Darth Vader helmet. I knew that it had got me into trouble the last time I wore it. So, I figured that it was probably a good idea to remove it before I started talking to the police. They walked up and said, "Why are you wearing that mask?" I said, "Its almost Halloween. I'm just having a little pre-Halloween fun, that's all." He said, "Do you mind if we have a look inside your vehicle?" I said, "Not at all. You'll love the interior of this car. Its state of the art inside." The policemen opened all the doors to my car and looked inside. One of them said, "Look at that dashboard." He was impressed by all the buttons and the little screen where the stereo controls were displayed. One of the policemen said, "Are you taking any kind of drugs tonight?" I said, "Yes, actually, but they're legal. It's a prescription medication from my doctor." I opened up the little compartment under the armrest in the middle of the front seats and showed him my prescription bottles. He looked at them and asked what they were for. I said, "I was diagnosed as bi-polar a while back. My doctor thinks that I need to take that stuff. I don't." He said, "Well, if you're out here wearing a Darth Vader mask and cutting down tree limbs, I think you should be taking whatever your doctor tells you to." I said, "I haven't actually cut down any limbs. I was just about to cut down that one limb there. That's it." He said, "Do you still live at the address on your driver's license?" I said, "Yes. I'm actually on my way back there now." He said, "Look, I don't feel like having to do a bunch of paperwork on you. Just get out of here and don't let me see you around here again. Go back to Polk County. Let them deal with you there, if you are wanting to get into trouble." I said, "I appreciate it. I'm not a troublemaker. I was just having a little fun." He said, "You're lucky that I'm not arresting you for vandalism to private property. Just get out of here and take the medication that your doctor has told you to take. Don't let me find you around here again." After that, I got back in my car and got back on the interstate.

On the way back to Gainesville, I decided that I should call Nanny. It was probably close to 11:00 pm by this time. I never called her that late at night, but I knew that she was usually up later than that. So, I called her. I told her that I was about to get married. I said that it was a real shame because I knew that she and Mom and Dad would not be able to see the wedding ceremony. Nanny said that she was sorry that she was going to miss the wedding. She didn't even ask about who I was getting married to. She just said, "Scott, its too late to be calling people right now." I said, "I'm sorry. I just thought that you might want to know that I'm about to get married." Nanny sounded very perturbed about my phone call. So, after telling her my news, I quickly got off of the phone. I didn't understand why everything I said to her or Mom and Dad always received such a strange response. I had thought that she might at least ask about the girl I told her I was about to marry. She didn't. I even thought that she might want to try to come to the ceremony, even though I had no idea of exactly where it was going to be held or what time it would take place. She never mentioned anything about wanting to come. She just apologized that she could not be there. I was a little surprised at her lack of interest in my big news. It made me feel like she didn't care about me anymore. I had already got that impression from Mom and Dad. Now I was pretty sure that the whole bunch of them had decided to just write me off. It made me sad and angry. I felt like I had sacrificed a lot to help them when they needed me. Now, when my life seemed to be full of so many wonderful, exciting things, they didn't want to hear the first word from me. I just told myself that I was better off without them. If they didn't want to be around me, then I didn't want to be around them. Even though I told myself this, I knew that I really still wanted nothing more than the approval of my parents and my grandmother. It was something I had strived for since I was a child. There was a long time where I thought I had their approval, even admiration. But now, I knew that for some reason, they had stopped caring about me.

I drove on to Gainesville. I was now used to the idea of getting into trouble with the police. This was now my second encounter with them in just a couple of days. I didn't worry about it. I figured that I still had the secret group on my side, I was not afraid of anyone, not even policemen. I knew that the secret group operated on a level that was above the law. Whenever I felt compelled to do something that bordered criminal behavior, I justified it by telling myself that what I was doing was something that the secret group had asked me to do. I wasn't always happy with the outcome of my actions, after doing things that I thought the secret group had told me to do.

On the way to Gainesville, I kept grumbling with The Voice in my head. I kept complaining how I had almost been arrested for trying to make a threat to the Middle Eastern people who ran the gas station. The Voice assured me that I just didn't know the whole story yet. It told me to continue on my way to Gainesville and at least appear at the ceremony that President Bush had supposedly set up. I was not excited about that idea either. For starters, I had no clue of exactly where to go in Gainesville. The Voice said it would tell me where the ceremony would take place, when I got there. I said, "I am so sick of everything being mysterious and confusing. Why can't you guys just show yourselves?" The Voice said, "Be patient. You will meet us in time. Just keep heading to Gainesville." I complained about how stupid the whole idea sounded. I couldn't believe that I was being asked to marry a girl who I had only seen for a few minutes at a gas station. I said, "I know that this is probably just another trick that you are playing on me. I'm going to stop in Gainesville, but if I don't see some real evidence that what you are talking about is true, then I am giving up on you guys. I've been running around like a maniac to the point that I am now exhausted. I can't keep this up much longer or I'm going to have a heart attack or something." The Voice didn't say anything. I just kept driving.

Chapter 57: Will the Real God and Heaven Please Stand Up

As I got into Gainesville, The Voice said, "Pull off on this exit." So I did. I saw a Publix Super Market down the street from where I was. The Voice said, "Pull into the Publix parking lot. That is where we will meet you to take you to the ceremony." So, I drove into Publix's parking lot and parked my car. I was so tired. I just laid back in my seat and closed my eyes. I opened them after a while and started looking around. I noticed that the parking lot was now almost empty. Publix had closed. Everyone had gone home. There were just a couple cars left in the parking lot. The Voice said, "The President's daughter is at the gas station over there." I looked in front of me and saw a 711 gas station. I had seen it earlier, so it wasn't like The Voice had mentioned the gas station without me seeing it first. I said, "Really?", with sarcasm. The Voice said, "Yes, she is waiting for you over there. Go over there and meet her." I said, "What am I supposed to do? Tell the girl that her dad wants me to marry her? This is the most retarded idea I've ever heard of." The Voice said, "Just go talk to her." I said, "I don't see any girl out there that looks like the girl I saw earlier." The Voice said, "Just go over there." So, I did.

I drove over to the 711 gas station. I looked around for the girl I had met briefly earlier that night. She wasn't anywhere that I could see. So, I went inside. I decided to get a Mountain Dew to wake me up. I bought the Mountain Dew and went back outside. There was a girl standing at a car there. She looked nothing like the girl I had seen earlier. I got in my car and The Voice said, "That is President Bush's other daughter. She's the one who wants to meet you." I said, "Yeah right. You said that the girl I met earlier was going to be here and she wanted to meet me. Now you're telling me that this girl is the one who wants to meet me. I don't know when to believe you anymore. I'm tired. I'm going to find a hotel. This has just been another waste of time." The Voice said, "Just go back to the parking lot. She's coming. Just wait a little longer." I said, "Fine. But I'm not talking to that girl over there." So I drove back over to the parking lot and waited a little longer.

I drank my Mountain Dew and stood around outside my car for a little while. I looked at my car and was just amazed that it now belonged to me. I walked around it, admiring what a nice car I now had. Then a new voice spoke to me through the little phone in my ear. The new voice said, "You've been led into a trap. You are actually about to be abducted by the followers of an ancient god. They are going to take you to their god and you will be killed." The Voice went on to explain that the "god" was actually a creature that usually drifted along in space. It was more of a machine than a living thing. The Voice told me that this machine looked like a squid. It floated in space and sometimes made a trip to Earth to gather people that it would devour to sustain itself. The Voice told me that this "squid god" actually devoured people for the ideas that were in their brains. The Voice said that the squid actually absorbed the ideas of the people that it consumed. It absorbed people's ideas and invented new ideas from them. The Voice told me that the squid had actually provided humans with a lot of our breakthrough technologies. It had spoken to secret members of the group that I was involved with for centuries and told them about things like: how to develop gun powder, the combustion engine, computers, and other things that were common items now and some things that I had only dreamed of. The Voice said that only recently, this squid had shown some people of the secret group how to achieve invisibility. The Voice told me that the new technology was always offered in exchange for more people. The Voice said that President Bush had actually tricked me into coming to this parking lot because that was where they planned to abduct me and take me to the squid, who was waiting at some location to receive a new batch of minds to devour. The Voice said that I had a lot of unique ideas in my head that President Bush realized would be of value to the squid. The Voice said that if I was abducted and taken to the squid, the process of being devoured was actually painless. It said that the process of being devoured by the squid was actually what Heaven was for some people. The Voice said that for the people who were devoured by the squid, Heaven was a place where they existed as a spirit inside of the great mind of the squid. The squid held the souls of all the people that it consumed and kept them eternally happy and unaware that they were now without a real body anymore. The Voice said that life with the squid would be painless and similar to the Bible's description of Heaven, as far as I was concerned.

I stood there by my car in absolute shock. All my beliefs about God had just been shattered again. The Voice had told me that the God that we all prayed to was actually a machine that drifted through space, collecting souls, to use like fuel, to develop new ideas. Heaven was just a state of consciousness that occurred after a person's actual body was consumed and all that was left were the ideas that were in the person's brain. Eternity was to be spent in the "brain" of some machine, as some spirit that was not aware of the fact that it was no longer a real being anymore, only a piece of information gathered and stored in some advanced computer "brain".

These were very depressing ideas to me. I felt devastated. I now thought that the secret group, the President, and even God, were all a bunch of liars. They had all tricked me into placing myself in a trap. I was now about to be consumed by a squid like machine, that was what we all called God. The machine only wanted me like a human wants a cow, to eat. The idea depressed me and also scared the hell out of me. I began to realize that the afterlife seemed a bit odd. I had always imagined Heaven being some magical place that was as real as life on Earth. Now I was being told that Heaven was nothing more than a virtual reality that was created by a machine that posed as a god. After realizing this, life seemed to lose all of its meaning. I thought that if the end game was to become nothing more than a meal for a squid, then life on Earth was now the most important thing of all, not Heaven and Eternity. I realized that my highest priority at that point was to stay alive on Earth as long as I could, because what came next didn't seem so appealing. Even though I was beginning to let The Voice work me into a panic again, I still had some doubts.

I asked the new voice, "So, how can I believe what you are saying? Nothing that I have been hearing lately has had any evidence to support it. Why should I believe you?" The Voice said, "I am a member inside of the secret group that is on your side. There are people here, like the President, that are not looking out for your best interest. George Bush is looking out for his own best interest. The squid wants him too, but George Bush keeps giving him other people to save himself. As long as the President continues to appease the squid, by giving him other people, he is safe." I said, "Is there any way that I can escape from this situation?" The Voice said, "Yes. That's why I have contacted you. You need to leave. There are some of us who will try to get you out of this mess that you are in. For now, just get out of there and keep heading south." So, I got in my car and drove away as quickly as I could. I believed the new voice. The threat that it had told me about was too scary not to believe him. I just wanted to do whatever it said. The old voice had led me straight into the jaws of Hell (or Heaven for some people). I just prayed, to whomever, that the new voice was actually telling me the truth and could save me from losing my soul to a monster that posed as a god.

As I drove south on I-75, I was now fully awake again. The thought of being taken to some monster that wanted to eat me had scared me out of my sleepiness. I was once again running on adrenaline. I kept watching for cars that were following me. The Voice said, "Drive to Wildwood. You'll be safe there. We have people there who will protect you." The Voice went on to explain that there was a group within the secret group. It told me that this group within the secret group was actually the ones who were now the only people on my side. The Voice said that most of the people within the secret group were dedicated to serving the squid. According to the new voice, the squid had been in contact with humans for hundreds of years. It had arranged for the rise of most of the world's leaders. It had also provided most of the technology that created the society we live in today. The Voice told me that the squid was a god, but was not God. That brought a wave of relief to me. The Voice said that there was actually a God. The Voice said that God was the one who had created the squid. The Voice said that the squid itself was actually more like a false god. The Voice said that the people who followed the beliefs of the Bible were actually following the message that had been created by this squid. The Voice said that all of the people who believed in the stories told in the coded version of The Bible were worshipping this squid and would all be consumed be this creature. The Voice explained that Heaven, for those people, would be the eternity that they spent as part of the brain of this squid machine. The Voice said that the only way to know the true message that God had spoken to His followers was to read the decoded version of the Bible. That made me think about what Pam from the BHC in Tallahassee had told me about there being a decoded version of the Bible that had been placed inside of every computer. I had never gone to the trouble of trying to find the correct key sequence to unlock the decoded version of the Bible. Now, I thought that finding the decoded version of The Bible should be a top priority, if I wanted to have a chance of knowing the real God and Heaven.

I drove on to Wildwood and turned off of the interstate on the exit there. The Voice told me that I was safe there. It said that I had escaped from the people who were planning to abduct me. I drove to a little motel and got a room. It was around 2:00 am at that point, I think. I was absolutely exhausted. When I walked into the room, The Voice said, "There are people in here that will guard you, but you can't see them." I was already familiar with the idea that invisible people were watching over me. So I thanked The Voice and went to sleep. I woke up the next morning around 7:00 am. I felt like I had just had a good night's sleep. It was less than 5 hours actually. The night before I had only slept for 2 hours, if that. And the nights before that, I might have slept 3 or 4 hours. I was just mainly running on adrenaline. In mania, once I woke up, I could not go back to sleep. My mind would start churning out plans that had to be carried out immediately. I never felt like there were enough hours in the day to do everything that I was supposed to.

So, after waking up, I got out of bed and took a shower. The Voice told me, "You should get used to taking cold showers. That's all your going to be getting in the near future after everything collapses." The old voice had already been telling me this too. I had been hearing about how the world was about to be taken back to the Stone Age. I had been told that once the real crap started to go down, there would be no more electricity, which meant no more hot water. The future that I imagined was filled with a lack of technology. The only people that would survive would be those who knew how to live with the most minimal of things. The future also was filled with strange new creatures. Soon the world would meet the dinosaurs again. There would also be aliens. They had been here all along, living beneath us in the Earth's core. Once Satan decided that it was his time to make Hell on Earth, the aliens would come out of the ground and roam among us. The future seemed like a scary place. I was afraid of what I might have to endure to win the battle against Satan. But I was still being promised that there was actually a God. He was still watching over me. I had just been confused about who he was. Now, I had met, or at least heard The Voice of, one of His true followers. The new voice assured me of this. And of course, I believed every word.

So, I took a cold shower. I stood there in the cold water for several minutes, imagining myself in the future, bathing in lakes and streams, always looking out for a predator that was waiting to eat me. After my cold shower, I decided that I would go eat breakfast. There was a restaurant attached to the motel. I decided that would be an easy place to eat. So I walked over to the restaurant.

Inside the restaurant were several strange people. They weren't actually strange. I just imagined things about them that made them strange to me. The first strange people I noticed were a man in his early 70's talking to a man in his 50's. I got the impression that they were father and son. The Voice said, "That is actually George Bush Sr. and George Bush Jr. They are in disguise so no one will notice them. They are here to check up on you. They are sorry for trying to give you over to the squid. They just wanted you to know that they hope you have no hard feelings towards them." I thought, "Well, I am totally scared to death of them now. But I better play nice towards them. I don't want to piss off someone as powerful as George Bush. That would only make my life harder." So, I decided to forgive Mr. Bush for trying to feed me to a space squid. (I know that this is sounding more and more ridiculous, but I swear this is all true. Bear with me. It only gets worse before it gets better.) I smiled at the older guys that were sitting at a table near me. I believed everything that The Voice said, just as I had blindly followed the old voice. The old guys smiled back at me. I thought it was a very nice exchange. I never said anything to them. I just thought that someone had done an incredible job developing their disguises, because those two guys didn't look anything like George Bush Jr. or Sr. There physique might have been close, but the faces didn't look anything like them. I just accepted everything, no matter how little sense it made. Then I got my first bit of "proof" that strange things were happening around me. I saw it with my own eyes.

The proof that I received that morning came from a girl who was my waitress. She had brought me my food and checked up on me. She was a red headed white girl. At one point I happened to glance at her when she was behind a counter doing something. She had her back turned to me. She looked over her shoulder so that I could see her face. The first time she did this, her face looked the way that it had every time I had seen her. Then she turned her head back to what she was doing. Then she looked back over her shoulder for just a second. I swore that her face had changed in that second that she glanced over her shoulder. In that quick glance, her face was dark skinned, like a Middle Eastern person, and her hair had turned black. She looked like an Indian girl, just for a second. I stared at the girl with total amazement. I couldn't understand what I had just seen. I wondered if she was one of the aliens. The Voice told me, "Welcome to the new world. You just saw our latest in camouflage. She can disguise her face in a split second. She is wearing a type of makeup that we can manipulate wirelessly to change her face instantly. You just saw our demonstration."

I smiled and just sat there in shock and awe. I had finally seen something. The Voice was confirming what I saw. At that point, I felt that I had moved into a closer relationship with the secret group. Now they had actually shown me something that I could believe. I now had total faith in the new voice. What had actually just happened was my first full visual hallucination. What had started as dots and flashes progressed into the silhouette of a person. The silhouette had convinced me of the existence of invisible people. Now my hallucinations progressed into actual images that were not there. The girl's face had changed before my eyes. It was scary as hell, but after getting an explanation from The Voice, I got comfortable with what had just happened. I had never had my eyes play a trick on me before. Just like my ears had never failed me before I started hearing The Voice. Now, my eyes and ears could not be trusted to tell me what was actually going on around me. In my mind though, I was developing more trust in the secret group. I had finally received proof that the things they had told me about were real.

I never spoke to the waitress about what I had seen her do. I assumed that I was not supposed to talk about those kinds of things. So, I just left her a big tip and thanked her before I left. When I left the restaurant, I realized that I had left my key card in my room. I had to go to the front desk to get a new one. Then I went back to my room and gathered my things to load up into my car.

As I was loading my car, I saw a guy standing outside near me. He reminded me of my dead uncle, Stan. I told the guy, "You look like someone I used to know." He said, "Yeah? I get that a lot. I must have a real common look about be." I said, "No. You just remind me of an uncle that I used to have." He said, "What's his name?" I said, "Well, his name was Stan Gann, but he died a couple years ago." The guy said, "Sorry to here that. The name doesn't ring a bell. Sorry." I said, "Well, it was nice to meet you anyway." And then I got in my car and drove off.

I drove back to I-75 and headed south. My plan was to go back to Lake Buffum and see how my parents' reacted to me showing up. I had only been gone for 4 or 5 days, but I felt like that was probably long enough for them to change their minds about me taking drugs that I didn't want to take.

As I drove down towards Polk County, I started to see more license plates that I thought had secret messages in them. I also saw several cars that made me believe that the secret group was communicating with me again. There was one car that said, "Just Married. Now into the cave." The words had been written in shoe polish on the windows of the car. There was a nice looking young couple driving in the car. They smiled at me as they passed by. I waved at them too. I thought that those people were actually two members of the secret group, playing a little joke about what had happened to me the night before. I thought about the girl who had called me her future husband. I still believed that she was Bush's daughter, but I still did not want to marry a girl that I never knew.

I also began to think that I was getting messages from the license plate of vehicles that passed me. The license plates that made me realize that the secret group was around were all number and letter combinations like XJ7 314 and things like that. The first one that caught my attention was a car that drove past me with a similar plate to the one that I just mentioned, the driver pointed up at the sky, when he was right in front of me. I looked up into the sky and saw a flash of an image. The flash looked like some sort of aircraft. It was similar to the flash of a person that I had seen a while earlier. I saw a white, translucent object for just a split second, and then it was gone. I immediately made the connection that the guy had pointed to the sky so that I would see the aircraft that his license plate identified. I assumed that the letter and number combination on his license plate was the actual name of the aircraft that I saw. I waved at the guy and was really excited. Now the secret group was showing more of their power to me. As I drove along I kept seeing more flashes of different aircraft in the sky. Each quick image was different from the others. Then, finally, I saw an enormous flash in the sky. The object that I saw this time was shaped like a flying saucer. It was huge, like the size of a city floating in the sky. I could tell that it was far away, but I knew that it was the biggest aircraft I had ever seen. It was awesome. Now I knew that I was in good hands. I figured that if the secret group had that kind of technology floating around in the sky, then I was always safe. The Voice told me, "That last aircraft is actually operated by aliens. They are also members of our group." I felt so excited. I realized that everything was starting to make sense. I was now seeing things and hearing the explanations for them. The Voice told me that there were several races of aliens, all from different worlds, who had found Earth long ago. The Voice said that some of the aliens were like care takers of us humans. Other aliens were out to destroy us all. Some of the evil aliens were Satan, and his demons. There were others, like the squid, who worked with humans, for a price, a sacrifice. And then there were aliens like the one we called God, and His angels, who actually wanted to protect us and offer us a way to live forever. The Voice said that fortunately, the aliens that had the most powerful technologies were the ones that we called angels and God. The Voice said that through their technology, they had actually created entire galaxies, just as the Bible mentions. The Voice said that the aliens that were out to destroy us had weaker technology and that was why they would end up losing to God and the angels in the end. These conversations with The Voice were comforting. It sort of put me back at peace again. After reeling from what I had learned the night before about God being a devouring squid floating in space and Heaven actually just being nothing more than something like the software of a computer brain, The Voice gave me comfort. I now felt like things were different, but really were the same as they had always been. So, some people were confused about which god to pray to. I was just glad that I had been shown the light. I was one of the lucky ones who had been chosen to spend eternity with the real God.

Chapter 58: The Road Back Home

I drove on to Lake Buffum. I got to Clermont on U.S. Hwy. 27 and stopped at a gas station there. I realized that I had not brushed my teeth in a couple of days. I wanted to use the bathroom at the gas station to brush my teeth. So, I went looking for my toothbrush and toothpaste and could not find it anywhere. There was so much crap in my car. I had buried it when I loaded everything into the Tribeca. I had thought about brushing my teeth many times when I had stayed at the hotel and when I had slept on the sidewalk in front of the church, but I never felt like digging through all my things to find my tooth brush and tooth paste. So, I went into the gas station and bought a new travel size tube of toothpaste and a toothbrush and went into the bathroom to brush my teeth.

After I came out, I saw some cigarette lighters that I thought looked neat. So I bought three different lighters. One was a lighter that had a green flame. It was a metal refillable lighter that had a frog on the side and made the sound of a frog croaking when you opened the top of the lighter. Another lighter looked like a poker chip. It was almost the exact size of a poker chip, except it was a little thicker. You could flip the top section of it over to make it shoot out a flame. It was pretty cool. The other lighter was another metal refillable lighter that I just thought looked nice. After I bought the lighters, I walked back outside.

There were several Middle Eastern guys sitting around a table that was right outside the door. I had an idea, after almost getting arrested at the gas station the night before. I thought that it might be my job to try to infiltrate the Middle Eastern terrorist groups by becoming friends with some of the gas station owners here in the U.S. So, when I saw those guys sitting at the table, I thought it looked like a perfect opportunity to try out my idea and see what I could learn from them.

I walked over to the guys and asked how they were doing and struck up a conversation. I don't remember what we talked about, but I felt like those guys were all very friendly. They never said the first thing that sounded threatening or suspicious. Imagine that. Middle Eastern guys who might not be terrorists. Yes, I might have been a little racist.

After talking with the guys, who I now thought could not be associated with terrorist activities, simply because I had a friendly conversation with them; I got back in my car. The Voice said, "You were just talking to the dead. Those guys are all people who were brought back to life after dying." I said, "They seemed like normal people to me." The Voice said, "They are normal people. They're no different from you. You were also brought back from the dead, remember?" I sat there for a minute, remembering my suspicion about what had happened that night at the PRC, the night when I had the terrible dream about being squashed by a giant foot. I was never sure that I had really died. But now, the new voice was confirming it. I had not thought of myself as actually being one of the undead. But now, The Voice told me that I was. It was a little depressing. I had still thought of myself as just another human, with some extra technology inside. Now, though, I realized that I was something different from the average human altogether. I was a zombie myself. The Voice said, "Our plan for you is to make you the leader of the undead army. You will be the one to lead them in the coming battle." I sat there and thought about that for a while. I had assumed that the undead would be a weapon used for evil. They were always evil in the movies. But now The Voice was telling me that they were no different from myself, and I certainly did not consider myself to be evil. The Voice told me that once Satan and his demons began to take over the Earth, God and the angels would need all the help that they could get to fight them. One of the things that they were planning on doing was creating an undead army. They were planning on bringing back all the people that had died in the past, and using them to fight Satan and his demons. This was a sort of neat idea to me. I imagined myself as the leader of all the famous people throughout history that had died. I told The Voice, "Alright, then I will be the leader of the undead." I said, "Rise undead soldiers. Rise from your graves and join me." And then I smiled at the idea of an army of monsters that would be at my command. The thought made me feel pretty important.

I made another stop not too far from the gas station in Clermont. It was at a newly opened Publix grocery store. I don't remember what I even stopped there for. I was so manic that I wanted to purchase all sorts of things that I did not need. The Publix trip was another one of those absolutely unnecessary shopping trips. I remember walking in and finding all sorts of items to purchase. I bought a few cheap toys, a few bags of bulk candy, and some personal hygiene items. I had no need for any of it.

As I walked outside to my car, I noticed two men and a small boy standing near my new car. The Voice told me that one of the men was the son of George Jenkins, the founder of Publix. The Voice said that the boy was the man's grandson. The Voice said that the men had come to see me because they had heard about me, and the grand future that was ahead of me. The Voice said that the men were also members of the secret group. I walked towards my car and smiled at the men as I walked by them. The Voice said, "Why don't you give some candy to the boy?" I thought that seemed like a nice gesture, seeing as how these men had apparently made a trip to that location just to see me. I never thought about the fact that I had decided to appear at Publix on a whim and that it would be impossible for anyone to know where I might show up at any time. I never knew what I would be doing five minutes into the future. I didn't try to analyze much of what The Voice said, I just believed almost everything. I figured that they were all involved with technology that I had no understanding of. So, if The Voice told me something, I usually tended to believe it.

I placed my bags of junk in my car and pulled out one of the bags filled with bulk candy. The bag was filled with about $10 worth of candy. I decided that it would be nice to give it to the little boy who was standing with the two men near my car. I hoped that once I gave the candy to the boy, they would begin talking to me and fill me in on some of the mysteries of the secret group. I walked over to the men and asked if it was alright if I gave the boy the bag of candy. One of the men asked the boy if he wanted it. The boy said that he did. So, I handed the bag to him. After that, my hope of starting a conversation was put to an end. The men thanked me for the candy and then walked on into the store without saying another word to me. I stood there and watched them walk off. Once again, things did not work out the way that I had expected them to. I had expected the men to begin thanking me for simply taking the time to speak with them. I expected that from there we would have a conversation that would answer a lot of the questions that I had about the secret group. I thought we would discuss the near future and the coming battles between the forces of good and evil. Instead, I simply got a thank-you for the candy and that was it.

After being let down at Publix, I drove on towards Lake Buffum. Then I got a call on my cell phone. It was from an attorney that Sara had hired to take care of our divorce. He was calling me, for the first time, to let me know that he had some papers for me to sign. He wanted to know if he could send a courier to meet me somewhere. I told him that I was about 1 ½ hours away from Bartow, but could meet his courier there a little after 12:00 pm. We agreed to meet at the Crisper's in Bartow, around 12:30 pm. So, I drove on towards Bartow.

On the way to Bartow, I called mom to see what she was up to. Mom said that she and Nanny were having a yard sale at Nanny's house. She asked me what I was doing and I told her that I was on my way back from Tallahassee. I didn't mention to her that I had bought a new car and a lot of other crap along the way. I thought I would let that be a surprise. I told mom that I was on my way to Bartow to meet with Sara's attorney to sign some divorce papers. Mom said that I could stop by Nanny's if I wanted to. I told her that I would. Then I hung up and kept on driving.

I got to Crisper's just a little after 12:30 pm. I pulled into the parking lot and it was packed. I thought, "I guess the word had gotten out that I'm going to show up here. These are probably all people who want to see me." I drove on through the parking lot and was stopped by a car that was backing out. I sat there for a minute of more, waiting for this guy to get on his way. Then I blew my horn at him. I thought, "O.K., you've seen me. Now let's move along. I've got other things to do aside from letting people gawk at me." The guy started moving. So, then I pulled into his spot. I got out and met the courier who was already there waiting for me. I had spoken to him on the phone earlier and told him what I was driving. I had said, "You won't be able to miss me. I've got a blue Subaru Tribeca with a bright orange kayak on top of it." When he walked up to me he said, "You were right. I couldn't miss that. That was quite an entrance." When I blew my horn, it was not just a little honk. I had kept my hand pressed on the horn for probably thirty seconds. It was very obnoxious, I'm sure. The horn honking was what the guy was referring to. I just said, "Yeah. Sorry about blowing my horn. I have just been running into idiot after idiot all the way down the state this morning. I'm just tired of the idiots. I had to blow my horn to relieve a little tension." He laughed and said, "Yeah. I don't know what that guy was taking so long for." Then he handed me a stack of papers. I said, "Do I need to sign these now?" He said, "No. We just hand deliver this kind of stuff. Read over it. Let us know if you don't agree with anything in there. Then stop by our office when you want to discuss it." I said, "Alright. We'll, I'm going to go in here and get some lunch. Do you want to come with me?" He said, "No. I've already eaten. I've got to get back to the office." I said, "Alright. Thanks for giving me this. I've been waiting for this for a long time. You just made my day." He laughed and went back to his car. I went on into Crisper's.

The place was packed. There were just a couple of empty tables left. I went into the line to order my food. As I was waiting in line, who should walk up, but Katherine Dunal. Katherine was a girl from high school who was on the swim team with me and had wanted me to date her in my senior year. I had turned her down, and always felt a little bad about it. Sara and I had run into her several times over the years since we graduated. Sara always got a little paranoid when Katherine came around, because she was always afraid that I would end up leaving her and getting together with Katherine. I never had any desire to do that. But Sara and I would usually end up in an argument after running into Katherine, because she would get so jealous. Even if I was just talking with Katherine for a few minutes, I was in trouble with Sara.

So, here was Katherine Dunal and she saw me. She said, "Scott! How are you doing?" I said, "Katherine Dunal. What are the chances of running into you here on a day like today." She asked what I meant. I said, "I'll tell you later. Are you eating here?" She said, "Yes. I'm eating with my boyfriend." I said, "Oh. Well, I'll sit with you guys, if you don't mind." She said, "Why would I mind? Of course. Let's catch up." So, I went to a table and Katherine and her boyfriend followed after me once they ordered their food.

Katherine introduced me to her boyfriend. We had actually already met a couple years earlier. Katherine had run into Sara and I and she was with this same guy that she was still dating. So, they were pretty serious, I figured. Katherine's boyfriend actually graduated with my younger brother Sam. Katherine's boyfriend had gone to school to become a civil engineer, like Sam was doing in the Air Force. So, we had a little in common. They asked about how Sam was doing. I told them how Sam was still in the Air Force, and how he had been to the Middle East several times. They wanted to know how Sara and I were doing. That's when I decided to let the cat out of the bag. I said, "Well that's why I'm here actually. I just had to meet with a divorce attorney to get some papers. Sara and I are getting divorced. That's why I said that it was funny to run into you on a day like today. The papers I got today are the first real thing we have done to actually get a divorce." Katherine said that she was sorry to hear about Sara and I splitting up. I said, "Its no problem to me. I'm tired of dealing with her. She has too many issues for me to figure out. We never really had a happy marriage. I'm just glad its over." After that little conversation, Katherine and her boyfriend told me about people from high school and what they were up to and so on.

As Katherine and her boyfriend were filling me in on some of our old high school buddies, I over heard a conversation between a group of guys that were all wearing suits and sitting near us. It sounded like they were talking about motorcycles. I thought I had heard one of them say, "Yeah, but we've got the special bikes. We've got the bikes you can't even see." I immediately thought that they were talking about some motorcycle that could become invisible. I have no idea of what they were really talking about, or if they really did say what I thought I heard. But I swore that I had overheard some people talking about invisible motorcycles. I thought about the aircraft that I had seen briefly flashing from invisible to visible and then back again. For some reason, I thought that these guys were connected to the secret evil group. I thought that they were wanting me to hear what they were saying so that I would be either impressed or scared. I said to them, "Well, you may have the invisible bikes, but we've got bigger things that are invisible.", and smiled at them. They looked at me like they had no idea what I just said, then turned back around and kept talking. Katherine and her boyfriend, I'm sure, were just as clue less as to what the hell I had just said as well. I think that little comment, and another thing that I did, gave them the quick impression that all was not right with me.

The other thing that I did was this: I had come to believe that I had found the way to communicate with the secret group on my phone and actually get a response from them. I had started dialing "1" or "2" or "3" on my phone and pressing the button that lets you talk in walkie-talkie mode on the Nextel phones. Whenever I pressed one of those numbers and then the button to send a call, someone would usually say something back to me on my phone. I thought that whenever I saw or heard something strange going on, something that I thought might be related to the activities of the secret evil group, all I had to do was press those buttons, and the secret group that I was with would know that I had just received some new information for them. I never tried to talk to whoever called me back on my phone. I just assumed that whatever they said was code for letting me know that they had received my message. By pushing the "secret" buttons, I had let them know that I had learned vital new information. I figured that they could take care of figuring out what that information was by either looking at video collected from the cameras that were always watching me, or possibly by somehow getting the information directly from the memory stored in my brain.

So, when I overheard the conversation about the invisible motorcycles, I got out my Nextel phone and dialed a number and pressed the walkie-talkie button. A person spoke to me on the other end. They said, "What do you want bitch?" The Voice talked over the speaker on my phone. Katherine and her boyfriend heard it. Katherine said, "Who was that?" I said, "Oh, it's a long story. Maybe I'll tell you about it one day." I was positive that The Voice on the phone was a secret group member letting me know that they had received my signal that strange new information had just been gathered about the secret evil group. "What do you want bitch?", I thought, was just a code way of telling me that they were listening. I figured that they talked this way so that other people would not know what was really going on. What really was going on was that I was dialing the walkie-talkie numbers of some poor people who were now getting very annoyed by an anonymous caller who dialed them and never spoke a word. I'm sure that they were very irritated because I had been doing this since a couple days after I bought the phone. Every time I saw strange things, I pressed the buttons. I had probably dialed these people 30 or 40 times already.

So, shortly after seeing my strange behavior, Katherine and her boyfriend let me know that it was nice to see me but that they had to go. I told them good-bye and never thought once about my actions being interpreted as odd. I was actually convinced that Katherine had probably heard that I was going to be at Crisper's that afternoon, even though the whole thing had only been planned less than 2 hours earlier, over a cell phone call between myself and the attorney's courier. I was convinced that so many people were always watching me, that word could spread that fast. I actually believed that Katherine was probably watching me on some secret website, and that's how she found out where I would be. The realization that most of my ideas were beyond ridiculous didn't come to me for another several weeks.

After lunch at Crisper's, I drove over to Nanny's house in Bartow. Just like Mom said, they were sitting out on the driveway, having a yard sale. I pulled up in my new ride, with the kayak on top. I thought that they would be gawking at the impressive new vehicle that I pulled up in. I got out and walked over to where they were sitting. Neither Mom nor Nanny said anything about my car. I asked them how they had been doing. They said that they were fine. I asked them what they thought about my new car. Mom said, "Is that your car?" I said, "Yes. I traded in the Forester for it." She said, "It looks like a very expensive car. Why did you trade in your old car?" I said, "It just reminded me too much of Sara. I couldn't look at it without thinking about her. I had to get rid of it." The truth was that I had bought it simply because I thought I needed something bigger to haul all the junk that I had been buying. I wasn't sure just how much more stuff I would have to buy before I found a place to unload it. So, I just bought a bigger vehicle so that I could carry more crap.

Mom and Nanny did not seem impressed with my purchase. I didn't care. I don't remember much else that we talked about during that time. After a while, Dad drove up. I showed him my new car. He didn't seem anymore impressed than mom or Nanny had been. I felt disappointed. I thought that they would be congratulating me for having such a nice vehicle. Instead, I'm sure what I was seeing was their realization that I had probably just spent all the money that was in the check that they worked so hard for me to get. They were probably regretting the fact that they had ever told me about that money. If they had not told me about that money, I never could have bought all the junk that I purchased during the time that I was away from them.

One of the things that The Voice had told me on my way back from Tallahassee was that my Tribeca could run on water. The Voice told me that my car could separate the hydrogen from the oxygen in the water and could run on the hydrogen. I had read a little about hydrogen fuel cells, so when The Voice told me that my car had the capability to run on water, it was just a pleasant surprise. I had not actually put any water in it yet. When I was at Nanny's house, I decided to try it out. I filled a 20 oz. bottle with water from her hose and poured it into the fuel tank.

I thought, "This is going to save me some serious money. Now, I don't ever have to buy gasoline again."

I told Dad about my car being able to run on water and how I had just put water in it. He said, "They don't make a vehicle that runs on water. They haven't found a way to convert water into hydrogen without spending more energy than what is required by the separation process yet. That technology does not exist for cars yet." I said, "Yes it does. The salesman at the dealership told me that my car could run on water. He said that he had not tested it yet, but that it could do it." Dad said, "You need to go to Discount Auto Parts and buy a chemical that will get rid of the water that you just poured into your fuel tank. That water is going to mess up your engine. You won't be able to run your car if you let that water get into the engine." I said, "The guy at the dealership said that this car had new technology that let it run on hydrogen. I think he knows what he's talking about." Dad said, "Suit yourself, but I think you're going to learn a hard lesson if you don't go get that product that they sell at Discount Auto Parts." I told him I would put some of it in my fuel tank, if it made him happy.

After showing Dad my new ride, we went inside. I remember thinking that this was going to be our first meeting since they had realized that I was something bigger than what they had ever imagined. I thought that once they saw my vehicle, and all the other stuff that I bought, they would have to realize that I was now connected to a pretty powerful group of people. As we sat around inside, we talked about a few things. I don't remember what exactly. I just remember thinking that Dad and I talking was probably similar to the way that George Bush Sr. and Jr. had probably talked to each other. I thought that they probably had secret conversations where they discussed the problems of the world and the agenda of the secret group that they served. I thought that my dad and I were like next generation members of that same group. When we were talking, I thought that maybe we were having our first meeting as members of the secret group.

After a while, Nanny said that they were all going out to eat. They asked me if I wanted to go with them. I said, "No, I've got plans with Justin tonight. I'll meet up with you guys some other time." I had thought that we might have been having our secret meeting at Nanny's house, but I didn't think that it went well. I don't remember what was said. I just remember getting the impression that Mom and Dad were less than thrilled that I was back. I realized that they probably didn't want to have me out at the lake house. So, I just decided that I would probably sleep at some hotel in Lakeland that night. My planning was always only a few hours into the future. I wasn't thinking about what I might be doing the next day or the day after that. With the way that the voices in my head were jerking me around, there was no way to know what to expect next. I just did all that I could do, until I was exhausted. Then I would find a place to sleep for a couple hours, and then start all over again. I just figured that I was in training. I assumed that all of the crazy running around, doing things that never turned out the way that I planned, was just like the frustration that comes from the Drill Instructors at Boot Camp. I believed that I was in some type of top-secret boot camp. Only I didn't have to show up at some place for training. The training was brought to me.

So, after Nanny and Mom and Dad decided to leave to go eat, I left to go to Lakeland. I called Justin White on my cell phone and asked what he was up to. He said that he was working at the bar at Chili's. I told him that I was on my way over to see him. He said that was good and maybe we could hang out after he got off work that night. On my way out of Nanny's neighborhood, I passed by the houses of some good friends of Nanny and Granddaddy and their son who lived next door to them. I saw their son outside. His name was Timmy Meeks. Timmy, and his parents Clarence and Alene Meeks had been members of Main Street Baptist since before I was ever born. Timmy was a few years older than me, so I never really knew him well growing up. But I did see him at church most Sundays as a child. When I saw him out in his yard, I decided that I wanted to say hello to him. I wanted him to see the cool new car I was driving around in mainly. I pulled up alongside his yard and rolled the window down. I said, "Hey Timmy! I'm Scott Gann. Do you remember me?" He said, "Hey! How are you doing?" I told him that I had just seen Nanny and was about to meet up with some friends in Lakeland. He asked me what I was driving. I said, "Oh this is my new car. It's a Subaru Tribeca. They just started selling them. This is one of the first one's that was sold at the dealership where I bought it." He said, "That is a really nice car." We talked about the car for a few minutes. While we were talking, I noticed the car vibrating a little. I thought, "This car is nervous. It's actually shaking because I'm talking to a new person." I heard the engine make a little strange sound. I said, "Easy girl." to the car. Then I said to Timmy, "This car had a mind of its own. It's almost like driving a living thing. It has some kind of computer in it that makes it do weird stuff." Timmy said, "Yeah, the technology that goes into some of these new cars is amazing." He didn't know that I was speaking very literally. I actually believed that the Tribeca was almost alive. I thought of it as a robot really, that just happened to look like a car.

The idea of my car being more than just a car, came to me first when I was driving out of the dealership, getting ready to leave town. I had noticed the strange sound of the engine. When I accelerated it sounded nothing like the Forester. It sounded more like an aircraft engine. It made a humming sound that was unlike any car I had ever heard. I thought, "This car has something special about it." The Voice told me, "Yes it does. We've added a lot of technology to this car. That's why we told you to get it. This car is more than just a car. It has a brain. It thinks." I thought that sounded pretty amazing, but totally believable. I knew that people had been building robots for many years and had been making a lot of progress with Artificial Intelligence. I just figured that my car had probably been modified with some hardware and software that allowed it to "think" a little more than the average car.

The next thing that happened that built on this idea was that I noticed a dash light come on when I lit up a cigarette inside of it. I had already told myself that I was not going to smoke in my new car. Thirty minutes later, I broke that promise. I was parked at a gas station and decided to light up a cigarette. I looked at the dashboard and a light came on shortly after I started smoking. I didn't recognize the symbol. I just remember thinking that it was the car's way of asking me not to smoke in it. So, I said, "I'm sorry for doing that to you. I'll put it out." I figured that the car must have some kind of sensors that detected the air quality and picked up on the smoke coming from the cigarette. I thought that the sensors must have triggered the car's brain to flash the light on the dashboard to tell me to put the cigarette out. So, after getting the message, I put out the cigarette and decided that if I was going to smoke, I would do it outside of the car, so that I wouldn't bother it. So, I came to believe that my car not only had a brain to control its many advanced features, but also to allow it to talk to me. I never believed that the car actually talked, I just believed that it communicated through its dashboard lights. Seeing that dash light come on was enough for me to believe that.

Later, The Voice told me that the Tribeca was just the first of a new generation of robots that would be coming into the public realm. The Voice told me that there would soon be robots taking over the jobs that people didn't like to do. I had seen enough science fiction movies that had similar ideas. So, when The Voice told me this, I wasn't particularly shocked. Granddaddy had actually bought a Roomba for Nanny as his last Christmas present to her. That little Roomba was the sorriest excuse for a robot that I had ever seen. It was supposed to go around the house and act like a little vacuum cleaner. The trouble was that it usually got confused by all the objects in the room and would end up going over areas that it had already vacuumed again and again. It was supposed to be able to travel all over the house and vacuum every surface. That never happened. So, I was not very impressed by the only real commercially available robot I had ever seen.

But The Voice assured me that the robots that were going to show up in the near future would be something far superior to anything that I had ever seen. It said that the robots would actually become self aware, like in the Terminator movies, and would one day be a force that humans would have to fight against. The Voice even said that the secret evil group was building a robot that was going to try to kill me, eventually. But The Voice said that it was nothing to worry about. The Voice said that there were more powerful allies on my side that would protect me from whatever the secret evil group threw my way. This whole conversation came about as I was driving down from Tallahassee.

Chapter 59: The End of a Friendship

After talking with Timmy for a few minutes, I told him that it was nice to see him and went on towards downtown Bartow. As I drove along I noticed my car jumping a little. I still thought that I was seeing the nervous reaction from my car, not something that might be related to that bottle of water that I dumped into my gas tank. I said, "Calm down girl. We're leaving."

After seeing the car behave strangely I thought that maybe it was a good idea to go ahead and buy the chemical that Dad had said would evaporate the water in my gas tank. I guess I wasn't totally sure that my car was simply nervous. I decided to go by the Discount Auto Parts store. I walked in and found the stuff that he was talking about. I bought it and poured the whole bottle into my gas tank. After I did that, I looked at the cars that were driving down the road by the store. I thought, "There sure are a lot of foreign people on the road today." I noticed a lot of Asians and Indians, more than I thought was usual for our area. I started to think that people around the world were coming to Bartow to see me. Or maybe they were people who had realized that something big was about to happen in our area. Maybe they were in on the secrets that I had come to discover. I started to think that perhaps Bartow was going to be at the center of some secret activity in the near future. I wasn't sure what exactly that would be, but I had an idea that maybe Bartow had a history that I had never heard about. Maybe there was something in town that was vital to the efforts of the secret forces of good and evil. After having this thought, I got back into my car and headed to Chili's in Lakeland, on South Florida Ave.

I got to Chili's and walked into the restaurant and went to the bar. There was Justin, just like usual, working behind the bar. I ordered a sweet tea and sat there and talked with Justin as he worked the bar. I stayed there until they closed that night at around midnight. What Justin and I talked about during the time he was working, I don't really remember.

One thing I do remember about that night was a couple of guys who sat down at the bar next to me. One guy was a fat, older man. The other guy was a tall, slim, older guy. Both of them seemed very friendly and we talked for a while. I don't remember what our conversation was about. What I remember was that at some point, I started to itch on my arms and chest. I immediately thought about that night at Wal-Mart when I had seen the weird guy who I thought was carrying some lethal virus. I had itched on my arms and chest that night after seeing him. I thought that he had transmitted his virus to me somehow. When I started itching after talking to those two guys at Chili's, I immediately realized that they had transmitted the virus to me. I said to the fat guy, "Have you just given me some kind of disease?" He laughed and said, "What are you talking about?" I said to Justin, "Justin, you need to get this guy out of here, he just tried to give me HIV or something?" Justin looked confused and said, "What?" I said, "Get this guy out of here. He has some contagious disease. I don't know what it is, but I'm itching all over. This guy touched me and now I'm itching. He has just given me some kind of disease." After that, I ran into the bathroom. On my way I patted my hand on the backs of everyone at the bar. As I walked down the bar and patted each person on the back, I said, "Here's some for you, and for you, and you." I thought I was giving the disease back to other people at the bar who were in on what had just happened. I assumed that the other people at the bar knew that the guy had intended to give me that disease. I thought, "Well then, I'll just give these bastards a little taste of their own medicine.", and I walked along, thinking that I was spreading the disease to all the people at the bar who were there waiting to see that I had contracted some deadly virus.

I walked past the bar and into the bathroom. I lathered my arms and chest with soap and hot water. I used paper towels to scrub my skin as hard as I could. I was hoping that by doing this, I would be able to kill the disease and stop it from spreading on my body. There were several people in and out of the bathroom while I was doing this. I just stood in front of the sink and scrubbed away. A few people commented about what I was doing. I just ignored them and kept on scrubbing. I thought that was the best chance that I had of not contracting the disease. The Voice had told me about tiny robots in my body that could fight foreign bodies, like the virus that the guy put on me at Wal-Mart in Tallahassee. But, I was not sure if this was the same thing, or something else. So, I scrubbed. Once I got myself all cleaned up, I dried off with more paper towels and then walked back out to the bar.

A girl at the bar stopped me and said, "Why did you just put your hand on my back when you walked by?" I said, "That was just a little love tap. I was just being goofy." She said, "O.K.", with a sarcasm in her voice that said, "Don't touch me again asshole." I sat back down where I had been sitting. The two guys that were there before were now gone. I said, "Justin, did you get rid of those guys?" He said, "Well, I told them that they had freaked you out and they left." Then he said, "So, what did you think that guy did to you?" I said, "Well, it's a weird story, but someone has created a virus that is more deadly than AIDS. It is spread through the air or by touch or something. I'm not really sure. But when that guy touched me, my skin started to itch right at the spot that he had touched. Then it quickly spread all up my arms and onto my stomach and chest. I don't know what he has, but I think it could be that virus. I just went in the bathroom and washed my arms and chest to try to get rid of it. I'm not itching anymore so I think I'm alright." Justin didn't say anything. He just looked totally confused. He said, "That guy is one of our regulars. He's a real nice guy. I don't think that he has any contagious disease." I said, "You would be surprised about some people. Not everyone is who you think they are these days." Justin didn't have a response. He just walked off and started making a drink for somebody.

After talking with Justin for a minute, The Voice said, "You need to get rid of that shirt. There are still germs on it." So, I went to my car and looked for a shirt to change into. I took off my shirt right there in front of the restaurant and put on my new one. There were lots of people standing around outside. They were probably wondering why in the world I had just changed from one T-shirt to another. I took the shirt that I had been wearing and threw it on the ground beside a building that was next to Chili's. I decided that it was better to just get rid of the shirt, rather than take a chance on spreading the disease onto other things in my car.

Another thing that I remember talking with Justin about that night was a girl that worked at Chili's. There was a girl there named, can you believe it, Jen. This Jen was also a beautiful girl. She was almost as beautiful as the Jen from Tallahassee. Only this Jen was a blonde, the other was a brunette. The Jen from Chili's was very good looking and also had a great body. Justin had actually introduced me to her one night when I had stopped by Chili's right after Sara had left. I had gone to Chili's one night after Justin and I had talked on the phone. Justin had said that we should go to a bar that was open later than Chili's, named Ted's, after he got off work one night. So, I drove up to Chili's and waited for Justin to get off work. I sat at the bar for about an hour while he worked. As I was talking to him, he said, "Hey, check out that girl over there. Is she awesome or what?" The girl that he pointed out was a waitress who worked there. She was wearing a tight little black shirt and tight black pants. She had a great body and nice long blonde hair. I said to Justin, "Damn! That girl is gorgeous. What's her name?" He said, "That's Jen. She's one of Danielle's friends." Danielle was Justin's wife. Justin said that Jen had been working there for about 6 months and that she was nice, but was melancholy. I said, "Why do you say she's melancholy?" He said, "Well, you never know what kind of mood she's going to be in. Sometimes she is really funny and talkative and sometimes she's very quiet." Justin said that most of the time she was a lot of fun to be around and that he wanted to introduce me to her. I said, "Thanks man. She's just what I need to get my mind off of Sara." Justin said, "Well, she does have a boyfriend, but who knows what could happen." I figured that it couldn't hurt to meet her. So Justin called her over to the bar and introduced us. We just said hello to each other and Justin told her that he and I had been best friends since junior high. After that she went back to waiting tables.

That night, after Justin got off work, he said, "Do you still want to go up to Ted's and hang out for a while?" I said "Of course, that's why I'm here." He said, "Jen's going to come up there with us." I said, "Sweet." So, Justin and I drove up to Ted's and walked into the bar. There were a few other people from Chili's who were already there. Jen was one of them. She was sitting at a table with a group of the people from Chili's. She wasn't really talking to any of them. Her boyfriend didn't seem to be around. Justin and I talked for a long time. I would glance over at Jen every now and then and find her looking at me. I mentioned it to Justin and he said, "Let's go over to her table and sit by her." She was at the end of a table that had a couple of empty chairs across from her. So, Justin and I sat down across the table from her. Justin had some conversations with her about work that night. And then I started asking Jen some questions myself. I asked her how long she had known Danielle. I told her about being in Justin and Danielle's wedding and other highlights from the years that I had known Justin. I also said, "So, Justin tells me that you have a boyfriend." She said, "Yes, but he's out of town." I said, "Does that mean that you are available for me to hit on you?" She laughed and said, "I didn't realize that you were hitting on me." I said, "I'm not. I'm just asking." She laughed and said, "No, I don't think my boyfriend would like it if you were hitting on me." I said, "Fine. Then, I'm just getting to know you." She said, "That's fine." So, we talked a little more. After a while, they announced last call, so we all left. I said bye to Jen and thought that I had made a good impression with her. That was my first meeting with Jen. This actually happened a while before I met the Jen in Tallahassee. After I met the Jen in Tallahassee, I put the Jen from Chili's on the back burner.

So, now, back to my more recent visit to Chili's. Back to the time that I was talking about earlier, after I had just had a disease placed on me by a Chili's regular:

I was sitting at the bar and I asked Justin about Jen. He said that she was still working there. That she still had the same boyfriend. He said that Jen had moved in with her boyfriend. He thought that they were getting serious. I said, "Damn. I really thought that I had a chance with her." Justin said, "Maybe you still do. Anything can happen. Just take it slow. She's pretty serious about the guy she's with though. I've met him. He's a nice guy. But, who knows, maybe she'll end up liking you more." I said, "Who knows."

I saw Jen a little while later. She was waiting tables. I said hello to her and she smiled and asked me how I was doing. We talked briefly before she went back to one of the tables that she was serving. I decided that I had to make a move on Jen. It was just another very bad idea. Actually, it was one of the worst ideas. What I decided to do was get her a ring. The Voice had already been having a little talk with me about how Jen really wanted to leave her boyfriend and marry me. Every girl I came across now, wanted to marry me. It never occurred to me that they probably would have wanted to know me a little better, maybe for a year or more, before ever thinking about the idea of getting married. Everything that happened to me had to have an aspect of the fantastic. If in the past I might have thought that a girl seemed a little interested in me, now that same encounter would provoke The Voice to tell me that the girl I had just met was dying to marry me. So, after already having a similar experience with a girl that I believed to be President Bush's daughter, I now thought about the possibility of getting married to Jen. I had spoken with Jen for a grand total of probably thirty minutes in my entire life, but compared to marrying a girl that I had hardly spoken two words to, The Bush Girl, I thought that Jen seemed like a better choice. So, I decided that I needed to buy her a ring, so that she could have a symbol to show her that I wanted to marry her as well. I thought that if she agreed to wear it, she would be telling me that she did in fact want to marry me. Like I said, it didn't matter to me that I didn't know this girl at all. I just knew that she was beautiful, seemed pretty nice, was a friend of Justin's wife, and The Voice had said that she wanted to marry me. That was all I needed at this point to jump on the opportunity to have a new beautiful wife. It was totally bizarre and unlike anything I had ever done before.

I tried to think of a place where I could buy a ring. It was already very late, probably after 11:00 pm. I decided that I would just buy her some cheap ring, if they sold one, at the gas station that was just a short walk up the street. Isn't that where everybody goes to get rings anyways?

So, I walked in and realized that they didn't happen to sell rings. Imagine that. What they did sell was belly button rings, the kind a girl might wear in her pierced navel. I thought that was even sexier than a crappy ring for her finger anyway. So, I bought a belly button ring from the gas station. It had a little jewel on it and cost about $15.00. I thought that made a perfect symbol to tell Jen that I wanted to marry her as much as she wanted to marry me. Really weird, I know.

I walked back over to Chili's and went back in with the ring. I found Jen and said, "Jen, this is for you?" She said, "What is it?" I said, "It's a ring for you to wear." She said, "Is that like a belly button ring or something?" I said, "Yes. I didn't know if you wore something like this, but I thought you might like it." I was hoping that at this point she would understand why I was giving her the ring, without me having to explain that I was trying to make the statement that I wanted to marry her. What she was probably thinking was something like, "You pervert. You know I have a boyfriend. Why would you give me something like this?" Instead she just smiled and said, "Well, I don't have any body piercings, so, I don't want that. Thanks though." I said, "Alright." and realized that the new voice could lie to me as well. I went back to my seat at the bar and waited for Justin to get off. There was one time when Jen walked by me after that weird little situation. I smiled at her and she winked back at me. I instantly felt like she had just let me know that she understood what I had just tried to do with the ring. It was all in her wink. With that one wink, she said, "Yes. I'll marry you." Of course, this all only happened in my mind.

After feeling like Jen was mine, I just sat there and felt a calm that I had not had for quite some time. I smiled at her every time she walked by me. She always smiled back. I imagined how great life was going to be with her at my side. Justin mentioned that a group was going to go back to Ted's, the bar that stayed open for an hour or so after Chili's closed. I asked Jen if she was going to Ted's. She said she was. Before I left for the employees to close the restaurant, I asked Jen if she wanted me to drive her to Ted's. I thought that she would surely say yes. Instead she said, "No. I'm riding up there with some of my friends." I was shocked. Why would the girl who wanted to marry me not want me to take her to the bar after Chili's closed. I just let it go. I thought that maybe I had just seen a little of her unpredictable side that Justin had mentioned.

One other odd little thing that happened that first night at Chili's was that I decided to go out to my car and get my Darth Vader helmet to show Justin. You might think that I would have realized that every time I put that thing on, it got me into trouble, but the thought never crossed my mind. I walked into the restaurant wearing my Darth Vader helmet. As usual, I expected people to be impressed. I went back to the bar, after getting several stares from people that I had passed. I sat back down in my spot. Justin said, "Dude! Take that thing off. You're going to get me in trouble. You aren't allowed to come in here wearing a mask." I laughed and said, "I never knew that so many people had something against a person wearing a mask." He said, "Give me that damn thing before I get in trouble." I took it off and said, "I'll put it back in my car. Geez!" So, I walked back to my car and put the helmet away.

After he got off work that night, I wanted to show Justin my new car. I had been telling him about it all night while he was working. Justin had asked how I could afford a new car without a job. I told him that I was receiving money from a group of people that I was working for. I told him that I couldn't really talk about what I was doing, but that I did have a job. I just told him that what I did was a little too sensitive to talk about in front of other people. I'm sure that had him wondering what the hell I was really up to. He probably suspected that I had become involved with a drug dealing operation or something.

So, after Justin got off work, we went out and I showed him my new car. I tried to crank it up to let him hear the engine. I turned the key and pressed the gas pedal. The car sputtered and wouldn't start. I thought about what Dad had said about water in the engine. I told Justin that my car was supposed to be able to run on water and he said that he had never heard of such a thing. I told Justin that the dealership told me that this car was the first of its kind. Justin said, "I don't think they know what they're talking about. I think you better get that water out of your fuel tank." I told him that I had already put a chemical in there to evaporate it. I sat there trying to get my car to start for several minutes and it finally cranked up. Justin and I had talked about going back to that bar called Ted's for a little while. So, when the car finally started he went to his car and I was going to follow him. I backed out of my parking space and drove maybe 20 feet through the parking lot and my car died again. I tried to start it back up and nothing would happen. I sat there trying to start my car until the battery went dead. Once that happened, Justin and his friend Danny helped me push my car back into a parking space. Little did I realize, that would be the last time I would drive that car for some time.

Justin asked me if I still felt like hanging out at Ted's for a while. I said, "Sure. I'm not going to be able to do anything about my car until tomorrow anyways. Besides Jen said that she was going up there. That will give me another chance to get to know her." Justin said, "Yeah, but remember what I said about taking it slow with her. She does have a boyfriend, remember? He's going to be up there at Ted's tonight. So, you probably want to play it cool with Jen." I said, "Yeah, but I can tell that she likes me. I'm not worried about her stupid boyfriend." Justin didn't say anything. I'm sure he was realizing that he had just set himself up for some trouble.

We went on over to Ted's and walked inside. There was Jen, sitting at a table with a small group of guys. Justin, Danny, and I sat at a table near her. We all talked for a little while and they drank a couple beers while I drank water. As exhausted as I always was, I never wanted to add alcohol to my system. I was always scared that it would make me so tired that I might fall asleep wherever I started drinking it.

So, Justin, Danny, and I talked; but what I was really doing was checking out Jen. I sat at the table in a chair that faced her. I kept watching her to see what she was doing. Every now and then she would look over at me and smile. That was all I needed. To add to my delusion, she got up and walked around a couple times. I thought I saw her look at people and make a squint with her eyes, like she was letting me know that she did not approve of whoever she was looking at. I thought, "Maybe

Jen is a spy like me. Maybe she is working for the secret group too. That must be why they want us to get together." After seeing her smile at me and give me, what I thought, were secret signals that she was aware that bad people were around us, I decided to make a move again.

I got up from the table that I was sitting at and walked over to her table. She was sitting in a chair. I stood right behind her and acted like I wanted to get in on whatever conversation was going on at her table. At one point, I put my hand on her shoulder. I wanted to let her know that I was standing there for her. She looked up at me and said, "How are you?" I said, "I'm good. How about you?" She said, "Please don't put your hand on my shoulder." So, I took it off. I continued to stand right behind her. I wanted to give the signal to everyone at the table that she was mine. Eventually, one guy at the table got a gutful of me. That guy happened to be Jen's boyfriend. He said, "Hey, buddy, why don't you go stand somewhere else. That's my girl you're standing next to. You're making her uncomfortable." I said, "Am I making you uncomfortable Jen?" She got up and walked off to the bathroom. As she walked off, I noticed that she looked scared. I said to her boyfriend, "I don't think you know who I am. I am the guy who Jen really likes. If you are her boyfriend, I think your time with her is over." He said, "Is that so?" I said, "Yes it is." Justin and Danny realized what was going on and walked over and said, "Scott, come on we need to leave." I said, "Hang on, this guy has a problem with me and Jen. We've got to have a little talk." Jen's boyfriend said, "I will kick your ass if you don't get out of here." That was all I needed to hear. I was ready to fight the guy right there. I said, "Well, do what you have to do, but Jen is still my girl now." At this point Jen had come back out of the bathroom and was standing about 15 feet away, watching nervously. I said to Jen, "Jen do you want to leave with me?" She said, "No. I'm staying here with my boyfriend. I told you I have a boyfriend. I'm sorry." Then Jen's boyfriend said, "There you go buddy. Now get the hell out of here or I will kick your ass." Justin and Danny grabbed my arms and said, "Scott, let's go." I walked out with them. I'm sure that Justin had no idea that I would end up putting him in such an awkward situation when he casually mentioned what a good looking girl Jen was and introduced me to her.

After that little incident, Justin and I drove back to his house. Justin had already asked me if I wanted to spend the night at his house. I had told him all about what had happened between my parents and I. I told him that I was planning on getting a room at some hotel in town that night. But then he asked me if I wanted to just save some money and stay with him instead. I said, "Yeah, if you don't mind, and if it's not a problem with Danielle, then I'll stay at your place tonight. I've been spending money on hotels and campgrounds since I left Mom and Dad's. If you'll charge me less than a hotel, then I'll stay with you tonight." I told him that I would just spend that one night with him. After that, I thought I would either go back to the lake or get another hotel.

So, Justin and I went back to his house. When we got there Danielle was already home with their little girl, Taylor. Danielle said that she was going out with some friends and would spend the night with them. So, after she left, it was just Justin and I. Taylor was asleep. It was after 1:00 am. Justin and I talked for a little while. He was telling me that I needed to leave Jen and her boyfriend alone. I changed the subject and talked a little about a few of the weird ideas that I had. One thing I told Justin was that someone had found a secret message within the Holy Bible. I said that someone had run the Bible through some decryption software on a computer and had discovered the actual meaning of the Bible. Justin said that he already knew about that. He went and got a book that was written specifically about what I had just talked about. He asked me if I had read it. I told him that I had never heard of it. He told me to take it and read it. After that, I assumed that Justin was also an operative with the secret group. I realized that I had known members of the secret group all along and just not been aware. I thought that Justin had just realized the same thing. So, I started telling him more about what I knew. I told him that I thought that God was actually an alien from another planet who had conquered all other beings in the universe to claim the title of being the one God. I told Justin that Satan was actually just a lesser alien who did not get along with God. God had punished him by placing him in a sort of prison in the center of the Earth. As I babbled on and on about all my new bizarre ideas, Justin sat and listened and seemed interested in my theories. After a while, we decided to get some sleep. I laid down on his couch with a blanket and pillow that he gave me. He went back to his room.

The next morning I was up by 6:00 am. We probably stayed up until after 3:00 am that same morning. So, I got another total of less than three hours of sleep. But, I felt great. I walked around his house for a while. I figured that he would be getting up soon. I went back to his office. He had shown me a room in his house where he kept all his high tech gadgets. His whole house was wirelessly networked. He had two laptops and two desktop computers. In his room, he had his television connected to one of the computers and could access his computer through the remote on his television. One of his laptops was a touch screen tablet PC. He had been showing it to me the night before. It was also on the wireless network. It was very cool.

I picked it up and opened a program that let you draw with the stylus. I started to draw a picture to tell Justin some of the things we had talked about the night before. I started to draw a picture of a cartoon looking alien. He had a little bubble shaped head. Out of his mouth, I wrote "Hello, Hello, Hello." I thought that I had drawn a picture of an alien who was greeting us for the first time. I looked at the picture and then decided that I didn't like it. I decided to draw a new one instead. I drew a picture of two tornadoes ripping through a town. I drew little pieces of buildings flying through the air. On top of one of the tornadoes, I drew a little cowboy hat. The picture was meant to be a symbol of what Justin and I would soon become. I imagined that Justin and I were about to become powerful secret agents; if Justin wasn't already one, and I just didn't know it. The tornadoes were Justin and I. We were ripping through the minions of the secret evil group. The tornado with the cowboy hat was me. I was still always wearing the cowboy hat. So I thought that if I drew it on the tornado, that would tip Justin off as to what the picture was about. I thought that seemed like a good picture, so I left it on the screen so that when Justin picked it up, he would see it. After drawing on his computer, I decided to draw a little picture on one of the sticky notes that I always kept in my pocket. I had started writing down little ideas on my sticky notepad as they came to me. I lost all those sticky notes somewhere during my last days in Lakeland.

On my sticky note, I drew a picture that showed a little boy watching television. A monster was coming out of the television. I drew the child's head exploding and his brain floating through the air towards the monster. I thought this picture was a good little reminder for how I felt about television. I had started to get the idea that the secret evil group might be brainwashing people through their televisions. I imagined that the way for the Anti-Christ to rise to power would be paved by the news stations praising some person to the point that everyone fell in love with them. I believed that person would be the Anti-Christ. The picture of the child's brain being sucked from his head, represented my idea about brainwashing.

After doodling on Justin's computer and my sticky notes, I started to wonder when Justin would wake up. It was now around 7:30 am. We had talked the night before about going back to my car and using a siphon to take out all the gas and put new gas in it. I wanted to do that as soon as Justin was ready. I was surprised that his little girl was still asleep. My kids always woke up at the crack of dawn, even on days when they didn't have to go to school.

So, around 7:30 am, I walked back to his bedroom. His door was open. So, I looked in and saw him laying there, with his eyes closed, and Taylor crawling around on the bed. The TV in his bedroom was on. So, I thought that he might be awake. I said, "Hey, Justin are you awake?" That woke him up. He looked at me and said, "No. I was still sleeping." I said, "I saw the TV was on, so I thought you were up." He said, "No, I sleep with the TV on all night." I thought that was weird. I said, "I was just wondering when you wanted to go over to Chili's." He said, "Let's wait just a little bit. Its still early." I said, "O.K." and walked back out to the living room. I waited maybe another hour for him to get up. Then we took Taylor to Danielle's mom's house. Justin said that he had already asked Danielle's mom to watch Taylor for a few hours.

We walked into Danielle's mom's house and The Voice told me some surprising news. It said, "This is a house of vampires. These people are all much older than they look. They drink human blood to keep themselves young." I never knew when The Voice was going to drop a bomb on me. That was a pretty big one. I looked over to a couch where Danielle's brother was sleeping. I thought, "Maybe they sleep all day. Just like in the movies." It was around 9:00 am. It's not like it was too late in the day to be sleeping. We walked past Danielle's sleeping, vampire brother; and went to Danielle's parents bedroom. In there was Danielle's mom. She was folding laundry. Justin introduced me to her. I said hello and shook her hand. I thought that I had just shook hands with a vampire. I felt slightly nervous, but by this point, so many wild ideas had already run through my head that this didn't seem that strange. I just assumed that if these people were in fact vampires, they were still decent people. I had heard stories about Danielle's parents over the years from Justin. He always seemed to think pretty highly of them. So, I figured that if these people were vampires, they must be good ones. By now I had come to believe that I myself was a sort of zombie. So, coming into contact with vampires didn't really scare me. I thought that there were probably good and evil versions of all the weird types of creatures that the voices had told me about.

Another thing that happened while we were at Danielle's mom's house was a situation with their television. When we walked in, the television was on one of the cable news channels. After meeting Danielle's mom, I walked back to their living room while Justin talked a few more minutes with her. I stood in the living room and watched the television. My mind had not been able to focus on TV for a while at that point. This time was no different. I saw footage of people in some foreign country dancing around and cheering about something. They were very excited about whatever was going on in their area. The Voice said, "Those people are excited because they have heard about you. They are praising you. People all over the world are hearing stories about the good things that they think you are about to do. You are a new world hero." I stood there and watched the images of the people cheering. I smiled at the television and thought, "You guys are giving me more credit than I deserve. I haven't even done anything great yet." I wondered what had been said about me and what they thought I was going to do that was worth getting so excited about. The Voice said that they had been adding some computer graphic special effects to some of the video that they had of me. The Voice said that they had taken a video of me walking down a sidewalk and disappearing into thin air. It said that there were other videos that showed me levitating off the ground and doing other miraculous things. The Voice said that I would soon be able to do those things for real, but that for now, they were building hype about me so that I would become a well known public figure. The Voice said that I would one day hold a political office and may even become the leader of the nation or the world. These ideas were fascinating to me and they helped continue to feed my out of control ego. I now believed that the world was watching me and loved me. Life seemed greater than I could have ever imagined. In reality though, I had burned almost every bridge that I had ever built, and was well on my way to burning another.

After dropping Taylor off with Danielle's mom, we drove back over to Chili's to check out my car. Justin had a siphoning kit that he brought with him. He put it in my fuel tank and started siphoning out the gas and chemicals that I had poured into it. He also brought a little gas container and he poured some gas back into the tank after he emptied it out. Then we used my jumper cables to try to get my car to start. I tried to crank it up, but it would never start running. It just kept sputtering and as soon as I let off of the ignition, it would die. So, after spending a half hour screwing around with my car, we gave up on it. I told Justin that I appreciated him helping me, but that I thought I better just call the Subaru roadside service people to have them look at my car. I asked Justin to just drive me back to Nanny's house, so that I could get a hold of my Dad and maybe have him look at it.

So, Justin and I headed back to Bartow. We talked about getting something to eat in Bartow and going by the auto parts store to get some more of that chemical that evaporated water in the gas tank. We went to the auto parts store first. I walked in and picked up another bottle of the chemical. Then I went to the register. At the register I saw a bunch of different key chains. I decided to get not one, but several. I bought one that was a little etched image of an angel inside of a glass cube. Another was a picture frame that had a picture of a baby with a birthday hat on. Another was a whistle that attached to a key chain. Another was a bottle opener that also attached to a key chain. All these things seemed like necessary items to me. After making my purchases, I went back to Justin's car, where he was waiting for me. Then we drove to Perkin's in Bartow before he dropped me off at Nanny's.

We walked into Perkin's and got a table. There were two girls sitting at a table near us. I said to Justin, "Do you see those two girls over there? They've been following me since I left Tallahassee." Justin looked a little surprised. He said, "Those two girls have been following you?" I said, "Yeah. But they don't always look like that. They are in disguise right now. Sometimes they have different colored hair. Sometimes they look a little fatter or skinnier, but I know that those two girls are the same ones that I have been seeing all the way back from Tallahassee." Justin asked me why they would be following me. I had my ideas about that too, but I didn't tell him. What I thought was going on was that I was being followed by the President's daughters. I thought that those two girls were the Bush girls and that they were still following me after that night when I had first met them on my way back from Tallahassee. I just told Justin that I didn't know who the girls were or why they were following me. I knew that what I actually thought might be too hard for anyone to believe.

Our waitress came to our table and asked what we would like to order. I said, "I hate this part." The waitress said, "I'm sorry?" I said, "You want to know what I want to eat. Don't you?" There is a little back-story to this comment as well:

There had been a few times when I was in New Orleans that I had ordered breakfast at a restaurant there. Every time I went in, I always had the same waitress. I remember asking her what she thought was good for breakfast one morning. She said, "I like grits more than anything. I'm a southern girl. You know what grits stands for don't you?" I said, "No. What?" She said, "Grits stands for Girls Raised In The South." I laughed and said, "Well, I like girls raised in the south too." She laughed. I thought she was flirting with me. Every time I came in to that restaurant, she was my waitress. She was always very friendly, and not bad looking. I would always make sure to order grits with everything I ate there. It was a brief little joke that I had going with her for a few days.

So, after meeting that girl in New Orleans, and after realizing that people could change the way that they looked; I started to think that every time I had a female waitress at a restaurant, it was probably that same girl from New Orleans, following me around. I thought that she was an agent of the secret group who made sure that my food was not poisoned. I thought that she traveled wherever I went and showed up at whatever restaurant I went to, making sure that my food was always safe. Of course, I never saw another waitress that resembled the girl in New Orleans. I just explained that problem by telling myself that she probably wore the same high tech makeup that I had seen on the waitress at the restaurant in Wildwood, the girl who's face I saw change before my eyes.

Now here was the poor waitress at Perkin's in Bartow, asking me what I wanted. My comment about "I hate this part.", was a reference to the fact that I was tired of always having to tell this girl what I wanted. I figured that she was the same girl who had been following me around for weeks. Why did I have to tell her what I wanted every time? I thought that by now, she should know that I usually ordered the same thing for breakfast, no matter where I was: eggs, grits, and bacon. I looked over to Justin. He looked totally confused. I smiled at him. He said, "I'll go ahead and order for him." I said, "Thank-you." The waitress was totally confused as well. Justin went ahead and ordered something off the menu. I don't remember what. He didn't even comment on what had just happened. I think he had seen enough to know that I had a serious problem. He had already heard my stories of how Sara and my parents had thrown me into rehab twice. I had always told him that they were the ones with the problems and he seemed to agree with me. Now, though, he had seen enough to know that I was the one with the problem. He just let me talk. I never picked up on this shift in perception until it was too late to do anything about it. Before I was done with Justin, I scared him so bad that we haven't had a conversation to this day.

After eating at Perkin's, Justin drove me to Nanny's house. The ride back to Nanny's house probably sealed the deal between Justin and I. I had already come to believe that Justin was indeed a secret agent for the group that I was associated with. I remember deciding to tell him about the device in my ear that let me hear the voices that always kept me in touch with the weird world around me. At this point, I also believed that I could simply think a thought, and it would be picked up by the secret group. I didn't need to talk to them anymore. I believed that the secret group and I had a telepathic connection. I didn't think of telepathy in some superstitious way. Everything had to do with technology for me. So, my explanation for mind reading was this: There was a device in my head, maybe the same device that let me hear the voices, that interpreted my brain activity into signals that were sent through the air, like cell phone signals. This brain activity was then picked up by a device, controlled by the secret group, that interpreted those brain signals into digital information that was used to rebuild the images that I saw with my eyes, or the thoughts that went through my head. I figured that if Justin was also a secret agent, he might have this technology too. I started to think of something to say to Justin, a simple message, that he might pick up with his communication device. I didn't want to speak. I just wanted to think something and see if Justin "heard" it in his head. I thought, "Justin, if you can hear me, give me a sign." Then I looked over at Justin. Justin looked back at me. I was smiling at him again. He said, "What are you smiling about?" I said, "You don't know?" He said, "No, what is it?" I said, "Maybe you don't have the technology that I have yet?" He said, "Dude, what the hell are you talking about?" I said, "You don't have the phone?" He said, "What phone?" I said, "The one in your ear?" He said, "I'm totally lost." I said, "I have a little cell phone in my ear. You can't see it. I've already looked in my ear and I don't see anything. But, there's something in there that lets me hear conversations between people. Sometimes, people talk directly to me. I've talked with some pretty important people through this thing. You wouldn't believe me if I told you who." Justin didn't even ask. I don't think he wanted to know. He just wanted to get me out of his car as quickly as possible. That was probably the incident that pushed Justin over the edge and far away from me.

By the end of that conversation we were at Nanny's house and we saw that my mom and dad were there, continuing the yard sale from the day before. Justin dropped me off. I got out and walked up to where mom and Nanny were sitting under the carport. I saw Dad walk out to Justin's car and they talked for a few minutes. I wondered what was being said. I found out later that the conversation taking place between Justin and my dad was about me. Justin was asking my dad what had happened to me. He couldn't understand what had caused his best friend to become a lunatic. Dad told me all of this years later. Dad said that Justin had tears in his eyes as he tried to tell my dad that he thought someone had to do something to help me before I did something terrible. At the time that I saw dad and Justin talking, I thought nothing of it. Little did I know, I had just ruined the best friendship that I have ever had.

Chapter 60: Ready for Re-Entry

After I got out of Justin's car, I walked on over to Mom and Nanny and started talking to them. The night before, I had a message from The Voice about Granddaddy. The Voice told me that Granddaddy was still alive, actually. The Voice said that Granddaddy would be making an appearance somewhere in Bartow that night. I imagined Granddaddy walking around Bartow in a black suit with black cowboy boots. Nanny had given me a pair of Granddaddy's old black cowboy boots. I thought that he would come back to town, wearing some boots like them. As I talked to Nanny, I asked her how she felt about Granddaddy being gone. Then I said, "What would you do if you knew that you could bring Granddaddy back from the dead?" Nanny's eyes watered up a little. She said, "Scott, Granddaddy is in Heaven. I wouldn't want to change that now, even if I could." I said, "Have you ever heard of The Human Genome Project?" She said, "No." I said, "Scientists are mapping human DNA. They are using super computers to identify all the parts of the DNA strand. When they have it complete they will be able to predict and cure all kinds of diseases. They have already found a way to bring people back to life. Granddaddy is alive. They have brought him back. I don't know how they do it. But the people that I work for now told me that Granddaddy is alive again." Nanny just repeated herself, "Scott, Granddaddy is in Heaven." She had long since realized that there was no way to reason with me. She didn't even try anymore. She just walked off and started talking to Mom and Dad.

Meanwhile, Mom and Dad started packing up the yard sale stuff. They acted like they wanted to leave as soon as I showed up. I was well aware of this. I asked Dad if he would mind driving over to Chili's to have a look at my car. He seemed very perturbed at this idea, but he agreed to take me back to my car, mainly just to get me away from them again. He and I got in his car and drove back to Chili's in Lakeland. I don't remember whether or not we spoke a word on the way over there. We got to Chili's and I poured in some more of the chemical, that I bought at the auto parts store, into my car. Then I tried starting my car again and got no result. Dad said, "Well, it looks like you've screwed it up good. You're going to have to have this taken to a mechanic to have this fixed. I can't do anything to help you." I said, "Well, I appreciate you coming over anyway. I'm going to call Subaru and have them come look at it." He said, "Alright, I'm going back to the house." and then he left. I was now alone again. I had no idea of what I was going to do next. I knew that Justin was supposed to work that night at Chili's. I figured that would be my plan for the night, hanging out at Chili's. The first thing I needed to do, though, was get my car looked at. So, I called a number for the Subaru roadside assistance. I got a guy to agree to come from Tampa to look at the car. He said that he would be there in a few hours. So, that took care of the afternoon too. I decided I would just stay right there at Chili's the whole day. That way, whenever the guy came to look at my car, I would be able to walk out of the restaurant and meet him.

So, after getting help from Subaru, I decided to go into Chili's and eat some lunch. I sat in the bar area at a little table. A good looking girl came up and took my order. I spoke with her briefly, asking her where she was from and that kind of thing. Chili's wasn't very busy at lunch, so the waitress at the bar had just me for her customer. She told me that she was from Brazil. That sounded exotic. She told me how beautiful her country was and how she wanted to go back. I thought that she seemed like a very nice girl, but I did not get wrapped up with her the way that I had about every other pretty girl I had come across lately. Instead, my mind was still on Jen. I had hoped that I would see her working that afternoon. It turned out that she wasn't working until later that day. Or maybe she was, I began to think, in disguise. I had already come to believe that Jen was a secret agent too. I thought that it was very possible that she may be there in disguise, watching me. So, I didn't want to screw up my chances with her by flirting with my waitress. Even though Jen had told me to my face that she preferred her boyfriend over me, I still was not convinced. I thought that maybe she was afraid of her boyfriend. I thought that maybe he beat her. Maybe he would have beat her if she said that she wanted to leave with me that night. That was my logic for Jen. The secret group had told me that she wanted to marry me. That was still the driving force that proved she loved me.

I noticed an older blonde headed woman working that day too. She sort of resembled Jen, but was much older. I didn't think much of her at first. My thoughts about who she was soon changed. It became the most grand idea I ever had. The idea that came from what I thought about the older woman was the craziest of all my ideas. That older lady changed my perception of who God was and what God wanted from me. But before that all happened, I got a call from the Subaru repair guy saying that he was outside. So, I went to meet him.

I walked out and told the guy what I had done to my car. I didn't explain my logic for putting water in my fuel tank. I just told him that some water had accidentally gotten into the fuel tank and now I couldn't get my car to start. He said he would take a look at it. The guy who came to fix the Subaru was a strange looking black man. I thought that something was odd about him. He was very friendly, but still, something wasn't right. I couldn't figure it out. Then The Voice said, "You have just met your first Martian. This man is actually an alien. He is wearing a disguise." At one point the repair guy went to his truck and started talking on the phone. The Voice said, "He is speaking with other aliens right now. He is telling them that he has found you. You might be in danger. Just stay calm. We'll help you." I walked over to the guy's truck, expecting to hear him speaking in some alien language. He smiled and kept talking. I understood every word. He was telling someone on the other end that he was not going to be able to fix my car and that he would have it towed to a service center in Tampa where they would perform the repairs." I thought, "Well, that doesn't sound like aliens on the phone to me." The Voice said, "He won't talk about what I said until he knows you can't hear him." I walked away and still believed The Voice, even though, once again, I had no proof of anything that it said.

After getting off of the phone, the repairman said, "Well, I can't do anything to fix your car here. You're going to need to have it towed to our service center in Tampa. They are going to have to look at your engine and see what they can do." I said, "Damn. I didn't realize that a little water could cause such a problem." He said, "Oh yeah. You've got a big problem. They're going to have to take your engine apart to find the water and get it all out. We're closed this weekend, so you won't be able to take it over there until Monday." It was Saturday when all this was going on. I remember because I still had two days before I could take care of my problem. So, I told the repairman to go ahead and schedule for a tow truck to take my car to Tampa on Monday. After that he left and I went back inside Chili's.

I went back in and saw that the older, blonde haired, lady was still working. I watched her walk out of the kitchen one time and go back in. A few minutes later, Jen walked out of the kitchen. She saw me and walked back into the kitchen. A few minutes later, the older blonde lady came walking back out. I sat there and watched as sometimes I saw Jen walking around, other times I saw an older woman, who resembled her, walking around. Neither of them ever talked to me. But both of them had looked at me several times. The Voice said, "You know that is Jen. The older lady is actually Jen in disguise. But Jen is not wearing the camouflage that other people have. Jen is different. She can actually change her shape without any special technology. She is not human. She is something else."

A little while later a group of young guys and girls came in. One of them was wearing a crown. Some of the girls were dressed in fancy gowns. I heard one of the guys say, "I am Zeus. Lord of all." I thought that was odd. I looked over at him. He actually had a beard kind of like a Greek god, except that he didn't have a moustache. The Voice said, "He actually is Zeus. All the gods that the Greeks worshipped are still around, living among us as humans. They are not human. They are aliens. They live forever." I believed everything from The Voice, as usual. It didn't phase me anymore to hear another wild idea. I didn't question anything. The Voice spoke facts. Whatever it said, was all that I needed to hear. I just sat there and thought how incredible it was to be in the presence of a once worshipped god. Then The Voice hit me with the wildest information it had ever told me up to that point.

The Voice said, "Have you figured out who Jen really is?" I said, "No." The Voice said, "Jen is God. She has come here to meet you personally. God wanted to have you as its personal companion. But God has realized that it has another plan for you instead. That is why Jen has become distant. She has realized that she cannot marry you. There is another plan now." I asked The Voice what that plan was. It said, "You will figure it out." I was once again, blown away by the information that The Voice said. Things couldn't get any weirder or more wonderful than realizing that God (herself, as it appeared) actually thought so much of me that she wanted to have me as her own companion for eternity. It was a weird love story.

My brain kept creating ideas that were more grand than its previous ones. The romantic relationship, for instance, began with an idea that a bartender whom, I met in Tallahassee, liked me. That was it. I simply had been told that a bartender liked me. But then, The Voice topped itself by telling me that The President's daughter wanted to marry me. That was a big leap to go from an average person liking me to the daughter of The President wanting to marry me. The only way to make a more grand scenario was what happened next, The Voice telling me that God had wanted to marry me. I guess my brain ran out of steam after that, because it never found a way to top that one.

So, God, herself, had wanted to marry me. It was the most fantastic idea that The Voice had ever told me. And I believed it all. The Voice explained that Jen could transform into anything because she was not at all human. She was actually the alien that had created our universe. She was the true God. She was the one who had been behind all that had happened up to this point. She was the one who was the true leader of the secret group. I was now told that the leader of the secret group was the one who actually thought so much of me that she had wanted to marry me. But now, The Voice had said that plan had changed and I would have to figure out what God's new plan was. There was always a mystery to unravel. This was just my next mystery, my next mission.

I walked out outside to try to get my head around the new information that I had just been given. I smoked a cigarette. I was no longer even nervous about the idea of cancer. I had already met the guy who had found the cure at the PRC. I figured that if cigarettes gave me cancer, the secret group would cure me of it with the technology that the guy at the PRC had helped create. After smoking the cigarette, I walked behind Chili's and sat on a pallet that was beside their dumpsters. I felt so tired. I wanted to sleep somewhere, but I had not reserved a room at any hotel yet. I decided to lay on a piece of cardboard that I put over two pallets, beside the dumpster. The smell of the dumpster didn't bother me. I was so tired. And I was in such a state of peace after realizing that God loved me so much that she had wanted to marry me. I thought that I must be the greatest human ever to be created, if I was in fact human at all. My ideas about my own humanity changed too. I started to receive information from The Voice that told me who I really was. But that all came a little later.

I laid down on the cardboard and closed my eyes. I started to fall asleep, but then I had a vision that kept me awake. With my eyes closed, I started to see the red spots and flashes that I had seen for several weeks now. Those spots and flashes began to change into beams of light. They looked like the lasers that spaceships in science fiction movies shoot out. Then, I saw what was creating the lasers. I started to see little white objects in a sea of black space. I realized that I was seeing something that was happening in outer space. What I was seeing was a battle between different spaceships in some far off section of space. The ships were firing at each other. There were hundreds of them. Every now and then, I would see flashes of light. These were explosions. Some of the ships were being blown up. I realized that I was seeing some battle and that one side was losing. I didn't know who the people were that were fighting. The Voice clued me in. It said, "This has been going on for hundreds of thousands of years. You are seeing the fighting that is going on between some of the aliens that are fighting for the control of your planet and people. There are much larger problems than the ones on your planet. The things that they are fighting about, you wouldn't even understand. But there are some humans fighting in some of the ships that you see. We have been training humans to help us for thousands of years. You will be one of them."

Now, it seemed that the big picture was finally starting to take shape. The Voice had explained to me that the ultimate goal was to train me to fight against the aliens who not only wanted to destroy life as I knew it on Earth, but also in other places that I never knew existed. The problems here on Earth, it seemed, were problems shared by other life forms on other planets. The Voice told me that a struggle had been going on for a time longer than I could comprehend. That struggle was between the forces that we describe as good and evil. The words "good" and "evil" are very subjective words though. The Voice said that there was a rationale for both sides and that once I learned the truth about each one, it may become harder to decide which side was right and which was wrong. I laid there on the cardboard sheet beside the dumpster for probably an hour or more. What started as an attempt to go to sleep, just turned into another mind blowing information session. My brain was getting so out of chemical balance that it could never turn itself off. Sleep was almost impossible for me. So, after realizing that I was not going to get any rest, I decided to go back into Chili's for a while.

I went into the restaurant and back to the bar. I was hoping to find Justin there by that point. It was some time in the middle of the afternoon. Justin was not there yet, though. I don't remember who was at the bar, but it wasn't anyone I knew. I think I ordered a glass of water and sat there for a couple hours, hoping that Justin would show up. At one point, I saw two really good looking girls come in and sit near the bar. They were at a table to my left. I watched them sit down and start talking on their cell phones. I could hear them telling someone about a trip that they had just got back from. The Voice said, "You know who those girls are don't you?" As soon as it asked that, I knew who they were. I was catching on to the game more quickly now. I thought, "That's the Bush girls. They're still following me." The Voice said, "That's right. George Bush still wants you to meet them. He is having them follow you until you agree to help them." I thought, "How am I supposed to help them?" The Voice said, "The President still wants your help to teach his daughters how to behave. They are still party animals. He knows that you could teach them how to live a decent life. He also knows that you can protect them." I already believed that all these things were true. I thought that I had lived a decent life. I thought I probably could give a couple of party girls a few pointers on what to do and what not to do. I also understood that if God herself had wanted me for a companion, then I probably had the power to protect people from harm better than most anyone else. How, exactly, I thought I would do that, I was not sure. I mainly just thought about all the invisible people who guarded over me and the fact that I had been resurrected from the dead. The combination of those two things made me think that I could probably do almost anything.

So, after seeing the Bush girls and realizing who they were, I looked over at them and smiled. They smiled back. I noticed that they were both very tan, almost too tan. The Voice said, "They got their tans from getting too close to the sun. They have actually been on a spaceship that took a trip to one of our bases on Venus. The sunlight is much more intense there. They got those tans because they weren't

wearing the right clothing when they were looking out the windows of their ship."
Just as usual, this all made perfect sense to me. I kept looking over at them. They
kept noticing. I rolled my eyes at them one time after I thought, "You girls are crazy.
You've seen things that no one else has ever imagined, and yet you like to come to
Chili's to get drunk." The girls were drinking some cocktails and doing a lot of
giggling. After they saw me roll my eyes, I heard one of them say, "I think that guy
thinks that he knows us." After hearing that, I decided to go outside and see if they
followed me. I thought that I might have a conversation with them in private if they
did. I waited around outside for several minutes, they never showed.

After waiting a while, I decided that it would be a good idea to get a room
somewhere. I thought about the Sheraton Four Points hotel that was just up the road.
It was just a few blocks north of Chili's, a short walk. So, I headed that way.

I walked to the Sheraton Four Points hotel and into the lobby. I then noticed
a really good looking girl who was the concierge. I asked her if she had any rooms
available with a single bed. She said that they did and that they were $80 per night. I
said, "I'd like to go ahead and reserve a room for tonight and tomorrow night." She
set me up and gave me a room key. I looked at what the girl was wearing. She had
on an outfit that almost looked like one of the French maid type get ups that you see
girls wear when they want to look very provocative. She definitely had the look
going for her. She was hot. There was also another girl working behind the front
desk. She was an Asian girl who was also pretty good looking. The Voice had
something to tell me about the two of them.

The Voice said that the two girls at the front desk were actually robots. The
Voice said that these two "girls" were actually some of the first of these robots that
would be secretly introduced into society. They looked real. They talked real. They
seemed very convincing as people to me. But The Voice assured me that these were
not real girls. The Voice said that these girls were actually going to be protecting me
while I was at the hotel. It said that these robot girls were actually trained assassins
that would kill any of followers of the secret evil group that might try to find me at
the hotel and harm me. As I talked to the girls, I tried to see if I could detect anything
unusual about them. The Asian girl spoke a limited amount of English. When she
talked, she often paused in between words. I wondered if this was a programming
flaw in the software that controlled her. Any other person would know that she was
just trying to find the right words to say. But I had to have fantastic explanations for
all ordinary things that happened around me. I talked with the two girls for a few
minutes. I don't remember what I said. I just remember that I was trying to figure
out if the girls were real or if they were machines that looked real. I guess my
troubled mind had taken in one science fiction movie too many. Now, all the crazy
ideas of the movies I had seen were becoming real, thanks to the voices and
hallucinations.

After failing to assess whether or not I had just talked to machines or people,
I decided to walk up to my room. I walked in and saw that the room had a nice bed, a
couple comfortable looking chairs, and even a desk that looked like an executive's
type desk. There was also a flat screen television and several mirrors around the

room. The room was on the fourth of fifth floor. It had windows that looked out over the back of the property, towards another wing of the hotel, and the parking garage. I thought it was a very nice room. It was one of the nicest rooms that I had ever stayed in. After checking out the bedroom, I walked into the bathroom. It was nice as well, though it was just a standard bathroom. It had a nice shower/bathtub and a large marble counter with a fancy sink in it. There was also a sheet of mirrored glass that ran along the length of one of the walls behind the sink. It was pretty fancy to me. After checking the place out, I decided to go back to my car and get some things to bring back to the room.

I walked back to Chili's to get some things out of my car. I grabbed as much stuff as I could carry. I had a bag of clothes and personal items, my pillow, and a few bags of crap that I had bought along the way. These bags were mainly filled with Star Wars toys that I had picked up at stores between Tallahassee and Lakeland. I had enough action figures to fill three or four Wal-Mart bags. I brought most of them back to the hotel with me. I got back to my room and decided to take a shower.

I started to get undressed to take a shower. As I was getting ready to take a shower, I thought that I could hear people talking from somewhere in the bathroom. It sounded like a conversation was going on behind the large mirror in the bathroom. I stopped undressing. The Voice told me that people were watching me from behind the mirror. It said that there were people from the secret group who were still analyzing me and that they were in some type of lab that was on the other side of that bathroom mirror. I looked into the mirror and said, "Can I please be left alone long enough to take a shower?" I got no response. But I still heard the sound of people talking. I pulled the shower curtain closed and got behind it and took off the rest of my clothes. As I was taking a shower, The Voice told me that there was a camera inside the showerhead. At that point I realized that the secret group had probably been watching me every time I took a shower or went to use a bathroom. I decided that modesty was now out the window, even though I still felt very awkward about the idea that someone could be watching me in the shower. I laughed a little and said, "I hope you guys are getting a good show. Why in the hell do you have to watch me take a shower?" Again, there was no answer and no explanation from The Voice. So, I finished taking my shower, with the realization that I was not even allowed to take a shower in private. So by that point, I realized that there was never a time when I was alone and not being watched. The effect of this was two sided. On one hand, it was comforting to know that I was never really alone. On the other hand, there were times when I wanted The Voice to shut up and leave me alone. The Voice kept me from sleeping when I wanted to, needed to. And not even being able to use the bathroom or take a shower without feeling like someone was watching me, made me feel like a prisoner or an exhibit in a science experiment. That's really what I thought I was most of the time, just an experiment. I thought I was the latest experiment of the secret group. I started to sometimes wonder just how much of what I was told was not true, but false information to see how I reacted to the secret group's little experiment.

After taking a shower, I decided to walk back over to Chili's and eat supper. I was hoping to find Justin there. I walked in and he was at the bar. So, I went on to the bar and sat down. I don't remember talking to him that much. I just sat there and drank water and ate something for dinner. Most of the time I was drawing little sketches on napkins and sticky notes. I was trying to make a record of the information that I had learned. The Voice had told me that the secret group was going to reform the Earth after all the major battles between God and Satan had been fought. The Voice asked me to come up with a design for the way the continents would be arranged on the new reformed Earth. I thought that sounded like an incredible honor. It did not seem impossible to me that the secret group could actually reshape the continents. With all of the technology that they had already shown me, it seemed like continent relocation and reshaping was a plausible idea. What good it would do, I didn't know. But this was like the ultimate design competition to me. I had enjoyed putting my own stamp on some of the small buildings that I had designed as an intern architect. Now I was being asked to design the shape of the continents themselves. The amount of work necessary to create whatever design I produced seemed unimaginable, but I believed that for the secret group, anything was possible. So, I started making a few sketches. They were all totally stupid, but that was about all I was able to do and produce, stupidity.

One sketch showed the continents arranged to form a giant smiley face. I thought that it would be funny if our planet was viewed from space as a giant smiley face. Another sketch showed a giant "W". This was for George W. Bush. I thought that since he was the leader of our nation, and would probably be the guy in charge during the coming battles between good and evil, it would be a nice gesture to rearrange all the continents on the planet in his honor. Another sketch showed two continents for the entire planet. I thought that this would be a way to separate the followers of good and evil. One continent would be a dwelling for the people who followed God and my secret group. The other was a much smaller continent. This would be where the people who had followed Satan and the forces of evil would live. I imagined that this would be Satan's Hell. One continent would be like a paradise. The other would be Hell. I drew a few other sketches, but I couldn't even tell you the logic behind them.

At one point, Justin introduced me to a red haired girl that was sitting at the bar with two rough looking older people. The girl was not that great looking. I could see that she had a tattoo on her back. I was never very attracted to girls with tattoos and the one on this girls back gave me the impression that she was probably someone to avoid. I don't remember what the design was, but it was big. It covered her lower back. The two older people beside her were her parents. They were all at the bar drinking beer. The girl also had a little boy with her. He looked like he was probably two or three. He was playing with a toy car at the bar while his mom and grand parents drank beer. I thought it was just a little on the inappropriate side. Justin introduced me to the girl and told me that we had gone to school with her sister. I don't remember the girl's name or her sister. I was not impressed with her and didn't want to know her. I was a little irritated with Justin for even introducing her to me. I thought, "If this is the kind of girl that you think I would be interested in, you must be crazy." After meeting the girl, I went outside to get away from the bar. I walked out and smoked a cigarette. There was a kid outside with his parents. He saw me smoking and I said, "Don't do this when you get to be my age. Cigarettes are very bad for you. I shouldn't be doing this." I put out the cigarette and the kid's dad thanked me and smiled. He seemed happy that I had just told his kid about not smoking. I felt guilty for being a bad example. I walked out to my car and thought about how I should stop smoking and become a more health conscious person.

I still hoped to hear from the Department of Health and Nutrition about the possible job that I thought had been offered to me while I was at the PRC. I had applied online before being kicked out of Mom and Dad's house. I went to the website for the Department of Health and Nutrition and found a link to job openings. I read through several descriptions and applied for one that sounded interesting. I don't even remember what it was. I was just sure that when The Department of Health and Nutrition saw my name on the application, they would hire me immediately. I figured that the secret group would have already arranged all that. They were the ones who I thought had set up the whole thing anyways. That day at the PRC, when the instructor had handed me a booklet about The Department of Health and Nutrition and said that if I was interested in applying for a job to go on their website, I just knew that was the secret group giving me an order. I knew that I needed to stop smoking if I was going to get a job with the Department of Health and Nutrition. I felt like the cigarette smoking was the only thing that I needed to do before they hired me. The fact that I had no training in health or nutrition didn't matter to me. I had a college degree. I figured that was probably enough for them. Besides, the main reason they would be hiring me would be because I was a member of the secret group. I figured that my job with The Department of Health and Nutrition would just be my cover so that the secret group could provide me with information that the government had classified as top secret.

As I sat in my car, I listened to Radiohead's *Hail to the Thief* album again. I was still hoping that someone would hear what I had heard and would realize the things that I had come to realize. I played the music loudly, so that people standing outside in the parking lot could hear it. At one point, I saw the red head from the bar come walking out. She walked right up to my car and smiled at me. I smiled at her and then closed my eyes. I laid there with my seat back for several minutes. When I opened them, she was gone. I was glad.

Another thing that happened that night at Chili's revolved around a new perception that I had of Justin. The Voice told me that Justin had actually been asked to play the part of a new devil that would replace Satan when he was destroyed. The Voice said that God realized that there had to be a balance of good and evil in the universe. "Without the presence of evil, no one would know what good really is." The Voice told me. The Voice said that God had actually asked Justin to begin practicing for this new role that he would play, once the battles between good and evil had been fought. The Voice said that Justin would not be like Satan, but that he was going to be the replacement for Satan once he was gone. The Voice said that God liked Justin and wanted to give Justin a portion of the Earth where he could deal with all the people who did not follow God. I guess this was another fantastic idea that came out of my subconscious. I had always thought that Justin being a bartender was kind of a bad thing. His job was to let people drink away their problems. To me, Justin was just a legalized drug dealer, in a way. He sold the drug that people used to change their perception of reality, if only for a short while. So, I guess The Voice telling me that Justin was going to become Satan's replacement, was just my brain spitting out information that I already believed, only on a fantastic scale. I had never thought that Justin was evil. I just didn't always think it was very cool that he was a bartender. But now that my brain was making up a supernatural explanation for everything around me, the Devil concept just popped out. I remember going back to the bar and watching Justin serve drinks. I remember watching his mannerisms and facial expression when he talked to people at the bar. I watched him and thought, "Yeah, Justin could make a pretty good Devil, I suppose." In a way, I felt a little sorry for Justin. I thought that he was being asked to do something that he might not want to do. I remember trying to talk to God and ask if he or she or whatever God is, wanted me to take on Justin's burden. I didn't think I got an answer. The next day I would.

After a while, I told Justin that I was going back to the hotel down the street. I told him that I had got a room there. I'm sure that he was relieved, but he said, "Well, you can stay at my house tomorrow if you want to." I told him that I didn't want to be a rogue. He said he understood. So, I left and walked back to the hotel.

On the way back to the hotel, The Voice told me that the secret group had come to the hotel where I was staying and was taking out people that were liberals. The Voice said that people who supported the Democrats were seen as a threat to me and they were being forced to leave the hotel so that I would be safe. The Voice said that the people were being taken out in body bags so that it appeared that they had been executed. The Voice said that some of the people in the secret group had ordered the people to be executed, but what was really happening was that the people were being put in body bags and placed in ambulances to make it appear that they were dead. What was really happening was that they were being relocated to some safe place where the people in the secret group couldn't harm them. You have to remember that The Voice that spoke to me at this point had told me that it was a member of a group within the secret group. The small group within the secret group was supposedly working for the true agenda of God. The Voice had said that most of the secret group was misled and was doing things that were in conflict with God's real plan. The Voice had described itself and its followers as the only one's who were looking out for my best interest and the best interest of everyone else on the planet.

So, The Voice had described a scene to me that sounded horrible. I imagined families being forced out of their rooms and being told to get inside of a body bag so that they could safely be carried out of the building and transported to a safe location. I imagined that there were other agents of the secret group who were watching over the whole process and being fooled into thinking that a group of Democrats had been executed, just as it had been ordered by some of their leaders.

I walked into the hotel and all seemed normal. I expected to find ambulances lined up outside the hotel. There were none. I walked around the lobby and didn't notice anything unusual. Then I walked towards the back of the lobby, to a hallway that led to a stairwell and some service corridors that went to other places in the hotel that were for employees only. I walked into the room that led to the stairwell. This was not a stairwell that was intended for guests to use. There was a grand staircase in the lobby that guests were supposed to use. This one was a fire escape stair that was probably just required by the building code as an emergency means of egress. It might have also been used by the staff when the service elevator was not working. The room was not decorated like the lobby. This was not a room intended for guests to see. I noticed the smell of chemicals in the room. I thought that I might be smelling some chemicals that were used during the evacuation of the Democrats that were staying in the hotel. I wondered if the secret group had used some chemicals to make the evacuees appear to be dead. I thought that they may have forced the people to take some type of chemical that caused them to go unconscious and reduced their vital signs so that, if they were examined, they appeared dead. The smell of the chemicals almost reminded me of formaldehyde. I know that formaldehyde is an embalming fluid and has nothing to do with the chemical I just described, but that smell reminded me of a science lab, or the way I imagined a morgue might smell. I looked around and thought that this room must have been where the secret group had placed the people in the body bags and carried them out of the hotel. It was a scary thought. I hoped that no one had actually been hurt. I also was afraid of what other things the secret group might have done that I didn't know about. I thought that if they had ordered the execution of innocent people just because they were of a different political party than the President, then they must be just as evil as the group that they supposedly were fighting against. I didn't agree with the views of the Democrats, but I didn't think that people should be killed or even forced from their hotel rooms, just because they had a different view than I did. I started to be afraid of the secret group. I wondered if President Bush was one of the people who had ordered the removal of the Democrats from the hotel. The Voice said that it had all been done to protect me and that this was just the beginning of many terrible things that I would witness before it was all over.

I went to my room and sat there on my bed for a while. I was hoping that I could wind down enough to get some sleep. But The Voice wouldn't let me do that. I looked at the mirrors in the room. The Voice had told me that all the mirrors were actually cameras that were watching me. So, I started to take the mirrors down. I took every one of them off the wall and turned it so that the mirror side was facing the wall. I was tired of feeling like people were watching me. I decided to see just what was inside of one of the mirrors. I placed one of the mirrors on my bed and turned it face down. It was in a frame and the back of the mirror was covered with a board and some paper over it. I tried to pry the board off of the frame so that I could see what was inside of the mirror. I pried the board away from the frame enough so that I could see what was behind it. I expected to find wires and camera equipment in there. There was nothing that I could see. I put the mirror back on the ground and turned it so that it faced the wall. The Voice said that all of the equipment was inside the frame so that it would be hard to find. I told The Voice that I didn't believe it. But I still kept all the mirrors off the wall and turned so that they were not looking at me. I felt like The Voice had tricked me again, but that didn't mean that I wouldn't fall for the next trick, just like I had for every other thing it said.

Another thing that was keeping me from sleeping was the noise that I thought was coming from the room next door. I could hear laughter and people talking loudly. The Voice told me that the people next door were a group of kids that had not been removed from the hotel, but whose parents were Democrats. The Voice told me that the kids were just typical spoiled Democrat kids who had no proper upbringing and were just being their usual obnoxious selves. I kept hearing people talk loudly and laugh every few minutes. Then, I decided to look at some of the toys that I had brought into the room with me.

I took out two figures that were identical. I bought two General Grievious action figures at some store along my way back from Tallahassee. General Grievious was my favorite character from the last Star Wars film, *Revenge of the Sith*. In the movie, General Grievious was the leader of the droid army. He was actually almost a machine himself. But at the center of a mechanical core, was an actual life form. General Grievious was actually the predecessor of Darth Vader. The machines that kept whatever was inside the robot body of General Grievious alive were supposedly a prototype of the machines that were used to create Darth Vader, after he was badly burned at the end of *Revenge of the Sith*. I liked the idea of machines keeping people alive after traumatic injuries. The Voice had told me that I had tiny little machines inside me that gave me the ability to hear its messages, see the weird things that I had seen, and fight off the diseases that the evil group had tried to infect me with. The Voice had told me that over time, more machines would be added to me. I wondered if I might eventually be more machine than human, like General Grievious and Darth Vader.

I took out the figures of General Grievious and placed them on a dresser that was in the room. I also took out a figure of a Clone Trooper and a new Yoda that I had bought. The Voice said, "Keep these with you, they will help protect you." The Voice was telling me that the little plastic toys, that I probably bought at Wal-Mart, were actually some type of little robot that could keep me out of harm, if the evil group tried to do anything to me. It was just another ridiculous statement that I took seriously. I looked at the little plastic figures and thought that they didn't look extraordinary to me but I put the figures in my pocket and decided to keep them there, just in case The Voice was telling me the truth. The Voice told me to take out some of the other figures and place them on the dresser in my room. It said that the toys would keep out members of the evil group, if they should try to come into my room when I was not there.

I decided to go back downstairs and check out the bar that was inside the hotel. I walked into the bar and saw the really good looking girl that was the concierge when I checked in. She was sitting at the bar, drinking a cocktail. Some guy was sitting near her and was talking to her. The bar had two sections that made an "L". I sat down at the end of the "L" that looked over to where she was sitting. I ordered a water and starting drinking it and checking her out. I was trying to see if she seemed interested in the guy who was sitting a couple chairs away from her and talking to her when I walked in. I started to think that maybe she was not too interested in the guy. I thought I would go over and talk to her myself. I still wasn't sure if she was human or machine, but I thought that even if she was a machine, she was a very good looking one. So, I went over to where she was sitting and asked if anyone was sitting in the chair beside her. She said that I could sit there if I wanted to. So I did.

I started talking to her. I don't even remember what I was saying. I just remember that I was still trying to figure out whether or not this girl was a real person or a machine. She seemed very nice. I don't remember anything in particular that she said. I do remember that I wanted to see what her reaction would be when I took out one of the Star Wars toys that were in my pocket. I reached in my pocket and pulled out the figure of the Clone Trooper. I sat it on the bar in front of me. I told the girl that the little figure was my good luck charm. I told her that I planned to take it with me wherever I went. She laughed a little nervously and said that she didn't know any grown men that walked around with kid's toys in their pockets. I said, "Well, I just realized that this guy is a good luck charm, so I'm going to take him with me wherever I go." I didn't show her the other three figures that were in my pocket. She didn't seem very impressed by the one that I had already taken out, so I figured that I should leave the others where they were. I talked to her for a little while longer and then she said that she was going to go home. The Voice said, "She wants you to come home with her." I asked her why she was leaving. She said, "Because it's late and I'm tired. I've got to be up early tomorrow. I've got to get some sleep." It was probably around 11:00 pm at this point. After she left, I went outside of the hotel and hoped that I would see her in the parking lot.

I stood outside in the parking lot and smoked a cigarette. After a few minutes, I saw the girl come walking out and head to her car. I walked over to where she would be passing. I said, "So, you are going home now?" She said, "Yes." I said, "I'd like to go out with you sometime if you want to." She said, "I can't. I've got to go home now. See you later." Then she got in her car and drove off. The Voice said that she wanted me to follow her. I said, "Well, I don't have a car. Thanks to me listening to the other voice, my car is out of commission, remember?" The Voice told me that the girl was an agent of the secret group. I said, "I thought she was a robot." The Voice didn't give any explanation. It went on to say that she was a trained assassin with the secret group and that the secret group had planned for us to become a couple. The Voice said that we would be working together in the future. I thought about all of the other girls that the voices had promised were involved with them some how and were interested in me. The Voice told me that it was O.K. to have multiple female partners. The Voice said that the secret group intended for me to have many female companions because I was going to be one of the last males left on the planet after all the battles between good and evil had been fought. The Voice said that I would have to help re-populate the Earth after everyone else had been destroyed or taken away.

The future that The Voice talked about sounded like living in the time of the caveman. In the future there would be no electricity, no cars, no technology other than what I could create for myself. The Voice said that once God and Satan had fought their final battle, I was intended to become one of the fathers of a new population that would worship God. The Voice never promised me that I would be spending eternity in Heaven. It talked about spending my time on Earth, after all civilizations had been wiped off the planet. I was going to have to create a new civilization, along with my many wives, and whoever else I could find that was suitable to bring into our little tribe. The Voice said that there would be dinosaurs, aliens, and other creatures who were all competing against us to control the planet and its resources. It sounded scary, but also exciting. I imagined myself running around in the ruins of a fallen world. I imagined having to escape from terrible creatures that would be out to get me. I thought about having to create a place of refuge where the people of my tribe would be able to flourish. The Voice had told me to get used to taking cold showers. I usually did take a cold shower, after The Voice made its request. But after a week or so of cold showers, I told The Voice that I would find a way to have hot water in the future. I told The Voice that I was not going to go without a hot shower for long. After the infrastructure that allowed electricity to be produced failed, I would just boil water over a fire for hot water, if that was all I could do. I also hoped that I would be able to receive technology from the aliens in the future, the same way that I had been told that people had been receiving technology from the giant squid for thousands of years. I was excited about the idea of being one of the last survivors in the new world.

After the girl drove off, The Voice also told me that she had been working at that hotel for the sole purpose of meeting me. The Voice said that she had been instructed by the secret group to meet me and see if we made a connection. I felt like we did. But, I felt that way about every pretty girl that gave me the chance to talk to her.

After the girl drove away, I walked down a little sidewalk than ran off of the hotel property and connected to a sidewalk that ran along South Florida Ave. I stopped about halfway down the sidewalk and lit another cigarette. I sat down on the edge of the sidewalk and smoked my cigarette. The Voice talked to me again. It said that there were aliens living in the sewers below me. It said that these were the aliens that were the spawn of Satan. The Voice said that the aliens had been making short appearances on the surface and that people had shot film of an alien walking around at night in the open. The Voice said that Satan and his minions were actually a race that lived on Mars long ago. The Voice said that they had all left Mars and come to Earth to live until there was a conflict with the alien we call God. God punished the Martians and forced them to live underground so that humans could inhabit the Earth. The Voice had told me a while earlier that some of the other creatures that had come to Earth from Mars were insects and reptiles. The Voice said that these creatures were actually all agents of Satan. It said that these creatures were actually the eyes and ears of the Martians and transmitted messages to the Martians, telling them about what they saw and heard. Every bug or reptile that I saw made me a little nervous because it made me aware that I was being watched by the eyes of the Devil. The insect and reptile connection to Satan was something that had been told to me by the old voice, shortly after I got out of the PRC for the first time.

Over the course of a few days, The Voice had told me a few things that made me sympathetic for the Devil. The Voice explained that Satan was just a less powerful alien than God. The Voice said that Satan had disagreed with God about many things and even tried to overthrow him at one point. Of course this is all in the Bible, but hearing it from The Voice made it legitimate for me. The Voice went on to explain that Satan had realized the error of his ways and really wanted to exist peacefully with humans, but God would not allow it. God had already passed a judgment on Satan and would never revoke it. God was tired of seeing the trouble that Satan caused for humans. The Voice said that Satan was really just a prankster. What might seem like a terrible tragedy to a human, might seem like a joke to Satan. God never found any of Satan's jokes to be very funny. God hated Satan for all the harm that he had done to His creations: humans and all the other creatures. The Voice said that Satan was the one who had created all of the problems that people have, and that God was the one always trying to fix everything and put things back the way He had originally intended them to be. The Voice said that was why God planned to destroy Satan, because He was tired of fixing problem after problem. So, hearing God and Satan described like two people with a long history of disagreements, made them seem a little less mysterious and scary. After The Voice had told me that Satan actually wanted to live in peace with humans, I began to wonder if I might act as a middleman between God and Satan. I wondered if I could help mend a relationship that had broken in a time farther back in history than I could comprehend.

As I sat on the sidewalk and smoked my cigarette, I heard what sounded like a large explosion in the distance. I jumped when I heard the loud boom. I stood up and tried to see if there was a fire somewhere nearby. The noise that I heard was definitely not my imagination, but I have no idea of what it was. I never watched the news or read the paper the next day, so I never got an explanation. But anyways, there was this explosive boom. The Voice said, "They have begun their attack! The military has just bombed a sewer where they have found aliens. The military wants to kill all of them." The Voice explained that the military had been following the activity of these aliens for years. It said that the aliens were recently becoming bolder and had been existing among us for thousands of years, disguised to look like us, so that they went undetected. The Voice said that now, they had stopped disguising themselves and were planning on making an attempt to live on the surface again. The Voice said that this would be the beginning of the end. The aliens below us would try to live with us and the alien above us, God, would destroy them for it. I felt sorry for the cursed aliens. The Voice told me how they hated the dark, hot environment where they had been forced to live. The Voice said that they just wanted another chance to try to coexist on the surface. It is funny how my philosophy and religion got wrecked every few days by something The Voice said. One day I was a fanatical Christian with traditional views, then I began to form my own little version of Christianity, and now I was reforming it again to have a little sympathy for the Devil and his demons.

After I heard the boom and The Voice's explanation of what had happened, I got nervous. I wondered if I might be attacked by a Martian that night in retaliation for what had just been done to them. Instead, The Voice told me some more information that actually scared the crap out of me at first, but then made me a little more comfortable with the idea of demons beneath my feet. The Voice said, "There is a Martian in the sewer below you. He is watching you through the storm drain hole behind your feet." I looked at the sidewalk and noticed the storm drain that I was sitting on top of. My feet were right in front of the hole. I'm sure that I had been subconsciously aware that the hole was there, but had not paid any attention to it.

396

After hearing The Voice, I got up and moved away form the storm drain. The Voice said, "The Martian doesn't want to hurt you. He actually would like one of your cigarettes if you gave him one." I thought that was odd, but The Voice said that the Martians like to smoke too. So, I lit a cigarette and tossed it into the storm drain. I looked into the black void of the drain and listened to hear any noises that might let me know that something was indeed down there. I listened and heard nothing. I said, "I hope you enjoy that. See you later." and walked away from the storm drain, back to the hotel.

I went back to my room and heard all the laughing and talking next door still. I decided that I still was not going to be able to get any sleep just yet, so I got a pad of graph paper that I had bought and decided to do some sketching in it. I decided to go back outside to an area in front of the hotel where they had some small tables. I had seen people sitting and smoking cigarettes and drinking wine there earlier. I walked out to the little covered patio area and there were still a few people sitting around out there. I sat at a table that was a little ways away from the nearest couple. I didn't want to talk to any of them. I just wanted to make some plans that The Voice had asked me to do.

The Voice had told me that Bartow was going to become a hub of activity for the forces of good and evil. The Voice said that I should try to design a type of fortress where innocent people could retreat to once the major fighting began. So, I got out the graph paper and some markers and began to draw a little fort. I don't remember exactly what it looked like. I just remember thinking that whatever I drew, was probably the greatest thing that had ever been designed and would surely be Bartow's most impressive structure. But in reality, it must have sucked pretty bad, because I don't even remember much about it. I remember basically drawing the representation of a small group of buildings that would function as the forts necessary service buildings. Then I drew a wall around the buildings and placed turrets every so often that would house the advanced weapons that the secret group would install there. The fort also had a dome roof over the entire structure that I intended to be constructed so that it would deflect a bomb or missile. I'm not sure what could actually do that besides some serious concrete and steel. I was thinking more along the lines of some advanced material that the secret group had yet to reveal to the public. I just imagined some type of translucent dome over the entire structure that might actually be some sort of energy field, rather than an actual material. I was trying to imagine something like the force fields that I had seen in science fiction movies.

After I finished sketching, I looked at the moon. It was coming up over the top of the buildings, across the street, to the East. It was a full moon. I stared at it for several minutes and thought that it appeared to be getting bigger. The Voice told me that the moon was actually getting closer to the Earth. The Voice said that the secret group had decided to transport me to the moon that night. The Voice said that they were going to take me to a base that was there on the moon. The Voice had already told me a couple days earlier that Granddaddy was living on the moon and that was where he had been taken after he died here on Earth. The Voice said that he had not actually died, but was taken out of his house when he appeared dead. The Voice said that his body had been transported to the moon and that he had been rehabilitated and cured of his cancer. The Voice had told me that Granddaddy had been a member of the secret group since he had served in the military when he was a young man. The Voice said that the special qualities that Granddaddy possessed also belonged to my mother and me. The Voice said that we were descendants of people who were actually not completely human. At some point in our family's history, the aliens had breed with one of our ancestors and produced a line of half alien half human creatures. The Voice said that the genes of the alien were still in our blood and that was one of the reasons that they had chosen me to include in their secret group. Again, another mind blowing idea seemed like no big deal at this point. I had already come to believe so many fantastic things that this was just more interesting information to me now, it didn't give me chills when I heard it though, like some of the other things that The Voice had told me in the past did.

So, I watched the moon and believed it was actually coming closer to the Earth. The longer I stared at it, the bigger it looked. My brain was so tired that simply staring at the moon long enough made it appear to grow. I would look away from time to time and then look back. Then it would seem like the size of the moon had not changed at all. The Voice explained that the secret group controlled a device that could actually move objects as big as the moon. It said that the device was being used to pull the moon towards the Earth and that people everywhere were noticing how close the moon was getting to the Earth. I thought about a Radiohead song on the *Hail to the Thief* album. The lyrics said, "Sail us to the moon." I had listened to that song many times and never really thought anything about it. But now it had a special new meaning. I thought that Radiohead had placed another secret message in a song that talked about people going to this secret base on the moon.

I realized that all this had been done for me. The moon itself was being moved, just so that I could be shown a secret base that was there. The Voice said that the news would tell the people that I was the one who had moved the moon. The Voice said that they wanted people to see me as a super human and that they were going to bestow upon me all of their technology so that I would be revered as a world hero. I looked around at the other people sitting outside. I wanted to see if any of them were noticing that the moon was getting closer. No one seemed to be picking up on that except me. I wondered if my eyes and The Voice were just playing another trick on me. I decided to go back inside and check on the moon a little later.

I went back inside the hotel and The Voice told me that secret agents were waiting to meet me in a room at the top of the hotel. I went to the elevator and went to the top floor. In the elevator was a girl dressed in a fancy gown and her brother and father who were also dressed up. They were going to a wedding reception, they told me. I said something to the girl that I don't remember. She asked me if I wanted to be her escort at the little party they were going to. I told her that I was not dressed for the occasion and she said that it didn't matter. She actually grabbed my arm when they got to the floor where they had to get off and tried to get me to come with her. I think she was probably drunk. I told her that I appreciated her offer but that I was very tired and needed to get some sleep. The truth was that The Voice had told me that she was just another Democrat who had not been forced to leave the hotel. The

Voice said that was why she was drunk, because all the Democrats liked to party and loved to drink their alcohol. After The Voice let me know that she was my opposition, I wanted nothing to do with her. It didn't help that she was not a very attractive girl to begin with. So, I stayed in the elevator and went on to the top floor.

I got out of the elevator and walked around, looking for some clue that would tell me where to find the secret agents. I walked down a corridor that had signs pointing to a pool. There was actually a pool on top of the hotel. But it had long been closed when I got there. At this point it was after 12:00 am. But I swore that I heard people talking outside, on the roof, where I thought the pool was. The Voice told me that I was hearing agents of the secret group who had captured the girl that was the concierge in the lobby. The Voice said that when they realized that she was interested in me, they took her and brought her up to the roof. The Voice said that they had her in the pool and were trying to get her to spill information about me or some other secret mission that she was involved in. The Voice said that she was involved with the same group within the secret group that I was talking to. Some of the members outside of that small clique had captured her and were interrogating her about something that she had done. The Voice told me not to interfere, that she would be alright, no one was planning to harm her. So, I felt sorry for her, but I walked away from the pool. I doubt that there ever was anyone up there. I think I was just hearing things in my head and mistaking it for actual sounds around me.

After leaving the pool entrance, I walked back down a corridor and came across a huge ballroom. The ballroom was all dark and empty except for the fancy tables and chairs that were within it. The Voice said, "They are waiting for you in there." So, I went in and walked around in the dark, sort of spooky, ballroom. I tried to see if I could make out anyone else in the room. I couldn't see anyone. Finally, I said, "I'm here. If you guys have something to say, please say it. I am running myself into the ground to do all the things that you keep telling me to do. Please come show yourselves to me at least." There was no answer. It was just me, in a big, dark, empty, room.

After realizing that I had just been led on yet another goose chase, I decided to check out one more thing before calling it a day. I complained to The Voice my whole way back to the elevator. I told The Voice that I was beginning to think that it was just like the old voice. It kept sending me on what seemed like important tasks, only to realize that nothing ever happened aside from me acting like an idiot. I told The Voice that I was too tired to listen to anymore of its crap that night. I told The Voice to please leave me alone and that I was exhausted.

I walked back to the elevator and went downstairs and back out of the lobby to the outdoor patio area. I wanted to check on the moon. I wanted to see if that was just another lie that I had been told. Just as I had thought, the moon was now much higher in the sky and was smaller than it had appeared before. I complained to The Voice again about the moon being another lie and another waste of my time. I decided to go back to my room and try to sleep. The realization that the new voice was no different from the old voice, made me sad. After coming to the realization that the new voice was as dishonest as the old voice, I also realized how tired I was.

I got back to my room and brushed my teeth and laid down on the bed. I turned off all the lights except for a wall sconce that had a very soft glow. I thought that would be enough light in case I had to go to the bathroom in the middle of the night. I was still hearing noises from the room next door. I laid there in bed and stared at the wall sconce. The wall and ceiling started to wobble a little. The longer I looked at the wall sconce, the more wobbling I saw in corners of my vision. It looked just like the wall and the ceiling were bending a little. It almost looked like little ripples were traveling across the wall and ceiling. I thought about another Radiohead song from the *Hail to the Thief* album. The words in that song said, "When the walls bend, when the walls bend, when you breathe in, when you breathe in." I was sure that this phenomenon was what the song was talking about. The Voice reassured this idea. It said, "You can walk through that wall or you can go right through the ceiling. You have the ability to pass through things now. All you have to do is walk right through things when you see them vibrating like this." I kept staring at the wall and watching the ripples that were traveling across it. I told The Voice that I had heard enough of its lies for one day. But I couldn't resist trying to do what it said that I could. So, after watching the wall and ceiling bend back and forth for several minutes, I decided to walk up to the wall and try out what The Voice said.

I walked up to the wall and put my hand on it. It felt like every other wall I had ever touched. I had expected that my hand would sink into the wall, just as if I had put my hand in water. But, that was not the case. It was firm, unlike the appearance it gave of something that looked almost like ripples on water. I stood there and looked at the wall. I could still see ripples traveling across it, though they were not directly in front of me. They were now on a new section of the wall that was a few feet away from me. I walked over to where I had seen the ripples and they disappeared as I approached them. Then I said, "Damn it! I'm tired of the tricks. I told you that I am too tired for this. Just let me sleep." I realized that my eyes were playing a trick on me. I wasn't sure if this was an optical illusion or if my eyes really had seen a wall that could bend. The Voice told me that I was never getting to the right spot on the wall in time. It said that if I could put my hand on a section of the wall when it was rippling, then I would be able to pass my hand through the wall. I gave up after trying a few times. I got mad and quit. I laid back down in bed.

I laid in bed and realized that I was still hearing the noises from next door. I decided that I could not sleep with all the racket they were making, so I got up and walked up to the door of their room and knocked on the door. It was probably after 1:00 am at this point. I knocked on the door and a young college aged guy opened the door. I said, "Hey, I'm trying to sleep next door. I was wondering if you guys would mind keeping it down a little." The guy said that he was sorry for keeping me up. He said that they had just come back from a wedding. I looked past him to see a girl in a wedding dress on a bed behind him. There were 4 or 5 other people in the room also. They were all drinking beer. They asked me if I wanted a beer and I refused it. I talked to him for a few more minutes and then went back to my room. After having the little discussion with the guy, I didn't hear any more noises from next door. Eventually, I went to sleep.

I woke up the next morning at some point after the sun had come up. I'm not sure what time it was, but I think that I actually slept more that night than I had in several days. I got up and went to the bathroom. I looked at myself in the mirror and decided that I needed to shave. I had long since started wearing a beard. The beard came about just before the time when I was thrown into the rehab center in Tallahassee. I decided that I liked the way I looked with a short beard, so I kept it. That morning I decided to do something a little different. I shaved a section of my face just below my cheek bones. When I was finished, I had long side burns on each side that ran down to my lower jaw bone. I also had a moustache and a little goatee. I thought it looked pretty cool. I thought I had just created another disguise. After shaving, I decided to go get some breakfast.

I walked out of the hotel and went to a Denny's that was just down the street. There was actually a line waiting to get in. I walked in and gave the girl my name and went back outside to wait. There were several people standing outside. The Voice said, "These are all your relatives. These are all Ganns from around the country who have heard about you and want to meet you. Most of the people in the restaurant are all Ganns." I looked around at the people standing outside. They were all different ages from little children to the elderly. I smiled at them when they looked at me, but I never said a word to any of them. After waiting several minutes, I was finally called inside and walked to a table. A waitress came up and took my order. I didn't do the weird thing where I acted like she should know what I wanted. This waitress was a middle aged woman with brown hair and looked nothing like the girl that I thought followed me around to every restaurant I went in. I told the lady what I wanted and she went off to turn in my order to the kitchen. The Voice said, "Your waitress is the mother of the concierge you met at the hotel yesterday. She is not really a waitress. She just wanted to meet you because her daughter had already told her all about you. She is very excited to meet you." The Voice had told me, on the night before, that the good looking concierge that I had talked to at the bar was actually distantly related to me. The Voice said that we were distant cousins, too far apart to matter. The Voice said that the girl was related to people on my dad's side of the family. So, there was this whole Gann connection growing in my mind. Now, I had met a beautiful distant relative and was surrounded by an entire restaurant of my relatives from all over the country. I kept looking around to see if I could recognize anyone. I could not. That didn't concern me though because I was not very familiar with many people on my dad's side of the family outside of his brothers. I looked around and saw several people that I thought could pass as relatives of mine.

There was one guy who was all dressed in black. He was an older man and he had a beard almost like Abraham Lincoln, except his came to a little point at the end and he was bald on top. I remember looking at this guy and thinking that there was something bad about him. The Voice said, "That man is actually a follower of Satan. He wants to persuade you to follow him and the secret evil group." The Voice said that a lot of the Gann family outside of my dad and his brothers were actually followers of the evil group. This idea probably came to me because my dad's family was not particularly religious, that I knew of. Dad's brothers, Mark and David, went to church; but I didn't think of them as deeply religious people like Granddaddy and Nanny. The Voice said that most of the distant family, the ones I didn't know, were all followers of Satan, and the man in black was one of their leaders. The Voice said that he was the one who had convinced most of them that Satan was the one to follow, not God. I watched that man and wanted to go and have a talk with him, but I never did. I was too scared that he might tell me something that changed my mind too.

Eventually, the waitress brought me my food. I ate it and didn't mention anything to her about the fact that I thought she was the mother of the beautiful girl that worked at the hotel. After I finished eating, I walked back to the hotel.

I went back to my room and made some more notes and sketches on my sticky pads. There was a desk there in the room. So, I just sat there and started drawing little sketches and writing weird notes to remind myself of all the information that I had gathered up to that point. One note that I remember in particular said, "Kill the Ganns. Rise Hollingsworths." This note was an order to the secret group to exterminate all the members of the Gann family that I thought worshipped Satan. The fact that I had actually felt sorry for Satan myself, just the night before, did not matter to me. I had just seen a bunch of people at the Denny's restaurant who I thought were Satan's followers. The Voice had told me that they would try to kill me if they could not convince me to change my views to match theirs. So, I was asking the secret group to just kill them before they killed me. I was not referring to anyone that I actually knew. I was only referring to the people in the restaurant whom I did not know, the man in black in particular. I didn't know if the secret group would actually kill any of them, or if they would just relocate them, the way they had supposedly relocated the people in the hotel the night before. I really didn't care. I just didn't want any of them to get me. It was an act of self-preservation. The part about "Rise Hollingsworths" was an order for the secret group to bring back all the Hollingsworths who carried the alien DNA that was supposedly in my blood. I wanted to be surrounded with people like me. I had been told that the alien genes in my body had come from the Hollingsworth side of the family. I was asking the secret group to bring my long dead relatives back to life. I don't know if my mom and dad ever saw the notes that I had in my room that day, but I'm sure that if they did, those notes would have scared the hell out of them.

After writing and drawing for a while, I decided to walk around the hotel a little. I walked downstairs and went to the pool outside. I walked around the pool and looked at all the little potted plants that were sitting around the edges of it. The Voice said that I should try some of the plants because some of them were poisonous and I needed to eat a little of each of them to give the little robots inside me a sample of the poison so that they could learn to produce the antibodies that would fight it. So, I pulled off a little piece of leaf on just about every plant out there. I would put a little piece of the leaf in my mouth and chew it for a while. Then I would spit it out. Each one had a little different taste to it. One tasted almost like green beans. I remember chewing on the different leaves and thinking that I was just giving information to the little machines inside me. I'm lucky that I didn't end up getting sick. I never swallowed any of the leaves, I just chewed on them a little and spit them back out. But I did swallow a little of the saliva in my mouth after chewing on each one. I figured that would give the robots all the poison that they needed.

After poisoning myself, I decided to check out the water temperature. It was a pretty cool day. The water was cold too. But The Voice told me that I needed to get in the water and test out another new ability that I had. So, I went back up to my room and put on a pair of shorts that I thought could be a substitute for a bathing suit. I walked back to the pool and jumped in.

The Voice had told me that I now had the ability to breath underwater. The Voice said that I could breathe water into my lungs and my body would be able to get enough oxygen out of the water to keep me going, as if I were part fish. The Voice said that the first few breaths would be very hard and that I would think I was drowning, but after a few tries, my body would adjust and begin to pull the oxygen out of the water. The Voice said that this was what the creature who became known as the ancient god, Poseidon, had done. He was worshipped as the god of the sea, because he had learned to breath water.

I put my head under water and tried to get the courage to breath in a little water. I sat there for a while holding my breath and wondering if this was just going to be another lie from The Voice. When I was almost unable to hold my breath any longer, I actually tried to breath in a little water. I couldn't do it. It was so unnatural for me to try to breathe in while I was under water. I came back up and gasped for air. I let my breathing return to normal and then tried again. This time I just kept my head above the surface and tried to breathe in with my mouth just on the surface of the water. I actually got a little water into my lungs and I started choking. I coughed and gagged for several minutes until I got all the water back out of my lungs. I told The Voice that if that was the process for learning to breathe under water, then I didn't want to learn how to do it just yet. I felt nauseous for several minutes after gagging on the water that I breathed in. I got out of the pool and laid in a chair that was beside it. After I felt recovered, I got back in and just swam around for a while until I got cold. The whole time I was in the pool The Voice was telling me that people were watching me from inside the hotel. A lot of the rooms of the hotel looked out onto the pool. There were people that I could see looking out their windows. They were probably wondering who in their right mind would swim on a cold day in a cold pool. I was sure that they were just more people who were amazed to see a major celebrity like me. After I got tired of swimming around the pool, I went back and laid in the chair again until I was dry enough to go back to my room.

I went back to my room and changed back into some dry clothes. After that, I went back downstairs and had planned to walk over to Chili's to eat lunch. On my way out of the hotel, I was stopped by the Asian girl who was working at the front desk the night before. She was on a break. She followed me outside. We sat down on a bench and started talking. She was very friendly. I don't remember much of what we talked about, but I remember her telling me that she was living with an older man that she did not like. She said that she lived with him because he had a nice house and gave her things, but that she thought he was actually a little repulsive. She said that he liked to drink all the time and she hated how he acted when he was drunk. I told her that I was sorry to hear about her situation. I told her that she should leave the guy if she didn't like him. She said that he wasn't that bad of a person and it wasn't worth moving out over until she figured out a better living arrangement for herself. After talking with her for a while, I decided to go on to Chili's and eat lunch.

I walked down to Chili's and went inside and sat at a table in the bar. Justin was not there. I got my food and started eating. After a while, someone I knew walked in. It was Angela Merick. She was actually my "girl friend" when I was in elementary school and we had been friends all through junior high and high school as well. I had run into her a few times over the years, oddly enough, right there at Chili's. I guess that she went there a lot. She and her boyfriend sat down at a table near me and she recognized me. We started talking and I couldn't help but bring up Sara. I don't remember what I said, but whatever it was it was bad enough that Angela later called someone and got Sara's number and told her that I wanted to kill her. Sara called me a while after all this had happened and told me that Angela had told her this. I don't know if Angela or Sara were exaggerating or not. I remember telling Angela that if someone took Sara out to a cow pasture and killed her, I wouldn't care. I don't remember saying that I wanted to kill her myself, though. I was just speaking figuratively. I didn't really want Sara dead. I was just using an expression to say that I cared about Sara so little, that if she died, it wouldn't bother me. And even that was not true. If something had happened to Sara, I don't know how I would have reacted, but I'm sure I would have been deeply saddened about it. I was angry with her, but not angry enough to do what I have been told that I said I would do. I talked with Angela for a while and never realized that I must have freaked her out. I don't remember anything else that I said to her. She and her boyfriend left at some point and I think I left shortly afterwards.

After leaving Chili's, I walked down to a plaza that had an Office Depot. I wanted to go in and see if I could find something to charge my Palm Pilot with. I had taken it out of the box and usually carried it in my pocket, even though I had never turned it on. In the box was an adapter that hooked the Palm Pilot up to a computer and charged its batteries. I was hoping to find something that I could plug into a wall or my car so that I could charge it up. As I walked to Office Depot, The Voice spoke to me again. It told me that God had decided that He or She wanted me to become Satan's replacement. After I had made the offer, apparently God had thought about it for a while, and had now decided that I would be the new Devil in place of Justin. The Voice said that was what God had wanted me to do when She had appeared to me as Jen and decided that She could not marry me. The Voice said that God had planned to ask me to become the new leader of "evil" in the world, after Satan had been destroyed, but felt like She had already asked a lot from me. So, The Voice said that God was reluctant to ask me to play the part of Satan, but since I had volunteered myself, God had changed Her mind. Now, I knew what my role really was. All the conversations explaining who God and Satan really were, all the unexplainable phenomenon that I had heard and seen, were all leading up to asking me to become a Devil. I said, "I would be happy to help God, in any way that I can, even if it means that I have to be the opposition." The Voice said that was the reason that God wanted me to be the Devil, because I was so unlike Satan. What God really wanted me to do was attract people to me, as the Devil, and then convert them into God's followers. I wasn't being asked to commit murder or other terrible acts. I was being asked to disguise myself as an evil being, so that I could attract followers and actually convert

404

them to worshippers of God. I was to become the dark that brought people to the light.

I walked towards Office Depot thinking of what I needed to do to play the part. I thought that I should probably just continue with the Darth Vader concept for a while. I thought that Darth Vader made a pretty evil character at times, so he was a good example of how I should behave. I walked along whistling the *Imperial March* song from Star Wars. I also remember taking out the lighter in my pocket that looked like a poker chip. I kept flipping it in the air and catching it. Every now and then I would light it and watch the flame coming out of it. I thought that the poker chip lighter was a nice accessory for someone who was about to become the Devil. It represented a lot of bad things: gambling, smoking, and the fire of Hell. I walked on into the parking lot where Office Depot was and saw a black girl come running out of a clothing store that was in the same plaza. She had a bunch of clothes in her arms and was running out towards the parking lot. A few employees came running out after her. I saw them catch up with the girl and physically restrain her. A few minutes later, a police car showed up. I realized that I had just seen a shoplifter get busted. I laughed and walked on towards Office Depot. I thought, "There is one of my new followers right there." and I watched as the girl was put in the back of the police car.

I walked up to the front door of Office Depot and realized that they were already closed for the day. An entire day had already almost passed by and, once again, I had not really accomplished anything. I looked in through the glass doors and saw a few employees walking around inside. I wondered if they might let me come in to look for an adapter for my Palm Pilot. I knocked on the glass but no one paid any attention to me. So, I started to walk off. Then a manager and another employee came out of the store. The employee was a good friend of my brother, Carter. The guy's name was Cory Watt. Cory and Carter had been friends since elementary school. I didn't know that he was working at that Office Depot. When I saw him, I asked how he was doing and we talked for a few minutes. I didn't want to tell him all the weird things that I had been up to lately. I just told him about Carter and my parents. We stood there talking for several minutes and each smoked a cigarette. I told Cory about my car breaking down at Chili's but I didn't tell him about pouring water in it. Cory asked me if I wanted him to give me a ride back to Chili's so that he could see my new car. So, I got in his car and we drove back to Chili's. I showed him my car and he seemed impressed. He left shortly after checking out my car. After Cory left, I decided to get a few more things out of my car to take back to the hotel. I don't remember what I grabbed, but I remember walking back loaded down with bags of junk that I thought might come in handy at the hotel.

I walked back to the hotel and saw that neither of the girls from the day before were at the front desk. Now, there was just an older lady working behind the desk. I went on to my room. I got back to my room and took a shower. I didn't bother hiding behind the shower curtain to get undressed. I figured that I was being watched everywhere that I went. So, I just tried to pretend that I wasn't under constant surveillance and jumped on in the shower. After taking a shower, I decided to go to Chili's and eat supper. So, I walked on back to Chili's and ordered supper.

Justin was there as usual. I sat at the bar and ordered some special that Justin recommended. We talked for a while. The place was a little less crowded than the previous two nights because it was Sunday. At one point, I noticed a guy that looked similar to my old boss, David Bartley. I looked at the guy and thought it was odd to see someone that looked so similar to David there at Chili's. The Voice said, "That is David Bartley, he is wearing a disguise so that people won't recognize him." I wondered why David would be there. The Voice said that he had come to see me. I didn't talk to him, because I was tired of falling for everything that The Voice said. I did tell Justin what I thought was going on. I said, "Justin, that guy over there looks like a guy I used to work for." Justin didn't have anything to say about it. I looked around the bar area and noticed another guy who looked like another David that I used to work with. This other guy looked very similar to David Barthowe from ETO/Architects. David Barthowe was the guy who had first interviewed me for my job at ETO. We had worked together on a lot of projects. I had thought about him many times since I left ETO. Once I saw the guy that looked like him, The Voice confirmed my suspicion. It said, "That is David Barthowe. He is also in disguise. He also wants to talk to you." I noticed that the guy who looked like David Barthowe was with two nice looking girls. I decided to go over and talk to him.

I walked up to his table and said, "You look just like my old boss. You aren't David Barthowe are you?" He smiled and said that he was not. He told me his name and asked me if I wanted to join him at his table. I said that I would. I started talking to the guy. I still thought that he really was David, and that he was just not admitting it for some reason. The girls at the table laughed every time I made a comment that let them know that I did not believe the guy when he told me that he was not David Barthowe. I said, "Well, I'm going to call you David, because I'm sure that's who you really are." The guy seemed willing to play along. I said, "David, you are supposed to be yelling at me and telling me to hurry up with what I'm working on." The guy said, "It sounds like David is an asshole." I told him that David was an asshole, but I really liked working with him. After a while, I finally started to believe that this guy might not be David Barthowe. I told the guy that I was sorry for not believing him. I told him that I had just had a lot of weird things happen to me lately and it wouldn't surprise me if people from my past started showing up there at Chili's. The guy didn't seem bothered by my weirdness. He kept talking to me and asking questions. He even ordered an appetizer and asked me if I would like to share some of it with him and the girls. I turned down the offer. I thanked him for putting up with me and I decided to leave the poor guy alone. Before I left, I told the guy where I was staying and wrote down my cell phone number and my hotel room number on a piece of paper and gave it to him. I told him that I would be back in my room later on that night if they wanted to stop by and hang out for a while. I was really hoping that he would bring the girls by my room, because they were very good looking and seemed interested in me. I never heard from any of them. My perception of people liking me was probably way off. They were probably just being polite and hoping to get me to leave them without any trouble. So, after giving the guy and his girls an invite to my room, I went back to the bar.

I told Justin that I had thought that guy was another guy I used to work with. Justin asked me why I thought people from Tallahassee would be there at Chili's on a Sunday night. I told him that I wasn't sure and that I didn't really think that those guys were the old Davids that I used to know. I was a little embarrassed about what I had just done with the guy that I thought was Davis Barthowe. I was also embarrassed that Justin now knew about it. I was afraid that I had made a fool of myself in front of him. So, after embarrassing my self at Chili's, I decided to go to a different bar that was just down the street from there. I got the impression that something was different between Justin and I at that point. I decided to get away from him for a while. Little did I know, that would be the last time I would ever see him.

I left Chili's and walked over to Sharky's Pool Hall. Sharky's was a pretty rough little bar and pool hall. They let people smoke inside. A lot of people came there on Friday and Saturday nights to get drunk and play pool. I walked in with the intention of just drinking some water at the bar and talking to the bartender that I noticed immediately after stepping inside. The bartender was a female who was pretty good looking. She had blonde hair and a nice body. I sat down at the bar and ordered a water. I talked with the bartender a little while as I drank my water. I don't remember what I said to her. I just remember The Voice telling me that the bartender was actually one of my relatives on my dad's side of the family. The Voice told me that the Ganns were working in places all over Lakeland and that most would be assisting the secret evil group in their future battles. The Voice said that this bartender was actually not working with those people and that she was actually helping the secret group that I was with. She seemed pretty friendly to me. I talked with her for a while then went outside for some reason. While I was outside The Voice gave me some new information about Sharky's. The Voice said that Sharky's was actually a place where a lot of the aliens that were living among us hung out. The Voice's description of Sharky's reminded me of the scene in the first Star Wars film where Obi Wan Kenobi and Luke Skywalker go to the bar on Tatooine. I imagined that Sharky's was a meeting place for extra terrestrials from all over the galaxy.

The Voice also told me that my cigarette smoking was something that would be useful once I arrived on the moon base. The Voice said that people on the moon base had been going outside and smoking cigarettes. They noticed that the smoke from the cigarettes and the secret buildings on the base were beginning to accumulate into an atmosphere on the moon that allowed for the existence of oxygen near the surface. The Voice said that the secret group had planned to form the moon into a planet that was capable of supporting life. The secret group had been creating oxygen on the moon for many years and there was now enough there that a person could go outside of the buildings for several minutes without a suit or breathing apparatus on. The Voice said that the smoke was somehow trapping the oxygen on the moon and keeping it near the surface. I know that this all sounds totally stupid, but at the time, I still fell for most of what The Voice told me. I lit up a cigarette and thought about how I might soon be on the moon doing the same thing. I walked back inside Sharky's and noticed a girl sitting at the bar who was not there when I walked out.

The girl was a slightly attractive blonde that resembled the girl that I had seen several days earlier in Gainesville at a gas station. She resembled the girl that The Voice had told me was one of the President's daughters. The Voice told me that this girl was the same girl I had run across earlier. She was the President's daughter and she was at Sharky's because her dad, George Bush, had told her to follow me until I agreed to look after her and her sister. I sat back down at the bar and watched the girl for a while. She was also sitting at the bar and had two guys with her. The Voice told me that the two guys were her bodyguards. One of the guys had a cowboy hat on and I kept hearing the girl call him Cowboy. The other guy was a younger Latino. I got the impression that he liked the girl. He probably was her boyfriend. The Voice said that he was just a bodyguard and that President Bush wanted me to replace the two guys that she was with. After watching the girl and listening to The Voice for several minutes, I decided to go talk to her. I wanted to acknowledge the President's daughter and see what she had to say.

I walked over to the girl and started a conversation by asking her where I knew her from. She said that she wasn't sure. I said, "You wouldn't be someone I have seen on television and in the papers would you?" She laughed and said that maybe she was. That was all I needed to hear to believe The Voice. I was sure that she was in fact the daughter of the President. I talked with her a little while. Again, I don't remember what we talked about. I just remember being so glad that I finally had some more proof that The Voice did tell the truth sometimes. I was sure that I was talking with the President's daughter. At one point, she and the Latino guy said that they had to go to the ATM that was just outside. I said, "Well, I need to go too. I'll go with you guys. That way you won't be alone. I'll help protect you." The girl laughed and probably thought I was just being weird or goofy. The truth is, I meant what I said. I thought that the President wanted me to protect his daughter. So, that was what I planned to do. Once I realized that the girl was George Bush's daughter, I was determined not to leave her side.

She and the Latino guy walked outside to the ATM and I walked right along with them. The two of them walked together, talking quietly so that I couldn't hear what they were saying. They were probably trying to figure out how to get away from me. The thought never crossed my mind. I stayed right behind them. I was sure that the girl wanted me to protect her. After they finished using the ATM, the guy said, "We're done. It's all yours." I said, "Well, I really don't need to use the ATM. I just wanted to make sure you guys were alright out here. You never know what might happen at night in Lakeland." I'm sure that little comment freaked them out. They walked on back into the bar without talking to me. I followed along behind them. When they sat back down at the bar, I sat right next to the girl. The Latino guy actually walked off for a while. The guy she called Cowboy, sat down beside me. He was talking to me for a while, but I wasn't really paying much attention to him. I was interested in talking with the daughter of the President. I kept asking her questions and talking to her about things that I don't remember. She seemed to like talking to me. At one point, she got a call from her mom and she said that she wanted me to talk to her mom. As she handed her phone to me, I thought that Laura Bush was on the other end. She handed me the phone and I said, "Hello?" The lady on the other end asked who I was. I told her that I was her daughter's new friend. I don't remember what else was said. I just remember that I was sure that I had just had a phone conversation with Laura Bush. At one point the girl took a picture of me with her camera phone. She said that she wanted a souvenir to remember me by. I figured that she would probably be showing my picture to important political figures and her friends. I already believed that I was more famous than she had ever been. People around the world had cheered for me. I had seen it on television. I thought that she wanted my picture like she might want a picture of her with a famous celebrity.

Later that night, the police came into Sharky's for some reason. I'm not sure why they were called up there. They were asking questions to the guy that the girl called Cowboy, and to some other people at the bar. I wouldn't be surprised if the Latino guy had called the police on me. But I'm not sure, because no one ever asked me any questions. I never saw them take anyone out of the bar that night. After walking around for maybe 15 minutes, they left.

After the police left, I continued talking to the girl at the bar. The Latino guy sat back down on the other side of her and started kissing her. I guess he wanted to give me the message that she was his girl. After seeing that, I still did not back off from her. I wasn't trying to start a relationship with her, I was just trying to get to know her, because I felt like I should know as much about her as I could if I was supposed to be protecting her and teaching her how to act properly, as her father had requested. Maybe thirty minutes after the police left, I was still rambling on to the girl at the bar, and Cowboy sat back down beside me. He started acting rude towards me. I don't remember what it was that he said, but he said something that let me know that he didn't appreciate how much attention I was giving to the girl at the bar. I figured that he was a body guard employed by the federal government and I didn't want to step on his toes. So, when I realized that I was irritating him, I backed off from the girl. I figured if President Bush wanted me to look after his daughter, he would at least have to get rid of her bodyguards himself. I was not going to go over their heads. So, I got up from my seat and went back over to the bartender and started talking to her again. I talked to her for just a few minutes and then decided that I did not want to be there anymore. I didn't like the tension that I was getting from Cowboy. He kept looking at me and it made me a little nervous. So, I decided to leave. I left a $100 bill on the bar for the bartender and walked up to the girl that I thought was the daughter of the President and told her I was leaving. She told me good-bye and I walked out. I got almost out of the parking lot and realized that I could not find my car keys. I thought that they were in my pocket when I had come in. Now they were not there. The Voice said that Cowboy had taken them. I was instantly furious. I thought that he had taken them just to pester me. I remembered him brushing up against me a few times as I was talking to the girl at the bar. I figured that he must have somehow taken them out of my pocket without me realizing.

So, I stormed back into the bar. I didn't care if he was a federal bodyguard. He had just messed with a larger power than himself. I was ready to fight the guy if I found out that he had my keys. I walked up to him and said, "I think you have something that belongs to me." He said, "Really. What?" I said, "Do you have my car keys?" He said, "No. How would I have your car keys?" I said, "They were in my pocket and now they're gone. Someone here has them! Who did you give them to?" He said, "Look dude, I don't know what you're on, but I don't think anyone here has your keys." I said, "I'm not on anything! I know you have my keys!" He said, "I think you need to leave." I said, "You think I need to leave huh?" He said, "Yes. Leave." I stood there for a minute and The Voice said, "Do what he says." I said, "Alright. If you want me to leave, then I will." So I did.

I walked back out and headed for the hotel. The whole way back I tried to remember where my car keys could have gone. I believed Cowboy when he said that he did not have them. Something about the way he talked sounded pretty honest. And he didn't get angry with me even after I accused him of taking them several times. I figured that he was probably a federal bodyguard and was not someone for me to mess with. So, I kept walking to the hotel. I couldn't figure out who had taken my keys.

I got back to my room and the first thing that I saw was my car keys sitting on top of the dresser. I complained to The Voice. I said, "Damn it! You just about got my ass kicked back there at the bar by telling me that guy had my keys! I am tired of this game you are playing! Stop screwing around with me! You are going to get me arrested or killed with this bull crap game you keep playing!" I laid down on the bed and thought about going to sleep. Then The Voice said, "We are going to take you to the moon base tonight." I said, "Yeah. I really believe it." with sarcasm. The Voice told me to look out the window at the rooms on the top floor of the hotel wing that was connected to my wing. I didn't notice anything unusual about the top floor. The Voice said, "See the expansion joint between the top floor and the floor below? The top floor rooms are actually spacecraft that can lift off of the hotel and travel into space. Your room is like that. You will be making a trip to the moon tonight when you are sleeping. When you wake up, you will be on the moon." I laid there in my bed, not even excited about what The Voice was telling me. I was becoming very tired of The Voice. It had told me so many lies and caused me so much trouble. I just wanted it all to end. I at least wanted a little break so that I could recuperate from all the weirdness of the last few weeks. Every day had become progressively more bizarre. Now everything was about aliens, monsters, God, Satan, the moon, and the rest of the universe. I had come to believe so many wacky ideas. I felt like I was going to die soon. I was so tired. My chest had been hurting for several days. I thought that I might end up having a heart attack before this was all over. But The Voice had no mercy. It kept on delivering more information, no matter how tired I was.

The Voice said that the idea of a compartmentalized building had actually been taken from one of my projects when I was I college at FAMU. I had designed a mall that had stores that could roll off onto an elevator and be placed at new locations within the mall. The Voice said that the secret group had seen my idea and used it when they built this hotel. The Voice said that all of the top floor rooms were individual compartments that could propel themselves into space.

The Voice freaked me out again when it told me that there were invisible children in my room who were going to be traveling with me. The Voice said that the children were sitting in the corners of the room and that I would not be able to see or hear them. I walked over to the corners of the room and tried to feel around to see if I touched anything. I never felt anything. The idea of little invisible kids in my room disturbed me for some reason. I laid there on the bed and wished that they would leave.

The Voice was not my only problem that night. The other thing that was bugging me was hearing noises that I thought were coming from the room next door. I kept hearing things banging against the wall and people talking loudly. I decided that I could not sleep at that hotel that night. I decided to go to my car. That would become my last act of madness as a free member of society.

I left my room and took with me several bags of junk that I had brought in with me. I decided that I was going to move out all my things and take them back to my car. I had gotten a gut full of that hotel. Too many weird things had happened there. It seemed like every time I was alone in the quiet hotel room was when The Voice was doing its best to keep me from sleeping. I didn't notice it as much during the day when I was away from the hotel. So, I hoped that if I got to my car and slept there, The Voice would leave me alone.

As I walked to the elevator, I decided that I was going to have a little revenge on the people in that hotel. I wasn't sure who it was that had caused me so much trouble, but The Voice had told me that the hotel was a monitoring station for people like me. The Voice had said that a lot of other people had come there before me and had been observed just the way that I had been observed while I was at the hotel. The Voice said that some of those people ended up working with the secret group, just like I was going to be doing. But The Voice also said that other people, ones who were deemed useless, were sometimes killed by the secret group. The Voice said that those types were usually people that didn't cooperate with the training. I told The Voice that I wanted to cooperate but I was just needing to rest and I would continue their training as soon as they let me get some sleep. I told The Voice that I hated the scientists who were watching me when I was in the bathroom and through the mirrors of my bedroom. I said that the hotel was too invasive of my privacy. I said that I was going to sleep in my car, if that meant that I was not cooperating, I didn't care.

I decided that I would have my revenge on the people of that hotel by making some noise there. It was around 2:00 am when I decided to leave. I had a whistle that I had bought somewhere along my little journey. I had been wearing it around my neck since I arrived in Lakeland. I decided I would walk down a hallway on each floor and blow my whistle as I walked down the hall. The whistle was very loud. I hoped that it would wake everyone up. So, I walked a ways down the hall on my floor and blew the whistle as loudly as I could. Then I decided not to take the elevator, but instead go down the stair. I blew my whistle in the stairwell. The bare concrete steps and walls created an amplifier that made the whistle echo even louder.

I walked out onto each floor and blew my whistle in the halls. I didn't hang around to see if anyone came out of their rooms. I just blew my whistle and kept on moving.

I walked out into the lobby with all my bags and the lady at the front desk asked what I was doing. I told her that I could not sleep in my room and that I was leaving to sleep in my car. She looked concerned.

I walked to my car and unloaded my bags into it. I saw my machete and decided to put it on my belt. The Voice had told me that I might be in danger. So, I thought the machete would be good protection against whatever came my way. I imagined myself decapitating a person or some creature that came out of the dark to attack me. I put on a hooded jacket and my Darth Vader mask and also grabbed a lantern that I had bought when I was camping. I turned the lantern on and walked back down South Florida Avenue to the hotel. I did not need a lantern. There was plenty of light from the streetlights. I just liked how freaky I probably looked as I walked down the road with my Darth Vader helmet, my lantern, and my machete. As I walked back to the hotel, The Voice told me that there were people stealing things out of my room at the hotel. The Voice said that these people were agents of the evil group. I had taken all of the toys that I had set up as my protectors, and placed them in a bag. The Voice said that since the toys were gone, the evil agents came into my room and wanted to take all the sticky notes that I had written information on. I started to hurry back to the hotel. I said in a loud voice, "Someone better stop me because I'm about to kill somebody!" I really meant it. I think if someone had happened to be in room when I walked in, there was a good chance that I might have just whacked them with my machete. I was fully convinced by what The Voice had said, even after so many blatant lies. I still fell for most everything The Voice told me. I thank God that I was stopped before I was able to get into my room.

I walked into the lobby with the Darth Vader helmet on, the machete on my belt, and my lantern still on. The lady at the front desk looked at me and she looked terrified. I didn't say anything to her. I just walked up the stairs to my room. I arrived at my door and realized that my key card would not open the door. I swiped it several times and got no response from the card reader. I decided to take off my helmet and go back down to the front desk. The Voice said, "I told you this would happen. You should have kept participating with the training. Now, there is no telling what they are going to do with you." I was a little scared by that comment. I walked back down the stairs.

When I arrived in the lobby, there were two policemen talking with the lady at the front desk. I walked up to the desk and told the lady that I could not get in my room. One of the police officers said, "Is this him?" The lady said, "Yes." I looked at the lady behind the desk and felt totally betrayed. I had not done anything to her, but I knew in that instant what was about to happen. The police officer said, "Sir, why do you have a machete on you?" I said, "I was taking my things to my car. I can't sleep here. It's too noisy in the room next to me. I just want to sleep in my car. I had the machete for protection because I didn't feel safe walking outside at night." The police officer said, "Do you know that it is illegal to carry a machete around?" I said, "If it's illegal, then why is it that I can carry it around at any state park and buy it at every Wal-Mart in the country?" He said, "The city of Lakeland had an ordinance against carrying a blade over 7" long." I said, "That sounds ridiculous to me. People can carry a concealed gun, but they can't carry a machete?" He said, "That's the law. Now please give me your machete." So, I took it off my belt and handed it to him. He said, "Can I see what is in your pockets?" I emptied out my pockets and he saw the Star Wars figures, the Palm Pilot, the cigarettes, the lighters, and everything else that I had been lugging around. He said, "What are you doing with those toys in your pocket?" I said, "They are just a good luck charm. I carry them with me wherever I go. Is that a crime in Lakeland too?" He said, "Alright, we're going to give you a ride to the hospital tonight. O.K." I said, "I don't need to go to the hospital." I knew what was about to happen. The police officer said, "I'm afraid I'm going to have to take you there to be evaluated. You are being Baker Acted. Do you know what that means?" I said, "Yes. This isn't the first time that I've been Baker Acted."

I begged the police officers not to take me to the hospital. I kept asking them what I had done wrong. They told me that I had upset the lady behind the front desk. She had told them about me leaving the hotel in the early hours of the morning. She might have mentioned me blowing my whistle in the halls too. The police said that she had told them several strange things about me, and that was why I had to be evaluated. I kept asking them to just take me to my car so that I could sleep. They told me that I would be able to get much better rest at the hospital. They asked me to put my hands behind my back and then they handcuffed me and led me to the police cruiser outside. I got in and we drove to Lakeland Regional Hospital. I don't think I said a word to them the whole way there. I kept trying to talk to The Voice telepathically. I kept asking The Voice what was going to happen next. The Voice finally said, "Don't worry, the police are taking you to the hospital because that is where you are going to meet up with some agents from the secret group. We have arranged transportation for you there. You will be taken from the hospital to Kennedy Space Center. A space shuttle is going to leave there tonight and take you to the moon base." After hearing that, I was actually excited. I then realized that I wasn't really being Baker Acted again, I was about to be taken aboard the space shuttle.

Chapter 61: The PRC, Round Two

We arrived at the hospital and the police gave me to a nurse who walked me back to a room where there were several hospital beds. She told me to lie down on one of them. It reminded me of the time that I was taken to the hospital in Tallahassee. I laid down on one of the beds that was propped up on the back, so that I could watch what was going on in the hall outside the room that I was in. I saw that there were two police officers standing guard outside my room. I remember telling them that they should let me go. I told them that they shouldn't listen to whoever was telling them to keep me there. I kept telling them that the real crazy people were the hospital workers who I thought were probably working with the secret evil group. The officers wouldn't acknowledge me. They just acted like I wasn't even talking to them. They would talk to each other, but not me. It made me angry. I remember telling them that they were cowards if they were following the orders of the hospital staff. Finally, a nurse came into my room and told me to lie on my stomach. I saw a needle in her hand. I said, "Don't tell me that you are about to stick that in me." She said, "Just roll over or we will have to force you to." I rolled over and she stuck me with the needle in my butt cheek. I remember saying, "Why do you guys love to drug everyone up. This is so ridiculous. I haven't done anything wrong and you're treating me like a rabid animal." The nurse gave me the shot and told me to just lie down and relax. The shot was apparently some kind of sedative. It wasn't long after she gave me the shot that I started feeling very tired. The last thing that I remember was The Voice telling me that there was a type of board on the roof of the hospital that was actually a vehicle that could take me to the moon.

The Voice said that this board looked like a surfboard, only it had an engine on the back that could propel it into space. I imagined myself riding a surfboard through the sky. That sounded like a pretty scary idea to me. What if I fell off? The Voice said that there were boots that my feet went into that kept me secured to the board. That still sounded pretty scary. The Voice also said that there was a suit that I had to wear that would keep me warm and supply me with oxygen. I was so tired that I told The Voice that they had better stick with the plan to transport me to the space shuttle. I told The Voice that I was too tired to fly myself to the moon that night. The Voice said that the space shuttle was no longer an option for me. I had to get myself on that board if I wanted to meet the secret group. I laid there, struggling to stay awake, just a little while longer. I realized that there was one more thing that I would have to do if I ever wanted to meet the secret group. I had to somehow get to the roof and get on that board. I watched the policemen who were standing guard over me. I kept hoping that they would walk off so that I could escape to the roof. Instead, they just kept standing there. My eyelids kept growing heavier. I felt totally panicked. I realized that my only option to escape and meet the secret group was rapidly slipping away. The drug was overtaking my system. Within minutes, the panic and anxiety were overcome by the power of the drug. The bed that I was laying in began to feel more and more comfortable. The warmth of the blanket against the cold hospital air made me want to stay where I was. The thought of getting out of that bed and climbing onto the roof quickly became something that seemed less important than just resting for a bit. I thought, "I'll just rest here for a minute, then I'll figure out how to escape." After that, I fell asleep.

I was awakened by a nurse who told me that she was going to take me to my room. She had me get out of bed and follow her to a room that was down the hall from where I had fallen asleep. There was no one else in the room. I walked in and laid down on the bed. I remember thinking, "Rest a little longer, then find a way to the roof." and went right back to sleep.

The next time that I woke up, it was light outside. I'm actually not sure if it was morning or afternoon. I sat in my bed and looked around the room. It was a much nicer room than any of the rooms at the PRC of the BHC. I wondered if I was now actually on the moon base. I could hear sounds outside my room. I could tell that I was hearing the conversation s of people walking around outside my room. I tried asking The Voice what was going on but I never got any response from it. I wondered if I had been abandoned. I kept trying to speak to The Voice, but it would not reply back. Eventually, I decided to walk out of my room and see what the heck was going on. I walked down a hallway to a window where a lady was sitting in an enclosed room. I asked her what I was supposed to be doing. She said to go back to my room and someone would come talk to me in a while. So, I went back to my room. I laid back down in my bed and began to wonder if I was at the hospital or if I was at the moon base. I started to wonder if I was just at the hospital, if nothing more had happened except the obvious, another Baker Act. The thought depressed me. I began to realize that The Voice may have just played its last trick on me.

After some time passed, a woman came to my room and asked me if I was hungry. I told her that I was and she brought me a tray of breakfast type food. She told me that I had a choice of staying at the hospital or being taken to Peace River Center in Bartow. I told her that I didn't want to go to either of those places. She said that those were my only two options. I was not going to be allowed to leave until a doctor had evaluated me and authorized me to leave. I told the nurse that I wanted to go back to the PRC. She said that she would have someone come pick me up shortly and take me there. I ate my breakfast and not long afterwards, two guys came to my room and told me they were going to give me a ride to the PRC.

I followed the guys to their van and we drove to the PRC in Bartow. I don't remember talking to the guys on the way there. I was starting to go into a little state of shock because it was becoming very apparent that I was definitely not at the moon base. I kept trying to keep the fantasy world alive. I told myself that perhaps the entire section of Polk County between Lakeland and Bartow had been transported to the moon. That was the only way that I could explain how I was in a van driving from Lakeland to Bartow. I kept trying to telepathically speak with The Voice, but it never answered. I was asking it if my theory about two entire towns being relocated to the moon, while I slept, was possible. The Voice would not respond. It made me sad. I started to realize that I actually was all alone again.

We got to the PRC and the guys took me to the same entrance that I had been led to by the police officers after my dad had Baker Acted me several weeks earlier. I was passed over to the PRC staff and the guys left. A nurse walked me on into the area where I had spent a couple weeks the last time I was there.

I walked into the dayroom and sat on a plastic couch there. I looked around at all the crazy people. There were a couple of people who were still there from the last time that I had been put in the PRC. One of them was Jose. I walked over to him and asked him why he was still there. He said that he had got into a fight with another guy after I left and they had forced him to stay. I had been out of the PRC for about three weeks. I was surprised to see him there still. There were a couple of others that I had seen before. One of the others was the girl that I thought was Jen, the girl from the bar in Tallahassee. She was still there and still looked disfigured. She told me that she lived in some state halfway house and had tried to run away and that was why she had been brought back to the PRC. I began to realize that I must have been wrong about her being the Jen from Tallahassee. She was just another poor mentally challenged person, not a host body for the brain of a beautiful girl that I had met in Tallahassee. It was upsetting for me to realize that I had been so wrong about her. The more I talked to her, the more I realized that she was definitely not who I had thought she was.

Most of the people there at the PRC were new faces to me. The crazy black lady who had claimed she was involved with a voodoo cult was not there. One new person that I came to enjoy talking to was a lady in her mid 40's with blonde hair and glasses. Her name was Michelle. She usually wore outfits that looked like something a dental hygienist might wear to work. What she wore was not exactly scrubs, but they were close to it. She told me that she actually was a nurse. She seemed very intelligent and was definitely all there. I felt comfortable talking to her because I thought she was about the most sane person there. She told me that she had been put at the PRC because a guy had been stalking her. She said that she called the police and told them that someone was following her everywhere she went. She said that the police came to her house and she became hysterical when she talked with them. She said that they Baker Acted her because she got so upset in front of them. She was very angry about being there. She never took the meds that they gave her. She would usually hide them under her tongue or between her teeth and gums in the back of her mouth. Then, after she walked off from the nurse who gave us our drugs, she would spit the pills out and throw them in a garbage can. She would tell me how stupid she thought all the people were who worked there. She reminded me of myself.

I had felt the same way until I met Dr. Barnes and she prescribed me an anti-depressant several months earlier. I knew that the anti-depressant helped pull me out my depression. So, I did have a little belief that some of the drugs they gave us could help a person. But, I still had stopped taking all my medication long before I went in the PRC the first time. I also stopped taking my meds as soon as I got out of the PRC the first time. I didn't like the way they made me feel. I was always tired. Even after sleeping for 10-12 hours, I would wake up and feel exhausted. The drug they had me taking, Zyprexa 20 mg twice a day, just totally zonked me out. I refused to let myself go through life feeling like a zombie. So, I would quit taking Zyprexa every time I got away from the doctors.

Michelle and I usually sat together at every occasion where we had to join the group of crazy people. That included all meals, all classes, and most of our free time. She was a very friendly lady. I remember telling her that I wished that she were younger because I thought she was a person that would make a great partner. But she was in her mid-40's. I thought that was too old of a person for me to think of as a girlfriend. Michelle told me that she had a long term relationship with two guys and they both died. One died in a car accident. I don't remember what happened to the other. But, Michelle said that she was no longer interested in finding a partner. She said she had felt like she was going to die from sadness each time those guys had died. She said she didn't want to ever have to go through something like that again. I understood. It sounded like Michelle had been traumatized too severely by losing her partner twice. I was actually relieved to hear her say that she was not interested in me as a boyfriend. That made it easy to talk to her and just think of her as a friend.

Another person that got my attention at the PRC was a guy named Travis. He was the scariest person that I had ever come across at any of my times in rehab centers. Travis had a big circular scar depression on his throat that looked like he had a tracheotomy at one time. When Travis talked it sounded like a raspy whisper. His was a scary sounding voice. When he talked he could only say a few words, then he would have to take a deep breath. When he breathed in, between words, it sounded like a struggle for him to take a breath. There was always a hoarse wheezing in his breaths. That alone was pretty scary. To add to it, he was violently insane. He was always angry about something and would make threats to the staff and the rest of us.

One day, I had just finished eating and Michelle and I were talking. I turned to look in the direction where I heard Travis yelling about something. Travis said, "What are you looking at mother f@$!er?" I said, "I'm trying to figure out what has you so upset this time Travis." He said, "I will kill your ass mother f@$!er!" and he marched up to me and head butted me as hard as he could. I was not prepared for him to do that. When his head banged against mine, I saw stars and blacked out a little. I lost my balance and fell back onto the table and then onto the ground. I laid there for just a couple seconds. I wanted to get back on my feet as soon as I could because I was afraid that he was going to start kicking me. I stood up and said, "Whoah! Travis! What the hell is wrong with you?" By that time, two orderlies had run into the room and grabbed Travis and dragged him off. Some nurses came up to me and asked what had happened. I told them that I didn't know. I said that I had just finished eating and was talking to Michelle when Travis walked up and head butted me for no reason. The nurses gave me an ice pack to put on my head. They told me that Travis was going to be put in isolation for a few days and that I wouldn't have to worry about him. I said, "Well, I really appreciate you guys putting me in here with a bunch of screwballs like Travis. You people are all real top-notch staff. I'm going to sue you guys for letting this happen to me."

That was my favorite threat to issue every time I was in a rehab center. I always talked about how I was going to sue the rehab center for mistreating me. Lots of people walked around talking about the same thing. I guess we were all a lot like criminals in prison. I've watched a lot of prison system documentaries and I've noticed a trend that almost everyone in prison claims that they are innocent and that they plan to retaliate by suing the system when they get out. We all liked to talk the same way in the rehab center. Most of us said that we had not done anything and were being mistreated in the rehab center. We all had plans to take the PRC to court for treating us so badly.

I can't really give a complete chronological report of what happened that second time at the PRC, because they were hitting me with serious drugs for most of the time I was there. I think I was taking 40 mg of Zyprexa when I first got put back in the PRC. A dosage that high made my perception of reality slip away in another direction. Now, instead of having racing thoughts and voices in my head, I just wanted to sleep all the time. The meds made it so that I could not talk right. I started slurring my speech and stuttering every time I talked. I also had trouble just piecing together the right words to say. So, most of the time, I didn't do a lot of talking.

I do remember one thing that happened shortly after I was admitted to the PRC. It occurred shortly after I arrived. I remember being very scared that something terrible was about to happen to me. I don't remember what caused me to believe that I was in danger. Like I said, my memory of that time has still not come back to me completely. It probably never will. I hope it stays that way. There are some things that are better off forgotten. Anyway, I was scared for my life for some reason. I begged the PRC staff to let me make a phone call. I wanted to call my dad and beg him to come get me. I was afraid that if I stayed much longer, I would end up dead. One of the orderlies finally gave in and walked me to a room with a phone. I picked up the phone and dialed my parents' cell phone. My dad picked up. I could hear a lot of people talking in the background. I didn't ask who they were. I thought that I already realized what I was hearing. I just went ahead and begged my dad to come get me. I told him that there were people there at the PRC who wanted to kill me. I told him that if he did not come get me, I might end up getting killed. It was the hardest thing for me to hear when I realized that he did not seem alarmed by my news. He actually sounded a little irritated with me for calling him. I was used to the tone. He always seemed irritated with me. But, I felt like this might be the last time that I ever spoke with him, unless he came and rescued me from the terrors of the PRC. I begged him to come get me. He told me that nothing bad was going to happen to me. He said that the people working there were only there to help me. He said that he could not come get me even if he wanted to because I was being held there for an evaluation. He said that the law would not allow him to take me away from the PRC because the police had put me there. He got off the phone shortly afterwards. I wanted to cry. I felt completely helpless and alone and was scared for my life. I don't remember what happened afterwards or why I thought my life was in danger. The PRC staff probably gave me some type of sedative to calm me down and shut me up. The rest of that event is a blur. I only remember the phone call to my dad and how helpless I felt after he got off the phone. There is one other thing that I remember about that call.

I remember where I thought my dad was and what I thought he was doing when I called him. I had heard several people talking and laughing in the background when I called him. I had already been told by The Voice that my parents were working for the secret evil group. I had not been given an explanation as to why they had become mixed up with them. I did not think that my parents were evil. I just thought that they were confused as to who they were working for. The Voice told me that my parents would become high-ranking government officials before all the battles between good and evil had been fought. When I heard all the people in the background, as I talked with my dad, I assumed that I was hearing my dad at some political gathering. The Voice had told me that my dad was going to try to become the next mayor of Bartow. The Voice said that my dad would begin his rise to power as the mayor of Bartow and would quickly climb the political ladder to become a powerful member within the United States government. When I heard the chatter in the background, I thought that I was hearing a party that my parents were hosting to gain support to get my dad elected as mayor of Bartow. I never mentioned this to my dad as we talked. I was too concerned about saving my own life. I didn't want to mention to him where I thought he was at and what I thought he was doing. I was afraid that if I mentioned it, he would only deny it and become angry. That would lessen my chance of having him rescue me. So, I never mentioned it to him.

There was a guy that caught my attention at the PRC. He was an orderly that worked there. He was a white guy that looked like he was in his late forties or early fifties. For, some reason, I got the idea that he was the father of the girl that I had met at Crisper's in Bartow a few weeks earlier, Rachel. The Voice was still talking to me briefly here and there. The Voice told me that this guy was her dad. I remember thinking that he had come to the PRC disguised as an orderly. The Voice said that he wanted to ask me to take care of Rachel because he knew that the end of the world was approaching and the secret group had told him that she was going to be one of my wives once the world had to be repopulated. I had come to think of Rachel as too immature to be someone that I was interested in.

Before I left for my camping trip at Rainbow Springs I had gone up to where Rachel worked at Beef O'Brady's. I remember sitting at the bar and seeing her working that day. I tried to get her to come talk to me, but she kept blowing me off and acting like she was busy. Then, at one point, she walked over to another guy at the bar and started talking to him. The guy she talked with was a pretty rough looking dude who was covered with tattoos and had piercings on his ears and on his eyebrow. I thought that if that guy was Rachel's type, then I didn't want anything to do with her. I remember her talking to the guy and he kept looking over at me and smiling. I got the point and left. I realized that Rachel must be his girl.

To further remove me from Rachel, I had a telephone conversation with her dad when I was driving up to Rainbow Springs. Rachel's dad called me and told me that his daughter had told him about receiving a strange note from me. He was talking about the note that I left that was attached to a list of items to bring on a campout and a beach ball. Rachel's dad asked me how old I was. I told him and he said that I was too old to be dating his daughter. He asked me if I had ever been married. I told him I was actually in the process of getting a divorce. He said that he wanted me to stay away from Rachel. I told him that I wasn't sure I would be able to do that, because I had a hard time being told what to do. He said, "I tell you what, you meet me at Beef O' Brady's anytime you want. I'll help you figure out that when I tell you not to do something, you had better not do it!" He said this as a threat. He also told me to call him when I wanted to meet him at Beef O' Brady's. It sounded like an invitation to a fight. I told him that I wasn't that interested in her and that I was sorry for getting him upset. He said it was no problem but that he didn't want me up at Beef O' Brady's again. I told him that it wasn't his business to tell me where I could and could not go. He said, "If I see you up there, you are going to have a problem!" and hung up. I called him right back. He answered and said, "What the hell are you calling me for?!? I told you to leave me and Rachel alone. Don't call here again!" and he hung up again. So, I let it go. I figured that a relationship with a girl, whose dad acted like a maniac, would be pretty miserable. So, I stopped thinking about Rachel.

But now here was a guy at the PRC who I thought was Rachel's dad. I remember thinking, "So, you figured out who I am and now you want to crawl back to me and beg me to take care of your daughter." Every time I saw or talked to that guy, I thought I was talking to Rachel's dad. He was very friendly towards me. I kept thinking that he was trying to be so nice because he felt bad for the way he had yelled at me on the phone. I never mentioned anything about Rachel to him. I had already made up my mind that Rachel was his problem, not mine. I had seen her hanging around with some rough looking people. I figured that she was probably pretty wild. I didn't want anything to do with her.

A girl that I still was interested in, though, was Jen from the Chili's in Lakeland. There was a girl at the PRC who I thought was related to her. I thought that the girl might be Jen's sister. She had blonde hair and looked a little like her. I remember talking with that girl and sitting by her in some of the classes we had to take. She was a nice girl, but there was something wrong with her. I could tell. The way she talked was not normal. I thought that she might be putting on an act because she wanted to blend in with the population at the PRC. I thought that she was really there to report back to Jen about what was going on there at the PRC with me. She was only there for a week or so and then she left. I figured that she had probably gone back to report to Jen.

I also still thought about the Jen from Tallahassee. I wondered if she was still watching me through the cameras that were all over the PRC. I thought that she was still keeping track of me and waiting for the right moment to show up and tell me that she loved me and wanted to be my wife.

There was a day when some of the employees were putting up a film on the windows of the room where we had our classes. The film made the windows look like stained glass. There was a pattern on the translucent film that looked like the different colored panes of glass that you might see in a cathedral. They gave the room a nice look. I thought that they were decorating the room for a ceremony. The Voice told me that the staff was preparing the room for a wedding. The Voice said that there was going to be a ceremony and that I would have to chose a wife at it. The Voice said that both Jen's were going to be there, as well as Rachel. I told The Voice that I intended to marry both of the Jens and tell Rachel that she could live with us after the world underwent the dramatic change, after the great battles between good and evil. I imagined that I would find myself in a world where the entire population had been wiped out. All that would be left were the girls and myself, and maybe a few others scattered across the planet. I imagined that I would be the leader of a new civilization that would emerge from my wives and I. I wasn't sure where the task of taking the place of the Devil fit into this whole picture. I thought that maybe I would be thought of as the Devil, by the other people who were left on the planet.

I watched the employees put up the stained glass patterned film and imagined myself at a wedding, perhaps that same day. The Voice told me that the wedding ceremony was going to take place within a couple days. Several days went by and there was no sign of any wedding. We just attended our classes and went about the usual routine. I finally realized that The Voice had lied to me again. There never was supposed to be a wedding. It was just another delusion. Once I realized this, it made me pretty sad. I realized that the girls that I had chased after and dreamed about had never wanted anything to do with me. Their love was all just a figment of my imagination.

One scary thing happened on an early morning shortly after I arrived at the PRC the second time. I was asleep in my bed in a room that I was sharing with four other guys. I remember hearing a buzzing sound that woke me up. I opened my eyes and a blinding light was coming from a light fixture in the room I was in. There was a nurse at the door. She had turned on the light. She said, "Scott, will you come with me please." I remember feeling heat from the light fixture and hearing a buzzing sound. It felt like I was standing in front of a heater. I wondered if that light was some special type of fixture that could actually burn people to death in their room. I remember following the nurse to a nurse's station and she gave me some pills and then I went back to my room and went right back to sleep. The next day I thought I got an understanding of what the PRC really did with that light.

That next day, I saw a patient go into a room. A few minutes later I heard that patient in his room screaming and yelling. The door was closed. A little while later, I saw a guy come walking down the hall with a cardboard box on a dolly. He went in to the room where I had heard the guy screaming earlier. He came back out a while later and I saw him pulling the cardboard box on his dolly and he left. I never again saw the patient that had walked into his room earlier. I thought that I had just seen a patient go in his room and get burned alive by that light fixture that had woken me up in the early morning hours of that same day. I thought he had walked into his room, the light had come on, and he disintegrated from the intense heat. I thought that the guy with the cardboard box had come in and swept what was left of that patient into the cardboard box and walked back out with his remains in the box. The thought scared me to death. I realized that the PRC staff could do the same thing to me if they felt like it. I was terrified.

I spent most of my free time drawing pictures of the weird information I had heard from The Voice and seen with my own eyes. I drew pictures of dinosaurs with robotic attachments on their heads and other parts of their bodies. I drew a design of a city for the future. It showed a tower that rose above the tops of the trees. On top of the tower was a giant platform. On the platform was a city that was covered by a translucent dome. I thought it would be necessary to build the cities of the future like fortresses. The elevated city kept all its occupants high above the mouths of the dinosaurs and other creatures that lived on the surface below. The domed roof over the city was there to protect it from chemical attacks and the weapons of the aliens that I imagined would be attacking us. I intended the dome to be made of some unknown advanced material or perhaps an energy field, like the ones in the Star Wars movies. Yes, even though the drugs were begging to slow me down, I still had not come out of my fantasy. The Voice still talked to me. That kept me going.

I drew other pictures that described the craziness in my head. One of the most terrible was a picture of people being sent down a conveyor belt. The people were strapped to a belt and were then dumped into a machine. On the other side of the machine, I drew Mc Donald's hamburgers, Taco Bell tacos, and KFC chicken coming out. I wrote a note at the top that said, "Humans. They taste like chicken." The drawing showed a machine that converted people into fast food. The Voice had told me that this was going on. The Voice said that the evil group had been gathering up homeless people, people deemed as having mental disabilities, and others; and taking them to a processing plant where they were turned into meat that was cooked at the fast food restaurants. The Voice said that was how the fast food companies kept their prices down. The Voice said that the agenda of the fast food companies was really to cause people to get a disease similar to Mad Cow Disease. By having humans eat humans, we would lose our sanity and become followers of the evil group. I drew lots of other pictures. Most were just as bizarre as the ones I mentioned.

Some of the things I drew were actually neat. I wish that I had saved them. I drew several houses while I was at the PRC. Some of them were bad, but some were pretty nice. I usually drew the houses three dimensionally. So, the drawings were pretty cool to me. I don't know what ever became of those drawings. I kept them all in a stack and carried them with me almost everywhere I went. But, somewhere along the way, they disappeared. I have never seen them since I left the PRC. I don't know if the staff took them, or if one of the patients took them.

One big let down for me happened shortly after I got to the PRC. I remember standing in the dayroom on a day when the sky was very overcast and looked like a major storm was approaching. I remember looking out the window and thinking, "Please send me a tornado to rip this building apart." I was asking the secret group to create a tornado with their weather controlling device. I hoped that the tornado would tear the roof off the building and I could escape. I stood there for a long time watching the clouds. They seemed to be circulating near the PRC. I was sure that a tornado was about to come at my request. A girl who worked at the PRC said, "Is there something funny outside?" I was smiling because I believed that the secret group had heard my request and was following my order. I told the girl, "No.

Nothing outside is funny. What's outside is dangerous. You might want to take cover because a tornado is about to rip this building wide open." The girl said, "What makes you think that a tornado is coming?" I said, "I just know. If you don't believe me, just stick around. You'll see." I was smiling the whole time I was talking. The girl said, "Well, I sure hope you're wrong about the tornado. That would be terrible." I said, "No it wouldn't because if a tornado hits this building, I'm leaving." She laughed and said, "You can't leave until the doctor says you can leave. Remember?" I said, "I work for people who are much more powerful than your doctors. If they want me to leave, I will." She laughed again and walked off. I stood there for a long time and stared at the sky. I was sure that a tornado would come down from the clouds and tear the building to pieces and leave me without a scratch, to walk away to freedom. The tornado never came. It was another reminder that The Voice and the secret group did not do what I wanted. I was their tool. They were not mine. I still believed that the secret group was real. But my faith in them was slipping away, day by day.

There was also a day when I realized that Jose was not who I had thought he was. I had thought that he was some agent of the secret group. I thought he was a doctor that performed the surgery on me to give me my special vision, the vision that had allowed me to see things that others could not. One day we were talking and Jose told me how he made his living. He said that he owned a company that sold prepaid minutes for cell phones. Jose said that he had a machine that printed the cards and he had agreements with service providers to sell airtime. He said that he also bought produce from South America and sold it in the United States. He said that he would buy enough produce to fill several semi trucks and then he would have it shipped to the U.S. for sale over here. He said that he sold the produce to local vendors who then sold it to their customers. I asked Jose how much money it took to get started in something like that. He said that if I invested $5,000 he could make me $10,000. I told him that I wanted in. I asked him to buy me $5,000 worth of produce and connect me with some sellers when we got out of the PRC. He said that he would be glad to. I told him that I would write him a contract that I agreed to pay him $5,000 and he would purchase the produce for me. I got out a piece of paper and wrote up some lame contract. I then went to the nurse's desk and asked them to make a copy of the contract for me. One of the nurses took my paper and read it. She said, "Oh no. You're not allowed to do this kind of thing in here. Where is Jose?" She came walking out and went over to Jose and started getting on to him. She said, "Jose, I have told you about trying to take advantage of people in here. Don't let me catch you trying to do something like this again." Then she tore up the contract that I had written and threw it in the trash. She said, "Scott, you need to stay away from Jose. He is trying to con you out of your money. Don't listen to anything he tells you. He is trying to steal from you." I let her walk away and said to Jose, "I'm sorry about that. I still want to give you the money when we get out. Who wouldn't want to double their money?" He smiled and thanked me.

After having that little talk, I began to think that Jose was not the doctor that I had believed he was. I realized that he was just a guy who was at the PRC for some reason that I didn't know about. He didn't make his money with the secret group. He made it selling produce and phone cards. He never talked about anything mysterious or related to any of the things that I had come to believe. He was just an average guy with some type of mental disorder. Even though I realized that he was not an agent of the secret group, I still liked him. We spent a lot of time together when I was at the PRC.

We all had to meet with a psychiatrist about once a week. One day I had a meeting with Dr. Chandry, one of the PRC psychiatrists who worked in the unit that I had been assigned to. Dr. Chandry was a middle eastern man in his early to mid 40's. I remember that I immediately hated him for several reasons. The main thing that I didn't like about him was his way of talking to me. He seemed very condescending and smug. He came across as a major asshole to me. The way he talked to me made me feel like he looked down on me. So, there was that. The other things I didn't like about him were the fact that he was middle eastern and the fact that he was a psychiatrist. I assumed that he was probably connected to some terrorist organization. I also thought of him as just another legalized drug dealer, as I thought all psychiatrists were.

In our meeting that day, I remember getting very snotty with Dr. Chandry. I don't remember what I said. I just remember what he said. He said, "I know what your problem is. The problem with you is that you think you are smarter than you really are." That comment pissed me off. I don't remember what my response to Dr. Chandry was, but I know it wasn't pretty. He ended up asking me to leave the room where we were having our meeting. I remember trying to shake his hand as I walked out and he said, "You should know that I don't do that." I couldn't believe that the guy was such an ass that he wouldn't even shake my hand. Maybe he was referring to a custom of his people not to shake hands. I've heard that some of the Arab countries do not shake hands and that it is actually an insult to try to have someone shake your hand. I've also heard the reason for that custom and I think it's a little too gross to talk about. Anyway, Dr. Chandry did not impress me in the least. I thought he was a typical psychiatrist, another idiot who was able to force medication on whomever he chose. I hated having to talk to him. Every time I saw him outside of his office, I gave him my meanest glare and never spoke a word to him.

One day, I was told that I was going to be making an appearance in court. I had a woman who acted as my legal guardian while I was at the PRC. She was my liaison between the people in my life outside the PRC and me. She gave me divorce papers to sign for Sara and she took care of the legal problem that dealt with me specifically. Apparently, it had been decided that I was going to be forced to attend a 5-week program at the PRC called SRT, which stands for Short Term Residency. I don't know why they don't call it STR. That's just one of many things that I thought were a sign that the people who ran the PRC were idiots. They couldn't even come up with the correct abbreviation for Short Term Residency, and yet they were supposed to be smart enough to tell me what my problems were.

My legal guardian told me that I was going to appear before a judge who would determine if it was necessary for me to attend the SRT program. I didn't know it, but my parents and grandmother had requested that I be put in the program in an attempt to straighten me back out. I had already been released twice from rehab centers and had relapsed both times. My parents and grandmother asked that I be kept at the PRC until it was clear that I could function in society again and was convinced to stay on my medication. I didn't find out that my parents and grandmother were actually the ones who had forced me to appear before a judge until years later.

I remember the strangest thing that happened that day was an episode that took place in the bathroom in my room. While I was at the PRC, one of the things I would do to pass the time was to take a shower several times a day. I did this mainly because it was always so cold in there. We had to wear the PRC issued clothes while we were in the unit that I had been taken to. All we had for clothing were thin cotton pants and a thin cotton shirt and some socks that didn't do a very good job of keeping my feet warm. The outfit that I had to wear looked like the clothes that inmates have to wear in prison, except my outfit was not bright orange or black and white, it was a sky blue color. I would take showers throughout the day whenever I got too cold. I usually took a hot shower. Sometimes I would take a cold shower because that was what The Voice wanted me to do. I was also told by The Voice to always take a shower with the lights out. That way I would get used to how I would have to shower in the future, when there was no more electricity.

On that day that I was supposed to see the judge, I took a shower in my bathroom. I turned out the light so that it was pitch black. I took a cold shower that day. As I was taking a shower, I started to hear noises that seemed to be coming from below me. I turned off the water and listened. I thought I could here moaning coming from the drain in the shower. The Voice told me that I was hearing the sounds of the aliens that were the minions of Satan. The Voice said that the aliens were right below me in the pipes that the drain fed into. I listened to the sounds. They were unlike anything I had ever heard. It terrified me. The Voice told me to get used to it because I would soon experience far more terrifying things than that. I got out of the shower and turned on the light. I half expected to find some creature in the bathroom with me when the light came on. To my relief, I was alone. I stood there and kept listening. I kept hearing the frightening sounds. They also seemed to be coming from the drain in the sink too. At one point I thought I heard a voice speak from the drain in the sink. It said, "Scott, we are coming for you." That was all I needed to hear to get the heck out of the bathroom. I dried off and got dressed and left the bathroom as quickly as I could. That was one of the last terrifying hallucinations that I had.

After getting freaked out in the bathroom, I walked around my room and did some exercises to warm up. Not long after I started trying to warm up, one of the orderlies came in my room and told me that I was the next person who was going to see the judge. So, I just kept exercising in my room until I was called, over the intercom, to the nurse's station.

I walked up to the nurse's station and was met by the guy who I thought was Rachel's dad. He walked me out of the unit that I was staying in and down a series of hallways that led us to a room where I was met by my mom, Nanny, my doctor, Dr. Chandry, his lawyer, my legal guardian, and a judge. They were all sitting around a big table. The judge was at the front of the table. My doctor and his lawyer were sitting across from me. My legal guardian sat beside me. Mom and Nanny sat at the end of the table, opposite from the judge. I remember walking in and not wanting to see my mom and Nanny there. I knew that they would have nothing but bad things to say about me to the judge. I sat down and my legal guardian said, "Let everyone else talk. You just sit here and be quiet until you are asked to speak." I told her I would do just that. Then the judge started asking my doctor what his recommendation was for me and why he felt justified to give his recommendation. My doctor told the judge that I had exhibited the behavior of someone with Schizoaffective disorder. He told the judge that I had been hearing voices and seeing hallucinations. He brought out photocopies of some of my sketches that I had done while I was in my room at the hotel in Lakeland. The judge looked them over. I burst out with my defense. I said, "Look, I know that this guy is viewed as a professional, but all he is really is a drug pusher. He wants to sell me a drug that will make me happy when I'm sad or a drug that will make me calm down if I get too happy about something. If I am sad, he says that I am depressed. If I am happy, he says that I am in mania. All he and his co-workers have done is create labels for people so that they can sell them drugs and make them think that they need those drugs to be normal. I have not done anything wrong. He is just trying to force me to take a drug that I don't need. He is nothing more than a legalized drug dealer." The judge made facial expressions as I was talking, like she agreed with some of what I said.

By the time I was done talking I was so angry that I was shaking. My legal guardian told me to be quiet and wait until I was asked to speak. My doctor sat across the table with a calmness that totally irritated the hell out of me. The judge asked my doctor a few more questions. I kept mumbling under my breath about what an idiot he was and made sarcastic remarks to everything he said. My legal guardian kept telling me to be quiet. After talking with my doctor, the judge turned to my mother and Nanny and asked them if they had anything to say about me.

I remember Nanny saying something about the fact that she thought that I had always been a good child, had done well in school, and even had a decent job after finishing school. But, then she said that something had changed me and that I was not like my old self anymore. She told the judge about the hurricanes, Granddaddy dying, Sara leaving, and a few other things that she thought had contributed to my current condition. I remember glaring at her the whole time she talked because I knew that she was condemning me to stay at the PRC for a much longer time than I had ever wanted to.

After talking with everyone at the table, the judge said that she recommended that I be placed in the SRT program. She asked me how I felt about her decision. I felt defeated. I realized that the SRT program was what my whole family wanted me to do. So, I told the judge that I didn't care one way or the other. I said, "Whatever you guys think is best, I'll do it. Apparently, I am not sane enough to know what is best for me." I said the last sentence with as much sarcasm as I could. I was totally pissed off at mom and Nanny. I felt like they had betrayed me once again, even after all the good things that I had tried to do for them. I felt let down. I had tried to earn their respect my whole life, and now I knew that they just thought of me as a mental case. I had about as much respect from them as I might get if I was a retard. It hurt to know that I was not respected by them. But, I guess things could have been a lot worse.

After the meeting was over, the guy who I thought was Rachel's dad said that it was time for me to go back to the unit. I got up and Nanny said, "Do I get a hug?" I said, "Not today." and walked out of the room. The guy who I thought was Rachel's dad said, "Scott, go give your grandmother a hug. Don't be like this." I said, "I don't feel like giving out any hugs right now. Sorry." He stopped me and said, "Your grandmother loves you. Please go give her a hug." So, I walked back in the room and gave Nanny a quick pat one the back and walked back out.

We walked back to the unit and I remember one of the guys that was a patient there asking me how everything went. I said, "It went great I guess. Apparently I am suffering from some new disease that they have come up with. You know that's all they do is make this crap up as they go along." The guy who was asking me about my court appearance was named Mark. We soon became pretty good friends. Mark asked me what the name of my disease was. I said, "They call it Greivious Cough" Of course, I just made up this name. I didn't want to tell anyone that I had just been diagnosed as schizophrenic. I knew that sounded too bad to share with anyone, even another person at a mental institution. So, I made up a name for my condition that I thought sounded kind of cool. The word "Greivious" had been taken from the Star Wars character, General Greivious. The "Cough" part was also taken from his character in the movie. General Greivious was a robot that went around coughing and wheezing.

Mark said, "Greivious Cough? I've never heard of that." I said, "Me neither. They probably make up new names for people all the time." I told Mark that I thought Dr. Chandry had just created a new label for me because the PRC was determined to find as many people to sell drugs to as they could.

A few days passed between the time that I was told that I was going to be put in the SRT program and when I actually began the program. The days passed by with the usual routine of going to classes, eating meals, and sleeping. The only thing that I remember about those days is a couple of guys who came into the unit that were even scarier than Travis. One of the guys was being brought to the unit from a prison. He looked scary, too scary for me to even try to talk to. I remember him having an outburst in several of the classes we were in. I avoided that guy at all costs. The other guy, actually had a confrontation with me. I was in the dayroom sitting on one of the plastic couches. I was talking with Michelle. Then the scary guy came into the room. He was a black guy with a foreign accent. I think he may have been from Africa. His accent sounded like some of the people I knew at FAMU that were from African countries.

Not long after he walked in, he started yelling at another black girl there. He was telling the girl that he was going to kill her. Then he started thrusting his pelvis towards her and acting like he was having sex with her. It was a very disturbing thing to see. For some reason, none of the orderlies were paying attention. The guy went on threatening the girl for probably a minute or more when I stood up and told the guy to calm down and leave the girl alone. He came stomping over to me and started threatening me. Michelle and the other girl ran out of the room and went to the nurse's station. The guy was right in my face and I knew he was about to try to beat the crap out of me when several orderlies came in and grabbed him and took him away. If Michelle had not been quick enough to get the attention of the staff, I probably would have just taken another beating. If that guy would have hit me, I probably would have hit back. Then I would have had more problems than I already did. I knew that if I got in a fight, I was probably taking a chance on further punishment. So, I tried to avoid people who seemed very aggressive.

As far as Travis was concerned, after he and I had our little scuffle, I made a threat to him that I thought would scare him. I didn't see him for several days after his attack on me. When I finally did see him, I said, "Well Travis, I hope you've got some money that you don't mind giving away because when I get out of here, I'm going to take you to court and sue you for assault. You might feel good about yourself for head butting me, but when I'm done with you, you're going to really regret what you did." I was half hoping that my threat would send Travis into another rampage and he would try to attack me again. I thought that if he tried anything this time, I would fight back. Fortunately all Travis did was cuss at me and tell me that there was no way I was getting any money from him because he didn't have any money to give me. I said, "Whenever you do get some money, get ready to hand it over to me because your ass is mine when we get out of here." I think I actually did scare Travis because after that threat he started trying to be nice to me. I think he was hoping that if he changed the way he acted towards me, I might let him slide. His trick worked. I ended up actually liking him a little before I went into the SRT program. I could tell that he had some serious issues, but he was not retarded or anything. He just had no self control. Travis would get up in the middle of almost every class and start cussing about something or do something to bring attention to himself. I would usually start laughing at Travis whenever he pulled one of his stunts in class. I thought it was sort of funny how he could always find something to get angry about. I'm sure Travis is now in some state mental institution, prison, or dead. He was definitely not someone who I could ever imagine functioning in the real world.

Another thing that happened during that time occurred one night when I was trying to sleep. I was in my room and was almost asleep when I heard a loud scream. It was the voice of a female and she was very upset about something. The Voice told me that the scream was that of a real witch that had just been brought into the PRC. The Voice was being literal. It actually meant that the girl who I heard screaming was a witch. The way she kept screaming sounded very scary. The Voice said that she was going to cast a spell on the workers at the PRC and that she would end up killing all of them. I had trouble sleeping that night because I kept thinking that I was going to wake up and find a witch standing at my door. I thought that she might try to kill me too. I assumed that witches were probably agents of the evil group. So it was assumed that she might try to harm me. I eventually slept at some point that night. The next day I remember asking Michelle if she had heard the screaming girl that night. Michelle said that it was one of the girls in the unit. She pointed the girl out to me. I remembered seeing her several times since I had been brought to the PRC. Seeing who I thought was the witch, eased my fears because I then realized that the girl who had been screaming was not what I had imagined. I quickly dismissed the witch idea as another lie from The Voice. I had just about had my fill of The Voice's lies. I still tried talking to The Voice occasionally, but my patience with it was growing thin.

One day an older lady came to meet with me and tell me about the SRT program. We sat down in the room where we had all of our classes. She gave me a little introduction about what the SRT program was like and told me about the differences between SRT and the unit that I was now living in. She said that people in SRT had more privileges than the people at the unit. She said that we were allowed to go outside everyday, several times a day. That was something that seemed really nice. We were never allowed outside at the unit. All day was spent in the prison like environment of the unit. I was always cold and miserable. The lady also said that we were allowed to smoke at the SRT. That also sounded nice because the unit was a no smoking facility. I had been there two weeks now and not had a cigarette. Even though I had told myself that I was quitting, I couldn't wait to be allowed to have a cigarette again. After hearing all the perks of the SRT, I still wanted to just be set free. I told the lady, "It sounds like SRT is a little better than this place, but I still don't want to go. Why can't you guys just let me get back to my life. This whole thing is so ridiculous. I haven't done anything wrong and you people are treating me like a criminal." The lady said that it was not up to her to decide whether or not I could leave. She said that the court had decided to put me in the SRT program and that was something that I would have to do before I could be released. I told her that I thought the whole thing was a waste of time and how tired I was of spending my days with crazy people. It had still not occurred to me that I was one of them. I still believed that the secret group was waiting for me to get out of the rehab center so that I could continue my training. Even though I been hearing less and less of The Voice, I still wanted to believe that something supernatural was taking place. The longer I stayed at the PRC, the less I believed that this was true.

Another meeting I had before leaving the unit, to begin the SRT program, was with a new doctor. I was introduced to a friendly Cuban man named Dr. Restrenno. I immediately liked Dr. Restrenno. Something about the way he spoke to me gave me a sense that he was a much better man than my other doctor, Dr. Chandry. Dr. Restrenno asked how I was doing at the unit and I told him that I hated it. I told him that I hated all the crazy people. I told him about Travis attacking me and the other guy who had wanted to attack me but was stopped. I told him that I hated Dr. Chandry. Dr. Restrenno said that a lot of people had problems with Dr. Chandry. I remember Dr. Restrenno saying, "I think the SRT will be good for you. This place has a way of draining people. You will like the SRT much better. You will have more freedom there." I told Dr. Restrenno that I just wanted to go home. He said that I would not be able to go home until it was clear that I was going to participate with the PRC and continue taking my meds after I left. I told Dr. Restrenno that I would take whatever they told me if they would just let me leave. He tried to tell me as kindly as he could that leaving was not an option for me. He said that the court had ordered me to complete the SRT program and that was what I had to do now. I told him that I understood, even though I still did not know why I was being forced to go through a program when I had never committed a crime. Dr. Restrenno just listened to me and said not to get upset because things would get better.

Chapter 62: The SRT

My first day at the SRT was a little bit of a shock. I was brought to the SRT after eating breakfast one morning. I was walked out of the unit, out of one building, across a parking lot, and into another building where the SRT program was housed. We walked in and I immediately realized that I was in a less harsh environment. Instead of having a nurse's station that was enclosed behind walls with little windows that could be slid open, the nurse's station was just an open area with a semi-circular counter that the nurses sat behind. That alone let me know that I had made a little step up. If the nurses did not have to be protected from the patients, then maybe, I hoped, the people here were not as crazy as the ones that I had been dealing with now for over two weeks.

I was walked up to the desk and a nurse started asking me questions. I had to fill out some paperwork and then they wanted to take my vitals. They took our vitals several times everyday at the unit and at SRT. After I had completed some forms and my blood pressure and heart rate had been checked, the nurse said that I needed to follow her to a room that was right next to the nurse's station. She and another nurse came into the room with me. They closed the door and she said, "O.K., here's the fun part. I need you to take off all your clothes." I said, "Are you serious?" She said, "Yes, I'm sorry but we have to make sure that you aren't bringing in any contraband and we have to see if you have any distinguishing marks on your body." I said, "Damn, this really is just like a prison, isn't it?" She said, "We aren't that bad are we?"

I felt really awkward about having to take off my clothes in front of two women. I took off my shirt and shorts and stood there in my boxers. I said, "Isn't this good enough?" The nurse said, "No. I'm afraid you have to take off your boxers too." I rolled my eyes and said, "This is too much." I couldn't believe that they were asking me to stand in front of them naked. It was so humiliating. I took off my boxers and she checked me out and asked me to turn around so she could see everything. I felt totally embarrassed. After checking me out for just a few seconds, she said I could get dressed again. I quickly put on my clothes and was glad to get that over with.

After my strip search, I was led to the room where all the classes were held. That room was also the equivalent of the dayroom that we had back at the unit. I walked in and saw that there were people walking around outside in a little fenced in yard that was outside of the dayroom. I saw people standing around outside smoking. Others were walking around the yard. Some people were just sitting by themselves in chairs and looked like they were relaxing. It looked like a much nicer setting than what I had just come from.

I walked into the dayroom and said hello to several of the people sitting in there. Most of them did not say anything back. One lady even sort of growled at me. That let me know that I was still amongst the screwballs. As I started trying to talk to people I began to realize that most of them were just about as messed up as the people back at the unit that I had just left. Still, there were a few who I realized could carry on a conversation and seemed pretty normal. The person that I talked to most of the time was Jose. He had been transferred to the SRT a few days before I was. Jose was the first person that I talked with at the SRT. I found him outside in the yard where everyone was walking around. He was smoking a cigarette. Jose told me that he would let me have a cigarette but that sharing cigarettes was against the rules. So, we just talked and I smelled the smoke of his cigarette and realized how badly I wanted one.

At the SRT we were allowed to purchase cigarettes. We had to place an order with one of the nurses and they would buy a pack of cigarettes for us every few days. We had to give them money to make the purchase for us. We were not allowed to have money on us. We had to have someone outside the PRC give money to the nurse and then they would set up an account for us. I usually kept about $20 in my account when I was there. We could also buy snacks from the vending machine at the SRT. We could buy a snack a couple times a day. We had to go to the nurse's station and ask for a couple dollars. They would give us the money and then we could buy a snack. We were supposed to give any change back to the nurse.

Another thing that was nice about the SRT was that we could wear our own clothes. I had my parents bring me enough clothes so that I could wear something different each day of the week. I had my parents bring me all of my Star Wars shirts. I usually wore them most days. I had two shirts with Darth Vader on them, one shirt with a Storm Trooper, and one that said, "Imperial Domination" on it. I loved those shirts. I still thought of myself as Darth Vader. I still believed that I would soon be feared and respected by all who knew me. But, as time passed, I slowly realized that I had been living in a fantasy world. I would soon transform from believing that everyone feared me, to being afraid of everyone myself. Before I was released from the SRT, I began to become aware of the fact that I had just spent several months as a different person. I had changed from my old self into a new personality. Before I left, I was changing back to my old self again. It took several weeks and a lot of medication, but it did happen, very slowly.

My parents and Nanny came to visit me regularly at the SRT. Someone from my family usually visited with me every evening. We would play cards and talk. I can't really remember any specific conversations. They were usually about what life was like in the SRT. I knew that any talk of the secret group would scare my family, so I had long since stopped talking about those kinds of things with them. I was starting to doubt if any of it had been real myself.

One thing I remember talking about with my parents was my car. I had left it at Chili's in Lakeland. Dad told me that he had it towed to a Subaru dealership there in Lakeland. He said that they fixed all the damage that I had done to it by pouring water in it. I think the bill came up around $1,000 for the repairs. He had my bank information so he was able to have it paid for from my account.

Another conversation we had was what I was going to do when I got out of SRT. I remember asking my parents if they would let me live with them. They were hesitant about this idea because of what had happened the last time that I lived with them. They told me to look into what type of living arrangement the SRT staff could find for me. I checked with the SRT staff and they told me about some half-way house type of living arrangement that I could stay at, but would have to pay rent every month. It was around $400 per month. After telling Mom and Dad about that option, they agreed that I could live with them when I got out, as long as I stayed on my medication.

Other people in the family visited me too. I hate to say it, but I always dreaded having people come to visit me at the SRT. I was beginning to realize what an idiot I had been. Once the drugs really took hold in my system, The Voice went away all together. I remember trying to talk to The Voice for weeks and never getting a response. My explanation, at first, was that the people at the PRC had somehow blocked the ability of the little phone in my ear. I thought that they had some device that prevented me from hearing the transmissions of the secret group. But as days became weeks, with no new information from The Voice, I began to lose faith. The lack of communication with The Voice, combined with the instructions of the teachers in the classes that we were required to take at the SRT, forced me to realize that there was a possibility that I had been very wrong about a lot of things. Before I left, I began to wonder if, perhaps, the world was not about to end. I began to wonder if I had been tricked, by my own brain, into believing in a lot of fantastic ideas that only existed in my head. So many things had been proven wrong already. The doubt of the existence of a secret group of people, who were controlling everything around me, was beginning to build. I still held on to the hope that once I left the PRC, The Voice would return and explain to me why it had been absent for so long. It never did. My last conversation with The Voice occurred before I was ever released from the SRT. The longer I went without hearing from it, the more depressed I became. The realization that I was not a secret agent, nor a world celebrity with super human abilities, caused me to begin to shut down. Once the realization of who I was, and what had really happened, registered with me, I saw myself as the idiot that I had become. My view of myself went from super hero to total loser in a matter of weeks. Once that happened, I went from an extremely high perception of myself to an all time low point in my life. But a lot of things happened in between the high and low.

The SRT program was a 5 level program. Each level represented one week. Each week had a set of requirements. If you failed to meet all the requirements of the week, you had to repeat the week. Once you passed everything in week one, Level One; you went to Level Two, and so on. To receive freedom and leave the SRT, a person had to meet all the requirements to get to Level 5. Level 5 was the last level. To complete all the requirements of Level 5, you had to perform all the tasks of the other levels, and also go on a couple of field trips with the SRT group, so that they could see how you might function once you went back to the real world. These trips were just simple outings, like, a trip to a store, a picnic lunch at a park, and so on. You also had to take a position of responsibility in the program. There were several positions you could choose from. You could be the President of the group, who made the final decision about where to take a trip to, and other very petty things. Or, you could be Vice President, who also had a big say in the decisions that we were allowed to make. You could be the Note Taker, who recorded the meeting minutes from all our group meetings. Or you could choose to be a helper with the cleaning staff. I ended up being the Note Taker.

Once you completed all the requirements of Level 5, they would tell you the day that you would be released from the SRT program. Once they let you leave, you were on your own again. A person would have to have made living arrangements outside of the SRT before they would let you leave. I don't know of anyone who they let leave who had planned to try to live on their own. Most people went to live with family or friends. A few went to half way houses.

The daily routine of the SRT was this: We had to wake up around 6:00 am every morning to go to the nurse's station and receive our morning doses of medications. For me, that meant 40 mg of Zyprexa. After our morning pills, we could go back to our room or hang out in one of the public areas. We had a room for watching television. We had a room where we ate our meals and could make phone calls. That room was also used as the meeting area when family or friends came to visit us. The other public room was the classroom area where we sat and listened to instructors who taught the various classes. That room was also where they would show movies when we had free time. We could also sit there and read, draw, or play games.

My morning routine was to take my pill and then go to the TV room and watch whatever was on the television. I never tried to make a call about what we should watch. I just watched whatever was on the channel that the television was set to. I hoped that I would receive a secret message from the television shows that I saw. I never did. I would listen to the news or the music videos (that's what was usually being watched) and try to find a hidden message in the words, but it never happened. The lack of secret communication helped create the doubt that was slowly building.

Someone usually already had the television turned to MTV before I ever walked in. That seemed to be everyone's favorite thing to watch. I remember seeing the videos of Shakira, Sean Paul, Madonna, Kelly Clarkson, Chris Brown, and others. I had not seen an actual music video on MTV since I was a teenager. I liked hearing the music, even though none of it was anything that I would go out and buy. Music had always been a big part of my life. I always had a new favorite band a few times every year. I liked music that had lyrics that seemed abstract and could be interpreted to mean many different things. That style of music fit me best because I could usually imagine a way that a particular song told a story about a part of my life. Certain songs from groups like; Pavement, Nirvana, REM, Pearl Jam, Tori Amos, and even Nine Inch Nails; to me, had meanings that talked about the way that I felt about things or just reminded me of good times that I had. Music has a way of doing that for me. I can hear certain songs from the past and they will jog a memory of something that I was doing at a time when I first heard that particular song. I might not be able to remember a lot of things, if it weren't for hearing certain songs that I might have been listening to during the time that those things happened.

Anyways, back to the daily routine. After watching videos for an hour or so, it was time for breakfast. Breakfast was usually pretty good. We would have eggs, grits, bacon or sausage, fruit, and milk and juice to drink. The thing I didn't like about breakfast, or any other meal, was the way people formed a line to get their food. Everyone always showed their true selfish nature when we formed our line. People would always try to cut in front of me and push their way to the front of the line. It was a stupid thing to do because our food was pre-arranged into trays that were assigned to each person. The SRT staff would call out a person's name when they saw their tray, and that person was supposed to get their food. I don't know why we even had to form a line. The whole food distribution process was a little wacky. It was always a matter of standing in a line, only to be cut in front of by all the greedy people who wanted to jump to the front and tell the SRT staff to find their tray.

The process of eating was always funny too. People would open their trays and start making barters with other people around them. "I'll trade you my grits for your toast and jelly." might be a typical trade offer. There were a couple of guys that were like garbage disposals. They would wait until most people had finished eating and then they would go around saying, "Are you going to eat that?" If the answer was "No.", Then they would ask if they could have whatever they were referring to and eat it themselves. A lot of people did not eat well. The SRT staff monitored what everyone was eating and tried to get some of them to eat more. I guess some people were either too nervous or too depressed to have an appetite. I was not one of them. I usually ate all of whatever came in my tray. I thought most of it was pretty good.

After breakfast, we would have a few minutes to take care of personal hygiene issues and then it was time for class. There was always someone talking on the intercom to let us know when the next activity was about to take place. You might hear something like, "Attention all clients, you have 5 minutes until class begins." There was also an announcement made to let us know that class had started and that we were now considered tardy. If you were tardy a few times, you did not receive credit for attending class. If you did not attend all classes in a given week, you did not progress through the system. You would lose your status of completing that week's requirements and would have to repeat the week.

Classes were usually about the importance of taking the medication that had been prescribed to us. The instructors usually talked on a level that a kindergartener could understand. They were trying to get the point across, to a bunch of people who could barely put together a logical statement, that the medication was the key factor in keeping them out of the mental institution. We also talked about the importance of proper nutrition, sleep, and exercise. We would have to complete worksheets and watch instructional videos. I had a bad attitude through most of the program. I usually tried to keep my mind off of anything that the instructor was saying. I would doodle on my papers, or just daydream. I was not in a state of mind to listen to someone talk who spoke as if they were talking to a kindergartener. The whole process was very degrading to me. I did not see myself as one of the people who needed help. Through most of my time in SRT, I was still convinced that the problem I had was that I was surrounded by a family who all misunderstood me. I still wanted to believe that all the crazy ideas that had popped in my head, thanks to The Voice, were real and that everyone else was simply in the dark, like cattle being led to slaughter. I still wanted to believe that I was the savior of all the ignorant people who had not been let in on the big secret that I had discovered. Even without the voice in my head, I tried to hold on to this belief until after I was released from the SRT program.

One of the things we had to do every morning, in our first class, was read a section of the newspaper out loud. We were supposed to find an interesting article and read to the class until the instructor told us we could stop. I would usually just glance at the paper and read the first thing I saw. I never tried to find anything that interested me, because by that point, nothing seemed to interest me. I was still unable to actually read and comprehend the newspaper. I had no problem reading out loud, I just was unable to comprehend what I was reading. To me, the newspaper was a source of secret information. I didn't want to read the paper. I wanted to read *through* the paper. I would look for patterns in the words or letters. I was trying to find a secret message that was hidden among the letters. Once I was in the SRT, I was unable to do that. All I could do was look at the letters and see them for what they were, just letters making up words that made sentences that told what was going on in the world. I still expected to pick up the paper one day and get some new information about what my next step was with the secret group, but it never happened.

The instructor for most of our classes was an older man named Tom. He was a very friendly guy. He was the one instructor that began to catch my attention and make me think that, perhaps, the medication was not such a bad thing after all. Tom spoke very slowly, but his voice was pretty firm. He had a bit of a Southern accent. I liked to hear him talk. Something about him reminded me of Granddaddy. He didn't look or sound like Granddaddy. But there was a wisdom in what he said that reminded me of the way Granddaddy spoke. After several weeks of basically ignoring every word he said, I began to listen, and realize that there could be some truth in what he had to say.

The things Tom usually talked about were the topics I already mentioned; medication, sleep, nutrition, and exercise. After hearing Tom repeat himself day after day, the messages finally began to sink in, even through my attempt to ignore him. Somewhere around week three or four, I began to listen to everything he said. I began to realize that Tom spoke the truth and that the voice in my head spoke in lies.

One of the instructors that I did not like was a skinny black guy who was my age or younger. He sometimes filled in on days when Tom was not there. His name was Carter. My problems with Carter began before I was ever put in SRT. I had met

Carter back in the unit one day. I met him on the one day that they let us go outside for a few minutes. Carter was watching over us with two other black girls who were also staff at PRC. I don't remember what exactly started a little verbal battle between Carter and I. It might have just been what he was wearing. He was wearing University of Miami shirt. I remember saying, "So I guess you think you're a pretty smart guy because you graduated from University of Miami." Carter said, "What makes you think that I graduated from UM?" I said, "Well, I see you're wearing they're shirt." He said, "That doesn't mean that I went there. I could just be a fan of their football team." I said, "So did you go there?" He said, "It's not really your business where I went to school." I said, "I'm just asking a simple question. I guess you probably think that you are too good to talk to me." Carter said, "No. I don't think I'm too good to talk to you. Its just not your business to know about my personal life." I said, "You know what? I hate people like you. All of you guys that work here think that you are better than all of us. You are nothing but an ignorant nigger!" Carter and the two girls standing beside him looked a little shocked that I had used the most offensive word a person could call a black person. Carter said, "Excuse me?" I said, "You heard me, you are just a dumb nigger!" Carter said, "Do you know what a nigger is?" I said, "Yes, a nigger can be a person of any race. I'm not slamming your race. I went to college at FAMU as a matter of fact. I have lots of black friends. I am not a racist. I am calling you a nigger because a nigger is someone who is ignorant and lazy. That's what you are. You have no idea of anything about me, but you have already passed a judgment on me, just because I have been sent here. I bet you don't do a damn thing around here besides walk around and act tough to all of us. You are a true nigger." Carter said, "Yep. You called me out. I don't do anything around here. They pay me good money too. I don't have to do anything except listen to people like you say stupid things like what you just said." The other two girls started laughing. I said, "Go ahead and call me stupid. I've been called a lot worse. But soon you are going to realize that some people might know about some things that you have never dreamed of." Carter said, "Really? Like what?" I said, "I don't have to share that kind of information with you. It's the same as you not having to tell me about your personal life. You guys think that you can make us answer every question you ask. You have totally taken away my personal life, and you want to tell me that your personal life is not my business. I don't have a personal life anymore, thanks to people like you! But I will tell you this, soon you are going to find yourself burning in the flames of Hell. Hell is the Earth and you will be left here when God takes away his followers. I'm going to be left here too. You had better hope that I don't find you." After that, I was taken away and put back inside. Threatening the staff was not tolerated. We could complain as much as we wanted to about how much we hated the place, how we were going to sue them all, and so forth. But if we made a direct threat to the staff, we usually got punished. My punishment was the loss of my outside privilege. I didn't care, because we were never allowed outside anyway. So, that was my first conversation with Carter.

Once I got into SRT, I saw Carter walking around the building almost everyday. He was one of the orderlies that assisted in watching us when we went outside. He also helped take our vitals on most days. I never got along with Carter. I don't think he ever got over our first encounter. Even after I made an apology to him for what I had said when we first met at the unit, I don't think Carter could really forgive me for using such a terrible word on him.

One day, after I had first arrived at SRT, I was in class and Carter was our instructor. My medications had been increased. I don't remember what the dosage was, but it was enough that all I wanted to do was sleep. I remember not caring about anything he was saying in class that day. I closed my eyes and fell asleep. Carter woke me up by calling my name. I opened my eyes and he said, "Scott, you can't sleep in this class. If I see you with your eyes closed again, I'm kicking you out and you'll lose credit for the class." I said, "Go to Hell Carter! I'm sleeping because the f@$!ing medication you are forcing me to take is making me so sleepy that I can't keep my eyes open! You idiots make us take drugs that you know make us drowsy and then you tell us we have to stay awake?!? You people are f@$!ing morons!" Carter said, "Leave the room Scott." An orderly came to the door and told me to get up and sit in a chair that was outside the classroom. I said, "Good. I can't stand these stupid classes anyway. This whole program is a total joke. You people are all a bunch of idiots and you think you're something special. You don't have anything to teach me. You don't know what you're talking about!" By this time, the orderly was walking over to me. I got up and walked to him. He said, "Calm down Scott. Just sit out here and relax. If you're tired, just close your eyes." I walked out and sat down in the chair and fell asleep. Zyprexa has a way of really knocking down a person, even a person as whacked out as I was.

Back to the daily routine: After our first class, we would usually get to go outside for thirty minutes. We were allowed to walk around a circular path that was in a big field outside the SRT building. We could also throw or kick balls with other people out there. Most of the time that I was outside, I was looking for an easy way to escape the facility. The whole field was fenced with a tall chain link fence that looked like it would take some time to climb over. There was one section of fence that had some trees that grew over it and some bushes in front of it. I thought about hiding in those bushes several times. I would walk over to them and look back to see if anyone was watching. There always was. They usually had 4 or 5 staff members out there with us. Escaping from the facility was not easy. There was one guy who did it. He was caught just a couple hours later. He had managed to run out to Hwy.17, which was about a mile from where we were. He was picked up by one of the staff members who got in a car and started patrolling the surrounding neighborhoods for him. They made him start the whole program over. He was in his 4th week when that happened. Seeing the punishment for trying to escape made me realize that it was not worth it. I decided the easiest thing to do would be to just participate in the program.

Most of the time I was allowed outside, I just walked the circle. I would walk laps until we were told we had to go in. Sometimes I jogged, just to pass the time, and so I could avoid talking to the people there.

After outside time, we went back to the classroom for another class. After that we had lunch. After lunch we had a little free time, another class, more free time, then dinner, another class, then the rest of the day was free time. Every four hours, we also got a chance to go outside and smoke a cigarette. The smoke break was my favorite part of the day. Smoking a cigarette took away the stress that I had from being in such an oppressive environment. The thing that really grossed me out about our smoke breaks were the people who would actually dig through the cigarette butt can and find a little piece of left over cigarette and start smoking it. The people that did this were the ones that were the most crazy. There were only a few people that I saw do this, but it really grossed me out to see them do it. I was glad that I was never that desperate for a cigarette. If I ran out, I just didn't smoke. A couple of times, Jose leant me one of his. We were only allowed to smoke two cigarettes at each smoke break. We were not supposed to share cigarettes. If someone ran out of cigarettes, that was just too bad. We were not allowed to give our cigarettes to each other. Jose did it anyway. He would ask for a cigarette and would have the nurse light it. Then he would walk around a corner, where she couldn't see him, and give it to me. We got caught one time, but there was no reprimand. The guy who saw us just said, "I know what you guys are doing over there. Don't share cigarettes. Scott, if I see you with a cigarette again, I'm taking away your smoking privileges for good." So, I stopped sharing with Jose. We only did that a few times anyway. He had given me a couple of his. I had given him a couple of mine. It was not a big deal. But for the SRT, everything could be a big deal if they wanted to make it out that way.

Another thing we had to do at SRT was our laundry. That was also a fun experience because you never knew if someone might try to steal your clothes from the washer or dryer. This was a problem that happened mainly with the girls. There were a couple of girls who liked to steal. Several girls complained about missing clothes. I usually hung around the laundry room when my stuff was getting washed. I didn't want to take a chance on losing one of my precious Star Wars shirts.

We were also allowed to shave at the SRT. They would not allow anyone to have a razor in the unit. Once I got to SRT, I finally got to shave again. I had gone two or three weeks without shaving before I arrived at SRT. It was nice to get to shave again. They still would not let us keep the razor. We had to give it back once we were finished. There were too many suicidal or violent people amongst us to let razors go out into the population.

The nicest thing that I got at SRT was the privilege to use headphones. Once I made it to Level 3, they allowed me to have headphones and sunglasses. I got my parents to buy me a radio head set so that I could listen to the radio in my free time. I spent most of my free time pacing up and down the halls, listening to the radio. I usually listened to 93.3 FLZ. It was one of the only stations that came in clearly enough for me to hear inside the building. I think my favorite songs were by Chris Brown, Sean Paul, and Akon. I had never liked that kind of music before, but when that was my only option, and I heard it several times a day, I started to tolerate it, and even like it. I wore my headphones during most of my free time and during most of my outside time.

The people that I spent my time with were Jose, a girl named Katrina, and a guy named Mark. Katrina was a blonde haired girl who I thought was very unattractive, but was nice and seemed normal. Jose tried to flirt with her a lot and she always tried to give him the cold shoulder. As unattractive as she was, she was the best looking girl there. She was quiet, but friendly. We usually just complained about all the things we disliked about the PRC. Katrina said that she ran a used car company that her dad had started. I don't remember what she did to get put in the PRC in the first place. She never seemed abnormal to me. She was always calling people on the phone in her free time. I overheard her talking about cars with people. It sounded like she was still trying to run her business from inside the SRT.

Mark was a guy who was younger than me. He and I had met back at the unit. He was the one who had asked me what the doctor had diagnosed me with. I had told him I had been diagnosed with Greivious Cough. I later told him that they labeled me as Schizoaffective. Mark didn't know what that was either. Neither did I. Mark was fun to talk to because he liked a lot of the same music that I liked. We would talk about our favorite bands and songs. Mark really liked Sublime. I liked them too. One of our first lengthy conversations was about what a shame it was that the lead singer of Sublime had overdosed on heroine. We both agreed that it was a shame because they had put out so many good songs before they ever got popular on the radio. By the time Sublime really got big, their lead singer was dead. Mark and I talked about what had happened to us to get us put in the rehab center. I told Mark that my parents were just not informed of some of the things that I knew about and that they would be proven wrong one day. I didn't go into any details about what those things that I knew were. I had already noticed how every person that I shared that kind of thing with was turned away or scared of me. I didn't want to have the same thing happen with Mark.

Mark told me that he had been doing some drugs with some friends of his and there was something about being on a boat and crashing it into a tree. Mark said that his parents had him Baker Acted because they thought he was crazy. After knowing Mark for a while, and hearing some of the strange ideas that he had, I began to see how his parents might think that he was crazy. Mark and I would get to talking sometimes, and out the blue, he would make a statement that made no sense at all. I can't remember exactly what he would say, but it was weird enough that I realized that there was a reason for him to be in the SRT program. Overall, I thought Mark was another of the least crazy people there. He was a very intelligent guy. Aside from his occasional weird statements, he was a good guy. When he read from the newspaper in class, he usually spoke with inflection in his voice at all the right places. He would also usually like to talk about what he thought the article he had just read was about. He was a good speaker when it came to that sort of thing.

Outside of Jose, Katrina, and Mark, I didn't speak with many of the other people there unless I absolutely had to. Most of the others had too many issues for me to deal with. There were several characters at the SRT who could have made good material for a comedy movie. My favorite totally crazy person was a guy named Conrad.

When I first met Conrad, on my first day in SRT, I listened to him talking to one of the staff members and I thought he was doing some kind of comedy routine. I listened to him talk and he reminded me of Norm Mc Donald from Saturday Night

440

Live in the 90's. Conrad was always dressed in some type of athletic wear. He usually wore the type of long pants you might see a person wear when they go out for a jog on a cold day. He also usually had on a wind breaker type jacket and a t-shirt on under that. On my first day in SRT, I heard a staff worker talking to Conrad. The worker was telling Conrad that he needed to change his clothes because he had worn the same outfit for a week. Conrad said, "I can't man. I've got a tennis match coming up, man." The worker said, "Oh, tennis?" Conrad said, "Yeah, man. I'm playing against Agasi tomorrow. I've got to do my SAT's too, man. You know last time I scored a 1100 on my SAT's, man." The SRT worker said, "O.K. Conrad. I know you're busy, but you need to change your clothes. You've got stains all over yourself and you smell bad. When was the last time you took a shower?" Conrad said, "I scored an 1100 on my SAT's, man. I've been practicing on my papers, man." Conrad held up a magazine that he had drawn columns of little bubbles all over. The magazine was just a typical magazine with photos and stories. Conrad had drawn little filled in circles all over the pages, as if he were bubbling in the answers on a multiple-choice test, like the SAT. That was a typical Conrad conversation. Everything in Conrad's world revolved around playing tennis and taking the SAT. No matter what someone tried to talk about with him, he always shifted the conversation back to tennis and the SAT. Conrad also usually walked around, swinging his arms as if he were swinging a tennis racket. He would tell whoever passed by him that he was practicing for some big game. To my friends at the SRT and I, Conrad was hysterical. We would purposely have a conversation with Conrad just so we could hear what was happening in his fantasy world of tennis and the SAT. We would often talk about what Conrad had said to us that day and laugh at each other's stories about poor Conrad. In reality, it was sad, because Conrad was just not all there. He had some type of mental disability that prevented him from being able to carry on a conversation with anyone. Still, Conrad usually seemed like a pretty happy guy. I guess its like they say: ignorance is bliss.

Another crazy guy there was named Carter. Unfortunately, he was not the funny kind of crazy. He was an obnoxious form of the problem. I usually did not speak to Carter because I had seen him lose his temper with a couple people in the SRT. One day, I sat down in a chair beside Katrina when class was about to start. I didn't even think about Carter sitting on the other side of me. He was already sitting in a chair that was one chair away from Katrina. I sat down in the empty chair between the two of them. I started talking to Katrina. Carter said, "Why do you have to sit in that chair? There are plenty of other chairs in here. Go sit in one of them." I turned to Carter and said, "Why can't I sit here?" He said, "Because, you are too close to me. I don't want your germs on me. Please sit somewhere else." I said, "Carter, I don't have anymore germs than anyone else here. This seat is here for someone to sit in. I have decided to sit here because I want to talk to Katrina. I'm sorry that's a problem for you, but I'm not moving." Carter got mad and started cussing at me. I cussed back at him and he finally got up and sat in a different chair on the other side of the room. I felt pretty good about getting him worked up enough to move. I thought he was weird for wanting me to move in the first place. After that day, Carter would always give me a mean glare when he saw me. He never spoke to me again. That was fine with me, because I thought he was pretty odd.

Another guy who bugged me was a guy named Robert. He was my roommate when I was first placed in the SRT. Robert seemed like a nice guy at first. We talked a little on the first few days that I was there. I soon realized that Robert had some kind of superiority complex. Every time we spoke, he usually made some condescending remark about me. One of the comments that really bothered me was a remark he made when we were talking about what medication we were taking. Robert named off three or four drugs that they were having him take. I told him that I was taking Zyprexa. He asked how much I was taking. I told him I was taking 20 mg twice a day. He said, "20 mg! That's a lot of Zyprexa! You must really have some serious problems. I've never met anyone that had to take that much before." I said, "Well, I don't feel like I have a serious problem. I just think that they are trying to get me hooked on a drug so that I will think I need it. Besides, I'm only taking one thing. You are taking several things. I think that you are the one with the serious problem." Robert just smirked and walked out of the room. Robert liked to walk up and down the halls, just like I did. We would pass each other many times every day as we walked the halls. Robert would always have this strut going when he walked. He also walked with one arm bent so that his lower arm was parallel to the ground and going across his waist, sort of like you might see a person walk if they were in some type of a procession or ceremony. The way he walked gave me the impression that he thought very highly of himself. It was odd.

Another crazy person was a girl named Theresa. She was a big fat girl with red hair. She was usually in a good mood and laughed a lot. The problem was that she would laugh at times when no one was talking. We might be in class and there might be a period where people were filling out worksheets and the room was dead quiet. Theresa would burst out in laughter and the instructor would ask her to calm down. She would sit there and laugh hysterically for several minutes, as if she could not control herself. Other times, I would see her staring off into space and shaking all over. She was very strange.

The weirdest thing that happened between Theresa and I happened outside in the yard one afternoon. Theresa came up to me and said, "You sure look familiar to me. What's your real name? I know its not Scott." I said, "Yes it is. I'm Scott Gann. I'm sorry but I don't remember ever meeting you before." Theresa smiled and said, "Yes you have. You used to be my boyfriend. Don't you remember?" I said, "No. I have never been your boyfriend. I think you have me confused with someone else." Theresa said, "Oh come on. We had a baby together. Don't you want to know about her?" I said, "No Theresa, you've got me mixed up with someone else." and I started to walk away. I wanted to get as far from her as I could. She was freaking me out, probably in the same way that I had freaked out several of the girls that I had met during my times in mania.

I walked back inside the SRT building and Theresa followed right behind me. She kept watching me and smiling at me. It bothered me. Finally, one of the SRT staff noticed that I was uncomfortable with Theresa and he said, "Theresa, leave Scott alone please. Go back outside." Theresa stood there right beside me for several seconds and then said, "But he's my boyfriend. We are just spending time together." I said, "Theresa, I am not your boyfriend. You have me confused with someone else." Theresa laughed and said, "I know you. You're just playing around." The SRT worker said, "Theresa, go back outside." She finally walked off. I thanked the SRT guy for saving me from her. She was really beginning to scare me. She was much bigger than me and I had already seen her doing this little stare into space and shaking uncontrollably all over. I didn't want to know what was going through her head during those times. I was afraid that if I was rude towards her, she might fly off the handle and hit me or something. Theresa definitely bothered me more than any of the other girls there at the SRT. Her size combined with her strange behavior made her a little frightening.

Another girl who was pretty weird was a girl who came in after I had been in the SRT for three weeks. This girl was actually slightly attractive. She was very slim and had long brown hair. I would try to talk to her every now and then, but she would always look at the ground, or a wall, and pretend that I wasn't even talking to her. When it came time for her to read her newspaper article to the class, she would always just sit there and wait for the instructor to skip her and move on to the next person. I never heard her speak the first word during the entire time I was there. I guess she must have had some kind of serious depression or something. She never came out to any of the public areas during free time. She always went straight back to her room and stayed there until she was forced to attend class or eat a meal. She could have been the most sane person there, for all I know. Maybe her strategy was to avoid getting to know any of us because she thought we were all too crazy to talk to. I'm not sure.

One other lady really disgusted me. She was a heavy, black woman who seemed pretty friendly most of the time. The thing that I could not understand was her bizarre behavior sometimes. There was more than one occasion where she would be sitting in her seat in class and she would start peeing in her pants. Urine would start dripping from her seat and she would just start laughing. I don't know if she thought that was her way of revenge on the SRT staff or what. It was totally disgusting. She would make a puddle of pee on the floor and once someone realized what she had done, they would make her leave the class. Then, SRT staff had to come in and clean it all up. I bet if they would have made her clean it up, she might have stopped doing that. This lady looked like she was probably in her 40's. I don't understand what would possess a 40 year old woman to do such a vile thing.

I think the strangest of all the people at the SRT was a guy whose name was Steven. Steven became my roommate after Robert left the SRT. This guy was only my roommate for about a week. He did enough strange things that they eventually relocated me to another room. Steven was one of the people who would dig through the cigarette butt can and pick up little pieces of cigarettes and ask people to light them with their own cigarettes. He never had his own cigarettes. He always dug through the left over butts until he found one that he liked. It was very disturbing to me. Steven always dressed in all black. His hair was also black. He never spoke to anyone. The only time I heard him talk was at night when we were supposed to be sleeping. He would lie in his bed and cuss at himself. I would hear him say things like, "You stupid f@$!ing idiot…" and "damn you stupid idiot". He would lie there in his bed, using every cuss word he could think of, to talk to himself in derogatory little blurbs. I would eventually ask him to be quiet as nicely as I could. I was scared of him. I was afraid that he might try to hurt me as I slept. I started telling the nurses about what he was doing at night. I also told them about the way he trashed the bathroom every time he went in there. He would go in the bathroom and soak every towel and washrag and throw them all on the floor. The floor would be covered with all the soaked towels and washrags and water. Sometimes there would be so much water on the floor that it would run out of the bathroom and into our sleeping area. The nurses finally responded to my complaints and moved me into a different room with a new roommate. I liked my other roommate much better.

That is the list of characters who really made an impression on me. There were lots of others who all had their quirks. I think there were probably around 25 people all together at the SRT when I was there. Every one of us had a reason for being there. We were all strange people in our own way. I avoided most of the people for one reason or another. Like I said, the only people I really made a point to talk to were Jose, Katrina, and Mark. Everyone else was too weird to associate with.

Another big event that happened at the SRT was a meeting with my girls, Liza and Gwen. They only saw me a few times while I was at the SRT. On our first meeting, I was half expecting them to show up with Sara. I think my mom had mentioned something about Sara possibly coming to see me. I actually got a little excited after hearing that. I thought that she might have decided to try to work things out with me one more time. After all the girl chasing I had done, I eventually came back around to the idea that maybe what I had done was a huge mistake. Now that I was alone in the SRT, with none of the girls I had previously tried to start a relationship with coming to my rescue, or at least visit me, I began to think about the possibility of trying to give Sara another chance. I thought that maybe I had been too harsh on her. I thought that it might be best to try and patch our relationship back together. We still had our two girls. I thought that Sara and I acting as husband and wife might be the best thing for them. But all those ideas were too little too late.

The girls came to see me one night, accompanied by my parents. They all walked in and I went up and hugged both of them and told them how much I had missed them. I asked Gwen if she had received the package that I had sent her for her birthday, the box of Star Wars crap that I know she cared nothing about. I had not seen my kids since I had left Mom and Dad's house to begin my last big adventure in craziness. I think that it had been at least a month since I last saw them. Liza came up to me and hugged me and started crying. I said, "Liza, what's wrong? Why are you crying?" She couldn't talk. She just kept crying. Liza was seven years old when I had my first trip to the rehab center in Tallahassee. She had always been told that I had a headache and had to go to the hospital to have it fixed. Now, she was 8 and I have no idea of what explanation she had been given for all the trouble she had been through. All she knew was that one day, I got a headache. Not long after, she had to leave her home and school in Tallahassee and move in with her grandparents. Now, her mom had left her dad and grandparents to live in an apartment. I'm sure that she knew that what she had experienced was not normal. When she saw me, she broke down. I stood there holding her for several minutes and wanted to cry myself. I realized that I had not even thought about how my actions had caused so much damage to my kids. It was for the best that Sara left, because if they would have had to see me when I was in mania, they probably would have abandoned me like most everyone else.

I asked Liza if her mom was going to show up. Liza said, "She's outside with Mr. Matt. She said she was coming though." I talked with Gwen and asked her how she had been doing. Gwen spoke to me as best she could. She was only four years old. She had not been impacted the way that Liza had. She was too young to remember what life was like before daddy lost his mind and caused the family to go to ruin. I talked with Liza and Gwen for a long time and then finally Sara walked into the room.

I saw Sara and I said, "Thank you for coming. It's good to see you." Sara said, "I didn't want to come. Liza begged me. That's the only reason that I'm here." Mom and Liza had already told me that Sara was seeing some guy named Mr. Matt. I didn't even ask Sara about her new pal. I could tell from her body language, and the silence, that she was not coming to mend a broken relationship. She was determined to follow through with what we had both agreed to do, divorce. Sara stood in the room for a few minutes while I talked with the girls. She didn't speak a word. She had nothing to say. No questions. Nothing. It was all very awkward for me. I had not seen the cold side of Sara in a while. We had our arguments in the past and she always came back around to my side after time passed. This time, it was different. Sara had moved on and found another person. It was over.

After Sara and the girls left, I remember a sadness coming over me that I had not felt in a long time. The realization that Sara was actually going to go through with the divorce finally sunk in. I had pitched fits about how I wished that she would hurry up with the divorce papers so that I could sign them. I was so happy when I finally got them. Nothing had been finalized yet, though. And the more time that passed, the more I began to think that I had wished for the wrong thing. Be careful what you wish for. That old saying held very true to my situation. I had wished for a divorce since Sara left me. Now that it was clear that it was going to happen, I regretted what I had said and done to her. I was just beginning to realize what an idiot I had been. I had treated Sara the worst of everyone around me. I held her responsible for my trips to the rehab centers. I had felt like she caused a lot of my stress and if I had not married her, none of this would have happened. Now, that I heard the mentioning of Sara with some new boyfriend, I regretted pushing her away. Too little, too late.

During my last couple weeks, I developed a new strategy for coping with life at the SRT. That strategy was to sleep as much as possible so that the days went by faster. We had a little Fall Festival at the SRT around Thanksgiving. We received coupons for volunteering for different responsibilities at the Festival. The festival was just a series of activities that friends and family members could come to the PRC and participate in. We had a few booths that sold caramel apples, popcorn, brownies, and so on. There were other activities such as singing, badminton, and other games. For every activity that we volunteered to help out in, we received a coupon that let us miss one class period. I volunteered for almost everything. I wanted as many chances to skip class as possible. I was pretty busy on the week that we spent preparing for the festival. I made signs and decorations. I helped prepare the brownies and caramel apples. I also volunteered to help run a couple booths during the festival and organize the badminton games. After the festival was over, we received our passes to skip class. I received 17 passes. That allowed me to miss almost every class for a week. Once I started having entire days filled with free time, I developed the sleeping strategy. I tried to sleep as much as possible, just to escape the monotony of the SRT.

The days at the SRT grew into weeks. The weeks kept accumulating until I reached Level 5. It was now approaching the end of December. There was a chance that I might get out in time to spend Christmas with my kids. I really wanted to have that happen. But I heard that I was going to have to stay until after Christmas. That was upsetting. The staff said that a lot of them would be taking time off for the holidays, and that might mean me staying an extra week. It bothered me, but I had already been knocked down so hard from the beginning of a realization that my whole perception of reality was wrong, that missing Christmas was really not that big a deal. I had already missed Halloween and Thanksgiving. It wasn't a major issue to miss one more holiday.

Once week five rolled around, my skip class tickets had run out. I had to attend all the classes again. Class time had become a total bore for me. Every class was just a repeat of information that I had already heard time and time again. Every week some people left, and new ones arrived. So, the information had to be repeated for the newcomers. We always had to hear about how important the medication was for a successful recovery from our illnesses. Some people there would never recover from their conditions. They were too far gone, as if they suffered from a mild form of mental retardation. I don't think that any medicine can cure that.

The other thing that had driven me nuts, by that point, was our Friday Bingo games. The simple game of Bingo was a major undertaking with the clowns who were the patients of the SRT. The game was set up to give a few people some responsibilities. There was one person who was selected to choose a number from a spinning barrel that was filled with numbered blocks. Another person was responsible for writing the numbers that had been selected on a board, so that everyone was aware of all the numbers that had been called out. Those two simple tasks created confusion for most of the people who got selected to perform them. A person would select a number, call it out, and then the other person was supposed to write that number on the board. It amazed me how many times the person recording the number wrote down an incorrect number or the person selecting the number called out a different number from what was actually in their hand. It was as if the simple act of seeing, hearing, and comprehending a number was just beyond the ability of many of the people at the SRT. That was when I began to think that I had been placed in a sea of morons. By week 5, I had seen this routine of incorrect number recognition every time we played Bingo. A simple ten minute game of Bingo usually drug on for 30 or 45 minutes because of the inability of these people to read, write, and hear numbers. It drove me nuts. I would make remarks to Mark, Jose, and Katrina about how we were surrounded by idiots. We usually all sat around and laughed at all the stupid things that went on during Bingo. At first, it was funny, but it ended up becoming very irritating to me. I hated Bingo by the beginning of week 5.

My last requirement for completion of Level 5 was a field trip. We had to plan the trip ourselves. Only Level 5 people could plan and attend the field trip. This was where the positions of responsibility came in. All of the Level 5 people voted for what we would do on our field trip, but it was ultimately the decision of the President of Level 5 to decide. I did not want to be President. The person who was President, was a guy named Bill. He had been the Level 5 President when I got there. He had no place to live at once he left SRT, so they would not let him go. He stayed at level 5 after I left. I have no idea of what happened to him.

My job was to record where we went and any other discussion that we had during our Level 5 meeting. We decided to go to a plaza in Lakeland that had a movie theater and several shops. We also planned to have a picnic lunch at a park in Lakeland.

The day of the field trip finally rolled around and the Level 5 people all gathered together to leave the SRT for an outing. It was the first outing for me. Some of the other people had been a Level 5 for a couple weeks and had already gone on more than one field trip. Bill had been on a field trip every week that I had been there. Some of the other people had made Level 5 status, but had done things to lose their privilege to be released from the SRT.

Once we were told we were about to take our field trip, we were walked out of the SRT building by a couple of the staff, and led to a van. There were 5 or 6 of us who were Level 5. We all piled in the van and drove to Lakeland. Our first stop was the plaza on South Florida Ave. We went to the plaza that was called Merchant's Walk. That was where the old AMC movie theatre used to be. There was also a Ross, and other stores in the plaza. We were told that we could walk wherever we wanted to, but we were given a time to meet back up. Jose and I were both Level 5. He and I hung out the whole time we were there. We just sat outside of Ross, while the others walked around in the store, looking at items they had no money to buy. One of the girls apparently did have some money. She came out with several bags of stuff from Ross. Most of that time, Jose and I sat on a bench and talked and smoked cigarettes.

About 20 minutes before we were supposed to meet back up with the SRT staff, Jose said he wanted to go to a restaurant, in the plaza, and get a beer. I told him that I didn't want to go because I didn't want to be late meeting up with the staff. Jose walked over to the restaurant and came back before we were ready to leave. I asked him if he had a beer. He said he had two. I laughed and said, "I guess you feel a little better now." He laughed and said that he did. He said he had been craving a beer the whole time he was at SRT. Fortunately for me, alcohol has never been something that I have craved. I'm thankful because I would hate to have another destructive habit, like cigarettes, controlling me. I do have major cravings for cigarettes. I have stopped many times in the past, but I always find my way back to them.

After leaving the plaza, we went to a park in Lakeland on Lake Mirror. Some of the people had the SRT staff buy them a lunch from a restaurant in Lakeland. I had opted to just have a bag lunch prepared by the SRT kitchen. I opened my bag to find a crummy bologna and cheese sandwich, an apple, a juice box, and a milk carton. I looked at the people eating their sandwiches and salads that had been bought at Salem's Gyros and Subs. I regretted my decision to eat more SRT food.

I walked down to Lake Mirror and sat on a bench in the sun. It was less than a week from Christmas. It was pretty chilly that day. I sat on the bench and quickly ate my food so that I could walk around again and warm up. The main thing that was on my mind that day was the future. I was unsure of what would happen next. I had already been told that there was a possibility of me getting out before Christmas. I was happy about that, but also felt a little uneasy about it. I knew how uncomfortable I felt in the short visits that I had with family members coming to visit me at the SRT. I was fine talking with the girls, my parents, and Nanny. It was the rest of the family that bothered me.

One of those visits that disturbed me was a visit with my mom's aunt, Susan Hoks. Aunt Susan and her daughter, Lauren Kellog, had come to visit me one day at the SRT. Aunt Susan started out asking me how I was doing and what life was like at the SRT. Then things took a little turn. Susan said, "Well, you know that you have scared the hell out of your parents and grandmother." I said, "Yeah. I figured that I did. But I never did anything that bad. I was just kidding around most of the time. They just didn't get my warped sense of humor." Susan said, "No they didn't. The stories I have heard didn't sound like a joke to me. You can't do those kinds of things after you get back out of here." Telling Susan that I had been playing a joke when I did some of the bizarre things to my parents (such as, pouring oil all over their driveway) was a poor attempt to lie and cover up the proof that I definitely had a major problem. I'm sure Susan knew that what I had done and said to my parents was no joke and that my actions were an indicator of major trouble with my brain.

The most disturbing part of that visit for me, was when she told me that she had brought me something. She handed me a book. I thanked her and then looked at the cover. The title was, *Don't Waste Your Life.* I looked at those words and felt a little anger building inside me. Aunt Susan went on to say that she had seen the book at a bookstore and thought of me. I looked at the cover and thought, "So, this is what you think I'm doing, wasting my life." The realization that people thought that my life was a waste really bothered me. I had not thought of my life in those terms. To realize that my family thought that I was wasting my life, was depressing. I'm sure Aunt Susan had the best intentions when she gave me that book, but it did not do any good for me. I have never read the first page of it. I could not get past the title. Those words, don't waste your life, just bothered me so badly that I could not even open that book. After she left, I put the book in a drawer in my room and never looked at it again. I still have it. Maybe I should see what it has to say. I have wasted a lot of my life. I just never thought of it that way, until now.

So, back to the field trip: I sat there on the bench at the lake and thought about how I was going to get my self out of the mess that my life had become. I had already been told, by my parents, that I could stay with them once I was released from SRT. They said that they were even in the process of buying a house in Bartow that I could live in. They said that they thought it would be a better arrangement than me having to live right under their wing all the time. The house they were in the process of buying was actually a house that we had looked at before Sara left. The weekend before she left me, Sara, my parents, and I had looked at this little 3 bedroom, 2 bathroom house that was near Nanny's house. My parents talked about buying it and letting Sara and I make payments to them, rather than a bank. Sara seemed very excited about it. I was too. The next week, Sara took the girls and left. I wonder if she realized that she was about to get roped in to another commitment with me and decided that she had better get out fast. I don't know.

So, anyways, I knew that there was a possibility that I would soon be living by myself. That actually scared me a little. I had begun to realize how much trouble I managed to get into during the short period that I was forced to live on my own. In those couple weeks that I was camping, and living out of hotels, I had run ins with the police several times. I was afraid of what I might do once I had to live by myself.

After eating lunch, we hung out at the park for a while. After that, we piled back in the van and headed back to the PRC. I had made it through the field trip without incident, so I passed that requirement. The field trip was designed to give us a taste of the real world. For me, it caused me to reflect on what I had done to get myself put in the PRC, and worry about my future. I think the field trip did exactly what it was designed to do. After the field trip, I just had a few more days and then I was free.

My last day at the SRT was very nice. I went to my classes, sat around at free time talking with everyone, and just enjoyed my last few hours with the screwballs. I got the contact information of the few people I thought I might associate with after I left: Jose, Mark, and Katrina. I have never contacted any of them. Jose called me once, after I left, and I didn't feel comfortable talking to him. I have never spoken with him since.

That last day, all I could think about was freedom. I was so excited, but nervous, about getting back to the real world. There was a lot to look forward to. My Dad had told me that my car had been fixed. I looked forward to driving around in it, even though I had no idea of how I was going to continue making the payments. I was still receiving the disability insurance payments, but they would only last another year or so. I knew that if I ever wanted to have a life for myself that resembled what I had at one time, I was going to have to go back to work. I had told my parents that I planned to go back into architecture. I said these things, but I was really unsure if I would be able to deal with the stress of that type of work ever again.

So, the time finally came when I was going to be released from my prison, the SRT. Mom and Dad showed up at the SRT and the staff started giving me all my personal items that had been taken from me. Mom handed me my car keys. She said my car was outside and that I could drive it home. I don't remember if I drove home by myself in my new car, or if my parents were with me.

After rounding up all my things, my parents and I left the PRC and went out to the lake house. I don't remember anything about that day. I think that the realization that I was not a member of some secret society had really started to settle in. This realization created a sadness in me unlike anything that I had ever experienced. I had not completely let go of the possibility that The Voice may still be trying to contact me, but as the days went on, away from the PRC, and I had no contact with The Voice; I was forced to lose faith in the bizarre things that I thought were happening around me. After I left the PRC, I hoped for a sign, anything, to let me know that the secret group was still out there, trying to contact me. Nothing ever came. Once the pills took hold of my system, the things that used to trigger a conversation with the voices never created the effect. I was left with only vague memories of little bits of information that The Voice had told me. The drugs had a way of ruining my memory for a long while. I would try to put together the story of what had happened in my head. Usually I could not focus on the act of remembering long enough to tell myself the story of what had happened. It was too painful. Once I realized that The Voice was some creation of my own brain, I wanted to forget everything. The realization that my own brain had tricked me, scared me to death. I was afraid of what it might do to me next. The fear of my own brain began to shut me down.

I know that we went back to the lake house on that first day after I was released from the PRC. I stayed at the lake house until Mom and Dad were able to close on the house that they bought in Bartow. I don't even know how long that whole process took. I was becoming very depressed during that time. The days began to pass in a blur. It wasn't the effect of the medication that caused the depression. It was all caused by the realization of what I had become. I was ashamed of what I was. I had been told that I had Schizoaffective disorder with Bi-Polar features. That label helped to destroy my self-image. I didn't know much about the disorder, other than what I had experienced myself. I knew what I saw in the other people at the PRC. I had not associated myself as being one of them, until after I was released and began to realize that I did have a serious problem. I began to understand that my brain was the problem. It was not the people around me who were wrong. It was me. I was wrong about everything. And I had done a lot of really stupid things. This understanding created the depression. The depression caused me to change into yet another personality. This new personality was a recluse. I became a recluse for about two years. It took months for the whole process to fully develop, but once it started, it took years to pull myself back out of it.

I think that I lived at the lake house for a couple months after I was released from the PRC. After that, my parents had bought the house in Bartow and fixed it up so that we could all live there together for a while.

A couple of things happened before I moved into the little house in Bartow. One major event was the finalization of the divorce. Sara had already completed all the steps to get our divorce finalized. When I was released from the SRT, the papers were waiting for me at her lawyer's office. All I had to do was show up and sign some legal documents. I remember calling Sara on the day that I was supposed to go sign the documents. I called and she picked up. I said, "Hey, I've just been thinking about this whole divorce thing. I just wonder if we are really doing the right thing." Sara said, "I think we are. I've thought about a lot too. I think this is the best thing to do." I felt a little nauseous after hearing those words. I said, "Alright, if this is what you want." She said, "Yes, this is what I want." I told her good-bye and hung up the phone. I had thought a lot about our situation over the last few weeks that I was at the PRC. I had come to hope that I might get one more chance. Sara had always told me that one day she was going to stop crawling back to me after every fight. She had said that one day she would give up and leave and I would be sorry for letting her go. I guess she was right. I did feel like I had made a big mistake. I knew that I had caused her a lot of grief over the years, and especially within the last year. I felt bad for her. I wanted to try to make up for my poor behavior by putting our broken relationship back together. I thought that would be the right thing to do. We had two kids together. I knew that they missed me. I didn't want to force my kids to be unable to see me when they wanted to.

Fortunately, though, Sara had a different plan. Her plan was to divorce. I say that it was fortunate because even though it hurt at first, in the long run, her absence allowed me to become a better person. To change from the weird recluse into who I am today took a long time. When we first divorced, I felt like I had just lost a major part of me. Now, though, I realize that the divorce removed a lot of stress from my life. Without the interactions with a person who was always disappointed in me, I was left to rebuild my own perception of myself. It took a long time. I didn't start to view myself in a positive light until recently. It took many years for me to overcome the loss of Sara and to realize that life is actually better without her. But now that I have made that realization, I would never want to go back. Some may say that divorce is sacrilegious. I say, in our case, divorce was good for the both of us. When we were married, we made each other miserable. That led to a lowering of my self-esteem. After we divorced, I got away from a person who, I think, unintentionally destroyed my confidence. After the divorce, I was allowed the time to rebuild myself, very slowly.

The other thing that happened before the big move into the little house, was a job offer. When I was still in the SRT, I told my parents that I wanted to go back into architecture. When it came to earning a decent paycheck, architecture was all that I knew how to do. I had told my parents about all the designing I had been doing while I was at the SRT. I had spent a lot of my free time sketching little houses. I usually drew elevations of the front of houses. Every now and then I might take the time to draw a floor plan that went with the elevation. I just drew everything free hand. I didn't have any drafting tools with me. All my work was just hand drawn. I enjoyed doing those sketches. They passed the time and let me use the creative side of my brain. I have no idea where those sketches ended up.

So, I was doing a lot of drawing in the SRT. That got me thinking about going back to a firm and getting paid to draw. Once I got out of the SRT, I put together a resume and sent it out to a few firms in Lakeland. I think every one of them wanted to interview me. I received a job offer from three of the four firms that I interviewed with. I decided to go with the guy who offered me the least amount of money. Money was not the primary thing I was interested in. What I wanted to avoid, if at all possible, was the office politics. I hated having to compete against other people for advancement and the admiration of my employer. My least stressful job had been the one where I worked as the only employee of an architect in Washington, D.C. I hoped that I could find that opportunity again in Polk County. I found it right there in Lakeland. It was with a guy named Sam Sheens. He owned Sam Sheens & Associates. His first-ever associate employee was me.

I interviewed with Sam and impressed him with my experience and portfolio. He offered me a job right away. I told him that he was the guy that I was most interested in working for because I had really enjoyed working in a similar environment to his own when I was in D.C. Even though his offer was the least amount of money I had worked for in years, I was still excited about working for him. I thought that if I could just work under one person, my life would be less stressful than if I had to deal with an entire office of people. My biggest fear was that someone would figure out that I had a mental disorder and call me out on it. I thought that if I just worked with one person, the chances of being discovered as the screwball, that I still believed I was, were slim. So, I took the job.

Chapter 63: Life in the Little House

The house in Bartow was a small home on Johnson Avenue. It was just a few blocks from Nanny's house. I could walk to her house in 5 minutes or less. It was a nice little home, although, not as nice as my old house in Tallahassee. It had a back yard with an old shed in it. The front yard was small and had a little flowerbed running along the length of the house. The flowerbed was mainly hedges with a few other plants in between. It had a covered carport. There was a nice concrete drive that went into the carport. It was wide enough that a car could be parked alongside the carport as well. I think the previous owner had parked an R.V. there. I had neighbors on both sides of me. On one side was a young couple around my age named Stan and Amy. I don't remember their last name. On the other side were The Mc Croals. I can't remember their first names. They were members of First Baptist Church in Bartow.

Before I was allowed to move in, my parents wanted to do some minor remodeling to the house. Dad put in some new tile in the bathrooms and put a bead board wainscoting on the kitchen walls. We also painted all the walls. I was not a part of any of the remodeling projects except painting and one other minor project. The only thing that I remember doing, aside from painting, was taking out a ramp that had been built inside the house. I have no idea of what I did with my time when all the other work was going on.

The ramp was built over two steps that were in the house. The ramp allowed the elderly woman, who had lived there, to travel from the living room to the bathrooms and bedrooms that were at a higher elevation than the rest of the house. The house had a change in elevation of about one foot. The ramp was maybe 10 feet long. The land that the house was built on sloped from one side of the property to the other. The steps inside the house were the result of a house built on a split-level pad.

I took out the ramp by simply pulling off all the carpet that had been placed over it and stripping it down to bare plywood. Then I simply picked up the ramp and drug it out of the house. We never got rid of that ramp. It sat alongside the house the entire time I lived there.

Once I started living in the house on Johnson Avenue, life changed for the worse. The main thing that brought about this change was my new job and how I dealt with it. After landing my job, I was very nervous about actually getting back into the daily grind of working. The interview process was somehow still fairly easy to me. I sailed through all but one of the interviews. The interview that bombed was with a firm that I had previously applied with a year earlier. They asked what I had been doing in the year since they last saw me. I told them that I had been taking care of my dying grandfather. I was sweating because I was so nervous about having to hide the big secret that I had been put in a mental institution twice since they had last seen me. I think my nervousness came across as weirdness to them because, once again, they did not give me a job offer.

So, just before moving into the Johnson Avenue house, I had started working for Sam Sheens. Sam was an extremely nice guy. He probably could have been my all time favorite boss, had I not done the things that I did while working for him. Sam was fairly soft-spoken and always cheerful. He greeted me every morning and was usually there before me and still there after I left. He was a hard worker who was determined to build his company. I was his only employee when I started, but he planned to grow into a much larger firm. Sam actually had one other guy who did some part time work for him from home. I was the first and only person that Sam had hired to work full time and in his office.

Sam's office was a small building on South Florida Ave. He shared his office with another tenant. The office was actually an old house that had been converted into a little office building. Sam and I shared a small room in the house. There was another room that we used to put a few of his things in after I started working there. The room where Sam and I worked had two desks and two computers. We didn't have a plotter. All the printing had to be done at a print shop that was across town, about 15 minutes away. We did our test printing at reduced scales so that we could print them from an 11" x 17" printer that we shared. Sam's operation was as small as Charles Mada, the guy I had worked for several years earlier in D.C.

I really liked Sam. He always complemented my work and the speed that I was able to produce it at. Sam said that I was one of the fastest draftsmen he had ever seen. I thought that was probably an overstatement, but it was nice to hear. When I first started with Sam, I was excited. I thought that I might become an architect some day after all. I imagined Sam taking me through the IDP process so that I got all my hours of training in all the required areas. I'm sure that if I would have lived up to my end of our agreement, he would have done just that. But I was a total failure with Sam. For reasons totally unrelated to him, I became the worst employee that I had ever been.

The first thing that started to drag down my motivation to work hard was child support payments. Sara and I had already gone to court for our divorce hearing by the time that I started working with Sam. At the hearing, a judge read to me the reasons that Sara wanted a divorce. "Irreconcilable differences", was the main reason for the divorce, as written by Sara's lawyer. I simply agreed to all the terms that the judge laid out. I was in a state of depression that made it hard for me to get concerned over anything. Sara had set up an arrangement where I was only allowed to see the girls every other weekend and only with supervision. I could not see the girls by myself. I agreed to that because I didn't want to be alone with the girls. I didn't trust my own judgment enough to take on that responsibility. I agreed to all of Sara's terms. I thought that her judgment was probably better than my own, so I just agreed to everything that she requested.

After the hearing, I was followed out by Sara and her lawyer. He said that he wanted to go ahead and talk about child support payments. I said that was fine and that I just wanted to get the whole thing over with. Sara's lawyer asked how much I was expecting to be making with my new job. I had not even started yet, but I did have the offer and I knew what I was going to get paid. Sam had agreed to pay me $17.00 per hour. That was a lot less than what I made with ETO/Architects. Sara's lawyer ran my income through some bull crap formula and said that my child support payments should be around $950 per month. I gasped at his number. I had already estimated that I would be making a little over $2,500 per month after taxes. This guy was telling me that I should expect to hand over almost half of my paycheck to Sara. I said, "I don't know how you just arrived at that number, but that is more than what I was expecting to pay." He said, "Well, its not a fixed number. Your child support payment will be whatever Sara and you decide." I said, "Alright how is $600?" Sara said, "That's a lot less than what he just said." I said, "O.K., $650. That's a lot of money. We never spent that much on the girls the whole time we were married." Sara said, "Yes we did. You don't realize how much it takes to take care of our girls." I said, "$650?" She said, "Fine. I just feel like you are Jewing me out of my money. I never asked you to give me anything the entire time that you were not working. Your mom told me that you got a lot of money from the insurance that Warren gave you. I never asked for any of that and I could have. Now you're acting like you can't afford to pay me what you should." I said, "How do I know where this magical number of $950 dollars came from. Of course this guy is going to try to get you the most money. He is your lawyer, not mine." Sara's lawyer just sat quietly with no response. Sara said, "Alright, $650 is fine." After that, her lawyer thanked me for saving him a bunch of headaches and paper work and they left.

So, now that I was working, I had to give Sara $650 of my money after taxes. That left me with around $1,500, if I worked a forty-hour week. Having to hand her that major payment every month was demoralizing. I didn't like having the freedom of when and how much money to spend on the girls taken away. Now, Sara was the sole provider for the girls, as far as they were concerned. She received a check from me for several months. I hated to give her every one of those checks. It wasn't because I didn't want to help my kids. It's because I started to believe that she was spending the money foolishly.

In March of 2006, Sara got married to Matt Henry. Our divorce was not finalized until January of that same year. In two months, she had made the switch from one husband to the next. Once she married him, I began to feel like she definitely did not need the child support money as much as I did. The girls would come to see me and tell me stories about all the wonderful things that they had done with their mom and Mr. Matt. I would hear about Sara taking them to have their fingernails and toenails painted at the beauty salon. The place she took them to was a pretty upscale beauty parlor. She would also take them there for expensive hair cuts. The thing that really aggravated me was when my mom told me that she had seen Sara and it looked like she had a boob job. I thought, "That bitch is out spending the money I'm giving her, for the kids, on new boobs for Matt. What a crock of crap this is!"

After they were married, Sara and Matt moved into a very nice two story house in an upscale neighborhood, north of Bartow. They also had a huge Ford quad cab truck, a Ford Expedition, and a Ford Mustang. All of these cars looked brand new. It really irritated me to see that she was living large, thanks to Matt, and I was still having to give her extra money, just so she could play harder. I'm sure that the money I gave her went straight to the excessive items that I always heard the girls talking about her buying. Every time that I saw the girls, they had a story about how mommy had taken them shopping at this store and that store. All the places they talked about were upscale stores with overpriced items. I thought it was unfair that Sara was able to decide how to spend my money, even if it was being spent on the girls. I thought that if I had been allowed to have a say in what the girls did and did not need, it would definitely have been under a budget of $650 per month. I thought the whole child support payment process was a joke. I should have hired my own lawyer and tried to force her to spend the money on a set of agreed items that fit within a smaller budget than what I had agreed to. Giving her that money every month took away a lot of my motivation to work. I felt like I was busting my butt so that she could have a great time and also look like a very generous mother to my girls. So, after only a few months of paying child support, I began to get so depressed about the whole situation that I quit wanting to work.

The other thing that made it hard to work was the medication. I still needed to sleep about 12 or 13 hours every day. By the time I came home from work, ate supper, and took a shower, I was exhausted and went right to sleep. I would wake up the next morning to the sound of the alarm clock and almost be unable to summon the strength to turn it off. I would try to open my eyes and they would feel so heavy that I could barely keep them open. Waking up with 40 mg of Zyprexa in the system is hard to do. At the PRC they would wake us up at one time and give us an extra hour just to actually wake up enough to stay out of bed for the rest of the day. Now that I was out and working again, I wanted to stick with my old routine of waking up with just enough time to get dressed, grab something to eat on the way to work, and be out the door. In the years past, that usually took 15 minutes or less. With the Zyprexa, I could not move as fast. I needed a lot more time to get myself together and get focused enough to get dressed and do the other things that had to be done before I could go to work.

I guess the main thing that caused my problems with my new job was the mental disorder itself, just playing another trick on me, in a new way.

Sam spent a lot of time out of the office. He was usually chasing new work or checking up on the few jobs we had going. That left me alone for a lot of the time. Whenever I was alone in the office, I would sit there and just stare at the computer screen, for thirty minutes or more sometimes, and do nothing. It was just as I had done before at Johnston Peachson. I could sit and stare at the computer and get lost in my thoughts. They were almost always flashbacks to moments at ETO/Architects, or flashbacks of all the crazy things that I had done since the time that I worked there. The more I tried to get myself to snap out of my condition, the more anxious I became. I would think to myself, "O.K., stop worrying about everything. Just focus on this freaking project. Focus. Focus." I knew that my behavior was abnormal. I knew that this must be just another symptom of my newly realized mental condition and that just made me more anxious. I knew that it was a problem associated with that terrible new label that I had been given, Schizoaffective disorder. I worried about how long it would take for Sam to realize that he had hired a maniac. I was convinced that I was indeed a maniac. The memories of the crazy behavior I had displayed, only a couple months earlier, let me know that I at least had moments of insanity. I tried hard to hide all the fear and anxiety that this caused. I worried that I might do or say something at work that would give me away.

At first, the anxiety just made me exhausted at the end of the day, after I left work. I would go home and just pass out. But soon, I started taking longer lunch breaks. I was allowed to take a one-hour lunch break every day if I wanted to. After letting myself get worked into a state of panic most mornings, I started trying to take a nap on my lunch break. I would drive to the same plaza where we had our little SRT field trip, The Merchant's Walk. It was just down the street from the office. I would park my car there and lie back in my seat and sleep, or just lie there and worry. My one hour lunch break started to turn into a 1 ½ hour lunch break and sometimes even 2 hours. I would go back to the office and tell Sam that I had to run a bunch of errands and that was why I was late. He never seemed bothered, at first. I was being paid by the hour. So, I didn't feel like I was cheating him out of anything, at first. Eventually, the stress got to where it wore me down before I ever walked in the door that morning.

The real trouble started when, one day, I woke up and realized that I did not want to go to work. I had not wanted to go to work every day for many weeks, but I kept forcing myself to continue trying to get back towards a life of self-dependence. I knew that my parents could not afford to pay for three houses forever. They had originally intended to buy the house for Sara and I to move into. After she left and I was put in the PRC, my parents and I talked about getting the house as a place where I could live by myself most of the time. My parents wanted to sell the lake house and move to Georgia. They had planned to keep the little house in Bartow as a place to stay for short visits when they came to see relatives in the area. I think they bought it with the hope that I would be able to take over the payments at some point. So, the more I stressed over how inadequate I was becoming at work, the more I also stressed myself over the fact that if I did not work, my living situation would probably have to change. Stress begat more stress. The snowball kept rolling down the mountain and grew into another avalanche that was too big for me to stop.

One day, I woke up and thought about staying home. I thought I might just call in sick. Then I convinced myself to go on to work. I got in my car and drove along thinking about how easy it would be to just call Sam and say that I was sick. I drove all the way to South Florida Avenue and was less than five minutes from the office when I thought, "O.K., its now or never. You can call in and have a day to relax, or you can drive another five minutes and start another stressful day. What's it going to be?" I pulled over into a gas station and called Sam's cell phone. He picked up. I said, "Sam, I'm really sorry, but I've got a cold and I don't think I better come in today." Sam said, "Oh, I'm sorry to hear that Scott. I hope you get to feeling better." I said, "Me too." Sam said, "Well, don't worry about it. I'll be O.K. without you today." I said, "I really appreciate it. I'll be there tomorrow, I hope." He said, "Alright, just rest up and get to feeling better." I thanked him and hung up. There was an instant feeling of relief. A great burden had just been lifted from me. I no longer had the responsibility of showing up for work that day. And it had been so easy. Sam believed everything that I said and even sounded like he felt sorry that I was not feeling well. I felt great! I now had the entire day to do whatever I wanted. I drove back to the house and started watching television. I think that was about all I did. I just sat around the house and watched TV. That was a great day to me. But it ended too quickly. Before I knew it, the time had come for me to show up for work the next day. I woke up that morning and thought, "I could just call in again and say that I am still sick." That was all it took. It had been so easy the day before. What harm could come from missing one more day? The day before had been so nice. There was no worrying about being a freak. No pressure from some project that needed to be completed. It was just me and the TV

So, I picked up the phone and called Sam. I told him that I was still sick and that I thought I had better stay out of the office one more day. He seemed fine with that idea. He said he didn't want to catch whatever I had. I told him that was my thinking exactly. I just wanted to stay out of the office so that he wouldn't catch my cold. The problem was that the "cold" I was suffering from was not contagious. My "cold" was really a combination of laziness, anxiety, and that terrible thing called Schizoaffective Disorder. I got off the phone with Sam and spent another totally productive day in front of the television. Again, the day seemed to just fly by. Time seemed to drag on and on at work. But at home, the days were never long enough. Before I knew it, it was time to show up for work again. I decided I had better make an appearance at the office on that day. I drove to work thinking about how much fun it had been to leave the stress of the office behind. I also thought about how easy it would be to just call in again. I decided against it and drove on to the office. I walked in and Sam said, "Welcome back! Are you feeling any better?" I told him that I was. I made up a story about having a fever and throwing up for two days. I told him that I thought I had gotten some virus that my kid had. I made the whole thing up. Sam seemed to believe everything. It was great, and so easy. I didn't care about the fact that missing work meant less money at the end of the month. I figured I was already used to not having much of a paycheck thanks to Sara sucking away a good chunk of it to spend on whatever stupid crap she felt she had to have. And I also still had the insurance checks coming to me every month. They were always the bulk of my income, $1,800 per month. I never made that much working for Sam.

After that first time of playing hooky from work, I wanted to do it again. I worked for maybe a week before I decided that I needed to do it again. I pulled the same routine with a new twist. This time I called in and said that I was having to stay home with a sick kid. I told Sam that my kid had come down with the same virus that she had contracted a week earlier. Sam said he was sorry to hear about my situation and that he hoped I could come in soon because work was beginning to back up. I told him that I would try to be there the next day. I think I ended up calling in the next day too.

I did the sick routine several times over the course of a couple months. Each time I called in sick, I would usually stay out of the office for at least a couple days. The last time I did it, I stayed out for an entire week. That was when the routine became too much for Sam. My mom happened to call Sam one day expecting to get a hold of me at the office. Sam told her that I had not been there all week. My secret was out. My parents came over to the house one day and had a talk with me about what Sam had told mom. Dad said, "Your boss says that you haven't been showing up at work in the last several days. Is everything alright?" I said, "I'm fine. I just haven't been going in because there have been a lot of slow days. Sam has sent me home early a lot of times because he runs out of work for me." Dad said, "It sounded like he has some stuff for you to do now. You need to go back up there. How are you going to pay all your bills?" I told Dad that I still had enough money coming in to pay my bills. That much was true. The lie was in the part about Sam sending me home early all the time because there was nothing to do. That actually had happened one time. I left early one afternoon because I had finished a project and Sam said that if I wanted, I could take the rest of the day off, because he needed some time to catch up with all the work he had, so that he could figure out what the next thing for me to do was. That only happened once. I made it seem like this was almost a daily occurrence. After Dad's little pep talk, I decided that I needed to try to pull myself together and get back to work.

I went to work that next week every day. Sam told me at the end of the week that he was going to give me a raise. He raised me to $18 per hour. I thanked him and asked him what I had done to deserve a raise. He said that I was a good worker, when I was there, and that he did not want to lose me. I thanked him for the compliment and told him that I would try to be there more for him, even if it meant working from home when I had sick kids to take care of. Of course that last bit was just another lie. There were never sick kids at home with me. I wasn't allowed to be near my kids unless I had my parents there to supervise the entire visit. Sam said that work was backing up because I had been gone so long and he was unable to do it all himself. I apologized and told him that I would try to reduce his load.

I worked for a few weeks almost everyday. I hated it. I still took the extra long lunch breaks in an attempt to get a power nap and convince myself to go back and finish the day. Sam said that I could work late or on weekends if I wanted to because things were so backed up. I never worked past 5:00 pm and I never came in on the weekends. I just did less than the bare minimum to get by and tried my best to stay motivated.

Sam ended up hiring a new employee to help out with all the work that was coming in. He hired a girl from the firm he had left to start his own business. It was the firm I had wanted to work at a year earlier: Lund, Prelor, Foler Architects. They had done a lot of nice work. I really liked their style and wanted to be a part of that firm. I never even got to the interview process though. They told me over the phone that they couldn't hire me because they had just hired two other people with my background and were only interested in picking up a licensed architect.

459

The new employee was a Puerto Rican girl named Norma. She was beautiful. She should have been a big motivation for me to show up at work everyday. She was very friendly and seemed intelligent. But, not even a pretty girl could help me overcome the misery of the office. Norma and I had a lot of time where it was just the two of us in the office. I never tried to flirt with her or really get to know her. I was too depressed and anxious. All I could think about was how long it would take her to realize that she was sitting right beside a lunatic. I remember being nervous the entire time I had to work with her. I didn't have to interact with her much. She had her projects and I had mine. It did not require communication between us. We just sat in the same room, a few feet apart from each other, and worked in our own little worlds.

During my last couple weeks at Sam Sheens & Associates, I was supposed to be creating construction documents for an office building. I remember sitting in front of the computer and staring into the monitor with all sorts of racing thoughts rolling through my head. I would think about anything except the task that was in front of me. I was supposed to be coming up with details for the office building. Instead I was replaying all the weird things that had happened up to that point. I worried about Sam and Norma realizing how little I was producing. I thought about Sara. I thought about all the conversations with the voices. And I thought about how this was exactly the way I had felt when I worked at Johnston Peachson while I was in my last semester at FAMU. I was experiencing the racing thoughts and anxiety that I had known when I was still in college. And just like when I worked for Johnston Peachson, I felt like I couldn't take another minute in that office. Even though there were no other people in the room but Norma and I, most of the time, I still felt like I was under more pressure than I could handle. I decided it was time for another break. I decided to use my car as an excuse to get away from the office.

I had damaged the rear bumper of my car by backing into a telephone booth at a gas station. The Subaru Tribeca sat high off the ground and the rear window did not give a good view of what was behind me. Still, I should have seen the telephone booth. It wasn't the big glass box type. This was just one of the little phones inside a small metal cover that was open on the front so you could get to the phone. I backed up from a gas pump and went right into the telephone box. I didn't hit it hard, but it put a small dent in the bumper. My dad had told me about a guy in Georgia, near their house, who did really good, cheap work on cars. They were planning to go up there for the summer. I decided that I would go up there for a week and see if I couldn't get the bumper fixed. I told Sam about my plans and he gave me no lecture about how important it was for me to stay. He just smiled and said that he hoped I had a safe trip and that my car turned out alright.

I went to Georgia with my parents. I dropped my car off with the guy my dad had recommended and he had it fixed by the end of the week. I think I paid him $200 for the repair. It looked great. As soon as that was taken care of, I drove back to Florida. I spent more in gas for the trip than I saved by going to that guy.

I called Sam and let him know that I had just returned from Georgia. He said that was great, but that he had hired a new employee while I was gone. He said that he wasn't sure if he had work for me at the time, but I was welcome to stop by the office on Monday and see what things were like.

When I showed up at the office, Sam introduced me to the new employee. He was sitting in my chair at my desk. After meeting the new employee, I realized that I had just been replaced. Sam said, "Yeah, I'm sorry, but I had to hire someone else because I just can't keep up with all the work. I would like to use you as a back up for when things get really hectic. Maybe you could work for me from home for a while. Who knows, maybe I'll have enough work to bring you back on full time soon." This was all said as if it were already understood that I had removed myself from a full time position and had asked to work from home on a part time basis. The truth was that I really had done just that, only I never said it. By not showing up several days of many of the weeks I had worked there, I had only been getting part time hours, usually between 20-30 hours per week on average. I had already told Sam that I was willing to work from home, if needed. So, he just took my words and turned them into something else. He basically fired me without ever saying that I was fired.

I left the office that day feeling a little shocked. I had left for Georgia thinking that I would go right back to the monotony of the office when I got back. Instead, I came back to realize that I had performed poorly enough to lose my job. After leaving that day, I went back home and wondered what I was going to tell my parents. I called Sam a few times to see if he had any work for me. I was hoping that there would be something, just so I wouldn't have to tell anyone that I had lost my job. Sam never had anything for me. The last time I called him, he told me that he would contact me if he had some work. The next time I heard from him was when he called to ask if I wanted him to mail my last paycheck or come by the office and pick it up. After that, I never heard from him again.

My last day working for Sam Sheens was around the end of May. After that, I sat around the house for about a month. My parents were in Georgia for the summer. I called and told them that Sam had run out of work for me and had to let me go. I'm sure they knew that was not true. Once I was let go from my job, I really had what I had been wanting, relaxation and freedom. I was glad to not have to show up at a job every day. I felt guilty for not doing anything to better my situation, but the lack of stress was more important to me than a paycheck. If I had no income at all, I probably would have tried to find a new job sooner. But, I had the insurance paychecks still coming in. It paid all my bills. Of course, I never worried about paying rent. The house belonged to my parents and they never asked me to pay them to live there. I knew that I should be paying them something, but after I stopped working, I didn't think that they were really expecting me to pay for my housing. I was taking advantage of them. I should have found a job and made an attempt to pay rent.

For about a month, I just sat around the house, all day, every day. I had no desire to go anywhere or do anything. The awareness that I was becoming a total slob added stress to a situation that should have been stress free. I didn't have a job to worry about, but I still found ways to keep myself stressed out. The main thing that kept me so far down was the little flashbacks of moments that had taken place before the last time I was admitted to the PRC. I could sit on the couch and just stare at the ceiling for hours. I would lay there with my eyes wide open and recall all the terrible thoughts and things I had done. Mostly, I wondered what my family thought of me. I knew that I had been a total nut job around them on several occasions. It was not my mom and dad that I was concerned about. I knew that they thought I was crazy. I had stopped worrying about what they thought. I was worried about what every one else thought of me; all my aunts, uncles, and cousins. I wondered just how much they had been told about all of the things that I had done. I knew that they did not know the worst of it, only because my parents were not around me during some of my wildest moments. But, I figured that my mom had probably told everyone just about everything she knew about what I had done. I wondered how it might have been presented and what the reactions of my family were when they heard the news. I feared that I would forever be the black sheep of the family. I hated the idea that I would probably always feel rejection from my family because of my actions. At one time, I had felt like a rising star within the family. Now, I believed that I was the lowest, most terrible person in the family. I was ashamed of myself for letting my brain trick me into doing so many weird things.

The main incident that replayed in my head over and over was the day at the lake house when we re-roofed the guesthouse. My uncles, Mark and David, had been there to help out. I had a lot of respect for both of them. I was a total idiot in front of them that day. That was the day that I poured the oil and anti-freeze all over the driveway and my parents' cars. That was the day that I had been taken away in a police car, right in front of my uncles. I thought back on that day and wanted to cry, but I couldn't. I guess the medication prevented me from getting that upset. I am not a crier under normal situations anyways. It takes something very traumatic to make me cry. Those memories were very traumatic, but for some reason, they never brought me to tears, though I wished they would have. I might have felt better had I been able to cry a little.

I also thought a lot about Warren Eto. I wondered what his life was like after I left. I'm sure that for him, I was just another employee who got a bad attitude and had to be let go. For me, those last few weeks at ETO/Architects were a nightmare. The way that I lashed out at many of the people I had enjoyed spending my days with, before my brain went haywire, made me very upset. I wanted to call and apologize to all of them, but I was afraid that if I did, I would find myself in an awkward position and come away from my apology feeling worse than I already did. Warren had been the most generous employer that I had ever worked for. He did a lot of things that boosted my self-esteem to a level it had never reached before. My last year at ETO was a high point in my career as an intern architect. I had left the man, who had treated me the best, in the worst possible way. I had made him so upset with me that he physically removed me from the building that last day that I worked there. I wondered how I would ever be able to get my confidence back after that episode. When I worked for Sam Sheens, my self-confidence was the lowest it had ever been. It would only go lower before I finally hit the bottom.

After laying around and felling sorry for myself for about a month, I decided to get another labor type job. Since my experience with Sam Sheens had turned out to be another disaster, I thought it would be best to take another shot at a job that required very little use of my brain. I applied with Labor Solutions in Lake Wales. That was the place that had given me the job with Arr Maz almost a year earlier. I had really enjoyed my time at Arr Maz and even tried to go back to work there before applying at Labor Solutions again. The receptionist said that she remembered me, but that they didn't have any openings at the time. So, I was forced to look elsewhere for work.

I filled out another application with Labor Solutions and filled out the part about the minimum acceptable salary as "no minimum". I did not want to find a job that immediately made me rich. I wanted to find something that I enjoyed doing and that caused me very little stress. I ended up with a job that I hated and gave me a new kind of stress.

Labor Solutions called me one morning and said that they had a job that I could start that afternoon if I wanted to. I asked what the job description was and they told me that I could start a job with DuPont Liqui-Box in Lake Wales. Liqui-Box, manufactured the 5 gallon plastic water bottles that fit into the water coolers you might find in most offices. They also made a couple other types of containers that were used for other things. Labor Solutions said that the pay was $8.50 per hour. They said that I would most likely be working on an assembly line. I told them I would take the job.

There had been a time, before I started working with ETO/Architects, when I had imagined that working on an assembly line might be fun. I thought that once you knew the routine of what you were supposed to do, it was just a mindless type of job. I imagined spending the day at a job where stress did not exist. I imagined myself standing in front of some conveyor belt, putting something together and sending it on down the line. In my imagination, it seemed like an assembly line job might be fun. Once I discovered the reality of that type of work, I realized that was the worst job I had ever had.

I showed up at Liqui-Box the afternoon that I had received the call from Labor Solutions. I was told that I would be working the shift that ran from 3:00 pm to 11:00 pm. That sounded great to me because it allowed me to have most of the day to do whatever I wanted. I always stayed up late anyways. 11:00 pm was way before my usual bedtime. I thought the shift I was on was just another great thing about the job, when I first started.

I was first introduced to the Human Resources and Safety Officer. She was a very friendly girl who was around my age. She ran me through all the safety rules. She told me that we were required to wear earplugs at all times because the machines that produced the bottles were very loud. She also showed me where to clock in and out everyday. After the introduction, she walked me over to a black guy who looked a little younger than me. His nickname was Amp. I think his real name was Anthony, but we all called him Amp. Amp greeted me and we talked for just a few minutes. He was on the assembly line. There was never a time for long conversations. Amp immediately started showing me what he was doing while we talked. Amp showed me how to set eight bottles, from the assembly line, and position them on a machine that rotated them around so that cellophane could be wrapped around them. The bottles went, spout first, onto a pin that was connected to a table that slowly spun in a circle. Amp would grab the end of a roll of cellophane that was also part of the machine. He pushed a button on the machine and the table started spinning. He would pull the cellophane around the bottles to make a loop around them and then let it go. The cellophane would stick to the bottles and the spinning table did the rest of the wrapping for him. The table spun around and around several times, until the cellophane had wrapped all the bottles tightly enough that they were now packaged into a bundle. After the machine had made the bundle of bottles, he took them to another machine that palletized them. He would get a pallet and set the bundle of eight bottles on it. Then he would go back and make another bundle. He would then stack that bundle beside the one he had just placed on the pallet. He would stack the next two bundles on top of the other two. These bundles were stacked perpendicular to the ones beneath them. The cross stacking made the palletized bundles more stable. He would stack the bundles so that they were four sets of bundles high. Then he would turn on another wrapping machine that worked similarly to the one that created the bundles. Only this machine was designed to wrap the entire stack of bundles together to make one pallet of bottles. The machine was started just like the other wrapping machine. Amp would press a few buttons and then pull the end of a roll of cellophane onto the stacked bundles. The pallet of bundles would begin to turn around in a slow circle. The cellophane would stick to the already wrapped bundles and would begin to tightly wrap them together. The roll of cellophane was on an arm that moved vertically, up and down the pallet. The pallet was spun around 10 or 15 times with the cellophane wrapping around it as it circulated. After completing its cycle, the machine would shut off. Then the pallet had to be pulled out of the machine and set aside for relocation via forklift. That whole routine, from stacking individual bottles on the assembly into bundles, and then into pallets, took about 15 minutes.

After watching Amp go through the process a few times, he asked me to give it a try. I did all the things that I watched him do, and he gave me a few pointers on ways to do things faster. After seeing that I was able to do the job he had just shown me, he walked off and left me to take care of the bottle wrapping myself. It was a very simple job. A first grader could do it. I wrapped bottles all day, every day for the first few weeks that I was there. It didn't take me long to realize that I hated that job. I hated it because it was so monotonous. The bottles ran down an assembly line of hangers that transferred the bottles to a machine that printed a label on them and sent them to a large table where I would take them and place them on the wrapping machine. The bottles never stopped coming. If I was ever distracted for more than a few minutes, the bottles would be so backed up that it would take 30 to 45 minutes just to catch back up and clear the table. The bottles came out of the labeling machine at a fast clip. It was all set up so that there was just enough time to wrap a group of bottles and place them on a pallet. By the time that was done, there would be at least eight more bottles already waiting to be taken off the table. When I had to stack the bundles up and make a pallet, that process took long enough that I would get back to the table and play catch up for 10 to 15 minutes to get the table cleared again. The work was not mentally challenging in the least, but it required speed and no time for daydreaming or chatting with other employees. After a few weeks of bottle wrapping, I started to realize that this was not something that I wanted to keep doing for very long. I hated it.

After a few weeks of wrapping and palletizing bottles, Amp said that the boss wanted to have me trained on the machines that actually formed the bottles. The bottles were formed in a machine that took small plastic pellets and melted them down into liquid. The liquid plastic was then injected into a mold that blew high pressure air into the mold with it. The liquid was forced to the outside of the mold and took the shape of a 5 gallon bottle. The machine would then open the mold and drop the bottle into a hopper that was just big enough to hold 3 or 4 bottles. If you let more than 4 bottles stack up in the machine, it screwed the whole process up and the machine would jam because the bottle in the mold had no where to go. So, this job required speed as well. My job was to take the bottles out of the mold, cut off any excess plastic that was around the edges of the bottle, insert the spout into a machine that sanded the inside of the spout so that it could not cut anyone, and then insert the spout end of the bottle into a clamp that carried the bottle on down the assembly line, where it would eventually meet the labeling machine and the table where I had been working. The trick with that job was similar to the old job. I had to be fast enough with the scraping and sanding so that I had the bottle hung up on the assembly line before the next bottle popped out of the mold. The trouble with that job always came when I had to sand the inside of the spout. The sanding was done by a machine. A lot of times the machine would end up chipping the spout. When that happened, we were supposed to throw that bottle onto another conveyor belt that carried the bottle to a grinder that chipped up the bottle back into little pieces that would then be fed back to the machine that melted it all back down and formed a new bottle. Every time the sanding machine screwed up a bottle, my work was slowed down because I had to put the bottle on the conveyor. By the time I did that there might be three more bottles waiting to be sanded. It was another fast paced job that required me to be constantly moving. The worst part of it was the heat. The machine had to heat the plastic into a liquid. So, there were very high temperatures around the machine. The bottles themselves were hot enough to blister my hands if I did not wear three pairs of gloves. Even then, my hands were always hot and sweaty inside the gloves. I would sweat like crazy the whole time that I worked at the bottle production station. I got two ten-minute breaks and one thirty-minute lunch break during my shift. I was always looking at the clock, counting down until my next chance to get out of the heat. I soon hated that job even more than the bottle stacking job.

After working at Liqui-Box for about a month, I convinced myself that the factory life was not for me. I couldn't stand the relentless pace that was set to produce the bottles and package them for transport. I worked for another month after I made the decision that I would soon quit. I still had the insurance checks coming in. So, the Liqui-Box job was not paying my bills. The money I received there was just blown on the gas to drive my fuel inefficient SUV and food. I decided that the job was not worth the time and money that it took from me. I was sick of the heat and sick of the monotony of that type of work.

The thing that made me decide to quit was an offer to work the shift that started when I left. Liqui-Box was a 24 hour operation. The day was split into three shifts. The shift that came in after us worked from 11:00 pm until 7:00 am. One day the head boss asked me if I might be interested in switching to the late shift. He said that they had lost some employees and needed some of the people from my shift to start working the late shift for a while, until they found replacements for us. He said that I would be able to return to my shift as soon as they found other people willing to work that late. I told him that I was not willing to work that late myself. I told him that I had kids and I did not want to get myself on a completely different schedule than they were on. He didn't seem very thrilled with my answer. I didn't care. I had no desire to play suck up to a boss that I didn't know and didn't care to know. I had no intention of becoming a long-term employee there. His request and his attitude in response to my answer helped seal the deal for me that I needed to quit soon.

A few days after getting pressured to work the late shift, I called Liqui-Box and told them that I had received a better job offer and that I was quitting. They didn't ask any questions. They were used to burning through employees. Most of the people that worked there left within a year. There were a few people that quit in the two months that I was there. There were other people, who were hired through Labor Solutions, that replaced them. Almost the entire staff of Liqui-Box was hired through the temp agency, Labor Solutions.

I was extremely happy about quitting Liqui-Box. I didn't have any great friends there. I didn't want any. I was still a recluse. The daily routine of Liqui-Box allowed me to work and still not have much contact with other people. The machines made too much noise for us to talk to each other. Besides that, there was never a moment for conversation, outside of our short breaks, because the assembly line was always churning out new bottles. The line never stopped. Neither could we.

After leaving Liqui-Box, I thought about getting another job. I thought about calling Labor Solutions to try another type of labor job. I thought about it, but never acted in on it. I quit Liqui-Box some time in July of 2006. I waited over a month before looking for a new job. I spent that time doing a lot more nothing. I slept until noon, or later, and stayed up until the early hours of the morning, sometimes until 3 am. I didn't leave the house except to buy food. I usually ate out at McDonald's or Taco Bell. I never went anywhere that required me to have to speak to a waitress. I didn't want any more contact with people than I was forced to have. Being around other people made me nervous. I didn't even speak to my neighbors. I usually looked out of all my windows before I went outside, to make sure that none of the neighbors happened to be out there. If I happened to be outside and saw them coming home or out of there houses, I immediately went inside. I avoided talking to everyone. I was ashamed of myself for too many reasons to count. The bulk of the shame was from the obvious: I was becoming too lazy to even hold a job.

Laziness is a funny concept though. It's another word like "crazy" to me. People say that someone is lazy when it appears that they don't want to do something.

I don't believe that people are born lazy. I think that there are factors that make a person become lazy. For me, laziness was caused by many factors. I think the main factor was the medication. I was still on a high dose of Zyprexa. I was taking 20 mg, twice daily. It was enough medication to make me have the sluggishness and tiredness that I felt on an increased level when I first began taking the 20 mg dose at the PRC. The medication still made me want to sleep a lot. Even after sleeping 9 or 10 hours, I would have trouble getting out of bed and functioning. The medication also still made me have trouble talking. I would have to speak slowly so that I did not stutter or slur my speech. Speech trouble made me depressed too. I hated not being able to say what I wanted. I hated most everything about me. So, naturally, I was severely depressed. The depression added to the laziness. The combination of medication, depression, and no motivation at work, led to the laziness. The realization that I was lazy just added to the depression and subtracted from my already low self-esteem.

As the days went on, each one seemed harder than the next. Days added into weeks and it all became just a blur. I don't remember any specific events from that period after working at Liqui-Box and the time that I took my next job. All I remember is the decline of motivation and the lowest self-esteem that I had ever had. I was beginning to think about putting an end to all the terrible days for good.

Mom and Dad came back from Georgia at some point before school started in August. When they got back, they started spending the night at the house with me, several times a week. I didn't like it when they spent the night because I didn't want anyone to know that I was staying up until 3:00 am and sleeping until 2:00 pm sometimes. When they spent the night, I would usually go to bed around 8:00 pm, just because I didn't want to have to be around people, not even my parents. Anything I could do to avoid people was what I did. That was my strategy for coping with my problems. I didn't want to talk to anyone. I didn't want to see anyone. My strategy was to be a recluse. When I was alone, I felt the best. I didn't have to worry about what other people thought of me.

I dreamed about running away to some deep forest or an island that was uninhabited by people. I actually thought about trying it. I thought that if I could just escape from all the people, I would solve all of my problems. The only thing that stopped me was that I enjoyed the comforts that all those people, who I could not stand, worked so hard to provide. I imagined how I would have to live if I left everyone behind. I thought about all the things I would have to have to be able survive. I would have to find some way to build a shelter, wherever I planned to go. I had no clue of how I would do that. I thought about how I would have to hunt for my food. I had no experience as a hunter. I didn't think that I had the skills to live off the land. So, that dream died as quickly as it came to me.

Another plan that I thought about trying was to live as a homeless person. That's really what I was anyway. Without my parents help, I would have been just another homeless person, wandering the streets and struggling to survive. Every time I saw a homeless person begging for a handout, I saw myself in the near future. I tried to imagine what life would be like as a homeless person. I had already had a little taste of it before I ended up in the PRC. Those couple of weeks in between the time I was kicked out of my parents' house, and then ended up getting Baker Acted, had been a small sample of how a homeless person might have to live. The difference between what I was and a homeless person is that I had money of my own. I never had to beg for a meal. Thanks to the insurance policy that Warren had provided for me, I at least had my own source of income.

I thought hard about just living out of my car. I had spent two weeks doing that. I really enjoyed it. I thought that might be my best option. The only thing that stopped me was that I knew I had to have an address to pick up my check from the insurance company. I could have just had it delivered to a Post Office Box, but I felt like that was even too much of a constraint on me. I didn't want to have anything that forced me to stay in one particular place any longer than I felt like it. I thought about taking a big trip to the west coast. I had heard about California being such a great place of opportunity. I thought hard about just disappearing from my family and moving there. I imagined myself establishing a new life, with new friends who didn't know me as a lunatic. That was my trouble with where I was. Everyone thought of me as a crazy person. I couldn't stand it. I had never felt "crazy", even though I had been. To me, the time when I hallucinated and heard voices, was something that had happened and now had passed. I was not having those problems anymore. I was pretty sure that The Voice was only a figment of my own imagination. I was deeply ashamed about it, but I hoped that it would never happen again. And if it did happen again, I planned to immediately see a doctor and tell them my problem. I was done playing games with The Voice and the secret group. I thought that even if it was all real, and not a figment of my imagination, I wanted no part of the plans that they had laid out for me. It had almost killed me to be under the stress that The Voice put on me. And there was never any real proof that anything it said was true.

After The Voice had stopped talking to me while I was at the PRC, I steadily lost hope that any of what I had imagined was real. At first I wanted to believe in what it had said. But after the drugs took effect and I was left with a slightly calmer state of being, I began to think that maybe life would be easier if I just forgot about The Voice and all that it had told me. After I got out of the PRC, I expected that I might start hearing The Voice again. I wanted to hear The Voice again, at first. But after many months of just my own thoughts rambling around in my head, I realized that life was better without The Voice. I wasn't going on wild goose chases to perform acts that The Voice compelled me to do. I wasn't suspecting other people of conspiring secretly to do evil things. I began to just see the world again as it had always been. I began to get back in touch with reality. The only problem was that once I realized what reality was, I also realized how I fit into it. I knew that if there was no secret group who had been communicating with me, then the communications must have come from within me. I realized that The Voice was just some weird product of my own malfunctioning brain. The visual hallucinations were just another product as well. Once I began to believe in this reality, my self-esteem took a major nose dive. All these transitions in my thinking slowly developed in the 5 or 6 months after I was released from the PRC. It didn't all happen at once. It took time. I had firmly believed in everything The Voice had said. It took a lot of convincing for me to realize that I had been wrong.

The way that I convinced myself that I was wrong was not through conversations with other people. I didn't talk to anyone. All the convincing came from inside me. It all came from the silence. The Voice didn't communicate with me anymore, so I began to doubt. Just as a person may doubt the existence of God, from lack of evidence to prove His existence; I began to doubt the existence of the secret group. It was a choice that I made. I chose not to believe in them anymore. I couldn't prove or disprove some of the things that The Voice had said, but I chose to disbelieve all of it. It made my life easier. I decided that even if there was some secret conspiracy going on and the world was about to end, I was not up for the challenge of preventing the crisis. The short time that I had spent running around, maniac style, had worn me so thin that I really began to fear for my life. There were many times when I had chest pains after learning some of the wild information that The Voice had shared with me. I half expected to fall over dead from a heart attack at some point if I kept letting The Voice run me ragged. I chose to stop thinking about The Voice. I chose to quit waiting to hear from it again. That choice was my first step back towards sanity. The problem was that by choosing to leave behind my theories about the end of the world, I was forced to realize how I fit into the real world. That was where the depression came from.

Once I accepted the fact that I was wrong about almost everything, I had to realize that I could not always trust my judgment. That is a pretty hard thing to have to do. To admit that you are wrong about something is one thing. To admit that you are wrong about everything is something all together different. I had to make that admission. I had been wrong about almost everything. For several months I went around piecing together crazy ideas about the world around me. My ideas changed my view of religion and my values of right and wrong. It even changed my value of human life. I reached a point where even the thought of killing people didn't seem that bad to me. I had never been the type of person who lacked good judgment of what was right and wrong before I started listening to The Voice. I thank God that The Voice never asked me to kill someone. If The Voice had told me to do that, there is a good chance that I might have tried to do it. I was very close to that point on the night that I was Baker Acted in Lakeland.

So, now that I had admitted being wrong about all of my religious beliefs and values, I had to figure out what to believe in again. That is something that I am still struggling with. I have trouble understanding why God would have put me in the position that I was in. If God is in control of everything, then, surely He allowed me to become what I was. If I had actually killed a person, some might say, "The Devil made you do it." I would say, "No. The Devil didn't make me do it. God made me do it." The Voice had told me that it was a true servant of God. So, I would have to say that God was connected to my wild thinking. Some might say that it was just the Devil in disguise. That is my problem with religion. It can be twisted to give an attempt to answer most every problem. The thing that I have noticed most, though, is that the religious leaders that I have known personally, have failed to solve my problems as they are happening. They are usually better talking about things in hindsight. They speak best when talking about things that have already happened, so that they can relate it to the Bible and find a way to explain the past. They are also good at giving strategies for how to behave in the future. But I have not ever met a pastor that can handle my problems as they happen. I never hear much talk about the present. I guess that I'm still bitter from my associate pastor in Tallahassee not coming to my rescue when I called him on that morning that my dad wanted me to see my doctor. I still wonder where I would be today, had he come over and talked with my dad and I. I hate to say it, but I think that had he tried to rescue me from my dad, he would have only made things worse.

I don't believe Christianity can solve all of life's problems. If it could, then why did I have to go to a mental institution to get myself back together. Why was I not sent to a pastor to have God's healing power used on me? I think that the answer is that because everyone in my family, at least, knows that there are some things that even God cannot change. Maybe this sounds heretical, but it is my view. I do not apologize for it. I don't know of anyone who would take a child who was born with Down Syndrome to a preacher and ask him to use God's power to heal the child and make it normal. That is how I think of my problem. I have a sort of retardation of the brain. This retardation is slight enough that it allows me to travel through society like a wolf in sheep's clothing. Most people would never suspect me to have a mental disability, especially now. But, it will always be with me, so I have been told. So, for me to expect God to heal me of my disease would be about as likely as Granddaddy being healed from his terminal cancer, or a Down Syndrome child being cured from it's defect, or a mentally retarded person becoming normal again. Maybe these things happen and I just don't ever hear about it. I have heard stories of people who have prayed for God to remove a tumor or some other life threatening disease and it actually happening. I have never met any of these people. I always hear about them in stories told by the pastors who have preached in the churches that I have attended. I guess what I'm trying to say is not that I don't believe in God. I do believe in God. I want to believe in God. I'm just saying that, perhaps, either we can't always have what we want or God just can't always perform miracles. I hope the former part of that statement is the truth. I would like to believe that God can perform miracles. It just sounds so nice to think that a power greater than myself is out there and might perform a miracle in my life. Maybe he just did, and I didn't even notice. I need to pay more attention.

Well, after the realization of reality kicked in and the depression increased as I tried to understand who I was, I spent a lot of time doing nothing. The depression kept keeping me down as the thoughts kept circulating that I was not a member of a secret group, but instead was just another crazy person who had to have his parents' support him so that he did not end up homeless on the street. I stopped trying to plan an escape from everyone. I knew that I needed to stay put, where I was. I realized that was the best place for me, right where I was. I knew that as long as I stayed there, I would receive my income and most importantly my medication. I was beginning to realize just how important the medication was. The more memories I had of my times in between and inside of the rehab centers, the more I realized that the medication was the only thing preventing that from happening again. I knew that if I left Bartow and ran off to California or wherever, I would probably run out of medication before I was able to connect myself with a new supplier. You see, as long as I continued to participate in the program at the PRC, I received my medication for free. Without the PRC, or insurance, the medication would have cost me close to $1,000 per month. So, I knew that the best thing to do was just stay where I was.

After Mom and Dad came back from Georgia and started spending the night with me, I had a couple of perks from their presence. Even though I didn't want them to be near me, there were a couple of nice things that resulted from them being there. The main thing was that Mom would always cook almost every day she was there. She would usually cook enough food so that there were leftovers for a couple days afterwards. Mom was always a good cook. I usually loved whatever she made. So having her there to cook meals was really nice. The other benefit of them being there was that it motivated me to look for another job. Mom had retired a year earlier and was at the house all day, every day, on the days that she and my dad spent the night. At first, I couldn't stand having to be around even my own mother that much. My mom was good at finding things for me to do to keep me busy. Whenever she was around, she would have me outside doing yard work or cleaning something inside the house. I thought that if I was doing chores around the house, I could probably handle getting paid to do chores. I didn't like how she always tried to keep me busy. I didn't want to be busy. I didn't want to do anything. But after a month or so of being my mom's chore boy, I decided to look for a job. So, I called Labor Solutions again. They called me in a few days with a job as a maintenance worker for a retirement community. The pay was $8.50 per hour. I told them I would take the job.

The retirement community was in Lake Wales. That meant another long commute to work everyday, in a vehicle that got around 20 mpg. My drive to my new job was actually farther than when I had worked at Liqui-Box. The retirement community was east of Lake Wales by another 6 or 7 miles. My total one way trip was around thirty miles. So, I was spending even more of an already ridiculously small paycheck on gas.

The retirement community was called Saddle Bag Lake Resort. It was a nice little gathering of pre-manufactured homes. It was basically a fancy trailer park. All the residents were elderly people. The retirement community had a pool, a clubhouse, tennis courts, a lake, and several other amenities. I thought that it was a pretty nice place for senior citizens to spend their days. The residents held meetings, classes, and played games throughout the day. The place seemed like a very busy, but peaceful place.

My first day on the job was a little shock from where I had last worked. The first major difference was the time that I had to start work. I had to be there at 7:00 am. I had not had to be at work that early since I had worked at a grocery store when I was in high school. I was not used to waking up so early that it was still dark outside. Waking up early was a big problem for me. I had to completely change my sleeping habits once I started working for Saddle Bag Lake Resort. The other big difference between Saddle Bag and the old job, was the people that I worked with. At Liqui-Box, I could tell that most of the people there were not the brightest people I had ever met. The guys who worked in the maintenance department, for the most part, seemed like pretty intelligent people.

On my first day, I got out of my car and walked towards a building that said, "Office" on it. I figured that was where I needed to go. I walked in and was met by several guys standing around talking. One of them was a gray haired guy who looked to be in his early 50's. He said, "You must be Scott. Hi, I'm John." and he shook my hand. John introduced himself as my new boss. He said he was the head of the maintenance department and would be getting me set to work that day. John introduced me to the other guys standing around beside him. There was Justin, Sammy, Arthur, and a big black guy whose name I can't remember. The black guy was one of the most intelligent and friendly of all of them. I wish I could remember his name. There were also two other guys who worked there who had not yet arrived. I got there about 20 minutes early on my first day. The other two guys showed up late. They were Dillan, and another guy whose name I can't recall. The other guy ended up getting fired a couple weeks after I started. He had a habit of showing up late or not at all. He reminded me of how I had been when I worked for Sam Sheens. The guys all said that he was an alcoholic. They said that he drank himself to the point that he would be too hung over to show up to work. John had a heart. He did not want to fire him. John said that he knew the guy had a lot of problems and that he thought the guy was really a very nice person, but people who were over John told him to get rid of the guy. So, after several warnings about missing work and showing up late, they canned him. I felt bad for the guy because I knew that he was probably very much like me.

After all the guys showed up on my first day, John told me to follow Justin to a truck and that I would be spending the day with him. We had three trucks and two Polaris off road utility vehicles. They were like a cross between an ATV and a golf cart. They were a lot of fun to play around with. I followed Justin to a truck and we drove on to the clubhouse. That was where we began every day. We always went to the clubhouse and received our orders for the first part of the day there.

On the drive from the office to the clubhouse, Justin told me about what the job would be like. He said that he thought this was the best job he had ever had because every day was different and the work was always easy. He said the work was physically demanding sometimes, but always mentally easy. I thought that sounded good to me. That was why I had applied for a labor job. I didn't want to have to think hard.

Justin was a guy who was a few years younger than me. He had a great personality. I could tell that he was probably a smarter guy than myself, but he never put that kind of thing in my face. After working there only a short time, I began to have a lot of respect for Justin. He had good leadership skills. He was intelligent, but not proud. He was always friendly and was complimentary of my work, no matter how simple what I had done was. If Justin still works at Saddle Bag, I'm sure he has moved up the ladder. He deserves to anyway.

That first day, we drove to the clubhouse and walked into a kitchen that was inside of it. We all stood around and listened to John assign tasks to each of us. After we were all given our jobs for that morning, we went into the main seating area of the clubhouse. There had been some event held there the day before. Our first job of the day was to fold all the chairs that had been set out and stack them against the wall. Then one of the guys, Arthur, began to vacuum the floors. The clubhouse was Arthur's turf. He spent most of everyday doing some type of maintenance on the clubhouse.

After stacking the chairs, I went to my next assignment. John had assigned me to work with Sammy and Dillan. The job was garbage pick up. The maintenance crew was responsible for gathering the garbage of all the residents of Saddle Bag. We were the trash collectors for the entire community. We collected trash twice a week. We drove a truck with a large trailer on the back and gathered all the trash that had been put in the trash cans along the street. When the truck was full, we drove to a dumpster, that was near the maintenance building, and dumped everything in it. Then we went back and gathered another load. The trailer was about 15' long. We usually had to fill it two or three times before we had gathered everyone's trash.

Sammy drove the truck and Dillan and I loaded the garbage from people's trashcans onto the trailer. It usually took about three hours to gather all the trash and deposit it into the dumpster. The retirement community was a pretty big place. In all, we probably disposed of the trash of a couple hundred homes.

I enjoyed playing garbage man. I got to ride on the back of the trailer as we cruised from house to house. Dillan and I stood on little plates that were welded onto the back of the trailer. We walked along side the trailer most of the time, until we saw that we might have to walk more than the length of a couple yards to get to the next trashcans. The job was just what I wanted, mindless activity.

Aside from trash collection, my other usual duties were pool maintenance, and general grounds keeping. The pool maintenance part was a little challenging. My job was to add the correct amount of chemicals to the pool everyday and clean the filters every few days as well. The process of adding the chemicals and cleaning the filters was only challenging because of all the plumbing that was in the room where we performed the maintenance. There were several different pipes that all had many valves that had to be shut or opened to perform different operations. Some of the pipes directed water to and from the pool. Other pipes directed water to and from the Jacuzzi. The Jacuzzi was another thing that had to be dealt with every few days. It had to be drained, scrubbed, and refilled every few days. The challenge with those tasks was to open and close the correct valves on the correct pipes. None of the pipes or valves were labeled. So, it was very confusing to me. I had Sammy show me how to change the filters, add the chemicals, and take care of the Jacuzzi several times; and I still could not remember how to do it all. There were about 50 things I had to remember in order to do all those tasks. If I had it in writing, I could have studied it and memorized it more easily. I wasn't bothered by the fact that I was not picking up the information quickly. Sammy said that the pool was always the toughest thing for anyone to learn there. Still, I did feel a little stupid after being run through the process three or four times, and still feeling clueless about which pipes did what and which valves needed to be opened and closed.

Grounds keeping duties at Saddle Bag Resort were usually things like digging up old plants that were no longer desired to be there, raking leaves, and spreading mulch. The biggest grounds keeping project that I did while I was there was the installation of a sprinkler system. Justin and I worked about a week on the project. We had to dig trenches for the sprinkler plumbing to be laid in. Then we had to connect all the PVC to make the system. I did most of that. While I was putting together all the pipes and connectors, Justin hooked up the sprinkler pump to a timer that ran the system at certain times everyday. I had not had much experience with PVC pipe-fitting. I really enjoyed it. Justin did the hard part though. He figured out how to program the timer and hook it up to the pump that he also installed. I just did the mindless work of measuring the pipes and cutting them to fit. I also attached all the sprinkler heads into the pipe work.

Another job that I enjoyed was road repairs. Dillan and I spent about a week driving around the community looking for potholes. We kept a supply of asphalt there at the maintenance building. Dillan and I would load up a pile of asphalt and drive around patching potholes all day. It was fun. All we had to do was get a shovel load of asphalt, put it in a pothole, and then tamp it down with a machine that vibrated the asphalt and packed it down solidly. I liked that job because it was physically demanding, but required the education of a kindergartener.

The thing that I did not like about working at Saddle Bag Lake Resort, was John. John was the head of maintenance. He was the kind of boss that wanted to always see everyone busy. I have no problem with always being busy. But John was ridiculous sometimes. One of those times happened as Justin and I were installing the sprinkler system. Justin was showing me what he was doing to connect the pump into the system. John drove by in his truck and saw me standing there listening to Justin tell me what he was doing. John pulled up and got out of his truck. He said, "Scott, what are you doing?" I said, "I'm putting these pipes together. Justin was just showing me how to connect the pump to the pipes." John said, "Well, there are a lot of people here who have nothing better to do than watch you guys. When they see you standing around, doing nothing, it makes them think that you are getting paid to do nothing. They will tell the office and then the office will jump on my ass for letting you guys take it easy. Always look busy. Don't ever stand around doing nothing." I understood what John was saying, but I had only been listening to Justin for maybe a minute or two. It aggravated me that the short time I had spent not busting my butt, caused me to get a lecture from John about looking busy. Justin told John that he had asked me to watch what he was doing, so that I would be able to do it in the future. John didn't care, he just repeated himself and told me not to let him see me standing around again. I thought he was being very anal-retentive. I thought John was too much of a micro manager. He worried too much about small things.

Another thing that I didn't like about John was that he caught on very quickly to the fact that I never talked. We would always spend our lunch breaks in the maintenance building. There were enough chairs in there for us all to sit around and chat while we ate our food. All the guys would usually be talking about something. I would just sit there quietly. I might laugh if someone said something funny, but I hardly ever added anything to the conversation. Just about every day

John would say, "Scott would you shut up over there. You're talking too much." and everyone would laugh. I hated that little joke he did. He would always give me a hard time for not ever talking. I would just say that I only spoke if I thought I had something worth saying. The truth was that I was still having a lot of difficulty in the communications department. I still found myself stuttering and slurring words whenever I talked. So, I just stuck with the strategy of not talking so as to not make a fool of myself.

The thing that really caused friction between John and I happened on a day a few weeks after I started working there. John had asked me to take his truck and go get a concrete cutting saw from the maintenance building. So, I drove to the maintenance building and picked up the saw. Then I drove back to a little building where John and I were going to be working that day. I went to back the truck into a spot near where it had previously been parked. I started backing up and I heard John yelling at me to stop. I hit the brakes and saw John walking away from the truck and cussing like crazy. John said, "G&! damn it! Go, forward a little!" I put the truck in gear and went forward as he asked me to. Then I turned it off to see what had got him so upset. I got out and he said, "Did you not see my tool bag when you were backing up?!?" I said, "No, where was it?" like an idiot, like I didn't already realize that I must have just run over it. John said, "It was right behind you! You just ran over the damn thing! I just bought that tool bag!" John walked off and cussed some more. He was very angry. That was the first I saw of his short temper.

John walked to the back of the truck and picked up the tool bag and threw it across the ground. Tools went flying all over the place. The tool bag was a fabric bag with some rigid support under the fabric. The rigid support had been bent when the truck ran over it. I just stood there stunned at John's little outburst. John walked around cussing for several more minutes. I thought about offering to buy him a new tool bag. I said, "John, just take the cost of the tool bag out of my check. I'm really sorry. I didn't see it." John said, "How could you not see it? It was right behind you. Damn it!" I said, "I don't know. I wasn't paying close enough attention. I'm sorry." John said, "Its alright. Just give me a minute to calm down." I thought he was getting a little too worked up over a fabric tool bag. None of the tools were even damaged. They were just scattered all over the grass from him slamming the bag down on the ground. John and I had to work together for the rest of the day. He didn't hardly speak to me except to give me an order. Eventually, John told some of the other guys about me running over his bag. That started a little joke with the guys that I was going to be the next one who got canned because I had run over John's favorite new tool bag. I didn't find anything funny about that joke. After the tool bag incident, I got the feeling that I had put myself on John's bad side.

About two months after working at Saddle Bag Lake Resort, my parents started telling me that I needed to apply for Social Security Disability benefits. They said that people at the PRC had told them that I was eligible for Disability because of my mental condition. I thought that sounded ridiculous. I didn't feel like I really had a condition anymore. Sure, I didn't really want to be around people, and I never had anything to say to the ones that I was forced to be around, but I didn't consider myself to have a problem that required me to be on Disability. My mom kept asking me to make an appointment with the Social Security office and see what I needed to do to receive Disability payments. My disability insurance coverage was about to run out. That meant that I soon would no longer receive my $1,800 check every month. I think that I still had a month or two left when my parents started telling me about checking out Social Security. I kept putting it off. I didn't mind receiving the checks from the ETO/Architects insurance policy. To me that was not really a bad thing. I felt like I was just taking advantage of one the perks that I had from working there. But, to begin receiving welfare was something different in my mind. I felt like I was lowering myself if I started getting Disability checks from the Federal Government. I knew that money was collected from people's paychecks. I didn't like the thought of living off of taxpayer's money. So, I just ignored my parents' request to get on Disability and continued working for a few more weeks.

One day, my mom asked me what the status was with Social Security Disability. I told her that I had called them and they had said that I made too much money to qualify. I told my mom that since I had worked three jobs since leaving the PRC, they did not consider me to be disabled and that I was not eligible for the Disability program. None of this was true. I had called and spoke with someone on the phone and set up an appointment. I couldn't bring myself to show up for the appointment. I was too proud to apply for Disability. I didn't want to be known as someone who received welfare. I knew that my family already thought very little of me. I figured that if I started receiving Disability payments, my reputation would sink even lower.

Mom said that she was going to set up an appointment to go up there with me to the Social Security office. She wanted to explain to them what I had been through and see to it that I got put on Disability. So, she called and made an appointment. We both went up there together and she told the people my story. She told them about me being put in several psychiatric facilities and how I was unable to hold a job. The person who took care of my claim asked me a bunch of questions and had me fill out a lot of forms. We had to make a few trips to the Social Security office before my parents' plan, to get me on Disability, was working. The main hold up was the fact that I was still working when we saw the Disability counselor the first time. The counselor had said that I made too much money at my job to be eligible for Disability. My parents' solution to that response was for me to quit my job. So, I did.

My last day at Saddle Bag Lake Resort was sometime in early November of 2006. I remember feeling a sense of relief when my parents told me that I should quit that job. I had worked for a couple months after the day that I ran over John's tool bag. I got along pretty good with everyone there except my boss, John. I think the incident with the tool bag just put me on his bad side and I was never able to get off of it. He always found something to complain about with whatever I did. He was not really mean. He just seemed unimpressed by anything that I did. I can't really say that I did anything to impress him. I never talked to him, or just about anyone else, unless I had to. I didn't try to ask him questions that were not absolutely work related. I didn't want to be friends with those people because I didn't want to have to tell anyone what I had just been through. I was still very ashamed about my recent past. It kept me very quiet. The fear of someone finding out that I was a screwball

476

made me a very silent person. All I wanted to do was blend in and be left alone. So, when my parents said that I should quit my job, I will admit, I felt relieved. I was tired of the stress of trying to hide from people that I had to spend all day with. I had a few good times working at Saddle Bag Lake Resort, I will admit, but most of those good times were not brought on by the people I worked with. The things I enjoyed were simple. I liked being outside on days when the weather was nice. I also liked having something to do that didn't require much thinking. I got a lot of both of those things when I worked at Saddle Bag Lake Resort. Even though I had a few good experiences, I was happy to leave.

I worked my last day knowing that it was probably the last time that I would ever see the people I worked with. I never mentioned to anyone that it was my last day. I didn't tell John or the office. I just kept it in my head that the next day I would not return to that place. I remember that on my last day, I worked with John most of the time. He was dumping loads of mulch on an area where we were making a little road. The road would not be paved. It was going to be surfaced with mulch. So, John kept using a little tractor with a bucket on the front for scooping up mulch from a big pile that we had delivered. John would scoop the mulch up and dump it on the road, which was nothing more than an area that we had previously cleared all the grass from with that same bucket attachment on the tractor. John would dump the mulch and I would spread it evenly over the cleared area with a rake. I raked the mulch all day. I kept thinking, "I am going to miss this." I really enjoyed a lot of the physical work we did. I felt like I was getting good exercise. I knew that once I quit working there, I would not get the same level of physical activity that I was getting when I worked there. After that day was done, I remember walking to my car and looking back at the little retirement community with a little remorse. I was a little sad that I would not be back the next day. But I was also relieved. I was the only one who knew that I would not be back. To everyone else, it was just the end of another day. For me, it was the end of my work life.

The next morning I called the office at Saddle Bag Lake Resort. Someone picked up the phone and I said, "Hi, this is Scott Gann from maintenance. I just wanted to let you guys know that I received a job that is closer to my house and I will no longer be working for you all." The person on the other end said, "Hang on a minute. Let me let you talk to John." John got on the phone and said, "Hello Scott." I said, "Hey John, I was just calling to tell you that I got a job close to my house. So, I won't be able to work with you anymore." John said, "That's fine Scott. Good luck with your new job." I thanked him and hung up. John did not seem the least bit bothered by the fact that I had just quit. I think he was probably glad. Like I said, I was never able to get on his good side. He never acted as if he disliked me. He just never acted like he was very pleased with anything I did. I was glad to get that phone call over with. After hanging up, I got another wave of relief, as if a great weight had been lifted from me. I knew that I now just had to get the Social Security office to approve me for Disability and I would have a source of income that did not require me to work.

By that point, my parents had convinced me that being on Disability was nothing to be ashamed about. They said that Disability was created for people like me, who had trouble keeping a job because of an illness or an injury. My parents, and my doctor at the PRC, convinced me that I had an illness. They said that was all that was wrong with me. I just suffered from an illness that was no different from any other illness. My doctor tried to explain to me that if a person had an illness or disease that caused a problem with some other organ in their body, like their heart, or lungs; and it prevented them from working, there would be no doubt that the person qualified for Disability. My doctor said that my brain suffered from a disease that prevented me from working, maybe not forever, but at least for a while. My doctor said that people with mental disorders actually had less trouble applying for Disability than people with other types of problems like a back injury or some other type of handicap.

Hearing my doctor say that I should take time off from working made me ashamed of myself, but also a little relieved. I was ashamed because I still did not believe that I really had a severe enough problem to prevent me from working and trying to support myself, even though I kept trying and failing at job after job. I really had not failed at my last two jobs. I hated Liqui-Box, so I quit. I didn't hate Saddle Bag Lake Resort, but I was not performing on the level that I should have. My desire to be as reclusive as possible prevented me from establishing the relationship, with my boss and co-workers, that I should have had. But my job with Sam Sheens was a total failure. I was so depressed that I could not bring myself to show up to work. And when I was there, I did a lot of staring into the monitor and remembering all the terrible events that had transpired to get me to where I was. So, I guess I might have had a problem. Was it enough of a problem to quit working for three years? I don't know. Maybe. The experts all thought that it was anyways. I guess that is what matters.

After quitting my job with Saddle Bag Lake Resort, my mom and I went back to the Social Security office and re-applied for Disability. That time I qualified. I went through all the invasive questions. Actually, my mom did most of the talking. I still hated having to talk about anything related to the new label that had been stamped on me, Schizoaffective disorder. The people at the Social Security office wanted me to tell them about what had caused me to be put into the psychiatric centers. I hated having to talk about that stuff. They would ask me questions and I would respond, "I'm sorry, I just don't have any memory of that time." My mom would try to answer their questions as best she could, but they would usually tell her that they wanted me to answer the questions. I got through the first interview and was then scheduled to meet with a federally approved psychologist who would make the final evaluation of my condition and determine if I was unfit to work and eligible for Disability.

A few weeks passed between my first interview and the interview with the psychologist. As the day approached I grew more and more anxious. I kept telling myself that he was going to see me and tell me that I did not have a problem and that I should go back to work. I had already become comfortable with the idea of not working and noticed how less anxious I was. Without the stress of dealing with people on a daily basis, I was able to control my anxiety and almost keep it at bay. I still had stress caused from worries about how I would pay my bills after the disability insurance dropped me. At the time I got through the first interview in January of 2007, I had already received my last check from them. I had quit working for Saddle Bag Lake Resort in November of 2006. My income was getting smaller and smaller and was now approaching zero.

As far as bills, I still had a cell phone contract, a car payment, insurance, and credit cards. I had racked up over $3,000 on one of my credit cards. I managed to spend all of the money that I had from the big $16,000 check I received from the disability insurance coverage, and then some. A lot of that money went to all the unnecessary things that I bought when I was manic. I had bought all kinds of useless garbage: things for my car, Star Wars toys, and all sorts of other miscellaneous items that I could not even bring myself to look at. The sight of those items brought back the memory of what had been running through my head when I bought them. I packed most of it into boxes and did not open them for years. It disturbed me too much to see it. I thought about burning it all, or giving it all away, but I thought that some of the stuff may serve some future purpose. So, I kept it.

Another thing that I blew my money on was alcohol. In the time that my parents were in Georgia that previous summer, I made many trips to a bar on South Florida Avenue. It was a place where I had previously thought I had run into George Bush's daughter. The bar was called Sharky's. That was the place that I had thought was a meeting place for extra-terrestrials. That weird idea had been planted in my head on the night that I was Baker Acted. Now, though, I knew that was just another product of my own imagination. I did not go to the bar searching for aliens or the daughter of the President. I went there to drink myself stupid so that I could forget what a terrible person I was, if only for a while. I would go to the bar four or five nights every week. I did this for most of the summer of 2006 and into the fall, from July until November. I was an employee of Liqui-Box and Saddle Bag Lake Resort during the time that I made my trips to Sharky's. I started going to Sharky's while I was working at Liqui-Box. I would get off work, go home and shower, change clothes, and then head to Sharky's for an hour or so. I got off at 11:00 pm at Liqui-Box, in Lake Wales. I would drive back to Bartow, and then head to south Lakeland. I usually had about an hour before they closed at 1:00 am during the week. On weekends they did not close until 2:00 am. So, I could really get drunk on Friday and Saturday night. I drove myself home on every one of those occasions. It's amazing that I did not get stopped for DUI. I passed many cops on my trips back to Bartow, after drinking 6 or more beers and leaving Sharky's at 1:00 am or 2:00 am. That was one of the stupidest things that I have ever done. I bet that I drove home drunk 50 times over the course of my alcoholic experience.

The reason that I was going to the bar was to see if I could make a new friend or meet a decent girl. I soon realized that Sharky's was not a good place to do either of those things. I saw many fights break out between people who were too drunk to have self-control. I saw girls who came there more than I did and knew most of the regulars by name. They didn't know me, because I never spoke to anyone unless I was first spoken to. I always just sat down at the bar and ordered a beer, drank it, and ordered another. I didn't even speak with the bartenders. I just stared at the big screen televisions and pretended to be interested in whatever was on. It was always sports, which I could not care less to watch, but I just wanted to look busy, so that other people would not talk to me. Sometimes I did want to try talking to people. That was the original intention for going there in the first place. The problem was, I could never think of anything to say. I had forgotten how to communicate with people. The medication still gave me speech trouble too. I was scared that I might try to say something and I would stutter or slur my speech. So, I just sat there and stared at the TV, wishing that I could be any one of the other people there who seemed to be enjoying themselves. As for me, I was miserable, as miserable as I had ever been. I felt trapped inside of my own brain. I was afraid to talk because of speech issues. I was also filled with the fear of a conversation developing that led to me giving away that I was mentally disabled. That was my greatest fear of all, the fear of someone realizing that I was retarded. I had heard the saying, "Its better to keep your mouth shut and have people think that you're an idiot, than to open it and prove it for them." That phrase had real meaning for me. I thought of myself as the biggest idiot that I had ever known. So, I thought it was best to keep my mouth shut, as much as possible.

I went to Sharky's several nights a week for many months. I blew a lot of money buying drinks. On average, I spent $20 to $30 a night on alcohol. The beer was not the expensive part. It was only $2.00 per bottle most nights. Some nights it was only $1.00. They made their money by selling mixed drinks and Red Bull. That was where I really spent the money. My favorite drink was called the Jager Bomb. It was a combination of Jagermeifter and Red Bull. It only took two Jager Bombs to equal the effect of about five beers. One Jager Bomb was $6.00. Some nights, I might buy three or four. On those nights, I would have to wait in the parking lot for a while, because I knew I was not fit to drive. Legally, I was never fit to drive, but I always did. I can't believe that I was not caught.

The thing that made me stop going to Sharky's was the realization of just how bad a place it was. There were several nights when the police came into Sharky's looking for drug dealers who were known to frequent that bar. There were also many nights when I heard that I had just missed an actual drug bust that took place at Sharky's. The night that helped me lose my desire to go there anymore was a night when I saw an actual drug deal take place. I walked into the bathroom and there were two guys with their backs turned to me. I looked over the shoulder of one of the guys as I walked by. He had several bags of pills that he was about to give to the other guy. I walked on over to the stall and heard the two of them talking. One guy was asking the other how much each bag cost and what it was. By the time I finished taking a leak, the transaction was over. I turned around and the guys were shaking hands and talking about some party that was happening at some person's house. After seeing that, I realized that I could have been associated with a drug deal, had the police happened to come crashing in at the moment I was in the bathroom. I decided that I did not want to take a chance on getting mixed up in that sort of thing. I will admit that the thought crossed my mind to ask the guy what he was selling. I was curious, because I had already rationalized that I was taking drugs anyway. What was the harm in taking some other drug, even if it was illegal? After having that thought, I realized that I should remove myself from temptation. I didn't really want to try any illegal drugs. It was just a fleeting thought that occurred at the moment that I saw the drug deal. I never acted on it, but I thought that I shouldn't put myself in a position where I might be tempted to try something like that. I already had an addiction to nicotine. I was afraid of what might happen if I tried some illegal drug and realized that it was so great that I wanted more of it. Thank God I have never let my will power slip enough to ever try any other drug aside from marijuana that one time when I was in college. I am sure that I am the type of person who could easily get hooked on a drug. Cigarettes have hooked me hard. I don't need any other bad habits.

Now, back to the to the story, back to the time when I lived in the little house in Bartow and was in the process of applying for Disability:

I knew that I was going to have a hard time paying my bills with no job and no check from the disability insurance that had been provided by ETO/Architects. I was hoping that Social Security would start paying me right away. The process took much longer than I had hoped for. I still had not met with the psychologist to get the approval for Disability. I was very nervous about that. I just knew that he was going to send me back to my old life and all of its struggles. I was sure that he would say that I was just fine and needed to be working.

On the day of my interview with the psychologist, I was so nervous that I threw up before I went to see him. I was in my house, getting ready to leave, when I realized I was about to throw up. I ran to the bathroom and hurled into the toilet. After that, the nausea went away, but I was still very anxious.

Mom and I met with the psychologist. He had an office in Bartow. The psychologist was a man who was very different from the other psychologists I had met. All the other shrinks were people who I thought were there to tell me that I had a problem. I thought that this guy was going to tell me that I did not have a problem. He was very short with my mom and I. He quickly told me that he was going to evaluate my mental state to see if I qualified for Disability. My mom started trying to talk to him and tell him what she had seen me do. He cut her off and said that the interview was between himself and I. She was not to be part of the process. He was not concerned with what she thought was wrong with me. He only wanted to see how I responded to a series of tests. That was all.

He said that he had already read over my history with the PRC and the rehab center in Tallahassee. All he wanted to do was ask a series of questions and have me answer them. I don't remember all of the questions he asked, even though there were only a few. One of the tests I remember was a memory test. He said, "I am going to give you three words. I will say them once. Then you repeat them back to me. I will ask you a little later to repeat them again." He said three things like, "Car, apple, dog." I repeated them back. Then he went on asking me other questions. One that I remember was a series of numbers. He said, "I am going to give you a series of numbers. I will say them to you and then you will repeat them back to me." He listed several numbers that had no pattern or relationship to each other, like, "One, seventeen, four, twenty eight, fifty". I repeated the series of numbers back to him. Then he said, "Alright, now repeat them to me in reverse order." I tried to think of the numbers that I had just said and panicked when I realized that I could only remember the last two numbers I had said. I named off the two I could remember and stopped. I said, "I am sorry. I can't remember the other numbers. My mind has gone blank. I think the medication I take has screwed my thinking up." He said, "Don't worry about it. Just try to think of the numbers that I just said." I sat there and could not think of anything except, "You idiot! You can't even remember a few numbers? What the hell?" I started feeling very hot. I was really nervous because that was the first time that I realized just how little information I could really take in. I told the guy, "I'm sorry. I can't remember anything else." He made a little note on his papers and said, "It's alright. Can you name the things that I mentioned when we first started the questions? The three words that I gave you?" I said, "Car". Then I thought really hard. I tried to pull something out of my retarded little mind, but nothing came to me. Finally, I said, "Car. That's it. I can't remember anything else. Sorry." He said, "It's alright. That is the point of this test. We have to see just how your brain is functioning. You did fine." I said, "That was fine? That was pretty sad. Normally, I think I could have told you all the numbers and the three words. It's the medication. It clouds my thinking. It messes up my speech too."

The psychologist said that I should take some time off of work. I could not believe what I heard. I was sure that he would say the opposite, until I started failing his tests, anyways. The psychologist said that I would be approved for Disability and that he would get his evaluation to the Social Security people promptly. I thanked him for his opinion. It was just what I had hoped for, even though it shamed me. I was now convinced that I was not fit to work. Two professionals had arrived at the conclusion that I was enough of a retard that I was unfit in the work world. The news was a two-sided blade that cut down my self-esteem on one side, and gave me a little relief on the other. I was glad that I did not have to worry about a job, but I was sad that I appeared to be an idiot. There was a time when I thought I was a pretty smart guy. When I managed to graduate with a degree in Architecture, I thought that I must have a little going on upstairs. When I was in mania, I was sure that I was the most intelligent person the world had ever known. After realizing just how far from the truth I had been, I began to slowly spiral into a new perception of myself. I began to realize that I might not be as smart as I had always thought I was. After receiving the evaluation from the psychologist and knowing just how poor my memory was, my self-image dropped even further.

After the meeting with the psychologist, life began to become a little routine. The days started to pass in a blur. Everyday was just another day of sitting around doing nothing. After my last check from the disability insurance came, I knew that I had better tighten up on spending because there was no telling when the money from Disability was going to begin. The application process was complete by the end of January of 2007. I did not receive my first check until May of 2007. During that time of zero income, many things occurred.

The main thing that filled my day was the television. Fortunately, my parents had cable TV installed at the Johnson Avenue house. I had not had cable television since I was in the fifth grade. We never had cable at the lake house because the cable company had never run the lines out to Lake Buffum. We always had antenna television and that was it. We usually received about 5 or 6 channels. There

482

was never anything on that I was interested in watching. So, I was never a television watcher. I spent my free time, as a kid, outside, playing with my brothers. At night we usually played video games on a television that we had dedicated to the Nintendo, or I would play around on our computer. When Sara and I got married and moved to Tallahassee, we had a very basic cable plan that let us watch all the major networks and included Animal Planet, and a couple other channels. I think we may have had 15 channels, if that. Now, though, I had a television with a full cable package. It had all the big cable channels, including: VH1, AMC, History Channel, Discovery Channel, and all the other usual suspects. The order that I listed the channels was my preference for what to watch. VH1 was my favorite of all the channels because of their late night music video program called *Nocturnal State*. That show had a lot of cool videos and introduced me to some new music groups that I liked to listen to. I discovered Fall Out Boy, The Shins, Regina Spektor, Panic at the Disco, The Killers, and others.

In all the time that had passed since I was released from the PRC, I had not wanted to listen to music. There was a period of about a year and half when I never listened to the radio, turned on a CD player, or anything. Once I started watching *Nocturnal State* on VH1, I began to like music again. In a way, that was my first step back towards being the person that I was before all the drama began. I had always loved music, not all music, just certain types of music. After having all the strange experiences listening to my Counting Crows and Radiohead CDs, I swore off music for a long time. I was afraid to listen to it for fear that a secret message might pop out and trigger some strange new thought. I especially hated to listen to anything that I had listened to during the times that I had been manic. Of course that included Radiohead, The Counting Crows, and others. I realized that those groups disturbed me because they created little flashbacks of what I had been thinking when I had listened to them while I was manic. I hated having to think about what had happened to me. A wave of depression came over me with every flashback.

I can remember being involved with a task and getting a flashback of something I had said, thought, or done while I was manic. Whenever this happened it was as if the world stopped around me. I could feel things changing inside me when I had these memories. I bet my heart rate quickened and my blood pressure went up during those early episodes. At first, there were times when I would get a flashback and I would quit whatever I had been doing. I would freeze up completely. I would find myself standing or sitting in the exact position for several minutes as the memories of the terrible things that had happened passed through my brain. When it was over, I would usually realize that my mouth was wide open. Sometimes, I would actually have a little drool coming out of my mouth. When that happened, I would usually snap back to reality. At night, in bed, was when I had the worst moments. My nighttime terrors occurred for several years and still occur sometimes. The effects of the flash backs and nightmares are the reason that I am writing all this down. I want them to stop. I am hoping that by forcing myself to put my recollections on paper, I will be able to let it all go. I am hoping that the nightmares will end.

So, music was the first old habit that came back to me. I remember listening to the songs of The Shins and Regina Spektor and thinking that I sort of liked them. It was new material that had no connection to the old me. I could listen to their songs and not have to think about the weird person that I was. Once again, music became a tool for distracting myself from the present. It was an escape. That was what it had always been for me. Whenever I was stressed, I had always listened to music to calm me down. Now I was able to find something new that did the same old trick. The problem was that *Nocturnal State* did not come on until 3:00 am. I made sure to adjust my sleeping habits accordingly. I would usually stay up until 4:00 am just so I could watch an hour of *Nocturnal State* and find some new material to distract my brain from all its negative thinking. Staying up until 4:00 am had its consequences. Since the medication still required me to sleep about 12 hours a day, I usually slept until 3:00 pm or 4:00 pm everyday. I knew that was a poor routine for getting through the day, but I had no job to show up at. There were no responsibilities that required me to keep a normal schedule. So, I just changed my schedule from that of a normal person to that of a night owl. I kept up this routine until I was no longer able to live at the Johnson Avenue house.

Almost every day after I had stopped working at Saddle Bag Lake Resort, I woke up between 3:00 pm and 4:00 pm. Waking up was the hardest part of the day. Almost everyday since I had been released from the PRC, the first thing that happened was the realization of who I had become. I woke up to realize that I was no longer a hard working guy with a wife and kids who loved him. No, now I was nothing more than a nuisance to society. The only way I survived was from taxpayer's money. I was not contributing to the world around me in any way. Instead, I was taking away from it. I was a parasite that sucked the blood of everyone around me. It was hard to make myself get out of bed and begin another day. I hated waking up. I hated being awake. From the minute I woke up, I counted down the hours until *Nocturnal State* would be on and I could end my misery for a short while and then go back to sleep.

I would usually wake up and walk into the living room and turn on the TV. Then I would sit in front of the TV until I got hungry. Whenever that happened, I usually got something out of the fridge and went right back in front of the TV. Usually, I spent almost all of my waking hours in front of the television. I had no desire to meet people. Actually I was afraid to meet people, even though I would put myself in a situation where I might meet someone when I was at the bar. The fear of having to tell someone about my time as a lunatic kept me very reclusive, and I stayed that way for several years.

After waking up and watching television for hours, I would sometimes want to get out of the house. This usually happened around 6:00 pm or 7:00 pm. I would usually drive to Lake Wales and go to the Eagle Ridge Mall. I enjoyed walking around there because I never saw anyone that I knew. I could walk around the mall and be invisible. I did not have to speak with anyone. I might smile at people I passed as I walked around the mall, but I never spoke to anyone except the people who I ordered an ice coffee from every time I went there.

Barnie's Coffee was a little store that got bought out by Starbuck's. How sad. Barnie's was so much better than anything Starbuck's has to offer. I loved Barnie's iced coffee drink, The Coffee Cooler. I always ordered a hazelnut Coffee Cooler every time I made my trip to the mall. The Coffee Cooler was really the only reason that I would drive all the way from Bartow to Lake Wales, which was over 20 miles from my house to the mall. It was a serious waste of gas. But, I justified it as something I had to do to get through the day. That was the hardest thing, finding ways to fill the hours that I used to spend as a productive member of society. Most of it was wasted in front of the TV. But there were several days a week when I made the trip to Barnie's, just to get away from the TV for a short while.

After a couple weeks of showing up at Barnie's on a regular basis, the people who worked there began to know what I was going to say I wanted: a medium hazelnut Coffee Cooler. After a couple months, several girls that worked there started kidding me about always ordering the same thing. They would always say, "Why don't you ever try anything besides the hazelnut Coffee Cooler?" I would say, "Because I like it. When I get tired of it, I'll try something else." After I began to realize that the people at Barnie's recognized me, I started to get nervous every time I went in there. I was afraid that one of them would start trying to talk to me. That would require me to talk back. I didn't want to do that. I was afraid I might say something and start stuttering or slurring my words. I usually tried to get my iced coffee and get out of there as quickly as possible, with as little conversation as possible. But interaction with the people there was inevitable. The more I showed up, the more the people there tried to talk to me. One girl, named Deseray, was the one who I finally decided to chat with a few times. We only had a few brief little conversations. She was a cute girl and always seemed glad to see me. I thought that if I had any confidence, I would have been able to start a relationship with her. But that was something that I had no interest in doing. I saw what I did to Sara. I knew how miserable I had made her. I didn't want to get involved with any girls, even cute, friendly girls who always knew my order at the coffee bar. Besides, I had no job and no income. I figured that no girl would want to have a relationship with a guy like me. I assumed that if I ever told anyone about what had happened to me, they would be afraid of me, the same way that everyone I knew was afraid of me. I thought it was better to just avoid making any new friends because I did not want to deal with the rejection I thought I would experience once I told them who I really was. My strategy for dealing with people was to be as silent as I could. At Barnie's, the only thing I said was what I wanted the people to make for me. With Deseray, I had a few short conversations about how much I liked Barnie's Coffee Cooler and how I wished they were not about to be bought out by Starbuck's. Deseray told me that she was from California and told me a few stories about things she missed there. Aside from those short conversations, which usually lasted less than a minute, we only said hello to each other. But there was something in the way that she greeted me, and had those little talks with me, that gave me the suspicion that I could have had a much deeper relationship with her.

The only way I was able to pay for the occasional trip to Barnie's was because I had saved a couple thousand dollars in my checking account and I still had another couple thousand in my savings account. Also, my parents would give me

$20-$40 dollars every couple weeks. I quickly burned through the money in my checking and savings. It was mostly spent between gas, iced coffee, alcohol, cigarettes, and trips to the movie theater.

The movie theater was another place where I wasted my time and money. On nights that I didn't go to the bar, I usually went to the movies. I did this a few times a week for several months. I would see movies that I didn't even really care to see. I would drive to Lakeside Village in Lakeland, to a movie theater there. They charged $8.00 for admission. By the time I bought a Coke and a pack of M & M's, I usually dropped about $15.00 every time I went there. I justified my movie theater expenses as just another way to cope with my mental state. The movie theater was another place I could go and be around people, but not have to talk to any of them. I could sit in the theater and be distracted from my self-hatred for a couple hours. It didn't bother me that between the bar, the mall, and the movies, I was spending way beyond my means. I justified it all as my coping strategy. My coping strategy was very expensive. I wish that I would have been smarter with my money. Instead of paying off my credit card debt, I was spending my last dollars on ridiculous trips for iced coffee, beer, and movies. If I had kept myself at home, I would have been able to pay off all my debt. I kept up the movie theater routine for several months. I stopped going when I realized that Social Security was not going to start paying me right away, and even when they did start paying, it would be much less than I had received from the disability insurance.

I was given a figure for my Disability income in the mail one day in February of 2007. The Social Security Department sent me a letter stating that I would receive around $1,000 per month from Disability. The letter said that I would begin receiving my checks in May of 2007. It said that my first check would cover the time period from January 2007 to May of 2007. After receiving that letter, I knew that I had better stop all the frivolous spending. I had made my last car payment in January of 2007. After that, I decided I would wait to see what Disability was going to pay me before I made another payment. I wanted to save all the money I had, in case I needed it for food. After seeing that I was not going to receive a Disability check until May of that year, I realized that I was going to have to get rid of my car. My parents told me to try to sell it. So, I put up a sign on the windows that said, "For Sale" and gave my phone number. I also ran an ad in the local newspaper for a couple weeks. I listed my asking price as $28,000. I still owed more than that, but I was hoping that someone would bite. The only call I ever received was from a guy who was wanting me to place an ad for my car in a magazine that he worked for. No one else ever called. After going about four months without making a payment, the bank sent me a letter saying that it was going to repossess my car. I was glad to see it go. The car was just another reminder of the time when I was out of my mind. I always felt like an idiot driving around in that thing. There I was, working at Liqui-Box and Saddle Bag Lake Resort, making just over minimum wage, and driving a $32,000 vehicle. Several people at both of those jobs asked me how I was able to pay for my car. I just told them that there was a time when I made really good money, and that I had most of the car paid off. That was all a lie. I had always just made the minimum monthly payment. That was it. I bought the car in September of 2006. I lost it in the summer of 2007. I didn't like the way that I lost my car, but it was a relief to see it go.

My car was repossessed in the summer of 2007 while my parents and I were in Georgia. I remember the day we left the lake house to drive to Georgia. I walked up to my car and looked at it. I opened the driver's side door and sat down in it. I looked at all the amazing features that were in the car. I thought, "This is the last time that I will ever sit in a car this nice again." I turned on the radio and watched all the lights come on in the neat display on the dashboard. Then I turned it back off and checked to make sure that I had not left anything in the car that I did not want to live without. After that, I locked the car and walked away from it, knowing that after that day, I would never see it again. Later that summer, when we were up in Georgia, I got a call from Nanny. She said that she had driven out to the lake house and that my car was gone. I said, "Yeah. I figured that they would have repossessed it by now." After that, I knew that I no longer had transportation. Now, I was totally dependant on my parents for everything. I had no house, no job, and now, no car. I was well on my way to becoming the homeless person that I had feared I would become. Before I lost my car, a few other things went away.

The lack of income led to the dwindling of my already tiny bank accounts. By March of 2007 I was almost broke. The frivolous spending to support my unnecessary routines of drinking alcohol, watching movies, and driving way to far for a $3.00 iced coffee, had taken its toll on my savings and checking accounts. I had stopped the trips to the bar and the movies around the end of February. But I still liked to drive to the mall to get my iced coffee. I felt like I had to get out of the house, if only for a couple hours, everyday. I was still very depressed. The lack of income only worsened the situation. As I watched my bank accounts get smaller and smaller, my depression grew larger and larger. I knew that I had blown a bunch of money on useless things. I wasn't spending in mania, I was spending to pass the time and to distract my brain from the terrible things it was thinking. I was not hearing voices anymore. I was just responding to reality, the reality that I was a total waste of a person. I felt like a rogue. I lived in a house that my parents had bought for me, in the hopes that I would be able to take over the payments. I received money from them as well. I usually spent that money on cigarettes. They usually only gave me $20 to $40 dollars every couple of weeks. That was just enough to support my smoking habit and also buy a few meals. I bought my gas and iced coffee with the small amount of money that was left in my bank accounts. I knew that routine would have to end soon, as well.

As I watched my bills come in and start piling up, I began to see what the future looked like for me. I knew that my credit was going to be ruined, but I didn't care. I hoped that once the Disability checks started arriving, I would begin to pay my bills again. The more the bills grew, the more my self-image shrank. I felt guilty about not paying my bills, but not guilty enough to stop wasting all my money on gas, cigarettes, and iced coffee. My car got 20 mpg on a good day. The drive to Eagle Ridge was at least 20 miles, if not more. So, every trip cost me two gallons of gas. I think that gas was approaching $3.00 per gallon at the time. So, lets just say that every trip to Eagle Ridge Mall cost me $6.00 in gas plus $3.00 for every iced coffee.

I usually made that trip 3 or 4 times a week, so that adds up to $27 to $36 for every week that I kept up my iced coffee habit. That would not be a big deal if I was working, like a normal person. But I had no income and I still kept spending the way I had always done. It was hard to take a step down in my life style. I had been gradually stepping down since I stopped working for ETO/Architects. Aside from the manic spending that I did during my time before my last trip to the PRC, I was pretty tight with money. But as I became more depressed, after that last trip to the PRC, I did not care what I was spending or what was in my bank accounts. I had started to make a new plan for the future. It was a very dark plan.

After the last check came from the disability insurance company, I decided to stop paying my bills. I knew my credit would be ruined, but I wanted to keep the little money I had for "emergencies". Like I said, that money all went to gas, cigarettes, alcohol, etc.; not emergencies. The things I had to let go of were my car and my cell phone. I didn't see the point in paying for a phone that I never used. The only people who ever called me were my parents and Nanny. I figured that if they wanted to tell me something, they could stop by and talk to me at the house. I had no need for a cell phone, so I got rid of it. I couldn't cancel the contract that I was in, so I just let the bills keep piling up until Sprint started sending me threatening letters that they were about to refer me to a collection agency. I didn't care. I kept throwing all of my bills right into the trashcan. If I suspected that a piece of mail was a bill, I would throw it in the trash without even looking at it. I did this with the cell phone bill, my credit card, and my car payments. I ignored all my responsibilities. I couldn't stand to even look at the rising dollar amounts that were shown on all my bills. The credit card was piling on interest as well as late fees. That bill was just under $3,000 when I stopped making payments on it. Before I was referred to a collection agency, the bill had grown to over $5,000. Once the collection agency took care of my account, they just sent me more threatening letters, but stopped adding late fees and interest to my bill. That relieved a little stress. Within a few months, all my accounts had been referred to collection agencies. So, all my bills were frozen and the late fees stopped accruing. At that point, I'm sure, my credit was totally ruined.

As the days dragged on between January and May of 2007, I got closer and closer to hitting the rock bottom of the downward spiral that I had been in since the time I married Sara. The end of the spiral only led to one thing, the end of me.

I had internet access at my house. Of course, my parents paid that bill. I never used it. I had no interest in anything. I had no desire to know about anything that the internet offered, except for one thing, suicide. Sometime in February, I began to research ways to end my life painlessly.

By that point, I had arrived at a point where I was tired of the way I was. I could not see anything positive about myself, or the way I interacted with other people. I was tired of always being nervous, afraid, or angry. I thought about who might be affected by my suicide. I could only think of two people who I thought might actually miss me, and I really didn't think that they would miss me for long. The people that I thought of were my two little girls, Liza and Gwen. My rational for them was that they would be better off without me. I got to see them every other weekend, but I never felt like I was able to be the father that I was supposed to be. I never spoke to them much in the time that they were with me. I was always too wrapped up in my own world of self-hate and self-pity. All I could think about, most of the time that they were with me, was how odd I must seem to them. I knew that Liza had to have some understanding that I was different from most people. I was not as concerned about Gwen, but I was bothered by my interactions with her as well. Gwen always wanted to talk about her new dad, Mr. Matt, and his kids. Both of my girls always had lots of stories about the fun times that they had with Mr. Matt and his kids. My girls started referring to Matt's kids as their brothers and sister. I felt like my kids had been taken away from me and they were drifting into a new life that their mother had created for them, a life that did not have much room for me. I saw the future with my girls as one where I was just some guy who they hung out with for a few hours, every other weekend. I felt cheated. I had spent a lot of time worrying about being a good father to my kids before Sara and I had divorced. There had been a time when I had worked very hard so that they might have a good future. There was a time when I thought that I was doing everything right. But now, everything had been pulled out from underneath me, and I had just watched as it happened.

At first I had fought very hard to prevent my current situation from happening. That night in Tallahassee, when Sara, my dad, and my brother; had all sat across from me at my kitchen table; I knew that was the moment to put up my best fight. I felt like after that night, after the failed attempt to prevent my diagnosis as a "crazy" person; my life had ended. After I was sent into the rehab center, I was never the same person. I went in fighting mad, but came out ready to surrender. After losing my job and my house, I really didn't think things could get much worse. But they did. The first trip to the rehab center in Bartow, just left me more upset with the people who had sent me there, my parents. After the last trip to the PRC, I came out ready to give up on everything. By that point, I had lost my wife and kids. I didn't feel like there was much motivation to do anything. It only took a little time for me to let things go so far down hill that I was not only ready to give away all that I had left, but also my own life.

So, I had reached a point where I had lost all motivation to do anything. Waking up every afternoon around 4:00 pm, to the fact that I was a child in an adult's body, gave me little reason to even try to get out of bed. Eventually I would crawl out and begin another dreary day. I moped around until even that just got old. I knew that my self pity was not doing me or anyone else any good. The only solution I could come up with was suicide. I thought that my kids would grow up to be better people if I removed myself from their life altogether. I knew that they seemed to have a lot of fun when they were with their mom and her new husband, Mr. Matt. I never felt like they enjoyed being around me. I didn't blame them. I couldn't stand me. I wasn't surprised that no one else could stand me either. So, after realizing that no one would even miss me, and everyone would probably be better off without me, I decided to investigate ways to kill myself.

The trouble with searching for suicide techniques on the internet is that when you type in "suicide", or "painless suicide", you get a list of websites that trick you into thinking you are about to find some great information about how to actually commit suicide. When you visit these sites, they all turn out to be websites from churches and other crisis organizations that put up all sorts of reasons why you should not commit suicide. I was disappointed that I could not find any good information about how to end my life with as little pain as possible. I was hoping that I might find some company that sold some pill that I could take that would just put me to sleep forever. It's a good thing that someone out there was already way ahead of me. I guess the regulators of the internet already realized that giving people easy access to information about suicide was not a good idea. I'm sure that if I had dug deep enough, I could have found something, but I only searched the internet a few times, for just a few minutes, and then I gave up. I didn't even have the motivation to stay focused on that task for very long. I figured that I already knew enough ways to kill myself. I just had to get the courage to do it.

I thought about driving my car into a telephone pole or a tree, but opted out of that because I thought that there was a good chance that I would survive the crash and wake up in some hospital only to realize that I was now paralyzed and would spend the rest of my life in a hospital bed, with tubes feeding me and keeping me alive for who knows how long. I thought about hanging myself, but that didn't sound pretty either. I imagined that might also result in me just paralyzing myself, because I wasn't sure how to correctly tie and hang the noose so that it actually did the job right. I finally came to the conclusion that the best thing to do would be to get a gun and blow my brains out. I knew that was probably the messiest way to go, but I thought it would be instant, and hopefully painless.

So, one day, after contemplating the effect of my suicide on every one else, and coming to the conclusion that it was the best thing to do; I began to search my parents' room for a gun. My parents slept in a room in the Johnson Avenue house when they stayed overnight. I knew that my dad had kept a pistol under the mattress of his bed at one time. I wondered if he might have a pistol under the mattress of their bed in the bedroom of the Johnson Avenue house. I walked into the bedroom and looked at the bed. I thought, "If the gun is here, I am going to use it. Then this will all be over. If there is no gun, then maybe God is trying to tell me something." I had goose bumps all over me as I had this thought. I knew that if there happened to be a gun under the mattress of that bed, then I would walk outside to the little shed in the back yard and end my life with it. I paused before lifting up the mattress. I was half hoping it was there and half hoping that it was not. Finally, I lifted up the mattress and saw that there was nothing there except the box spring frame below. I went to the other side of the mattress and lifted it up. Nothing. Then, I looked around in the closet of their room, and then through the dressers. Still nothing. So, after searching every place I could think of where my dad might have hidden a gun, I gave up. I was a little relieved, but also a little disappointed. On one hand, I thought that perhaps that was God's way of telling me that he did not intend for me to die at that time. I know that suicide is a sin, according to the Bible, but I figured that God would cut me some slack. I had prayed for Him to forgive me if I killed myself. I felt like I had made my peace with Him. But, after realizing that there must not be a gun in the Johnson Avenue house, I wondered if He had purposely set up those conditions to prevent me from taking such drastic measures. On the other hand, I thought that it was pretty crappy that I couldn't even find a way to successfully kill myself. Sure, I could think of many other ways of attempting it, but I was not positive that any of those ways would actually complete the act of suicide, or if they would just leave me still alive, but in much worse shape than I had been beforehand. So, after failing to find a gun, I gave up on the idea of suicide, but not altogether. I still thought that there might come a time when I was able to get my hands on a gun and use it. I just thought that I had better wait until the timing was right. I was sure that there was a gun at the lake house, but my parents were there. I didn't think that I could sneak in and take a gun without being caught. So, I just waited and hoped that there might come a time when I was able to get my hands on one of Dad's guns.

I think that time when I actually had myself convinced that the world would be a better place without me was the low point of my life so far. I hope I never again allow myself to think of doing such a thing. I know that it was not a good solution for my problem. But I had just followed a series of thoughts that led me to believe that suicide was the right thing for me to do. Shame is the justification for suicide in other cultures, just not ours. I have heard that Japanese Shoguns often killed themselves if they lost a battle or did some other act that brought shame on themselves or their family. I have heard that it was considered an honorable thing to do. There was a time when I thought that suicide was the honorable thing for me to do. I felt like I only brought shame to my family and myself. I was tired of being ashamed of myself, and felt guilty for the way I had treated my family. Suicide seemed like the correct response for a life of letting people down. I did not want to see a future where my kids either hated me or were just so ashamed of me that they never spoke to me. I wanted out before those things became a reality.

Fortunately, I never had an opportunity to get a hold of one of Dad's guns. Mom had retired from work and was usually out at the lake house. So, I did not try to get a gun, for fear that she would catch me with the gun and have me sent back to the PRC. By the time I had the opportunity to get a gun, I had lost the desire to use it. There were only a few months when I really thought seriously about killing myself. I guess I was not motivated enough, because after the attempt to find a gun in the Johnson Avenue house, I never made another attempt to take my life. After a few months of having suicidal thoughts, I began to see that perhaps suicide was not the best thing for me to do. After having those suicidal thoughts, my attitude began to slowly change from one of altogether hopelessness to something a little less severe. I slowly began to shift from hopeless to just lackadaisical. Even though I was really only back to the way I had felt before the desire to kill myself had come along, this shift from suicidal to just having no care or desire for anything was a major step in the right direction. That shift was the first step back out of the downward spiral.

I suppose that the first thing that began to turn things around in my mind was the music that I listened to. I began to listen to The Shins, Regina Spektor, and The Killers, a lot. Those bands were my favorite discoveries from watching *Nocturnal State*. There weren't a lot of heavy lyrics in their music, just sounds that I enjoyed hearing. I have no idea of what any of the songs from The Shins are even about. I have trouble understanding what the lead singer is even saying. But I really like their sound. It's a little mellow most of the time. I could almost listen to their music with my parents. That's one thing, my parents can't stand most of my music. I guess that's probably typical of every generation.

Anyway, Regina Spektor, I like her songs as well. I can understand everything that she says, though I don't always know what she really means. I really liked her album, *Begin to Hope*. I guess that was what I was starting to do. I was beginning to hope that somehow, something good might come from the mess that was my life. I liked the songs, Better, and Fidelity, the best. Neither of those songs had some life changing lyrics. I just liked them in the same way that I liked The Shins. Listening to her voice was soothing to me somehow. She has a great voice. Something about the way she sings makes me wish that I could meet her. Her voice makes her beautiful to me. She's not bad looking to begin with, but her voice makes her more attractive to me.

The Killers were the band that I liked to listen to if I wanted to feel a little energized. I know the name sounds a little scary. With a name like, The Killers, you might think that I am talking about listening to some death metal band. But if you have listened to the radio stations that play pop music like Brittany Spears and Rhianna, then you have probably heard a Killers song and just not been aware of it. Their music is not death metal. It's far from it. It is really just a throw back to the 80's type of pop music, with a little rock spin put on it. I bought their album, *Sam's Town*, after hearing the single *When You Were Young*. I listened to the rest of the album and became an instant fan. They also had another hit single from that album called *Bones*. I really liked that song as well. My favorite songs from the album were not the singles, but songs like *Read My Mind* and *Bling*. Again it was not really the lyrics that got my attention, it was just their sound that I liked. They had a retro-pop style that I thought was very cool. Listening to those bands gave me a distraction from the mundane life that I lived. I could listen to their music and get away from all the bad thoughts that constantly rolled through my mind when it was unoccupied or not distracted by other things. That was all I wanted to do was distract myself from thinking terrible things about myself. That was the reason for the drinking, the movie and television watching, the driving across the county for iced coffee, and the music. It was all just a distraction. I hoped that I could keep myself distracted long enough for my depression to pass. I hoped that one day I would experience something that made me realize that life was still worth living. Those things were already all around me. I just couldn't see them through the fog that was clouding my judgment.

During the time when my depression was at its worst, I neglected everything. I didn't do my usual personal hygiene routine. I brushed my teeth once a day, just before I went to bed at night. In the morning I skipped tooth brushing. I didn't eat breakfast. I didn't see the point in brushing my teeth in the morning anymore. So, I stopped. I also stopped wearing deodorant. I didn't have anyone to impress. I didn't care if I smelled a little funky every day. The only people I ever saw were my parents and Nanny. I didn't care what they thought of me. I knew they thought I was crazy, so I just figured I would play the part. I did usually take a shower everyday. I still liked to take a shower because the hot water took away some of the tension that was in my muscles. I guess the anxiety was having physical effects on me still. I also hardly ever did laundry. I might wear the same clothes for two weeks without changing or washing them. Even after wearing them for two weeks, I would usually just hang them back up in the closet when I decided to change my outfit.

Another place where my mental problems manifested themselves was in my pets. I didn't take care of them either. I still had Blue and I still had an iguana named Licky. I had bought Licky back in 2001, just before Gwen was born. Licky was 6 years old at the time I was living in the house on Johnson Avenue. He was a typical iguana. He would let you hold him when he was cold, but if he was already warm, watch out! He would slap the crap out of you with his tail or bite. I still liked him. He required very little attention and food. I always fed him vegetables, usually squash and carrots. His favorite was yellow squash. During the time that I was most depressed, I began to neglect feeding him. It wasn't that I stopped caring about him. The problem was that I spent so much time worrying about myself that I never thought about him. I had put him and his cage in the little shed in the back yard. I never went outside except to smoke a cigarette. I did that in the front of the house, under the carport. So, the little shed was usually out of sight and out of mind. I hardly ever saw the shed or thought about the poor little lizard who was inside it. I would go days sometimes without feeding him. All the years before, I had fed him twice daily. He went from a healthy looking lizard to a skeleton of his former self, within a matter of a few months. One day, Liza was over for a visit and she came in the house crying. I said, "What's wrong Liza?" She said, "Licky is dead. He's not moving. His eyes are closed." I immediately tried to remember the last time I had fed him. It had been several days, once again. He had lost a lot of weight over the past few months. I had noticed and I tried to get myself to remember to feed him regularly, but it never happened. I would be so wrapped up in myself that I could not break away for the time it took to remember to feed him. I walked out to the shed, sure that Liza was right about him being dead. I walked over to his cage and saw him laying on the bottom of it. He never stayed at the bottom of his cage. He was always on the side or in his little perch. I reached in and picked him up. He was stiff as a board. His food bowl was empty. I had starved the poor creature to death. I felt terrible for being so selfish that I let my poor little lizard die such a terrible death. I told Liza that he probably died of old age. I realized that I was unfit to take care of anything. The death of Licky was an indicator of just how sorry of a person I had become. It was also a reason why I was afraid to have my kids by myself. I figured that if I could not even take care of a creature who only required a few pieces of squash every day, then there was no way I was fit to take on the challenge of taking care of my kids.

My dog, Blue, was another sign of neglect. Blue had always been well taken care of before the last time I was put in the PRC. After I got out and moved into the house on Johnson Avenue, I put up a fenced area in the backyard and kept her there. The idea was to give her a 20' x 20' place in the backyard where she could run around. The problem was that she always dug under the fence and got out. She never went roaming around the neighborhood. She usually just sat by the side door of the house and waited for someone to come out and play with her. I would find her there when I went outside to smoke a cigarette. When I saw her, I would put her back in the fenced area and tie her to a cable that was attached to a tree. After many escapes from the fenced area, I decided to keep her on the cable permanently. She hated it.

She would always manage to get herself tangled around the trunk of the tree. I would check on her every day and usually find that she had wrapped herself around the tree to the point that she only had a couple feet of cable to move around on. She might spend an entire day and night wrapped around the tree. I would usually hear her barking and whining from inside the house when that happened. Her barking was the only thing that saved her from me forgetting about her entirely. Once I heard her bark, I would remember that she was out there and was probably tangled up in the cable again. I would go out and straighten her back up, but she would get the cable wound back around the tree within hours of my repair.

The main thing that showed that she was not being properly cared for was the fact that she was also losing weight and was infested with fleas. Before my last stay at the PRC, I always fed her and gave her Frontline flea medication to prevent her from getting fleas. After being released, I fed her when I thought about it. That was not everyday. I also stopped giving her Frontline. Eventually, my dad said that he was going to take Blue out to the lake so she could have a place to run around. It was a good thing that he did that because had he not, she might have been my next dead pet. After Blue moved back to the lake house, she put her weight back on and my dad treated her for fleas. So, once Blue got away from me, her life improved. I figured that everyone's life was probably improved when I was not around.

Chapter 64: Back to Lake Buffum

In April of 2007, my mom came to visit me one day at the house on Johnson Avenue. Mom visited regularly, usually several times a week. She almost always cooked a meal for me when she was there. If she had not done that, I probably would have just eaten frozen dinners or fast food for every meal. I was too lazy to cook for myself. I had nothing to do but sit around, and my mom still came over and cooked supper for me, like I was still a little kid. That's all I was really, just a little kid hiding inside of the body of an adult. As some little kids are afraid of the dark and the monsters that hide there, I was afraid of people. I could stand the dark, but it was the people that I feared most. All the people were the monsters that terrorized me. I was so scared of what people thought of me, or what they would think of me if they ever caught wind of the fact that I was a schizophrenic. Anyways, back to the story...

Mom came over one day and told me that my dad was contemplating on either renting the Johnson Avenue house to someone other than myself, or selling it. Mom said that they wanted me to move back to the lake house. When she said this, time slowed down a little. I knew that the day would come when my parents would tell me that they could not afford the house I lived in, but I just never expected it to come so soon. They had only bought the house just a little over a year earlier. I had grown comfortable living on my own, even though I was not really living on my own. My parents paid the rent, the utilities, and even most of the grocery bills. I was not living on my own, I was just living by myself, and I had become comfortable with that arrangement. When Mom told me the news that I was about to have to go back to living with them again, it really bothered me. Mom said that they just could not afford to pay for three houses. They were still making payments on the lake house and their house in Georgia. Mom said that between the house payments and the rising insurance costs, they were going broke.

A few days later Mom said that Dad had decided to just sell the house, so I needed to start packing my things because they needed to get it ready to sell. I felt miserable about the idea that I was going back to live with my parents again. I had just started to establish a routine that filled most of my day, and didn't cost much money. I had stopped driving to Lake Wales for iced coffee. Instead, I drove a few miles north of Bartow, to a Dunkin Doughnuts and started buying a regular coffee a few times a week. That switch reduced my drive from a previous total of over forty miles to less than fifteen. The price of the coffee at Dunkin Doughnuts was also less than half of what I had been paying for iced coffee.

The other habit that I had started was jogging. I would go to the Bartow High School track and jog for over an hour, every other day. Once Mom told me that I was going to have to move back to the lake, I realized that my jogging days at the track were over. I had only started the routine about a month before she told me this news. The jogging was my first attempt to do something about the fact that I had gained over twenty pounds in the last few years since I was first diagnosed with a mental disorder. After I moved back to the lake house, I stopped jogging, and switched to just walking. When I started jogging, I began to realize that physical activity was very beneficial to my mental well being. I remember sitting in my car after a long jog, and feeling pretty good about myself. I began to feel like I had a new goal. My goal was to get back in shape. I had let myself go when the depression and mania controlled my life. Now that I had been taking my medication for over a year, the downward spiral path that I had traveled on for so many years, was beginning to go in reverse. But, the move back under my parents' wing was a bump in the path. Having to live with them took some adjustment. I had become very comfortable with being by myself all day, almost everyday. I knew I would have to make some big changes to my routine once I started living with them again. The thought of being with my parents all the time really bothered me. As the day approached when I had to move back under their roof, I became more and more anxious. I was afraid of what might happen when I had to be around them all the time. I was afraid that I might do or say something that angered them enough to kick me out again. I was afraid that if that ever happened again, there would be no more chances to redeem myself. I would end up as another homeless person on the street. I figured it would only take one misstep and then I would be thrown out to survive on my own.

Moving day occurred only a couple weeks after my mom first delivered the news that I would have to relocate. I spent those couple of weeks packing boxes and cleaning. Mom was there most days too. She was busy packing up the kitchen and cleaning all sorts of things as well. Once everything was packed up, all that was left was to load it all up and drive it out to the lake house. There were a few moments of nostalgia where I looked around the rooms of the house and thought about things that had happened there. I remembered spending time with my girls in the room that we had set up for them to sleep in. I remembered laying on their bed with them and watching Sponge Bob Squarepants. That was Liza's favorite show at the time. I thought about the incident where I tried to find the gun in my parents' room. I looked around my bedroom and thought of all the days that I had slept until 4:00 pm. I walked into the living room and remembered all the hours that I had spent staring at the TV, but not actually watching it; instead just staring into space, and being haunted by my recent past. Yes, there were a lot of memories from that little house, most of them very unpleasant.

After everything had been taken back to the lake house, I was officially back under my parents' wing. I felt miserable about it. I missed being able to do what I wanted, when I wanted. I knew that there would be no more late nights, watching *Nocturnal State* until 4:00 am. There would be no more iced coffee runs either. Now, my schedule would be determined by my parents. I would have to do what they thought I should do, and when they thought I should do it. My mom took up that job immediately.

I guess mom thought that it would be best if I were kept busy. It was probably the best thing for me. I don't know how I would have passed the hours, had she not planned most of them for me. Mom liked to work outside in her flowerbeds. She said that she loved to work outside, but her back gave her too much trouble if she bent over for very long. So, she started giving me little chores to do. She would have me pull weeds, trim plants, spread mulch and weed blocking fabric on the flowerbeds, water plants, etc. Every day she found things for me to do in the yard. I would usually hesitate when she first told me what she had planned for me to do each day. I didn't like being 31 years old and having my mother give me chores. It wasn't that I minded doing whatever she came up with. I just didn't like her telling me what to do. It made me feel like a child, or a slave. But, I know that was immature. After all, my parents were giving me free room and board. The least I could do was the few chores that she found for me to do every day. The realization that I was still totally dependant on them was what always kept me motivated to do whatever she said. I didn't want to do or say anything that might upset her. I was afraid that she might get angry and decide to kick me out of the house again, and I did not want that. I knew that soon, I would not even have a car. I didn't want to find out what true homelessness was really like.

At night, Dad was in control of the TV, so I watched whatever he wanted. There was no cable TV at the lake house. So, the option of watching VH1 or History Channel was not available. The selection of channels at the lake house included: NBC, ABC, CW, My Network TV, V32, and occasionally PBS. Those stations rarely had any programming that interested me. The only shows that I cared to watch came on NBC and PBS on the rare days when it came in. I spent most of my nights over in the other house, the guesthouse. That was where I set up my computer. I started to spend a lot of time in front of the computer at night. I also spent a lot of time with my XBOX and PS2. At night, I played a lot of video games. It was just a way to pass the time.

Dad usually went to bed around 11:00 pm, that was when I would stop playing video games and go back to the main house. After he went to bed, I would turn on the TV and watch the news on NBC and wait for *The Tonight Show* to come on. After *The Tonight Show* was over, *Late Night with Conan O' Brien* came on. Conan was the guy I had been waiting all night to see. After moving back to Lake Buffum, his show was the highlight of my day. I thought Conan O' Brien was hilarious. Watching his show was a habit that I had formed when I used to stay up to watch *Nocturnal State* at the Johnson Avenue house. I really enjoyed watching Conan every night. It was so nice to have a little comedy in my life. Before Conan became part of my routine, I went over a year, never smiling or laughing at anything. I had several people pick up on that and it bothered me when they would tell me, "Scott, we never see you smile anymore." Sara was one of those people. She would tell me that she wished I would at least fake a smile every now and then. But I could never find anything to smile about. All I could do was wallow in self-pity and anxiety. But after finding Conan O' Brien, from 12:30 am until 1:30 am, I did a fair amount of laughing. After listening to all the crazy things that Conan came up with, I felt a little better. Conan amazed me with his wit. He must be a very intelligent guy. His hilarious way of retorting to his guest's comments is just genius to me. Jay Leno on *The Tonight Show* is a little funny, but, to me, Conan blows him away. Watching Conan O' Brien was another little step back up the spiral, for me. I was at the very beginning of a long road back out of the darkness. A little music, a little laughter, and a little exercise, helped begin to push me away from the bottom of the downward spiral. I was just beginning to find things in life that I could enjoy and appreciate. I was beginning to climb back up.

After watching Conan O'Brien, I would make an attempt to go to sleep. It was hard at first. I was used to staying up another 2 ½ hours after Conan went off the air at 1:30 am. At first, I would lie there in bed and watch the clock until 2:30 am. I would usually doze off after that. I slept until 10:30 am every morning. I went from getting 10-12 hours of sleep every night to just eight. The way I compensated for the lack of sleep was to take a nap from 1:00 pm to 4:00 pm. Sometimes I even slept as late as 5:00 pm. I was still on a high level of Zyprexa, so I still required a lot of sleep.

So, my days began to set themselves up into a new routine. The routine was: wake up and do chores for a couple hours, eat lunch, take a nap, eat supper, play video games, watch TV, and then go back to sleep. That was my routine for a long time. I stopped getting exercise, except when I was doing chores. I think that had a negative impact on me. I should have kept up my jogging routine. I think that if I had done that, I would have made faster progress towards finding some level of peace and happiness. The days began to go by faster as I adjusted to my new routine, and quickly grew into weeks. When I moved out to the lake house, it was only a few weeks until summer.

Chapter 65: Little Steps

The summer of 2007 was the first summer I had spent in Georgia since I was a kid. The last time I had been to Georgia for the summer was before I ever started working and driving my own car, I guess I was either 14 or 15. I went to Georgia that summer because I knew that my car was about to be repossessed. If I stayed at the lake house by myself, I would have no transportation and no way to get groceries. So, I left for Georgia with my parents.

Before we began to spend the summer in Georgia, my parents planned a trip to Connecticut to visit my brother, Carter, who had moved there with his girlfriend, Sue. My brother and his girlfriend had just had their first baby, a little girl whose name was Helen. My parents wanted to visit my brother because he had just had his first child and we had not yet seen her. So, around the end of May, we made a trip to Connecticut to see my brother, his girlfriend, and their new baby.

That trip was the first time that I really enjoyed myself, a little, since I had been released from the PRC. We had previously taken a trip to Las Vegas to see my other brother, Sam, who was stationed there with the Air Force. That trip was nice too. But I can't say that I really enjoyed myself there. Yes, there were a lot of interesting things to see, but I really felt uncomfortable the whole time I was there because I just could not bring myself out of the depression enough to really appreciate what was around me. For some reason, the trip to Connecticut was different.

I think the main difference was a slight shift in my attitude. By the time of that trip, I had done away with the idea of killing myself, even though I still hated who I was severely. But the hate had resided enough to allow me to stop being so caught up in myself that I could not interact with my brother. I guess I was also a little more comfortable around him because he had already seen me at a time when I was manic. I knew that he had experienced a little of the worst of me. So, I didn't feel like I had a lot to hide from him. That allowed me to be a little less anxious when I was there.

We drove from Georgia to Connecticut in my parents' van. Dad and I took turns driving. We broke the trip up into two days. We spent a little time each day just sight seeing at a few of the places we passed on the way to Connecticut. I really enjoyed the drive to Connecticut. We followed the Blue Ridge Mountains into the Shenandoah Mountains and continued to follow the same mountain range for most of the drive. It was very scenic.

We arrived in Connecticut and went straight to my brother's apartment to meet his new little girl, Helen. Helen was only a couple of weeks old when we met her. She was a typical new born, chubby and very small. She was a cute baby. We spent most of that first day just visiting with Carter and Sue, and of course, Helen. The next day Dad and I decided to rent a couple of scooters and ride them along the coast near the town where we were staying. The scooter rental inspired me to make a decision that would have a very positive impact on me in the coming months.

Dad and I rented a couple scooters from a little shop in Old Saybrook, CT. I had never ridden a scooter before. My dad had let me drive his Honda VTX motorcycle one time, years earlier. So, I had almost no experience driving anything motorized with two wheels. The guy who rented us the scooters gave us some safety rules and a couple helmets and sent us on our way. Dad suggested that I practice riding the scooter around the parking lot before we got on the road. The rental guy had shown me the controls and told me how to use them. So, I got on the scooter, turned on the ignition, and opened the throttle. It was so cool to open the throttle and have the thing start moving. I fell in love with the idea of two wheeled transportation right there. I had driven my dad's VTX and the thing had scared me to death. I was so nervous about possibly wrecking his bike that I did not enjoy or appreciate the experience of driving it. But this little scooter was different. We were already covered with a little insurance from the fee we paid the rental guy. So, I was not as nervous about destroying the scooter as I had been about wrecking my dad's bike. Plus, the scooter was a tiny little thing. My dad's VTX was an 1800 cc motorcycle with lots of power and lots of weight. The scooter was light. Maneuvering was a breeze. I zipped around the parking lot a few times and soon became comfortable enough to try taking it out on the road.

Dad and I began heading west on U.S. 1 in Old Saybrook. At first, I was a little nervous, but the nervousness quickly passed and was replaced by awe. It was so exhilarating to feel the wind blowing around me as I drove down the road. Passing cars or being passed by cars was also really neat. It was so different than anything I had ever experienced before. We were only doing 30-35mph most of the time, but it seemed so much faster on that little scooter. Passing cars, with nothing separating me from them but the air between them and I, was so exciting to me. The scooter made driving more like a game or sport. I felt much more connected to the space around me. In a car, you are closed off from the space you pass through. The closed windows and air-tight interior really lack something that you can only experience on a motorcycle. When I was on the scooter, I could feel the air and notice the subtle changes in temperature as we passed from one area to another. I could also smell the salt air coming from the ocean. I could feel the sun's heat coming down on me. It was all so nice. Dad and I drove our little scooters for 6 hours. I loved every minute of it. My parents and I had already had a discussion about how I would be able to get a new car after my Subaru got repossessed. My parents said that they would sign on to a loan if I wanted to get something that I could afford to make payments on, once I started getting my checks from Disability. After having the scooter experience, I began to think of ditching the idea of some four wheeled transportation and dropping down to two. I began to imagine myself driving a motorcycle. At first, it was just a little thought that I had while I was riding on that little scooter, but as the days went on, after that little ride, I began to think seriously about getting around on a motorcycle. That little decision would turn out to be a very positive choice for me.

The other positive thing that happened on the Connecticut trip was a daytrip to New York City. I had spent a week in New York City when I was in college. A group of the Consortium students from the school in Washington, D.C., and myself, all spent a week long field trip in New York city to study some of its greatest art and architecture. On that trip, we met with several different architecture firms, and schools in the city. I became slightly familiar with all the big attractions of New York City during that week because we had a lot of free time to explore on our own. My friend, Johnson, and I spent all of our time going to all the tourist attractions, such as: The Empire State Building, The World Trade Center, The Statue of Liberty, etc. So, when my dad and brother said that they wanted to take a trip to New York, I told them that I would be glad to take them to all the places that I had been. So, I played tour guide for most of that trip. I found a really good map of the city that showed the subway lines and all their stops. Without that, I would have been lost. But, as it turned out, I made a pretty decent tour guide. We made it to several of the big attractions in one day. We saw Central Park, St. Peter's Cathedral, 30 Rock, Empire State Building, China Town, Little Italy, Wall Street, Battery Park, and The World Trade Center Ground Zero Construction Site. The only thing we ran out of time for was The Statue of Liberty. I think we managed to see quite a bit for one day. We were exhausted by the time we left. It was a lot of fun. The responsibility of touring my dad and brother around made me feel a little important, if only for a short while. That little bit of responsibility was the first I had taken on since I had stopped working. It felt good to know that my brain could still function well enough to at least escort my dad and brother around New York City. I could tell that they really enjoyed the trip. My dad even made the comment that he would have been lost and frustrated if I had not come along to show them how to get to all of the things that we saw. I felt a little pride in knowing that I had helped my dad and brother have a good time. That was the first time I felt I had done anything to make someone happy since before I was put in the rehab center in Tallahassee. Up until that point, I thought that I usually just made people miserable. That made me miserable. The New York City experience was another small, but significant boost to my still very low self-esteem.

After the scooter experience and the New York City trip, we stayed in Old Saybrook for a day or two and then headed back to Georgia to spend the rest of the summer. The thing that I remember most about the rest of that summer was sleeping. I tried to sleep the summer away because I was uncomfortable having to spend all day, every day with my parents. It was very awkward for me to have to be around them all day. I just felt like it was so wrong for me to be living with them at 31 years old. I had been able to pretend that I was independent when I lived by myself in the little house in Bartow. Now, I had to face the fact that I was an adult who lived with his parents. It was very depressing. My parents found projects for me to work on to keep me busy. But when I was not doing some chore for them, I tried to sleep the time away. It was the same strategy that I had used when I was in the SRT program at Peace River Center. I hoped that by sleeping, time would fly by. I thought that I would keep up that strategy until we were back to Florida and Dad went back to work. For some reason, it didn't bother me as much when it was just Mom and I. I think it was only because I had become used to her visiting me at the Johnson Avenue house. I had also grown a little comfortable with her being home all day at the lake house, after I moved back out there. Having Dad home all day too, was a new part of my daily routine. Any change in the routine brought stress to me. So, since I had both of my parents around me all day, I felt very stressed by the change in routine. The strategy was to sleep as much as possible until the routine again became what I was familiar with.

I usually woke up around 10:30 am. I would walk around the house and usually end up in front of the TV, unless my parents had something they wanted me to do. I would watch TV for an hour or so. Then I would eat lunch. After lunch, I might sit in front of the TV again for another hour. By that time, it was around 1:00 pm. At that point I would go back to my room and crawl back in bed. I was never tired. I would just lie there and wish that my life was different. I would think about all the things I would need to do in order to get my life back together. I would try to think of some type of job that I could work that I might enjoy. I could never think of anything that seemed interesting. Sometimes I would begin to come up with a plan, but then I would shoot it down with reasons why my plan was no good. I would lie there and think myself in circles until I got tired enough to fall asleep. I would usually end up sleeping until 5:00 pm. Then I would get out of bed, sometimes after one of my parents came in to wake me up. By the time I got out of bed, it was usually time for dinner. I would eat dinner and then go back to sit in front of the TV. I would usually stay in front of the TV from 6:00 pm until 1:30 am. 1:30 am was when Conan O'Brien's show was over. Sometimes I stayed up later. We had cable TV at the Georgia house. So, it was possible to watch *Nocturnal State*. Sometimes I got a little taste of my old routine. I stayed up until 4:00 am on some nights, just so I could catch an hour of *Nocturnal State*. Staying up until 4:00 am and waking up at 10:30 am had the effect of making the mid day nap a necessity. So, looking back on that summer, the thing I remember most was all the sleeping I did.

There was one big project that summer that took a little of my time, only for a few days though. That project was the sanding of the deck that wrapped around the front of the Georgia house. My parents had painted the entire deck a forest green color years earlier. The sun, rain, and snow, had taken their toll on the paint and it began to crack and peel off in several places. The deck looked pretty bad. So, my parents decided to just strip off all of the paint so that the decking was just bare wood. That task proved a little more challenging than we first expected. The first attempt to remove the paint was with chemicals. Dad bought some paint remover. He and I poured it over some spots on the deck. We let it sit for a few minutes and then began scraping at the paint with tools made for the job of removing paint from surfaces. We scraped and scraped with not much result. After applying the paint remover, and scraping, several times; we gave up on that approach. The next idea that Dad had was to rent a floor sander and try to sand off the paint. We got a sander from an equipment rental store, and brought it back to the house. Dad sanded over a portion of the deck and quickly realized that the sander was not going to do the job either. Finally, Dad resorted to using a little hand sander that he had at the house. The little hand sander proved to be the most effective way of removing the paint. The sander took off all the paint, but it was small and took a lot of time to cover the huge area that had to be sanded. My dad and I took turns sanding the deck. It took several

502

hours a day for several days to complete the job. After the deck-sanding project, I really didn't have any other major tasks to do that entire summer.

The only other thing I can remember about that summer was a couple who my parents became good friends with. Their names were Jan and William. They were a couple who had bought a house just up the hill from my parents' house. They were from Winter Haven, Florida, which was less than 20 miles away from my parents place on Lake Buffum. My parents really enjoyed spending time with Jan and William. They would go over to their house and play Mexican Train Dominoes some nights. Other nights, Jan and William would come over to my parents' house. Those nights that my parents' new friends came over is what I remembered about that summer. Mom would usually give me a few hours of advance notice that their friends would be coming over that night. I would begin to count down the hours until they arrived. I dreaded the idea of having to speak with any new people. I felt trapped and knew that I could not get away from the situation. I had no car. So, I couldn't make an excuse to leave. I knew that I would have to sit in the house and interact with my parents' new friends. I figured that my mom had already told them all about me and my times at the rehab centers. I couldn't stand to face people who I did not know, who I thought already knew all about me. The shame and fear of how they might react to me made me very anxious. I would count down the hours and become more nervous with each passing minute.

When Jan and William finally did show up on that first night that they came over to visit my parents, I tried to hide for as long as I could. My plan was to stay in the TV room for as long as possible. The TV room was the farthest room from the kitchen, where my parents and their friends sat and played dominoes. Mom finally walked back to the TV room and said, "Scott, Jan and William are here. Why don't you come say hello to them." When Mom said that, I knew that I was going to get dragged into a conversation that I had tried so hard to avoid. I was afraid that they would ask me questions that I did not want to answer, or say something to make me feel worse about myself than I already did. Reluctantly, I walked into the kitchen and greeted them and introduced myself. They both said hello and asked me if I wanted to join the game that they were playing. I said, "No thanks. I'm just going to watch TV. But thanks for offering." and I walked back to my pacifier, the television. I sat there in the TV room the entire time that my parents' friends were there. I did not want to go near them and take a chance on getting brought in on some conversation. I was so nervous that I knew if I tried to speak much, I would surely stutter and slur through my words and come out of the conversation looking like an idiot. So, I tried my best to avoid them. I just stared at the TV and tried to listen to the conversations that were going on in the kitchen. I was expecting to hear some negative statement made about me. It never happened.

At the end of the summer, Liza and Gwen came up to spend a week with me. My brother, Carter, had asked me to come back to Connecticut for a baptizing ceremony for his little girl, Helen. So, the girls, Mom, and I; all rode back up to Connecticut for the baptizing ceremony. I was nervous about having to be in a ceremony. I wasn't sure exactly what I would have to do, but I knew that even if I only had to stand in front of a church full of people, that would make me very nervous. When my brother first asked me to be in the ceremony, my first thought was to make up an excuse for why I could not come. Carter and Sue asked me to be Helen's godfather. Carter said that was a tradition that Sue's denomination always did. I can't remember what denomination Sue's family is, but it is very similar to the Baptist faith. Anyways, my brother had asked me to be in Helen's baptizing ceremony because I was the godfather. I thought that Carter choosing me to be Helen's godfather was a very nice gesture. So, I felt like I had to show up to the ceremony.

The girls, mom, and I all arrived in Connecticut a couple days before Helen's ceremony. We all stayed in the hotel that my parents and I had stayed in at the beginning of the summer. Over the course of the four or five days that we visited my brother and his family, we took the girls to several places around the area where Carter lived. We saw Gillet's Castle and we went to a place called Rocky Neck State Park. Rocky Neck was my favorite place near Carter's apartment. It was a beach that had a large rock formation that you could climb all over. The girls and I climbed up the rocks and walked around the tops of them. The top of the rock formation was probably 40 feet from the ground. So, the girls really enjoyed getting to do something that seemed a little dangerous. It really wasn't that dangerous. The rocks all sloped gently enough that a person could climb up them without much skill at all. I had to lift Gwen up over a few steep places, but other than that, it was pretty safe climbing. When we got to the top, the girls really enjoyed being able to walk around and look down on all the people below. That little excursion to the rock formation at Rocky Neck was the first time that I had spent any quality time outdoors with my kids since I had been released from the PRC. I had been outside with them, to places like Cypress Gardens, but it was never what I would call quality time. I was always in a daze from the negative thoughts that swirled through my head constantly. But that day at Rocky Neck, there was a moment where I realized that I was doing something that I had not done in a long time. I realized that I was enjoying spending time with my kids and they were enjoying being with me. That moment of realization was another little step forward, away from the bottom of the downward spiral.

I guess it was around the time of that trip to Connecticut, at the end of the summer of 2007, that I realized that my girls might not have stopped loving me after all. I had feared that I had been replaced by my ex-wife's new husband, Matt. Matt was very successful with his contracting company and he seemed to be making good money. I would always hear stories from the girls about all the fun things that they had done with their mom and Mr. Matt. They always had a story about riding four wheelers, riding in a boat on Crooked Lake, or going to some beach house for the weekend. I felt like I was unable to compete with the level of spending that my ex-wife and her new husband were doing for the girls. I felt inadequate as a father. My kids would always come over in clothes from their mom's house. Their clothes were always expensive name brands that had been purchased by my wife or Matt at some high-end kid's clothing store in Lakeland. I began to believe that my girls would not appreciate me because I could not give them those kinds of things. On top of it all was my piss poor attitude. I was always so miserable that I had trouble focusing on my kids when they were around. I would catch myself pretending to listen to what they were telling me, but actually drifting along in my own thoughts, with no clue of what they had been telling me. The only way that I would get jarred from my inward focus, was if they asked me a question pertaining to what they had been talking about. Then I would have to ask them to explain what their question was about, because I had no clue of the context of the question, since I had not been listening to a word they said beforehand. Liza or Gwen would repeat enough of what they told me so that I could make an attempt to respond to their question. I would respond with some vague answer that made it seem like I had been listening to their every word. I would usually try to listen to what they were saying after I realized that I was ignoring them, but within minutes, I would be back in my own little world, lost in the negative thoughts that ruled over me. That was how I spent most of my time with my kids on all the weekends that they came over, up until that trip to Connecticut. But on that trip, something changed. Somehow, I realized, I had been able to pull myself out of the negative thoughts for long enough that I was able to actually listen to my kids when they talked to me. I was just beginning to realize that my kids seemed to like me still. Even though I had basically abandoned them.

After Sara left, back in August of 2005, I had spent very little time with my girls. At first the neglect was a product of mania. I had been so wrapped up in the conspiracy that I thought I was a part of, that thoughts of my kids never made their way into my brain. Then, after the trips to the rehab center, the mania was replaced by a depression that was equally destructive to my relationship with my kids. So, for about two years my kids went without having me as a real father. I was present with them physically from time to time, but mentally, I was never around. As I began to realize my problem, the depression only worsened when I realized that I would probably be replaced by a guy who was a better dad than I was. It really bothered me to think that I might soon have two little girls who could care less whether I was around or not. I wanted to try to prevent that from happening, but I had no idea of what it would take. I knew that I couldn't compete on a monetary level. I figured that was the most important part to gaining the respect of my kids. Thank God, it does not appear that is the case.

After the Connecticut trip, I thought back on what had happened in those few days with my girls. I began to realize that it was not the money being spent that was what had caused a change. The change that I had noticed was from inside me. I began to realize that all I needed to do was spend time with them, and listen to them. I realized that attention was what my girls needed most, not fancy things. Of course, this is not a new idea, but it was new to me. I had been convinced that my kids would be more influenced by the power of money than by anything that I could ever provide for them. If I had to tell one thing that I think I learned from this whole experience, this journey from sanity to insanity, and back again, I think I would have to say that I have learned that money isn't everything. I think that God blessed me by showing me that money is not everything. That was the first big lesson that I began to learn from what had happened to me. I'm not saying that I would not love to be rich. What I think I learned was that money is not what makes a person happy. I always knew that this was true for me, but I was not sure that was the case for other people. The way my wife had left after I was unable to pay all of our bills, convinced me that for some people, money was very important. I assumed that would be the case for my girls as well. I know that money is a necessity in our culture. I know that the lack of money did cause a lot of problems between my wife and I. But, I have less money now than I have ever had, and I find myself happier than I have ever been. So, money is definitely not the solution for happiness. I'm sure that it helps to have more money, but I don't believe that a person can find happiness through wealth. I was never rich, but I was the most miserable at the time when I made the most money. I'm not saying that there is a connection between money and unhappiness either. I don't think that it was the money that made me unhappy. What made me miserable was the time that I had to spend to make the money. It was the missing out on all the little things that happened with my family that made me unhappy. I did not like to come home from work and have my wife tell me that I had missed some special moment with the girls because I had been working late. The lack of quality time with the people you are most attached to, is one of the things that causes unhappiness, I think.

Chapter 66: Big Improvements

The summer came and went and soon I was back at the lake house and back to my old routine. Dad went back to work and the days became something more familiar to the way life had been before we went to Georgia. My Social Security Disability checks started coming in May of 2007. The first check was another lump sum check to make up for all the missed payments. The check covered the time, starting in January of 2007 when Disability approved me, and went on to May. The check was almost $5,000. I used a little of that money to help with expenses on the trips to Connecticut. I used the rest to help pay off the balance that I still owed on the Subaru Tribeca.

When the Tribeca was repossessed, it was then auctioned off to the highest bidder at a car auction. The car was sold for $22,000. I still owed over $29,000. So, the bank referred me to a collection agency, which threatened to take legal action if I did not quickly pay off the bill. The collection agency said that if I paid the balance off in full, by a certain date, they would reduce my bill by almost half. So, I ended up taking my Disability check and using it to pay off the balance I owed for the Tribeca.

Another major debt that I had to settle was with the IRS. They sent me a letter saying that I owed taxes on the disability insurance checks that I had been receiving. I assumed that I would not have to pay taxes on that money, since I had been receiving it due to the fact that I was unemployed. But the IRS wanted their money. They said that I owed $2,500 in taxes for the money that I had received. I didn't have that much. So, I asked my dad if he could take out a loan and let me repay him. He agreed to take out the loan and I paid off the IRS. After that, I started paying my dad $200 a month to repay the loan. That was my first and only bill that I had for a couple months. I actually still had other bills, but I did not pay them. I still have several debts that all together total about $6,000. The majority of these bills are from a credit card that I maxed out when I was in mania. To this day, I have not paid a dime to that credit card bill. Paying off that bill is the first thing I plan to do once I begin working again.

So, with my credit screwed, I knew that there was no way that I could buy a car or any other transportation until I saved the money to pay for it without having to finance any of it. My dad said that he would help me get a car if I wanted to find something I could afford. I thought about the scooter I had ridden in Connecticut and how much I had enjoyed it. I told Dad that I was seriously thinking about getting a motorcycle.

After coming back from Connecticut, Mom had started back with her routine of finding little chores for me to do around the house. That routine went on for several weeks. Then one day, Mom told me that she was thinking about joining the YMCA in Lake Wales. She asked me if I would be interested in joining with her. Mom said that she wanted to see if the YMCA could become a new part of her routine. She wanted something to do that gave her an excuse to get out of the house and get some exercise. I thought about how I had enjoyed working out at a gym in Tallahassee years earlier. I thought that the YMCA sounded like a good idea, though I was not thrilled about having to be around other people. I was familiar with the gym culture though. I knew that there were ways of working out at a gym and not having to interact with other people there. So, I told Mom that I would go up there with her and at least check the place out. That was another little decision that ended up having a big impact on me.

Mom and I went up to the YMCA and asked if we could look around at their facilities. We walked past the front desk and down a hall. On the right was a weight room. I walked into the weight room and looked around. I noticed all the cardio and weight training equipment. There was another room off of the main weight room that was dedicated to free weights. I saw all the equipment and thought that it was not as nice as the gym I had worked out at previously, but it was nice enough. I walked out of the weight room and followed a sign that said "Pool". I walked out to the pool and met Mom. She was standing out there talking to one of the lifeguards. The pool looked very nice. It had six swimming lanes that were 25 meters long. There was also a diving well. I thought that the pool was also not as nice as the pool at my old gym, but nice enough. After Mom and I scoped out the place, we went back to the front desk and asked about prices for a membership. The girl at the front desk told us that it was $35 per month for individuals and $50 for a family membership. I asked if I could join with my mom on the family plan because I was her dependant. They said that was fine as long as I showed proof of income and that I was their dependant. Mom and I signed up for the family membership. That little decision to join the YMCA started out as a whim, but ended up forming a new routine for me. Exercise played a key role in transforming me both physically and mentally.

After Mom and I joined the Y, we started going there every morning to swim in the pool. It was August. So by 11:00 am, when we usually showed up, it was hot and the water felt great. Mom joined a water aerobics class, shortly after starting her YMCA routine. I just swam laps in the pool while she went to her water aerobics class.

When I first started my member ship at the Y, I weighed over 200 pounds. When I was first put in the rehab center in Tallahassee, I weighed around 180 pounds. I gained all that weight from a combination of lack of exercise, poor eating habits, and the medication that I was prescribed, Zyprexa. One of the side effects of Zyprexa is that it makes you gain weight. With the high dosage they had me on, I began to quickly put on the pounds. Within two years, I gained over twenty pounds. It all went to my abdomen. I started to develop a potbelly. I hated it. It made me look like an alcoholic or something. I'm sure that all the beers I consumed when I made my frequent bar visits, during the time I lived in the Johnson Avenue house, did not help

508

my situation either. Before I had to move out to the lake house, from the Johnson Avenue house, I bought a scale. That was my first move to take charge of my weight. I got in the habit of stepping on the scale each morning and night. I began to see a little weight loss when I started jogging the track while I lived in Bartow. But, after moving back to the lake house, I got out of the exercise routine and my weight either stayed the same or increased slightly. After I joined the YMCA, I really began to make weight loss a priority. After I began to swim, I slowly started losing weight.

When I first started going to the YMCA, all I did was swim. I would swim when my mom wanted to go up there. That was every day for the first couple weeks. Then she decided to start going every other day. We first started swimming in the morning. Then she changed her schedule to go in the afternoon, once Dad got off work, so that he could go with us. The evening swim became our routine for several months. When I started swimming, I usually only swam about 10 laps, 20 lengths of the pool. By the time the water got too cold to swim in, I was up to 30 laps, 60 pool lengths. That equaled one mile. I started breaking my swimming into 3 sets of 10 laps, with a several minute break between each set. Once I began to swim seriously, the weight began to drop.

In September of 2007, I started looking at different motorcycles. I was positive that I did not want a car. Sara still had me restricted from seeing my kids by myself, so I felt that there was no need for a car. I was not allowed to drive my kids anywhere, unless my parents or grandmother was with me. So, there was no need to worry about transporting anyone but myself. I thought about the rising cost of gasoline. I knew that even the most fuel-efficient car would not compare with a motorcycle. I asked my dad how much his insurance was for his VTX. He told me that he paid about $50 a month for insurance. As I started to think about how much cheaper a motorcycle would be than a car, I became sure that a motorcycle was the thing for me.

I looked at a Harley Davidson dealership that was not far from the lake house. I saw the prices and they were just as Dad had told me, outrageous. So, I went over to Sky Power Sports, a Kawasaki & Suzuki dealer in Lake Wales. I looked at several Sport bikes. I liked the style of a couple of them, but I was a little nervous about buying one and then later feeling like an idiot for riding on a kid's motorcycle. I started to think that the Cruiser style of motorcycle best fit what I wanted. I didn't want to look like a stunt pulling speed freak on one of the crotch rockets that I had seen at Sky Power Sports. I liked the image that was associated with The Cruiser, just a general bad ass. I wanted to have a bike that said that about me, even though I really thought the opposite about myself. So, I went to the Honda dealership in Winter Haven.

I walked into the dealership and started looking at the Honda bikes. Honda makes the CBR Sport Bike. It looks really cool to me. I looked at the CBR for a while and tried to imagine myself riding on a crotch rocket. I just couldn't see myself on it. I liked the way it looked and the salesman promoted it very well, but I just couldn't see myself riding on one of those things. So, I moved over to the bike my dad had, the VTX. I looked at the 1800 cc VTX's. They looked awesome. There were three variations of the VTX: The Classic, The Retro, and the Standard. At first, I really liked The Classic the best, but the more I looked at The Retro, the more I began to like it as well. I liked the 1800 C because that was my dad's bike. I had ridden it only once, but I always thought he had the coolest bike that I had ever seen. So, I went into the dealership with the expectation of falling in love with a VTX Classic. But before I left, I had come to like another bike better. The salesman walked me to the back of the store to show me some 2007 and 2006 bikes that were reduced because they were about to start selling the 2008 models. He showed me a 2007 1300 cc VTX Retro that had a manufacturer's rebate of $500. The price of the VTX was only $8,500 already. Compared to $14,000 for the 1800 cc VTX, I thought that seemed like a very good deal. So, after seeing that there was very little difference between the look of the 1800 and the 1300 VTX, I decided that I would go with the deal that the salesman had shown me. I came back with my dad the next day.

Dad and I went to the Honda dealership in Winter Haven one October day and bought the 1300 VTX Retro. I loved it. It was all black and chrome. Very nice. Dad signed as the prime person on the loan and I co-signed for it. Dad told me that I would just pay him whatever the monthly bill totaled. My credit was so screwed that there was no chance of me qualifying for a loan. So, after an hour of paper work, the VTX was mine, technically Dad's.

Dad said that he would drive the VTX home from the dealership because I had no real driving experience. I was glad to let him do that because I was still very nervous about the idea of driving a big bike. The little scooter was nothing like the VTX. The VTX had serious power and serious weight. I didn't want to chance wrecking the motorcycle on my first ride. So, Dad drove home and I followed. When we got about two miles from the house, Dad pulled over and got off the bike. I got out of the van. He said, "Alright, its yours from here." Dad showed me how to operate the throttle, brakes, clutch, and shifter. Then I was on my own to get myself back to the house without crashing my new motorcycle. I was excited but also very nervous. I just knew that I was going to end up dropping the bike or wrecking it in those two miles.

First, I sat down on the bike. I had sat on it in the dealership, so that part was nothing new. What was new was that I now had to actually make this thing run. I turned the ignition key, flipped the stop switch, and pressed the ignition button. The motorcycle came to life and began to roar. I felt very cool at that point, but still very nervous. Dad had already put the bike in first gear. So, I eased off on the clutch and the bike lurched forward and stalled. That scared me a little. I had no idea of how to smoothly let out the clutch. So, the next time I let off the clutch easier than I had done the first time. I stalled out the second time trying to switch from first to second gear. Eventually, after stalling many times, I made it home. I was nervous about riding the motorcycle, but I knew that there were good times ahead, if I could just figure out how to properly operate it. After a few days of practice on the motorcycle, I became familiar with shifting, braking, and turning. I was still shaky, but I was improving. The next thing I had to do was get my motorcycle license.

I had already received a temporary motorcycle license that was good for 60 days. I had to take a written exam for that. I passed it with only one incorrect answer. That was another little self-confidence booster. The people at the Honda dealership had told me that was the easiest way to get through the driving exam was to take a motorcycle-training course. They said that the course ended with the driving exam. If I passed the exam at the course, I would be given a voucher that I could take to the DMV to receive my motorcycle license. So, that is what I did.

I signed up for a one-day course with a motorcycle training company called MST, Motorcycle Safety Training. The course was a breeze. They let us use motorcycles that they provided. The bikes that they had us use had little 300 cc engines. The bikes were so light and easy to maneuver that the test was a piece of cake. If I had taken the test with my VTX, I never would have passed the test because a portion of the test involved a very tight turn and maneuvering through a series of closely spaced cones. My VTX had a very wide turning radius. I never would have been able to make it through the turning part of the test had I used the VTX.

After passing my test and receiving my motorcycle license, I started to have a little more confidence in myself. I realized that if I was still able to learn something new, like how to ride a motorcycle, then I might be capable of learning other new things as well. Before I passed the tests to get my license, I was sure that my brain was so far gone that I would never be able to work again. I believed that since I had been unable to repeat the series of numbers and words that the psychologist gave me, at the test to see if I was eligible for Disability, I was no longer able to function in a way that would allow me to work. But, after realizing that I could read and retain information, I began to have a little hope that I might one day return to the workplace. That small hope was the true beginning of my rebuilding process. Once I realized that I did still have a brain worth using, I began to raise my self-image. The motorcycle only added more self-esteem. The more I rode it, the more confident I became in myself. It may seem odd that something like a motorcycle could have such an impact on a person, but for me, that is what it did.

With the motorcycle, it was the little things that began to improve my perception of myself. For one, it is the way that all motorcyclists wave at each other as we pass each other on the road. I began to feel like I was a member of a little group of people who never would have acknowledged each other, if it were not for the fact that we all had motorcycles. I really liked the way that every motorcyclist I passed waved at me. At first, I thought I was just coming across a few friendly people who happened to be on motorcycles. But I soon realized that the wave was a motorcycle custom. So, I started waving at every motorcyclist I passed. It was nice to feel like I had people who at least acknowledged me enough to give me a little wave. Of course, I didn't know any of them. I didn't want to know any of them. It was just nice to wave and be waved at. Something about that made me feel less alone in the world. I felt like I had little friendships that occurred for only a few seconds as I passed and waved at all the motorcyclists on the road.

Another thing that helped my self-esteem was the way little kids lit up whenever they saw me pull into a parking space near them, or start putting on my gear when I was about to take off on my bike. For some reason, little boys all love my motorcycle. I have had many short conversations with kids as I am getting off or getting on my motorcycle. The conversations are usually with little boys who are fascinated by my motorcycle. They usually want to know how fast my motorcycle goes and if I like my motorcycle. I always enjoy talking with the kids who like my bike. Every time I talk with little kids, I feel better about myself. They are usually very easily excited and always appreciative of my attention. Having those little encounters with kids who loved my motorcycle gave me a little boost of confidence. I began to realize that at least children still liked me, even if the rest of the world could not stand me.

There were conversations about my motorcycle with adults as well. At first, I was uncomfortable talking with adults about my motorcycle. But I soon began to anticipate the typical questions everyone asked. The usual questions were about gas mileage, the make and model of my bike, and what was required to get a motorcycle license. I ran into a lot of admirers who really seemed to love my bike. I got a lot of compliments from people who told me that I had the nicest bike that they had ever seen. Those types of comments made me proud of my decision to ditch the idea of the automobile and start driving on less. I felt smart for driving around something that had serious horsepower, but ran on less fuel than the most fuel-efficient car.

Gasoline prices were another thing that boosted my self-perception. I knew that gas was getting expensive when I bought my bike, but by the summer of 2008, gas went from expensive to ridiculous. I was paying $4.09 per gallon for a part of the summer for regular unleaded. Every time I stopped to fill up, someone would ask me how much I had just spent on gas. I would smile and say, "About $10.00". They would gasp because they were typically spending between $60 to $80 to fill up their gas guzzling automobiles. Every trip to the gas station made me more thankful that I had been smart enough to break out of the routine of using a car to get me from A to B. The high price of gas caused my self-esteem to rise higher.

So, there were many benefits that came from the simple purchase of the Honda VTX. Between the forced social interactions and the fact that I was paying less for gas than anyone I knew, my self-esteem slowly began to rise. I received a little boost every time someone complimented my bike or told me how they wished they could get away with paying as little as I did for gasoline. I was coming further out of the downward spiral. I was beginning to pick myself up again.

The other thing that was boosting my moral was the YMCA. After I got the motorcycle, I had freedom, once again. I was no longer reliant on my parents to chauffer me around. I could come and go as I pleased. That was a huge deal to me. I was miserable during the time that I had no transportation. It made me feel even more like a little kid. With no car of my own, I could only leave the house when my parents decided to go somewhere. But with the motorcycle, I could go anywhere I wanted, at any time. The only place I went was the YMCA. I began to set up a routine of going to the YMCA every Monday, Wednesday, and Friday. I quit just going to the pool and began a workout routine in the weight room in September of 2007. By November, I was only working out with weights. The pool was closed in

November because the water temperature got too cold. Once I began to take working out seriously, the weight just kept coming off.

My workout routine included only my upper body. I began my routine by doing three sets of ten reps of each exercise that I performed. I did exercises that worked out my shoulders, neck, back, chest, and arms. I used free weights and the machines to work out those muscles. After each work out, I would come away with the little boost that comes from the release of endorphins that physical activity creates. I began to notice how energized I was after working out. I liked the feeling. It was a little natural high. Not only did I begin to feel better physically, I also began to notice a sharper mind developing. I began to regain the ability to think clearly and even talk, at times. Even though there were moments when I felt I could speak almost as well as I had before I was put on the medication, there were still times when I would catch myself slipping up my words. These moments usually happened at the only time that I had interaction with people other than my parents, at the YMCA. One example was a guy who said, "Hello." when I walked into the weight room. I said, "How's it doin' man?" I immediately realized the stupid thing that had just slipped out of my mouth. I mixed, "How's it going?" with "How are you doing, man?" I felt like an idiot. So, I just kept walking back to the equipment that I planned to use and hoped that he did not catch the stupid thing that I had just said. Mentally, I was improving, but was still far from my old self. But the more I worked out, and stuck to my new routine, the better I felt. As my self-perception became more and more positive, I began to regain more ability to communicate properly. This process took about a year. By the summer of 2008, I would say that I was well on my way to becoming a version of my old self that had not existed in over 10 years. There were several things that happened shortly after joining the YMCA that allowed me to begin to become my old self again.

The main thing was that Mom went back to work. Mom started teaching as a substitute teacher at different schools in Polk County. She was able to work just about any day that she wanted to, and she usually worked every day. So, with Mom and Dad both gone all day, I began to have even more freedom. With my parents out of the house, it almost felt like I was living on my own again. But with my new freedom came new responsibility. Mom began having me do all of the cooking and house cleaning. She was busy at work all day and was too tired to come home and cook. So, I took over as the new housewife. I began to refer to myself as "The Cabana Boy". I became the person in the house who did all of the housework. Those new duties began to shape a new routine for me.

Once mom started working, my new routine was as follows: Wake up around 10:00 a.m., do whatever chores mom had asked me to do for the day, go to the YMCA every Monday, Wednesday, and Friday, come back home and goof off for an hour, cook supper, watch TV with my parents for an hour or so, put up the food, clean up the kitchen, walk for an hour, and then go over to the guesthouse to play video games until 11:30 pm, at 11:30 pm watch *The Tonight Show* and *Late Night With Conan O'Brien*, then go to sleep. Repeat. Tuesdays and Thursdays I usually spent the time that I would spend at the YMCA on every other weekday, taking little rides on my motorcycle to either Sebring, Lakeland, or just around Lake Wales. I usually would ride to a mall and walk around for an hour or so, just to break up the day. The mall was a good place to walk when it was too hot or cold to be outside. On nice days, I sometimes just rode to Lake Wales and walked around the lake.

The positive impact that came from my mother going back to work was that it allowed me to feel like I was contributing something to the household. By having the small responsibility of cooking and cleaning, I felt like I was at least doing something to help out my parents. I hated how much I depended on them. That was why I always wanted to avoid them as much as possible. I wanted to avoid them for the same reason that I wanted to avoid everyone else, shame. Before I was asked to do the cooking and cleaning, I felt like I only took from my parents, without ever giving anything back. But once I was able to cook for them and clean their house, I felt like I was doing something that benefited them. They always complimented the food I cooked or the chores I did. It made me feel good. I felt like I was finally doing something to show a little gratitude to them. That also made me feel good. Once I began to have a little pride in my ability to cook decent meals and take care of the chores that Mom asked me to do, my self-image took another jump, and I stepped further from the bottom of the downward spiral.

One other important thing that boosted my self-esteem happened at a doctor's office. Sometime in February of 2008, I qualified for a health insurance plan that was created for people with low incomes. The health insurance plan let me see a regular doctor who prescribed my medication, Zyprexa. I loved the fact that I could just see a regular doctor, instead of having to see a psychiatrist at a psychiatric institution. It allowed me to feel a little less ashamed of the fact that I needed to see a doctor for my mental stability. I knew that the hardest thing would be having to tell my doctor my history with the PRC and explain to him why I needed the medication that I took. I was very nervous about that first appointment.

I remember the day that I went to see my new doctor, Dr. Acuna, for the first time. It was a day filled with shame. First, there was the shame of telling the medical billing girl that I had insurance with Polk County Health Plan. I knew that would mark me as a person with little or no income. The Polk County Health Plan was the insurance that I had received because I had such a small income. I got over that little bit of shame though. I think that my nervousness about having to tell my doctor my medical history made the fact that I was viewed as low class seem not so hard to deal with. I knew that the worst part was yet to come.

After getting the payment arrangements squared away, I was called back to a room where I would meet my new doctor. I was very ashamed to have to tell anyone about my condition, Schizoaffective disorder, but I thought that it would be worth it if it meant that I would no longer have to see a psychiatrist for my medication. I waited in the room for a few minutes and then a nurse came in. She introduced herself as Nancy. She seemed very friendly. She had me sit in a chair across from a chair that she sat down in, which was in front of a computer. Nancy opened up a file in some medical software that she used on the computer. Then, Nancy started asking me questions. Some questions were no problem, but others were very hard to answer. The first tough question was, "Do you work?" I said, "No." Nancy checked a box on the form she was filling out on the computer. A few questions later, Nancy hit me with the question that I had been dreading having to answer for over two years. Nancy asked, "Do you have any mental health problems?" I said, "Yes." and just sat there. I knew that I would have to talk about this subject, but it was so hard. I had not told anyone about my condition. I didn't talk about it with my family and I had no friends to worry with. So, until that day at Dr. Acuna's office, I had never been forced to talk about my mental state outside of my visits with my psychiatrist.

When Nancy asked about my mental health status, I thought I would cry before I was able to tell her my complete answer to her question. I sat there for probably a minute, trying to get the lump out of my throat. Finally, I said, "I was diagnosed as Schizoaffective." and then I couldn't make eye contact with her. I just stared at the ground. I didn't want her to see the fact that my eyes were watering up, and I just couldn't bring myself to see the reaction on her face once she had heard what I had just said. I didn't want to see the subtle sign of disgust that I assumed I would probably see after I told anyone about who I was. To my surprise, Nancy said, "Hey, it's O.K. I just had to ask you that question because I see that you are taking Zyprexa." Then she said, "Don't feel bad about it. Lots of people have to take the kind of medicine that you take. I had to take Zyprexa myself for a while." Suddenly, I was able to look at her again. Those few words that she spoke about taking Zyprexa were all that I needed to beat down the shame enough that I could look at her as she talked to me. I realized that if she had taken the drug that I took, and she was able to live a possibly normal life, then maybe I was not as terrible of a person as I thought I was.

Nancy went on to tell me that she had gone through a bit of depression after her grandmother died. Nancy said that she went for months in a very depressed state and was unable to stop herself from crying all the time. Nancy said that she told her doctor about her problem, and they prescribed the same drug that I was taking, Zyprexa. After hearing Nancy's story, I immediately felt a sense of immense relief. Nancy was the first person I met who seemed very normal, but had to take Zyprexa. I was so overwhelmed with a sense of comfort from her that I can't remember much of anything else that happened that day. She asked me a lot of other questions, and I answered each one without any sense of shame. By relating herself to me, she made me feel so calm that I was able to instantly snap out of the fear and shame. After meeting Nancy that day at the doctor's office, I began to realize that there were other people like me, who had been through a difficult time, but were able to get themselves back together and continue living a normal life. I thank God for allowing me to meet Nancy that day. I know that she had no idea of how big of a difference she made in my life with that simple story she told me, but I am very grateful for her decision to share that piece of information with me. I thought about Nancy for a long time after that first meeting. After that chance encounter (maybe not chance at all), I began to feel a little less ashamed of myself. I had finally found someone who I felt I could relate with.

Just before the summer of 2008, I was still keeping my routine of staying up late and sleeping late, but I had stopped the afternoon naps. Those afternoon naps stopped after I got my motorcycle. Once I had my motorcycle, and freedom, there was no longer a need to try to hurry the days along by sleeping through them. After the motorcycle came, I began to appreciate life a little. The longer I had the bike, the more I appreciated not only it, but everything around me. I stopped waking up and dreading the fact that I had another day to make it through. I started to wake up and become excited about what the day might bring. I had not looked forward to the future in several years. Once I began to appreciate all the little things, I think, I was becoming the person I had not been in over 10 years. All the stress of getting a girl pregnant before marrying her, raising the babies that came afterwards, while trying to survive architecture school, and work; all added up to a very miserable time in my life. I regret saying that my children caused my to be miserable, but it is true. It was not my children's actions that brought the misery. It was the shame of having kids too soon. That was what created the misery. It was the shame and knowing that I had let down my parents and grandparents by not living up to the way that I had been raised. That created the misery. So, after my wife left, took the kids away, and left me to fend for myself, I slowly began to improve. But I had to hit rock bottom before I was able to begin rebuilding myself. The rebuilding of my self-image was well under way by the summer of 2008.

The end of my daily routine, in May of 2008, involved watching *The Tonight Show with Jay Leno*. *The Tonight Show* usually ends with a performance from a music group. One night I saw two weird looking girls walk out on stage and start singing a song. I listened to their song and thought that they sounded pretty good. Their style of music was a little different than most of what I listened to, and yet it was similar in ways, as well. They sang a song called, "Back In Your Head". I didn't really pay attention to the words. I just liked the sound of their music and I loved their voices. There was something very unique about their voices. The uniqueness of sound was all I looked for in music after I started to like music again once I had been released from the PRC. I liked their sound. I liked it enough that I went to a music store at the Eagle Ridge Mall the next day to find their CD. I looked through the Rock section and found it. The CD was titled Tegan and Sara, *The Con*. I picked it up and scanned it on one of the music players that allowed me to listen to samples of the album. I was instantly blown away by their album. I knew that what I was listening to was something better than anything I had heard in a long time, maybe ever. But again, it was not the words that grabbed me at first, it was just their music.

After a couple weeks of going to the music store and listening to the Tegan and Sara CD, I decided that I should buy it. That CD was the first album I listened to and fell in love with since I had bought the Radiohead and Counting Crows albums years earlier. For me, there is something special that happens when I discover really good music. For me to classify something as really good music, it has to contain very well designed sounds, but also well written lyrics that speak to me and say something that I had thought before, or introduce me to new ideas that I have never thought. The Tegan and Sara album, *The Con,* had all those qualities. The more I listened to it, the more I identified myself with those strange little girls that I had seen on *The Tonight Show* a couple weeks earlier. Their album, The Con, became the soundtrack of my summer. I listened to it constantly from the time I bought it, in May of 2008, right up through the end of the summer. It is one of my new all time favorite albums.

The main songs that spoke to me were title track, "The Con", and "Dark Come Soon". Those two songs talked about a few thoughts that had played in my mind for several years. "The Con" has a line that says "Nobody likes to, but I really like to cry. Nobody likes me. Maybe if I cry." For me, that small statement spoke volumes about the way I had been feeling since I was released from the SRT program at the PRC. I believed that no one liked me anymore because I had been diagnosed as Schizoaffective. I believed that because of all my strange behavior, all the people I knew had written me off as a lost cause, not worthy of caring about. The part about the crying was something that I wished I had been able to do many times. There were a lot of times when I felt like crying, but the tears never came. When Sara left, every time I was forced into a rehab center, as I saw all the people I knew begin to act different around me; all those times, I wanted to cry. But I was unable to do it. Instead, the sadness just grew inside of me and caused the shame that shut me down. Hearing Tegan and Sara Quin say that they really liked to cry and that nobody liked them, were statements that I could totally relate to. It felt good to know that I was not the only person in the world who felt the way that I did. Their simple words helped me so much.

The other song, "Dark Come Soon", had a statement that I could relate to as well. Tegan Quin says, "Dark, you can't come soon enough for me. Saved, from one more day of misery. Everything I love, get back from me now. Everyone I love, I need you now." Again, those were words that hit home with me. I had waited for the dark every day for several years. Dark meant that soon I would be asleep. When I was asleep I could dream. I always hoped for good dreams. Every now and then, I would actually have one. But waking up from a good dream was actually worse than waking up from a nightmare because once I woke up, I realized that I was back to the reality of being labeled as Schizoaffective, and all the misery that came with it. I remember waking up from dreams that Warren Eto had asked me to come back to work in Tallahassee. In my dreams I would be crying because I was so happy. I knew that if Warren had asked me back to work, my life would go back to the way it had been. I would wake up from those dreams and realize that it was all another fantasy. I would lie in bed and feel like crying because I knew that my fantasy was so far from my reality. My reality was that I had lost my wife, children, house, and car; and I now lived with my parents because I was too pathetic to take care of myself. Waking up from a good dream was usually a very hard experience for me. But I always looked forward to dreaming. My dreams were the best parts of my day, even if waking from them was difficult. I would wake up in the morning and count down the hours until I could go back to sleep. Being conscious of my present situation was so hard that all I wanted to do was sleep. "Dark, you can't come soon enough for me." was a thought that had passed through my depressed little brain many times.

After hearing *The Con* album, I fell in love with Tegan and Sara Quin. I would still love to see them in concert some day. I rate them as my newest favorite band. I place them on a level with REM, Radiohead, and The Counting Crows. Those are the only bands that I have liked as much as I like Tegan and Sara. Their lyrics are very straight-forward most of the time and that is what I love about them. I listen to a lot of groups who write very abstract lyrics that could be interpreted to mean many different things. I like that style of writing as well, but Tegan and Sara speak to me. I am still stuck on my latest album of theirs. I think it was their third, *If It Was You*. I also own *So Jealous*. That album filled my listening time towards the end of the summer, after I ordered it online. The first song on *So Jealous* says, "I feel like, you wouldn't like me if you met me. I feel like, I wouldn't like me if I met me." That song is just another blatant statement about the way I felt for several years. I loved hearing Tegan and Sara put my exact thoughts to music. I was positive, for a long time, that no one would ever want to be around me. Fortunately, I was proven wrong about that idea. I don't believe that there was ever a time when no one liked me. There was a long time when I'm sure my parents had a tough time dealing with me, but I don't think they ever stopped loving me. I can't imagine ever not loving my girls. So, I can understand when they tell me that they never stopped caring about me, even though I was a frightening person to be around.

I love all the songs on *So Jealous*. *So Jealous* and *If It Was You* are both equals to *The Con* in my opinion. They all deal with the same troubles of rejection and depression that were such a major problem for me. I think that their music makes for great therapy. For me, it allowed me to feel less alone. By hearing two girls talk about their problems, I felt like I knew them and we had something in common. I would love to thank Tegan and Sara Quin for creating music that was so helpful to me.

After I bought my first Tegan and Sara album, I decided that I wanted to be able to listen to music wherever I went. So, I bought an MP3 player. I bought a little Sansa Clip for $40 at Wal-Mart. I loaded it with all my favorite songs and began to listen to them whenever I rode my motorcycle, took my evening walks, or whenever I wanted. The MP3 player allowed music to become a larger part of my life than it had been in a long time. After buying the MP3 player, I soon began to find other groups that I liked. Radiohead put out their album, *In Rainbows*. I discovered Vampire Weekend, The French Kicks, and Goldfrapp. Those albums were the first to find their way onto my MP3 player, along with Tegan and Sara. Once I loaded my player with several hours of music, I began to listen to it often. I started to appreciate music again, the way I had years earlier. I think that appreciation of music marked the point when I really began to become more like the person I had been before I married Sara. Through music, I began to find an identity for myself again. I no longer felt as weird or alone as I once did. I was able to listen to the lyrics of some of my new songs and find comfort in them.

Chapter 67: The Reawakening

The reawakening of my old self really started to come around during the summer of 2008. That summer, my parents planned a trip where they drove from Georgia to Connecticut. From Connecticut they headed west across the northern states around the Great Lakes, and into Canada. Then they went on to California. From California they drove east and returned to the Georgia house. They drove the whole trip in about 5 weeks. That five weeks, I stayed at the house in Georgia by myself. It was a wonderful time for me. It was the first chance that I had been allowed to live completely on my own for that long, ever.

Mom and Dad left the Georgia house for Connecticut in June. After that, I was on my own. I was so excited. I knew that being on my own would be a big improvement over the way I had lived for the last several years. Even though it was only for a short time, it was long enough for me to realize that being on my own was the way that I preferred to live. I always felt so uptight around my parents. The guilty feelings that came from knowing that I was rouging off of them made me very uncomfortable around them. Once they left for their trip, I felt free. Once they left, I was responsible for taking care of myself. That included buying all my own food and cooking for myself. Of course, I didn't have to come up with money for rent. So, I still was not completely back in reality, but it was the closest thing to it that I had experienced in several years.

After my parents left, I set up a routine for myself. The first thing that I did was join a gym that was only 8 miles from their house. That was a big improvement over my 16 mile drive to the YMCA in Florida. Another nice thing about that gym was that it was free. It was paid for by property taxes. So, residents of the county could all use the facilities for no charge. The nice thing was that not many people took advantage of it. I never had to wait to use any of the equipment. The gym was the anchor of my weekly routine. I went to it three times a week, just as I did in Florida. I also added some calisthenics to my work out routine, and started taking whey protein to supplement my protein intake. My weight kept going down. By the summer of 2008 I had dropped to 165 pounds from over 200 pounds just a year earlier. I lost all my weight from working out and watching what I ate.

My daily routine that summer was as follows: I would usually wake up around 10:00 am. Then, I would do push-ups and sit-ups on my workout days: Monday, Wednesday, and Friday. After doing my calisthenics, I would ride up to the gym and work out for about an hour. After that, I would usually go back to the house and eat lunch, watch TV for an hour or so, or take a ride on my motorcycle. In the evening, I usually called either Carter, Sam, my parents, my girls, or Nanny. After my evening phone conversation, I would watch TV until I was tired, usually around 12:30 am. That was the flow of a typical day during those weeks that I got to pretend that I was independent.

I did a lot of riding on my motorcycle that summer. I explored all the surrounding towns near my parents' house. Getting out and planning small adventures was something I had not done since Sara and I were married. I loved taking a half-day ride to places like: Helen, GA, Franklin, NC, Elligay, GA, The Nantahala River, NC, and others. Those little trips were a lot of fun. I did more exploring that summer than I had ever done in my life. The explorations led to activities that I would not have done otherwise. I hiked to the top of Brasstown Bald. I went tubing down a stream in Helen, GA. I watched people paddle their kayaks through the white water of the Nantahala River. I hiked to several waterfalls. I did all kinds of things that I had enjoyed doing in the past. The small adventures that I went on that summer were just another indicator that my self-esteem was rising. I did all those trips alone. There were times when I actually wished that I had someone with me to enjoy the moment. The desire to share my time with another person was something that had not existed until that summer. After I realized that things were more fun when shared with other people, I knew that I was returning to my old self. I was returning to the version of me that actually liked people, instead of fearing or hating them. That desire to find someone to share my time with started as just a small thought that occurred at times when I realized that I was actually having fun. After that summer, the desire began to grow. I realized that I wanted to find a friend, someone who I could go places with or just talk with about nothing. I wanted to find an outlet, someone I could vent all my frustrations to, someone who could vent frustrations to me. I realized that I wanted to begin building new bridges and stop tearing down all the ones that I had.

The first attempts to build bridges came in the form of telephone conversations. I began to make the telephone part of my daily routine. Since I had been put in the rehab center in Tallahassee, I never talked to anyone on the phone, unless I was forced to. That included my brothers, my girls, and my grandmother. That summer, it all changed. I decided that it was time to reach out to my family again. So, I began calling one member of my family every night. I would usually talk on the phone for an hour. I began to look forward to my telephone chats. They soon became one of the highlights of my day. My phone calls were never serious discussions about anything. They were just simple chats about what I had been doing since my last call. I would also get to find out what my brothers, Nanny, and my girls were up to. I especially liked to hear from my girls. I began to feel guilty for leaving them again.

As the summer went on, and I had no contact with my kids, I began to feel like I had made a bad decision to go so far away from them. I did not see them from the time we left, at the end of May, until they came to visit at the end of the summer in August. That was the longest I had gone without seeing my kids since the last time that I was released from the PRC. I decided to go to Georgia, for the entire summer, in the first place because my parents were going to take their van to Georgia. I was afraid that I would not be able to buy all of the groceries that I needed if I had only my motorcycle to get them with. I also knew that with the van gone, I would have no way of picking up my kids. So, even if I were to stay in Florida, I would not get to spend my weekends with my girls. Still, the longer I went without seeing them, the more I regretted making the decision to be without them. I really enjoyed talking to them on the phone every few days, but it was not the same as seeing them in person. By the end of that summer, I told myself that I didn't want to ever be away from my kids that long again. It made me feel too guilty to leave them for that long.

My girls were really the two people that I first realized really cared about me. Aside from my girls, I thought that my dog, Blue, was the only companion and friend that I really had. She never asked questions and she always loved to be around me, no matter how weird I might be. For several years, Blue was my only friend. I tried talking to Blue, as I might talk to a person. It was my way of practicing how to communicate. Sometimes I would tell Blue little thoughts that passed through my head. A lot of the times, I had trouble even talking to her. There were a couple of years where I just couldn't put together my words right. The art of speaking left my brain. I guess the medication affected me that way for a while. But eventually, I began to realize that I could talk again. Some of my first decently arranged sentences went to Blue. Once I realized that I could speak to her correctly, I began to talk to my kids. Once I felt comfortable talking with them (that took a long time), I began to speak with my parents. That whole process of learning how to communicate again took several years. I've only had the ability to speak my thoughts clearly for about a year now. Since I have been able to talk right, my life has changed dramatically.

During that brief period of five weeks that summer in 2008, when I pretended to live on my own, my self-esteem soared. I realized that I was capable of supporting myself. That gave me a lot of confidence. I had lived by myself at the little house on Johnson Avenue, but I did not take care of myself. My mom bought most of my groceries and did most of my cooking. So, even though I had a brief period where I lived alone, I was not really doing the things that I should have been doing to support myself. But that summer, I really felt like I was living on my own. I realized that I might have a future where I was able to live on my own someday.

My parents came back around the middle of July. After they returned, life went back to the old routine that existed when they were around. I no longer could decide what I was eating that night or what I wanted to watch on TV. But I kept to my work out schedule and short motorcycle rides. I continued doing my push-ups and sit-ups. I also continued to take the whey protein supplement. So, I established some new activities that became part of my routine. Even after my parents returned, I did not feel depressed or uptight about their presence. I had begun to dream of a potentially decent future. I began to have hope that I might one day be independent again. That dream motivated me and kept me from back sliding into the negative thinking that had controlled my every waking moment for so many years. I was tired of letting depression beat me. I wanted to give myself another chance to go back into the real world. I had the dream. I just had not yet worked out the details of how to achieve it.

Summer ended several weeks after my parents came back from their big cross-country adventure. We went back to Florida and I picked up the old Florida routine where I had left off. I began to work out at the YMCA again. I also went back to doing all the cooking and cleaning. My parents went back to work. Life returned to normal again, only it was not what it had been before the summer. My attitude had changed. Life was more exciting, even though there was no new excitement in it. The excitement came from within me. I felt like I might be on the verge of doing something good. I just was not sure what that would be. The only tangible bit of good that I could see was the change in the quality of the time that I spent with my two girls, Liza and Gwen.

In Christmas of 2007, my girls had gone to Georgia to spend a week with my parents and I at their house in Georgia. Something very strange happened that Christmas that brought me a terrible vision of the future. The strangeness came from my oldest daughter, Liza. Liza appeared to not want to have anything to do with me or my family that week that she spent with us. She did not want to talk to me or be near me. She spent a lot of her time talking on the phone to her mother. If she talked with anyone at all that week, it was usually my cousin, Alice, who was 20 years old and probably seemed very cool to Liza, who was 10. I had never seen Liza seem so distant from me. Every time I tried to talk to her, she seemed very strange. She acted as if she was irritated to have to talk to me. It scared me.

I began to realize that my inward focus and all of my self loathing and pity had resulted in turning away the little girl who used to light up every time I walked in the door from work. The thought that she might be beginning to resent me or dislike me made me very afraid. I had spent most of her young life thinking of her and her sister as a burden. When I was working, I always cringed at how much money was spent on daycare, diapers, clothes, food, etc.; for my two girls. I spent too much time worrying about how I would ever afford to take care of them properly and not enough time worrying about what I needed to do to ensure that they grew to be loving, caring individuals who shared my values and had respect for their parents as I always had for my own.

After seeing Liza's odd new behavior that week at Christmas, I was afraid that I was seeing a future that had no place for me in it. Liza would talk on the phone to her mom and step dad for an hour sometimes and then have nothing to say to me. I began to think that I had been replaced by Sara's new husband, Matt. I figured that I deserved it. I knew that I had basically been a terrible father towards my girls for the majority of their lives, especially since my stints in the rehab centers. I had let two years go by, hardly ever sharing a loving moment with my two girls, and now I was beginning to pay the price. My oldest was showing me that she no longer cared to have anything to do with me. Surprisingly, after years of basically ignoring her, once she ignored me, I felt a sense of hurt unlike anything I had ever felt. I had taken my daughter's love for granted and never cared much about it. But when it seemed to be diminishing, it sounded an alarm bell that motivated me to attention. I knew that I had to do something to get her back. For some reason, it took that small experience of her lack of caring to make me begin to care more.

Liza ended that week with the hardest blow of all. She said that she wanted to go home early. She left with Alice a few days before she was originally supposed to. Gwen stayed with me and my mother for a few more days and then we all drove back to Florida. But Liza's absence made a lasting impression on me. After that week, I told myself that I would do whatever I could to let her know that I really cared about her.

The first thing I did was call Sara and tell her about what I had witnessed that week with Liza. I couldn't think of anyone else to talk about the problem with and I wondered if she had noticed anything similar happening between her and Liza, though I doubted that would be the case after all the telephone calls I had seen between her and Liza. Sara said that she had not seen Liza acting the way that I had described her when she was with Sara. I asked her to please have a talk with Liza about at least being more respectful to my parents. Sara agreed that that was important. She said she would have a talk with Liza about being rude towards my family. I think that was a little lame of me to call and basically tattle on Liza to her mom, but it was the only thing I could think to do. After that phone call, I knew that if I was going to have any luck with changing Liza's behavior, I would have to do more than just report her to her mother. I knew that what I really needed to do was give Liza a motivation to want to be around me. At first, I thought that the best way to get my kids to want to spend time with me would be to take them to fun places and spend money on them. It was not until that trip to Connecticut, in the summer of 2007, when I began to realize that perhaps, money was not the thing that I needed to re-establish a proper relationship with my girls.

In January of 2008, I bought annual passes for Liza, Gwen, and I to Busch Gardens in Tampa, FL. I thought that if I started taking them there that they would have a lot of fun and would begin to enjoy being with me more. As it turned out, I was right. The only thing was, I soon realized that it was not Busch Gardens, with all its exciting rides and shows, that made my girls seem to love me more. No, what I finally realized was that they seemed to love me more because I was spending more time with them and was actually devoting my attention to them. Every time we went to Busch Gardens, it was just the girls and I. Before those weekend trips to Tampa, we always spent all of our time with my parents. Everywhere we went, my mom and dad were with us. But after we started going to Busch Gardens, we had a lot of time where it was just the three of us. It took over 1 ½ hours to get from the lake house to Busch Gardens. So, we had a lot of time in the car ride over there to talk. That was where the magic began to happen. Liza and Gwen had at least three hours, on each trip to Busch Gardens, to do nothing but talk to me about what was going on in their lives. It was their new opportunity to talk to me that, I think, began to bring us all closer together.

Liza and Gwen started telling me about their friends, things that happened at school and home, and all sorts of other subjects. I got the chance to tell them things about my childhood and other topics that I thought they might find interesting. The more time we spent talking to each other, the closer I began to feel to my kids. At first, I was blown away at just how little I really knew about the two little girls that I had helped raise. I realized the result of my ridiculous waste of time, focusing on myself, had caused me to miss out on a lot of things that had happened in the girls' lives. In just two short years, I had ignored them entirely and almost lost their desire to think of me as a father. I watched the process of them slipping away from me without any remorse for a long time. I had convinced myself that they would be better off without me in their lives. But that previous Christmas, when it became obvious that they were in fact slipping away, through Liza's lack of desire to spend any time with my family or myself, I had a quick change of heart. The feeling of rejection from my own children was not something that I was prepared for. Even though I had told myself that they would be better off without me, once they seemed to lose the desire to be around me, the pain was more than I was ready to deal with. Now, I was fighting to win back their attention. I had realized that, even if they might be better off without me, I definitely would be worse off without them. I realized that I needed them more than they needed me. They were the only two people I could spend time with and not feel the weird nervousness that I experienced when I was around everyone else. My girls were the ones who never asked questions that I felt uncomfortable answering. I guess someone had told them not to talk about what had happened to me at the rehab centers because they never asked about those times. I'm sure that they have questions that need to be answered. In time, I will tell them everything. But for now, they are too young to deal with the bizarre details of exactly what I thought and did during that time.

After Liza, Gwen, and I started taking our trips to Busch Gardens, I started to notice little things, like the way they always wanted to be around me whenever we were together, no matter who else was around. It was just small things like the way they always wanted to sit next to me at the table when we ate our meals at my parents' house and when we went to church with my parents on Sunday. Those trips to Busch Gardens were the beginning of a great repair to my relationship with my kids. After the annual passes expired in December of 2008, I knew that Busch Gardens was only a place that we went, not a magical force that brought my kids closer to me. What had brought us closer together did not come from the money that I spent, the rides, the shows, or the food. The closeness came from the shift in my attitude about my kids. Each weekend I spent with them, I realized more and more, that what they needed was my attention. The more attention I gave them, the more I learned about who they were. They also got to see who I was. They seemed to like it. I was able to crack jokes and act goofy with them. They loved that. They had not seen that side of me through most of their lives. Finally, after years of worrying about how I could properly raise my girls, I felt like I was becoming a good father for them. It is funny to me that even though I had less money to spend on them, I felt like I was providing them with more than I ever had. In the years I had spent stressing about my job and the money I was earning, I had always worried that I was not doing enough. I would come home so stressed out from work that I could not spend quality time with my kids, even when we were together. I could only think about the stressful things that happened at work and the deadlines that I had to meet. So, even though Sara and I did a lot of fun things with the girls over the years that we were married, I cannot say that I was ever a good father, because I was never a good listener. I was always too wrapped up in my own little world to effectively spend time with my wife and kids. I had to lose my job, my income, my wife, my house, and everything else to realize just how important my kids really were. I would not recommend that scenario to anyone else. I would recommend that parents make a special effort to listen to their children and really focus on what they are saying. That is where a real relationship begins.

Chapter 68: And Life Goes On

I knew that I wanted to return back to work. I figured that would be the first step toward establishing a new life for myself that resembled the one that I had lived that summer, when my parents left. I began to research what my options for work would be without losing my Disability benefits. I didn't want to take a chance on losing my benefits because I was afraid that if I lost them, and was unhappy with whatever job I took, I would have no income again. I couldn't afford to let that happen because I was obligated to pay my dad for the motorcycle loan and the money he let me borrow to pay off my taxes.

I had spent a lot of time that summer thinking about what type of work I might enjoy doing. Every time I tried to imagine myself in a job, I always ended up with the same predicament. The predicament was that I did not want to be around people. Even though I was able to keep my mood up, I still had not developed the courage to speak to other people. Sure, I might say hello to people as I passed them at the gym, but, aside from my immediate family, I did not have conversations with anyone. I was still too scared of the possibility that a conversation would develop that would lead to me spilling the beans about my schizophrenia. That was the thing I still feared most. I was afraid that if I started working, I would find myself in some setting where people would question my past and I would have to tell them about the strange path that I had been down. So, every time I imagined myself working, I imagined the people who would be prodding me with questions that I did not know how to answer. I would run myself in circles, trying to dream up a job that had little to no contact with other people. I could not think of one that existed. So, I came to my next best option, The Ticket To Work Program.

The Ticket To Work Program is a federal program for returning people with disabilities to the work place. Once a person is on Disability, they receive a Ticket To Work. That ticket can be given to an Employment Network to help them find a job, receive vocational training, and learn skills that they might need to find employment. The Employment Network is a job search company, authorized by the federal government, to find a job that best suits a particular person with a particular disability. Some EN's specialize in finding jobs for people with certain types of disabilities, such as, the deaf, blind, physically impaired, etc.

So, I had to find an Employment Network that would serve my disability. I found out that unless a person uses the Employment Network to find them a job, they are responsible for reporting to the Social Security Administration about all their income. This requires a lot of paperwork and it made me fear that I might end up losing my Disability benefits if something got screwed up with the reporting process. So, I decided that it would be best for me to use the Employment Network to find me a job. I also hoped that the Employment Network might handle the difficult task of explaining my situation to a potential employer. I thought that if the Employment Network did that, it would be worth whatever trouble I had to go through to use their services.

In October of 2008, I finally got to a point where I had found a local Employment Network that I could use to find me a job. I called a phone number for a person who dealt with people with disabilities. I called several times and only got the person's voicemail. So, I left a brief message and asked them to return my call. That same day, I got another phone call that ended up changing my plans for job hunting.

The phone call was from Nanny. She asked me if I could drive her to her doctor for a colonoscopy appointment. I told her that I had no problem taking her there. It wasn't like I had anything in my schedule that prevented me from doing that. The only place I ever went, routinely, was the YMCA. So, I drove Nanny to her colonoscopy appointment the next day. I assumed it would be just a routine check up and I would get back on with my research of the Employment Network as soon as I was finished helping Nanny.

Nanny and I went to her doctor and he performed the colonoscopy evaluation. After the test was over, Nanny was brought to a room where she could wake up from the anesthesia. After she started waking up, her doctor walked up and said, "I have some bad news dear. You have some problems with your colon." At first I thought that he might just give her some warnings about something he had learned from his examination of her colon. But instead he went on to say that he had found a large growth that might potentially be cancerous. He said that he was unable to remove it and she would have to have it surgically removed by a specialist. After Nanny received that news, she seemed a little nervous. She had been through several colonoscopies and there had been several times where her doctor removed cists that formed in her colon. But she had never been told that she had something that would require surgery to remove it. Her doctor told her that she would probably have to be hospitalized while she recovered from the surgery. I immediately realized that my job hunt would have to be postponed. I knew that if Nanny was going to have surgery, then I be the most likely candidate to help her while she recovered.

A few days after her initial evaluation with her doctor, Nanny had an appointment with a specialist who would actually perform the surgery on her intestines. The doctor started talking about the different stages of cancer and how the growth that had been discovered in her colon might hold a low stage cancerous tumor. Up until that point, the word "cancer" had not really held much significance in my mind. But after hearing the surgeon talk about the potential of a cancerous tumor being in Nanny's intestine, I got a little nervous, and thought about the terrible experience with cancer that I had witnessed with Granddaddy. The surgeon went on to give the details of exactly what he would need to do to remove the growths. There were actually three different areas that were of concern, I think. The surgeon had to remove all of them. That required him to remove a section of her intestines that was almost a foot long. The surgeon said that Nanny would be hospitalized for about two weeks. After that, if all went well, she would be able to return home. He said that once she was home, she would still require assistance because she would be very weak and still in pain. The surgery would require an abdominal incision to reach the intestines. Basically, he would have to cut Nanny open with a large cut across her abdomen, then cut out the cancerous portion of her intestine, sew the two sections of her intestines back together, and then sew her abdomen back together. That sounded like a lot of cutting to me. I realized that this would not be a simple operation. She was going to be out of commission for a while. I realized that the job hunt would need to be postponed indefinitely. I began to think that I might be entering a new care-giver type situation similar to the one I had taken when Granddaddy was dying from cancer.

Nanny had the operation scheduled a couple weeks from her first visit with the surgeon. She was sent to Lakeland Regional Hospital, the same place where Granddaddy had spent many days and nights before finally being given the news that he had terminal cancer. Lakeland Regional Hospital held bad memories for me. I prayed that I would not see a repeat of what happened to Granddaddy.

Nanny was scheduled to have her surgery in the morning one day in October of 2008. There was a mix up with the scheduling at the hospital and she ended up having her surgery around 5:00 p.m. She had to spend the whole day without food or water and had already been fasting for over a day before the surgery. She was not placed in her hospital room until sometime that night. My parents wanted to stay at the hospital with her that first night, so I went on home. I went back to the hospital the next day and gave my mom a break from being at the hospital all night. Mom went home just long enough to take a shower and then she came back. We started to set up a schedule where I stayed with Nanny during the day, and my mom slept in Nanny's hospital room with her at night. We didn't want Nanny to be alone in the room. We were afraid that she might get upset or scared if she was allowed to be by herself. One night, Mom came home and left Nanny by herself. We found out the next day that Nanny had a panic attack that night. So, after that, we always had someone sleep in the room with her.

Nanny stayed in the hospital for about two weeks, recovering from her surgery. The first day that I visited her after her surgery, she looked like death. She had tubes going in her nose and a couple of I.V. bags hooked up to her arm. The I.V. bags were filled with pain medication and nutrients to feed her damaged body. On that first day after surgery, she slept most of the time. She didn't talk more than a few words at a time, which came out in weary whispers. She looked and sounded horrible. Nanny's skin was a pale grayish color and her face looked drawn. I'm sure that she was suffering quite a bit, but she didn't really complain, just like Granddaddy when he was suffering from his cancer. The first few days she just laid in bed and slept through most of the day. After the first day, the tube in her nose was taken out. That improved her sickly look a little. Each day she was in the hospital, she was required to get up and walk around as much as possible. The process of getting out of and back into bed was the most painful part of her day. I guess the strain of the abdominal muscles as she lifted herself out of bed really hurt. She moved very slowly as she pulled herself out of bed. She also made lots of groans and grunts as the pain registered when she moved to get up or lay back down. The first day after surgery, she walked up and down a hallway outside her room one time. It took about 10 minutes for her to make the whole trip, which was maybe a 1/16 of mile, if that. Each day after that, she made a little more progress with her walks. She began to walk further and longer each time. After going for 4 or 5 days without food or water, they allowed her to begin a liquid diet. She began drinking chicken broth, juice, water, and coffee. During her second week, she progressed to a solid diet. They allowed her to leave the hospital when it was clear that her digestive system was working, as indicated by the fact that she had gas and a bowel movement. The day that Nanny was allowed to leave the hospital and return home was a big deal for Nanny. She was so glad to return to her home. She said that the hospital was wearing on her because she was not able to sleep through the night. Nurses were in and out of her room throughout the night checking on her. So, she never got a full night's sleep. During the day, she had visitors who kept her from sleeping. So, by the end of her stay, she was pretty exhausted.

Once Nanny was able to come back home, I kept with the routine of spending my day with her. My parents came over at night and slept with her so that she never felt alone. We kept up that schedule for a couple weeks and then let Nanny see if she was able to take care of herself.

My days with Nanny reminded me of the time that I had spent taking care of Granddaddy. Nanny slept in bed for a good portion of the day for the first few days I was there. She was so exhausted from her hospital stay that she needed a few days to recuperate. I spent most of the day in front of the TV or reading the newspaper. I did this not to keep my mind off of negative thoughts, as I had when Granddaddy was dying, but just to give me something to do. My attitude had gone through a major shift since the time that Granddaddy had died. I was no longer wallowing in fear and self-pity. I was able to forget about my problems and actually focus on someone other than myself. I tried to be as helpful to Nanny as I could. I hope I was a help, even though I don't really feel like I did that much. About the only thing I did for Nanny was to fix her something to drink or eat when she wanted it. I only had to do that a few times because she was trying to be as independent as possible, even though she had a huge incision in her abdomen. Nanny told me that she appreciated me just being there. The idea was to have someone with her at all times, just in case something terrible happened, such as a fall, or a tear in her stitches. Thank God, nothing ever happened. Nanny had a swift recovery. After a couple of weeks of sitting around Nanny's house as a security blanket, Nanny said that she thought she would be fine on her own. So, I went back to my usual routine.

Chapter 69: Full Circle

After finishing my job as Nanny's helper, I thought about looking for a job again. The only problem was that just as I finished helping Nanny, my mom told me that she had an important announcement about my brother, Carter. Mom said that Carter and his long time girlfriend, Sue had decided to get married. Mom said that the wedding would take place just after Thanksgiving of 2008. It was only two weeks away. Carter and Sue made the decision to have a quickly put together, small ceremony; just to make it official that they were married. They had been living together for several years already. Their little girl, Helen, was almost 1 ½ years old. I guess they were tired of hearing comments from their family and friends about having a child and not being married. So, they decided to tie the knot, probably just to shut everyone up, if for no other reason. I had always thought that they made a good couple. They seemed to genuinely appreciate each other. I never heard them speak negatively of each other in front of other people. I thought that said a lot. Sara and I made rude jokes about each other many times in front of our families. I hated doing that, but I think that Sara just thought she was being funny whenever she started making little jokes about me. After she started insulting me in front of other people, I would usually feel like I needed to have a come back. So, I would find a way to slam her back with some little insult of my own. I never saw Carter and Sue do that. I thought that was a good indicator that they really liked each other. So, when I heard that they were getting married, it was no big surprise. It was just a way of making official, what had already existed for several years, the fact that they really loved each other.

When my mom told me that they were planning on going to Connecticut for Thanksgiving to attend Carter and Sue's wedding, my first thought was "I am not about to show up in front of a bunch of strange people at some damn wedding." I instantly imagined myself surrounded by Carter and Sue's family and friends and being so nervous that I could barely stand to be in the same room with all of them. I was sure that I probably seemed odd to all the people who met me. I didn't like having contact with the few people that I was forced to see routinely at the YMCA. I definitely did not want to place myself in a setting where I would be forced to talk to strangers. I was sure that I would have to introduce myself to a bunch of people and I knew the question that would eventually come up, "So, what do you do for a living?" That was the question that I feared almost as much as a question about my medical history. I hated having to answer that question because it made me either tell a lie, like, "Oh, I am a draftsman. I do work for an architect in Lakeland from my house." or it forced me to tell someone that I was unemployed. I knew that if I told someone that I was unemployed, I would feel compelled to explain why I was unemployed and that would lead to me talking about getting diagnosed as Schizoaffective. The fear of having to talk about unemployment and my mental disability was the driving force that made me a recluse. I was so scared to talk about those kinds of things with anyone. I was so afraid of the rejection that I thought would surely come whenever I started the conversation that led to me talking about schizophrenia and joblessness. It was the rejection and disappointment that I feared most. I figured that it would be better to live my life without human contact, than to live knowing how much people disapproved of me.

So, when my mom told me that they were going to Carter's wedding and it was assumed that I would go along, I was stressed. I wanted to tell my parents some excuse for why I could not go. Even though I hated the idea of going to Carter's wedding, I knew that I would regret not going. So, even though I hated the idea of showing up in front of a large group of people and appearing to be an idiot, I decided that I would go. The whole process took just a few minutes, but I stressed out about the coming wedding for days. I kept trying to get myself ready to appear in front of people who might ask the questions that I hated to answer. I told myself that I would probably just lie and tell them the story about working as a draftsman from my house. I thought that sounded pretty good. I figured that if I lied about having a job, then I would be able to avoid talking about my mental condition. So, once I got my story straight about what I did for a living, I felt more comfortable with the idea of being around a group of strangers.

My parents and I drove to Connecticut during the Thanksgiving holiday. My parents decided to stay at a hotel there in Old Saybrook. I was supposed to sleep with Carter and Sue at their apartment. I was a little nervous about having to spend my evenings with Carter and Sue. I was afraid that we would not have anything to say to each other and I would feel very awkward. As it turned out, Carter and I had a lot to say to each other. In fact, the conversations between Carter and I are what inspired me to begin writing this story.

Each night that I spent with Carter and Sue, there was a lot of conversation. We all talked about light topics for most of the time that Sue was awake. It was after she went to bed that Carter and I got into some serious conversations. I don't remember how the subject came up, but I eventually began to tell Carter about some of the strange ideas that I had during the time that I was insane. The topic was heavy on my mind because Carter and I had never talked about it. Since the time he sat in my kitchen, in my house in Tallahassee, on the night before I was first Baker Acted; we had never spoken a word about all the weirdness that developed after that time. I never talked about it with anyone. When it came to talking with people in my family, I always felt most comfortable around Carter for some reason. I guess it was because we had so much in common. He was always very artistic and I was as well. I guess that gave us a common ground that allowed other things to be built on.

So, the first person who got to hear some of the details of my crazy times in and out of the rehab centers was Carter. I told him about hearing voices and the explanation that I had come up with for that. I told him all about the secret group and all the troubles that they got me into. I told him about my visual hallucinations and how I thought that the secret group had implanted a device in my eye that gave me some improved form of vision. I told him about my ideas about God and Satan being aliens.

Carter listened to all of my wild tales and seemed very interested in them. He actually seemed amazed at some of the bizarre ideas that I had come up with. Carter was very supportive and told me that he had a lot of respect for me. For me, it was just what I needed to hear. Carter said that he didn't think that too many people had the experience that I had and that there were probably a lot of people who might have had my experience and wound up committing suicide. I didn't tell him that I had thought very hard about doing the same thing myself. Carter and I spent several hours on several nights talking about what had happened during my time of bizarre behavior. I feel a little guilty because we actually stayed up until 3:00 a.m. on the night before his wedding, talking about all the crazy things I had done and thought. Still, we both agreed that it was worth it. I think Carter appreciated hearing my stories as much as I appreciated him listening to them. I had been dying to tell someone about my craziness, I just couldn't bring myself to do it. Carter caught me at just the right moment when I was just getting up the courage to talk to someone about what I had been through. Having those hours where it was just Carter and I made the perfect setting for me to get a lot of my fears off my chest.

After that week in Connecticut, I felt like I had released a huge weight off of myself. I realized that it felt good to talk to my brother about my problems. Having him there to listen and respond to the things I said lifted a lot of stress off of me. Carter told me that he had always wanted to talk with me about the times when I was sent to the rehab centers. He said that he wanted to talk about those things, but was afraid that I was not ready to talk about them. So, we went a few years without ever speaking about the 900 pound gorilla that was always in the background whenever we talked. The silence about the subject made for some awkward moments. But after having those conversations, I felt like Carter and I had become much closer. I really appreciated him for taking the time to listen to me. Those nights that we spent talking were the first conversations I had with anyone at that length. Being able to talk about my fear and shame brought me great relief and the realization that I was beating my problems instead of letting them control me.

By the end of those days in Connecticut, I began to realize that, perhaps, I was not an idiot. I had effectively communicated with my brother for the first time in a long time. I began to think of myself as a normal person, who just happened to live through a series of stressful events that brought on some very bizarre symptoms. The key word is normal. I began to doubt that I was an idiot and I began to see myself as normal, at least as normal as I had ever been.

The catalyst for this story being written on paper happened during the conversations between my brother and I. After hours of me telling Carter some of the bizarre things that I did and thought, Carter asked if I had ever thought about writing any of my thoughts down, in case I were to ever forget them. I told Carter that I had thought about writing some of it down, but I just never did. I told him that I was afraid it might be too hard for me to dwell on those memories long enough for me to write them down. I knew that I wanted to make a record of my experiences with the illness that I suffered from. I just wasn't sure that I would ever be able to actually do it. I told Carter that I thought it would probably take about 100 pages to write down all the things that I had experienced in my most crazy times. I told Carter that was the reason why I had never started to write it all down. I was afraid that I might get too wrapped up in my terrible memories. I usually tried to distract myself from thinking about all the weird things that had happened. I knew that to write about it would require me to spend a lot of time reliving moments that I wished had never happened. I was afraid that all the time I spent remembering the past might lead to me having a relapse of mania and that I might end up back in another rehab center. So, I just thought about the idea of writing for a while after we got back from Connecticut. The thought began to slowly grow into a desire. The more I thought about writing, the more I wanted to give it a try. This story began as an idea to create a series of outlined statements that told about some of the most bizarre things I had thought and acted on. I thought that I might fill twenty or thirty pages if I just wrote a brief record of my most bizarre behaviors. But as I began to write my outline, things quickly changed into more of a story format. That is what led to the story you are reading right now.

The big event of the Connecticut trip for me, of course, was the talks that Carter and I had. But the reason for being there in the first place was the wedding. Carter and Sue had a very nice, small little ceremony. I was actually supposed to be the best man. So, I had a part in the ceremony. I gave the rings to the Justice of the Peace, who performed the marriage ceremony. Other than that, my only part was to stand there and watch the ceremony. I had been stressing about how I might appear awkward and nervous in front of the crowd of friends and family that gathered for Carter and Sue's wedding, but I actually made it through the event without feeling too out of place. There were a few moments where I felt a little nervous, but for the most part, I think I did alright. No one asked me about my situation or my job. That was a big relief. I talked with a few of the people there at the wedding. It was all small talk about what a beautiful area they lived in and the weather. I think I made it through all of my conversations without coming across as nervous or weird. Over all, I would say that Carter and Sue's wedding was a success for me. That was the first time in several years that I had been to a major gathering of people and not come away feeling like I had just made a fool of myself. The wedding was just another step up and out of the downward spiral. I realized that it was now possible for me to deal with large groups of people again. That just brought back more confidence that I had a good chance of being successful as an employee again. My confidence in myself rose, once again.

It was also around this time that another minor decision ended up having a major impact on me. The minor decision was the choice to read a book by Stephen King called *Duma Key*. In that book, there is a side story that tells of a little girl who suffers a major head injury and loses her ability to communicate. After many years of living in silence, with no way of speaking about the things she thinks and desires, the little girl picks up a pencil and begins to draw some lines on a paper. She soon realizes that through drawing, through the creation of art, she begins to find a way to communicate again. Through the process of using a new part of her brain, the little girl soon regains her ability to associate the correct words for the things in the world around her. Thanks to art, the process of creation, the little girl fully regains her ability to speak to her family again and goes on to live a normal life, at least for a short while. It is a Stephen King story, after all, so things can never be normal for long. But the point is that I read this wonderful story about how the process of creating brought back lost abilities for this poor little girl. The story inspired me. It led me to think about doing some creating of my own. And, would you believe it, after only a short while of using this creative part of my brain, I found that the exact thing that happened to that little girl also happened to me.

It all began one night shortly after we got back from Connecticut, it was only a few weeks until Christmas of 2008. I thought that I would put the job hunt on hold until after Christmas. Then, one Sunday night, December 7, to be exact, I broke away from my usual routine of television and video games. I walked over to the guesthouse and turned on my computer. I had decided to write the outline that would describe some of the things that Carter and I talked about. The first few words came very slowly. I had never written about any of the things that happened to me during my times of mania and depression. I had not ever written much of anything except papers for school projects. I had never been one to keep a diary or anything like that. So, it was very awkward, at first, to write about my feelings and thoughts. The first few points came out very slowly. I spent a lot of time trying to figure out what to say and how to say it. After a couple hours, I had a short list of items that were some of the strange moments that had happened as I made my journey in and out of the rehab centers. After writing a short list, I began to think that I might want to write down my experiences in my own way of speaking, rather than just list things that happened. Once I made that transition in thinking about how to write, the words began to flow. I realized that it might be important to begin with an introduction that talked about who I was before all the weirdness began. So, a structure began to develop. I had developed an introduction and knew that what I wanted to do was make a record of what had led up to being put in a psychiatric facility. After writing many pages and devoting many hours to the project, I started to think about my story as something more than just a personal record. I began to think of my story as a piece of literature that other people might be interested in reading.

I thought about letting my brother, Carter, read it, once it was completed. Then I began to wonder if anyone else might be interested. I thought that my parents and grandmother might be interested in seeing my work as well. Once I began to think of my project as becoming a potential book, I began to take my work seriously. Writing took over all of my free time. I replaced all the time that I spent playing video games and watching TV with writing. I soon realized that the writing was therapeutic. The more I wrote, the more excited I became about what I was doing. I had never thought of myself as a writer, but that was what I was beginning to feel like. I began to realize that the more I wrote and used the part of my brain that allowed me to communicate in that fashion, the better speaker I became. It wasn't long after I started writing that I realized how much easier the words came out of my mouth when I had something to say. At first, it was only conversations with my parents and my girls. But soon, another person entered my life. Once again, a small event occurred and everything changed.

During the few weeks between Thanksgiving and Christmas break, I had some out of the ordinary experiences at the YMCA. It started with some simple chats with the receptionist who always worked at the front desk during the time that I was at the YMCA. The receptionist would usually ask me a question or make a comment that required me to talk to her. She started by asking me about my motorcycle one cold day, as I was leaving. She said, "Aren't you cold out there on that motorcycle?" I said, "No, it's not really that bad if you wear the right clothes." After that, I walked out of the building and thought nothing of her question. A few days later, I was leaving the YMCA again and she asked me, "So, do you come up here on your lunch break?" There it was, a reference to working. I knew that I could either tell her that I never had a lunch break because I didn't have a job (My life was one big lunch break.), or I could tell her a lie and say that I was on my lunch break when I was at the YMCA. I said, "Yes. I'm on break most days when I come up here, not today though." and then I walked out of the building, feeling very bad for lying about my situation.

I just didn't want to get into my personal life with people at the YMCA, especially the employees. I told the lie that I worked as a draftsman from my home for an architect in Lakeland to a couple of the people there who had asked me what I did for a living. I felt bad about lying to them, but I just did not want to get into a conversation where I had to tell anyone who I really was and what I really did with my time when I was outside of the YMCA. So, when the receptionist asked if I was on my lunch break, I hesitated for a second and then decided to just continue with the lie that I had already told to a couple of other people there.

The next time I was at the YMCA, I walked up to the front desk and swiped my card in the little card reader that let them know that I was a paying member. As I swiped my card, the receptionist said, "Wait!" I realized that she was entering in some information for some people, who were just joining the YMCA, on the computer that was connected to the card reader. When I swiped my card, it messed up what she was doing. I said, "Oh! I'm sorry. Did I just mess you up?" She said, "Yes, but that's O.K. Its no big deal." I walked on back to the weight room and did my usual routine. I thought about how oblivious I had just been as I walked into the building. I had noticed the two people that the receptionist was dealing with and I saw her asking them to stand in front of the little camera that took their picture and processed it into the computer that created the new member profiles. It just didn't register to me that swiping my card would mess up what the receptionist was doing until it was too late. As I was leaving that day, the receptionist said, "Have a good day." I said, "Thanks. You too. Next time I mess you up on your computer, just slap me!" She laughed and I walked on out of the building. I felt pretty proud of myself for being able to crack a little joke. That was the first time I had made anyone, aside from my girls, laugh in a long time. It felt good to hear the receptionist laugh at my little comment.

After leaving the YMCA, I went to Wal-Mart. That was my usual routine. I usually went to Wal-Mart after going to the YMCA because there was a Dunkin Doughnuts inside of Wal-Mart. I would go from the YMCA to the Dunkin Doughnuts and order an iced coffee. I would usually walk around the store for 30 minutes or so while I sipped on my iced coffee. That particular day, after leaving the YMCA and making my rounds to Dunkin Doughnuts, I happened to stumble across the receptionist from the YMCA as I walked out of one of the aisles there. Seeing her surprised me. She said, "Hey! What are you doing here?" I said, "I'm just following you around, apparently." She laughed and I walked on past her. I did not want to get into a conversation with her because I had already started to tell her the lie that I was self-employed. Telling that lie made me very uncomfortable around whomever I told it to. So, I made another quick little joke and hurried away from her. I thought to myself, "What are the chances of running into her here? Especially after just having the awkward little incident with the computer at the Y." After that little encounter, the thought of the receptionist slipped away from my mind and I went on about my usual routine.

The next day that I went to the YMCA, I walked into the building and was met, not by the usual receptionist, but by another girl that I had seen at the YMCA. The girl said, "Are you Scott Gann?" I said, "Yes." She said, "This is for you." and handed me a white envelope with my name on it. I thanked her and walked on into the weight room. My first thought was that I had just received a bill or some letter from the YMCA. Then I thought, "If this is a bill, why wasn't it just mailed to the house?" I began to suspect that the envelope did not contain a letter, but something else. I left the weight room and went into the bathroom and walked into a stall and closed the door behind me. I opened the envelope. Inside there was a note. It read:

"Instead of following me, you can just give me a call or send me a text sometime. Maybe we can have lunch sometime."

Michelle,
Michelle's phone number

I read the note and immediately felt a sense of panic. I knew that there was no easy way to get out of what had apparently happened between the receptionist and I. I had a feeling that she was a little interested in me from the way that she usually asked me a little question or made a comment to me every time I left the YMCA. Now that I had the note, there was no doubt that she was interested in getting to know me. It freaked me out because I could not think of a good way to avoid the situation that was developing. I thought that I had three options: I could either stop going to the YMCA, so that I never had to see her again, or I could call her and tell her some lie that would stop her from wanting to get to know me, or I could call her and tell her the truth about me and face what I thought would be the rejection that I had worked so hard to prevent myself from having to deal with. I went on through with my usual work out routine and hoped that there would be a moment when Michelle stepped away from the front desk so that I could leave the building without having to talk to her. I wasn't sure what I wanted to say to her. I was so nervous about having to talk to her that I just wanted to leave and have some time to plan how I would deal with her note and suggestion for me to call her or go out for lunch. Luckily, I saw

Michelle step away from the front desk. So, I quickly made my exit out of the building and avoided any uncomfortable situation.

After returning to the lake house, I debated my options for dealing with the Michelle situation for several hours. The more I thought about what to do or what to say, the more nervous I got. Finally, I decided that the best thing to do would be to offer to go to lunch with her. I thought that would be the nicest thing to do. I decided that I would tell her everything about my condition. I assumed that once she found out who I was, that would be the end of it. I decided that I would rather tell her the truth about me than tell her a lie and then be very uncomfortable every time I passed by her on my way in and out of the YMCA. There was no way for me to avoid her unless I just quit the YMCA all together. I didn't want to do that. So, I decided that honesty was the best policy for that situation. Once I made up my mind to tell Michelle the truth, a sense of calm came over me. Then I thought about what to say when I called her. I came up with a little punch line to open our first conversation. I grabbed my dad's cell phone and entered in her number. Then I sat there for a minute. I thought, "Once I press "Send", I change everything." I knew that this would be my first attempt to establish a new relationship outside of my immediate family. All my friends from the past had either been abandoned by me or vice versa. I had spent the past three years with no friends. My closest thing to a friend was my dog. She was the only thing that I ever spoke to. Now, I was about to try to reach out and form a new friendship, even though I knew that the relationship may only last for a few hours, possible even minutes. Still, I thought that it was time for me to at least try to tell someone my story and see what happened. I decided that if Michelle's reaction was what I assumed it would be, at least I had tried to do something that I had been afraid to do for years, form a new relationship.

So, I pressed "Send" on the cell phone and listened to the rings. After a couple rings, Michelle picked up. She said, "Hello?". I said, "Is this Michelle?" She said, "Yes." I said, "Michelle, this is Scott Gann. I got your note. So, do you often leave notes with your phone number to strange guys who ride motorcycles?" She laughed and said, "Maybe." I laughed and said, "Well, alright." We talked briefly and I told her that I would be glad to go out to lunch with her some time if that was what she wanted to do. But I gave her a little forewarning. I said, "I will tell you this, you may not want to waste a whole lot of time on me because I am damaged goods." Michelle laughed and said, "What does that mean?" I said, "It means just what I said. I am damaged goods." She said, "Why do you say that?" I said, "I can't tell you all my secrets when I don't even know you yet. We can talk when we go out for lunch." Michelle said that was fine and we set a date for Friday of that week. That was the day that my parents were leaving to go to their house in Georgia for the Christmas holiday.

I spent the next few days thinking hard about what I would say to Michelle on our lunch date. I didn't want to come across as weird or scary. I wanted to give her a sense that she was dealing with a normal person who just happened to be diagnosed as Schizoaffective. So, the first thing I thought I would do was give her a sample of some of my architectural work. I thought that might impress her and lead to a conversation about who I had been before I received the label of mentally disabled. I wanted to start with my past, the same way I had started to tell my story when I started writing it on the computer. I thought that would be the best way to introduce myself to her. So, I gathered one of my old portfolios of college projects and I grabbed a CD that had some of my best work from ETO/Architects. I thought that if she saw some of the things that I produced, she might be impressed enough to make it through my story about who I was in the present. I decided that I would hand Michelle my collection of work and then go work out for an hour, as usual. I hoped that she would look through my work and find it interesting enough to ask a question about it. I thought that might be a good way to start us talking. Then, she would get off work, and we would go on our lunch date and she would find out who I was.

So, on the Friday that we were supposed to have our date, I walked into the YMCA and handed Michelle my portfolio and CD. I said, "This is a little of what I used to do to make a living. I thought you might find it interesting." She said, "O.K." and took the portfolio and CD from me. Then, I walked on back to the weight room and did my usual routine. I was pretty nervous the whole time that I was there. I was afraid that I might be about to walk into a disaster. But, I convinced myself that the worst thing that could happen would be that Michelle did just what I thought she would do. I thought that once I told her who I was, she would find an excuse to end our date, give me the cold shoulder, and never speak to me again. I told myself that would be fine. I wasn't ready to begin a romantic relationship yet anyway. The only thing that I wanted from Michelle was just a test. I wanted to see how she would react to my story. Beyond that, I had no expectations of any future with her. I hoped that there might be a chance of us becoming friends. I had spent a lot of time wishing that I had someone to talk to. It was nice to talk to my brother, Carter, but he was far away in Connecticut. What I wanted was someone that I could hang out with from time to time, the way that I had once hung out with Justin White. I just wanted a friend. I hoped that Michelle might become that person.

After finishing my workout, I nervously walked up to the front desk where Michelle worked at. She was getting ready to leave as I walked up. I said, "So, are you ready to go?" She said that she was. I had told her that she could decide where we would go for lunch. She had asked me what I liked to eat. I told her that I liked to eat food. Anyplace that served food was fine by me. When we left I said, "So, did you decide where we should go yet?" She said, "Is Chili's alright?" I said, "That sounds good to me. I was just hoping you wouldn't say that you wanted to go to some expensive place like Chalet Suzanne." She laughed and said that was not her style. She liked things simple. The first awkward moment came when she asked how we were going to get there. I said, "Well, I drove my motorcycle. If you don't mind riding on the back of that, I'll be happy to take you there on it." and laughed. She said, "No, I had a bad experience with a motorcycle. I can't do that." I laughed and said, "Well, I guess we have to go in your car then." She said that was fine. So, we hoped in her van. She drove a maroon Chrysler mini-van, just like my parents' van. I would have driven my parents' van that day, but they had already taken it that day because they were on their way to Georgia. As we walked to Michelle's van, I said, "So, do you have any kids?" I realized that the van was a dead give away to the answer for that question. Michelle said, "Yes. I have three. I have a four year old, a three year old, and a 1 ½ year old." I said, "Three kids! You must have your hands full!" and laughed. She said, "Yes. They keep me busy."

Michelle and I got into her van and started to head out for Chili's. The first thing Michelle said was, "So, that stuff you gave me, the CD and this book, what is this?" I said, "Its architecture. That's what it pretends to be anyways. That is what I used to do for a living. I thought I would impress you with who I used to be because who I am now is not that impressive." Michelle said, "Oh. So, what did you mean by the comment about being damaged goods?" I decided that I would go ahead and drop a bomb on her before we even got out of the parking lot. I paused for a few seconds. I had been thinking about how to begin this type of conversation for three years. I was still not sure what the best way to begin it would be, but I went ahead and gave it my best shot. I said, "Damaged goods. Well, let me tell you why you won't want to waste much time with me: First of all, I live with my parents. I have no house of my own. I drive a motorcycle because I have no car of my own. I have no job. That is why I have no house or car. I don't have a job because I was diagnosed with Schizophrenia. Are you ready to turn the car around yet? It won't hurt my feelings if you do." She said, "No." I said, "I can't believe it." Then there was a few seconds of silence. Then Michelle said, "Well, I live with my parents too." I said, "Really?" She went on to explain that she had a house but it burnt down in a fire. She said that she and her husband had divorced and she moved into her mom's house. She said that she had lived there ever since she and her husband divorced.

So, Michelle and I had a little common ground. We both had kids and both lived with our parents. After telling Michelle that I was schizophrenic, I felt like I had told her the worst thing about me. She said that the weirdest thing about her was that she still maintained a close relationship with her ex-husband. She said that they were still very good friends. I didn't pry because I was not in the mindset that I was on a date. I thought of our first outing as just two people getting to know each other. I still believed that I would probably never hear from Michelle again after our lunch discussion. I had only told her that I was schizophrenic. I had not yet told her any of the details that caused me to receive that diagnosis. I believed that once she heard some of the details, she would get scared or just disgusted with me, and that would be the end of it.

We had lunch at Chili's. Over lunch we talked about our pasts. I felt like I did most of the talking. I realized right away that Michelle was more of a quiet person than my ex-wife had been. So, I filled the silence with stories about myself. Most of my time was spent unloading some of the details about my times in and out of the psychiatric centers. Those stories were what I believed would end up turning Michelle away from me. But I told them anyway. It was part of the test, the test to see just how a person would respond to the strange stories that I had to tell about myself. I talked and talked. Michelle just listened. I think she would make a great therapist. She was a very good listener. After we finished our lunch, we headed back to the YMCA. When we got out of Michelle's van, I walked over and gave her an awkward little hug. I thought that it was the appropriate thing to do. She had given me the opportunity to test my theory that most people would be revolted by what I was. It seemed like maybe I was wrong because she hugged me back and thanked me for the lunch date. I was stunned. I couldn't believe that I had not completely repulsed her. It seemed like she could at least tolerate me. I thought that she may have even still been interested in knowing me better.

After that first lunch date, Michelle called me the next day and thanked me for going to lunch with her. She said that she had a really nice time. I was shocked. I thought that I would have surely turned her away with the stories I had told her. But for some reason she seemed to at least still find me interesting. We ended up talking on the phone several times. Each phone call lasted for over an hour. As on our first date, I did most of the talking. I tried to let her talk, but she would give brief responses to my questions and then come back at me with another question that would give me an opportunity to rattle on for several more minutes. We had a few phone calls and then it was time for me to drive Nanny up to Georgia to meet my family there at my parents' house for Christmas.

That Christmas of 2008, I drove Nanny, Liza, and Gwen up to Georgia in Nanny's car. We drove up on Christmas day because I wanted to give the girls a chance to spend Christmas morning with their mother. The ride up was nice. We all talked most of the 11 hour drive from Bartow, FL to Young Harris, GA. I was in a great mood because I was beginning to realize that I was doing something big by writing this story. The writing gave me confidence that I had not possessed in over a decade. On top of it, I had met Michelle. She added to my confidence, because she seemed to like to hear what I had to say. She also brought me a little confusion because I was not ready for a girlfriend, but I did like her as a friend. She helped me to realize that there were people out there who were willing to involve themselves with people like me. So, by the time we all arrived in Georgia, the stage had been set for me to have the best Christmas I had since a time before Liza was born. I was a little high from the excitement of writing this story and my new friend, Michelle. In addition to that, my girls seemed to love me more than ever. I had spent a lot of time making sure that this Christmas would be one they would appreciate. I wanted to be sure that I did not experience another Christmas like the one the year before, when Liza seemed so distant and acted like she would rather be with her mother than have to spend time with me. I made a point to show the girls how much I appreciated them.

That Christmas was the best I time I had in a long time. My brothers were there. My girls were there. And, of course, Nanny and my parents were there. In addition, my dad's brother, David, and my aunt, Pam, were there as well. We had a house full. It was a great time. It is unusual for me to say that, because for most of the Christmas holidays that had occurred over the ten years prior to that one, I would have come away with gripes and irritations about things that happened during the holiday. But that Christmas, I cannot think of one thing that bothered me. I'm sure that there were things that would have irritated me in the past, but my attitude had made such a drastic shift that nothing seemed to be able to bring me down. There were a few reasons why some of the other people might not have considered that Christmas to be their favorite, but for me, it was the best one in a long time.

The first great event happened on the night that we all arrived. We opened presents since it was Christmas Day, after all. I was so excited for Liza and Gwen because I had bought them a gift that I thought they would really enjoy. I bought them each a GameBoy Advance SP. That was the last generation of GameBoy before Nintendo started making the Nintendo DS. So, I wasn't buying them the most expensive portable video game system, but to me it was the best value. The GameBoy had been around for several years and there had been hundreds of games already made for it. I could buy most of the games for less than $10 on line. I only paid $60 for each GameBoy. The DS cost $120 a piece. So, I felt like I was saving a lot of money by getting the older style GameBoy. The thing that I liked most about the GameBoy was that Nintendo had released a lot of the best games that were created for the original Nintendo, the Super Nintendo, and the N64; for the GameBoy. All of my favorite games that I had played as a child and teenager were available for the GameBoy SP. So, I bought a few of my favorite games for Liza and Gwen. I hoped that they would appreciate them the way that I had when I was a child. As it turned out, they were very excited when they opened the boxes that contained the GameBoys and the video games. I had never seen them act so appreciative of any thing I had ever given them. Seeing the joy that those little GameBoys brought to my girls made me very happy. I knew that I had done a good job, once again. I was very pleased with myself because I had managed to give my girls something that they wanted and I had been able to do it with very little money. I told the girls that the GameBoys were their big present that year and that I did not plan to renew our annual passes to Busch Gardens. I told them that in the coming year, we would find new things to do. As it would turn out, I ended up realizing that the girls were happy doing whatever I came up with. It was not the money that I spent on them that brought them happiness. It was the fact that wherever we went or whatever we did, I let them know that they were special to me by listening to them and just generally trying to be a good father for them.

That Christmas, the event that probably brought a lot of grief for many people in our house was the fact that 7 out of the 12 people in the house all caught a stomach virus that led to them all vomiting and having severe diarrhea. The combination of the two most disgusting things that a person has to suffer through made all the people that caught the virus very sick for a couple days. It was weird because the virus hit almost everyone in the house within a few hours.

On the first night that all the people came down with the illness, there were so many people throwing up, and having diarrhea, that some of them actually had to go outside and throw up off of the deck because all three of the bathrooms were already occupied. The whole event was very strange. I made a little joke the next morning, after realizing that I had slept through the whole puking ordeal, as it mainly started in the middle of the night. I said, "So, I guess I slept through Puke Fest 2008." It didn't get many laughs at first. But soon, my brother, Sam and I were cracking jokes about all the puking that was going on. We kept using the Puke Fest 2008 theme to build a series of jokes that involved all the pukers as members in a rock band. Sam said that the anthem of Puke Fest 2008 was "Rock it, then Puke it!". I said, "Thank you Young Harris! You make a great crowd! We love you! Good-Night!", and then made the sound of someone puking. Sam and I got a lot of laughs with our Puke Fest jokes. Uncle David said, "Puke Fest 2008 is all fun and games until you become one of the pukers." We all laughed. So, even though we had some serious illness going around the house, the healthy people managed to still have a pretty good time. The only people who didn't get sick were: my Dad, Sam, Uncle David, Gwen, and myself. We were the ones, who, I guess, probably had the most fun that Christmas. Everyone else spent a lot of time in the bathroom for several days.

Another fun thing that we did was Disc Golf. Disc Golf is a sport similar to golf, except that instead of playing with a ball and clubs, you play with a Frisbee like set of discs. Instead of playing towards a hole, you throw to a basket. The sport is a lot of fun to me. The best part about it is that, in the surrounding area around my parents' house, all of the courses are free. We played Disc Golf several times over the Christmas break. The thing that I noticed that was different about those games, from the ones in years past, was that I did not feel nervous or awkward. In the past, I usually got tense if I made a bad throw. I would get nervous about my poor Disc Golf skills and then my game would go to crap. The nervousness would lead to more mistakes. But that Christmas, I made a couple of bad throws and that was the end of it. I never got worked up or nervous after screwing up a throw. I realized that I had a strong sense of calmness that had developed from the realization that I might not be as terrible of a person as I had once thought that I was. My shift in attitude affected everything from my ability to communicate right down to my ability to play Disc Golf. I ended up playing better than I ever had. With the nervousness at bay, I was able to make a lot of really good throws. I came away from those Disc Golf games feeling very pleased with my new found confidence and the way it was improving everything about me.

So, by the time that Christmas holiday was over, I felt like I was fully able to deal with the challenges that I would have to face once I entered the workplace again. I had spent many hours in conversations with my brothers, Aunt Pam, Uncle David, Nanny, and my parents, and my girls. Not once did I feel I said or did something that made me appear weird. I came away from that holiday ready to return to work. I only had one last thing that I wanted to do before I began to search for a job. I wanted to finish writing this story. By the time the Christmas holiday had rolled around, I was beginning to believe that this book might be of value to people other than my immediate family. I decided that something good might come from the effort to write down my story. I had started to think of writing about more than just a description of the weird things that had happened to me. I wanted to write something that might be helpful to a person who may be experiencing or may know of someone who is experiencing the kinds of things that I did. I told myself that I would not get distracted with a job until I had finished my story.

Christmas ended and I came back to Florida in January of 2008. I went back to the usual routine, only now there were two new items on my daily agenda, the writing, and Michelle. I filled all of my free time, between the gym, the chores, and Michelle; writing this story. I usually spent 4 to 6 hours a day working on this project. I found the process of writing down my experiences to be very good therapy. The writing exercised a part of my brain that had not been used in a long time, not since I had stopped working as an architectural intern had I spent so much time focusing on a specific task. I thought of the writing as my new job. I tried to spend the amount of time that I might spend at work, writing this story. At first, I wrote, on average, between 8 to 10 hours a day. But then Michelle involved herself with me and I began to spend some of my free time with her. After I began to spend time with Michelle, my daily writing time dropped back to 4 to 6 hours a day. That has been the average for most of this story. I think it is a reasonable amount of time for me to dedicate to this project.

As far as Michelle is concerned, we started seeing each other a few times a week, usually for a couple hours at a time. I also called her several times a week, at night, and talked with her. Michelle and I started having little outings after I got back from the Christmas holiday. We usually walked Lake Wales or Eagle Ridge Mall for a couple hours. She came out to the lake house a couple times as well. We spent most of our time just talking, although, I usually felt like I did most of the talking. After spending many hours talking to Michelle in person and on the phone, I began to feel like I was talking too much. I had gone so long without having anyone to talk to that I felt like I was unloading the last three years of my life on her too quickly. There was so much that I had wanted to tell someone. Poor Michelle just happened to cross my path at a time when I felt like I really wanted to talk to someone. That was why I had decided to tell Michelle the truth about me in the first place.

So, with Michelle seeming to be interested in what I had to say, I just kept talking. After several years of silence, it was very nice to have someone who seemed to want to hear what I had to say. The problem was that the more time I spent telling Michelle all the dark secrets about my past, the more I began to realize that I was sharing a lot of myself with someone who I knew very little about. Michelle had told me a few things about herself, but she was always brief. Her style of talking was very minimalist.
Still, I am very grateful that Michelle was willing to devote so much of her time with me. Even though I felt like our conversations were usually a little one sided, I still appreciated just having someone to hear what I had to say. I had not had a good listener in my life in a long time. Sara was a good listener, but she had been gone for over three years. Michelle helped fill a void that had existed since my wife and my old friend Justin went away.

Michelle has become the catalyst for change in my life. Once I made the decision to give one person a chance to really know me, it allowed me to break through the wall that I created between myself and the rest of the world. After realizing that Michelle did not reject me, I began to wonder whether she was unique or if I might find others who would not reject me as well. Through Michelle, I have been able to build the beginnings of a new network of friends. Having people whom I consider friends has drastically improved my self-image. The realization that I still have the ability to socialize has given me great hope for my future. Thanks to Michelle, I feel more like a "normal" person again. She has allowed me to test the waters of social networking and realize that I still have the skill to communicate with new people and establish new relationships. That is something that, for many years, I thought I would never be able to do again. Had Michelle simply decided that I was not worthy of creating a friendship with, I might still have that belief. I am very grateful to have met Michelle.

One last song that I stumbled on not long ago made a little impression on me. I think it sums up my whole experience as a schizophrenic. The song is by My Morning Jacket. It is on their album, *Evil Urges*. The song is titled, "Smokin From Shootin". The song says, "Do you see my smoking guns? They're smokin' from shootin' at nothing dear... Do you live your life on the run? Losing out on lovin. Asking for nothing. Running from something that isn't there."

I think that pretty much sums up a lot of what I went through between my times in and out of the rehab centers. I spent a lot of time, in mania, running around, following the orders of people who did not exist. Once the depression settled in, I spent a lot of time in fear of things that might not have been completely real either. I had an unnatural fear of people. Just as the song says, I spent a lot of my life on the run. I jumped from job to job, never feeling comfortable with the people I worked with. For at least a decade of my life, I did a lot of shooting, in my mind, at imaginary enemies that were really only the products of a deranged mind. The shooting, for me, was worrying. I spent far too many years worrying about things that had happened at work, at school, with my family, and friends. The culmination of all that worry caused me to suffer from the anxiety that led to my times of depression, mania, and delusions. If I would not have allowed myself to spend so much time worrying, I might not have ever needed to see a psychologist or psychiatrist. I think that worrying about things that have already happened and cannot be changed is a complete waste of time, though I'm sure we all do it. Worry does nothing but create stress. Stress produces all kinds of health problems, both mentally and physically. If you can find a way to relieve your stress, you can defeat my type of mental illness.

Chapter 70: The Present

So, that brings us to the present. At the present I am still jobless, homeless, and without a car. But, even though I lack a lot of material things that most people find very important, I am happier than I have been since I was a teenager in high school. I have an established routine that keeps me busy. I stick to my medication so that I am able to function normally. I am trying to rebuild the bridges that I have burned between myself and my family. I have even made my first new good friend in Michelle. Making a friend with Michelle has led to me now having a new circle of friends, who I know through her. My circle is new, and just barely formed, but it is there, and growing. As for Justin White, my old best friend, I tried to call him not long ago and he hung up once he realized that it was me on the other end. It hurt a little to realize that he still has some big issues with me, but there is nothing I can do aside from try to communicate with him. If he has made up his mind that I am a lost cause, then that is his problem. I have moved on past the people who have written me off. I have learned to find confidence from within myself. I would prefer to continue making new friends and meeting new people who will be supportive of me. I would prefer to leave behind all those people who I feel helped tear me down. But there is still a part of me that wants to reach out to them as well.

As for the job search situation, that is something that is becoming debatable. After writing this story, I have realized that I have found something that I am passionate about. I have thoroughly enjoyed writing all that you have read. I think that I may have just stumbled onto something that I may continue to do into the future. My plan is to look into publishing this story and then begin promoting it. Once I feel that I have done all that I can do to help propel this book to its final destination, wherever that may be, I may begin to write a new story. I already have ideas for future stories. They will all be fictional, if they are ever written into existence. They will be based on some of the things that I have discussed in this book. I have no idea where this path that I have just begun to travel down will take me, but I know that I have enjoyed my journey so far.

As for what really motivates me these days, my two girls, Liza and Gwen, are the center of my world. They mean more to me than anyone else. They were the only two people who I never felt judged by. They were so young and probably so well protected from me during my early struggles with schizophrenia, that they have never seemed phased by any of it. Aside from the Christmas of 2007, my girls have always acted like they really love to spend time with me. They helped me through my darkest days without even knowing it. Their innocence and unconditional love were what first began to bring me out of the dark downward spiral that I had walked down. I pray that I can return the favor some day.

Another thing, that just happened very recently, was that I found a church that I feel comfortable at. I have spent a lot of time, over the past few years, attending a church that has never really moved me, at least not the way that I felt moved at times when I attended TRBC in Tallahassee. I only recently began to play volleyball with a group of people from the YMCA at a church not far from there. The idea to play volleyball came from Michelle. She invited me to play with her, so I did. I realized that I enjoyed the interaction with people at the volleyball games. The combination of physical exercise and spending time with good people, have been a great bonus to my life. So, after realizing that I enjoyed spending time with the people that I played volleyball with, I decided to try out their church. I have only attended one service so far, but that one service moved me more than anything I have experienced since I left TRBC in Tallahassee. I can see from that one service that this church may be a place where I might learn more about a meaningful relationship with God. I plan to attend that church again very soon. My latest addition to my schedule is Tuesday night volleyball and Sunday morning at church. I might possibly attend every Sunday, as opposed to my old routine of just showing up at church when I have my two girls with me. I have high hopes for my future with this church.

My last major battle that I have to fight is with cigarettes. I have not stopped smoking since I was released from the PRC. I have used cigarettes as a crutch. At first, I smoked whenever I felt stressed. There was a time when I was stressed easily and very often. Now, they are just a bad habit, an addiction, that have too much control over me. I smoke now just out of routine. I usually smoke around 10 cigarettes a day. Sometimes I will cut back to four or five a day, but usually, unless I have my girls, I smoke around 10 a day. I know full well how harmful they are in the long term. I keep telling myself, "Just one more, then I'll quit." But one more cigarette becomes another. Then I tell myself that I will just buy one more pack or one last carton, and the cycle continues. Cigarettes have a hold on me. I know that they are dangerous and I am fully aware of how they plan my day. I wake up on some days, when I have lots of time around my family or my girls, and try to plan times when I might get a chance to smoke. It is ridiculous and it must stop before it kills me. I don't notice any negative effect from smoking other than the fact that running seems to be a little harder than it used to. I guess the years of inhaling the toxic smoke has probably done some damage to my lungs. Once I do quit, I plan to begin a serious cardio-exercise program to get my lungs and heart back in shape. But that is step two and I have yet to begin step one. I hope that I can find the motivation to end the cycle that will eventually lead to my premature death. I have given myself the deadline of quitting smoking once I am done with this story. I have set other deadlines in the past and let them slip on by without ever making a real effort to quit. I hope I can muster the strength to beat the habit this time. We shall see.

Chapter 71: How to Defeat Schizoaffective disorder

As I have said, I hope that this story will be of some educational use to someone who reads it. I will end by summarizing what I think are the important lessons that I learned from my ordeals in an out of psychiatric facilities. Before going into the details, let me say that there are some groups of psychiatric professionals who will tell you that they do not believe that schizophrenia can develop from stressful circumstances. I have my doubts as to whether or not these people really know what they are talking about. Perhaps, not every person with schizophrenia can point to specific stressful events and see how they might cumulatively affect them. Maybe some people really are born with a different type of brain that is naturally disposed to schizophrenia. Evidence suggests that physical differences in the brain of a schizophrenic person do play a major part in the onset of the illness. I just have doubt that those physiological differences are the only thing that causes schizophrenia. I believe it could be a combination of physiological and environmental factors that cause the full effects of schizophrenia. I say this because, for me, I never had a problem with the disease until major stressors were introduced into my life.

Another point that I find myself in disagreement with the professionals is the idea that a person with schizophrenia cannot affect their outcome by positive thinking and taking positive actions. It is a fact that only 25% of people with Schizophrenia go on to live a life free from anti-psychotic medication once the illness has manifested itself. Another 25% go on to live productive, relatively independent lives with the help of medication. The rest of people affected by schizophrenia find themselves living a life heavily dependent on others, hospitalized, or dead, mostly from suicide. Presently, I would place myself into that 25% that lives productively with the help of medication. I would like to find myself in that 25% that doesn't require medication, but, for now, that is not the case. My point is that I wonder how many people can move themselves from the 50% who need ample amounts of assistance to the 50% that does not, simply by taking the steps that I will describe next. I have hope that people who suffer from schizophrenia can improve their situation by taking the steps that I describe below. It just seems so self defeating to think that people have no hope of finding the ability to take control of their situation. I know that the steps I took had a positive effect on me. Had I not done these things, I think I would find myself another member of the 50% who is either heavily dependent on a support group, hospitalized, or dead. Please don't lose hope that you can change your condition. At least try taking the steps I list here. They did me a world of good. I pray that you will find the same results that I did.

With that said, I'll list what I think are the most important steps a person can take to try to beat the illness.

I think that the most important thing that a person with a mental disability can do is first acknowledge the fact that they have a problem. To get the person to realize that they need help is also the most difficult step to accomplish. It requires the use of skilled professionals who know how to deal with crisis stabilization. The problem with mental illness is that it is, of course, a disease of the mind. The part of the body used to make decisions is the very part of the body that is affected. So, it's a difficult task to get a malfunctioning brain to realize that it is actually having a problem. For a small number of people, this step of realization never occurs. They unfortunately end up spending their lives in and out of rehab centers, permanently hospitalized, or worse. But fortunately, the majority of people with mental illnesses do eventually realize that there is a problem. The job of getting a person to understand that they have a problem is one that is best left to professionals who deal in this matter. I am, of course, biased to The Peace River Center in Bartow, Florida. Without their patience and understanding, I would be just another homeless person wandering the streets, in prison, or dead. It is essential to find the proper facilities with trained doctors and staff who can evaluate and respond to the crisis before it is too late. Once the problem is acknowledged, the road to recovery can begin.

I strongly recommend Baker Acting an individual who needs help but refuses to get it. The Baker Act is a tool created just for the purpose of forcing someone to get help for their problem. The hardest thing you will ever have to do will be the day you commit a loved one into a psychiatric facility against their will. Be prepared for arguments, accusations, anger, possibly even violence. But the results are worth the agony.

I had to be Baker Acted three times before I would admit that I indeed had a problem. The admission of my problem was the hardest thing for me. Once I was finally convinced that I did in fact have a problem, everything else good followed and my condition slowly improved. It was not an easy process to transition from denial to realization of the fact that I did have a mental disability. It was even harder to transition from the realization of my problem to the solution for how I would deal with it. As I have said, that process took a few years of my life away, but in the end, I am better for it. Had I been allowed to continue to live my life without realizing that I was the cause of my troubles, I would have probably ended up in prison, or dead. So, the most important step of dealing with a mental health crisis is to find a way to get the person with the problem to realize and firmly believe that they actually have a problem. Again, I strongly recommend seeking professional help.

The hardest part of getting them to realize their condition will be getting them to deal with the stigma that is associated with mental disorders. I hope that my story will shed a little light on the fact that at least some of us who have mental disabilities are no different than any, so called, "normal" people. We just have to have medication to help us fight our disease. It is no different than a person with a heart condition needing heart medication to improve and prolong their life. That leads me to my next subject.

The medication is the next important step. Once a person has realized that they do have a condition that prevents them from living a normal, healthy life; and

548

after they have been stabilized, they must be convinced that the medication is the only thing that will prevent them from relapsing back to their old self and all of the problems that come along with that old self. I thank God that He has allowed people to understand enough about the human brain that they have been able to develop drugs that combat the irregularities in the brain that cause the different types of mental illness. For me, taking the medication was an admission that I had a problem. I did not take my medication until I was fully convinced that there was something wrong with me. People who abuse alcohol and other illegal drugs are only self medicating themselves from a deeper problem that can only be resolved with the proper, legal, medication prescribed by their doctor. You have to convince the person to have faith in the medical establishment enough to take the medication that they prescribe. I think that it helps to refer to psychologists and psychiatrists as doctors. There is too big of an inappropriate stigma surrounding the field of psychology. They really are just doctors who specialize in matters dealing with one specific, very important, organ, the human brain. I used to believe that psychologists and psychiatrists were all just as flaky as anyone else. A lot of them probably are. But there are some who seem genuinely interested in improving the mental health of their patients. A person must have faith in their psychiatrist enough to take the medication that they prescribe. The field of psychiatry is not as exact as other medical fields. It took several different trials with several medications before I found the drug that worked best for me, Zyprexa. A person who has a mental disability must be convinced that the medication is the key to their successful return to a normal life.

The next most important thing is sleep. It is recommended that most people receive 7 to 8 hours of continuous sleep every night. I try to get at least 8 hours. Once I have slept for 8 continuous hours, I can wake up and feel ready to begin my day. If I get less than that, I notice a dullness in my mind. Without proper sleep, I am not as sharp and have more trouble in conversation. I also notice that without proper sleep, I lack the ability to focus my attention. I believe that all people should take sleep very seriously. It was the lack of sleep that first caused my symptoms to develop. Before I began to do all nighters in college, I had routinely slept for 7 to 8 hours a day. In college I began to go 24 or 36 hours without sleep. That was when my real troubles first began. The lack of sleep is more dangerous than people give it credit for. I truly believe that the lack of proper sleep was a key factor to developing the strange symptoms that led to the strange behaviors that I performed. A person who has made the steps of admitting their disability and takes their medication seriously will still have problems if they do not get the proper amount of sleep. People with mental disabilities must be convinced to get at least 7 to 8 hours of sleep a day. One way of ensuring good sleep is to maintain a proper amount of exercise every day. This leads to my next point.

Exercise is key to keeping a sound body and mind. It is old information but is very relevant to the subject of mental health. Before I began working out, I was sluggish, both physically and mentally. After I began to work out at the gym and walk everyday for at least 30 minutes, I began to notice the first signs of the lifting of the depression that had reigned over me for two years. It was not until I started exercising that I began to improve my mood. There is a strong relationship between the health of the body and the health of the mind. In the years that led up to my progressive mental collapse, I was very sedentary. I spent all day sitting in front of a computer monitor, only to go home and sit on a couch in front of another screen, the TV. My whole life, up until I began working as an architectural intern, I had been a very physically active person. The lack of exercise made an immense contribution to the failure of my brain. I am positive of this. A person must motivate themselves to begin an exercise routine that challenges their muscles and gets them doing the things that they were made to do. People were not created to sit in front of computers and TVs their whole lives. We were once hunters and gatherers. We all still need proper physical exercise to keep our body and mind in check. For people with mental disabilities, this is crucial for their mental well-being.

Another critical piece of the puzzle is family. For me, without my family, I would have surely ended up destroying my own life and the lives of others. Thankfully, I was blessed to be born into a loving family that loves me unconditionally. As I said in the beginning, I am a lucky child. I have loving parents who have seen me through the darkest of times and still, for some crazy reason, keep loving me. Without the support of my parents, my grandmother, my brothers, my girls, and all the rest of my family, I would never have made it to where I am today. I am not saying that I have accomplished anything special, but I have made some incredible progress for my own mental well-being. I never could have done it on my own. It took years of my parents waiting patiently for me to come out of my self-created shell. It took the love of my two girls to show me that I still had a purpose on this Earth. Without them, I might have committed suicide. It took the wisdom of my grandmother to convince me that I really did have a problem, but it was no big deal. She and my parents told me that my problem was only going to be as big of a deal as I allowed it to be. I allowed it to almost ruin my life. But thanks to their support, I slowly picked up the broken pieces of my old life and turned them into something new. Without family, a person with a mental disability has a very hard road ahead of them. It takes the effort of a special group of people who genuinely love the disabled person, for whatever reason, to successfully progress a disabled person from a state of uncontrollable thoughts and actions to a state of normalcy. I thank God for my family. Without them, I would not be alive today.

The last big factor is nutrition. I think that in order to keep a healthy mind and body, a person must eat properly. For me, that means following the FDA guidelines for a healthy diet. I try to eat vegetables and fruit several times a day. I probably don't eat them as much as I should, but generally, I eat some form of fruit or vegetable at least three times a day. Protein is also very important, especially once a person begins a serious exercise program. Protein helps to rebuild and grow muscles. It also strengthens the body's immune system and is a natural appetite suppressant. Body builders recommend that a person consume 1 gram of protein for every pound that they weigh. I have not managed to stick to levels of protein that high. To take in that kind of protein requires a lot of eating and supplements. I take a whey protein supplement that provides 26 grams of protein per serving. I also make a point to eat meat several times a day. Of course everyone thinks that carbohydrates are a big no-no, but a person must consume a certain level of carbs everyday for proper nutrition. Body builders recommend a ration of 60% carbs to 40% protein for a typical meal. I don't follow that ratio. I think carbs make up about 40% or less of my diet. I try to avoid a lot of carbs because I know that the bread leads to the fat that accumulates on my body. Since I started reducing my carb intake, I have lost a lot of weight. The combination of exercise and carb control helped me lose the majority of my excess fat. I now weigh 160 pounds. I am 5'-10". So, that is an acceptable weight for me. Nutrition is critical to maintaining a healthy body. A healthy body leads to a healthy mind. So, for people with mental disabilities, nutrition is critical.

That completes my list of things that I think are critical for a person to make the transition from being oblivious to the fact that they have a mental disability towards becoming a successful member of society.

Chapter 72: Closing Thoughts

Now, let me begin to close by leaving you with my views on the following subjects: money, work, religion, and family.

First, let me tell you how much I value money. I think that money is not the root of all evil. I think that the lack of money leads people, acting out of desperation, to do things that they might not ordinarily do. Obviously, it takes a certain amount of income for a person to survive in the world we live in, unless they want to live as a homeless person, begging for their next meal. I myself am nothing more than a homeless person who has been given, through the grace of God, a set of people that have helped to support me financially. Without my parents allowing me to live with them, I would have no place to sleep at night other than a homeless shelter. I realize that I am forever in my parents' debt for allowing me to live with them, even though I am 32 and possibly capable of supporting myself. If I was not eligible for Disability, I would not have any income. I live off of the taxpayer's dollar. I feel very guilty about that. I was once a taxpayer myself and I hated having to give a portion of my paycheck to the Federal Government. Now, I am very grateful that someone had the foresight to establish a system that takes care of people like myself. I would have survived without my Disability checks, but my life would definitely have been much harder. I doubt that I would be writing this story now, had I not been given those checks.

The flip side of money, for me, is excessive amounts of money. I live off of less than $13,000 per year. I don't have to pay rent to my parents. So, all of my money goes to the few bills I have, my two girls, and some frivolous things like the almost daily trip to Dunkin Donuts for iced coffee. I usually budget around $200 for myself every month to spend on whatever I want. That includes: clothing, personal hygiene items, food, and of course, cigarettes. Cigarettes alone usually take away about $35 dollars of my income every month. My point here is that I live off of very little. I don't buy lavish things because I can't afford them. Does that make me a less happy individual? No. I have less money and less material things than I have ever had, but I am now happier than I was in the time when I did have a decent income and lots of material things. When I had a lot of possessions, I worried about what might happen if I lost all of them. Now that most of them are gone, I have learned the answer. You learn how to live without them. And I have to say that I am a better person from learning that fact. Now, I don't worry about losing all my material items. I know that they do not bring me happiness. Money does not bring happiness. Happiness only comes from within. For me, it comes from the realization that I am doing something good in the world. Right now, the good that I am doing is helping to raise my two girls to be decent human beings. Also, I feel that writing this book may become something that does some good for someone, someday. I don't believe that money can make a person feel that they have a sense of true self worth. For me, it took the lack of money for me to realize that money was not the most important thing in life. I think it is great if a person finds themselves in a situation where they become wealthy, but I don't think that wealth can create true happiness.

As far as my views on the importance of having a job go, I believe staying busy is very important for all people. If you must have a certain amount of income, then, naturally, you must have a job to attain it. If you just want to stay busy, a job is another way to fill your day. For me, it is important to stay busy. I would like to return to the standard of living that I attained when I worked as an intern architect, but it is not so important to me that it will drive me to work the way that I did when I was an employee at ETO/Architects. When I worked there, I worked too much. I hope that once I return to the workplace, I will find a way to balance my career with the other things in my life. I don't ever want to find myself in another job that requires me to miss sleep or stop getting the right amount of exercise or nutrition. I think that working is very important for most people. It is the workforce that gives our country its strength. If everyone sat around and did nothing all day, the way that I have for the last two years, this country would become a third world nation. We would have the struggles with poverty and starvation that those kinds of countries have to deal with. No, I think that any American who can work, should work. I think that is an integral part of being an American citizen. We should all pitch in and do our part to help lift our country out of the current state of depression that it is currently in. People say recession right now, but the real word is depression. I just hope that there will be a job for me when I do try to find one. Working is very important for me. When I have a job, I feel like I am contributing to my country. Not having a job has been very hard for me. I don't want to get comfortable with the idea of not working. I think that is a dangerous road to go down. I don't want to go down that road. I don't think that anyone who can work should go down that road either. Laziness only leads to other problems. Laziness is probably what led to the current state of our economy now. It was the greed that came from the laziness of the people who allowed our country to fail that I think started this whole mess that our country is facing.

Religion. That is a topic that is always in the back of my mind. Is the Holy Bible actually the word of God? Or is it just the writings of some very wise individuals? Those questions have plagued me with doubt for most of my life. I think that the Bible contains a lot of valuable information for how to live a good and decent life. But, was it written by God, through the hands of mere humans? I will never know. That is where faith comes in. I guess I will just have to have faith in the fact that the Holy Bible is the actual final word from God. It is just so hard for me to do that after reading and hearing about how the Bible was created. After having my own little episode of belief that I was in direct contact with God him or herself, I can see how it is possible for people to lose their sanity and believe that they are actually in the presence of or at least communicating with God. My episodes of total mania have made it difficult for me to simply have faith in the way that the Bible came to be created. I have often wondered if some of the Bible's writers and characters would be diagnosed with a mental disorder today. If some of the events from the Bible took place today, I think that some of the people from those events would receive a diagnosis of mentally disabled. That realization has caused me to have a problem with both my religion and the field of psychology. In some areas, it seems that psychology almost replaces religion. There is actually a clinical condition called Religiosity. That is a term used to describe a mentally disabled person who has a condition that involves a serious religious tone to their mania like symptoms. I think that if I had told my psychiatrist about some of my wild ideas about religion, he would have diagnosed me as having the problem of Religiosity. I wonder how many people in the Bible would have received the label of mentally disabled, had psychology existed in their time. It seems to me that stories about angels appearing and speaking to people, God talking to people through burning bushes, and other similar situations; all have the possibility of being stories about people who hallucinated. I have no idea of what mental state these people were in at the times when they thought that they were in contact with heavenly entities. Maybe they were all having some form of mental disorder. Maybe not. I would like to believe the latter. I would like to believe in the thing that I was taught as a child, that the Bible is God's holy word. It just seems that there are so many other religions that all make the same claim about their texts. Muslims, Jews, and Christians all choose to believe in certain parts of the Bible. It seems that the disagreement over what is truth and what is not has caused so much evil in the world. The fact that planes flew into buildings in New York City and Washington D.C., all stemming from a drastic cultural difference that was created by a difference in faith, has caused me to do a lot of pondering. If God really has intended for us to know Him by reading scriptures, why has He allowed there to be so many different factions that all have their own spin on a similar theme? Who is right? Who is wrong?

Because of my family, and my own upbringing, I feel compelled to believe in the Holy Bible. I have never read the texts of the Muslims or the Jews. I know that they both believe in certain parts of the Holy Bible. Each religion has set parameters for what they do and don't believe about the Holy Bible. Christians say that Jesus is the Messiah. Jews say that is not true, the real Messiah has not yet come. Muslims say that Mohammed is the way to salvation. I have never fully read the Bible. I only know what I have gleaned from the reading that I have done, and what I have learned from years of Sunday School, and from listening to preachers speak about the Word of God. I hate to admit it, but I come away from all that time spent trying to find the right answer, just as confused as I was when I first started. The more I learn about the Bible, the more questions I have that are met with the answer, "You just have to have faith." It seems to me that faith is the same thing that Jews, Muslims, Buddhists, and all the other religious believers have. They all just have faith that what they have been taught is the truth. So, what really is the truth? I don't know.

I have come to the realization that faith is a conscious choice. If I am ever to feel comfortable with a religion, it will require me to stop trying to understand, "Why?" and just simply let go of my doubt and replace it with faith. I would like to believe that there is a God. I would like to believe that He created me. So, I choose to believe that. It seems just as likely that some awesome being could have created the universe as it is that it was created by a series of natural process that are just like the natural forces that we see on Earth. I choose to believe that God exists. I have many doubts about particular details that cause the tension between all the world's religions. I wonder if there is a greater truth that envelopes all of the world's religions. Maybe that seems like too liberal of an idea for a true Christian to have, but I still wonder. It just does not seem fair to believe that there is only one way to spend eternity with God in Heaven. It seems more fair to me that God allowed different cultures to develop their own way of describing Him. It seems to me that religion is just a way of describing things that cannot be explained through science. I wonder if one day, science will replace religion. I know that a lot of Christians feel that it already has, to an extent, in this country.

I want to believe in God. I want to be a faithful Christian. I think that my lack of faith prevents me from fully appreciating what it is to be a firm believer. I pray for God to give me the understanding that I need to put my doubts aside and just follow the teachings of Jesus and the Holy Bible. I know that in order for that to happen, I need to become more involved with a church. I need to do more than just show up for the Sunday morning worship service every other week, when my girls visit. I also need to spend time studying the Bible, so that I can really understand what it has to say. I pray that God will give me the motivation to do that. My current stance for religion is that I am a Christian. I believe in God. I believe that Jesus was God in the form of a human. I believe that Jesus died for my sins. I believe that, because I believe Jesus to be the Son of God, I will enter the kingdom of Heaven. I am trying hard to believe those things anyways. I pray that God will give me faith and understanding.

My final topic that I want to discuss is my family. I have already said a lot about them. I just want to take a little space to thank them for all that they have done for me. Without all of them, I would never have been able to write the book that I have written. My girls are the most important people in my life. Not far behind them are my mom and dad, my brothers, and my grandmother. I love them all dearly and hope that I have many more wonderful years with them. They have all worked hard to lift me up from the fall that I took that led me into the psychiatric centers. I put my parents through hell and they still continued to love me. I neglected my daughters for the better part of their lives, and still they loved me. I lashed out at my grandmother and my brother, Carter. They still love me too. If these people had not continued to turn the other cheek, I would probably be dead by now. I owe all of them my life. I think the only way to pay back a debt like that is to live everyday to the fullest, and try to help them all any way that I can. I thank God for the wonderful family that He has given me. They are all the greatest people that I know.

Chapter 73: All Apologies

To close this story, I would like to make a few apologies and also include a prayer.

To Sara:

Thank you for all of the time that you spent with me. Thank you for all the energy that you spent trying to figure out how to help me with my problems. Thank you for giving me our two wonderful daughters. I am sorry for the way that I treated you through most of our marriage. I am sorry that things ended so terribly. I don't blame you for what happened between us. I think that most of what happened was my fault. I have thought about you often since we parted. At first, I blamed you for most of the things that went wrong in my life. As time passed, I realized that you were not really the problem. The problem was myself. You happened to marry a person who already had a distorted view of reality. I blamed you for problems that I helped create. I am sorry for that. I am sorry that it took so long for you to get the courage to leave. I hope that you are happy in your new marriage. You deserve to be. You are a wonderful person. I wish you and Matt all the best of life and love. I'm not sure that it was God's plan for things to work out the way that they did, but I think that we are both better for it. I just hope that our children can understand, one day, what happened between us and that none of it was your fault. I know I can't ever make up for some of the things that I said and did to you in the time that we were together. I think that the only way to make amends is to be a supporting father for our children. I hope that God will continue to bless you and your new family.

To Liza and Gwen,

I hope that you do not get a chance to read this too soon. I am afraid that you are both still too young to learn about the terrible person that I once was. I hope that your memories of me, when you were both younger, are not as bad as I sometimes fear that they might be. I want you to know that I think that I neglected you both for many years. I am sorry for that. I have tried to make up for lost time by being the best person that I know how to be, when you are around. I hope that I have been able to provide you with a decent example of how a person should behave. I know that there are a lot of things about me that you do not understand: Why I don't have a job. Why I live with my parents. Why I don't have a car. Why I only get to see you once a week and every other weekend. I can't imagine how hard your life must be at times. I never had to live through my parents divorce. My parents had disagreements, but they always worked through their problems. Don't be upset with your mother for what happened. She is not the guilty one. I am. I hope that one day, you will realize that all the hard times have made you stronger. I hope you both know that you are the most important people in my life. Without the two of you, I would be lost. You lift my spirit every time I am with you. You are both the smartest, most beautiful little girls I know. Thank you for always loving me. You have no idea of how powerful you both are. Even though you are small and young, you both possess the power to change people. It happens every time you are with me. I may be having a good day before we get together, but once I am with you, it only gets better. There were times in my life that the only good part of my life was the time that we spent together. Had I not been able to spend time with you, during those dark days, I might not be alive to write this letter to you now. In a way, I owe you my life. That is why I dedicate to you. Your love is worth more to me than anything else. I love you both dearly in return. Know that whenever a time comes when you feel that you are alone or in more trouble than you can deal with, I will be here for you.

To Mom and Dad,

Thank you for all the times you have saved me from myself. Without you, I would be lost. Without you, I would be homeless. Without you, I would have to beg for my food. You both provide me with the basic things that a person needs to survive. You also provide so much more. Thank you for listening to me at times when no one else would. Thank you for your patience. Thank you for putting up with all the days that I let go by without speaking a word to you. Thank you for providing me with the environment that allowed me to heal from the self inflicted wounds that I gave myself. Thank you for raising me to be strong enough to bring myself out of the darkness, and back into a life that has meaning and purpose. Thank you for making your home my home as well. I am sure that I have caused you both many stressful days and nights. I am sorry for that. There are too many incidents for me to list where I was wrong and you were both right. I know that I have not done too many things to make you proud to call me your son, but I still have hope that, one day, I will be able to make that happen. I know that words can only do so much. I know that the only way that I can truly show you my appreciation is do live a life that demonstrates how much I care about the both of you. I try to do the little things, like the cooking and cleaning. That is my way of showing you that I care. I know it is not much. I know that I take a lot more from you than I give to you. I am sorry that this is the way that my life has turned out. There are times when I regret letting things get so abnormal, but I really can't see how things could have worked out any better. If I had decided to live on my own, after leaving the Peace River Center, I never would have been able to make it. The only thing that kept me from living some miserable life on the street was you. Without you, I would have lost contact with Liza and Gwen. My life would have continued to spiral out of control, probably to the point of death. I thank you for giving me life, and for saving my life. As I have written to the girls, I owe you my life. The only way that I can repay my debt is to live a life that honors the way you raised me. I love you both. Thank you for all that you do and all you have done.

Finally, I would like to close my story with a prayer:

Dear God,

Thank you for all that you have given me. I know that I am not your most devoted follower, but I do appreciate all that you have allowed me to experience, both the good and the bad. I know that there have been many times when I doubted your existence and cursed you if you did exist. I apologize for my behavior in those times and hope that you will forgive me.

Thank you for surrounding me with people who have lifted me up in times when I have fallen. Thank you for giving me the ability to speak and think again. Thank you for letting me walk in the darkness. It was the darkness that allowed me to see the light. Before my life was turned up side down, I had no idea of just how good I had it. Now, you have allowed me to appreciate the little things. Thank you.

Thank you for giving me the strength to continue living. Thank you for giving me the realization that I am not alone or worthless. Thank you for making me the person that I am today.

Please God, use me to give peace and understanding to people who need to know that they are not alone, or worthless. Please allow this book to impact a person who needs to hear this story. Please use it to better the understanding of what mental illness is, how it develops, and how it can be resolved. Please continue to bless me with your love and grace. Please help me continue to grow in my knowledge of you and your desires for my life. Please bless my family and help them continue to grow in their love for you. Again, I thank you for all that you have done. All that I do, I do for you.

A disclaimer from the author:

To protect the privacy of the people in my story, all of their names have been changed to fictitious names. I didn't want to take a chance on dealing with repercussions from the information in my story offending any of the people that I have mentioned. Aside from the changing of names, all other content is fact, and is to the best of my recollection.

Contact the Author:

You may contact Scott Gann for any and all inquiries at: scot.tg@live.com

Need to order additional copies?

For additional copies, please go to **Lulu.com** and search *For a Minute, I Lost Myself: The Past and Present of a Schizophrenic*, by Scott Gann. Lulu.com will print and deliver your copy as soon as you order it. Printing usually takes from 3-5 days. Shipping time depends on what method of shipping you choose.

or

Contact me at scot.tg@live.com and I'll order a copy for you. If you enjoyed reading my book, be sure to tell a friend about it!

The following information was obtained from research and inquiries to those believed to control the lyrics from which the excerpts in this book were taken.

Permission was granted for use of the excerpted lyrics for the following songs:

1.　　　Excerpts from "The Con " first appeared at page 603, written by Tegan and Sara Quin, Copyright 2007 by Sire Records

2.　　　Excerpts from "Dark Come Soon " first appeared at page 604, written by Tegan and Sara Quin, Copyright 2007 by Sire Records

3.　　　Excerpts from "You Wouldn't Like Me " first appeared at page 605, written by Tegan and Sara Quin, Copyright 2004 by Vapor Records

4.　　　Excerpts from "Smokin From Shootin " first appeared at page 634, written by Jim James, Copyright 2008 by ATO Records

No response was received to requests for permission in respect to the excerpts from the following songs:

1.　　　Excerpts from "The Well and the Lighthouse " first appeared at page 5, written by The Arcade Fire, Copyright 2006 by Merge Records

2.　　　Excerpts from "Miami " first appeared at page 279, written by Adam Duritz, Copyright 2002 by Geffen Records

3.　　　Excerpts from "Good Time " first appeared at page 306, written by Adam Duritz, Copyright 2002 by Geffen Records

4　　　Excerpts from "New Frontier " first appeared at page 306, written by Adam Duritz, Copyright 2002 by Geffen Records

5.　　　Excerpts from "Carriage " first appeared at page 307, written by Adam Duritz, Copyright 2002 by Geffen Records

6.　　　Excerpts from "Black and Blue " first appeared at page 279, written by Adam Duritz, Copyright 2002 by Geffen Records

7.　　　Excerpts from "Up All Night (Frankie Miller Goes to Hollywood)" first appeared at page 308, written by Adam Duritz, Copyright 2002 by Geffen Records

www.ingramcontent.com/pod-product-compliance
Lightning Source LLC
Chambersburg PA
CBHW020329270326
41926CB00007B/102